KB186211

한국의 토익 수험자 여러분께,

토익 시험은 세계적인 직무 영어능력 평가 시험으로, 지난 40여 년간 비즈니스 현장에서 필요한 영어능력 평가의 기준을 제시해 왔습니다. 토익 시험 및 토익스피킹, 토익라이팅 시험은 세계에서 가장 널리 통용되는 영어능력 검증 시험으로, 160여 개국 14,000여 기관이 토익 성적을 의사결정에 활용하고 있습니다.

YBM은 한국의 토익 시험을 주관하는 ETS 독점 계약사입니다.

ETS는 한국 수험자들의 효과적인 토익 학습을 돕고자 YBM을 통하여 'ETS 토익 공식 교재'를 독점 출간하고 있습니다. 또한 'ETS 토익 공식 교재' 시리즈에 기출문항을 제공해 한국의 다른 교재들에 수록된 기출을 복제하거나 변형한 문항으로 인하여 발생할 수 있는 수험자들의 혼동을 방지하고 있습니다.

복제 및 변형 문항들은 토익 시험의 출제의도를 벗어날 수 있기 때문에 기출문항을 수록한 'ETS 토익 공식 교재'만큼 시험에 잘 대비할 수 없습니다.

'ETS 토익 공식 교재'를 통하여 수험자 여러분의 영어 소통을 위한 노력에 큰 성취가 있기를 바랍니다.

감사합니다.

Dear TOEIC Test Takers in Korea,

The TOEIC program is the global leader in English-language assessment for the workplace. It has set the standard for assessing English-language skills needed in the workplace for more than 40 years. The TOEIC tests are the most widely used English language assessments around the world, with 14,000+ organizations across more than 160 countries trusting TOEIC scores to make decisions.

YBM is the ETS Country Master Distributor for the TOEIC program in Korea and so is the exclusive distributor for TOEIC Korea.

To support effective learning for TOEIC test-takers in Korea, ETS has authorized YBM to publish the only Official TOEIC prep books in Korea. These books contain actual TOEIC items to help prevent confusion among Korean test-takers that might be caused by other prep book publishers' use of reproduced or paraphrased items.

Reproduced or paraphrased items may fail to reflect the intent of actual TOEIC items and so will not prepare test-takers as well as the actual items contained in the ETS TOEIC Official prep books published by YBM.

We hope that these ETS TOEIC Official prep books enable you, as test-takers, to achieve great success in your efforts to communicate effectively in English.

Thank you.

입문부터 실전까지 수준별 학습을 통해 최단기 목표점수 달성!

ETS TOEIC® 공식수험서
스마트 학습 지원

토익기출
by YBM

구글플레이, 앱스토어에서
ETS 토익기출 수험서 다운로드

구글플레이

앱스토어

ETS 토익 모바일 학습 플랫폼!
ETS® 토익기출 수험서 어플

교재 학습 지원
1. 교재 해설 강의
2. LC 음원 MP3
3. 교재/부록 모의고사 채점 및 분석
4. 단어 암기장

부가 서비스
1. 데일리 학습(토익 기출문제 풀이)
2. 토익 최신 경향 무료 특강
3. 토익 타이머

모의고사 결과 분석
1. 파트별/문항별 정답률
2. 파트별/유형별 취약점 리포트
3. 전체 응시자 점수 분포도

ETS TOEIC 공식카페 ▾

etstoeicbook.co.kr

ETS 토익 학습 전용 온라인 커뮤니티!
ETS TOEIC® Book 공식카페

강사진의 학습 지원   토익 대표강사들의 학습 지원과 멘토링

교재 학습관 운영   교재별 학습게시판을 통해 무료 동영상
강의 등 학습 지원

학습 콘텐츠 제공   토익 학습 콘텐츠와 정기시험
예비특강 업데이트

---

www.ybmbooks.com에서도 무료 MP3를 다운로드 받을 수 있습니다.

토익,

실력과 점수를 한 번에!
출제기관이 만든
진짜 문제로 승부하라!

왜
출제기관에서
만든 문제여야
할까요?

2,300명의
시험개발 전문가!

교육, 심리, 통계, 인문학, 사회학 등
2,300여 명의 전문 연구원이 모인 ETS.
토익 한 세트가 완성되려면 문제 설계 및 집필,
내용 검토, 문항의 공정성 및 타당성 검증,
난이도 조정, 모의시험 등 15단계의 개발공정에서
수많은 전문가의 손을 거쳐야 합니다.

2,300

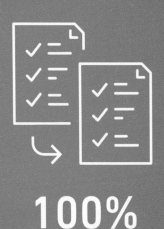

싱크로율 100%

ETS TOEIC 교재의 모든 예문과 문항 및 해설은
100% ETS TOEIC 정기시험 개발부서에서 개발
및 검수되었습니다.
그러므로 사진, LC 음원, 문항 유형 및 난이도 등
모든 면에서 실제 시험과 싱크로율 100%입니다.

100%

최고의 정기시험
적중률!

기출 문항을 변형한 복제 문항이 아닌,
ETS 토익 출제팀이 만든 원본 문항 100%로,
시중의 어느 교재와도 비교할 수 없는 압도적으로
높은 적중률을 보장합니다.

최고의 적중률!

| 발행인 | 허문호 |
| 발행처 | YBM |

편집	이선주
디자인	DOTS
마케팅	정연철, 박천산, 고영노, 김동진, 박찬경, 김윤하

| 초판발행 | 2021년 12월 20일 |
| 6쇄발행 | 2024년 8월 1일 |

신고일자	1964년 3월 28일
신고번호	제 1964-000003호
주소	서울시 종로구 종로 104
전화	(02) 2000-0515 [구입문의] / (02) 2000-0564 [내용문의]
팩스	(02) 2285-1523
홈페이지	www.ybmbooks.com

ISBN 978-89-17-23859-4

ETS TOEIC

토익 정기시험 RC 기출입문서

PREFACE

Dear test taker,

Here is a test preparation book created to help you succeed in using English as a tool for communication both in Korea and around the world.

This book will provide you with practical steps that you can take right now to improve your English proficiency and your TOEIC® test score. Now more than ever, your TOEIC score is a respected professional credential and an indicator of how well you can use English in a wide variety of situations to get the job done. As always, your TOEIC score is recognized globally as evidence of your English-language proficiency.

With the ETS TOEIC® Starter Reading, you can make sure you have the best and most thorough preparation for the TOEIC® test. This book contains key study points that will familiarize you with the test format and content, and you will be able to practice at your own pace. This book exclusively contains a number of actual items which are carefully selected according to the beginners' level. Beginners can familiarize themselves with the characteristics of the actual TOEIC® test.

> The ETS TOEIC® Starter Reading includes the following key features.
> · A number of actual items which are carefully selected according to the beginners' level
> · Analyses of the TOEIC question types and preparation strategies
> · Specific explanations for learners

Use the ETS TOEIC® Starter Reading to help you prepare to use English in an ever-globalizing workplace. You will become familiar with the test, including the new test tasks, content, and format. These learning materials have been carefully crafted to help you advance in proficiency and gain a score report that will show the world what you know and what you can do.

출제기관이 만든
국내 유일 기출 토익 입문서!

토익 입문자들에게
최적화된 구성

토익을 처음 접하는 입문자들이 학습에 어려움을 느끼지 않도록
수준별, 단계별 학습을 제공합니다.

기출 문제 국내 유일
독점 수록

입문자도 풀 수 있는 엄선된 기출 문제를 통해
진짜 토익을 접하고 실전에 대비할 수 있습니다.

ETS만이 제시할 수 있는
체계적인 공략법

토익 각 파트에 대한 이해를 높이고
원하는 점수 달성을 위한 체계적인 공략법을 제시합니다.

토익 최신 경향을 반영한
명쾌한 분석과 해설

최신 출제 경향을 완벽하게 분석하고 반영하여
고득점을 달성하게 해줄 해법을 낱낱이 제시합니다.

CONTENTS

PART 7 기초쌓기

WHAT IS THE TOEIC?

TOEIC은 어떤 시험인가요?

Test of English for International Communication (국제적 의사소통을 위한 영어 시험)의 약자로서,
영어가 모국어가 아닌 사람들이 일상생활 또는 비즈니스 현장에서 꼭 필요한 실용적 영어 구사 능력을 갖추었는가를
평가하는 시험이다.

■ 시험 구성

구성	Part		내용	문항수	시간	배점
듣기(LC)	1		사진 묘사	6	45분	495점
	2		질의 & 응답	25		
	3		짧은 대화	39		
	4		짧은 담화	30		
읽기(RC)	5		단문 빈칸 채우기 (문법 / 어휘)	30	75분	495점
	6		장문 빈칸 채우기	16		
	7	독해	단일 지문	29		
			이중 지문	10		
			삼중 지문	15		
Total	7 Parts			200문항	120분	990점

■ TOEIC 접수는 어떻게 하나요?

TOEIC 접수는 한국 토익 위원회 사이트(www.toeic.co.kr)에서 온라인
상으로만 접수가 가능하다. 사이트에서 매월 자세한 접수일정과 시험 일정 등의
구체적 정보 확인이 가능하니, 미리 일정을 확인하여 접수하도록 한다.

■ 시험장에 반드시 가져가야 할 준비물은요?

신분증 규정 신분증만 가능
　　　　(주민등록증, 운전면허증, 기간 만료 전의 여권, 공무원증 등)
필기구 연필, 지우개 (볼펜이나 사인펜은 사용 금지)

■ 시험은 어떻게 진행되나요?

09:20	입실 (09:50 이후는 입실 불가)
09:30 - 09:45	답안지 작성에 관한 오리엔테이션
09:45 - 09:50	휴식
09:50 - 10:05	신분증 확인
10:05 - 10:10	문제지 배부 및 파본 확인
10:10 - 10:55	듣기 평가 (Listening Test)
10:55 - 12:10	독해 평가 (Reading Test)

■ TOEIC 성적 확인은 어떻게 하죠?

시험일로부터 약 10-11일 후, 인터넷과 ARS(060-800-0515)로 성적을 확인할 수 있다. TOEIC 성적표는 우편이나 온라인으로 발급 받을 수 있다(시험 접수시, 양자 택일). 우편으로 발급 받을 경우는 성적 발표 후 대략 일주일이 소요되며, 온라인 발급을 선택하면 유효기간 내에 홈페이지에서 본인이 직접 1회에 한해 무료 출력할 수 있다. TOEIC 성적은 시험일로부터 2년간 유효하다.

■ TOEIC은 몇 점 만점인가요?

TOEIC 점수는 듣기 영역(LC) 점수, 읽기 영역(RC) 점수, 그리고 이 두 영역을 합계한 전체 점수 세 부분으로 구성된다. 각 부분의 점수는 5점 단위이며, 5점에서 495점에 걸쳐 주어지고, 전체 점수는 10점에서 990점까지이며, 만점은 990점이다. TOEIC 성적은 각 문제 유형의 난이도에 따른 점수 환산표에 의해 결정된다.

학습 플랜

20 일 완성

- 하루 3~4시간 학습
- 매일 '문제 풀이 전략 → 연습용 문제 → 실전형 문제'의 단계를 밟아가며 학습하는 단기 집중형 스케줄

1주	☐ Day 1	☐ Day 2	☐ Day 3	☐ Day 4	☐ Day 5
	Part 5 Unit 1-2	Unit 3-4	Unit 5-6	Unit 7-8	Unit 9-10
2주	☐ Day 6	☐ Day 7	☐ Day 8	☐ Day 9	☐ Day 10
	Unit 11-12	Unit 13-14	**Part 6** Unit 1-2	Unit 3-4	Unit 5
3주	☐ Day 11	☐ Day 12	☐ Day 13	☐ Day 14	☐ Day 15
	Part 7 Unit 1-2	Unit 3-4	Unit 5-6	Unit 7	Unit 8
4주	☐ Day 16	☐ Day 17	☐ Day 18	☐ Day 19	☐ Day 20
	Unit 9	Unit 10	Unit 11	Unit 12	ETS 실전모의고사

40 일 완성

- 하루 1~2시간 학습
- 매일 부담 없는 학습량을 꼼꼼히 학습하는 심화 학습형 스케줄

1주	☐ Day 1 **Part 5** Unit 1	☐ Day 2 Unit 2	☐ Day 3 Unit 3	☐ Day 4 Unit 4	☐ Day 5 Unit 5
2주	☐ Day 6 Unit 6	☐ Day 7 Unit 7	☐ Day 8 Unit 8	☐ Day 9 Unit 9	☐ Day 10 Unit 10
3주	☐ Day 11 Unit 11	☐ Day 12 Unit 12	☐ Day 13 Unit 13	☐ Day 14 Unit 14	☐ Day 15 **Part 6** Unit 1
4주	☐ Day 16 Unit 2	☐ Day 17 Unit 3	☐ Day 18 Unit 4	☐ Day 19 Unit 5	☐ Day 20 **Part 7** Unit 1
5주	☐ Day 21 Unit 2	☐ Day 22 Unit 3	☐ Day 23 Unit 4	☐ Day 24 Unit 5	☐ Day 25 Unit 6
6주	☐ Day 26 Unit 6	☐ Day 27 Unit 7	☐ Day 28 Unit 7	☐ Day 29 Unit 8	☐ Day 30 Unit 8
7주	☐ Day 31 Unit 9	☐ Day 32 Unit 9	☐ Day 33 Unit 10	☐ Day 34 Unit 10	☐ Day 35 Unit 11
8주	☐ Day 36 Unit 11	☐ Day 37 Unit 12	☐ Day 38 Unit 12	☐ Day 39 ETS 실전모의고사	☐ Day 40 ETS 실전모의고사

점수 환산표 및 산출법

점수 환산표 이 책에 수록된 Final Test를 풀고 난 후, 맞은 개수를 세어 점수를 환산해 보세요.

LISTENING Raw Score (맞은 개수)	LISTENING Scaled Score (환산 점수)	READING Raw Score (맞은 개수)	READING Scaled Score (환산 점수)
96 – 100	475 – 495	96 – 100	460 – 495
91 – 95	435 – 495	91 – 95	425 – 490
86 – 90	405 – 470	86 – 90	400 – 465
81 – 85	370 – 450	81 – 85	375 – 440
76 – 80	345 – 420	76 – 80	340 – 415
71 – 75	320 – 390	71 – 75	310 – 390
66 – 70	290 – 360	66 – 70	285 – 370
61 – 65	265 – 335	61 – 65	255 – 340
56 – 60	240 – 310	56 – 60	230 – 310
51 – 55	215 – 280	51 – 55	200 – 275
46 – 50	190 – 255	46 – 50	170 – 245
41 – 45	160 – 230	41 – 45	140 – 215
36 – 40	130 – 205	36 – 40	115 – 180
31 – 35	105 – 175	31 – 35	95 – 150
26 – 30	85 – 145	26 – 30	75 – 120
21 – 25	60 – 115	21 – 25	60 – 95
16 – 20	30 – 90	16 – 20	45 – 75
11 – 15	5 – 70	11 – 15	30 – 55
6 – 10	5 – 60	6 – 10	10 – 40
1 – 5	5 – 50	1 – 5	5 – 30
0	5 – 35	0	5 – 15

점수 산출 방법

아래의 방식으로 점수를 산출할 수 있다.

자신의 답안을 수록된 정답과 대조하여 채점한다. 각 Section의 맞은 개수가 본인의 Section별 '실제 점수 (통계 처리하기 전의 점수, raw score)'이다. Listening Test와 Reading Test의 정답 수를 세어, 자신의 실제 점수를 아래의 해당란에 기록한다.

	맞은 개수	환산 점수대
LISTENING		
READING		
총점		

Section별 실제 점수가 그대로 Section별 TOEIC 점수가 되는 것은 아니다. TOEIC은 시행할 때마다 별도로 특정한 통계 처리 방법을 사용하며 이러한 실제 점수를 환산 점수(converted[scaled] score)로 전환하게 된다. 이렇게 전환함으로써, 매번 시행될 때마다 문제는 달라지지만 그 점수가 갖는 의미는 같아지게 된다. 예를 들어 어느 한 시험에서 총점 550점의 성적으로 받는 실력이라면 다른 시험에서도 거의 550점대의 성적을 받게 되는 것이다.

▼

실제 점수를 위 표에 기록한 후 왼쪽 페이지의 점수 환산표를 보도록 한다. TOEIC이 시행된 때마다 대개 이와 비슷한 형태의 표가 작성되는데, 여기 제시된 환산표는 본 교재에 수록된 Test용으로 개발된 것이다. 이 표를 사용하여 자신의 실제 점수를 환산 점수로 전환하도록 한다. 즉, 예를 들어 Listening Test의 실제 정답 수가 61~65개이면 환산 점수는 265점에서 335점 사이가 된다. 여기서 실제 정답 수가 61개이면 환산 점수가 265점이고, 65개이면 환산 점수가 335점 임을 의미하는 것은 아니다. 본 책의 Test를 위해 작성된 이 점수 환산표가 자신의 영어 실력이 어느 정도인지 대략적으로 파악하는 데 도움이 되긴 하지만, 이 표가 실제 TOEIC 성적 산출에 그대로 사용된 적은 없다는 사실을 밝혀 둔다.

RC

기초 학습
READING PRESTUDY

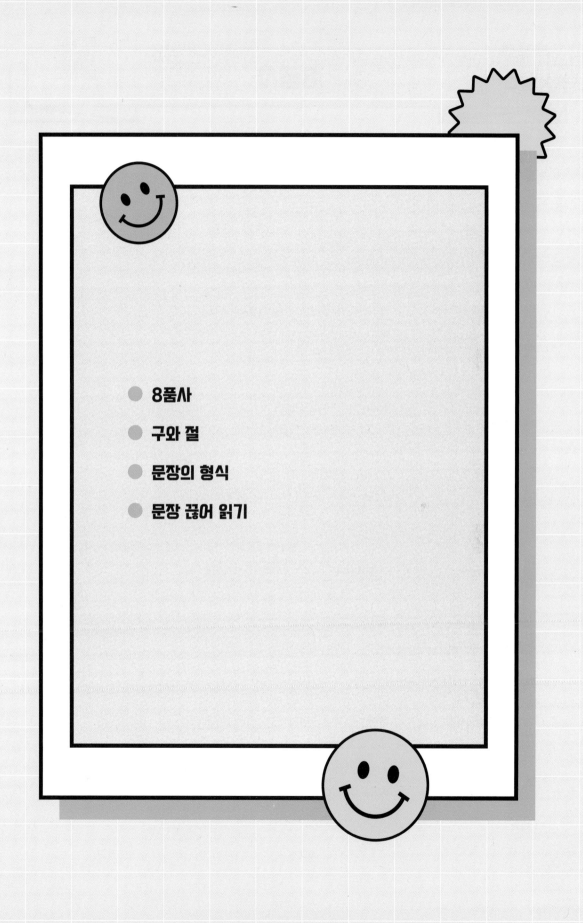

- 8품사

- 구와 절

- 문장의 형식

- 문장 끊어 읽기

8품사

단어를 기능이나 형태의 특징에 따라 나눈 종류들을 '품사'라고 합니다. 영어에는 모두 **8개**의 품사가 있는데, 각 품사들의 특징은 다음과 같습니다.

명사
Noun

우리는 이름을 통해 서로 다른 물건, 사람을 구별하게 되는데요. 명사는 바로 그 이름에 해당하는 품사입니다.

student 학생　**bank** 은행　**air** 공기　**success** 성공

대명사
Pronoun

명사를 대신해서 쓰는 품사를 대명사라고 해요.

he 그　**they** 그들은　**his** 그의　**them** 그들을

형용사
Adjective

명사의 생김새나 특징을 꾸며주는 말이 형용사입니다.

young 젊은　**wise** 현명한　**short** 짧은　**helpful** 유익한

동사
Verb

동사는 우리말로 '~하다, ~이다'로 끝나는 말로, 동사는 사람이나 사물 등의 움직임 또는 상태를 표현합니다.

drink 마시다　**write** 쓰다　**be** ~이다　**look** 보다, ~하게 보이다

부사
Adverb

부사는 다른 품사나 문장 전체를 꾸며 의미를 풍성하게 해주는 역할을 합니다.

beautifully 아름답게　**late** 늦게　**really** 정말로

전치사
Preposition

전치사는 우리말 '~에서, ~에, ~으로' 등에 해당하는 품사로서 명사와 함께 사용됩니다.

at ~에　**from** ~부터　**on** ~(위)에　**to** ~로

접속사
Conjunction

단어, 구, 절을 이어주는 역할을 하는 품사라는 점을 알아 두세요.

and ~와, 그리고　**but** 하지만, 그러나　**or** ~나, 또는　**so** 그래서

감탄사
Exclamation

감탄사가 있어서 기쁨, 슬픔, 놀라움 등의 감정을 나타낼 수 있어요.

Wow 우와!　**Oops** 아이고　**Ouch** 아야

구와 절

구와 절은 둘 이상의 단어가 합쳐진 말 뭉치입니다. 구는 둘 이상의 단어가 [단어 + 단어]의 형태로 쓰이며 [주어 + 동사]의 형태를 갖지 않습니다. 절은 둘 이상의 단어가 [주어 + 동사]의 형태로 하나의 품사처럼 쓰입니다.

As we discussed, you will receive a 10% discount on your rent for six months.
절(주어 + 동사)   구   구   구

논의한 바와 같이, 6개월 동안 임대료를 10퍼센트 할인 받으실 겁니다.

구와 절은 단어와 마찬가지로 문장 안에서 하나의 품사, 즉 명사, 형용사, 부사 역할을 할 수 있습니다.

● 명사구/명사절   명사처럼 주어, 목적어, 보어로 쓰입니다.

명사구 I enjoy playing games. 나는 게임하는 것을 즐긴다.
                   목적어

명사절 He said that the game was called off. 그는 경기가 취소되었다는 것을 말했다.
                   목적어

● 형용사구/형용사절   명사를 수식하거나 설명합니다.

형용사구 We provide games for children.
                   └─── 명사 수식

저희는 아이들을 위한 게임을 제공합니다.

형용사절 We provide games that are popular among children.
                   └─── 명사 수식

저희는 어린이들 사이에서 인기 있는 게임을 제공합니다.

● 부사구/부사절   동사, 형용사, 부사, 절 전체를 수식합니다.

부사구 The game was called off because of the rain.
                   └─── 절 전체 수식

비가 와서 경기는 취소되었다.

부사절 The game was called off because it rained a lot.
                   └─── 절 전체 수식

비가 많이 와서 경기는 취소되었다.

문장의 형식

문장 요소들이 모여 하나의 문장을 이룹니다. 영어 문장이 구성되는 방식에는 총 다섯 가지가 있는데, 이 다섯 가지를
영어에서는 다섯 가지 문장 형식이라고 해서 '5형식'이라고 해요.

● 1형식　주어 + 동사

주어와 동사만으로도 완전한 구조의 문장이 됩니다. 목적어가 필요 없는
동사가 쓰입니다.

The chicken ran away.　그 닭이 달아났다.
　　　주어　　　　동사

She sang beautifully.　그녀는 아름답게 노래 불렀다.
주어　동사　수식어: 부사

● 2형식　주어 + 동사 + 보어

보어 자리에는 대개 형용사나 명사가 옵니다.

　몸의 감각이나 상태를 나타내는 동사가 2형식에 많이 쓰입니다.

감각 동사	**sound** ~처럼 들리다	**look** ~처럼 보이다	
	seem ~처럼 보이다	**taste** ~한 맛이 나다	
	feel ~처럼 느끼다	**smell** ~한 냄새가 나다	
기타 동사	**be** ~이다	**become** ~이 되다	
	get ~이 되다		

The car looks expensive.　그 차는 비싸 보인다.
　주어　　동사　　보어: 형용사

Lucy became a teacher.　Lucy는 선생님이 되었다.
주어　　동사　　　보어: 명사

● 3형식　주어 + 동사 + 목적어

의미상 목적어가 필요한 동사가 쓰입니다.

He wants some tea.　그가 차를 원해요.
<u>주어</u>　<u>동사</u>　　<u>목적어</u>

I picked up the phone.　나는 수화기를 들었다.
<u>주어</u>　<u>동사</u>　　　<u>목적어</u>

● 4형식　주어 + 동사 + 간접목적어 + 직접목적어

간접목적어는 '~에게'라고 해석하며, 직접목적어는 '~을[를]'이라고 해석합니다. 간접목적어가 직접목적어보다 먼저 나와요.

물건을 주는 행위를 나타내는 동사가 4형식에 많이 쓰입니다.

give 주다	**offer** 제공하다	**ask** 묻다	**award** 수여하다
send 보내다	**show** 보여주다	**teach** 가르치다	**buy** 사주다

Tom gave his girlfriend a present.
<u>주어</u>　<u>동사</u>　　<u>간접목적어</u>　　<u>직접목적어</u>
톰은 여자친구에게 선물을 주었다.

Ms. Brown bought her son some bread.
　<u>주어</u>　　　<u>동사</u>　　<u>간접목적어</u>　<u>직접목적어</u>
브라운 씨는 아들에게 빵을 좀 사주었다.

● 5형식　주어 + 동사 + 목적어 + 목적격 보어

'~을(를)'로 해석되는 목적어 다음에 목적어의 상태를 보충 설명하는 목적격 보어가 나옵니다.

5형식에 많이 쓰이는 동사는 다음과 같습니다.

make 만들다	**leave** 두다	**keep** 유지하다
call 부르다	**find** 알다	**consider** 여기다, 생각하다

You make me happy.
<u>주어</u>　<u>동사</u>　<u>목적어</u>　<u>목적격 보어: 형용사</u>
당신이 나를 행복하게 해요.

They found the girl honest.
<u>주어</u>　<u>동사</u>　　<u>목적어</u>　　<u>목적격 보어: 형용사</u>
그들은 그 소녀가 정직하다는 것을 알게 되었다.

문장 끊어 읽기

효율적인 직독직해를 하기 위해서는 문장 구조를 이해하고 문장을 끊어서 읽는 훈련이 필요합니다.

● 긴 주어는 동사 앞에서 끊어 읽기

주어와 동사 사이에는 수식어구나 수식어절이 끼어서 긴 주어를 만드는 경우가 많은데, 이런 경우에는 동사 앞에서 끊어 읽는 것이 좋습니다.

- [At least / five years of] advertising sales experience / is preferred.
  최소 / 5년의 광고 판매 영업 경험이 있으면 / 더욱 좋습니다.

- The newest model / [of this attractive bike] / debuted / from Roadwell Motorcycles / in October.
  최신 모델이 / 이 멋진 오토바이의 / 첫선을 보였다 / 로드웰 오토바이 사에서 / 10월에

- The fact / [that he already had a deep knowledge of the store] / was a definite plus.
  사실이 / 그가 이미 백화점에 대해 깊은 지식을 가지고 있다는 / 확실한 장점이었다.

● 긴 동사구는 동사 뒤에서 끊어 읽기

긴 동사구나 수동태의 뒤에서는 끊어 읽는 것이 편리합니다.

- It has been in print / continuously / for the last two decades.
  그것은 출간되었습니다 / 꾸준히 / 지난 20년간

- An article / may be exchanged / without a receipt / for the same product / in a different size or color.
  물품은 / 교환될 수 있습니다 / 영수증 없이 / 동일한 제품으로 / 다른 크기나 색상의

● 수식어구 앞에서 끊어 읽기

전명구, to부정사구, 동명사구, 분사구와 같은 수식어구 앞에서는 끊어 읽는 것이 좋습니다.

- I was initially hesitant / to sign up / to spend my Friday nights / in a pottery studio / instead of with family and friends.
  저는 처음에는 내키지 않았습니다 / 강좌에 등록해 / 금요일 저녁을 보내는 것이 / 도예 공방에서 / 가족, 친구와 보내는 대신

- Employees / can access / the fitness center / using their Trifecta Laboratories ID cards.
  직원들은 / 이용할 수 있습니다 / 헬스클럽을 / 트라이펙터 연구소 신분증을 이용해

● 절 앞에서 끊어 읽기

절은 that, if, when 등과 같은 접속사로 이어집니다. 따라서 접속사 앞에서 끊어 읽는 것이 좋습니다.

- I / am confident / that we can solve this problem / well in advance of the deadline.
  저는 / 확신합니다 / 우리가 이 문제를 해결할 수 있다고 / 마감일 훨씬 전에

- Below is a list / of our team members / and the type of calls and e-mails / that will be directed to each person.
  아래는 명단입니다 / 우리 팀원들의 / 그리고 전화와 이메일 유형입니다 / 각 사람에게 전달될

- The security deposit of $750 / will be refunded / within 30 days / after the tenant vacates the premises.
  임대 보증금 750달러는 / 반환된다 / 30일 이내에 / 세입자가 집을 비운 후

● 등위접속사 앞에서 끊어 읽기

and, or, but과 같은 등위접속사는 구와 절을 이어주는 연결어 역할을 합니다. 따라서 등위접속사 앞에서 끊어 읽는 것이 편리합니다.

- I / vacated Unit 7 / last month / and just received / my security deposit.
  저는 / 7호를 비웠습니다 / 지난달에 / 그리고 방금 받았습니다 / 제 임대 보증금을

- Employees / visiting from other Trifecta offices / may also access the facility / but need to sign in / at the reception desk.
  직원들은 / 트라이펙터의 다른 근무처에서 방문하는 / 역시 시설을 이용할 수 있습니다 / 하지만 기록을 하고 들어가야 합니다 / 안내 데스크에서

다음 문장을 끊어 읽기에 유의해 읽어보세요.

1 Refunds are only possible / if the item is returned / within 30 days of purchase / and is accompanied / by the original sales receipt.

2 If the 30-day period has expired / or you do not have a receipt, / you may return the item / for store credit, / which can be applied / toward a future purchase.

3 Your photograph Coastline in Winter / has been chosen / as the third place winner / in the "Views of Our World" landscape photography contest / sponsored by Mintner Photography Magazine.

해석

1 환불은 가능합니다 / 물품이 반품되고 / 구매일로부터 30일 이내에 / 함께 제시되는 경우에만 / 판매 영수증 원본이

2 30일 기간이 경과되었거나 / 영수증이 없는 경우에는 / 물품을 반품하실 수 있으며 / 매장 포인트를 받는 식으로 / 이는 적용될 수 있습니다 / 향후 구매 시

3 귀하의 사진 '겨울 해안선'이 / 선정되었습니다 / 3위 수상작으로 / 풍경 사진 콘테스트 '우리 세상의 풍경'에서 / 〈민트너 포토그래피 매거진〉에서 후원한

RC

PART 05

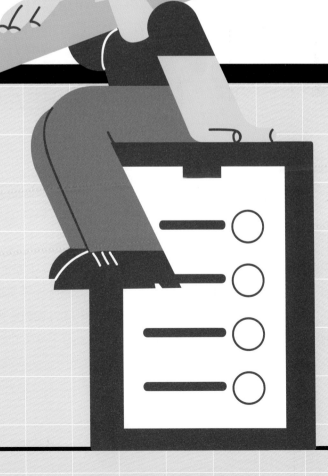

UNIT 01

문장 구조

무료인강 바로가기

다양한 성분들이
어우러져 완성되는 문장!

The foxes sing.

여우들이 노래한다.
　주어　　　　동사

여우들이 / 부른다 / 노래를
　주어　　　　동사　　　목적어

여우들은 / ~이다 / 즐거운
　주어　　　동사　　　보어

문장의 뼈대를 이루는 성분은 〈주어＋동사〉입니다. 따라서 '무엇이(foxes) 무엇하다(sing)'처럼 주어와 동사만으로 문장을 만들 수 있어요. 이 뼈대에 '무엇을(노래를)'에 해당하는 목적어가 오기도 하고, 다른 성분을 보완하는 보어(즐거운)가 오기도 해서 문장의 의미가 더 풍성하게 완성됩니다. 그럼 문장을 구성하는 이 4가지 핵심 성분에 대해 알아봅시다.

● 주어와 동사

주어는 상태나 동작의 주체로 문장에서 '무엇이', '누가'에 해당합니다. 주어가 될 수 있는 품사는 명사와 대명사이며 이 밖에 명사 역할을 하는 것들도 주어가 될 수 있습니다.

명사	대명사	명사 역할을 하는 것
fox	you	to sing / singing / that the foxes sing

All employees / must wear / a uniform.

모든 직원은 / 입어야 한다 / 유니폼을

동사는 움직임이나 상태를 나타내는 말로 문장에서 '~하다', '~이다'에 해당합니다. 동사의 종류로는 일반동사와 be동사 가 있으며 동사에 의미를 더해주는 조동사와 함께 쓰이기도 합니다.

일반동사	be동사	조동사 + 동사
sing	are	can sing

Mobile phones / are very useful.

휴대전화들은 / 매우 유용하다

● 목적어와 보어

문장에서 동사의 대상이 되는 말로 '누구를', '무엇을'에 해당합니다. 주어처럼 명사, 대명사 또는 명사 역할을 할 수 있는 것들이 목적어가 될 수 있습니다.

명사	대명사	명사 역할을 하는 것
fox	you	to sing / singing / that the foxes sing

This brochure / contains / detailed information.

이 안내서는 / 담고 있다 / 상세한 정보를

문장에서 주어나 목적어의 상태를 보충 설명해 주는 말로 주로 명사 또는 형용사가 보어가 될 수 있습니다.

명사	형용사
fox	busy

The business proposals / seem / promising.

그 사업제안서는 / ~처럼 보인다 / 전망이 좋은

기초 QUIZ

1. 다음 중 주어가 될 수 있는 것을 <u>모두</u> 골라보세요.

   (A) manage   (B) are   (C) manager   (D) you

2. 다음 중 보어가 될 수 <u>없는</u> 것을 골라보세요.

   (A) happy   (B) happily   (C) easy   (D) baby

주어가 될 수 있는 것은 명사, 대명사 등 명사 역할을 하는 것입니다. (A) 동사 (B) be동사 (C) 명사 (D) 대명사   정답: (C), (D)

보어가 될 수 있는 것은 명사 또는 형용사입니다. (A) 형용사 (B) 부사 (C) 형용사 (D) 명사   정답: (B)

① 주어 자리

주어 자리에는 명사, 대명사, to부정사, 동명사 그리고 '~하는 것'으로 번역되는 구나 절이 올 수 있습니다.

명사	The (management, ~~manage~~, ~~managing~~) / will create / a special team. → 동사와 형용사는 주어가 될 수 없습니다. 경영진은 / 만들 것이다 / 특별 팀을
대명사	They / conduct / a survey / every year. 그들은 / 실시한다 / 설문 조사를 / 매년
to부정사 / 동명사	To handle[handling] a budget deficit / is not easy. = It is not easy / to handle a budget deficit. 예산 적자를 해결하는 것은 / 쉽지 않다
명사절	That the company will go out of business / is not true. = It's not true / that the company will go out of business. 그 회사가 파산할 것이라는 것은 / 사실이 아니다

② 동사 자리

하나의 문장에는 반드시 하나의 동사가 있어야 합니다. 동사 자리에 들어갈 수 있는 것은 다음과 같습니다.

일반동사	The management / created / a special team. 경영진은 / 만들었다 / 특별 팀을
be동사	The prices / are / reasonable. 가격이 / ~이다 / 합리적
조동사 + 동사원형	The company / will go out of business. 그 회사는 / 파산할 것이다
명령문	Please contact / Mr. Loren / as soon as possible. 연락주세요 / 로렌 씨에게 / 가능한 빨리

③ 동사 자리에 올 수 없는 것

〈to + 동사원형〉, 〈동사원형 + -ing〉, 과거분사는 동사 자리에 올 수 없어요.

- The management / (created, ~~creating~~, ~~to create~~) / a special team. 경영진은 / 만들었다 / 특별 팀을
- The prices / (are, ~~be~~, ~~being~~, ~~to be~~, ~~been~~) / reasonable. 가격이 / ~이다 / 합리적

ETS 문제로 **훈련하기**

STEP 01

(A), (B) 중 알맞은 것을 고르세요.

1 Jarwin Pharmaceuticals ------- participants to meet certain eligibility criteria.

(A) requires   (B) requirement

2 All ------- will be donated to the public library.

(A) profited   (B) profits

3 Your letter will ------- to our customer service department.

(A) sends   (B) be sent

4 ------- is a form of exercise that has been recommended by doctors.

(A) Walks   (B) Walking

5 A service engineer ------- the broken copy machine in the lobby.

(A) repairs   (B) repairing

6 When you ------- to access your account, please type your password.

(A) want   (B) wanting

STEP 02

빈칸에 가장 알맞은 것을 고르세요.

7 Weather forecasters ------- that heavy rain would come to this region.

(A) predicted   (B) predictably
(C) predictable   (D) prediction

8 ------- from *Megavision Monthly* may sometimes include special offers from third parties.

(A) Correspond
(B) Corresponds
(C) Corresponded
(D) Correspondence

9 The White Fountain Inn will ------- reservations only for parties of six people or more.

(A) accept   (B) accepts
(C) accepting   (D) accepted

10 The ------- of athletic equipment at Ready-Set-Go Sporting Goods is impressive.

(A) various   (B) vary
(C) variety   (D) varied

| WORDS | 1 pharmaceuticals 제약 회사 participant 참여자 eligibility criteria 자격 기준 require 요구하다 requirement 요구 2 donate 기부하다 3 department 부서 4 form 방식, 유형 exercise 운동 5 service engineer 수리[서비스] 기사 broken 깨진, 고장 난 copy machine 복사기 at the moment (바로) 지금 6 access 접근하다, 접속하다 account 계정, 계좌 7 weather forecaster 기상 캐스터 region 지역 8 third party 제3자 9 reservation 예약 10 equipment 장비, 기기 impressive 인상적인

✎ 목적어와 보어

① 목적어 자리

목적어 자리에는 명사, 대명사, to부정사, 동명사 그리고 '~하는 것을'로 번역되는 구나 절이 올 수 있다.

명사	Anderson / needs / (advice, ~~advise~~, ~~advisable~~) / from his supervisor. → 동사와 형용사는 목적어가 될 수 없습니다. 앤더슨 씨는 / 필요로 한다 / 조언을 / 그의 상사의
대명사	The manager / will welcome / you / at the airport. 매니저가 / 맞이할 것이다 / 당신을 / 공항에서
to부정사 동명사	The purchasing manager / agreed / to order appliances. 구매 부장은 / 동의했다 / 전자제품을 주문하는 것을 Mr. Duncan / is considering / resigning his position. 던칸 씨는 / 고려하고 있다 / 그의 자리를 사임할 것을
명사절	The notice / mentions / that the construction will start tomorrow. 통지문은 / 밝히고 있다 / 내일 공사가 시작될 것임을

② 보어 자리

보어 자리에 올 수 있는 것은 명사 종류와 형용사입니다. 보어에는 주격 보어와 목적격 보어가 있으며 주어나 목적어와 동격일 때는 명사를, 상태나 성질을 나타낼 때는 형용사를 사용합니다. 토익에서는 형용사 보어 자리 문제가 주로 출제됩니다.

❶ 명사 보어

주격 보어	Mr. Winsor / became / the right candidate / for this position. 윈저 씨는 / 되었다 / 적임자가 / 이 직위에
목적격 보어	Trent / considers / Mr. Hearst / a good employer. 트렌트 씨는 / 생각한다 / 허스트 씨를 / 좋은 고용주라고

❷ 형용사 보어

주격 보어	The sports complex / is / (available, ~~availably~~) / now. 그 종합운동장은 / ~하다 / 이용 가능한 / 지금
목적격 보어	The music / made / the performance / (impressive, ~~impress~~, ~~impressively~~). → 동사와 부사는 목적격 보어가 될 수 없습니다. 음악은 / 만들었다 / 공연을 / 감명 깊게

ETS 문제로 **훈련하기**

(A), (B) 중 알맞은 것을 고르세요.

1 Mr. Sharma predicts that Clearfoto's latest camera will be a great ------- in the retail marketplace.

(A) succeed   (B) success

2 The president of Cuddly Toys, Inc., has announced ------- to expand the company's production facility.

(A) will plan   (B) plans

3 The agreement becomes ------- once both parties have signed the documents.

(A) effectively   (B) effective

4 The survey asked respondents whether they enjoy ------- a walk in the morning.

(A) taking   (B) took

5 The new software has made the design team more -------.

(A) productive   (B) productively

6 Wang and Associates will be interviewing ------- for the managerial position next week.

(A) applicants   (B) apply

빈칸에 가장 알맞은 것을 고르세요.

7 Please send ------- for the logo design contest to Alicia Chang in the communications department.

(A) submitting   (B) submitted
(C) submissions   (D) submissible

8 It is ------- to make hotel reservations at least three weeks in advance.

(A) necessary   (B) necessarily
(C) necessitate   (D) necessity

9 Mr. Gallos renewed the ------- on the company automobile one week before it expired.

(A) to register   (B) registered
(C) register   (D) registration

10 The Fornsworth Transportation Council will look over the amended fee structure to make sure the changes are -------.

(A) reason   (B) reasonably
(C) reasoning   (D) reasonable

| WORDS | 1 retail 소매(의) 2 expand 확장하다 facility 시설, 설비 3 agreement 계약, 합의 once 일단, 한 번 party (계약 등의) 당사자 document 문서, 서류 4 survey (설문) 조사 respondent 응답자 6 managerial position 관리직 8 in advance 사전에 9 renew 갱신하다 expire 만료되다 10 transportation 교통 look over ~을 검토하다 amend 개정하다 fee structure 요금 구조

수식어

주어, 동사, 목적어, 보어를 제외한 나머지는 수식어입니다.

① 형용사와 부사

형용사는 주로 명사를 수식하는 역할을 하며, 부사는 형용사, 부사, 동사, 또는 절 전체를 수식하는 역할을 합니다.

형용사	The keynote speaker / gave / an impressive speech. ↑ 명사 기조연설자는 / 했다 / 인상적인 연설을
부사	Ms. Turner / was extremely happy / to receive the award. ↑ 형용사 터너 씨는 / 아주 기뻤다 / 상을 받게 되어

② 전치사구

구는 단어와 단어가 합쳐져서 한 덩어리로 쓰이는 것을 말하며, 전치사구는 주로 문장 내에서 명사를 수식하는 형용사구나 동사, 형용사, 또는 문장 전체를 수식하는 부사구로 쓰입니다.

형용사구	You / can get / some information / about new products. 명사 ↑ 당신은 / 얻을 수 있다 / 정보를 / 신제품에 관한
부사구	The tourists / arrived / at their destination / in time. 동사 ↑↑ 관광객들은 / 도착했다 / 그들의 목적지에 / 제때

③ 수식어절

절은 '구'보다는 큰 개념으로 주어와 동사를 갖춘 형태, 즉 흔히 '접속사 + 주어 + 동사'의 형태로 명사를 수식하는 형용사 또는 동사, 형용사, 문장 전체를 수식하는 부사절로 쓰입니다.

형용사절	The clerk / recommended / some dress shirts / that would go well with the suit. 명사 ↑ 점원은 / 추천했다 / 와이셔츠를 / 그 양복에 잘 어울릴
부사절	Since the hotel overlooks the sea, / you / will have / a nice sunrise. ↑ 그 호텔에서 바다가 내려다보이니까 / 당신은 / 볼 것이다 / 멋진 일출을

ETS 문제로 **훈련하기**

STEP 01

(A), (B) 중 알맞은 것을 고르세요.

1 WRX Express ------- opened three new rail lines last year.

(A) successfully   (B) success

2 Belton's shipbuilding industry provides a ------- market for local steel manufacturers.

(A) size   (B) sizable

3 Temperatures are ------- warm in Dulang City, even in winter.

(A) consists   (B) consistently

4 ------- rising fuel prices, Fleetstand Trucking plans to restructure some of its divisions.

(A) Owing to   (B) Even if

5 Hamilton City traffic information is -------- accessible online.

(A) readily   (B) ready

6 The best-selling item in Ronie Fashion's new line is a ------- sweatshirt.

(A) reversible   (B) reverses

STEP 02

빈칸에 가장 알맞은 것을 고르세요.

7 The Transit Association operates an ------- network of bus routes between Clifton and Lawville.

(A) extend   (B) extends
(C) extensive   (D) extensively

8 The dental office remodel was delayed ------- the flooring was back-ordered.

(A) whether   (B) because
(C) as well as   (D) with reference to

9 *The Springlea Times* recently published a list of area doctors who ------- keep blogs.

(A) activating   (B) actively
(C) active   (D) activate

10 Krowip employees must submit their time sheets ------- the end of the day today.

(A) by   (B) or
(C) then   (D) to

| WORDS | **2** shipbuilding 조선 manufacturer 제조자[사] **4** owing to ~ 때문에 restructure 구조조정하다 division 분과[부/국] **5** accessible 접근할 수 있는 **8** delay 미루다 flooring 바닥재 back-ordered 주문이 밀려 있는 **9** recently 최근에 publish 발표[발행]하다 actively 활발히 **10** time sheet 근무시간 기록표

기출 명사 어휘 1

QR코드로 발음도 들어보세요

아래 토익 필수 어휘들을 표현과 함께 익혀 보세요.

plan	계획	inventory	재고, 물품 목록
application	지원서, 신청서	precaution	예방 조치
merchandise	상품, 물건	reliability	신뢰성
duration	(지속되는) 기간	registration	등록
influence	영향(력)	specialty	전문, 전공
operation	운영, 작동	perception	지각, 인식
quality	품질	method	방법, 방식
reputation	명성, 평판	guide	안내 책자; (여행) 안내인, 가이드
committee	위원회	accessory	부대용품
experiment	실험	warehouse	(물류) 창고

어휘 표현 익히기   위의 단어들을 외우고 아래 표현을 완성해 보세요.

1. return the defective _____   결함 있는 **상품**을 반품하다
2. hours of _____   **영업** 시간
3. remaining _____   남아 있는 **재고**
4. change the initial _____   처음 **계획**을 변경하다
5. a safety _____   안전 **예방 조치**
6. _____ of the meeting   회의 진행 **시간**
7. _____ control   **품질** 관리
8. build a _____   **평판**을 쌓다
9. payment _____   지불 **방식**
10. improve product _____   제품 **신뢰도**를 높이다

| ANSWERS | 1. merchandise 2. operation 3. inventory 4. plan 5. precaution
                 6. duration 7. quality 8. reputation 9. method 10. reliability

ETS 문제로 훈련하기

STEP 01 (A), (B) 중 알맞은 것을 고르세요.

1 The board of directors will vote on the ------- to merge with Fray Publishing.

(A) plan   (B) summary

2 As a safety -------, all employees must wear goggles in the experiment room.

(A) specialty   (B) precaution

3 Mr. Yost has decided to rent an apartment for the -------- of his stay in Manchester.

(A) collection   (B) duration

4 The company has a -------- for producing stoves of the highest quality.

(A) reputation   (B) perception

STEP 02 빈칸에 가장 알맞은 것을 고르세요.

5 The membership -------- should include a letter explaining your reasons for wanting to join us.

(A) guideline   (B) inventory
(C) application   (D) committee

6 Damaged ------- must be documented and returned to the warehouse immediately.

(A) information
(B) establishments
(C) services
(D) merchandise

7 Advance ------- is required for all technical staff who wish to attend the conference.

(A) registration   (B) influence
(C) operation   (D) significance

8 In his new role, Mr. Oh will be responsible for ensuring the ------- of all products.

(A) procedure   (B) layer
(C) accessory   (D) quality

| WORDS | 1 board of directors 이사회 vote 투표하다 merge 합병하다 2 safety 안전 goggles 보안경 experiment room 실험실 3 rent 빌리다, 임차하다 stay 체류, 방문 4 produce 생산하다, 제작하다 stove 가스레인지 6 document 기록하다, 입증하다 warehouse (물류) 창고 7 advance 사전의 technical staff 기술직 직원들 8 be responsible for ~에 책임이 있다 ensure 보장하다

1 The Evonton Library has a digital ------- of more than 1,500 business journals and periodicals.

(A) collects
(B) collecting
(C) collection
(D) collected

2 Upon entering the building, please ------- at the front desk.

(A) registration
(B) register
(C) registering
(D) registered

3 Research suggests that Termal, a popular allergy medicine, may ------- sleep.

(A) induce
(B) induced
(C) inducing
(D) will induce

4 It is the ------- of Hyde-Cooper, Inc., to continue providing the highest level of customer satisfaction.

(A) intentional
(B) intention
(C) intend
(D) intended

5 The range of research studies presented on the first day of the conference was very -------.

(A) impressed
(B) impress
(C) impressively
(D) impressive

6 ------- in medical technology have allowed doctors to diagnose illnesses with greater accuracy.

(A) Advanced
(B) Advancing
(C) Advancement
(D) Advances

7 As the audience ------- waited for the actor to appear onstage, he surprised them by marching down the aisle.

(A) expectant
(B) expect
(C) expectantly
(D) expectation

8 To secure the floorboards to the porch framing, ------- large decking screws spaced at 12-inch intervals.

(A) to use
(B) use
(C) useful
(D) using

9 The new printer ------- reduced the amount of waste produced by the accounting department.

(A) great
(B) greater
(C) greatest
(D) greatly

10 In its advertisements, Filmore Furniture emphasizes the strength and ------- of its products.

(A) rely
(B) reliable
(C) reliably
(D) reliability

Questions 11-14 refer to the following e-mail.

To: Alexa Kyros
From: Ronald Bergsma
Subject: February Conference
Date: November 15
Attachment: Contract

Alexa:

Because I will be on vacation, you will be the contact person for the trade conference that will be held here at the Teanon Hotel, February 5–10. I want to make sure that you have the ------- beforehand. The conference chair is Pari Kumar. I will send her an e-mail ------- you. The **11**   **12** conference is a large one, requiring the use of the Grand Ballroom. Ms. Kumar will give you the final count of attendees in early January. After that, you can ------- with the catering **13** department regarding the menus and number of meals.

I am attaching the contract for you to review. ------- . **14**

Ron Bergsma
Event Manager

11 (A) payment
   (B) issue
   (C) information
   (D) service

12 (A) to introduce
   (B) introduction
   (C) will introduce
   (D) introductory

13 (A) coordinating
   (B) coordinator
   (C) coordinates
   (D) coordinate

14 (A) This was the list of the electronic equipment that Ms. Kumar sent.
   (B) I suggest we meet in person next week to go over it together.
   (C) The same conference last year had about 350 attendees.
   (D) Please be aware that my e-mail address has changed.

| WORDS | 1 periodical 정기 간행물 2 register 등록하다 3 induce 유발하다 4 intention 의도 customer satisfaction 고객 만족 5 range 범위, 다양성 present 발표하다 6 diagnose 진단하다 with accuracy 정확하게 7 aisle 통로 8 secure (단단히) 고정시키다 floorboard 마룻장 porch 현관 framing 틀, 뼈대, 테 decking screw 목재용 나사못 space 간격을 두다 interval 간격 9 reduce 줄이다 10 emphasize 강조하다 strength 내구력 11-14 attachment 첨부 trade conference 통상 회의 beforehand 미리 chair 의장 attendee 참석자 catering department 연회 부서 regarding ~에 관하여

UNIT 02

명사

무료인강 바로가기

명사, 존재하는 모든 것의 이름!

사람, 사물, 심지어 어머니의 사랑처럼 눈에 보이지 않는 것까지
세상에 존재하는 모든 것에는 이름이 있죠.
바로 그 이름에 해당하는 품사를 '명사'라고 합니다.

꽃이 폈다.

나는 커피를
마신다.

가족의 토대는
사랑이다.

위에 열거한 첫 번째 문장처럼 명사는 문장에서 동작을 하는 '주체(꽃)'가 되기도 하고, 두 번째 문장처럼 동작의 '대상(커피)'이 되기도 합니다. 또한 세 번째 문장처럼 다른 말을 보충하고 보완하는 역할(사랑)을 하기도 합니다. 이처럼 명사는 문장에서 주어, 목적어, 보어 같은 중요한 자리에 모두 쓰이는 꼭 필요한 품사입니다. 영어에서 명사는 어떠한 형태이며 어떠한 특징이 있는지 살펴보고 토익에서 출제되는 포인트들을 하나씩 배워봅시다.

● 명사의 형태

아래의 단어들은 끝의 형태(어미)를 보면 명사임을 알 수 있습니다.

품사	주요 형태		
명사(Noun)	location 위치 movement 이동 storage 저장	happiness 행복 expense 비용	distance 거리 society 사회
사람 명사	employer 고용주	inventor 발명가	

● 셀 수 있는 명사와 셀 수 없는 명사

영어에서는 명사를 셀 수 있는 명사(가산 명사)와 셀 수 없는 명사(불가산 명사)로 구분합니다. 보통 물건이나 사람처럼 하나, 둘, 개수를 셀 수 있는 명사는 '셀 수 있는 명사'인 반면에 물, 설탕처럼 개수를 셀 수 없는 것이나 지명이나 인명, 눈에 보이지 않는 추상적인 개념은 '셀 수 없는 명사'입니다.

셀 수 있는 명사	book 책	doctor 의사	computer 컴퓨터	discount 할인
셀 수 없는 명사	water 물	London 런던	money 돈	information 정보

● 명사의 단수와 복수

셀 수 있는 명사는 반드시 하나(단수)인지 여럿(복수)인지 표시해야 합니다. 명사가 하나일 때는 앞에 a나 an을 붙이는데, 명사의 발음이 [a, e, i, o, u]로 시작될 경우 발음을 편하게 하기 위해 a 대신 an을 붙입니다. 명사가 여럿일 때는 단어 끝에 대체로 -(e)s를 붙입니다.

단수 명사	a book 한 권의 책	an accident 하나의 사고	a bus 버스 한 대
복수 명사	books (여러 권의) 책들	accidents (여러) 사고들	buses (여러) 버스들

기초 QUIZ

1. 다음 중 명사는 무엇일까요?

   (A) add   (B) addition   (C) additional   (D) additionally

   > 단어가 -tion의 형태로 끝나면 명사입니다. (A) 동사 (C) 형용사 (D) 부사   정답: (B)

2. 다음 중 복수 명사를 골라보세요.

   (A) money   (B) changes   (C) designer   (D) success

   > 명사 뒤에 -(e)s가 붙으면 복수입니다.   정답: (B)

✎ 명사의 쓰임과 위치

① 명사의 역할

명사는 문장에서 주어, 목적어, 보어로 쓰입니다. 특히 목적어는 타동사 뒤나 전치사 뒤에 위치한다는 것을 알아두세요.

주어: 동사 앞
The management / **will create** / a special team.
운영진은 / 만들 것이다 / 특별 팀을

목적어: 동사 뒤
Mr. Anderson / **needs** / advice / from his supervisor.
앤더슨 씨는 / 필요로 한다 / 조언을 / 그의 상사로부터

목적어: 전치사 뒤
Most employees / take part / **in** the competition.
대부분의 직원들은 / 참가한다 / 대회에

보어
Mr. Bacon / **was** / a consultant / at a hospital.
베이컨 씨는 / ~이었다 / 상담가 / 한 병원에서

② 명사의 위치

위와 같이 문장에서의 역할에 따라 명사 자리를 찾을 수도 있지만 앞에 a(n), the, 소유격, 형용사, 전치사를 보고도 뒤에 명사가 와야 함을 알 수 있습니다.

a(n), the + 명사	Candidates / should meet / **the** qualifications / for the job. 후보자들은 / 갖추어야 한다 / 자격 요건을 / 그 일자리를 위한
소유격 + 명사	Each participant / is required / to sign / **his or her** application. 각각의 참가자는 / 요구됩니다 / 서명하도록 / 그의 또는 그녀의 지원서에 **Mr. Kevin's** strength / in sales / makes / him / the leader. 케빈 씨의 강점이 / 영업에서의 / 만든다 / 그를 / 리더로
형용사 + 명사	**New** employees / will receive / training / for a week. 신입 사원들은 / 받을 것이다 / 교육을 / 일주일 동안
전치사 + 명사	All staff / attend / a meeting / **on** Mondays. 전 직원은 / 참석한다 / 회의에 / 월요일마다

ETS 문제로 **훈련하기**

STEP 01

(A), (B) 중 알맞은 것을 고르세요.

1 ------- for the fund-raiser normally begin in February.

(A) Preparations (B) Prepare

2 Sales of compact cars have surpassed industry analysts' -------.

(A) predicted (B) predictions

3 In ------- with their contract, Keller Automotive Company charges rental fees on an hourly basis.

(A) accordance (B) accordingly

4 To order replacement parts for broken machines, please contact the -------

(A) manufacturer (B) manufactured

5 This is a ------- that all employees should submit telephone service work orders.

(A) remind (B) reminder

6 The hotel cost included shuttle service to the airport, making it an excellent -------.

(A) value (B) valuable

STEP 02

빈칸에 가장 알맞은 것을 고르세요.

7 The Museum of Natural History will be closed for six months for a complete -------.

(A) renovation (B) renovate
(C) renovated (D) renovates

8 You may adjust the ------- of your monitor so the image on the screen is suitable for viewing.

(A) brightness (B) brighter
(C) brighten (D) bright

9 Basic ------- for the editor position include a journalism degree and knowledge of publishing software.

(A) qualifying (B) qualifications
(C) qualifies (D) qualify

10 After five years in -------, Empress Chemical plans to expand by opening a second site.

(A) operate (B) operated
(C) operation (D) operational

| WORDS | **1** fund-raiser 모금 행사 normally 보통은, 통상적으로 **2** compact 소형의, 간편한 surpass 능가하다, 넘어서다 prediction 예측, 예견 **3** charge 부과하다 rental fee 사용료, 임대료 on an hourly basis 시간당으로 **4** replacement part 교체 부품 broken 고장 난, 부러진 **5** employee 직원 submit 제출하다 work order 작업 주문서 **6** value 가치 **7** complete 전면적인, 완전한 **8** adjust 조절하다 brightness 밝기 suitable for ~에 적합한 viewing 보기, TV 시청 **9** editor 편집자 degree 학위 publishing 출판(업) **10** expand (사업을) 확장하다 site (건물이 들어설) 장소, 지점

셀 수 있는 명사와 셀 수 없는 명사

① 셀 수 있는 명사(가산 명사)

일반적으로 토익에 출제되는 명사는 셀 수 있는 명사이며, 셀 수 있는 명사는 단독으로 쓰일 수 없습니다. 즉, 명사가 하나(단수)일 경우 앞에 a(n)을, 여럿(복수)일 경우 끝에 -(e)s를 붙여야 합니다.

discount 할인	machine 기계	document 문서
increase 증가	chance 기회	employee 직원

- The manager / decided / to hire (an employee / ~~employee~~).
  부장은 / 결정했다 / 직원 한 명을 고용하기로

- (~~Machine~~ / Machines) / will arrive / tomorrow.
  기계들이 / 도착할 것이다 / 내일

② 셀 수 없는 명사(불가산 명사)

셀 수 없는 명사는 하나 또는 여럿으로 구별할 수 없으므로 앞에 a(n)을 쓰거나 끝에 -(e)s를 붙일 수 없습니다.
따라서, 단독으로 쓰일 수 있어요. 다음은 토익에 자주 나오는 셀 수 없는 명사이므로 꼭 익혀두세요.

advice 조언	equipment 장비	information 정보
access 접근 (권한)	merchandise 상품	permission 허가

- The Web site / provides / (advice / ~~an advice~~) / for gardening.
  그 웹사이트는 / 제공한다 / 조언을 / 원예에 관한

- Power Gym / installed / new (equipment / ~~equipments~~).
  파워 짐은 / 설치했다 / 새로운 장비를

③ 형태가 유사한 명사

아래와 같이 형태와 의미가 비슷하지만 셀 수 있는 명사와 셀 수 없는 명사로 나뉘는 경우가 있습니다.

가산 명사	불가산 명사	가산 명사	불가산 명사
permit 허가증	permission 허가	certificate 자격증	certification 증명, 증명서 (교부)
manufacturer 제조업자	manufacturing 제조업	competitor 경쟁 상대	competition 경쟁
adviser 고문	advice 조언	employer 고용주	employment 고용, 채용

- We / need / a (permit / ~~permission~~) / to enter the factory.
  우리는 / 필요하다 / 허가증이 / 공장에 들어가기 위해서

- He / will work / directly with key clients / as an (~~advice~~ / adviser).
  그는 / 일하게 될 것이다 / 직접 주요 고객들과 함께 / 고문으로서

ETS 문제로 **훈련하기**

STEP 01

(A), (B) 중 알맞은 것을 고르세요.

1 Retail sales in apparel declined in August after a significant ------- in July.

(A) increase   (B) increases

2 The library will accept donations of used ------- by March 31.

(A) computer   (B) equipment

3 Obtaining ------- to be a medical assistant usually requires a high school diploma.

(A) certification   (B) certificate

4 Markon Airway passengers can claim lost ------- at the airline counter.

(A) baggage   (B) suitcase

5 Discount ------- for the jazz concert are available in Ms. Klein's office.

(A) ticket   (B) tickets

6 ------- in the automotive industry is expected to increase in the years ahead.

(A) Competition   (B) Competitor

STEP 02

빈칸에 가장 알맞은 것을 고르세요.

7 As stated in our memo, equipment should not be used for non-work-related -------.

(A) purposes   (B) purpose
(C) purposely   (D) purposeful

8 Han Airport is seeking an experienced air-traffic controller for long-term -------.

(A) employer   (B) employed
(C) employs   (D) employment

9 Candidates must demonstrate a high ------- of expertise in international policy.

(A) level   (B) levels
(C) leveling   (D) leveled

10 Beth's Bazaar has received ------- from customers on the beautiful displays in the store window.

(A) compliments
(B) compliment
(C) complimented
(D) complimentary

| WORDS | 1 retail sales 소매 판매 apparel 의류, 의복 decline 감소하다 significant 상당한, 현저한 2 accept 받다, 접수하다
donation 기부, 기증 used 중고의 3 obtain 얻다 medical assistant 의료 보조원 require 필요로 하다
4 claim 요구하다, 요청하다 5 available 구할 수 있는 6 automotive 자동차의 in the years ahead 향후 몇 년 간
7 equipment 장비, 용품 non-work-related 업무와 관련되지 않은 8 seek 구하다, 찾다 experienced 숙련된, 경험이
있는 air-traffic controller 항공 교통 관제사 long-term 장기간의 9 candidate 후보자, 지원자 demonstrate (실례를
들어) 보여 주다 expertise 전문 지식 10 display 전시, 진열

✏️ 명사 앞에 쓰이는 수량 표현

① 셀 수 있는 단수 명사 앞

다음 표현들은 의미에 상관없이 뒤에 셀 수 있는 명사의 단수 형태가 와야 합니다.

each 각각의	**each** (guest / guests) 각각의 손님
every 모든	**every** (guest / guests) 모든 손님

② 셀 수 있는 복수 명사 앞

다음 표현들은 뒤에 셀 수 있는 명사의 복수 형태가 와야 합니다.

several 여럿의	**several** (product / products) 여러 상품들
various 다양한	**various** (product / products) 다양한 상품들

③ 셀 수 있는 복수 명사 / 셀 수 없는 명사 앞

다음 표현들은 뒤의 명사가 셀 수 있는 명사의 복수 형태이거나 셀 수 없는 명사 형태 두 가지 모두 가능해요.

	셀 수 있는 복수 명사	셀 수 없는 명사
any 어떤	any employees 어떤 직원들	any information 어떤 정보
some 일부의	some employees 일부 직원들	some information 일부 정보
most 대부분의	most employees 대부분의 직원들	most information 대부분의 정보
all 모든	all employees 모든 직원들	all information 모든 정보

→ any는 셀 수 있는 단수 명사 앞에도 올 수 있어요.

• Please contact / us / if you have any question.
연락을 주세요 / 저희에게 / 만약 당신이 어떠한 질문이라도 가지고 있다면

④ 주의해야 할 수량 표현

다음 표현들은 서로 같은 의미이지만 뒤에 오는 명사의 종류가 서로 다릅니다. 이들 중 a few의 경우 a만 보고 뒤에 오는 명사로 단수 명사를 고르지 않도록 주의해야 합니다.

	셀 수 있는 복수 명사	셀 수 없는 명사
많은	many customers 많은 고객들	much information 많은 정보
조금 있는	a few customers 소수의 고객들	a little information 약간의 정보
거의 없는	few customers 거의 없는 고객들	little information 거의 없는 정보

ETS 문제로 **훈련하기**

STEP 01 (A), (B) 중 알맞은 것을 고르세요.

1 Ms. Dalton will face many ------- in her new position.

(A) challenge   (B) challenges

2 The new car will consume less fuel while emitting fewer -------.

(A) pollutant   (B) pollutants

3 Despite some earlier ------- regarding the opening date, we will be ready by October 1.

(A) confusion   (B) confuse

4 ------- employees should attend the safety training meeting.

(A) All   (B) Every

5 Each ------- must have a valid driver's license.

(A) applicant   (B) applicants

6 Laforn Transit's drivers have ------- influence on policies affecting fare increases.

(A) few   (B) little

STEP 02 빈칸에 가장 알맞은 것을 고르세요.

7 The new restaurant has generated ------- excitement because of the reputation of its chef.

(A) many   (B) few
(C) much   (D) little

8 Several recent ------- provide proof that the XK1Ultra motorcycle is quieter than its competitors.

(A) test   (B) tests
(C) testing   (D) tested

9 In order to ensure a timely response, please include your account number on all -------.

(A) are corresponding
(B) correspondence
(C) corresponds
(D) correspond

10 ------- employee interested in participating in the seminar should contact Dan Bezel.

(A) Both   (B) Any
(C) Few   (D) All

| WORDS | 1 face 직면하다 2 consume 소비하다 fuel 연료 emit 내뿜다, 배출하다 3 despite ~에도 불구하고 regarding ~와 관련하여 opening date 개장일, 개업일 4 safety training 안전 교육 5 valid 유효한 6 have influence on ~에 영향을 미치다 fare 요금 7 generate 만들어 내다, 발생시키다 excitement 흥미, 흥분 reputation 명성, 평판 8 proof 증거 motorcycle 오토바이 competitor 경쟁사, 경쟁 상대 9 timely 시기 적절한 account number 계좌[계정] 번호 correspondence 서신 10 participate in ~에 참가하다

아래 토익 필수 어휘들을 표현과 함께 익혀 보세요.

confidence	자신감, 신뢰	pressure	압박, 압력
requirement	필요 조건	qualification	자질, 자격 요건
acquisition	인수, 획득	itinerary	여행 일정표
compliance	(법 등의) 준수	assistance	도움, 지원
statement	명세서, 성명서	variety	다양함
occasion	경우; 행사	opportunity	기회
recognition	인식; 인정	audience	청중, 관중
invention	발명(품)	position	직책, 직위
burden	부담, 짐	sequence	연속, 순서
association	협회, 연계	residence	거주, 주택

어휘 표현 익히기   위의 단어들을 외우고 아래 표현을 완성해 보세요.

1. a _____ of colors   다양한 색상
2. a detailed _____   자세한 **여행 일정표**
3. under _____   **압박**을 받는
4. _____ with new regulations   새로운 규정을 **준수함**
5. on special _____   특별한 **경우**에
6. a _____ for the job   일자리의 **필요 조건**
7. merger and _____   **인수** 합병
8. the _____s of candidates   후보자들의 **자격 요건**
9. provide additional _____   추가적인 **지원**을 제공하다
10. an _____ to meet with recruiters   채용 담당자들을 만날 **기회**

| ANSWERS | 1. variety 2. itinerary 3. pressure 4. compliance 5. occasion
                6. requirement 7. acquisition 8. qualification 9. assistance 10. opportunity

ETS 문제로 **훈련하기**

STEP 01

(A), (B) 중 알맞은 것을 고르세요.

1 The ability to gain the ------- of your clients is essential in a sales job.

(A) confidence   (B) liability

2 The cafeteria in the Rowles Building serves a ------- of sandwiches.

(A) variety   (B) type

3 The ------- for Mr. Ogawa's trip includes stops in London and Paris.

(A) position   (B) itinerary

4 The ------- should turn off mobile phones for the duration of the concert.

(A) residence   (B) audience

STEP 02

빈칸에 가장 알맞은 것을 고르세요.

5 Toynik Stores' profits have decreased recently, so the chain is under ------- to cut costs.

(A) pressure   (B) burden
(C) weight   (D) load

6 Your résumé shows excellent -------, and we would like to arrange a time for an interview.

(A) recognition   (B) qualifications
(C) scheduling   (D) invitation

7 Henry Allen will deliver a presentation on his ------- of a new manufacturing process.

(A) sequence   (B) decision
(C) invention   (D) situation

8 The community housing authority gives limited financial ------- to first-time home buyers.

(A) division   (B) assistance
(C) statement   (D) association

| WORDS | 1 gain 얻다 essential 필수적인 2 cafeteria 구내식당 3 stop (잠시) 머묾, 체류 4 turn off ~을 끄다 for the duration of ~동안, ~내내 5 profit 수익, 이윤 decrease 감소하다 cut costs 비용을 줄이다 6 arrange 마련하다, 정하다 7 deliver a presentation 발표하다 manufacturing process 제작 공정, 제조 과정 8 authority 당국 financial 재정적인

1 The ------- of the deadline allowed the Tobin Group to finish its proposal on time.

(A) extended
(B) extend
(C) extendable
(D) extension

2 Valgor Corporation has adopted innovative marketing ------- for its latest products.

(A) approach
(B) approaches
(C) approached
(D) approaching

3 Visitors to Farnhem Garden will be delighted to discover an incredible ------- of annual flowering plants.

(A) varied
(B) variety
(C) varies
(D) vary

4 Given the ------- of certain fashion trends, Ms. Zheng believes we will be able to sell some of our overstock next summer.

(A) durable
(B) durably
(C) more durable
(D) durability

5 ------- informational packet will include the conference schedule as well as local hotel information.

(A) Every
(B) Few
(C) Whole
(D) Many

6 According to Ms. Lee's -------, 150 square meters of hardwood flooring are needed to complete the project.

(A) calculate
(B) calculated
(C) calculations
(D) calculates

7 If you are interested in the ------- of Chief Managing Editor, submit your cover letter and résumé no later than Friday.

(A) position
(B) positioning
(C) positioned
(D) positions

8 Contact the IT department if any software ------- arise during the online meeting.

(A) complicated
(B) complications
(C) complicate
(D) complicates

9 Geraldo Guiterez has just been appointed to a prestigious position in ------- at Cardero Advertising.

(A) management
(B) manager
(C) managing
(D) manages

10 Ms. Gleason does not have the ------- to hire new employees, but her recommendations are highly valued.

(A) authority
(B) authorize
(C) authored
(D) author

Questions 11-14 refer to the following memo.

To: First Shift Employees
From: Santosh Gulati
Date: April 13
Subject: Revised shift times

Next month, West Side Grocery will begin selling bread and pastries from Rayford's Bakery. ------- . Our customers have frequently requested that we carry these items.
     11

The only time slot they have available in their daily delivery route is 6:00 A.M. ------- ,
     12
starting May 1, the first shift will begin at 5:30 A.M. instead of 5:45 A.M. Employees must be ready to greet the driver and accept the delivery. This will leave enough time to ------- the baked goods and open the store at the usual time.
     13

Thank you for your ------- .
     14

Santosh Gulati, Manager

---

11 (A) Please contact your manager immediately.
(B) They are meeting the targets they have set.
(C) Their products sell very well in this region.
(D) It is important to arrive on time.

12 (A) Accordingly
(B) Likewise
(C) As usual
(D) Since then

13 (A) test
(B) make
(C) cool
(D) display

14 (A) cooperative
(B) cooperation
(C) cooperated
(D) cooperate

| WORDS | **1** proposal 제안(서) on time 제때에 **2** adopt 채택하다 latest 최신의 **3** delighted 기뻐하는 incredible 믿을 수 없는, 대단한 annual 한 해의, 일년생의 **4** given ~을 고려할 때 overstock 과잉재고 **5** packet (특정 용도로 제공되는 서류의) 꾸러미 conference 회의 **6** according to ~에 따르면 hardwood flooring 경재 마룻바닥(재) complete 완성하다 **7** managing editor 편집장 submit 제출하다 cover letter 자기소개서 no later than 늦어도 ~까지 **8** contact 연락하다 arise 발생하다 complication 문제 **9** appoint 임명하다 prestigious 고급의, 일류의 **10** recommendation 추천 highly valued 높이 평가받는 **11-14** grocery 식료품 잡화점 frequently 자주 carry (가게에서 품목을) 취급하다 time slot 시간대 accept 받아들이다 immediately 즉시 region 지역

UNIT 03

대명사

무료인강 바로가기

대명사, 명사를 대신하여
활약하는 아바타!

사람, 사물을 의미하는 명사가 반복될 때,

대명사가 아바타처럼 명사 대신 쓰입니다.

대명사는 문장 내 역할이나 상황에 따라 다양하게 변신하기도 합니다.

민수는 공부를 하고 있다.

그는 문제를 풀고 있다.

꿈에서 그를 보았다.

이 점수는 그의 것이다.

위 문장들에서 '그'는 맨 첫 문장의 '민수'임을 알 수 있어요. 대명사는 앞에 가리키는 명사가
여자인지, 남자인지, 사물인지 또는 하나인지 여럿인지 등에 따라 형태가 달라집니다. 또한 명
사를 대신하기 때문에 명사처럼 주어, 목적어, 보어로 쓰일 수 있어요. 토익 시험에 출제 빈도
가 가장 높은 대명사는 사람을 가리키는 인칭대명사예요. 그럼 인칭대명사를 중심으로 다양한
대명사를 배워봅시다.

● 인칭대명사

인칭대명사는 문장 내 역할에 따라 모습이 달라집니다. '나는(I)'처럼 문장의 주어로 쓰일 때 주격, '나의(my)'처럼 소유의 뜻으로 쓰일 때 소유격, '나를(me)'처럼 목적어 자리에 쓰일 때 목적격이라고 합니다. 격에 따라 형태가 다르지만 같은 형태도 있으므로 주의하여 암기해 두세요.

격		주격	소유격	목적격	소유대명사	재귀대명사
인칭		~은, ~는	~의	~을, ~에게	~의 것	~ 자신
1인칭	나	I	my	me	mine	myself
	우리	we	our	us	ours	ourselves
2인칭	너	you	your	you	yours	yourself
	너희(들)	you	your	you	yours	yourselves
3인칭	그 (남성)	he	his	him	his	himself
	그녀 (여성)	she	her	her	hers	herself
	그것 (사물)	it	its	it	-	itself
	그들/그것들 (사람, 사물)	they	their	them	theirs	themselves

● 지시대명사

사람이나 사물을 가리키는 대명사이며 가까운 것은 this나 these, 멀리 있는 것은 that과 those로 칭합니다.

단수	this 이것	that 저것
복수	these 이것들	those 저것들

● 부정대명사

'정해지지 않은' 수량을 나타내는 대명사를 부정대명사라고 합니다.

some 몇몇   most 대부분   all 모두   many / much (수/양이) 많은 것[사람]

지시대명사와 부정대명사는 명사 역할 외에, 명사를 수식하는 한정사로 형용사처럼 쓰이기도 한다.

기초 QUIZ

1. 빈칸에 들어갈 올바른 인칭대명사를 골라보세요.
   Submit _____ application.
   (A) you   (B) your   (C) yours   (D) yourself

   '너의'라는 뜻의 인칭대명사 소유격은 your입니다. 정답: (B)

2. 다음 중 부정대명사를 골라보세요.
   (A) she   (B) all   (C) this   (D) itself

   (A)와 (D)는 인칭대명사, (C)는 지시대명사입니다. 정답: (B)

✏️ 인칭대명사

① 인칭대명사의 쓰임

주어 자리에는 주격, 명사 앞에서 소유 관계를 나타낼 때는 소유격, 동사나 전치사 뒤 목적어가 와야 할 때는 목적격을 써야 합니다.

주격 They / conduct / a survey / every year. 그들은 / 실시한다 / 설문 조사를 / 매년

소유격 Our service / is reliable. 우리의 서비스는 / 믿을 만하다

목적격 The manager / will welcome / you / at the airport. 매니저가 / 맞이할 것이다 / 당신을 / 공항에서

  Mr. Jones / will send / the report / to him. 존스 씨는 / 보낼 것이다 / 보고서를 / 그에게

② 소유대명사

소유대명사는 '~의 것'이라는 뜻으로 〈소유격 + 명사〉를 결합시킨 형태입니다. 소유의 의미가 있지만 소유격과 다르며 명사의 의미가 함축되어 있으므로 명사처럼 생각해야 합니다. 따라서, 주어, 목적어, 보어 자리에 단독으로 쓰입니다.

주어 Customers / like / our **products** / because ours are durable.

  (ours = our products)

  고객들은 / 좋아한다 / 우리의 제품을 / 우리의 것(제품)이 내구성이 있기 때문에

목적어 Of the three **ideas**, / the judge / chose / mine. (mine = my idea)

  세 가지 아이디어 중에서, / 심사위원은 / 선택했다 / 내것을

보어 The **document** / on Ms. Paik's desk / is hers. (hers = her document)

  서류는 / 백 씨의 책상 위에 있는 / 그녀의 것이다

③ 재귀대명사

주어와 목적어가 같은 대상을 가리킬 때 쓰는 것이 재귀대명사입니다. 목적어 자리에 쓰이는 재귀용법과, 주어를 강조하기 위해 쓰이는 강조용법이 있습니다. 관용표현은 통째로 암기해두세요.

재귀용법 스스로를, 스스로에게	He / devoted / himself / to charity work. (생략 불가) └────── = ──────┘ 그는 / 헌신했다 / 자기 자신을 / 자선 사업에
강조용법 바로 자신이, 직접	Eva / (herself) / issued / the certificate. (생략 가능) 에바는 / 그녀가 직접 / 발급했다 / 인증서를 = Eva / issued / the certificate / (herself).
관용표현 스스로, 혼자서	The hiring manager / will interview / the group / by himself. 채용부장은 / 면접할 것이다 / 그 집단을 / 혼자

ETS 문제로 훈련하기

STEP 01

(A), (B) 중 알맞은 것을 고르세요.

1 Mr. Martinez will be available to sign copies of ------- new book.
(A) his   (B) he

2 Mr. Randall asked us to fix the broken fence by -------.
(A) our own   (B) ourselves

3 New hires must fill out all employee paperwork by the end of ------- first week.
(A) them   (B) their

4 Ms. Williams has given ------- a detailed construction schedule.
(A) us   (B) our

5 Employees should verify the calculations -------.
(A) their   (B) themselves

6 Mr. Erikson has submitted his sales report, but Ms. Wyman has not yet submitted -------.
(A) her   (B) hers

STEP 02

빈칸에 가장 알맞은 것을 고르세요.

7 Ms. Kim will oversee operations, and all group leaders will report back to -------.
(A) she   (B) herself
(C) hers   (D) her

8 All Dokgo Design employees should update ------- timesheets daily.
(A) theirs   (B) them
(C) their   (D) they

9 As an account manager, ------- need to ensure that Ms. Han receives your budget reports.
(A) yours   (B) your
(C) you   (D) yourself

10 Mr. Roberts took Ms. Taylor's portfolio because he mistakenly thought It was -------.
(A) him   (B) himself
(C) his   (D) he

| WORDS | 1 available (시간이 비어) ~할 수 있는, 시간이 있는 copy (책의) 한 부 2 fix 수리하다 fence 울타리 3 new hire 신입사원 fill out ~을 작성하다 4 detailed 상세한 construction 건설, 공사 5 verify the calculations 검산하다 6 submit 제출하다 7 oversee 감독하다 operation 운용, 작업 8 timesheet 근무시간 기록표 9 account 고객, 거래처, 계정 ensure (that) 반드시 ~하게 하다 budget 예산 10 portfolio 작품집, 포트폴리오 mistakenly 실수로

지시대명사

① this / these와 that / those

지시대명사 this의 복수는 these, that의 복수는 those입니다.

- This[That] / **is** the main cause / of their success.
  이것은[저것은] / 주요한 이유이다 / 그들의 성공의

- These[Those] / **are** confidential files.
  이것들은[저것들은] / 기밀 파일들이다

cf. • This[That] policy / **is** effective / immediately.
  이[저] 정책은 / 효과가 있다 / 즉시

  - These[Those] results / **are** completely unexpected.
  이[저] 결과들은 / 전혀 예상하지 못했다

② that과 those

that과 those는 비교 대상이 되는 명사의 반복을 피하기 위해 씁니다. 비교 대상이 단수 명사라면 that, 복수 명사라면 those를 쓰며, 그 뒤에는 〈of + 명사〉 형태인 수식어구가 주로 옵니다. this와 these는 이러한 쓰임이 없어요.

- Your **advertisement** / is similar / to that of E&P Law Firm. (that = advertisement)
  귀사의 광고는 / 비슷하다 / E&P 법률회사의 그것(광고)과

- **The features** / of the new computer / are better / than those of the old model.
  (those = the features)
  특징들은 / 그 신형 컴퓨터의 / 더 낫다 / 구형 모델의 그것들(특징들)보다

③ those (~한 사람들)

those는 those who, those with 등의 수식 표현과 함께 자주 어울려 쓰입니다. 지시대명사 중 토익에 가장 많이 출제되니 반드시 기억해두세요.

- Those / (who are) interested in the seminar / should register / in advance.
  사람들은 / 그 세미나에 관심 있는 / 등록해야 한다 / 미리

- Those / (who are) on duty / cannot make personal calls.
  사람들은 / 근무 중인 / 사적인 전화를 할 수 없다

- Those / with camping permits / are allowed / to stay on the park grounds / past 8:00 P.M.
  사람들은 / 캠핑 허가증을 가진 / 허용된다 / 공원에 머물도록 / 오후 8시 이후에

ETS 문제로 **훈련하기**

STEP 01

(A), (B) 중 알맞은 것을 고르세요.

1 ------- mechanic has worked at Mr. Kim's Auto Shop for years.

(A) This   (B) These

2 FQX Tech's customer service is better than ------- of Applebaum Tech.

(A) this   (B) that

3 Although Mia Cheung is new to the sales team, her skillful presentations seemed like ------- of an experienced salesperson.

(A) these   (B) those

4 Only ------- with valid photo identification may enter the building.

(A) this   (B) those

5 ------- employees affected by the plan should watch the online presentation.

(A) Those   (B) Which

6 ------- who are planning to move to a new house need to consider hidden costs such as insurance.

(A) They   (B) Those

STEP 02

빈칸에 가장 알맞은 것을 고르세요.

7 Since Ms. Rahman has withdrawn her application, ------- analysts will be interviewed for the position.

(A) they   (B) these
(C) this   (D) that

8 The screen of the latest computer is 15 percent larger than ------- of the previous model.

(A) which   (B) those
(C) whose   (D) that

9 ------- who have not received the form should report to the registration desk.

(A) These   (B) This
(C) Those   (D) That

10 This year's revenue figures are remarkably similar to ------- of the preceding four years.

(A) those   (B) that
(C) them   (D) this

| WORDS | **1** mechanic 정비사 auto shop 정비소 **2** customer service 고객 서비스 **3** sales team 영업팀 skillful 능숙한 experienced 경험이 풍부한 **4** valid 유효한 photo identification 사진이 부착된 신분증 **5** affect 영향을 미치다 presentation 발표, 프레젠테이션 **6** insurance 보험 **7** withdraw 철회하다 application 지원(서) analyst 분석가 **8** previous 이전의, 앞의 **9** form 서식, 양식 registration desk 등록 창구 **10** revenue figures 수익 (수치) remarkably 현저히, 놀랍게도 be similar to ~와 비슷하다 preceding 이전의, 먼저의

부정대명사

① 부분을 나타내는 부정대명사

부정대명사 중 '~ 중에서'란 의미의 of 이하의 수식을 받으며 부분을 나타내는 대명사들을 알아두세요.
참고로, of 이하는 전치사 수식어구이므로 생략할 수도 있어요.

one 하나	each 각각	both 둘 다	several 몇몇	
few 거의 없는 것	many 많은 것	some/any 일부, 몇몇	most 대부분 all 모두	of the 가산 명사 복수

little 거의 없는 것	much 많은 것	some/any 일부, 몇몇	most 대부분 all 모두	of the 불가산 명사

- Each / [of the products] / has / its own serial number. 각각은 / 상품들의 / 가지고 있다 / 고유의 일련번호를
  가산 명사 복수
- Many / [of the products] / are currently in stock. 다수는 / 제품의 / 현재 재고가 있다
  가산 명사 복수
- Some / [of the furniture] / is currently out of stock. 일부는 / 가구의 / 현재 재고가 없다
  불가산 명사 (단수)

② another와 the other의 차이

cf. other는 대명사가 아니며 뒤에 명사가 와야 합니다.

- There are **two entrances**; / one is for visitors / and the other is for our employees.
  두 개의 출입문이 있다 / 하나는 방문자용이다 / 그리고 나머지 하나는 우리 직원용이다

- **Among all the candidates**, / only Jim / answered / the questions / while the others / failed.
  모든 후보자들 중에 / 짐만 / 답했다 / 질문에 / 반면에 나머지 후보자들은 / 답하지 못했다

③ each other / one another

대명사 each other와 one another는 '서로'란 의미를 가지고 있으며 주어 자리에는 쓰이지 않아요. 뒤에 명사가 오지
않는다는 점도 기억해두세요.

- The team members / should help / each other. 팀원들은 / 도와야 한다 / 서로

ETS 문제로 **훈련하기**

STEP 01

(A), (B) 중 알맞은 것을 고르세요.

1 Irena Laboratory decided to hire ------- of the technical analysts.

(A) both   (B) much

2 ------- of the passengers on flight 246 missed connecting flights in Dublin.

(A) Everybody   (B) Several

3 ------- of our employees in guest services will arrange the meeting rooms for the seminar.

(A) Some   (B) Much

4 ------- of the new employees were able to attend the orientation.

(A) Most   (B) Other

5 Of the three parking garage plans, two are unacceptable, while ------- is possible.

(A) the other   (B) other

6 ------- of the musicians in the group attended Japler School of the Arts.

(A) The one   (B) One

STEP 02

빈칸에 가장 알맞은 것을 고르세요.

7 Customers can visit the Web site to find reviews of ------- of Yantar Manufacturing Company's most popular products.

(A) so   (B) such
(C) ones   (D) some

8 Cency Apparel has ------- of the most loyal customer bases in the fashion industry.

(A) instead   (B) still
(C) one   (D) those

9 As they trained together, the athletes challenged -------, and the team became stronger overall.

(A) one another   (B) each
(C) its own   (D) other

10 Although many tourists plan a day at the local history museum, ------- simply want to go shopping.

(A) another   (B) anyone
(C) other   (D) some

| WORDS | **1** laboratory 연구소, 실험실 hire 고용하다 technical analyst 기술 분석가 **2** passenger 승객 connecting flight 연결 항공편 **3** arrange 준비하다 **4** employee 종업원, 직원 attend 참석하다 **5** parking garage 주차장 plan 계획, 설계도 unacceptable 받아들일 수 없는 **7** review 논평, 비평 product 제품 **8** loyal 충성스러운 customer base 고객층 **9** athlete 운동선수 overall 전반적으로 **10** local 지역의

기출 명사 어휘 3

QR코드로 발음도 들어보세요

아래 토익 필수 어휘들을 표현과 함께 익혀 보세요.

increase	증가	development	발달, 개발
duty	의무, 업무	conservation	보존, 보호
notice	통지, 공고문	colleague	동료
result	결과	consideration	고려, 숙고
demand	수요, 요구	procedure	절차, 순서
expense	비용	supervision	감독, 감시
form	서식, 양식	attendance	참석, 참여
stage	단계; 무대	advantage	이점, 장점
statistic	통계 자료	attention	주의
reward	보상, 보답	evaluation	평가

어휘 표현 익히기   위의 단어들을 외우고 아래 표현을 완성해 보세요.

1. meet the _____   **수요**를 충족시키다
2. an _____ in software sales   소프트웨어 매출액의 **증가**
3. under the _____ of the manager   매니저의 **감독**하에
4. fill out the_____   **서식**을 작성하다
5. until further _____   추후 **공지**가 있을 때까지
6. the _____ of a study   연구 **결과**
7. under _____   **고려** 중인
8. follow the _____   **절차**를 따르다
9. work well with _____s   **동료**들과 협업을 잘하다
10. wildlife _____   야생 동물 **보존**

| ANSWERS | 1. demand 2. increase 3. supervision 4. form 5. notice
6. result 7. consideration 8. procedure 9. colleague 10. conservation

ETS 문제로 훈련하기

STEP 01 (A), (B) 중 알맞은 것을 고르세요.

1 Big Fields, Ltd., is committed to the ------- of natural resources.
(A) conservation   (B) suggestion

2 Milgrove Township continues to experience a 4 percent annual population -------.
(A) expense   (B) increase

3 All participants at the seminar are asked to complete the evaluation -------.
(A) form   (B) claim

4 I am attaching a copy of my résumé for your -------.
(A) explanation   (B) consideration

STEP 02 빈칸에 가장 알맞은 것을 고르세요.

5 The prices listed in the Silesian Sun Tour catalog are effective until further -------.
(A) mark   (B) notice
(C) ability   (D) attention

6 The bank has introduced a variety of banking products to meet the ------- of its customers.
(A) demands   (B) rewards
(C) duties   (D) advantages

7 The department has been under the ------- of Jane Harden for the past three years.
(A) attendance   (B) supervision
(C) sight   (D) provision

8 All factory employees should follow standard ------- when operating heavy machinery.
(A) procedures   (B) developments
(C) categories   (D) qualifications

| WORDS | 1 be committed to ~에 헌신하다, 전념하다 natural resource 천연자원 2 township (행정 구역 단위) 군구 population 인구 3 participant 참가자 complete 작성하다, 기입하다 evaluation 평가 4 attach 첨부하다 résumé 이력서 5 effective 효과적인, 유효한 6 introduce 내놓다, 도입하다 a variety of 다양한 7 department 부서 8 operate 가동하다, 조작하다 heavy machinery 중장비

1 Ms. Pamu has scheduled a meeting with ------- chief financial officer, Mr. Chambers.

(A) her
(B) she
(C) herself
(D) hers

2 A weekly rail pass is the most economical option for commuters, but ------- are available.

(A) other
(B) others
(C) the other
(D) another

3 Due to unusually high demand, ------- of our lawn supplies need to be restocked.

(A) some
(B) something
(C) other
(D) each other

4 Although employee participation in community-service projects is strictly voluntary, ------- are encouraged to join in.

(A) everything
(B) nowhere
(C) theirs
(D) all

5 Ms. Chan worked on the budget summary by ------- until Ms. Sumardi was free to help.

(A) her
(B) herself
(C) she
(D) hers

6 The Rowleigh Company has once again increased ------- quarterly profits.

(A) itself
(B) its
(C) it
(D) us

7 In order to finish the candidate interviews, Ms. Asaki believes that ------- will need to stay in New York another day.

(A) her
(B) hers
(C) herself
(D) she

8 Ms. Lu's administrative assistant will mail a copy of the annual report to ------- who cannot attend the meeting.

(A) them
(B) this
(C) those
(D) then

9 ------- are the accounts that need to be updated by Matt Jepsen in the Sales Department.

(A) These
(B) Something
(C) Another
(D) More

10 Brookton Furnishings has transformed ------- into a competitive company through an aggressive marketing campaign.

(A) it
(B) its
(C) itself
(D) its own

Questions 11-14 refer to the following memo.

Date: September 14
To: Henderson Store 195
From: Alex Sitton
Re: Final days at Henderson

Hello Henderson 195 staff. It is with a heavy heart that I announce that I will be leaving the store later this month. ------- final day will be September 30. I have decided to take a
11
position as general manager at the Henderson Store in Plains City.

I have thoroughly enjoyed my time as your manager here at store 195. The opportunity in Plains City, ------- , was one I could not pass up.
12

Emily Linares from store 196 will take over as your general manager beginning on October 1. Emily will be a great fit for this store. ------- .
13

Thank you for a fantastic experience ------- the past few years. I will miss seeing you all.
14

11 (A) My
    (B) Her
    (C) Our
    (D) Their

12 (A) therefore
    (B) for example
    (C) comparatively
    (D) however

13 (A) Actually, I was born in Plains City.
    (B) Call me if you have any additional questions.
    (C) She looks forward to joining the team here.
    (D) You may have heard this news already.

14 (A) except
    (B) despite
    (C) besides
    (D) throughout

| WORDS | 1 financial 재무의, 재정의 2 economical 경제적인, 절약이 되는 commuter 통근자 available 이용할 수 있는
3 unusually 평소와 달리, 대단히 lawn supplies 잔디 관리 도구[장비] restock 새로 구입하다, 재고를 다시 채우다
4 participation 참여 strictly 전적으로 voluntary 자진해서 하는 encourage 독려하다 5 budget 예산 summary
요약, 개요 6 increase 늘리다 quarterly 분기의 profit 수익 7 candidate 지원자 8 administrative assistant 사무
업무 보조(원) 10 transform 변형시키다 competitive 경쟁력 있는 aggressive 공격적인
11-14 thoroughly 아주 opportunity 기회 pass up 놓치다 fit 적임자 additional 추가의

UNIT 04

형용사와 부사

무료인강 바로가기

문장을 풍요롭게 만드는 형용사와 부사

형용사는 명사가 가지고 있는 특징을 분명하게 드러내면서 꾸며줍니다.
주로 명사의 모양이나 상태, 성질 등을 표현합니다.
부사는 언제, 어디서, 어떻게, 얼마나 등 구체적인 정보를 전달해 의미를
더욱 풍성하게 해줍니다. 주로 '~하게'라는 의미로 해석합니다.

붉은 당근   당근은 붉다.   달팽이는 느리게 움직인다.

형용사와 부사는 모두 꾸며주는 역할을 담당하는데 꾸미는 대상을 사이좋게 나누어 가졌어요.
형용사는 오로지 '명사'만을 따라다니며 꾸며주고, 부사는 명사를 제외한 나머지를 꾸밉니다.
형용사가 명사를 꾸밀 때는 명사 앞에서 바로 꾸미기도 하고 뒤에서 보충설명하는 방식으로
꾸미기도 해요. 위의 예시에서 '붉은', '붉다'가 위치는 다르지만 모두 '당근'이라는 명사를 꾸미
고 있죠. 반면에 부사는 '느리게'처럼 주로 동사를 수식합니다. 형용사와 부사 모두 꾸미는 역
할을 하지만 이처럼 꾸미는 대상이 다르기 때문에 이 둘을 구별하는 문제가 토익 시험에 자주
출제됩니다.

● 형용사와 부사의 형태

아래의 단어들은 끝의 형태(어미)를 보면 형용사 또는 부사임을 알 수 있습니다. 부사의 주요 형태는 '형용사 + -ly'이며, 이외에도 정해지지 않은 다양한 형태가 있어요.

품사	주요 형태		
형용사(Adjective)	comfortable 편안한 natural 자연스러운 dramatic 극적인	active 활동적인 useful 유용한 easy 쉬운	famous 유명한 confident 자신감 있는
부사(Adverb)	rapidly 빠르게 very 매우	easily 쉽게 just 막, 방금	usefully 유용하게 quite 상당히, 꽤

● 형용사의 역할

명사 수식	Mr. Kim / owns / a big supermarket. 김 씨는 / 소유하고 있다 / 큰 슈퍼마켓을
명사 보충(보어)	Her job / is difficult. 그녀의 일은 / 어렵다

● 부사의 역할

부사는 명사 외에 나머지 품사를 수식해줍니다.

동사 수식	She / suddenly / changed / her opinion. 그녀는 / 갑자기 / 바꾸었다 / 그녀의 의견을
형용사 수식	This business / is extremely successful. 이 사업은 / 대단히 성공적이다
부사 수식	He / solved / problems / very easily. 그는 / 해결했다 / 문제를 / 아주 쉽게

기초 QUIZ

1. 다음 중 형용사를 찾아보세요.

   (A) vary   (B) variously   (C) variety   (D) various

   > 단어가 '-ous'의 형태로 끝나면 형용사입니다. (A) 동사 (B) 부사 (C) 명사 정답: (D)

2. 다음 중 부사를 찾아보세요.

   (A) reliable   (B) reliably   (C) rely   (D) reliance

   > 형용사 뒤에 -ly가 붙으면 부사입니다. (A) 형용사 (C) 동사 (D) 명사 정답: (B)

형용사와 부사의 쓰임

① 형용사의 쓰임

❶ 명사 수식

• Green Kitchen / offers / fresh dishes. 그린 키친은 / 제공한다 / 신선한 음식을

❷ 명사를 보충

주어 보충 동사(2형식)	be ~이다 become ~이 되다 remain ~인 채로 남다

목적어 보충 동사(5형식)	make 만들다 find 알다 consider 여기다, 생각하다 keep 유지하다

• The prices / are reasonable. 가격이 / 합리적이다
    주어   2형식 동사   형용사 – 주어 보충

• The CFO / found / the contract / successful. CFO는 / 생각했다 / 그 계약이 / 성공적이라고
    5형식 동사   목적어   형용사 – 목적어 보충

② 부사의 쓰임

❶ 동사(구)를 수식

부사는 동사의 앞이나 뒤에서도 수식하지만 다양한 동사의 형태 사이에서 수식을 하기도 합니다.

[부사＋동사/동사＋부사]　The director / immediately approved / the plan.
　　　　　　　　　　　　이사는 / 즉시 승인했다 / 그 계획을

　　　　　　　　　　　　Interest rates / have fallen sharply. 이율이 / 급격히 떨어졌다

[be＋부사＋p.p./-ing]　Apartment prices / **are** dramatically **changing** / in the downtown area.
　　　　　　　　　　　　아파트 가격이 / 급격히 변동하고 있다 / 시내 지역에서

[have＋부사＋p.p.]　Air traffic / **has** considerably **increased**. 항공 교통량이 / 상당히 증가했다

❷ 형용사, 부사, 구나 절을 수식

[형용사 수식]　　　　The agreement / is mutually beneficial.
　　　　　　　　　　그 합의는 / 상호간에 이익이다

[부사 수식]　　　　　Refunds / were made / surprisingly promptly.
　　　　　　　　　　환불은 / 이루어졌다 / 놀라울 정도로 신속하게

[구를 수식]　　　　　The cookbook / can be purchased / only in specialty stores.
　　　　　　　　　　그 요리책은 / 구입할 수 있습니다 / 오직 전문점에서

[절 전체를 수식]　　Unfortunately, / the book is out of print.
　　　　　　　　　　안타깝게도 / 그 책은 절판되었다

ETS 문제로 훈련하기

 STEP 01

(A), (B) 중 알맞은 것을 고르세요.

1 The redecorated lobby will feature ------- chairs.
(A) comfortable   (B) comfortably

2 The cinema is -------- located near a major shopping district.
(A) convenience   (B) conveniently

3 --------, our sales have increased for the past three months.
(A) Fortunately   (B) Fortunate

4 The display of Mexican crafts will remain -------- for a limited time only.
(A) openly   (B) open

5 The banquet facility is the ------- venue for business luncheons.
(A) idealize   (B) ideal

6 This special offer is available ------- to employees of Moriyama Association.
(A) exclusionary   (B) exclusively

 STEP 02

빈칸에 가장 알맞은 것을 고르세요.

7 When studies are -------, Deni Contracting Group will make a bid on the project.
(A) complete   (B) completion
(C) completeness   (D) completely

8 Training will enable employees to respond ------- to customer service concerns.
(A) appropriate
(B) more appropriate
(C) appropriately
(D) appropriateness

9 Affirmatis, Inc., ------- made the scope of the research broad during its initial stage.
(A) intend   (B) intention
(C) intentional   (D) intentionally

10 New employees may find themselves -------- on their coworkers for advice.
(A) dependence
(B) dependent
(C) dependently
(D) depend

| WORDS | **1** feature (주요 요소로) 포함시키다   **2** district 지역, 지구   **3** sales 매출(량)   **4** craft 공예(품) remain 남아 있다, 계속 ~이다 for a limited time 한정된 기간 동안   **5** banquet facility 연회 시설 venue (행사를 위한) 장소 luncheon 오찬   **6** available 이용 가능한   **7** make a bid 입찰하다   **8** enable A to부정사 A가 ~할 수 있게 하다 respond 대응하다 concern 관심사   **9** scope 범위 broad 넓은 initial 초기의   **10** coworker 동료 직원

형용사와 부사의 주의해야 할 형태

① 끝말에 따라 의미가 달라지는 형용사

어떤 끝말이 붙는가에 따라 뜻이 달라지기도 하므로 주의해야 합니다.

considerable 상당한	considerate 사려 깊은	confident 확신하는	confidential 기밀의
respectful 예의 바른	respective 각자의, 각각의	successful 성공한	successive 연속의
reliable 믿을 만한	reliant 의존하는	sensible 분별 있는	sensitive 민감한

- The pricing strategy / is based / on (reliable, ~~reliant~~) information.
  그 가격 전략은 / 근거를 두고 있다 / 믿을 만한 정보에

- The information / in the file / is strictly (~~confident~~, confidential).
  그 정보는 / 파일 속의 / 엄격하게 기밀이다

② 주의해야 할 부사

❶ 형태가 비슷하지만 의미가 다른 경우

형용사/부사	부사	형용사/부사	부사
close 가까운/가까이	closely 밀접하여, 면밀히	late 늦은/늦게	lately 최근에
hard 어려운/열심히	hardly 거의 ~ 않는	near 가까운/가까이	nearly 거의
high 높은/높게	highly 매우	short 짧은/짧게	shortly 곧
deep 깊은/깊게	deeply 몹시, 깊이	large 큰/크게	largely 주로

- The construction of a bridge / is (~~near~~, nearly) complete. 다리 공사가 / 거의 완료되었다
- Dr. Nakamura / is a (~~high~~, highly) regarded economist. 나카무라 박사는 / 매우 존경받는 경제학자이다

❷ 숫자 앞에 오는 부사

다음 부사들은 뒤의 숫자 표현과 어울려 쓰입니다. 숫자 앞에 빈칸이 있다면 선택지에서 아래 부사들을 골라주세요.

nearly/approximately/about 대략, 거의	over/more than ~ 이상	at least 최소한, 적어도

- JC Services / has / nearly 100 corporate clients. JC 서비시즈는 / 보유하고 있다 / 거의 100곳의 기업 고객을

❸ 부정부사

다음 부사들은 '~하지 않다'란 부정의 의미를 가지고 있는 부사들입니다. 해석에 유의하세요.

never 결코 ~ 않다	hardly/scarcely 거의 ~ 않다	seldom/rarely 좀처럼 ~ 않다

- The firm / never charges / a delivery fee. 그 회사는 / 결코 청구하지 않는다 / 배송 요금을

ETS 문제로 **훈련하기**

STEP 01

(A), (B) 중 알맞은 것을 고르세요.

1 Customer service employees should be ------- to customers.
(A) respectful   (B) respective

2 Mr. Robinson's flight from Kuala Lumpur was delayed for ------- three hours.
(A) more than   (B) still

3 Mr. Himura has been ------- involved in the development of Visetrix wireless headsets.
(A) deep   (B) deeply

4 All passengers should be ------- of others by speaking softly when talking on mobile phones.
(A) considerable   (B) considerate

5 Most managers ------- examine applicants' educational backgrounds.
(A) close   (B) closely

6 ------- Ms. Lacombe has been working overtime to meet the deadline.
(A) Late   (B) Lately

STEP 02

빈칸에 가장 알맞은 것을 고르세요.

7 We expect there will be -------- 250 people attending the convention.
(A) approximately   (B) approximate
(C) approximation   (D) approximated

8 Kananga Electric's project to develop solar-powered home appliances has been --------.
(A) successful   (B) successive
(C) success   (D) succeed

9 Penter Electronics' newest machines require ------- any additional equipment.
(A) hardest   (B) harder
(C) hardly   (D) hard

10 Ms. Falconi is ------- responsible for the increase in sales of team uniforms.
(A) largely   (B) largest
(C) larger   (D) large

| WORDS | 2 flight 항공편, 항공기 3 headset 헤드셋(마이크가 붙은 헤드폰) 4 mobile phone 휴대 전화 considerate 배려하는
5 applicant 지원자 educational background 학력 6 work overtime 초과 근무하다 7 attend 참석하다
convention 컨벤션, 대규모 회의 8 develop 개발하다 solar-powered 태양열로 작동되는 home appliance 가전제품
9 additional 추가의 equipment 장비, 도구 10 largely 크게, 주로 be responsible for ~에 책임이 있다

기출 명사 어휘 4

QR코드로 발음도 들어보세요

아래 토익 필수 어휘들을 표현과 함께 익혀 보세요.

account	계정, 계좌; 설명	direction	지휘, 감독; 방향
average	평균	policy	정책, 방침
capacity	용량, 수용 능력	estimate	견적(서)
value	가치	objective	목적, 목표
detail	세부 사항	obligation	의무, 책임
amount	양, 총계	charge	요금; 책임
field	분야, 현장	reference	참조, 참고
responsibility	책임, 업무	delay	지연, 지체
tenant	세입자, 거주자	modification	수정
location	위치	agreement	합의, 계약

어휘 표현 익히기   위의 단어들을 외우고 아래 표현을 완성해 보세요.

1. for your _____   참고용으로
2. a seating _____   좌석 수, 수용 인원
3. review the repair _____   수리 견적을 검토하다
4. a recent _____ change   최근의 정책 변경
5. in the _____ of science   과학 분야에서
6. for more _____s   더 많은 세부 정보를 원하면
7. the main _____ of this meeting   이 회의의 주목적
8. shipping _____   배송 요금
9. on _____   평균적으로
10. _____ in delivering a replacement   교체품 배송 지연

| ANSWERS | 1. reference 2. capacity 3. estimate 4. policy 5. field
6. detail 7. objective 8. charge 9. average 10. delay

ETS 문제로 **훈련하기**

STEP 01

(A), (B) 중 알맞은 것을 고르세요.

1 On -------, Mr. Jarvela takes two business trips a month.

(A) average   (B) norm

2 Dr. Cha has been one of the most respected researchers in her -------.

(A) field   (B) account

3 The engineering team has not yet finalized all the ------- of the design.

(A) details   (B) policies

4 New tenants have no ------- to pay for any damage before moving in.

(A) promise   (B) obligation

STEP 02

빈칸에 가장 알맞은 것을 고르세요.

5 There will be ------- in implementing repairs to the Chicago assembly line.

(A) places   (B) inclusions
(C) oppositions   (D) delays

6 The purchase of additional land will allow Montauk Logistics to double their warehouse -------.

(A) modification   (B) ability
(C) qualification   (D) capacity

7 Health-conscious parents restrict the ------- of sugar their children consume.

(A) reason   (B) total
(C) location   (D) amount

8 For your -------, we have included a copy of your purchase order with this shipment.

(A) reference   (B) learning
(C) direction   (D) meaning

| WORDS | 1 business trip 출장 2 respected 훌륭한, 높이 평가되는 researcher 연구자 3 engineering team 기술팀 finalize 마무리하다, 완결하다 4 tenant 세입자, 거주자 damage 손상, 훼손 5 implement 시행하다 assembly 조립 6 additional 추가의 double ~을 두 배로 하다 warehouse 창고 7 health-conscious 건강을 의식하는 restrict 제한하다 consume 소비하다, 섭취하다 8 purchase order 주문서 shipment 발송(품)

1 Ms. Hirai and Ms. Byrd have ------- strategies for conducting consumer research.

(A) differ
(B) different
(C) difference
(D) differently

2 Ms. Jeong has requested a prompt response, ------- within the week.

(A) preferable
(B) preferably
(C) preference
(D) prefer

3 The area around Lake Clamonde is ------- accepted to be among the country's most scenic.

(A) widely
(B) wide
(C) widen
(D) wider

4 Mr. Phillips will discuss -------- approaches for the promotion of our merchandise.

(A) addition
(B) additions
(C) additional
(D) additionally

5 An updated telemarketing database could provide a ------- advantage to the firm's sales team.

(A) distinct
(B) distinctly
(C) distinction
(D) distinctively

6 To ensure safe swimming conditions, employees of ST Pool Systems must add chemicals to the pools --------.

(A) regularly
(B) regular
(C) regularity
(D) regularize

7 The training program on writing ------- policies and procedures starts on Monday.

(A) effect
(B) effects
(C) effective
(D) effectively

8 The readers' response to the updated magazine format has been ------- positive.

(A) overwhelming
(B) overwhelmingly
(C) overwhelmed
(D) overwhelm

9 Although Ms. Gutierrez has been working as a trader for only two months, she is ------- regarded by clients.

(A) high
(B) highly
(C) higher
(D) highest

10 Ms. Wang works ------- with city officials to ensure that her neighborhood is served well.

(A) cooperate
(B) cooperated
(C) cooperative
(D) cooperatively

Questions 11-14 refer to the following e-mail.

To: Abdul James <ajames@gesondcellular.com>
From: Rebecca Quinn <rquinn@vhobitech.com>
Subject: Thank you for the interview
Date: November 14

Dear Mr. James,

Thank you again for taking the time to speak to me about the office manager position. I would like to provide you with a professional reference. ------- . We have worked together for five years. In particular, she supervised my ------- work during Vhobi Tech's move.
11 **12**
She can comment knowledgeably on my ------- . Please let me know if you have any other questions or would like me to send you any further information. I hope my résumé
13
demonstrates how ------- I have pursued a career in this industry. I look forward to hearing
14
from you.

Sincerely,

Rebecca Quinn

---

11 (A) I do not have any names to give you right now.
  (B) I would like to learn more about the pending merger with Mobi Denwa.
  (C) You can speak with Erin Gover, my team lead at Vhobi Tech.
  (D) I can be reached by e-mail or by phone.

12 (A) extend
  (B) extensive
  (C) extending
  (D) extends

13 (A) display
  (B) agenda
  (C) operation
  (D) performance

14 (A) seriously
  (B) consequently
  (C) cautiously
  (D) firmly

| WORDS | 1 conduct 수행하다 consumer 소비자 2 prompt 즉각적인 response 응답, 답장 3 scenic 경치가 좋은
4 approach 접근법 promotion 홍보 merchandise 상품 5 advantage 장점, 우위 6 ensure 보장하다, 확실하게
하다 condition 환경, 상태 chemicals 화학 약품 7 policy 정책, 방침 procedure 절차 8 format 구성 방식
9 trader 거래자, 중개인 regard 여기다, 평가하다 10 neighborhood 지역 (주민) 11-14 reference 추천인, 추천서
supervise 감독하다 knowledgeably 지식이 많아서 pursue 정진하다 pending 임박한 merger 합병

UNIT 05

비교

무료인강 바로가기

자기 PR 시대, 비교도 잘해야 해!

'다른 건 몰라도 이건 남보다[남만큼] 잘한다'는 게 있죠?
그럴 때는 비교하는 말을 써서 표현해 주세요.
둘 이상의 대상을 서로 비교하는 방식으로는 원급, 비교급, 최상급이 있습니다.

민수는 *키가 크다*.
민수는 유진이 **만큼** *키가 크다*.   원급
민수는 유진이**보다** *키가 더 크다*.   비교급
민수는 친구들 **중에서 가장** *키가 크다*.   최상급

위 예문에서 첫 문장을 보면 비교 대상 없이 단독으로 '키가 크다'라고 표현하고 있어요. 그러나 아래 문장들처럼 비교 대상이 생기면 비교 구문을 쓰게 됩니다. 비교 구문에는 두 대상이 비슷할 때 쓰는 '원급 비교'와 어느 하나가 더 우월하거나 열등할 때 쓰는 '비교급 비교'가 있습니다. 또한, 비교해 보니 그중 최고일 때는 최상급 비교를 쓸 수도 있어요. 토익에서는 비교급 비교가 가장 많이 출제된다는 점을 유념해서 공부해 봅시다.

● 원급·비교급·최상급의 형태

원급인 형용사나 부사를 비교급과 최상급으로 만들 때는 규칙적으로 변하는 형태와 불규칙적으로 변하는 경우 두 가지가 있습니다.

형용사/부사의 형태	원급		비교급		최상급	
1음절의 짧은 단어	cheap	저렴한	cheaper	더 저렴한	cheapest	가장 저렴한
2음절 이상의 긴 단어	important	중요한	more important	더 중요한	most important	가장 중요한
불규칙 변화	good / well	좋은/잘	better	더 좋은/더 잘	best	가장 좋은/가장 잘
	bad / ill	나쁜/아픈	worse	더 나쁜	worst	가장 나쁜
	many / much	수/양이 많은	more	더 많은	most	가장 많은
	little	적은	less	더 적은	least	가장 적은

● 원급·비교급·최상급 비교 문장

위의 형태를 바탕으로 만들어진 기본 비교 구문은 아래와 같습니다.

원급 비교	The film / is as exciting as the original novel.
	그 영화는 / 원작 소설만큼 흥미진진하다
비교급 비교	The film / is more exciting / than the original novel.
	그 영화는 / 더 흥미진진하다 / 원작 소설보다
최상급 비교	The film / is the most exciting / of all the action movies.
	그 영화는 / 가장 흥미진진하다 / 모든 액션 영화 중에서

기초 QUIZ

1. 다음 단어들의 비교급 형태와 최상급 형태를 쓰세요.
   1) expensive – _____ – _____
   2) well – _____ – _____

   규칙 변화의 형태와 불규칙 변화의 형태를 알아두세요.
   정답: 1) more expensive, most expensive 2) better, best

2. 빈칸에 알맞은 단어를 고르세요.
   This pen is longer (as, than) that pen. 이 펜은 저 펜보다 더 길다.

   비교급 longer와 어울리는 표현은 than입니다. 정답: than

원급 비교와 비교급 비교

① 원급 비교 : as + 원급 + as

as와 as 사이에 들어가는 품사를 묻는 문제는 양쪽의 as를 빼고 문장 구조를 살펴보면 됩니다. 주어를 설명하는 보어 자리이면 형용사를 쓰고, 동사를 꾸며주는 부사 자리이면 부사를 씁니다.

- The hydrogen car / **is** as reliable as the gasoline car. 〈as + 형용사의 원급 + as〉
  형용사: 주격 보어로 주어를 보충
  수소 자동차는 / 휘발유 자동차만큼 신뢰할 수 있다

- This device / can process / data / as quickly as a supercomputer. 〈as + 부사의 원급 + as〉
  부사: 동사 process 수식
  이 기기는 / 처리할 수 있다 / 데이터를 / 슈퍼컴퓨터만큼 빠르게

② 비교급 비교 : 비교급 + than

비교급 비교는 형용사나 부사의 비교급 형태에 '~보다'란 의미의 than을 붙여 만듭니다. 문장에 than이 있다면 그 앞에는 반드시 비교급의 형태가 있어야 해요. 문맥상 비교 대상을 알 수 있는 경우 than 이하는 생략이 가능합니다.

- The new community center / was larger / than we expected.
  새 주민센터는 / 더 컸다 / 우리가 예상한 것보다

- Online advertising / is more effective / than print advertising.
  온라인 광고는 / 더 효과적이다 / 인쇄 광고보다

- They / will measure / productivity / more accurately / (than in previous years).
  그들은 / 측정할 것이다 / 생산성을 / 더 정확하게 / (전년도들보다)

③ 비교급 강조 부사

다음은 비교급 앞에서 '훨씬, 더, 상당히' 등의 의미로 비교급을 강조해 주는 부사들입니다. 부사 very는 원급을 수식하는 부사로서, 비교급을 수식할 수 없어요.

much / even / still / far / a lot 훨씬, 더욱 더	considerably / significantly 상당히

- Online shopping / is (much, ~~very~~) more popular / than in-store shopping.
  온라인 쇼핑이 / 훨씬 더 인기가 있다 / 매장에서 쇼핑하는 것보다
  → 부사 very는 원급만 수식하며 비교급은 수식하지 못함

- The price / was considerably higher / than he expected.
  가격은 / 상당히 더 비쌌다 / 그가 예상한 것보다

ETS 문제로 **훈련하기**

STEP 01

(A), (B) 중 알맞은 것을 고르세요.

1 Bonus payments will be ------- than they were last year.

(A) smaller　　(B) small

2 The renovated break room is as ------- as the cafeteria on the tenth floor.

(A) spacious　　(B) space

3 The Slenderline mobile phone is smaller ------- other models.

(A) at　　(B) than

4 Employees should feel free to consult the on-site physician as often ------- needed.

(A) than　　(B) as

5 The Piazza Bridge is ------- wider than the bridge over the Lucca River.

(A) more　　(B) even

6 According to Coville Deli, orange juice sells ------- well as coffee in the morning.

(A) more than　　(B) just as

STEP 02

빈칸에 가장 알맞은 것을 고르세요.

7 We believe that a job applicant's work history is ------- important as his or her education.

(A) like　　(B) much
(C) as　　(D) less

8 Winblaze running shoes are not quite as ------- as comparably priced brands.

(A) light
(B) lightly
(C) lightest
(D) lightness

9 Even though ------- than forecast, rain caused the tennis tournament to be delayed by an hour.

(A) light　　(B) lighter
(C) lightly　　(D) lightest

10 Our European markets have grown ------- stronger since the company's launch.

(A) consideration
(B) considerate
(C) considerable
(D) considerably

| WORDS | **1** payment 지불(금) **2** renovated 개조된 break room 휴게실 **3** mobile phone 휴대폰 **4** feel free to 부담 없이[편하게] ~하다 on-site 현장의 physician 의사, 내과 의사 **5** wide 넓은 **6** according to ~에 따르면 **7** job applicant 구직자 **8** running shoes 운동화 comparably 비교할 만하게, 비슷하게 priced 가격이 매겨진 **9** forecast 예보, 예측 **10** grow strong 강해지다

✏️ 최상급 비교와 비교 구문 관용표현

① 최상급 비교

최상급 비교는 앞에 'the 또는 소유격'이 오며 '~ 중에서'라는 범위를 나타내는 표현과 함께 어울려 씁니다. 또한 ever나 possible과 같은 표현이 최상급 강조 표현으로 쓰이기도 합니다.

- This year's book fair / was the largest one / of all other similar events.
  올해의 도서 박람회는 / 가장 큰 행사였다 / 모든 다른 비슷한 행사들 중에

- **Of all the staff**, / Mr. Booth / works / the most carefully.
  모든 직원들 중에서 / Booth 씨가 / 일한다 / 가장 조심성 있게

- This / is the biggest change / that we have **ever** experienced.
  이것은 / 가장 큰 변화이다 / 우리가 이제껏 경험한 것 중에

② 비교 구문 관용 표현

다음은 원급, 비교급, 최상급을 이용한 대표적인 관용표현들입니다.

the same + (명사) + as ~와 똑같은	**as + 원급 + as possible** 가능한 ~하게
배수사 + as + 원급 ~보다 몇 배나 …한	**no later than** 늦어도 ~까지
rather than ~보다는, ~ 대신에	**the + 비교급 + of the two** 둘 중에서 더 ~한
the + 서수 + 최상급 ~번째로 …한	**one of the + 최상급 + 복수 명사** 가장 ~한 것 중 하나
the + 비교급 ~, the + 비교급 … ~할수록 더 …하다 **비교급 + than any other + 단수 명사** 다른 어떤 ~보다 더 …한	

- Mr. Yang / will work / on the same project as his colleagues.
  양 씨는 / 진행할 것이다 / 그의 동료들과 똑같은 프로젝트를

- Workmen / delivered / the fragile items / as carefully as possible.
  작업자들은 / 배달했다 / 깨지기 쉬운 물품을 / 가능한 한 조심스럽게

- The longer / you work, / the more / you get paid.
  더 오래 / 당신이 일할수록 / 더 많이 / 당신은 급여를 받는다

- This ceremony / is the second most important event / in the year.
  이 기념식은 / 두 번째로 중요한 행사이다 / 한 해 중에

- We / will start / construction / in May / rather than July.
  우리는 / 시작할 것이다 / 공사를 / 5월에 / 7월이 아니라

ETS 문제로 **훈련하기**

STEP 01

(A), (B) 중 알맞은 것을 고르세요.

1 Attendance figures at this year's environmental summit were the ------- on record.

   (A) higher   (B) highest

2 The route of the new high-speed train will provide ------- access to the resort towns.

   (A) ready   (B) readiest

3 Applications for the accounting position must be received no ------- than April 19.

   (A) later   (B) further

4 Our support staff receives the ------- salary increase as the managerial group.

   (A) same   (B) as

5 A recent customer poll suggests that Heirloom Seating is the ------- of the two sofa brands.

   (A) more durable (B) most durable

6 Of all the candidates, Mr. Wang appears to be the ------- promising.

   (A) most   (B) much

STEP 02

빈칸에 가장 알맞은 것을 고르세요.

7 Our accessory packages offer telephone customers the ------- selection of carrying cases and covers in the marketplace.

   (A) wider   (B) widest
   (C) more widely (D) most widely

8 The X200's crisp images prove that it is the most ------- advanced digital camera on the market.

   (A) high   (B) higher
   (C) highly   (D) highest

9 Developing work schedules that are both effective and fair is one of the toughest ------- faced by managers.

   (A) challenge   (B) challenges
   (C) challenging   (D) challenged

10 Mr. Yamaguchi wants to order the ------- possible lamps for all employee offices.

   (A) bright   (B) brightest
   (C) brightens   (D) brightness

| WORDS | 1 attendance 출석, 참석 figure 수치 summit 정상회담 2 high-speed train 고속 열차 access 접근
3 application 지원(서) accounting position 회계직 4 managerial 경영자의, 관리인의 5 customer poll 고객 의견
조사 6 candidate 지원자, 후보자 promising 유망한 7 selection 선택(의 폭) marketplace 시장 8 crisp 선명한,
바삭한 highly advanced 첨단의 on the market 시장에 나와 있는 9 effective 효과적인 fair 공정한 challenge
도전

아래 토익 필수 어휘들을 표현과 함께 익혀 보세요.

attendee	참석자	site	현장, 장소
support	지지, 지원	material	재료, 자료
fee	수수료, 요금	matter	문제, 상황
conclusion	결론	exception	예외, 제외
decision	결정, 판단	profit	이익, 이윤
permission	허락, 허가	standard	표준, 수준
expertise	전문 지식	priority	우선순위
failure	실패; 고장	distribution	배분, 배포
solution	해결	possibility	가능성
advancement	진보, 발전	repetition	반복

어휘 표현 익히기   위의 단어들을 외우고 아래 표현을 완성해 보세요.

1. a top _____   **최우선 순위**
2. technical _____ services   기술 **지원** 서비스
3. charge higher _____   더 높은 **수수료**를 부과하다
4. make a _____   **결정**을 하다
5. increase a _____   **이윤**을 증가시키다
6. building _____s   건축 **자재**
7. important _____s   중요한 **문제들**
8. on a construction _____   공사 **현장**에서
9. pay _____ to details   세부 사항에 **주의**를 기울이다
10. _____ method   **배분** 방식

| ANSWERS | 1. priority 2. support 3. fee 4. decision 5. profit
6. material 7. matter 8. site 9. attention 10. distribution

ETS 문제로 훈련하기

STEP 01

(A), (B) 중 알맞은 것을 고르세요.

1 Our Web site informs you about all related ------- and costs.
(A) shapes   (B) materials

2 Ms. Idassi needed to take care of personal -------- before returning to the office.
(A) matters   (B) conclusions

3 Click, Inc., has announced that its ------- have risen 16 percent in the last six months.
(A) employees   (B) profits

4 Due to unexpected system -------, the workshop is postponed until next month.
(A) failures   (B) components

STEP 02

빈칸에 가장 알맞은 것을 고르세요.

5 Mr. Blondell tried to protect his family from media ------- during his run for the National Assembly.
(A) attention   (B) payment
(C) possibility   (D) registration

6 Musicflux will reduce its ------- for access to its digital music files by 20 percent.
(A) entrance   (B) fees
(C) earnings   (D) decision

7 The ------- for the proposed complex is at the intersection of Gaskins Road and Patterson Avenue.
(A) belief   (B) advancement
(C) travel   (D) site

8 Advance Limited is involved in the manufacture, sale, and ------- of its products.
(A) solution   (B) distribution
(C) exception   (D) repetition

| WORDS | 1 inform 알리다 2 take care of ~을 처리하다 3 announce 발표하다, 알리다 rise 상승하다, 오르다 4 unexpected 예상치 못한 postpone 연기하다 5 protect 보호하다 run for 입후보하다 National Assembly 국회 6 access 이용, 접근 7 intersection 교차로, 교차 지점 8 be involved in ~에 관여하다 manufacture 제조, 생산

1 In your search for an architect, you could not hope to find a ------- designer than Ms. Lopez.

(A) more accurately
(B) most accurately
(C) more accurate
(D) most accurate

2 Less expensive laundry detergents can be just ------- effective as the more expensive products.

(A) more
(B) as
(C) very
(D) much

3 Red Badge has been gaining market share and is now Talo Security's ------- competitor.

(A) strongly
(B) strength
(C) strongest
(D) most strongly

4 Reimbursements will be paid as ------- as possible after all forms have been received.

(A) quick
(B) quickly
(C) quicker
(D) quickest

5 Edwards Plumbing earned the ------- ratings for customer satisfaction in this year's Best Businesses survey.

(A) higher
(B) highest
(C) more highly
(D) most highly

6 Plastic is now a ------- more versatile construction material than it was in the past.

(A) much
(B) so
(C) very
(D) really

7 Sky Miles Airlines canceled more flights ------- any other North American airline in July.

(A) as
(B) while
(C) than
(D) whether

8 The general contractor expects Mountain Office Park to be ready for occupancy no ------- than next month.

(A) late
(B) later
(C) latest
(D) lately

9 Sorin's Lakeview Grill is the largest restaurant ------- to be built along the shores of Lake Swensen.

(A) usually
(B) ever
(C) always
(D) constantly

10 Researchers are working on a new material that will be twice as ------- as ordinary concrete.

(A) durably
(B) durable
(C) durability
(D) durableness

Questions 11-14 refer to the following notice.

At Mitiwa Publishing House, we are always looking for the next best-seller for our readers.
To encourage more submissions, we have recently changed our online manuscript
submission process to be ------- for writers. This new system also allows our editors
11
------- and provide constructive feedback on your work more quickly. If you are ultimately
12
given a contract, you will be assigned an editor to help publish and promote your new

------- .
13

If you have any questions about using the updated system, please e-mail the help desk at
help@mitiwaph.org. ------- .
14

11 (A) easier
(B) braver
(C) sharper
(D) broader

12 (A) reading
(B) read
(C) to read
(D) have read

13 (A) music
(B) site
(C) book
(D) show

14 (A) Mitiwa has an excellent reputation for publishing.
(B) Our editing staff members have a lot of experience.
(C) Our template was developed to increase our efficiency.
(D) You will receive a response within three days.

| WORDS | 1 search 찾기, 탐색 architect 건축가 2 laundry detergent 세탁용 세제 effective 효과적인
3 gain 얻다 market share 시장 점유율 competitor 경쟁자 4 reimbursement 환급금 form 서식, 양식
5 plumbing 배관 (작업) rating 평가, 평점 customer satisfaction 고객 만족 6 versatile 다용도의 construction
material 건축 자재 7 cancel 취소하다 flight 항공편 8 general contractor 시공사, 종합 건설업자 expect A to *do*
A가 ~할 것으로 예상하다 occupancy 점유, 점거 9 shore 해안, 물가 10 researcher 연구원 ordinary 일반의, 보통의
concrete 콘크리트 11-14 encourage 격려하다 submission 제출(물) recently 최근 manuscript 원고 process
과정 editor 편집자 ultimately 최종적으로 contract 계약(서) assign 배정하다 promote 홍보하다 reputation 평판
template 템플릿, 견본 양식 increase 높이다 efficiency 효율성 response 답변

UNIT 06

동사의 형태와 수 일치

무료인강 바로가기

동사, 변화무쌍한 카멜레온!

움직임이나 상태를 나타내는 동사는 쓰임새에 따라 동사원형(현재형), 과거형,
과거분사형, 현재분사형, 3인칭 단수형 등 여러 가지 모습을 취합니다.
또한 주어가 단수이면 동사도 단수형을 쓰고, 주어가 복수이면 동사도 복수형을 씁니다.

They **change** color. 현재형
바꾼다

They **changed** color. 과거형
바꿨다

It **changes** color. 3인칭 단수형
바꾼다

동사는 어떤 시점을 나타내는지에 따라 동사원형(현재형), 과거형, 과거분사형으로 형태가 달라지며 진행의 의미를 나타내는 현재분사형도 있습니다. 또한 주어가 하나 또는 한 사람일 때 동사의 현재형에 '-(e)s'를 붙이는데 이런 동사 형태를 3인칭 단수형이라고 합니다. 동사는 문장에서 필수 요소이므로 동사의 다양한 형태와 쓰임을 확실히 익히도록 합니다.

● 동사의 형태

동사는 문장에서 동사원형, 과거형, 과거분사형, 진행형 등으로 형태가 바뀌어 쓰입니다.

종류	형태	규칙동사	불규칙동사
동사원형(현재형)	동사원형	finish 끝내다	rise 오르다
3인칭 단수(현재형)	동사원형 + (e)s	finishes	rises
과거형	동사원형 + (e)d / 불규칙한 형태	finished	rose
과거분사형	동사원형 + (e)d / 불규칙한 형태	finished	risen
현재분사형	동사원형 + ing	finishing	rising

● 수 일치

수 일치란 주어와 동사의 단수와 복수 형태를 맞추는 것을 말합니다. 이때, be동사를 제외하고 동사는 현재형일 때만 변화합니다. 과거나 미래의 경우 주어의 단수, 복수 여부에 상관없이 같은 형태를 씁니다.

주어	be 동사	have 동사	일반동사
단수	is / was	has	동사원형 + (e)s
복수	are / were	have	동사원형

The shop / has / great reviews. 그 상점은 / 받고 있다 / 좋은 평가를
단수 주어　　단수 동사(현재)

The shops / have / great reviews. 그 상점들은 / 받고 있다 / 좋은 평가를
복수 주어　　복수 동사(현재)

The shop[shops] / had / great reviews. 그 상점은[상점들은] / 받았다 / 좋은 평가를
단수[복수] 주어　　　과거 동사

The shop[shops] / will have / great reviews. 그 상점은[상점들은] / 받을 것이다 / 좋은 평가를
단수[복수] 주어　　　미래 동사

기초 QUIZ

1. 다음 동사의 형태를 써보세요.
   - have → 과거형: _____ 과거분사형: _____
     현재분사형: _____

   have는 과거와 과거분사의 형태가 같습니다.　정답: had, had, having

2. 알맞은 동사의 형태를 고르세요.
   The documents (was / were) thoroughly reviewed.

   주어 The documents가 복수이므로 be동사의 복수형이 정답입니다.　정답: were

동사의 형태

① 동사원형

현재 시제
Many contractors / contact / the director's office / for proposals.
많은 도급업자들이 / 연락한다 / 이사의 사무실에 / 제안을 하기 위해

조동사 뒤
The company / must revise / its security policy.
회사는 / 개정해야 한다 / 보안 정책을

명령문
Please bring / the receipt / if you want / to exchange an item.
가져오세요 / 영수증을 / 원하시면 / 제품 교환을

② 3인칭 단수 현재형

현재 시제를 나타낼 때 주어가 3인칭 단수이면 동사 끝에 '-(e)s'를 붙여야 합니다.

- Bank of Rickville / specializes / in the credit card business.
  릭빌 은행은 / 전문으로 한다 / 신용카드 사업을

③ 과거형

동사의 과거형은 '-(e)d' 형태의 규칙 동사와 그 외에 불규칙하게 변하는 형태가 있습니다.

- The research team / evaluated / the quality of the dishwashers / **last week**. (규칙 동사)
  연구팀은 / 평가했다 / 식기세척기의 품질을 / 지난주에

- The motor show / took place / **last month**. (불규칙 동사)
  자동차 전시회가 / 개최되었다 / 지난달에

④ 현재분사(-ing)와 과거분사(p.p.)

현재분사와 과거분사는 단독으로는 동사로 쓰이지 못하지만, be동사나 have동사와 어울려 동사로 쓰입니다.

be + -ing (진행)	Ms. Kraus / (is editing, ~~editing~~) / the quarterly expense report. 크라우스 씨는 / 수정하는 중이다 / 분기별 지출 보고서를
have + p.p. (완료)	Beatle Book / has published / numerous best-sellers / since 1984. 비틀 북은 / 출간했다 / 수많은 베스트셀러를 / 1984년 이래로
be + p.p. (수동)	The faulty product / (was returned, ~~returned~~) / immediately. 결함이 있는 상품은 / 반품되었다 / 즉시

ETS 문제로 훈련하기

STEP 01

(A), (B) 중 알맞은 것을 고르세요.

1 The Darlingstone Hotel is ------- a complimentary breakfast to all of its guests.

(A) offered   (B) offering

2 Adion Airlines cannot ------- that all flights depart on time.

(A) guarantees   (B) guarantee

3 The Desorbo Company will be ------- its new leather boots in the fall catalog.

(A) introducing   (B) introduced

4 The information should be ------- carefully in the space provided.

(A) written   (B) wrote

5 The workers have ------- the batteries in the fire alarm system.

(A) replaced   (B) replacing

6 A survey technician ------- mapping the property lines at 10 Mulberry Drive last Monday.

(A) finishing   (B) finished

STEP 02

빈칸에 가장 알맞은 것을 고르세요.

7 Our company must ------- contacts quickly to build new trade relationships.

(A) establish   (B) establishing
(C) to establish   (D) establishes

8 The holiday travel brochures ------- by registered mail this morning.

(A) arriving   (B) arrived
(C) arrival   (D) to arrive

9 Café Rouge's manager is continually -------- to improve the dessert menu.

(A) have strived   (B) strive
(C) been striving   (D) striving

10 Please -------- the owner's manual before using your Klvl Craft oven for the first time.

(A) consulting   (B) consulted
(C) consults   (D) consult

| WORDS | **1** complimentary 무료의 **2** depart 출발하다, 떠나다 on time 정시에 **3** leather 가죽 introduce 소개하다, 내놓다 **4** carefully 주의 깊게 **5** fire alarm 화재 경보 **6** survey 조사, 측량 property line 대지 경계선 **7** build 세우다, 형성하다 trade relationship 교역 관계 **8** brochure (광고, 안내를 위한) 소책자 registered mail 등기 우편 **9** continually 계속해서, 끊임없이 **10** owner's manual 사용자 설명서 consult 참고하다, 찾아보다

✏️ 주어와 동사의 수 일치

① 단수 주어 + 단수 동사

단수 명사	The **company** / (~~produce~~, produces) / heavy machinery. 가산 명사 단수 그 회사는 / 생산한다 / 중장비를 Protective **clothing** / (was, ~~were~~) made / for the factory workers. 불가산 명사(단수 취급) 보호복은 / 제작되었다 / 공장 작업자들을 위해
동명사/to부정사	**Visiting[To visit] the headquarters** / (~~motivate~~, motivates) / new employees. 본사를 방문하는 것은 / 동기를 부여해준다 / 신입사원들에게
명사절	**What customers like best** / (is, ~~are~~) our great service. 고객들이 가장 좋아하는 것은 / 우리의 훌륭한 서비스이다

② 복수 주어 + 복수 동사

복수 명사	The **representatives** / (~~is~~, are) negotiating / a deal. 대표자들이 / 협상하는 중이다 / 계약을
A and B	**John and his assistant** / (organize, ~~organizes~~) / weekly meetings. 존과 그의 비서가 / 준비한다 / 주간 회의를

③ 주어 + [수식어] + 동사

주어와 동사 사이에 주어를 꾸며주는 수식어가 있을 때는 주어가 단수인지, 복수인지 한눈에 파악되지 않으므로 주의해야 합니다. 이때는 수 일치에 영향을 미치지 않는 수식어 부분을 제외한 후에 주어의 단수형, 복수형을 판단해야 합니다.

• The **opportunity** / [to attend the seminars] / (is, ~~are~~) open / to the public.
  기회는 / [세미나들에 참가할 수 있는] / 열려 있다 / 일반 대중에게

• **Passengers** / [who possess a first-class ticket] / (~~boards~~, board) / the plane / first.
  승객들이 / [일등석 티켓을 소지한] / 탑승한다 / 비행기에 / 먼저

ETS 문제로 훈련하기

PART 5 | UNIT 06

STEP 01

(A), (B) 중 알맞은 것을 고르세요.

1 Our updated Web site now ------- users to upload images and audio files.

(A) allowing　　(B) allows

2 Sending a letter of thanks after a job interview ------- highly recommended.

(A) are　　(B) is

3 The documents in the filing cabinet ------- to be organized alphabetically.

(A) need　　(B) needs

4 Our research ------- were published in the July issue of *Breakthrough*.

(A) result　　(B) results

5 The sales figures of the Gamma Company ------- in many newspapers.

(A) was reported
(B) were reported

6 What the survey results show ------- that tourism to Jeju Island has significantly increased.

(A) is　　(B) are

STEP 02

빈칸에 가장 알맞은 것을 고르세요.

7 Salary ------- are determined after performance reviews by area managers.

(A) increases　　(B) increasing
(C) increase　　(D) increasingly

8 The approved ------- for the new city park features flower gardens, benches, and a picnic area.

(A) design　　(B) designs
(C) designed　　(D) designers

9 Event organizers ------- an increase in the number of vendors at this year's art festival.

(A) anticipate　　(B) anticipates
(C) anticipating　　(D) to anticipate

10 The final installment in the popular mystery series ------- due to arrive in stores yesterday.

(A) is　　(B) are
(C) was　　(D) were

| WORDS | 　1 updated 개편된, 개정된　2 highly 매우, 강력하게　3 organize 정리하다　alphabetically 알파벳순으로　4 issue (잡지나 신문 같은 정기 간행물의) 호　5 sales figures 매출액　6 tourism 관광업　significantly 상당히, 크게　7 determine 결정하다 performance review 인사 고과　8 approve 승인하다　feature 특별히 포함하다　9 organizer 주최자, 조직자　vendor 노점상, 판매　10 installment (전집, 연재물 등의) 1회분, 한 권　be due to ~할 예정이다

주의해야 할 수 일치

① 수량 표현의 수 일치

❶ 단수 취급

one, each, every + 단수 가산 명사 one, each + of the + 복수 가산 명사 (* every of the는 쓰이지 않음)	+ 단수 동사

- (One, Each, Every) room / **has** / Internet access. (한, 각각의, 모든) 방은 / 갖추고 있다 / 인터넷 접속을
                          단수 가산 명사   단수 동사
- (One, Each, ~~Every~~) of the rooms / **has** / Internet access.
                               복수 가산 명사   단수 동사

❷ 복수 취급

many, a few, few + (of the) + 복수 가산 명사	+ 복수 동사

- Many (of the) options / **are** available. 많은 선택 사항들이 / 이용 가능하다
                   복수 가산 명사   복수 동사

❸ 단수 / 복수 둘 다 가능

some / half / most / all + (of the)	+ 불가산 명사	+ 단수 동사
	+ 복수 가산 명사	+ 복수 동사

- All (of the) merchandise / **was** tested / carefully. 제품 전부가 / 점검되었다 / 면밀히
                  불가산 명사   단수 동사
- Most (of the) vehicles / **have** / a navigation system. 차량들 중 대부분이 / 갖추고 있다 / 내비게이션 시스템을
                  복수 가산 명사   복수 동사

② a number of / the number of

a number of (많은) + 복수 명사	+ 복수 동사
the number of (~의 수) + 복수 명사	+ 단수 동사

A number of suitcases / (is / **are**) missing. 많은 여행용 가방들이 / 없어졌다
                복수 주어   복수 동사

The number / of foreign investors / (**is** / are) on the rise. 수가 / 외국인 투자자의 / 늘고 있다
단수 주어   단수 동사

ETS 문제로 훈련하기

STEP 01 (A), (B) 중 알맞은 것을 고르세요.

1 Every security camera installed in the laboratories ------- 24 hours a day.

(A) record   (B) records

2 All of the ------- for the laboratory technician position possess the necessary training.

(A) applicants   (B) application

3 Roughly half of the employees at Century Photo Labs ------- to work by bus.

(A) commutes   (B) commute

4 A number of vehicles ------- parked illegally despite the city's strict regulations.

(A) is   (B) are

5 The number of smartphone users -------- expected to increase by 30% this year.

(A) is   (B) are

6 -------- vendors are required to register with the receptionist when entering the building.

(A) All   (B) Each

STEP 02 빈칸에 가장 알맞은 것을 고르세요.

7 The number of toy ------- has remained steady nationwide, except in the board-game sector.

(A) manufacture   (B) manufactured
(C) manufacturers   (D) manufacturing

8 One possible ------- is that bigger projects receive more funding and are therefore more successful.

(A) conclusive   (B) conclude
(C) conclusion   (D) concluding

9 Because of the economic upturn, most of the business leaders ------- to make a big profit.

(A) hoping   (B) hopes
(C) hope   (D) to hope

10 According to the policy, each team member ------- an annual performance review.

(A) receive   (B) to receive
(C) have received   (D) receives

| WORDS | 1 install 설치하다 laboratory 실험실, 연구실 2 possess 소유하다, 보유하다 training 교육 3 roughly 대략, 거의 photo lab 현상소 commute 통근하다 4 vehicle 차량, 탈것 illegally 불법으로 strict 엄격한 regulation 규정, 규제 5 expect 예상하다, 기대하다 increase 증가하다 6 vendor 판매상, 판매 회사 register 등록하다, 기재하다 receptionist 접수 담당자 7 nationwide 전국적으로 8 funding 자금 9 economic upturn 경기 호전 make a profit 수익을 내다 10 policy 정책, 방침 annual 매년의, 연례의 performance review 인사 고과

정답 및 해설 p.62

89

아래 토익 필수 어휘들을 표현과 함께 익혀 보세요.

install	설치하다	implement	실행하다
import	수입하다	experience	경험하다
grant	주다, 수여하다	submit	제출하다
exceed	초과하다	notify	~에게 알리다
accept	수락하다	conduct	(업무 등을) 수행하다
modify	수정하다	attend	참석하다
address	다루다, 처리하다; 공식 언급하다	respond	응답하다 (to)
obtain	얻다, 획득하다	excel	뛰어나다 (in)
define	정의하다	attach	첨부하다
recall	상기하다	advance	진전시키다

어휘 표현 익히기 위의 단어들을 외우고 아래 표현을 완성해 보세요.

1. _____ a new system — 새로운 시스템을 **설치하다**
2. _____ a strategy — 전략을 **실행하다**
3. _____ an offer — 제안을 **수락하다**
4. _____ our goals — 우리의 목표를 **초과하다**
5. _____ the contract — 계약서를 **수정하다**
6. _____ the problem — 문제를 **처리하다**
7. _____ an access code — 접속 코드를 **획득하다**
8. _____ failure — 실패를 **경험하다**
9. _____ staff of the schedule — 직원들에게 일정을 **알리다**
10. _____ a training session — 교육에 **참석하다**

| ANSWERS | 1. install 2. implement 3. accept 4. exceed 5. modify
6. address 7. obtain 8. experience 9. notify 10. attend

ETS 문제로 **훈련하기**

(A), (B) 중 알맞은 것을 고르세요.

1 Construction costs for the tunnel are expected to ------- $300 million.

(A) excel   (B) exceed

2 The mayor will ------- the issue of road improvement in today's speech.

(A) address   (B) educate

3 Emone Motor has not ------- any delays in production this quarter.

(A) submitted   (B) experienced

4 Ms. Gupta wishes to ------- the terms of her employment contract.

(A) respond   (B) modify

빈칸에 가장 알맞은 것을 고르세요.

5 Most public telephones in France and Italy only ------- telephone cards, which are for sale at post offices.

(A) include   (B) import
(C) accept   (D) enter

6 The new laser printer arrived yesterday, but it has not been ------- yet, so please continue using the old one.

(A) conducted   (B) installed
(C) admitted   (D) posted

7 It is important that all members of the project team ------- tomorrow's meeting.

(A) attend   (B) belong
(C) commit   (D) arrive

8 All visitors must sign in with the receptionist and ------- a visitor's identification tag.

(A) obtain   (B) define
(C) recall   (D) inquire

| WORDS | 1 construction cost 건설비, 공사비 2 mayor 시장 issue 문제, 사안 improvement 향상, 개선 speech 연설, 담화 3 delay 지연 quarter (4분의 1) 분기 4 terms (계약) 조건 employment contract 고용 계약(서) 5 public telephone 공중전화 6 install 설치하다 8 sign in (들어가기 위해) 서명하다 receptionist 접수 담당자

1 The current system ------- users to access their online banking accounts by entering a password.

(A) allowed
(B) allows
(C) allow
(D) allowing

2 Ms. Chiodo, our chief financial officer, is pleased that annual ------- have been rising steadily.

(A) profit
(B) profits
(C) profitable
(D) profiting

3 The lightweight trailer by Tow-Well Manufacturing can ------- almost any kind of small boat.

(A) accommodate
(B) to accommodate
(C) accommodates
(D) accommodating

4 Weathervane LLC, a research firm based in Denton, ------- clients understand consumer trends in the region.

(A) helpful
(B) to help
(C) helping
(D) helps

5 The time needed to acquire all of the necessary materials ------- on several factors.

(A) depend
(B) depends
(C) depending
(D) to depend

6 Any questions or concerns about the revised meeting schedule should be ------- to Ms. Lee.

(A) direction
(B) director
(C) directs
(D) directed

7 Palor Corporation's annual operating costs at the Fukui plant ------- steady.

(A) is remaining
(B) have remained
(C) to remain
(D) remaining

8 The number of transport companies competing for government contracts ------- decreased sharply.

(A) have
(B) has
(C) having
(D) to have

9 Last year's restructuring of the Anyang Industries plant ------- in enhanced worker safety.

(A) to result
(B) has resulted
(C) result
(D) resulting

10 The employees at Topso Lumber ------- to wear company uniforms and identification badges at all times.

(A) expecting
(B) expects
(C) to be expecting
(D) are expected

Questions 11-14 refer to the following advertisement.

Jiffy Fleet Office Supply

As improved technology makes online shopping easier than ever, consumers generally
------- purchases to arrive quickly and reliably. For more than 25 years, Jiffy Fleet Office
  11
Supply has been providing timely service to help your business operations run ------- .
                                                                    12
Furthermore, smart office managers know that maintaining a stock of essential supplies
is important. It is what keeps your team ------- . From desk chairs and whiteboards
                                                  13
to business cards and printer paper, we have you covered. ------- . Discover more at
                                                                              14
jiffyfleetoffice.com.

---

11 (A) expect
    (B) expecting
    (C) expectations
    (D) are expected

12 (A) largely
    (B) smoothly
    (C) eagerly
    (D) notably

13 (A) productive
    (B) attractive
    (C) original
    (D) exclusive

14 (A) Our desk chairs are designed for your comfort.
    (B) We also carry a full range of computer accessories.
    (C) Prices for printer paper have gone up recently.
    (D) Overnight delivery requests will incur an additional fee.

| WORDS | **1** current 현재의 **2** chief financial officer 최고재무관리자 annual profit 연간 수익 **3** lightweight 경량(의) accommodate 수용하다 **4** research firm 리서치 회사 consumer 소비자 region 지역 **5** acquire 입수하다 material 자료 **6** concern 관심사 revised 수정된, 변경된 **7** operating cost 운영비 plant 공장 **8** transport 운송 compete 다투다, 경쟁하다 contract 계약, 도급 decrease 감소하다 sharply 급격히, 날카롭게 **9** restructuring 구조조정 result in 그 결과 ~가 되다 enhanced 향상된, 강화된 **10** identification badge 신분 확인 명찰, 사원증 **11-14** office supply 사무용품 consumer 소비자 purchase 구매(품) reliably 확실히 timely 적시의 operation 운영 furthermore 게다가 maintain 유지하다 essential 필수적인 productive 생산적인 range 범위 accessories 부속품 a full range of 모든 종류의 overnight 하룻밤 사이의 incur (비용을) 발생시키다 additional 추가의 fee 요금

UNIT 07

시제

무료인강 바로가기

시제, 시간에 따라 변하는
동사의 모습!

'마시다'라는 동사는 언제 행동이 이루어지는지에 따라
'마셨다', '마실 것이다'라고 표현하죠?
이처럼 시제란 시간에 따라 변하는 동사의 모습을 나타내는 것입니다.

He drank milk.　He is drinking milk.　He will drink milk.

그는 매일 우유를 마신다.
그는 어제 우유를 마셨다.
그는 내일 우유를 마실 것이다.
그는 5년째 우유를 마시고 있다.

우리말 동사도 '매일', '어제', '내일' 같은 시간에 따라 동사의 끝부분이 변하듯이 영어도 시간에 따라 동사의 형태가 바뀝니다. 현재, 과거, 미래 외에도 자주 쓰는 시제로 '과거부터 지금까지', 즉 '5년째'처럼 쭉 지속되는 시간도 있는데요 이를 '현재완료'라고 합니다. 이 네 가지는 토익 시험에 가장 자주 출제되는 시제입니다. 토익에서 시제 문제는 시간을 나타내는 표현과 어울리는 시제를 익혀두면 어렵지 않게 풀 수 있습니다.

● 시점을 나타내는 단순 시제

현재 동사원형 동사원형 + (e)s	현재의 상태, 습관적인 동작	They / use / computers. 그들은 / 사용한다 / 컴퓨터를 Dan / uses / a computer. 댄은 / 사용한다 / 컴퓨터를
과거 동사원형 + (e)d	과거의 동작이나 상태	They / used / computers. 그들은 / 사용했다 / 컴퓨터를
미래 will + 동사원형	앞날에 대한 추측, 의지, 계획	They / will use / computers. 그들은 / 사용할 것이다 / 컴퓨터를

● 당시 벌어지고 있는 일을 나타내는 진행 시제

현재진행 am / are / is + -ing	현재 진행 중인 일	The man / is meeting / his client. 남자가 / 만나고 있는 중이다 / 그의 고객을
과거진행 was / were + -ing	과거의 특정 시점에 진행되고 있던 일	The man / was meeting / his client. 남자가 / 만나는 중이었다 / 그의 고객을
미래진행 will be + -ing	미래의 특정 시점에 진행되고 있을 일	The man / will be meeting / his client. 남자가 / 만나고 있을 것이다 / 그의 고객을

● 시점과 시점을 잇는 완료 시제

현재완료 have / has + p.p.	불특정한 과거에 시작되어 현재까지 계속되는 일	Neil / has worked / here / for five years. 닐은 / (지금까지) 일해 왔다 / 이곳에서 / 5년 동안
과거완료 had + p.p.	과거의 시점보다 더 이전에 일어난 일	Neil / had worked / as a deliveryman / before he joined this company. 닐은 / (그 당시) 일했었다 / 배달원으로 / 이 회사에 입사하기 전에
미래완료 will have + p.p.	미래의 시점에 끝나거나 그 시점까지 영향을 미치는 일	Neil / will have worked / here / for 10 years / next month. 닐은 / 일하게 될 것이다 / 여기시 / 10년 동안 / 다음 달이면

● 기초 QUIZ ●

1. 다음 시제의 이름을 쓰세요.

   1) is meeting _____   2) have met _____

'be + -ing'는 진행, 'have + p.p.'는
완료 시제입니다.
정답: 1) 현재진행 2) 현재완료

2. 다음 동사를 미래완료 형태로 바꿔보세요.

   1) finish _____   2) make _____

미래완료 시제는 'will
have + p.p.'입니다.   정답: 1) will
have finished, 2) will have made

단순 시제와 진행 시제

① 현재 시제

현재 시제 시간 표현	always 항상	often 자주, 흔히	usually 보통, 대개
	frequently 빈번히, 자주	generally 일반적으로	regularly 정기적으로
	every 매 ~, ~마다	now/currently/presently 현재, 지금	

- John / **usually** / leaves / the office / at 6:30 P.M. 존은 / 보통 / 떠난다 / 사무실을 / 오후 6시 30분에

　　　　습관　　　현재 시제

② 과거 시제

과거 시제 시간 표현	yesterday 어제	last week[month, year] 지난주[달, 해]
	시간 표현 + ago ~ 전에	previously 이전에

- We / hired / temporary workers / **last month**. 우리는 / 고용했다 / 임시 직원들을 / 지난달에

　　과거 시제　　　　　　　　　　　과거 시점

③ 미래 시제

미래 시제 시간 표현	tomorrow 내일	next week[month, year] 다음 주[달, 해]
	shortly/soon 곧	this (coming) Thursday 오는 목요일에
	the upcoming year 다음 해	at the end of + 미래 시점 ~의 말에

- Mr. Kim / will resign / as president / **next month**. 김 씨는 / 사임할 것이다 / 사장직에서 / 다음 달

　　　미래 시제　　　　　　　　미래 시점

④ 현재 / 과거 / 미래진행 시제

진행 시제들도 시간의 단서들에 맞는 be동사의 현재, 과거, 미래 형태를 갖습니다.

- Highway 12 / is **currently** undergoing repairs. 〈현재진행〉

12번 고속도로는 / 현재 수리되고 있는 중이다

cf. 현재진행 시제가 가까운 미래를 표현하기도 합니다.

　We / are arriving / at our destination / on schedule.

　우리는 / 도착할 것이다 / 목적지에 / 예정대로

- The executives / were discussing / the expansion project / **yesterday**. 〈과거진행〉

임원들은 / 논의 중이었다 / 확장 계획을 / 어제

- The technician / will be fixing / the heaters / **tomorrow morning**. 〈미래진행〉

그 기술자는 / 수리하고 있을 것이다 / 난방기들을 / 내일 아침에

ETS 문제로 **훈련하기**

 STEP 01 (A), (B) 중 알맞은 것을 고르세요.

1 Mr. Hirose -------- at First Street Financial five years ago.
(A) works (B) worked

2 The factory president --------sometime during the next three years.
(A) will retire (B) retires

3 At 9 P.M. last night, Mr. Holbroke ------- to his client on the phone.
(A) was talking (B) is talking

4 Cartford Museum opens at 9 A.M. and -------- at 5 P.M. on weekdays.
(A) closed (B) closes

5 The visitors ------- touring our production facilities at 10 A.M. tomorrow.
(A) were (B) will be

6 Aviaty Airlines ------- free snacks on all of its flights starting next January.
(A) will be offering (B) are offered

 STEP 02 빈칸에 가장 알맞은 것을 고르세요.

7 Mei Watanabe ------- anticipates changes in consumer behavior with surprising accuracy.
(A) very
(B) early
(C) fast
(D) often

8 Next month the employee cafeteria -------- closing at 2:00.
(A) was (B) are
(C) has been (D) will be

9 Mr. Melniczak ------- the minutes of this afternoon's client meeting before the end of the day.
(A) distribute
(B) to be distributed
(C) will distribute
(D) has been distributing

10 Ms. Diaz ------- a template last year that can be reused for the new database project.
(A) create (B) created
(C) has created (D) will create

| WORDS | 1 financial 금융의, 재정의 2 sometime 언젠가 3 client 고객, 의뢰인 on the phone 전화로 4 on weekdays 평일에, 주중에 5 tour 견학하다, 둘러보다 facility 설비, 시설 6 snack 스낵, 간식 7 anticipate 예상하다 behavior 행동 accuracy 정확(성) 8 employee cafeteria 직원 구내 식당 9 distribute 배포하다 minutes 회의록, 의사록 10 reuse 재사용하다

✎ 완료 시제

① 현재완료 : have[has] + p.p.

현재 완료에 자주 쓰이는 시간 표현	for/over/in the last[past] + 기간 지난 ~ 동안에 since + 시점 ~ 이래로, ~부터 recently/lately 최근에 just 방금 already 이미 yet 아직

- I / have worked / for this company / **since 2010**.
  나는 / 근무해 오고 있다 / 이 회사에 / 2010년부터

② 과거완료 : had + p.p.

과거완료에 자주 쓰이는 시간 표현	before + 주어 + 동사의 과거형 ~이 …하기 전에 by the time + 주어 + 동사의 과거형 ~이 …했을 때쯤

- **Before I arrived** / at the airport, / I had confirmed / my flight reservation.
  　　　　　　　 ② 공항 도착 (과거)　　　　　 ① 공항 도착 전의 일 (과거완료)
  나는 도착하기 전에 / 공항에 / 확인했다 / 내 비행기 예약을

  = After I had confirmed / my flight reservation, / I arrived / at the airport.
  　　 ① 공항 도착 전 (과거완료)　　　　　　　　　　 ② 공항 도착 (과거)
  나는 확인한 후에 / 내 비행기 예약을 / 도착했다 / 공항에

③ 미래완료 : will have + p.p.

미래완료에 자주 쓰이는 시간 표현	by + 미래 시점 ~까지 by the time + 주어 + 동사의 현재형 ~이 …할 때까지

- The team / will have finished / the project / **by the time the CEO returns**.
  　　　　　　　　　　　　 미래에 완료되는 일
  그 팀은 / 끝낼 것이다 / 프로젝트를 / CEO가 돌아올 때까지는

ETS 문제로 **훈련하기**

 STEP 01

(A), (B) 중 알맞은 것을 고르세요.

1 The warehouse ------- used to store Yetla Fertilizer since 1999.

(A) was   (B) has been

2 The 10:17 A.M. train ------- already left before Mr. Abaki's team arrived at the station.

(A) has   (B) had

3 The manufacturer ------- the warranty on its latest camera models by twelve months.

(A) extend   (B) has extended

4 Feltlove Charity ------- enough money to build a library by the end of the year.

(A) will have raised (B) have raised

5 Several Tiger Gym health clubs ------- recently in the city center.

(A) have opened
(B) will have opened

6 Ms. Jameson has ------- begun working on resolving the problems with the client.

(A) quick   (B) already

 STEP 02

빈칸에 가장 알맞은 것을 고르세요.

7 For the last fifteen years, Matlock, Inc., has ------- among the nation's leading toy manufacturers.

(A) rank   (B) ranked
(C) ranking   (D) ranks

8 By the time the technicians discovered the computer problem, several files -------.

(A) are disappearing
(B) will have disappeared
(C) disappear
(D) had disappeared

9 Because the warranty ------- already, the store is not obligated to replace the product.

(A) is expiring   (B) will expire
(C) expires   (D) has expired

10 Arten Publishing ------- an average annual growth of 7 percent since it went public twenty years ago.

(A) experiences
(B) has experienced
(C) will experience
(D) experiencing

| WORDS | 1 warehouse (물류) 창고 store 보관하다 fertilizer 비료 2 station 역, 정거장 3 warranty 품질 보증 latest 최신의 4 charity 자선 단체, 구호 단체 5 several 여럿의 recently 최근에 6 work on ~에 애쓰다 resolve 해결하다 7 leading 선두적인 8 by the time ~할 무렵에 technician 기사, 기술자 9 be obligated to ~할 의무가 있다 replace 교환하다 expire 만료되다, 만기가 되다 10 average 평균(의) annual growth 연간 성장 go public 상장하다, 공개하다

아래 토익 필수 어휘들을 표현과 함께 익혀 보세요.

reduce	줄이다, 감소시키다	indicate	~임을 나타내다
attract	끌어들이다, 유치하다	purchase	구입하다
handle	다루다, 처리하다	appear	~인 것 같다; 출연하다
consume	소비하다	register	등록하다 (for)
postpone	미루다, 연기하다	approve	승인하다
load	(짐을) 싣다	deliver	배송하다
promote	홍보하다; 승진시키다	assemble	조립하다
permit	허가하다	produce	생산하다
decline	거절하다	equip	장비를 갖추다
schedule	일정을 잡다	continue	지속하다, 계속하다

어휘 표현 익히기 위의 단어들을 외우고 아래 표현을 완성해 보세요.

1. _____ a music concert — 음악회를 **홍보하다**
2. be _____ted to park in the area — 그 지역에 주차하는 것이 **허용되다**
3. _____ the meeting — 회의를 **미루다**
4. _____ boxes onto a truck — 상자들을 트럭에 **싣다**
5. _____ new customers — 신규 고객들을 **유치하다**
6. _____ a product — 제품을 **구입하다**
7. _____ the price — 가격을 **인하하다**
8. _____ for the course — 그 강좌에 **등록하다**
9. _____ that the medicine is effective — 그 약이 효과가 있다는 것을 **나타내다**
10. _____ customer complaints — 고객 불만 사항을 **처리하다**

| ANSWERS | 1. promote 2. permit 3. postpone 4. load 5. attract
6. purchase 7. reduce 8. register 9. indicate 10. handle

ETS 문제로 **훈련하기**

STEP 01

(A), (B) 중 알맞은 것을 고르세요.

1 These chemicals are hazardous and should be ------- with care.
(A) handled
(B) dislocated

2 The new botanic garden will ------- tourists during the summer.
(A) appeal
(B) attract

3 The shipping department ------- products onto twenty trucks this morning.
(A) loaded
(B) served

4 For security reasons, only authorized personnel are ------- to use this room.
(A) permitted
(B) written

STEP 02

빈칸에 가장 알맞은 것을 고르세요.

5 Michael Keller, president of Teekman Financial, ------- on a special broadcast of *The Frances Ting Show*.
(A) appeared
(B) seemed
(C) approved
(D) numbered

6 The new projections show that we will need to ------- next year's production by 15 percent.
(A) decline
(B) consume
(C) arise
(D) reduce

7 All construction materials will be ------- to the loading dock at the rear of the building.
(A) produced
(B) assembled
(C) equipped
(D) delivered

8 Because of poor weather conditions, the outdoor concert has been ------- until next week.
(A) expected
(B) scheduled
(C) continued
(D) postponed

| WORDS | 1 chemical 화학 제품[약품] hazardous 위험한 with care 주의해서 2 botanic garden 식물원 3 shipping 발송, 배송 4 security 보안 authorized personnel 인가 받은 직원 5 appear 출연하다 6 projection 전망, 예측 7 construction material 건축 자재 loading dock 하역장 rear 뒤쪽 8 weather condition 기상 상황 outdoor 야외의

1 Businesses on Ellory Avenue ------- early yesterday to allow work crews to repave the street.

(A) are closed
(B) to close
(C) closing
(D) closed

2 MO Hardware ------- free flashlights to the first 50 customers during its grand opening next Friday.

(A) is offering
(B) having offered
(C) was offered
(D) to offer

3 Ms. Choi described the proposed project while she ------- a lunch meeting with the new clients.

(A) was having
(B) having
(C) has
(D) will have

4 Last year the quality control team ------- several new policies designed to improve efficiency.

(A) implementation
(B) implements
(C) implemented
(D) implementing

5 Effective next Monday, Ms. García ------- responsible for keeping track of staff vacation time.

(A) was
(B) will be
(C) to be
(D) had been

6 Dr. Suzuki arrived for the ceremony on time even though her train ------- twenty minutes late.

(A) is leaving
(B) will leave
(C) to leave
(D) had left

7 With advance notice, the restaurant is ------- able to accommodate parties of ten or more.

(A) ahead
(B) currently
(C) enough
(D) before

8 Seeking new sources of income, many regional orchards ------- catering to tourists in the last few years.

(A) will begin
(B) have begun
(C) will have begun
(D) to begin

9 The lights suddenly went out while the audience ------- a musical performance of *Man of La Mancha*.

(A) was watching
(B) is watching
(C) watches
(D) will watch

10 After Noriko Tamaguchi ------- the skills for her job, her manager asked her to help train new employees.

(A) is mastering
(B) has mastered
(C) masters
(D) had mastered

Questions 11-14 refer to the following article.

TEMA, GHANA (10 April)—Ghana Aluminium Company (GAC) is pleased to announce the appointment of Madhu Quaye as chief operating officer of its Mozambique division effective 1 July. His 30 years of experience in the ------- made him the obvious choice for the position,
11
according to company spokesperson Gladys Ayambe. Mr. Quaye graduated with a master of science degree in mining engineering from the National University of Ghana. He then -------
12
his career as a process design engineer at Accra Mining Industries (AMI). Two decades ago, he left AMI for GAC. ------- . In Mozambique, Mr. Quaye will oversee day-to-day operations at
13
Maputo Aluminium, Inc., over ------- GAC has acquired a controlling interest.
14

11 (A) license
(B) industry
(C) outset
(D) program

12 (A) began
(B) had begun
(C) was beginning
(D) will begin

13 (A) The company also has a division in
Guinea.
(B) He developed an interest in mining at a
young age.
(C) Most recently, he has served as GAC's
vice president of development.
(D) The downsizing came after reports of
huge financial losses.

14 (A) when
(B) that
(C) what
(D) which

| WORDS | **1** work crew 작업반 repave 재포장하다 **2** hardware 하드웨어, 철물(류) flashlight 손전등 grand opening 개장, 개점 **3** proposed 제안된, 발의된 **4** quality control 품질 관리 implement 시행하다 efficiency 효율성 **5** effective 유효한, 발효되는 keep track of (지속적으로) ~을 파악하다 **6** ceremony 기념식 on time 제시간에 **7** advance 사전의 accommodate 수용하다 **8** sources of income 수입원 orchard 과수원 cater 음식을 제공하다 **9** go out (불·전깃불이) 나가다 **10** train 훈련[교육]시키다 master 숙달하다 **11-14** appointment 임명 chief operating officer 최고 운영 책임자 spokesperson 대변인 master of science degree (이학) 석사 학위 mining engineering 광산 공학 decade 10년 day-to-day operation 일상 업무 acquire 획득하다, 얻다 controlling interest 지배 지분(회사의 경영권 행사에 충분한 주식 보유) downsizing 규모(인원) 축소, 감원 financial loss 재정 손실

UNIT 08

능동태와 수동태

무료인강 바로가기

입장 차이를 나타내는 태!

주어가 동작을 행하는 입장인지 당하는 입장인지를
나타내는 동사 형태를 '태'라고 합니다. 주어가 동작을 스스로 행하면
능동태, 주어가 동작을 당하는 입장이면 수동태로 표현합니다.

He pushes a cart.
A cart is pushed by him.

그는 카트를 민다.
카트를 미는 능동적 입장

카트는 그에 의해 밀린다.
밀리는 수동적 입장

위 예문에서 보듯 능동태는 '누가, 무엇을, 어떻게 했는지'를 나타내는 반면, 수동태는 '누구에
의해' '어떻게 되었는지'를 언급합니다. 따라서 능동태와 수동태 중 어떤 태를 쓸지는 문장의
주어가 '하는' 입장인지, '당하는' 입장인지 판단하면 됩니다. 또한 위 두 번째 수동태 예문에서
주어(카트)는 되는(밀리는) 입장이므로 동사 뒤에 '무엇을'에 해당하는 말이 따로 없습니다. 토
익에서 수동태는 문법뿐 아니라 독해 파트에서도 필수적인 부분이니 형태와 의미 모두 잘 익
혀두시기 바랍니다.

● 능동태를 수동태로 바꾸기

동사의 수동 형태는 〈be + p.p.〉이며 능동태가 수동태로 바뀌는 과정은 아래와 같습니다.

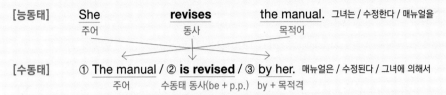

[능동태]　　She　　　　**revises**　　　　the manual. 그녀는 / 수정한다 / 매뉴얼을
　　　　　　주어　　　　　동사　　　　　　목적어

[수동태]　① The manual / ② **is revised** / ③ by her. 매뉴얼은 / 수정된다 / 그녀에 의해서
　　　　　　주어　　　수동태 동사(be + p.p.)　 by + 목적격

① 능동태의 목적어(the manual)를 수동태의 주어로 보내기
② 능동태의 동사(revises)를 〈be + p.p.〉 형태로 주어와 수 일치시켜 is revised로 바꾸기
③ 능동태의 주어(She)를 〈by + 목적격 대명사〉의 형태로 by her로 바꾸기

● 수동태의 형태

수동태는 현재, 과거, 미래가 있으며 동작의 주체가 중요하지 않을 때는 by 이하는 생략 가능해요. 미래 수동태의 will 대신 다른 조동사를 쓸 수도 있어요.

현재 수동태	과거 수동태	미래 수동태
am / are / is + p.p.	was / were + p.p.	will be + p.p.

The room / is prepared. 객실이 / 준비되어 있다
　　　　　 현재 수동태

The room / was prepared. 객실이 / 준비되어 있었다
　　　　　 과거 수동태

The room / will be prepared. 객실이 / 준비될 것이다
　　　　　 미래 수동태

The room / can be prepared. 객실이 / 준비될 수 있다
　　　　　 조동사 + 수동태

The room / should be prepared. 객실이 / 준비되어야 한다
　　　　　 조동사 + 수동태

기초 QUIZ

1. 다음 문장을 수동태로 고쳐보세요.
   Scientists / wrote / a paper. 과학자들이 / 썼다 / 논문을
   A paper / _____ _____ / by scientists.
   논문이 / 쓰여졌다 / 과학자들에 의해서

   과거 시제 동사를 〈be + p.p.〉 형태의 수동태로 만들려면 be동사를 was나 were로 바꾸면 됩니다. 　정답: was written

2. 다음 동사를 수동태로 바꿔보세요.
   • change → 과거 수동태: _____ 미래 수동태: _____

   수동태 형태 〈be + p.p.〉에서 be동사를 과거, 미래로 씁니다. 정답: was / were changed, will be changed

✎ 능동태와 수동태의 구분

① 단순 수동태 be + p.p.

능동태는 동사 뒤에 목적어(명사)가 있으나, 수동태는 동사 뒤에 목적어가 없거나 수식어가 옵니다. 수동태 뒤에는 행위자 by 이하를 생략 가능하며 문맥에 따라 by 이외의 다양한 전치사가 쓰일 수 있어요.(p.108 ② 참조)

• The maintenance staff / (inspected, ~~was inspected~~) / the assembly line.
　　　　　　　　　　　　　　　능동　　　　　　　　　　　　목적어

　정비 직원들은 / 점검했다 / 조립 라인을　　　　　　　→ 수동태 뒤에는 목적어가 오지 못합니다.

• All the fabrics / (~~manufactured~~, were manufactured) / [in South America (by people)].
　　　　　　　　　　　　　　　　　　수동　　　　　　　　　[수식어]

　모든 직물들은 / 제조되었다 / 남미에서　　　　　　　→ 수동태 뒤에 수식어나 'by + 행위자'가 옵니다.

② 진행 수동태 be being p.p.

진행 수동태는 진행형(be + -ing)과 수동태(be + p.p.)가 결합된 형태로 '~되고 있는 중이다'란 의미로 해석됩니다. 종류는 현재진행 수동과 과거진행 수동 두 가지가 있으며, 미래진행 수동태는 없어요.

[능동태]　　Mr. Kim / is cleaning / the room. 김 씨가 / 청소하는 중이다 / 그 방을
　　　　　　　　　　　　　　　　　목적어

[수동태]　　The room / is being cleaned / [by Mr. Kim]. 방이 / 청소되고 있는 중이다 / 김 씨에 의해 〈현재진행 수동태〉
　　　　　　　= is being + is cleaned　　　[수식어]
　　　　　　　　현재진행형　　수동태

③ 완료 수동태 have been p.p.

완료 수동태는 완료 동사(have + p.p.)와 수동태(be + p.p.)가 결합된 형태로 '~되어 왔다 / ~되었다'란 의미로 해석됩니다. 현재완료 수동태, 과거완료 수동태, 미래완료 수동태가 있으며 만들어지는 과정은 아래와 같아요.

[능동태]　　The manager / has changed / the room. 매니저가 / 바꾸었다 / 객실을
　　　　　　　　　　　　　　　　　　　목적어

[수동태]　　The room / has been changed / [by the manager]. 객실이 / 바뀌었다 / 매니저에 의해 〈현재완료 수동태〉
　　　　　　　= has been + was changed　　　[수식어]
　　　　　　　　현재완료형　　수동태

• The room / had been changed / [before we came]. 〈과거완료 수동태〉
　객실이 / 바뀌어 있었다 / 우리가 오기 전에

• The room / will have been changed / [by tomorrow]. 〈미래완료 수동태〉
　객실이 / 바뀌어 있을 것이다 / 내일까지는

ETS 문제로 **훈련하기**

STEP 01 (A), (B) 중 알맞은 것을 고르세요.

1 Jindo Industrial ------- a $15 million addition to its Singapore factory last week.

(A) opened　　(B) was opened

2 The Phaliya Hotel is ------- in the Bangkok business district.

(A) locating　　(B) located

3 Companies can always ------- better marketing strategies.

(A) develop　　(B) be developed

4 The use of flash photography is ------- in this building.

(A) prohibited
(B) prohibiting

5 An increase in competition last year ------- a significant drop in sales.

(A) has caused　　(B) is caused

6 The computer training guidelines were ------- by Rita Chen and Deborah Woo.

(A) revising　　(B) revised

STEP 02 빈칸에 가장 알맞은 것을 고르세요.

7 The career fair will be ------- on July 2 in the Human Resources building.

(A) holds　　(B) holding
(C) hold　　(D) held

8 The committee unanimously ------- Anuja Ganguli's *To the Mountain* as the Book of the Year.

(A) select　　(B) selecting
(C) selected　　(D) was selected

9 Your belongings should ------- safe at all times when you travel around the tourist attractions.

(A) keep　　(B) kept
(C) be kept　　(D) be keeping

10 Please visit Klara Cosmetics on Bauer Street while the East Avenue location is being -------.

(A) renovates　　(B) renovated
(C) renovating　　(D) renovations

| WORDS | **1** addition 추가된 것, 증축물 **2** business district 상업 지구 **3** strategy 전략, 계획 **4** photography 사진 촬영 (기법) **5** competition 경쟁 significant 커다란, 중대한 **6** guideline 가이드라인, 지침 **7** career fair 취업 박람회 Human Resources 인사부 **8** unanimously 만장일치로 **9** belongings 소지품 attraction (관광) 명소 **10** renovate 개조[보수]하다

✎ 주의해야 할 수동태

① 자동사의 수동태

1형식과 2형식 자동사는 뒤에 목적어가 올 수 없으므로 수동태를 만들 수 없어요.

1형식 **동사**	go 가다	come 오다	arrive 도착하다	rise 오르다
	expire 만료되다	take place 개최되다		

2형식 **동사**	be ~이다	become ~이 되다	seem ~처럼 보이다	remain ~인 채로 남다

- The train / (arrived, ~~was arrived~~). 기차가 / 도착했다
- The regional meeting / (will take place, ~~was taken place~~) / on Thursday.
  지역 회의는 / 개최될 것이다 / 목요일에
- The factory / (remains, ~~is remained~~) operational.
  그 공장은 / 여전히 운영 중이다

② by 이외의 전치사를 쓰는 수동태 표현

be p.p. with	be satisfied[pleased] with ~에 만족하다	be concerned with ~에 관심이 있다
	be equipped with ~을 갖추다	be associated with ~와 연관되다
be p.p. in	be interested in ~에 흥미가 있다	be involved in ~에 개입하다
be p.p. at	be surprised at ~에 놀라다	be disappointed at ~에 실망하다
be p.p. to	be exposed to ~에 노출되다	be related to ~와 관계가 있다
be p.p. for	be known for ~로 유명하다	be scheduled for ~로 예정되어 있다

- The lab / is equipped / with the advanced tools.
  그 실험실은 / 갖추고 있다 / 고급 장비들을
- Mr. Barkley / is interested / in starting his business.
  바클리 씨는 / 관심이 있다 / 자신의 사업을 시작하는 데
- Shareholders / are surprised / at the earnings report.
  주주들은 / 놀랐다 / 수익 보고에
- These policies / are related / to accounting.
  이 정책들은 / 관련이 있다 / 회계와
- Staff members / at the Kubla Khan Hotel / are known / for being especially helpful.
  직원들은 / 쿠블라 칸 호텔의 / 알려져 있다 / 특히 기꺼이 돕는 것으로

ETS 문제로 **훈련하기**

PART 5 | UNIT 08

STEP 01

(A), (B) 중 알맞은 것을 고르세요.

1 Skin ages fast if it is exposed ------- the sun too much.

(A) to
(B) with

2 Momoko Masaoka's paintings of the sea are inspired ------- her childhood in the Matsushima region.

(A) by
(B) to

3 One of the most promising candidates was ------- with the company's competitors.

(A) embarrassed
(B) associated

4 The marketing department is somewhat related ------- the advertising department.

(A) to
(B) by

5 Employees were ------- at the board's decision to make Ms. Vasilev the new vice president.

(A) surprising
(B) surprised

6 All orders placed online will be ------- from our Santa Cruz warehouse within 24 hours.

(A) shipped
(B) arrived

STEP 02

빈칸에 가장 알맞은 것을 고르세요.

7 Ms. Drake ------- with the service the subcontractor provided for Ormsby Industries.

(A) satisfies
(B) was satisfied
(C) will satisfy
(D) satisfied

8 Highvale Restaurant is ------- to using only the freshest ingredients in all of its dishes.

(A) commit
(B) committed
(C) to commit
(D) committing

9 The board of directors' meeting is ------- for the first Monday of every month.

(A) schedule
(B) schedules
(C) scheduled
(D) scheduling

10 The newly renovated laboratory is equipped ------- state-of-the-art research equipment.

(A) by
(B) with
(C) in
(D) to

| WORDS | **1** age 늙다, 노화되다 expose 노출시키다 **2** inspire 영감을 주다 childhood 유년시절 region 지역 **3** promising candidate 유력한 후보자 competitor 경쟁자, 경쟁업체 **4** somewhat 다소, 약간 advertising 광고 **5** board (of directors) 이사회 decision 결정 vice president 부사장 **6** ship 발송하다 warehouse (물류) 창고 **7** subcontractor 하도급 업체 **8** ingredient 재료, 구성 요소 dish 요리 **9** schedule 일정을 잡다 **10** newly 새로, 최근에 renovate 개조하다, 혁신하다 state-of-the-art 최첨단의

정답 및 해설 p.82

109

아래 토익 필수 어휘들을 표현과 함께 익혀 보세요.

access	접속하다, 접근하다	evaluate	평가하다
collaborate	협업하다 (with)	prevent	막다, 예방하다
restore	복구하다	specialize	전문으로 하다 (in)
complete	완료하다; 작성하다	feature	특징으로 하다
enforce	집행하다, 강요하다	report	보고하다
guarantee	보장하다	advise	조언하다
inquire	문의하다 (about)	seek	찾다, 구하다
recommend	추천하다	replace	교체하다, 대신하다
renovate	수리하다	organize	조직하다
apply	지원하다, 신청하다	contact	연락하다

어휘 표현 익히기   위의 단어들을 외우고 아래 표현을 완성해 보세요.

1. _____ your online bank account   당신의 온라인 은행 계좌에 **접속하다**
2. _____ in art lesson   미술 수업을 **전문으로 하다**
3. _____ historic sites   유적지를 **복원하다**
4. _____ all the courses   (교육 등의) 모든 과정을 **마치다**
5. _____ a rule on all visitors   모든 방문자들에게 규칙을 **적용하다**
6. _____ next-day delivery   익일 배송을 **보장하다**
7. _____ making a reservation   예약하는 것을 **추천하다**
8. _____ sculptures and paintings   조각품과 그림을 **특징으로 하다**
9. _____ a significant rise   상당한 증가를 **보고하다**
10. _____ an experienced designer   경력이 있는 디자이너를 **구하다**

| ANSWERS | 1. access 2. specialize 3. restore 4. complete 5. enforce
6. guarantee 7. recommend 8. feature 9. report 10. seek

ETS 문제로 훈련하기

STEP 01

(A), (B) 중 알맞은 것을 고르세요.

1 All employees are required to ------- annual evaluations every December.

(A) complete   (B) agree

2 The accountants have been authorized to ------- our databases.

(A) solve   (B) access

3 It will be difficult to ------- the safety regulations without effective monitoring.

(A) enforce   (B) imply

4 Markos Industries is pleased to ------- a 10 percent rise in quarterly earnings.

(A) report   (B) advise

STEP 02

빈칸에 가장 알맞은 것을 고르세요.

5 Companies often ------- with their contractors to find solutions to shared concerns.

(A) collaborate   (B) evaluate
(C) conduct   (D) support

6 Nova Appliances ------- that all of its washing machines are free of mechanical defects.

(A) prevents   (B) organizes
(C) controls   (D) guarantees

7 The popular television series *On the Fences* ------- a very talented cast.

(A) applies   (B) senses
(C) marks   (D) features

8 The Rogers family of retail stores is ------- experienced managers for several northeast locations.

(A) seeking   (B) looking
(C) entering   (D) inquiring

| WORDS | **1** require 요구하다 annual 매년의, 연간의 evaluation 평가, 사정 **2** accountant 회계사 authorize 권한을 부여하다 **3** safety regulation 안전 규정 effective 효과적인 monitoring 감시, 관찰 **4** quarterly earnings 분기별 수익 **5** contractor 계약 업체, 도급 업체 solution 해결책, 해법 shared 공유하는, 공통된 concern 관심사 **6** appliance 가전제품 washing machine 세탁기 free of ~이 없는 mechanical defect 기계적 결함 **7** talented 재능이 있는 cast 출연자들 **8** retail store 소매점 location (영업) 장소

1 Payment on the latest shipment is due and must ------- within five days.

(A) to receive
(B) receive
(C) be received
(D) received

2 The new lighting fixtures arrived this morning and will be ------- tomorrow afternoon.

(A) installed
(B) installing
(C) installment
(D) installation

3 If you correspond with the company president regarding this matter, a copy of your letter should ------- to his secretary as well.

(A) send
(B) sent
(C) to send
(D) be sent

4 Fluctuations in the price of corn usually ------- to changes in the region's weather.

(A) tied
(B) can be tied
(C) will have tied
(D) are able to tie

5 The new advertisement has been -------- to reflect your company's image.

(A) customized
(B) customize
(C) customizing
(D) customizes

6 Kinghorn Publicity Press ------- for creating advertisements that leave a strong impression on viewers.

(A) will know
(B) is known
(C) to know
(D) has known

7 Nearly half of the Scortflex Corporation's distribution centers ------- in major coastal cities.

(A) are situating
(B) situate
(C) are situated
(D) situates

8 Last week, senior managers at Alameda Hardware ------- to begin a review of safety procedures.

(A) were instructed
(B) instructed
(C) instructing
(D) will instruct

9 An exhibition of Andrea Lenin's paintings ------- in the Noya Gallery.

(A) holds
(B) has held
(C) is holding
(D) is being held

10 The delegation will depart from the embassy at 9 A.M. and ------- to the airport by the Minister of Sports.

(A) will accompany
(B) accompanied
(C) will be accompanied
(D) being accompanied

Questions 11-14 refer to the following letter.

June 30

Peter Mazzie
14 Wyndmoor Court, Apartment A
Edinburgh, EH5 2TU

Dear Mr. Mazzie:

Your subscription to *Financial News Weekly* will expire on October 30. That's still four months away, but if you ------- before July 21, we will add one extra month to your subscription. All you have to do is complete and return the enclosed card. You do not need to enclose your ------- at this time. We will send you an invoice, and you can send your money later. ------- . You will not miss a ------- copy of *Financial News Weekly*, and you will receive an extra month for free!

Sincerely,

Sharon Oakman
Circulation Manager

11 (A) renew
(B) renewing
(C) had renewed
(D) will be renewed

12 (A) rent
(B) bill
(C) résumé
(D) payment

13 (A) Carry the card at all times.
(B) So mail the card today.
(C) We have charged your credit card.
(D) Your next copy will arrive shortly.

14 (A) single
(B) recognized
(C) treatable
(D) lonely

| WORDS | 1 payment 결제, 대금 shipment 수송품 be due 결제일이 되다 2 lighting fixture 조명 기구[장치] 3 correspond with ~와 서신을 주고받다 copy 복사(본), (서류 등의) 한 부 4 fluctuation (급격한) 변동 tie 결부시키다 5 reflect 반영하다 6 impression 인상 viewer 시청자 7 nearly 거의 distribution 유통 major 주요한 coastal 해안의 situate 위치시키다 8 hardware 철물 procedure 절차 instruct 지시하다 9 exhibition 전시회 10 delegation 대표단 depart 출발하다 embassy 대사관 minister 장관, 각료 11-14 subscription 구독 expire 만료되다 extra 추가의 complete 완료하다, 작성하다 return 반송하다 enclose 동봉하다 invoice 송장, 청구서 miss 놓치다 circulation (신문·잡지의) 보급, 판매 부수 at all times 항상 charge 청구하다 shortly 곧

UNIT 09

to부정사와 동명사

무료인강 바로가기

만능 재주꾼 to부정사 vs. 명사로 변신한 동사, 동명사!

〈to + 동사원형〉 형태인 to부정사는 문장 내에서 명사, 형용사, 부사의 역할을 합니다.
역할이 하나로 고정되어 있지 않다고 해서 '부정사(不定詞)'라는 이름이 붙었어요.
동명사는 동사에 -ing가 붙어 명사처럼 쓰이는 말로, '~하는 것, ~하기'라는 뜻을 나타냅니다.

I want <u>to take</u> a taxi.
<u>Walking</u> makes you feel better.

나는 택시를 <u>탄다</u> 원한다.
  동사

나는 택시 <u>타기를</u> 원한다.
  동사를 명사로

위 예문에서 보듯이 우리말에서도 하나의 문장에 두 개의 동사를 그대로 쓸 수는 없어요. 문맥에 맞게 하나의 동사를 다른 형태로 바꿔야 합니다. 영어에서도 마찬가지로 동사를 쓰임에 맞게 바꾸는데 대표적인 것이 바로 to부정사입니다. to부정사는 명사, 형용사, 부사라는 여러 가지 역할을 하는 만큼 문장에서 활용도가 아주 높답니다. 반면, 동사가 변해 명사 역할만 하는 것이 동명사입니다. 하지만 둘 다 공통점이 있어요. to부정사와 동명사 모두 동사가 변해 새로운 쓰임새가 생겼지만 동사로는 쓸 수 없다는 점 꼭 기억하세요.

● to부정사의 형태

to부정사는 〈to + 동사원형〉의 형태를 갖습니다. to부정사의 의미를 부정할 때는 to 앞에 not이나 never를 붙입니다. 또한 to부정사의 주어가 따로 있을 때는 to부정사 앞에 〈for + 목적격〉 형태를 써서 '의미상 주어'를 나타냅니다.

기본형: 〈to + 동사원형〉	He / decided / to take the subway. 그는 / 결정했다 / 지하철을 타기로
부정형: 〈not[never] + to + 동사원형〉	He / decided / not to take the subway. 그는 / 결정했다 / 지하철을 타지 않기로
to부정사의 의미상 주어	This book / is hard / for me / to understand. 　문장의 주어　　　　　　to부정사의 주어: 이해하는 주체 이 책은 / 어렵다 / 내가 / 이해하기에

● 동명사의 형태

동명사의 기본적인 형태는 〈동사원형 + -ing〉입니다. 동명사의 의미를 부정할 때는 to부정사와 마찬가지로 앞에 not이나 never를 붙입니다.

기본형: 〈동사원형 + -ing〉	She / is afraid / of making speeches. 그녀는 / 두려워한다 / 연설하는 것을
부정형: 〈not[never] + 동명사〉	Kate / apologized / for not coming to the meeting. 케이트는 / 사과했다 / 회의에 오지 않은 것에 대해

● 기초 QUIZ ●

다음 중 알맞은 것을 고르세요.

1. The restaurant / recommends / (reserve, reserving) a table.
   그 식당은 / 추천합니다 / 테이블을 예약하는 것을

2. She / is afraid of / (to make, making) speeches.
   그녀는 / 두려워한다 / 연설을 하는 것을

문장의 동사인 recommends가 있으므로 동사가 또 올 수 없습니다. 따라서, 명사처럼 목적어 역할을 하는 동명사가 와야 합니다.
정답: reserving

전치사 뒤에는 to부정사가 올 수 없습니다. 정답: making

✎ to부정사의 쓰임

① 명사 (~하는 것, ~하기)

[주어]
To handle a budget deficit / is not easy.   예산 적자를 해결하는 것은 / 쉽지 않다

= It is not easy / (for us) to handle a budget deficit.
　가주어　　　　　　　　　　　　진주어

→ to부정사가 주어인 문장은 'It(가주어) ~ to부정사(진주어)'로 바꾸어 쓸 수 있습니다.

[목적어]
The purchasing manager / **agreed** / to order appliances.
구매 부장은 / 동의했다 / 전자제품을 주문하는 것을

We / found / it difficult / to keep up with the record sales.
　　　　　가목적어　　　　　　　진목적어
우리는 / 알게 되었다 / 힘들다는 것을 / 작년의 매출 기록을 계속 유지시키는 것이

to부정사를 목적어로 취하는 동사	agree 동의하다	refuse[decline] 거절하다
	decide[choose] 결정하다	want[wish, hope] 원하다, 희망하다
	plan 계획하다	expect 기대하다

[보어]
Ms. Watson / appears / to be the next speaker.
왓슨 씨가 / ~ 같다 / 다음 연설자인 것

② 형용사 (~할, ~하는)

to부정사는 형용사 역할을 하기도 하며 주로 아래와 같은 명사를 뒤에서 수식해요.

way 방법	attempt 시도	effort 노력	ability 능력	decision 결정

[명사 수식]
Consultants / are offering / a way / to maximize profits.
컨설턴트들은 / 제시하고 있다 / 방안을 / 수익을 극대화할

③ 부사 (~하기 위하여 등)

to부정사는 부사의 역할을 하기도 하며, 이 경우 동사, 형용사, 문장 등을 수식합니다.

[동사 수식]
Brochures / were sent / to describe product features.
브로슈어가 / 발송되었습니다 / 제품의 특징을 설명하기 위해

[형용사 수식]
The theater / is proud / to present more performances.
그 극장은 / 자부심을 느낀다 / 더 많은 공연을 상연하게 되어

[문장 수식]
To guarantee your reservation, / please contact / us / within 24 hours.
예약을 보장하기 위해서 / 연락해 주십시오 / 우리에게 / 24시간 이내에

ETS 문제로 **훈련하기**

STEP 01

(A), (B) 중 알맞은 것을 고르세요.

1 The team is doing everything possible to ------- the deadline.
(A) meet
(B) meeting

2 One of your tasks as a computer programmer is -------- our Web site.
(A) updates
(B) to update

3 Travelers should call the airline ------- confirm their flights 24 hours before departure.
(A) for
(B) to

4 The team decided ------- the project because of budget constraints.
(A) cancel
(B) to cancel

5 It is effective ------- a meeting agenda to the attendees in advance.
(A) circulated
(B) to circulate

6 Mr. Woo declined to ------- on rumors that he is planning to retire.
(A) commenting
(B) comment

STEP 02

빈칸에 가장 알맞은 것을 고르세요.

7 The Benson Investment Group plans to ------- stock in more than 300 companies worldwide.
(A) purchased
(B) purchases
(C) purchasing
(D) purchase

8 ------- fine furniture, Mr. Taylor uses special wood that is not available in stores.
(A) To build
(B) Build
(C) Built
(D) Has built

9 In an effort ------- sales, we have sent a questionnaire to previous customers.
(A) to improve
(B) improved
(C) has improved
(D) improving

10 In order to ------- more tourists, the Henly Museum is offering free admission in July.
(A) attraction
(B) attracting
(C) attractive
(D) attract

| WORDS | 1 deadline 마감(일) 2 task 일, 직무 3 confirm 확인하다 departure 출발 4 constraint 제약 5 effective 효과적인 agenda 의제, 안건 attendee 참가자 in advance 사전에, 미리 6 decline 거절하다 rumor 소문 retire 은퇴하다 7 stock 주식 purchase 구입하다, 매입하다 8 available 입수할 수 있는 9 sales 매출, 매상 questionnaire 설문지 10 attract 유인하다, 끌어들이다 tourist 관광객 admission 입장

동명사의 쓰임

① 동명사의 쓰임

주어
Boosting sales volume / **is** the goal / for this quarter.
판매량을 증가시키는 것이 / 목표이다 / 이번 분기의

동사의 목적어
The sales manager / **suggested** / (~~to change~~, changing) the current supplier. 영업부장은 / 제안했다 / 현 납품업체를 바꾸는 것을

동명사를 목적어로 취하는 동사	finish 끝내다	give up 포기하다
	avoid 피하다	enjoy 즐기다
	delay[postpone] 미루다	suggest 제안하다
	recommend 추천하다	consider 고려하다

전치사의 목적어
We / can save / time / by (~~to cooperating~~, cooperating) with each other.
우리는 / 절약할 수 있다 / 시간을 / 서로 협력함으로써

보어
Our main concern / **is** / maintaining our market share.
우리의 주 관심사는 / ~이다 / 시장 점유율을 유지하는 것

② 동명사와 명사의 차이점

동명사는 문장 내에서 명사 역할을 하므로 명사처럼 주어, 목적어, 보어로 쓰일 수 있습니다. 하지만 동명사는 동사적 성질을 가지고 있기 때문에 명사와는 차이점이 있습니다.

동명사 + 목적어	He / reviewed / the report / before (submitting, ~~submission~~) it. 목적어 그는 / 검토했다 / 보고서를 / 그것을 제출하기 전에 → 동명사는 뒤에 목적어가 올 수 있으나, 명사인 submission 뒤에는 목적어(it)가 올수 없음
부사 + 동명사	Wilson Fashion / is famous / for (**skillfully**, ~~skillful~~) making / leather belts. 윌슨 패션은 / 유명하다 / 솜씨 있게 제작하는 것으로 / 가죽 벨트를 → 명사를 수식하는 것은 형용사, 동명사를 수식하는 것은 부사
관사(a, the) + 명사	The (reviewers, ~~reviewing~~) / should e-mail / the document / to the client. 검토자들은 / 이메일로 보내야 한다 / 서류를 / 그 고객에게 → 명사 앞에는 관사가 필요한 반면, 동명사 앞에는 관사가 올 수 없음

ETS 문제로 **훈련하기**

 STEP 01 (A), (B) 중 알맞은 것을 고르세요.

1 Ms. Pieraccini has nearly finished -------- the budget report.

(A) to edit   (B) editing

2 ------- yourself to the audience is the first step of your presentation.

(A) Introduction   (B) Introducing

3 The train company has decided to reduce fares as a way of ------- customers.

(A) attraction   (B) attracting

4 The dieticians recommend ------- a well-balanced breakfast daily.

(A) eating   (B) eaten

5 Our new method of ------- rubber for tires is still being tested in the lab.

(A) to produce   (B) producing

6 Forty hours of training in machine operation is a ------- for new product assemblers.

(A) requirement   (B) requiring

STEP 02 빈칸에 가장 알맞은 것을 고르세요.

7 For many years the local government has considered ------- Red Valley as a wilderness park.

(A) designate   (B) designates
(C) designating   (D) designation

8 After -------- interviewing a number of applicants, we are pleased to offer you a position.

(A) carefully   (B) to care
(C) careful   (D) most careful

9 Because of his success in -------- the merger, Mr. Rivera was promoted to vice president.

(A) organize   (B) organization
(C) organizer   (D) organizing

10 In ------- for her years of service, the company threw Ms. Parida a retirement party.

(A) appreciating   (B) appreciative
(C) appreciate   (D) appreciation

| WORDS | **1** nearly 거의 budget report 예산 보고서 **2** audience 청중 presentation 프레젠테이션, 발표 **3** reduce (가격을) 낮추다 fare (교통) 요금 as a way of ~의 한 방법으로 **4** dietician 영양사 recommend 권장하다, 추천하다 well-balanced 균형 잡힌 **5** method 방식 rubber 고무 lab 연구실, 실험실 **6** requirement 필요조건, 요건 assembler 조립 기술자, 조립공 **7** wilderness park 야생 공원 **8** applicant 지원자, 신청자 position 일자리, 직위 **9** merger 합병 **10** appreciation 감사 throw a party 파티를 열다 retirement 은퇴, 퇴직

✎ to부정사와 동명사 표현들

① 동사 + 목적어 + to부정사

| advise 조언하다 | encourage 격려하다 | allow[permit] 허락하다 | ask 요청하다 | + 목적어 + to 동사원형 |
| invite 초대하다 | expect 기대하다 | require[request] 요구하다 | | |

The president / encouraged / employees / to increase productivity.
사장은 / 장려했다 / 직원들이 / 생산성을 높이도록

② be + p.p. + to부정사

위의 동사들은 수동태의 형태로 아래와 같이 자주 쓰입니다. 토익에 자주 출제되는 아래 형태들을 외워두세요.

be encouraged to do ~하도록 장려되다	be expected to do ~할 것으로 예상되다
be advised to do ~하도록 권고되다	be required to do ~하도록 요구되다
be allowed to do ~하도록 허락되다	be asked to do ~하도록 요청되다

• Employees / were encouraged to increase / productivity / (by the president).
　직원들은 / 높이도록 장려된다 / 생산성을 / (사장에 의해)

③ 자주 쓰이는 to부정사 구문

| too + 형용사[부사] + to 동사원형
너무 ~해서 …할 수 없다 | 형용사[부사] + enough + to 동사원형
~할 정도로 충분히 …하다 |

• This place / is (too / ~~very~~) small / to hold a job fair.　이곳은 / 너무 좁다 / 취업 박람회를 열기에는
• This place / is large (enough / ~~too~~) / to hold a job fair.　이곳은 / 충분히 크다 / 취업 박람회를 열 만큼

④ 전치사 + 동명사[명사]

lead to ~을 초래하다	contribute to ~에 기여하다	be committed to ~에 헌신[전념]하다
object to ~을 반대하다	be accustomed to ~에 익숙하다	be dedicated to ~에 헌신[전념]하다
be subject to ~ 될 수 있다	be used to ~에 익숙하다	be devoted to ~에 헌신[전념]하다
by -ing ~함으로써	look forward to ~을 고대하다	upon[on] -ing ~하자마자

• Our recruiters / are devoted / to (providing, ~~provide~~) the best career opportunities.
　우리 채용자들은 / 헌신하고 있다 / 최고의 취업 기회를 제공하는 일에

• By using this coupon, / members / can get free admission / to the museum.
　이 쿠폰을 사용함으로써 / 회원들은 / 무료 입장할 수 있다 / 박물관에

ETS 문제로 **훈련하기**

STEP 01

(A), (B) 중 알맞은 것을 고르세요.

1 Ms. Park has asked her assistant ------- the report tomorrow.

(A) will type   (B) to type

2 The newspaper's circulation department is committed to ------- excellent service.

(A) provided   (B) providing

3 The corporate charter requires its executives ------- in the best interest of the company.

(A) acting   (B) to act

4 The shipment is ------- big to load into our delivery van.

(A) too   (B) very

5 Mr. Saito is used to --------- presentations to international clients.

(A) give   (B) giving

6 Guests are asked to register at the front desk ------- entering the main lobby.

(A) upon   (B) in order to

STEP 02

빈칸에 가장 알맞은 것을 고르세요.

7 Mail carriers are encouraged to ------- comfortable shoes while on duty.

(A) wearing   (B) wore
(C) wear   (D) worn

8 You are invited ------- the third annual conference for digital sound engineers.

(A) attending   (B) to attend
(C) attend   (D) attended

9 The president stated that he was looking forward to -------- work on the construction project.

(A) begin   (B) began
(C) begins   (D) beginning

10 All advertising at the National Textile Convention is subject to -------- by the board of directors.

(A) approve   (B) approvingly
(C) approving   (D) approval

| WORDS | **1** assistant 조수, 비서 **2** circulation department (신문사의) 판매국 be committed to ~에 전념하다, 헌신하다
3 corporate charter 기업 설립 강령 executive 이사, 중역 in the interest of ~을 위해서 **4** shipment 배송(품)
load (짐을) 싣다 van 화물용 트럭 **5** international 해외의, 국제적인 **6** register 등록하다 **7** mail carrier 우편 배달원
encourage 권장하다 on duty 근무 중인 **8** invite 초대하다, (요)청하다 annual 매년의, 연간의 **9** state (정식으로)
말하다 look forward to ~을 고대하다 construction 건설, 공사 **10** textile 직물, 옷감 be subject to ~을 받아야
한다, ~될 수 있다

아래 토익 필수 어휘들을 표현과 함께 익혀 보세요.

additional	추가적인	accessible	접근 가능한, 이용 가능한
relevant	관련 있는, 적절한	competent	유능한
outstanding	뛰어난; 미해결의	brief	(시간이) 짧은; (말, 글이) 간단한
adequate	충분한; 적절한	multiple	많은, 다수의
substantial	상당한, 많은	essential	필수적인
temporary	임시의	previous	이전의
upcoming	곧 있을	valid	유효한; 타당한
responsible	~에 책임이 있는	initial	처음의
possible	가능한	beneficial	유익한, 이로운
probable	개연성 있는	mutual	상호 간의, 서로의

어휘 표현 익히기   위의 단어들을 외우고 아래 표현을 완성해 보세요.

1. _____ funds — **추가** 자금
2. _____ achievement — **뛰어난** 업적
3. _____ opportunities — **상당한** 기회
4. _____ workers — **임시** 직원
5. _____ documents — **관련** 서류들
6. _____ to disabled people — 장애인들이 **이용할 수 있는**
7. _____ for damage — 손상에 대해 **책임이 있는**
8. a _____ identification — **유효한** 신분증
9. a _____ secretary — **유능한** 비서
10. a _____ description — **간략한** 설명

| ANSWERS | 1. additional 2. outstanding 3. substantial 4. temporary 5. relevant
6. accessible 7. responsible 8. valid 9. competent 10. brief

ETS 문제로 훈련하기

PART 5 | UNIT 09

STEP 01

(A), (B) 중 알맞은 것을 고르세요.

1. Highway 140 is not ------- by Exit 2A due to road construction.
   (A) accessible   (B) possible

2. A ------- identification card is required before entering the plant.
   (A) severe   (B) valid

3. Waldman Graphics will increase its workforce by 15 percent in the ------- year.
   (A) previous   (B) upcoming

4. Versatility and flexibility are ------- to getting a good entry-level job.
   (A) essential   (B) initial

STEP 02

빈칸에 가장 알맞은 것을 고르세요.

5. The monitor was damaged in shipping because the packaging was not -------.
   (A) adequate   (B) likely
   (C) intended   (D) expected

6. Until the central heating can be repaired, portable heaters will be used as a ------- measure.
   (A) brief   (B) summary
   (C) temporary   (D) perishable

7. The managerial position would offer ------- flexibility in scheduling and a higher salary.
   (A) fixed   (B) multiple
   (C) hopeful   (D) additional

8. Mr. Yoo was ------- for the successful completion of the downtown hotel renovation project.
   (A) probable   (B) trusting
   (C) powerful   (D) responsible

| WORDS | 1 due to ~ 때문에 construction 건설, 공사 2 identification card 신분증 require 요구하다, 필요로 하다 3 workforce 인력 4 versatility 다재다능함 flexibility 유연성, 융통성 entry-level job (경험이나 자격이 크게 필요하지 않은) 초보적인 일 5 packaging 포장재, 포장 6 central heating 중앙 난방 장치 portable 휴대 가능한 measure 조치 7 managerial position 관리직 8 renovation 수리, 보수

정답 및 해설 p.96

123

1 Dental patients are advised to ------- to our office every six months for a checkup.

(A) return
(B) returns
(C) returned
(D) returning

2 They delayed ------- the offices so that the meeting could continue without disturbance.

(A) clean
(B) cleaned
(C) to clean
(D) cleaning

3 After ------- the tire on Ms. Hoven's rental car, the mechanic advised her to replace it.

(A) inspected
(B) inspection
(C) inspecting
(D) inspects

4 Stow University offers online programs to help mid-level managers who wish to ------- in their careers.

(A) advance
(B) advancement
(C) advances
(D) advancing

5 The Internet has made it easier for vehicle buyers ------- for banks that offer the best loans.

(A) to search
(B) search
(C) have searched
(D) searches

6 Ms. Peng called this morning ------- Mr. Torres of the latest changes to plans for the Gineon project.

(A) will inform
(B) to inform
(C) was informing
(D) has been informed

7 Syna Corporation's earnings were not impressive ------- to attract more investors.

(A) enough
(B) fully
(C) quite
(D) rather

8 The entire sales team must meet the annual target ------- qualify for performance bonuses.

(A) in order to
(B) instead of
(C) even if
(D) so that

9 Combro Electronics, Inc., made the decision to ------- production of their latest mobile phone due to design flaws.

(A) suspend
(B) suspended
(C) suspends
(D) suspending

10 Youth Networking is a nonprofit organization that is committed to ------- part-time job opportunities for students.

(A) arranging
(B) arrangement
(C) arrangements
(D) arranges

Questions 11-14 refer to the following article.

New Fusion Restaurant Headed for 47th Street in Omaha Park neighborhood

Veteran chef Ned Sheehan is bringing fusion food to Omaha Park. "Neighborhood residents say that they have to go downtown to enjoy bold, innovative eateries," he said. "------- ."
    11

Sheehan, a former chef at the downtown restaurant Carlotti's Café, expects ------- Fusion
    12
Eats at the old site of Dio's Pizzeria, 13 West 47th Street, in late autumn.

"I've already prepared more than 30 ------- for Fusion Eats," Sheehan said. "They all
    13
feature a mix of familiar and exotic ingredients." Menu items will include duck curry, shrimp dumplings, and mushroom pies. Sheehan, an Omaha Park native, said he evaluated 20 other potential ------- for the restaurant before choosing the 47th Street
    14
storefront.

---

11 (A) But I want them to have creative dining options nearby.
(B) As a result, there is less traffic in the downtown area.
(C) I was surprised because I have never lived in Omaha Park.
(D) In fact, few people will attend those cooking classes.

12 (A) opened
(B) to be opened
(C) to open
(D) being open

13 (A) bowls
(B) recipes
(C) instructions
(D) personnel

14 (A) renovations
(B) investors
(C) managers
(D) locations

| WORDS | 1 dental 치과의 patient 환자 checkup 검사, 검진 2 delay 미루다, 연기하다 disturbance 방해, 소란 3 mechanic 정비공 replace 교체하다 4 advance 승진하다 career 직장 생활 5 vehicle 차량 6 latest 최근의 7 earnings 수입, 수익 impressive 인상적인, 감동적인 attract 끌어들이다 investor 투자자 8 meet (요구 등을) 충족시키다 qualify for ~의 자격을 얻다 performance bonus 성과급, 실적 보너스 9 due to ~ 때문에 flaw 흠, 결함 suspend 유예[중단]하다 10 nonprofit organization 비영리 단체 be committed to ~에 전념[헌신]하다 11-14 head for ~으로 향하다 bold 대담한 innovative 혁신적인 eatery 식당 former 이전의 feature ~을 특징으로 하다 familiar 친숙한 exotic 이국적인 ingredient 재료, 성분 dumpling 중국식 만두 mushroom 버섯 native 토박이 evaluate 평가하다 potential 잠재적인 storefront 거리에 면한 가게 자리

UNIT 10

분사

무료인강 바로가기

동사가 변신해
형용사처럼 쓰이는 분사!

동사에 -ing나 -ed가 붙어 형용사처럼 쓰이는 말을 '분사'라고 합니다.
형용사 역할을 하므로 분사는 문장 안에서 명사를 꾸밀 수 있습니다.

잠자는 도마뱀!　　　　**씻어 놓은 접시!**

앞마당에 쿨쿨 잠자는 도마뱀이 있어요. 이럴 때 '잠자다'란 동사 sleep을 '도마뱀'이라는 명사를 수식하도록 '잠자는', 즉 sleeping으로 바꾼 것이 분사입니다. 즉 분사는 동사를 가지고 만든 형용사입니다. 부엌에는 누군가 씻어 놓아 반짝반짝 빛나는 접시가 있네요. 접시가 씻고 있을 수는 없죠? 따라서 누군가 씻어 놓은 접시라는 수동의 의미가 어울려요. 이럴 때는 동사 wash에 -ed를 붙여 washed로 만들어 접시를 꾸밉니다. 이처럼 분사와 분사가 꾸미는 명사의 관계가 능동이면 현재분사(-ing), 수동이면 과거분사(-ed)를 써요. to부정사나 동명사는 형태가 한 가지인 반면, 분사는 이렇게 형태가 두 가지이므로 어떤 형태를 쓸지 구분하는 것이 토익의 핵심입니다.

● 분사의 종류

현재분사	〈동사원형 + -ing〉 능동, 진행을 의미	carry → carrying 운반하는 중인 update → updating 업데이트하는 중인
과거분사	〈동사원형 + -(e)d〉, 불규칙 형태 수동, 완료를 의미	use + -d → used 사용된 〈규칙 형태〉 pay → paid 지불된 〈불규칙 형태〉

● 분사의 쓰임

분사는 형용사와 쓰임이 같습니다.

명사 앞 수식	the updated handbook 업데이트된 지침서
명사 뒤 수식	the event / [introducing a new line of products] 행사 / 신제품군을 소개하는
주격 보어	The results of the survey / are disappointing. 설문 조사 결과는 / 실망스럽다 2형식 동사
목적격 보어	He / found / his coworkers / motivated. 그는 / 알았다 / 동료 직원들이 / 의욕적임을 5형식 동사

● 분사구문

형용사 역할을 하는 분사와는 달리, 분사구문은 시간, 이유 등을 나타내는 부사 역할을 합니다.

분사 형용사 역할	The man / [carrying an umbrella] / is a bank teller. 남자는 / 우산을 들고 있는 / 은행원이다
분사구문 부사 역할	Carrying an umbrella, / I strolled / around the castle. 우산을 들고서 / 나는 거닐었다 / 성 주변을

기초 QUIZ

1. 다음을 현재분사와 과거분사의 뜻을 생각하며 해석해보세요.
   1) a falling leaf: _____
   2) a fallen leaf: _____

현재분사 falling은 '떨어지고 있는', 과거분사 fallen은 '(이미) 떨어진'이란 의미입니다.
정답: 1) 떨어지고 있는 나뭇잎
2) 이미 떨어진 낙엽

2. 다음 문장에서 분사에 밑줄을 치고 문장을 해석해보세요.
   The man driving the truck is my cousin.

분사 driving은 명사 The man을 꾸며주는 형용사 역할을 합니다.
정답: driving, 트럭을 운전하는 남자가 내 사촌이다.

현재분사와 과거분사

① 현재분사

❶ 능동, 진행의 의미일 때

〈동사원형 + -ing〉의 형태로, 분사가 꾸미는 명사가 행위를 하는 주체일 때 씁니다. '~하는'이라고 해석합니다.

- Due to rising costs, / the publisher / decided / to raise its subscription rates. 〈능동의 의미〉
  '상승하는' 주체 (능동)

  상승하는 비용 때문에 / 그 출판사는 / 결정했다 / 구독료를 인상하기로

- I / am writing / to express my interest / in your internship program. 〈진행의 의미〉

  나는 / 쓰고 있습니다 / 관심을 표현하기 위해 / 귀사의 인턴십 프로그램에

❷ 현재분사 + 목적어

분사가 명사를 뒤에서 수식할 때 분사 뒤에 목적어가 있으면 현재분사가 옵니다.

- The manager / [interviewing applicants] / reviewed / the applications / in advance.
  '인터뷰하는' 주체   목적어

  그 매니저는 / 지원자들을 인터뷰하는 / 검토했다 / 지원서들을 / 미리

② 과거분사

❶ 수동, 완료의 의미일 때

〈동사원형 + -ed〉의 형태로, 분사가 꾸미는 명사가 행위를 당하는 대상일 때 씁니다. '~된'이라고 해석합니다.

- Please submit / the revised proposal / for final approval. 〈수동의 의미〉
  '수정되는' 대상 (수동)

  제출해주십시오 / 수정된 제안서를 / 최종 승인을 위해

- He / has just completed / the application form. 〈완료의 의미〉

  그는 / 막 작성했다 / 지원서를

❷ 과거분사 + (수식어)

분사가 명사를 뒤에서 수식할 때 뒤에 목적어가 없거나 수식어가 있다면 과거분사가 옵니다.

- *Cornerstone Magazine* / frequently publishes / articles / [written by outside contributors].
  '쓰여진' 대상   수식어

  코너스톤 잡지는 / 자주 게재한다 / 기사를 / 외부 기고자에 의해 쓰여진

ETS 문제로 훈련하기

STEP 01

(A), (B) 중 알맞은 것을 고르세요.

1   The deposit is not refundable if a ------- reservation is canceled.

(A) confirmed   (B) confirmation

2   Please place your payment in the ------- envelope and mail it by April 20.

(A) enclosed   (B) enclosing

3   Research has shown that consumers prefer ------- advertisements over those aimed at the general public.

(A) personalized   (B) personalizing

4   Adequate storage space is important to companies ------- large quantities of materials.

(A) produced   (B) producing

5   Mr. Nam is an excellent employee and completes work ------- to him quickly and thoroughly.

(A) assigned   (B) assigning

6   Next week, the candidates will be on television ------- their ideas.

(A) introduced   (B) introducing

STEP 02

빈칸에 가장 알맞은 것을 고르세요.

7   Notify our office if you cannot open the ------- workshop schedule.

(A) attach   (B) attached
(C) attaching   (D) attachment

8   It is imperative that all employees attend the annual sales meeting -------- for March 21.

(A) has been scheduled
(B) schedules
(C) will schedule
(D) scheduled

9   The pamphlets were redesigned to include photographs of the hotel's ------- interior design.

(A) updating   (B) update
(C) updates   (D) updated

10 A banquet ------- the appointment of the new president was held yesterday at the Aston Hotel.

(A) celebrating   (B) celebration
(C) celebrates   (D) celebrated

| WORDS | **1** deposit 보증금 refundable 환불할 수 있는 reservation 예약 cancel 취소하다 **2** place 두다, 놓다 envelope 봉투 **3** consumer 소비자 aim at ~을 겨냥하다 **4** adequate 충분한, 적절한 storage 저장, 보관 large quantity 대량 **5** assign 할당하다 thoroughly 철저히 **6** candidate 출마자, 후보 **7** notify 알리다 attach 붙이다, 첨부하다 **8** imperative 반드시 해야 하는 attend 참석하다 annual 매년의, 연례의 sales meeting 영업 회의 **9** pamphlet 팸플릿, 안내 책자 **10** banquet 연회 appointment 임명, 지명

주의해야 할 분사

① 감정을 나타내는 분사

감정을 나타내는 동사의 경우 대체로 감정을 일으킬 때는 현재분사, 감정을 느낄 때는 과거분사를 씁니다.
주로 사물이 현재분사, 사람이 과거분사와 어울려 쓰여요.

interesting 흥미로운	interested 흥미를 느끼는	confusing 혼란스럽게 하는	confused 혼란스러운
exciting 흥분시키는	excited 흥분한	exhausting 지치게 하는	exhausted 지치는
pleasing 기분 좋게 하는	pleased 기분 좋은	disappointing 실망스러운	disappointed 실망한
satisfying 만족스러운	satisfied 만족한	embarrassing 난처하게 하는	embarrassed 난처한
overwhelming 압도적인	overwhelmed 압도된	frustrating 좌절하게 하는	frustrated 좌절한

- The handbook / contains / some confusing information.
  소책자는 / 포함하고 있다 / 일부 혼란스럽게 하는 정보를   information이 감정(혼란스러움)을 일으킴

- New employees / seem confused / about what to do.
  New employees가 감정(혼란스러움)을 느낌
  신입사원들은 / 혼란스러운 듯하다 / / 무엇을 해야 할지에 관해

② 형용사로 굳어진 분사

어떤 분사는 자주 쓰이다 보니 명사를 수식하는 형용사로 굳어져 쓰이기도 합니다. 이런 분사의 경우 현재분사와 과거분사를 구분하지 않고 쓰이므로 통째로 암기해 두세요.

현재분사		과거분사	
leading company	선도적인 기업	complicated procedures	복잡한 절차
demanding task	어려운 과제	detailed descriptions	자세한 설명
challenging project	어려운 프로젝트	limited resources	한정된 자원
lasting impression	지속되는 인상	preferred means	선호하는 수단
missing luggage	분실된 수하물	accomplished writer	뛰어난 작가
existing system	기존의 시스템	experienced manager	경험 있는 매니저
remaining job	남아있는 업무	skilled worker	숙련된 직원
outstanding performance	뛰어난 성과	qualified employee	자격을 갖춘 직원

- The mobile phone / is the (preferring, preferred) means of communication.
  핸드폰은 / 선호되는 의사소통 수단이다

ETS 문제로 **훈련하기**

(A), (B) 중 알맞은 것을 고르세요.

1 The speech made a ------- impression on participants at the banquet.

(A) lasted
(B) lasting

2 The sales representative is ------- in the negative feedback from his customers.

(A) disappointed
(B) disappointing

3 New construction, including additions to ------- buildings, requires the acquisition of a permit.

(A) existed
(B) existing

4 La Cantina Han offers the most ------- dining experience in the city.

(A) surprised
(B) surprising

5 Some students have complained that Physics 301 is too ------- for them.

(A) demanded
(B) demanding

6 If you are ------- in attending tomorrow's workshop, please let your supervisor know.

(A) interesting
(B) interested

빈칸에 가장 알맞은 것을 고르세요.

7 *Fan Musica* is one of the ------- international journals on classical music.

(A) led
(B) leads
(C) leader
(D) leading

8 Inoue and Hisakawa Ltd. is seeking ------- applicants for a legal assistant position.

(A) qualify
(B) qualification
(C) qualifies
(D) qualified

9 The city's rigid building codes have become too ------- for Mr. Cooper to accommodate.

(A) frustrated
(B) frustration
(C) frustrate
(D) frustrating

10 Many consumers think that the instructions for assembling furniture are overly -------.

(A) complicates
(B) complicate
(C) complicated
(D) complication

| WORDS | 1 make an impression 감명을 주다 banquet 연회 2 representative 담당 직원, 대표자 negative 부정적인 feedback 의견 3 existing 기존의 acquisition 취득, 획득 4 dining 식사 5 complain 불평하다 physics 물리학 6 supervisor 감독, 상사 7 journal (전문 분야를 다루는) 신문, 잡지 classical music 고전 음악 9 rigid 엄격한, 융통성이 없는 building code 건축 규정 accommodate 수용하다 10 instruction 설명, 지시 overly 너무, 몹시

분사구문

① 분사구문 만들기

분사구문이란 부사절에서 〈접속사 + 주어〉를 생략하고 '동사 + -ing'를 붙여 절을 구로 간단하게 바꾼 것을 말합니다.
수동의 경우 Being이 생략 가능하며, 의미를 분명히 하기 위해 〈접속사 + 분사구문〉 형태로 쓰기도 합니다.

- When consumers shop online, / they / should check / the refund policy.
  접속사 + 주어 생략

→ Shopping online, / consumers / should check / the refund policy.
  동사 + -ing

→ When shopping online, / consumers / should check / the refund policy.
  접속사 + 분사구문

  온라인에서 쇼핑할 때 / 소비자들은 / 확인해야 한다 / 환불 정책을

- Because the author's book is written / in difficult English, / it is hard to understand.
  접속사 + 주어 생략

→ (Being) Written / in difficult English, / the author's book is hard to understand.
  동사 + -ing (Being 생략 가능)

→ Because written / in difficult English, / the author's book is hard to understand.
  접속사 + 분사구문

  그 작가의 책은 쓰여졌기 때문에 / 어려운 영어로 / 그것은 이해하기 어렵다

② 분사구문의 여러 가지 뜻

분사구문은 시간, 조건, 이유, 동시 상황, 연속동작 등의 다양한 의미로 해석됩니다.

[시간]   Noticing the error, / the editor-in-chief / reported it / to the proofreader.
           (= When he noticed the error,)
           오류를 발견했을 때 / 편집장은 / 그것을 알렸다 / 교정자에게

[동시 상황] Watching the fashion show, / the audience / filled out / an evaluation form.
           (= As they watched the fashion show,)
           패션쇼를 지켜보면서 / 관객들은 / 작성했다 / 평가서를

[연속 동작] The bus tour / starts / at noon, / lasting about 3 hours.
                                    (= and it will last about 3 hours.)
           버스 투어는 / 시작된다 / 정오에 / 그리고 약 세 시간 동안 계속될 것이다

[이유]   Impressed by the product demonstration, / buyers / ordered / several items.
           (= Because they were impressed by the product demonstration,)
           제품 시연에 감명을 받았기 때문에 / 구매자들은 / 구입했다 / 몇 개를

ETS 문제로 **훈련하기**

STEP 01

(A), (B) 중 알맞은 것을 고르세요.

1 ------- a survey last month, the polling firm visited every resident in town.

(A) Conducted　　(B) Conducting

2 ------- in plain language, the magazine is easy to read.

(A) Written　　(B) Writing

3 ------- three decades ago, the exhibition hall needs to be renovated.

(A) Constructing　　(B) Constructed

4 ------- the draft of the contract, Mr. Kelvin found some errors in it.

(A) Reviewing　　(B) Reviewed

5 When ------- your salary, it is important to consider regional pay scales.

(A) negotiating　　(B) negotiation

6 Stormy weather led to power outages last night, ------- some residents without electricity.

(A) leaves　　(B) leaving

STEP 02

빈칸에 가장 알맞은 것을 고르세요.

7 ------- in proximity to the airport, the Tominski Hotel is an ideal choice for business travelers.

(A) Locating　　(B) Located
(C) Locates　　(D) Locate

8 The stock market rose again yesterday, ------- a weeklong trend.

(A) continuing　　(B) continual
(C) continues　　(D) continually

9 The company earned 150 million euros, ------- it to fund its planned expansion.

(A) allowing　　(B) allows
(C) allowance　　(D) allowably

10 As ------- in the agreement, the maintenance staff will respond to all service requests within 48 hours.

(A) notes　　(B) note
(C) noted　　(D) noting

| WORDS | **1** polling 투표, 여론 조사 resident 주민 **2** plain 평이한, 알기 쉬운 **3** decade 10년 exhibition hall 전시장 renovate 보수하다, 개조하다 **4** draft 초안 contract 계약(서) **5** important 중요한 regional 지역의 scale 등급, 체계 negotiate 협상하다 **6** stormy 폭풍우 치는 lead to ~을 초래하다, 야기하다 power outage 정전 electricity 전기 **7** proximity 가까움, 근접 ideal 이상적인, 가장 알맞은 **8** stock market 주식 시장 **9** earn (돈을) 벌다 fund 자금을 대다 expansion 확장, 확대 **10** note 언급하다 agreement 합의, 계약(서) maintenance 유지 보수

아래 토익 필수 어휘들을 표현과 함께 익혀 보세요.

comprehensive	포괄적인, 종합적인	potential	잠재적인
considerable	상당한	rapid	빠른, 신속한
impressive	인상적인, 감동적인	confidential	기밀의
steady	꾸준한	key	주요한, 핵심적인
reliable	믿을 수 있는	minor	사소한
authorized	공인된; 위임된	frequent	잦은, 빈번한
mandatory	의무적인	capable	할 수 있는
spacious	(공간이) 넓은	available	이용 가능한; 시간이 있는
sufficient	충분한	limited	제한적인
former	예전의, 전임의	complete	완성된, 완전한

어휘 표현 익히기   위의 단어들을 외우고 아래 표현을 완성해 보세요.

1. a _____ review   **종합적인** 검토
2. _____ business trips   **잦은** 출장
3. _____ information   **기밀** 정보
4. a _____ company   **믿을 수 있는** 회사
5. an _____ agent   **위임된** 대리인
6. a _____ dining room   **넓은** 식당
7. _____ clients   **잠재** 고객들
8. _____ factors   **주요** 요소들
9. _____ modifications   **사소한** 수정 사항들
10. _____ economic growth   **꾸준한** 경제 성장

| ANSWERS | 1. comprehensive 2. frequent 3. confidential 4. reliable 5. authorized
6. spacious 7. potential 8. key 9. minor 10. steady

ETS 문제로 **훈련하기**

STEP 01

(A), (B) 중 알맞은 것을 고르세요.

1 The agency can help young businesses identify ------- customers.

(A) potential   (B) improved

2 If you experience a problem with this product, take it to any ------- service center.

(A) sufficient   (B) authorized

3 Good Health Hospital has offered ------- services of health care.

(A) comprehensive
(B) unaccustomed

4 Since many people want to attend the show, extra buses will be made ------- to the public.

(A) frequent   (B) available

STEP 02

빈칸에 가장 알맞은 것을 고르세요.

5 Documents of a ------- nature should be stored in locked file cabinets at all times.

(A) confidential   (B) limited
(C) former   (D) mandatory

6 Ongoing training can be the ------- element in maintaining a productive workforce.

(A) key   (B) handy
(C) marginal   (D) complete

7 Our latest product brochure had to be reprinted to correct several ------- errors.

(A) overdue   (B) minor
(C) reliable   (D) rapid

8 Jefferies Electronics has enjoyed ------- sales since the start of this fiscal year.

(A) steady   (B) detailed
(C) renewable   (D) complete

| WORDS | 1 agency 대행사 identify 알아보다, 발견하다 2 experience 겪다, 경험하다 3 health care 건강 관리 서비스, 보건 4 the public 일반 대중 5 document 서류 nature 성질, 본성 store 보관하다 locked 자물쇠로 잠긴 6 ongoing 지속적인, 진행 중인 maintain 유지하다 productive 생산성이 높은 workforce 노동력, 직원 7 latest 최근의 reprint (책의) 재판을 찍다 correct 바로잡다, 수정하다 8 sales 판매, 매출 fiscal year 회계 연도

정답 및 해설 p.108

135

1 Since storage space is -------, all employees are asked to discard unwanted items.

(A) limit
(B) limitingly
(C) limited
(D) limitations

2 ------- employment contracts will be distributed at the end of the month.

(A) Revising
(B) Revision
(C) Revised
(D) Revise

3 Frontier University is seeking ------- individuals to participate in a survey.

(A) interest
(B) interests
(C) interested
(D) interestingly

4 Working so many hours of overtime to meet the deadline has left the design staff feeling -------.

(A) exhaust
(B) exhausting
(C) exhausted
(D) exhaustive

5 Any person ------- in a legal case is advised to consult a lawyer.

(A) involving
(B) involves
(C) involve
(D) involved

6 A trip to Robin Island will leave visitors quite ------- about its beauty.

(A) exciting
(B) excited
(C) excite
(D) excitement

7 Chin Industrial Supply is a ------- distributor of auto parts internationally.

(A) leading
(B) leader
(C) leads
(D) leadership

8 When ------- the lamp from the carton, slide it out by the base and avoid pulling on the electric cord.

(A) removing
(B) removes
(C) removed
(D) remove

9 Submit the deposit within the ------- time frame to avoid losing the reservation.

(A) allot
(B) allotted
(C) allotting
(D) allotments

10 ------- just six months ago, Fin's Grill has become one of the most popular restaurants in Delton.

(A) Opened
(B) To open
(C) Been opened
(D) Had been opening

정답 및 해설 p.110

Questions 11-14 refer to the following article.

Packaging and Transferring Flammable Liquids

All vehicles and containers that transport flammable liquids must be clearly identified. Specific requirements for the ------- can be found on page 6 of this document.
11

As a general rule, red diamond-shaped stickers with white text should be used. Please note that details may vary from region to region. If you are ------- of the exact
12
requirements for your area, always contact the National Transportation Bureau directly.

While the sender must supply the correct stickers for each container ------- , it is the
13
carrier's responsibility to make sure they are properly affixed to the containers. Vehicles carrying flammable liquids must also display a placard that is readily visible to other drivers. ------- .
14

---

11 (A) labels
(B) studies
(C) catalogs
(D) transactions

12 (A) unheard
(B) unsure
(C) independent
(D) incapable

13 (A) transports
(B) transporting
(C) being transported
(D) having been transported

14 (A) There are several possibilities for parking.
(B) It has been placed there for your convenience.
(C) This is an option when the loading area is occupied.
(D) No exceptions are to be made under any circumstances.

| WORDS | **1** storage space 저장 공간 discard 버리다, 폐기하다 **2** revised 개정된, 수정된 employment 고용 contract 계약(서) distribute 배포하다 **3** individual 개인 participate in ~에 참가하다 **5** legal case 소송 consult 상담하다 **7** distributor 판매[유통] 회사 part 부품 **8** electric cord 전기 코드 **9** submit 제출하다 deposit 보증금 allot 할당[배정]하다 **11-14** package 포장하다 transfer 이동하다, 운반하다 flammable 인화성의 liquid 액체 vehicle 차량 transport 운송하다 identify 식별하다 specific 구체적인, 특정한 requirement 요건, 요구 사항 as a general rule 대개는 vary 다르다 region 지역 transportation 교통, 운송 bureau (관청의) 부서, 국 directly 직접, 바로 supply 제공하다 responsibility 책임 properly 적절하게 affix 부착하다 placard 플래카드, 현수막 visible 보이는, 알아볼 수 있는 convenience 편의, 편리 under any circumstances 어떠한 경우에도

UNIT 11

전치사

무료인강 바로가기

명사를 한발 앞서는 전치사!

전치사는 말 그대로 앞에 놓인다고 해서 붙은 이름입니다.
주로 명사나 대명사 앞에 놓이며 하나로 묶인
〈전치사 + 명사〉 덩어리는 문장에서 수식어 역할을 하게 됩니다.

나는 출발했다 / 정오에 / 버스로

'나는 출발했다'라는 문장에 '정오에, 버스로'라는 말을 붙여 언제, 어떻게 출발했는지 자세히
이야기했군요. 이때 우리말의 조사 '~에, ~로'와 같은 기능을 하는 말이 영어에서는 전치사입
니다. 우리말은 조사가 명사 뒤에 붙는 반면 영어는 'at noon, by bus'처럼 명사 '앞에 위치'
하기 때문에 '전치사'라고 부릅니다. 이처럼 〈전치사 + 명사〉 덩어리는 시간, 수단 등 다양한 의
미를 나타낼 수 있습니다. 토익에서 전치사 문제를 풀 때는 빈칸 뒤의 명사가 시간을 나타내는
지 장소나 수단을 나타내는지를 먼저 확인하는 것이 좋습니다.

● 전치사 뒤에 올 수 있는 형태

전치사 뒤에는 명사(구), 대명사, 동명사 등의 명사의 형태가 올 수 있어요.

전치사 + 명사(구)	**at** school 학교에서	**under** the tree 나무 아래에
전치사 + 대명사	**like** this 이처럼	**with** him 그와 함께
전치사 + 동명사	**by** increasing the price 가격을 인상함으로써 **before** leaving the office 사무실을 나서기 전에	

● 전치사구의 쓰임

〈전치사 + 명사〉 덩어리는 문장에서 수식어 역할을 해요. 즉 형용사나 부사처럼 쓰입니다. 따라서, 명사를 수식 보충하거나 절 전체를 꾸미는 등의 역할을 합니다.

명사를 꾸밈	The results of the survey / will be released / next week. 설문 조사의 결과는 / 발표될 것이다 / 다음 주에
주어를 보충	Our staff / is on duty / 24 hours a day. 　　　　　　　보어 우리 직원들은 / 근무 중이다 / 하루 24시간
절을 꾸밈	For safety reasons, / inspectors / visit / the factory / every month. 안전상의 이유로 / 조사관들이 / 방문합니다 / 공장을 / 매달

기초 QUIZ

1. 다음 중 전치사 뒤에 **잘못된** 요소가 들어간 것을 고르세요.

   (A) during the vacation　　(B) for explain

   (C) at the seminar　　(D) by using the Internet

전치사 뒤에는 명사(구), 대명사, 동명사가 올 수 있습니다. explain (설명하다)은 동사이므로 전치사 뒤에 올 수 없습니다.　정답: (B)

2. 아래 문장에서 전치사구의 역할을 쓰세요.

   This item is **on sale**. 이 제품은 할인 중이다.

be동사 뒤에 쓰여 주어인 This item을 보충하고 있습니다.
정답: 보어

시간을 나타내는 전치사

① 시점을 나타내는 전치사

in ~에	연도, 계절, 분기, 월	in 2018 2018년에	in winter 겨울에
		in the third quarter 3분기에	in January 1월에
on ~에	날짜, 요일	on June 27 6월 27일에	on Saturday 토요일에
at ~에	시각, 시점	at 7 o'clock 7시에	at night 밤에
		at the beginning of the month 매월 초에	

from ~부터	시작하는 시점	from May to July 5월부터 7월까지
since ~부터, ~ 이래로	과거부터 현재까지 계속되는 기간	since 2001 2001년부터 (지금까지)
		since adopting the new policy 새로운 정책을 채택한 이래로

until ~까지	동작이나 상태가 계속될 때	The inspection process / **lasted** / until mid-September. 검사 절차는 / 지속되었다 / 9월 중순까지
by ~까지	동작이나 상태가 특정 시점에 완료될 때	We / should **recruit** / a manager / by November 30. 우리는 / 채용해야 한다 / 매니저를 / 11월 30일까지

before ~ 전에	before the presentation 발표 전에
after ~ 후에	after 3 P.M. 오후 3시 이후에

② 기간을 나타내는 전치사

for + 숫자 기간 ~ 동안	for three weeks 3주 동안
	for the last two months 지난 2개월 동안
during + 행사/사건 ~ 동안	during the vacation 방학 동안
	during the performance 공연하는 동안

within ~ 이내에	within 30 days 30일 이내에
	within a year 일년 이내에
throughout ~ 내내	throughout the week 일주일 내내

ETS 문제로 **훈련하기**

STEP 01

(A), (B) 중 알맞은 것을 고르세요.

1 Judith Cooke has been working in the sales department ------- 1999.
(A) on
(B) since

2 Updates to the database are scheduled to begin ------- 5:00 P.M.
(A) against
(B) after

3 Lecro Industries' customers may request refunds ------- thirty days of purchase.
(A) by
(B) within

4 The security badge needs to be activated ------- tomorrow.
(A) before
(B) on

5 All branches will be closing at 4 P.M. ------- Friday because of the holiday.
(A) on
(B) at

6 At the Highbridge Tech Symposium, refreshments are served ------- the day in the lobby.
(A) throughout
(B) within

STEP 02

빈칸에 가장 알맞은 것을 고르세요.

7 Williamstown Borough Bikes is open on weekdays ------- 10 A.M. to 5 P.M.
(A) from
(B) since
(C) by
(D) until

8 The construction on Highway 12 is expected to continue -------- next month.
(A) until
(B) across
(C) down
(D) onto

9 Mr. Desai has been president of Southern Horizons Bank ------- over ten years.
(A) in
(B) for
(C) up
(D) from

10 All departments must submit statistical reports ------- 4:00 P.M. on Monday.
(A) beside
(B) to
(C) between
(D) by

| WORDS | 1 sales department 영업부 2 update 갱신, 업데이트 3 request 요청하다 4 security 보안 badge 배지, 명찰 activate 작동시키다, 활성화시키다 5 branch 지점 6 refreshments 다과 7 weekday 평일 8 construction 건설, 공사 9 president 사장 10 submit 제출하다 statistical 통계의

장소를 나타내는 전치사

① 위치를 나타내는 전치사

in ~ (안)에	넓은 장소나 공간의 내부	in New York 뉴욕에서	in the hall 홀 내에
on ~ (위)에	표면에 접촉해 있을 때	on the floor 바닥 위에	on the shelf 선반 위에
at ~에	특정 지점을 나타낼 때	at the store 상점에서	at the airport 공항에서

between (둘) 사이	between the two companies 그 두 회사 간에 between A and B A와 B 사이에
among (셋 이상의) 중에	among the residents 주민들 중에서

within ~ 내에	within the department 부서 내에
next to ~ 옆에 = by, beside	next to / by / beside the stadium 경기장 옆에
near ~ 근처에	near the exit 출구 근처에

in front of ~ 앞에	in front of the counter 계산대 앞에
behind ~ 뒤에	behind the fence 담장 뒤에
opposite ~ 맞은편에	opposite the hotel 호텔 맞은편에

② 방향을 나타내는 전치사

to + '목적지나 대상' ~로	to America 미국으로	to my coworker 내 동료에게
toward + '일정한 방향' ~을 향해	toward the south 남쪽을 향해	toward the suburbs 교외를 향해

through ~을 통해	through the forest 숲을 통과하여	through the crowd 인파를 통과하여
along ~을 따라	along the beach 해변을 따라	along the border 국경을 따라
across ~을 건너, ~에 걸쳐	across the street 길을 건너	across the country 전국에 걸쳐

ETS 문제로 **훈련하기**

(A), (B) 중 알맞은 것을 고르세요.

1 Randy will be doing a product demonstration ------- the convention.

(A) at　　　　　　(B) across

2 The maintenance supplies are kept in Room 132, ------- the security desk.

(A) next to　　　　(B) among

3 Rail service ------- Montreal and New York was suspended due to heavy snowfall.

(A) between　　　(B) against

4 Dr. Kim's office is located ------- the tenth floor of the building.

(A) of　　　　　　(B) on

5 The new store will be located somewhere ------- the south coast.

(A) among　　　　(B) along

6 The area's harbor contains the second-largest port ------- Europe.

(A) under　　　　(B) in

빈칸에 가장 알맞은 것을 고르세요.

7 Guests can find additional linens and towels ------- the closet.

(A) with　　　　　(B) across
(C) for　　　　　(D) in

8 The 502 bus travels ------- the city, stopping at Broad Street and the Medical Center.

(A) between　　　(B) with
(C) next　　　　(D) through

9 The tourism office is ------- the convention center, across from the hotel district.

(A) throughout　　(B) against
(C) next　　　　(D) near

10 Ginnis Co. plans to hold seminars to promote better communication ------- its staff.

(A) under　　　　(B) past
(C) among　　　　(D) behind

| WORDS | **1** demonstration 실연, 시연 convention 컨벤션, 대규모 회의 **2** maintenance supplies 유지 보수용 자재 security 보안 **3** suspend 중단하다 **4** be located 위치하다 **5** somewhere 어딘가에 coast 해안 **6** harbor 항구, 항만 **7** linen 리넨 제품(침대 시트, 베갯잇 등) closet 옷장 **8** travel 이동하다, 다니다 **9** district 지구, 지역 **10** promote 촉진하다

그 밖의 전치사

① 수단 / 동반을 나타내는 전치사

by ~에 의해 (수단)	수단이나 방법 또는 행위자를 나타낼 때	by the senior executive 최고 중역에 의해 by adjusting the volume 음량을 조절함으로써
through ~을 통해 (수단)	매개체나 수단을 나타낼 때	through the Internet 인터넷을 통해 through an e-mail 이메일을 통해
with ~와 함께	함께하거나 도구를 쓸 때	with the coupon 쿠폰을 소지하고
without ~ 없이	없거나 하지 않음을 나타낼 때	without further notice 추후 통보 없이

② 기타 전치사

about, on, over ~에 대해 (주제)	the movie about an entrepreneur 한 기업가에 대한 영화 the lecture on global warming 지구 온난화에 대한 강의 concern over inflation 물가 폭등에 대한 우려
as ~로서 (자격)	as your tour guide 여러분의 관광가이드로서
for ~을 위해	for further information 추가 정보를 위해 for employees 직원들을 위해
like ~처럼	like other stores 다른 가게들처럼
unlike ~와 달리	unlike other competitors 다른 경쟁업체들과 달리

③ 이유 / 양보를 나타내는 (구)전치사

due to, because of ~ 때문에 (이유)	due to a power failure 정전 때문에 because of overbooking 초과 예약 때문에
despite, in spite of ~에도 불구하고 (양보)	despite the decreased sales 감소한 판매량에도 불구하고 in spite of traffic congestion 교통 정체에도 불구하고
regardless of ~에 상관없이	regardless of time and location 시간과 장소에 상관없이

④ -ing 형태로 끝나는 전치사

concerning, regarding ~에 관해	concerning the policy 그 정책에 관해
following ~ 이후에, ~을 따라	following the instructions 지침을 따라
considering ~을 고려하면	considering the current situation 현 상황을 고려하면
including ~을 포함해	including dates and locations 날짜와 장소를 포함하여

ETS 문제로 **훈련하기**

STEP 01

(A), (B) 중 알맞은 것을 고르세요.

1 ------- Le Deux cookware, Weir cookware is dishwasher safe.
   (A) Unlike　　　(B) Without

2 The conference site in Lanesville is easily accessible ------- car or train.
   (A) in　　　(B) by

3 At Pizza Delight, we want to provide our customers ------- the best service possible.
   (A) from　　　(B) with

4 Ms. Nelson was hired to lead the company ------- an organizational restructuring.
   (A) above　　　(B) through

5 ------- the speech, there is a question and answer session.
   (A) Following　　　(B) As

6 ------- bad weather, the event organizers didn't cancel the outdoor charity event last night.
   (A) In spite of　　　(B) Instead of

STEP 02

빈칸에 가장 알맞은 것을 고르세요.

7 Beginning on May 1, Jasper Clothing will operate ------- an online-only retailer.
   (A) into　　　(B) as
   (C) since　　　(D) during

8 KSD's Web site conveniently lists the prices of goods and details ------- shipping options.
   (A) about　　　(B) along
   (C) until　　　(D) into

9 ------- the completion of 30 days of employment, employees are entitled to paid vacation.
   (A) Follow　　　(B) Follows
   (C) Followed　　　(D) Following

10 You may not reproduce the photographic material ------- the written permission of the copyright owner.
   (A) into　　　(B) until
   (C) among　　　(D) without

| WORDS |　1 cookware 조리 기구 dishwasher safe 식기세척기에 사용 가능한 2 accessible 접근할 수 있는 3 provide ~을 제공[공급]하다 customer 고객 4 lead 이끌다, 안내하다 organizational restructuring 조직 개편 5 speech 연설, 담화 session (특정 활동을 위한) 시간, 기간 6 organizer 주최자 outdoor 야외의 charity 자선 7 operate 영업하다, 운용되다 retailer 소매점 8 shipping 배송 9 completion 완료, 완성 be entitled to ~의 자격이 되다 paid vacation 유급 휴가 10 reproduce 복사[복제]하다

기출 구전치사 어휘

QR코드로 발음도 들어보세요

아래 토익 필수 어휘들을 표현과 함께 익혀 보세요.

regardless of	~와 상관없이	as a result of	~의 결과로
according to	~에 따르면	on behalf of	~을 대표하여
along with	~와 함께	instead of	~ 대신에
prior to	~ 전에	in favor of	~을 찬성하여
contrary to	~와 반대로	in terms of	~의 측면에서
such as	~와 같은	in case of	만일 ~한다면
pertaining to	~에 관하여	in the event of	만약 ~하면
in addition to	~뿐만 아니라	in preparation for	~을 준비하여
because of	~ 때문에	in spite of	~에도 불구하고
rather than	~보다는, ~ 대신에	due to	~에 기인하는, ~ 때문에

어휘 표현 익히기   위의 단어들을 외우고 아래 표현을 완성해 보세요.

1. _____ restructuring — 구조조정의 **결과로**
2. electronic devices _____ mobile phones — 휴대 전화**와 같은** 전자 장비
3. _____ the departure — 출발 **전에**
4. _____ the company — 회사를 **대표하여**
5. submit it _____ the receipt — 영수증**과 함께** 그것을 제출하다
6. _____ making a payment — 비용을 지불하는 **대신에**
7. _____ constructing a stadium — 경기장을 만드는 것에 **찬성하여**
8. _____ industry reports — 업계 보고서**에 따르면**
9. _____ previous experience — 이전 경력**에 상관없이**
10. _____ profitability — 수익성 **측면에서**

| ANSWERS | 1. as a result of 2. such as 3. prior to 4. on behalf of 5. along with
6. instead of 7. in favor of 8. according to 9. regardless of 10. in terms of

ETS 문제로 **훈련하기**

STEP 01

(A), (B) 중 알맞은 것을 고르세요.

1 In the event ------- rain, the outdoor concert will be rescheduled.

(A) of   (B) with

2 Additional details ------- the workshop will be sent to all team members.

(A) pertaining to   (B) in spite of

3 The magazine selected Appler as the best agency ------- terms of customer loyalty.

(A) in   (B) without

4 Article submissions must be submitted one week ------- to publication.

(A) before   (B) prior

STEP 02

빈칸에 가장 알맞은 것을 고르세요.

5 Gessen Contractors guarantees customers top-quality handiwork on every job, ------- of how small.

(A) in case   (B) regardless
(C) whether   (D) rather than

6 In the event of rain, the reception will be held in the main banquet hall ------- the garden.

(A) instead of   (B) because
(C) despite   (D) when

7 ------- a report in the *Financial News*, Han Bank posted a net profit of $9.5 million for the second half of the year.

(A) According to   (B) Nevertheless
(C) Even though   (D) As if

8 I am writing ------- behalf of Mr. Johnson to inform you of the change in the date of our upcoming conference.

(A) for   (B) on
(C) to   (D) at

| WORDS | **1** outdoor 야외의 reschedule 일정을 변경하다 **2** additional 추가의 details 세부 사항 **3** agency 대행사
customer loyalty 고객 충성도 **4** article 기사 submission 제출(물) publication 출판, 발행 **5** handiwork 일[작품]
6 reception 리셉션, 환영 연회 banquet hall 연회장 **7** post (재정 관련 정보를) 발표하다 net profit 순이익
the second half of the year 하반기 **8** inform A of B A에게 B를 알리다

1 The Southeast Accounting Conference will be held ------- the Valmor Convention Center.

(A) with
(B) for
(C) at
(D) from

2 We recommend that you keep the original store receipt ------- proof of purchase.

(A) off
(B) except
(C) as
(D) through

3 Ms. Murata requests that this month's sales totals be submitted ------- the end of the day.

(A) within
(B) if
(C) that
(D) by

4 ------- a recent drop in sales, the Talvidia laptop remains the most popular one on the market.

(A) Due to
(B) Despite
(C) Not only
(D) Although

5 The Vehicle Licensing Agency sends notices to all commercial truck drivers 90 days ------- their license expiration date.

(A) due to
(B) prior to
(C) far from
(D) outside of

6 Customer service responded very quickly to our complaint ------- the fish tank that was broken during shipment.

(A) to
(B) from
(C) within
(D) about

7 To request a transfer to another department ------- the company, employees should contact Mr. Castillo in the human resources office.

(A) among
(B) whereas
(C) within
(D) since

8 The prime minister's speech will be broadcast live ------- the nation this evening.

(A) opposite
(B) regarding
(C) across
(D) after

9 On our Web site, online shoppers can find information on our new products ------- ease.

(A) with
(B) to
(C) for
(D) from

10 Claire Smith will be out of the office until next Tuesday ------- her attendance at a corporate retreat in Los Angeles.

(A) as well as
(B) moreover
(C) since
(D) because of

Questions 11-14 refer to the following article.

Automobile Sales on the Rise

The Commerce Board predicts that by the year's end national automobile sales will have reached 910,000 units. This figure is 15 percent higher than the ------- year's number and
11
is just short of the all-time high of three years ago. The Board attributes these gains to several factors, ------- the availability of lower interest rates on car loans. In contrast to
12
the general demand for automobiles, the market for minivans has shown little to no -------
13
these past five years despite intensive advertising efforts. ------- .
14

---

11 (A) following
    (B) current
    (C) previous
    (D) final

12 (A) include
    (B) includes
    (C) included
    (D) including

13 (A) growth
    (B) competition
    (C) value
    (D) interruption

14 (A) Another factor is the changes in consumer preferences.
    (B) It is even expected that some models will not be renewed next year.
    (C) The success of the advertisements took the Board by surprise.
    (D) Consumers prefer minivans because of their utility.

| WORDS | **1** be held 열리다 **2** receipt 영수증 as a proof of ~의 증거물[증빙]으로 **3** submit 제출하다 **5** vehicle 차량 notice 공고, 통지 commercial 상업용의 expiration 만료 **6** respond 대응하다 complaint 항의 shipment 배송 **7** transfer 이동, 전근 human resources office 인사과 **8** prime minister 총리 be broadcast live 생방송으로 중계되다 **9** product 제품, 상품 **10** be out of the office 사무실을 비우다 attendance 참석 corporate 기업의, 회사의 retreat 수련회 **11-14** predict 예측하다 reach ~에 도달하다 figure 수치 all-time high 사상 최고치 attribute A to B A를 B의 탓으로 여기다 factor 요인, 요소 car loan 자동차 구입자금 대출 in contrast to ~와는 대조적으로 intensive 집중적인 effort 노력 consumer preference 소비자 선호(도) renew 새로 교체하다, 갱신하다 utility 유용성

UNIT 12

등위접속사와 명사절 접속사

무료인강 바로가기

고리처럼 양쪽을 이어주는 접속사!

접속사는 문장 내에서 말과 말을 서로 이어주는
연결 고리 역할을 합니다. 길고 복잡해 보이는 문장도
접속사를 알고 있으면 쉽게 이해할 수 있어요.

나는 좋아해 / 사과와 바나나를
나는 알아 / 네가 과일을 좋아한다는 것을

영어의 대표적인 접속사로는 등위접속사와 종속접속사가 있습니다. 등위접속사는 '사과, 바나나' 같은 단어부터 구나 절까지 다 연결하는데, 접속사로 연결된 양쪽이 서로 동등한 지위에 있습니다. 반면 종속접속사는 '나는 알아'와 '네가 과일을 좋아한다'처럼 절과 절을 연결하되, 어느 한쪽이 주가 되는 절(주절), 나머지 한쪽이 주절에 딸린 절(종속절)이 됩니다. 종속접속사가 이끄는 절은 문장에서 명사, 부사, 형용사처럼 쓰이므로 명사절, 부사절, 형용사절(관계사) 접속사라고도 부릅니다.

● 접속사의 종류

영어에는 동등한 것들을 연결하는 등위접속사, 두 단어 이상이 짝을 이루어 쓰이는 상관접속사, 주절과 종속절(명사절, 부사절, 관계사절)을 연결하는 종속접속사가 있어요.

등위접속사	Ms. Yoon / is diligent / and patient. 　　　　　　　형용사　　　　　형용사 윤 씨는 / 부지런하다 / 그리고 안내심이 많다
상관접속사	You / can either save or spend / the money. 　　　　　　　동사　　　동사 당신은 / 저축하거나 쓰는 것 둘 중 하나를 할 수 있다 / 그 돈을
종속접속사	She believes / that she will get a promotion. 　　주절　　　　　　종속절 그녀는 믿는다 / 그녀가 승진할 것을

● 명사절 접속사

대표적인 종속접속사인 명사절 접속사의 종류는 아래와 같습니다. 명사절이므로 문장에서 주어, 목적어, 보어로 쓰여요.

종류	that ~라는 것	if / whether ~인지 아닌지	의문사 who 누가, what 무엇이 등

[주어]　　Who will be promoted / is not certain.
　　　　　　　명사절: 주어 역할
　누가 승진할지는 / 확실하지 않다

[목적어]　I / do not know / if she will be promoted.
　　　　　주절 동사　　　　명사절: 목적어 역할
　나는 / 모르겠다 / 그녀가 승진할지 아닌지는

[보어]　　The truth / is that she will get a promotion.
　　　　　　주절 동사　　　명사절: 보어 역할
　사실은 / 그녀가 승진할 것이다

◦ 기초 QUIZ ◦

1. 다음 문장에서 or가 연결하는 단어에 표시하세요.
   I will either visit or call you.

2. 아래 문장의 성분을 분석해보세요.
   We know that you are a reliable person.
   주어 (　　)　　　　　(　　　　　)

등위접속사는 앞뒤에 문법적으로 같은 형태를 연결해요. 따라서, or는 앞의 visit와 뒤의 call을 연결합니다.　정답: visit, call

문장의 주어는 We, 동사는 know, 목적어는 that 이하의 절인 3형식 문장입니다.　정답: 동사, 목적어

등위접속사와 상관접속사

① 등위접속사

등위접속사는 문법적으로 동등한 단어, 구, 절을 연결해주며, 이를 병렬구조라고 합니다. 아래 예문을 보면서 이 등위접속사의 특징을 다시 한번 살펴보세요.

and 그리고	but / yet 그러나	or 또는	so 그래서

[단어+단어] The research and development department / conducted / a survey.
　　　　　　　　　　명사　　　　　　　명사

연구 개발 부서가 / 실시했다 / 설문 조사를

[구+구] The city government / will create / theme parks / by the river or on the hill.
　　　　　　　　　　　　　　　　　　　　　　　　전치사구　　　　　전치사구

시 정부는 / 만들 것이다 / 테마파크들을 / 강가 또는 언덕 위에

[절+절] The secretary made a backup of the files, / so the information was recovered
　　　　　　　　　　　　　　　　　절(주어 + 동사)　　　　　　　　　　절(주어 + 동사)
successfully.

비서가 그 파일들을 백업했다 / 그래서 정보가 성공적으로 복구되었다

② 상관접속사

상관접속사는 두 단어 이상이 짝을 이루어 쓰이는 접속사입니다. 등위접속사와 마찬가지로 단어, 구, 절을 이어줍니다.

both A and B	either A or B	neither A nor B
A와 B 둘 다	A나 B 둘 중 하나	A와 B 둘 다 아닌
not A but B	not only A but (also) B	B as well as A
A가 아니라 B	A뿐만 아니라 B도	A뿐만 아니라 B도

- The toys / were sold / not by children / but by adults.

  장난감들은 / 판매되었다 / 아이들에 의해서가 아니라 / 어른들에 의해서

- Online shoppers / get / not only a 10% discount / but also free delivery service.
  　　　　　　　　　　　　　　　　　　　A　　　　　　　　　　　　　　B

= Online shoppers / get / free delivery service / as well as a 10% discount.
　　　　　　　　　　　　　　　　　　B　　　　　　　　　　　　　　A

  온라인 쇼핑객들은 / 받는다 / 무료 배송 서비스도 / 10% 할인뿐만 아니라

- You / may request / either a refund or a replacement.

  당신은 / 요청할 수 있습니다 / 환불 또는 교환을

ETS 문제로 훈련하기

STEP 01

(A), (B) 중 알맞은 것을 고르세요.

1 Heavy rain ------- snow is expected to affect the region today.
(A) because
(B) or

2 Ms. Noguchi's flight was delayed, ------- she arrived in time to attend the meeting.
(A) both
(B) but

3 The town of Monkark has ------- natural beauty and attractive architecture.
(A) both
(B) either

4 The company will raise prices ------- lower discounts on January 1.
(A) and
(B) again

5 Rava Metals became ------- a profitable business but also a multinational corporation.
(A) as well as
(B) not only

6 Payment is accepted either at the time of purchase ------- upon delivery of the merchandise.
(A) and
(B) or

STEP 02

빈칸에 가장 알맞은 것을 고르세요.

7 Neither the president ------- his press advisor was available for comment.
(A) either
(B) nor
(C) and
(D) but

8 Thanks to the chemists' hard work and -------, the product development stage has been successfully completed.
(A) dedicated
(B) dedication
(C) dedicating
(D) dedicates

9 Tickets to the art museum can be purchased either online ------- by phone.
(A) but
(B) yet
(C) and
(D) or

10 The survey can help a company to identify potential customers ------- analyze its competitors.
(A) as well as
(B) instead
(C) while
(D) for example

| WORDS | **1** heavy rain 폭우, 큰비 affect 영향을 미치다 region 지역 **2** delay 지연시키다 **3** architecture 건축, 건축 양식
4 lower 낮추다 **5** profitable business 수익성이 좋은 사업 multinational corporation 다국적 기업
6 purchase 구입; 구입하다 upon delivery of ~을 인도하는 즉시 merchandise 상품 **7** press advisor 언론
자문[조언자] available for ~을 위한 시간이 있는 **8** chemist 화학자 hard work and dedication 성실과 헌신
development 개발 **9** art museum 미술관 by phone 전화로, 전화상으로 **10** identify 확인하다, 찾아내다 analyze
분석하다 competitor 경쟁자

that과 if/whether

① 명사절 접속사 that

명사절 접속사 that은 '~라는 것'이라고 해석합니다. 확실하고 단정적인 사실을 나타낼 때 씁니다. 명사절 접속사 that은 목적어 자리에 쓰일 경우 생략이 가능해요.

[주어]   That the company will go out of business / is not true.
그 회사가 파산할 것이라는 것은 / 사실이 아니다

[목적어]   Mao Co. / announced / (that) it will expand its business into the European market.
마오 사는 / 발표했다 / 유럽 시장으로 사업 확장을 한다는 것을

[보어]   The problem / is that we don't have enough funds for the advertisement.
문제는 / 우리가 그 광고에 쓸 충분한 자금이 없다는 것이다

② 명사절 접속사 if / whether

❶ if와 whether

if / whether는 '~인지 아닌지'라고 해석되며, 불확실한 상황을 나타냅니다. whether는 주어, 목적어, 보어가 되는 절을 모두 이끌 수 있지만, if는 '동사의 목적어'가 되는 절만 이끈다는 점에 주의하세요.

[주어]   (If, **Whether**) the investment will make a profit / remains to be seen.
그 투자가 이익을 낼 것인지 아닌지는 / 두고 볼 일이다

[목적어]   The residents / want / to know / (**if**, **whether**) the city will widen the road.
주민들은 / 원한다 / 알기를 / 시에서 그 도로를 확장할 것인지 아닌지

[보어]   The issue / is / (if, **whether**) or not the national economy will recover.
문제는 / ~이다 / 국가 경제가 회복될 것인지 아닌지

❷ whether만의 쓰임

접속사 whether는 전치사의 목적어로 쓰이며 to부정사와도 쓰일 수 있으나 if는 쓰일 수 없습니다.

전치사의 목적어	Participants / asked / **about** whether the new medication will cure the disease. 참가자들은 / 질문했다 / 신약이 병을 고쳐줄지 아닌지에 대해
whether to + 동사원형	Employees / have not decided / whether **to follow** the management's decision. = whether they will follow the management's decision 직원들은 / 결정하지 못했다 / 운영진의 결정을 따라야 하는지 아닌지

STEP 01

(A), (B) 중 알맞은 것을 고르세요.

1 We ask ------- you please refrain from bringing food inside the museum.
(A) unless
(B) that

2 The commission concluded ------- funding is needed to repair the dam.
(A) if
(B) that

3 When asked ------- she will retire soon, Ms. Johannsen said that she will never stop working.
(A) while
(B) whether

4 Gladsock employees do not know ------- they will receive a bonus this year.
(A) if
(B) what

5 ------- the business model will attract new clients is assumed.
(A) That
(B) If

6 There is disagreement about ------- the prototype will be ready in time for the conference.
(A) if
(B) whether

STEP 02

빈칸에 가장 알맞은 것을 고르세요.

7 One frequent complaint air travelers make is ------- the overhead compartments are too small.
(A) then
(B) to
(C) whether
(D) that

8 Chef Alice Grissom says she must decide ------- to open an additional restaurant in Strasbourg or to remain only in Colmar.
(A) for
(B) if
(C) whether
(D) over

9 Before using this product for the first time, ensure ------- you read the instructions carefully.
(A) that
(B) how
(C) what
(D) them

10 Mr. Nam inspects the landscaping work to determine ------- it conforms to company standards.
(A) because
(B) so
(C) whether
(D) while

| WORDS | 1 refrain from -ing ~하기를 삼가다 2 commission 위원회 conclude 결론을 내리다 funding 자금 제공, 재정 지원 3 retire 은퇴하다 4 employee 직원 bonus 상여금 5 be assumed ~이라고 추정되다 6 disagreement 의견 충돌, 이견 prototype 원형, 시제품 in time 시간 맞춰 conference 콘퍼런스, 회의 7 frequent 빈번한 complaint 불평 overhead compartment 머리 위 짐칸 8 chef 요리사, 주방장 additional 추가의 9 ensure 반드시 ~하게 하다 instructions 설명서 10 inspect 점검하다 landscaping 조경 conform to ~에 부합하다, 따르다

의문사와 that/what의 구분

① 의문사

의문사는 크게 의문대명사와 의문부사로 나뉘며 해석으로도 구분할 수 있지만 뒤에 이어지는 절이 완전한지 불완전한지 여부로도 구분할 수 있어요.

의문대명사 + 불완전한 절	who 누가	what 무엇이	which 어느 것이	
의문부사 + 완전한 절	when 언제	where 어디서	why 왜	how 어떻게

[주어]   (Who, ~~How~~) will be elected as the next mayor / is everyone's concern.
누가 차기 시장으로 선출될 것인지가 / 모두의 관심사이다

[목적어]   The new vacuum cleaner / reflects / (~~that~~, what) our customers need.
신형 청소기는 / 반영한다 / 우리 고객들이 무엇을 필요로 하는지를

[보어]   This / is / (how, ~~what~~) we deal with computer malfunctions in the office.
이것은 / ~이다 / 우리가 사무실에서 컴퓨터 오작동을 처리하는 방식

② that과 what의 구분

접속사 what은 의문사로 '무엇'이란 의미 외에 '~라는 것'이란 의미도 가지고 있어, 같은 의미의 명사절 접속사 that과 비교가 됩니다. that은 뒤에 완전한 절이, what은 뒤에 불완전한 절이 옵니다.

- The notice / mentions / (that, ~~what~~) the construction will start tomorrow.
  <u>that + 완전한 절</u>

공지문에 / 언급하고 있다 / 공사가 내일 시작될 것이라고

- (~~That~~, What) makes the product so unique / is its fabulous design.
  What + 불완전한 절

그 제품을 그토록 독특하게 만드는 것은 / 아주 멋진 디자인이다

ETS 문제로 **훈련하기**

STEP 01 (A), (B) 중 알맞은 것을 고르세요.

1 The voters have to decide ------- candidate has the greater appeal.

(A) whom   (B) which

2 A local magazine asked people to describe ------- their jobs involve.

(A) what   (B) which

3 ------- customers would suggest to us will be considered seriously.

(A) That   (B) What

4 Harbor Fish Restaurant will continue to offer ------- has sold well in the past.

(A) what   (B) whose

5 ------- should impress passengers most is the comfort of the seating at Liverpool Airport.

(A) What   (B) When

6 We do not know ------- will attend the awards ceremony.

(A) where   (B) who

 STEP 02 빈칸에 가장 알맞은 것을 고르세요.

7 At the workshop, Mr. Aryl will explain ------- you can protect your computers from viruses.

(A) how   (B) who
(C) what   (D) which

8 ------- pleased the clients most was the effective customer service Moradon Bank provided.

(A) Who   (B) That
(C) What   (D) This

9 The employee directory has a section that tells users ------- can answer questions.

(A) if   (B) how
(C) who   (D) he

10 The product development team cannot say ------- the new line of products will be released.

(A) which   (B) who
(C) what   (D) when

| WORDS | **1** voter 투표자 appeal 매력 **2** describe 설명하다, 묘사하다 involve 포함하다, 관련시키다 **4** in the past 과거에
5 impress 감동시키다, 깊은 인상을 주다 comfort 편안함, 안락함 seating 좌석 **6** awards ceremony 시상식
7 protect A from B A를 B로부터 보호하다 **8** please 기쁘게 하다 effective 효과적인 **9** directory 명부 section
부분, 구획 user 이용자 **10** release 출시하다

기출 부사 어휘 1

QR코드로 발음도 들어보세요

아래 토익 필수 어휘들을 표현과 함께 익혀 보세요.

recently	최근에	approximately	대략, 거의
frequently	자주, 빈번하게	nearly	거의, 대략
closely	면밀히, 밀접하게	currently	현재
shortly	곧	tightly	단단히, 꽉
highly	매우, 대단히	completely	완전히, 전적으로
definitely	분명히, 확실하게	proudly	자랑스럽게
urgently	긴급하게	extremely	극도로, 극히
relatively	상대적으로	previously	이전에, 앞서
newly	새로	lately	최근에
exactly	정확하게	usually	대개

어휘 표현 익히기　위의 단어들을 외우고 아래 표현을 완성해 보세요.

1.	have _____ become popular	**최근** 유명해졌다
2.	_____ examine the documents	서류를 **면밀하게** 검토하다
3.	will return _____	**곧** 돌아올 것이다
4.	_____ need security guards	**긴급하게** 보안 요원들이 필요하다
5.	_____ two hours	**대략** 2시간
6.	be still _____ low	여전히 **상대적으로** 낮다
7.	be _____ on a business trip	**현재** 출장 중이다
8.	Rules change _____.	규정이 **자주** 바뀐다.
9.	_____ reach the goal	**확실하게** 목표에 도달하다
10.	as _____ stated	**이전에** 말한 바와 같이

| ANSWERS |　1. recently[lately]　2. closely　3. shortly　4. urgently　5. approximately[nearly]
6. relatively　7. currently　8. frequently　9. definitely　10. previously

ETS 문제로 훈련하기

STEP 01

(A), (B) 중 알맞은 것을 고르세요.

1 The two companies worked together on a ------- profitable development project.

(A) highly   (B) tightly

2 Plumville Library ------- announces the launch of a brand-new Web site.

(A) extremely   (B) proudly

3 The ------- formed client advisory division is now hiring financial specialists.

(A) currently   (B) recently

4 The company's stock price is ------- low compared to its annual earnings.

(A) relatively   (B) anonymously

STEP 02

빈칸에 가장 알맞은 것을 고르세요.

5 Emergency equipment is tested ------- to ensure that it is in good working condition.

(A) lately   (B) frequently
(C) truly   (D) relatively

6 Volunteers are ------- needed to prepare a large book order for shipping before Friday's deadline.

(A) closely   (B) tightly
(C) urgently   (D) exactly

7 Our division leader announced that the new sales team will ------- reach its goal for this year.

(A) freely   (B) extremely
(C) definitely   (D) usually

8 Investors believe that Star Mining's growth will be stronger than ------- expected.

(A) completely   (B) previously
(C) positively   (D) newly

| WORDS | **1** profitable 수익성이 높은 development project 개발 사업 **2** announce 발표하다, 공지하다 launch 출시, 개시 brand-new 아주 새로운 **3** formed 구성된 advisory division 자문 부서 financial specialist 금융 전문가 **4** stock price 주가 compared to ~에 비교하여, ~에 비해 earnings 소득, 수익 **5** emergency equipment 비상 장치 condition 상태 **6** shipping 발송, 배송 deadline 마감 기한 **7** division leader 부서 책임자 **8** investor 투자자

1 Both Ms. Liu ------- Ms. Schultz are attending the international business conference in Jakarta next week.

(A) either
(B) or
(C) and
(D) nor

2 Hua Husing's achievements were remarkable considering ------- he was only twenty-six at the time.

(A) that
(B) what
(C) since
(D) whether

3 Greenlove Publishing specializes in books about environmental challenges ------- successes.

(A) those
(B) when
(C) onto
(D) and

4 The company's final decision on whether or not ------- Ms. Johnson depends on the result of a reference check.

(A) hire
(B) hiring
(C) to hire
(D) will hire

5 We have been given specific instructions on ------- Ms. Crane wants this task to be completed.

(A) who
(B) how
(C) that
(D) whoever

6 Primo Publishing has not yet decided ------- they will introduce their new software's advanced features.

(A) which
(B) who
(C) what
(D) when

7 The purpose of this survey is to find out ------- our performance meets customers' expectations.

(A) neither
(B) whereas
(C) although
(D) whether

8 Currently, Skypoint Fashions does not have any vacancies, ------- the company expects to be hiring later this year.

(A) or
(B) once
(C) that
(D) but

9 Traces of ------- Caribbean music and traditional jazz can be heard in Kendra Bauden's new recording.

(A) already
(B) fewer
(C) both
(D) ever

10 Clients are reminded ------- the law offices will be closed on Monday for the holiday.

(A) if
(B) yet
(C) still
(D) that

Questions 11-14 refer to the following e-mail.

To: Bee Goh Pon
From: Passaro Dental Group
Date: 13 January
Subject: Your teeth

Dear Mr. Pon,

Your smile is ------- to us. It is time for you to schedule an appointment for a checkup
        11
and cleaning. Your last ------- with us was more than fifteen months ago. At Passaro
                    12
Dental Group, we recommend ------- you get a routine cleaning every six months and an
                        13
examination every year.

We look forward to hearing from you and serving your dental needs. ------- .
                                                    14
Sincerely,

Barbara Ong, Hygienist
Passaro Dental Group
4587 Jaunty Road, Suite B
Singapore 168938
Phone: 65 6324 0112

11 (A) important
   (B) polite
   (C) available
   (D) similar

12 (A) course
   (B) reunion
   (C) visit
   (D) stay

13 (A) what
   (B) each
   (C) most
   (D) that

14 (A) It has been a pleasure doing business
      with your firm.
   (B) Please contact us if you have any
      questions or concerns.
   (C) This is your final opportunity to change
      your mind.
   (D) We are happy to welcome new
      patients to our practice.

| WORDS | **2** remarkable 놀라운, 주목할 만한 **3** publishing 출판 specialize in ~을 전문으로 하다 challenge 도전
4 reference check 추천인 조회 **5** specific 구체적인, 명확한 instructions 설명, 지시 **6** advanced 최신의 feature
기능, 특징 **7** performance 성과, 실적 meet 충족시키다, 부응하다 expectation 기대 **8** vacancy 공석 **9** trace
자취, 흔적 **11-14** checkup 검진 cleaning 치석 제거 routine 정기적인 dental 치과의 practice 개업 장소

UNIT 13

부사절 접속사

무료인강 바로가기

다양한 부가 정보를
알려주는 부사절 접속사!

부사절 접속사는 문장에서 부사 역할을 하는 절을
이끌어 시간, 조건, 이유 등
다양한 부가 정보를 전달하는 역할을 합니다.

Marry me if you love me.

만약 당신이 나를 사랑한다면 결혼해주세요.

그냥 '결혼해주세요'라고 말할 수도 있지만 '만약 당신이 나를 사랑한다면' 하고 조건을 붙일 수도 있습니다. 이럴 때 '~한다면'에 해당하는 말이 부사절 접속사입니다. 부사절은 이처럼 '조건' 외에도 '시간', '이유' 등 다양한 의미를 전달하는데, 일상대화에서 자주 쓰이는 만큼 토익에서 출제 빈도가 높습니다. 다양한 부사절 접속사의 의미를 잘 익히는 것이 중요합니다.

● 부사절 접속사

부사절은 〈부사절 접속사 + 주어 + 동사〉의 형태로 문장 내에서 부사 역할을 하는 수식어절입니다.
주절(접속사가 없는 절)과 부사절의 위치는 서로 바뀔 수 있어요.

[Although organic vegetables are expensive], / they are popular.
　　　종속절: 부사절 (부사절 접속사 + 주어 + 동사)　　　　　　　　주절

= Organic vegetables are popular / [although they are expensive].
　　　　　주절　　　　　　　　　　　　　　부사절

유기농 채소는 비싸지만 / 인기가 있다

● 부사절 접속사의 종류

부사절 접속사는 문장에서 시간, 조건, 이유 등을 나타내는 수식어 역할을 하는 부사절을 이끕니다.

시간	Please turn off the light / before you leave. 전등을 끄세요 / 당신이 떠나기 전에
조건	We will give a discount / if you buy two. 저희는 할인을 해드립니다 / 두 개를 사시면
이유	Heather was sad / because she lost the game. 헤더는 슬펐다 / 그녀가 게임에서 졌기 때문에
양보 / 대조	Although it was raining, / we went out for a walk. 비가 오는 중이었지만, / 우리는 산책을 나갔다

기초 QUIZ

주절과 종속절을 표시하고, 주절과 종속절의 위치를 바꿔 써보세요.

1. When he applied, Edgar was working as a designer.
　　(　　　　) 　　　　　　(　　　　　)

2. _____

부사절 접속사 When이 이끄는 절이
종속절입니다.　정답: 종속절, 주절

종속절과 주절은 그 위치를 바꾸어
쓸 수 있습니다.
정답: Edgar was working as a
designer when he applied.

시간/조건을 나타내는 부사절 접속사

① 시간을 나타내는 부사절 접속사

when ~할 때	as ~할 때, ~하면서	while ~하는 동안	once 일단 ~하면
before ~ 전에	after ~ 후에	until ~까지	since ~이래로, ~부터
as soon as ~하자마자	everytime ~할 때마다	by the time ~할 때까지	

- Once fruits / are packaged, / farmers / distribute / them / directly to retail stores.
  일단 과일들이 / 포장되면 / 농부들은 / 유통시킨다 / 그것들을 / 직접 소매점들에

- The meeting / continued / until everyone expressed their views on the agenda.
  회의는 / 계속되었다 / 모든 사람이 안건에 대한 자신의 의견을 표시할 때까지

② 조건을 나타내는 부사절 접속사

if 만약 ~라면	unless 만약 ~가 아니라면 (= if not)	as long as ~하는 한
in case (that) ~하는 경우에 대비해	provided[providing] (that) ~라는 조건으로, 만약 ~한다면	

- The swimming pool / should be closed / unless a trained lifeguard is on duty.
  수영장은 / 문을 닫아야 한다 / 훈련된 안전 요원이 근무하지 않는다면

- Provided that there is no damage / to the apartment, / you will receive / your full deposit.
  만약 아무런 하자가 없다면 / 아파트에 / 귀하는 수령하게 될 것입니다 / 보증금 전액을

- Extra chairs / have been prepared / in case there are more participants than expected.
  의자가 추가로 / 준비되었다 / 예상보다 많은 참가자가 있을 경우에 대비해

③ 시간과 조건을 나타내는 부사절의 시제

시간이나 조건을 나타내는 부사절에서는 현재 시제로 미래를 나타냅니다.

- We / will have / a vacation / when the project (is, will be) over.
  우리는 / 보낼 것이다 / 휴가를 / 그 프로젝트가 끝날 때

- The project / will be completed / soon / if everything (goes, will go) well.
  프로젝트는 / 완료될 것이다 / 곧 / 만약 모든 것이 순조롭게 진행된다면

ETS 문제로 훈련하기

STEP 01 (A), (B) 중 알맞은 것을 고르세요.

1 Please arrive at the conference center by 8:00 A.M. ------- you are a presenter.
(A) if (B) until

2 ------- the building has been inspected, the tenants will be able to move in.
(A) While (B) As soon as

3 The new auditorium will be opened ------- the building inspection is complete.
(A) whether (B) once

4 Center Financial will consider all applications, ------- they are received before May 15.
(A) if not (B) provided

5 ------- seafood processors have cleaned the fish, they package it for sale.
(A) Because (B) Once

6 Durham Tax Partners will be closed for two days ------- a new electrical system is installed.
(A) while (B) that

STEP 02 빈칸에 가장 알맞은 것을 고르세요.

7 Mr. Gaber, who dislikes air travel, only attends professional conferences ------- they are held nearby.
(A) or (B) if
(C) still (D) unless

8 ------- you have calculated your travel expenses, please inform Ms. Murakami by e-mail.
(A) In addition to (B) As well as
(C) In regard to (D) As soon as

9 Customers can write a check ------- they have two pieces of identification.
(A) in case of (B) providing for
(C) together with (D) as long as

10 Personal information will remain confidential ------- permission is given for it to be released.
(A) whether (B) as if
(C) except (D) unless

| WORDS | 1 presenter 발표자 3 auditorium 강당 inspection 검사, 점검 4 application 지원(서) 5 processor 가공업자 package 포장하다 6 install 설치하다 7 attend 참석하다 8 calculate 계산하다 expense 지출, 경비 9 write a check 수표를 끊다 identification 신분 증명(서) 10 confidential 기밀의 permission 허락, 허가 release 공개하다, 발표하다

이유/대조 등을 나타내는 부사절 접속사

① 이유를 나타내는 부사절 접속사

이유	because / as / since ~이기 때문에	now that ~이므로

- The accountant / left the office / early / since he had an appointment with his client.
  그 회계사는 / 퇴근했다 / 일찍 / 고객과 약속이 있었기 때문에

- Now that you have completed the internship, / you / are eligible / for the benefits package.
  당신은 인턴 과정을 마쳤으므로 / 당신은 / 받을 자격이 있습니다 / 복지 혜택을

② 양보/대조를 나타내는 부사절 접속사

양보	though, although, even though, even if ~에도 불구하고, 비록 ~이지만
대조	while / whereas ~인 반면에

- Although nobody likes the dress code, / all personnel / should comply / with it.
  아무도 그 복장 규정을 좋아하지 않음에도 불구하고 / 모든 직원들은 / 준수해야 한다 / 그것을

- While their camera has a better memory chip, / our model / has a higher resolution.
  그들의 카메라가 더 좋은 메모리 칩을 갖고 있는 반면에 / 우리 모델은 / 해상도가 더 높다

③ 그 밖의 부사절 접속사

목적	so (that) / in order that ~하도록 하기 위해서
결과	so + 형용사/부사 + that 매우 ~해서 ⋯하다

- Visitors / should wear / safety gear / so (that) they can enter the plant.
  방문자들은 / 착용해야 한다 / 보호 장비를 / 공장에 들어갈 수 있도록 하기 위해

- The idea / was so revolutionary / that the company needed more discussion / to implement it.
  그 아이디어는 / 매우 혁신적이어서 / 그 회사는 / 더 많은 논의가 필요했다 / 그것을 실행하기 위한

ETS 문제로 **훈련하기**

STEP 01

(A), (B) 중 알맞은 것을 고르세요.

1 ------- money has been budgeted for the program, the director is reluctant to proceed.

(A) Because of   (B) Although

2 Suits must be worn in the office, ------- casual dress is allowed in the workshop.

(A) so that   (B) while

3 Mr. Medina was unable to speak with reporters ------- his flight arrived late.

(A) as   (B) while

4 ------- I have changed offices, I wanted to update my contact information.

(A) Since   (B) After

5 Mobile phones have become ------- prevalent that service is available even in remote areas.

(A) so   (B) still

6 Ms. Lim will attend the meeting in person, ------- Mr. Parker will attend remotely.

(A) moreover   (B) whereas

STEP 02

빈칸에 가장 알맞은 것을 고르세요.

7 ------- Ms. Flores is not available right now, she may be able to help us next week.

(A) Whenever   (B) In order that
(C) Once   (D) Even though

8 Please update your time sheets by Friday ------- we can process your paycheck in a timely fashion.

(A) even   (B) also
(C) yet   (D) so

9 Register your new product online ------- you will have access to technical support information.

(A) rather   (B) in case of
(C) as to   (D) so that

10 ------- the meeting began late, we were able to discuss the entire agenda.

(A) Nevertheless   (B) Still
(C) Although   (D) However

| WORDS | **1** budget 예산을 세우다 be reluctant to ~하기를 꺼리다 proceed 진행하다 **2** suit 정장 casual 격식을 차리지 않는, 평상시의 allow 허용하다 **4** contact information 연락처 **5** prevalent 널리 퍼져 있는 remote 외딴, 먼 **6** in person 직접 (만나서) remotely 원격으로 **7** available 시간이 되는 **8** paycheck 급여 **9** register 등록하다 have access to ~에 접속하다 technical support 기술 지원 **10** agenda 안건

접속사와 전치사의 구별과 접속부사

① 의미가 같은 접속사와 전치사

같은 뜻이지만 접속사를 써야 할 때와 전치사를 써야 할 때를 구별해야 합니다. 뒤에 절(주어 + 동사)이 오면 접속사를 쓰고, 명사(구)가 오면 전치사를 씁니다.

	접속사	전치사
시간	while ~ 동안에 before ~ 전에/after ~ 후에 since ~ 이래로, ~부터/until ~까지	during ~ 동안에 before ~ 전에/after ~ 후에 since ~ 이래로, ~부터/until ~까지
이유	because, as, since, now that ~ 때문에	because of, owing to, due to ~ 때문에
양보	though, although, even though, even if 비록 ~이지만, ~에도 불구하고	despite, in spite of 비록 ~이지만
제외	except that ~을 제외하고	except for ~을 제외하고

- They / missed / the deadline / (even though, ~~despite~~) they worked overtime.
  그들은 / 지키지 못했다 / 마감일을 / 초과 근무를 했음에도 불구하고   주어 + 동사

- The flight / has been canceled / (~~because~~, due to) a mechanical problem.
  비행편이 / 취소되었다 / 기계적인 결함 때문에   명사구

cf. 부사절에서 주어와 be동사의 생략

부사절의 주어가 주절의 주어와 같은 경우 주어와 be동사를 함께 생략할 수 있습니다.

While you are shopping online, / you / should check / the refund policy.
당신이 온라인에서 쇼핑하는 동안 / 당신은 / 확인해야 한다 / 환불 정책을

→ **While shopping** online, you should check the refund policy.

② 접속부사

접속부사란, 접속사가 아닌 부사로서 두 개의 문장 사이에 위치해 의미를 자연스럽게 연결하는 역할을 합니다. 부사절 접속사와 의미가 비슷해서 선택지에 자주 출제되므로 주의하세요.

therefore 그러므로	however 그러나	moreover 게다가
otherwise 그렇지 않으면	as a result 그 결과	in addition 게다가
meanwhile 그동안	nevertheless 그럼에도 불구하고	for example 예를 들어

- Customers / should follow / our return policy. / Otherwise, / they / won't get / a refund.
  고객들은 / 따라야 한다 / 우리의 반품 정책을 / 그렇지 않으면 / 그들은 / 받을 수 없다 / 환불을

ETS 문제로 훈련하기

STEP 01 (A), (B) 중 알맞은 것을 고르세요.

1 Mr. Ono has all the documents that were passed out ------- the presentation.

(A) while　　　(B) during

2 ------- budget constraints, all employees will receive a salary increase.

(A) Despite　　　(B) When

3 ------- the new product is complete, Dr. Seong's team will work overtime.

(A) Until　　　(B) During

4 The younger staff look up to Ms. Itoh ------- her years of experience in the field.

(A) because of　　　(B) because

5 ------- sales figures are strong, we still expect to see a decline in profits for the year.

(A) Even if　　　(B) In spite of

6 ------- Ms. Kinder finishes her graduate degree, she will look for a job.

(A) Due to　　　(B) After

STEP 02 빈칸에 가장 알맞은 것을 고르세요.

7 The committee meeting was moved ------- a problem with the heating system.

(A) provided that　(B) because of
(C) throughout　　(D) even though

8 The office will be closing at 3 P.M. on Friday ------- the holiday weekend.

(A) due to　　　(B) while
(C) since　　　(D) as if

9 ------- the weather is getting cooler, it is important to keep doors shut in order to conserve energy.

(A) However　　(B) Whatever
(C) Because of　(D) Now that

10 ------- arriving at the airline terminal, Ms. Ortiz learned that her flight was delayed.

(A) Because　　(B) After
(C) Now that　　(D) Even if

| WORDS | 1 document 서류, 문서　pass out 배부하다　2 budget 예산　constraint 제약　salary 봉급, 급여　3 complete 완료된 work overtime 초과 근무하다　4 look up to ~을 존경하다　5 sales figures 매출액　6 graduate degree 석사 학위 look for ~을 구하다　7 heating system 난방 시스템　8 holiday weekend 연휴 주말(휴일이 낀 주말)　9 conserve 아끼다, 보존하다　10 learn 알게 되다

QR코드로 발음도 들어보세요

아래 토익 필수 어휘들을 표현과 함께 익혀 보세요.

regularly	정기적으로	partially	부분적으로
widely	널리, 폭넓게	temporarily	임시로
carefully	조심하여, 주의 깊게	annually	일년에 한 번, 매년
hardly	거의 ~ 않다	accurately	정확히
strictly	엄격히	specifically	분명히; 특히
separately	따로, 별도로	sharply	날카롭게; 급격히
promptly	즉시; 정각에	probably	아마도
immediately	즉시	narrowly	좁게; 가까스로, 간신히
professionally	직업적으로	extensively	광범위하게
objectively	객관적으로	surprisingly	놀라울 정도로

어휘 표현 익히기   위의 단어들을 외우고 아래 표현을 완성해 보세요.

1. attend conferences _____   회의에 **정기적으로** 참석하다
2. _____ stated on the label   라벨에 **분명하게** 적힌
3. read the agreement _____   계약서를 **주의 깊게** 읽다
4. take place _____   **일년에 한 번씩** 개최되다
5. be handled _____   **별도로** 처리되다
6. _____ change   **거의 바뀌지 않다**
7. _____ closed for renovation   개조보수를 위해 **임시로** 문을 닫은
8. _____ limited quantities   **엄격히** 제한된 양
9. _____ recognized   **널리** 인정받는
10. drop _____   **급격히** 떨어지다

| ANSWERS | 1. regularly 2. specifically 3. carefully 4. annually 5. separately
6. hardly 7. temporarily 8. strictly 9. widely 10. sharply

ETS 문제로 **훈련하기**

STEP 01

(A), (B) 중 알맞은 것을 고르세요.

1 The elevators in the north wing will be closed ------- for maintenance next week.

(A) annually   (B) temporarily

2 The number of prizes is ------- limited; only a few will receive the recognition.

(A) strictly   (B) tensely

3 Ensure that all office-related expenditures are recorded ------- in the database.

(A) rightly   (B) accurately

4 The new computer has been ------- advertised, but demand for it is still low.

(A) sharply   (B) widely

STEP 02

빈칸에 가장 알맞은 것을 고르세요.

5 The contents of the packages are perishable so they must be delivered --------.

(A) promptly   (B) specifically
(C) extensively   (D) objectively

6 In order to accommodate the dramatic increase in traffic, a new bridge is needed -------.

(A) broadly   (B) immediately
(C) easily   (D) professionally

7 Mr. Sosa, the area manager, visits all the offices under his management -------.

(A) regularly   (B) widely
(C) recently   (D) brightly

8 Read the safety procedures ------- before operating the machine for the first time.

(A) carefully   (B) harmlessly
(C) extremely   (D) hardly

| WORDS | 1 wing (건물의) 동, 부속 건물 maintenance 정비, 유지 보수 2 recognition 포상, 표창 3 ensure 반드시 ~하게 하다 office-related 사무와 관련된 expenditure 지출, 비용 record 기록하다 4 demand 수요 5 contents 내용물 perishable 잘 상하는 6 accommodate 수용하다 dramatic 극적인, 급격한 7 management 관리, 운영 8 safety procedure 안전 절차 operate (기계를) 조작하다, 가동하다

1 Tourism has flourished in South Joree ------- the world has learned more about its beautiful beaches.

(A) still
(B) as
(C) rather
(D) than

2 The client canceled her order ------- the coffee table she wanted was no longer available.

(A) because
(B) however
(C) for example
(D) as a result

3 ------- the success of his restaurant, chef Sook Yong wrote a best-selling cookbook.

(A) Because
(B) When
(C) After
(D) Already

4 ------- new employees can begin working, contracts must be signed.

(A) Without
(B) Before
(C) Until
(D) Except

5 ------- admission to the violin recital is free, we welcome donations of any amount.

(A) Despite
(B) Except
(C) While
(D) Equally

6 The automobile title transfer will not be official ------- signed by the seller and buyer.

(A) without
(B) until
(C) between
(D) against

7 ------- you have registered with Select Software, you will receive a customer identification number.

(A) Once
(B) Soon
(C) As well
(D) Next

8 Werlin Paper will not add a new product line this fiscal year ------- this would require hiring more staff.

(A) as
(B) which
(C) until
(D) but

9 The museum is closed to the public ------- the heating system is being renovated.

(A) during
(B) while
(C) after
(D) along

10 Stonefair Park will close early this Friday ------- park workers can begin setting up the art festival.

(A) for example
(B) as if
(C) even though
(D) so that

Questions 11-14 refer to the following memo.

To: All Kirbling Sales Associates
From: Tania Chow
Date: April 15
Re: Summer sales promotion

I want to remind all of you of the upcoming summer promotion at our store. To celebrate the summer ------- , we are offering special discounts on outdoor grills, garden supplies, and patio furniture. This three-day promotion ------- on May 20. ------- we plan to
11   **12**   **13**
promote the event with signs and newspaper advertisements, we will still need word-of-mouth advertising by you to generate interest among our customers. ------- . As always, I
14
appreciate your outstanding work and dedication!

11 (A) success
   (B) release
   (C) season
   (D) completion

12 (A) begin
   (B) will begin
   (C) began
   (D) beginning

13 (A) In summary
   (B) Whether
   (C) In case
   (D) Even though

14 (A) Please mention the sale to your customers before they leave the store.
   (B) If you are interested in sales, we are now hiring for our busy summer period.
   (C) Our new patio furniture features a modern design.
   (D) Prices will be increasing, so make your purchases now!

| WORDS | 1 tourism 관광업 flourish 번창하다, 번성하다 2 cancel 취소하다 no longer 더 이상 ~ 않다 4 contract 계약(서) 5 admission 입장료 donation 기부(금) 6 title transfer 명의 변경 official 공식적인 7 identification number 식별 번호, 고유 번호 8 fiscal year 회계 연도 9 heating system 난방 설비 renovate 보수하다 10 set up 준비하다 11-14 promotion 판촉 upcoming 다가오는 patio 테라스 word-of-mouth 구두의, 입소문의 mention 언급하다 outstanding 뛰어난

UNIT 14

관계사

무료인강 바로가기

두 문장을 자연스럽게 연결하는 관계사!

두 문장에 동일한 요소가 있을 경우, 반복되는 요소를 대신하면서 두 문장을
이어주는 것이 관계사입니다. 관계대명사는 〈접속사 + 대명사〉의 역할을 하고,
관계부사는 〈접속사 + 부사〉의 역할을 합니다.

나는 어떤 남자를 만났어. 그는 영화배우야.
= 나는 영화배우인 어떤 남자를 만났어.

맨 위처럼 두 문장으로 말해도 괜찮지만 아래처럼 한 문장으로 말해도 좋습니다. '어떤 남자'
와 '그'는 같은 인물이므로 두 번째 문장에서 '그는'을 생략하고 '영화배우인 어떤 남자'라는 덩
어리가 되어 좀 더 간단한 문장이 됐죠. 영어에서는 이럴 때 요긴하게 쓰는 말이 '관계대명사'
입니다. '가까운 관계로 이어주는 대명사'라고 생각하면 돼요. 영어의 인칭대명사에 주격, 목적
격, 소유격이란 격이 있으므로 관계대명사 역시 이 세 가지 형태가 있습니다. 토익에서는 주격
관계대명사가 자주 출제되므로 주격 관계대명사를 중심으로 공부해봅시다.

● 관계대명사의 종류

관계대명사는 앞에 오는 명사(선행사)가 사람인지 사물인지 여부에 따라 아래와 같이 나뉩니다. 이때 주의할 것은 that 은 소유격이 없으며 콤마 뒤에 쓰이지 않는다는 것입니다.

선행사	주격	목적격	소유격
사람	who, that	whom, that	whose
사물, 동물	which, that	which, that	whose, of which

● 관계대명사절의 이해

관계대명사는 〈접속사 + 대명사〉이며 관계대명사가 이끄는 절을 '관계대명사절'이라고 합니다.

I watched a movie. + The movie was very touching.

→ I watched a movie / and it was very touching. 나는 영화를 보았다 / 그리고 그것은 매우 감동적이었다.
접속사 + 대명사

→ I watched / a movie which was very touching. 나는 보았다 / 매우 감동적인 영화를
선행사 (사물)   관계대명사절

● 관계부사절의 이해

관계부사란 〈전치사 + 관계대명사〉를 대신하는 접속사로, 관계부사를 포함하고 있는 절을 '관계부사절'이라고 합니다.

The city held the job fair. + I lived in the city.

→ The city in which I lived / held the job fair.

→ The city where I lived / held / the job fair. 내가 살았던 도시에서 / 개최했다 / 취업 박람회를
선행사   관계부사절

기초 QUIZ

1. 다음 두 문장을 관계대명사를 써서 연결해 보세요.

   We will purchase the copier. + It is on sale this week.

   → _____

   문장에 the copier와 대명사 It이 반복되며 the copier가 사물이므로 관계대명사 which[that]로 두 문장을 연결합니다.
   정답: We will purchase the copier which[that] is on sale this week.

2. 관계부사에 O표, 선행사에 밑줄을 치세요.

   There are different reasons (which / why) sales are slow.

   선행사 reasons를 꾸며주는 관계부사절에서 why가 관계부사로서 앞뒤 절을 연결하고 있습니다.   정답: why(관계부사), reasons(선행사)

✎ 주격 관계대명사

① 주격 관계대명사 + 동사

주격 관계대명사는 관계사절에서 주어 자리를 대신하므로 뒤에 동사가 옵니다.

- Participants who[that] have questions / should remain seated.
  선행사 (사람)　　주격관계대명사 동사

  질문이 있는 참가자들은 / 계속 앉아 있어야 한다

- She designs / clothes which[that] attract young people.
  　　　　　선행사 (사물) 주격관계대명사　　동사

  그녀는 디자인한다 / 젊은 사람들을 매혹시키는 옷을

② 주격 관계대명사 + 동사의 수, 시제, 태

주격 관계대명사 뒤의 동사는 앞의 선행사와 수 일치를 하며, 시제, 태를 맞추어 쓰입니다.

- The new air conditioner that (was, ~~were~~) released [last week] / has an automatic timer.
  　　　선행사 (단수)　　　　　　　　단수 동사 / 수동태 / 과거 시제

  지난주에 출시된 신형 에어컨은 / 자동 타이머 기능이 있다

③ 〈주격 관계대명사 + be동사〉의 생략

〈주격 관계대명사 + be동사〉의 형태가 생략될 수 있어요. 이때 선행사 뒤에는 be동사 뒤에 올 수 있는 형용사나 -ing, p.p. 형태가 남아 있으니 형태에 주의하세요.

- The crew [(that were) inspecting the goods] / found / that some units are badly damaged.
  　선행사　　　　　　　　　　-ing

  물품을 검사하던 작업반원은 / 발견했다 / 몇 개가 심하게 파손된 것을

- The monthly meeting [(that was) scheduled for May 15 / will take place / on May 23.
  　　　선행사　　　　　　　　　p.p.

  5월 15일에 예정되었던 월례 회의는 / 열릴 것이다 / 5월 23일에

ETS 문제로 **훈련하기**

STEP 01

(A), (B) 중 알맞은 것을 고르세요.

1 This report includes a chart ------- summarizes the company's profits.

(A) which　　(B) who

2 Sun Airlines offers special discounts to customers ------- fly more than once a month.

(A) who　　(B) which

3 Please confirm receipt of the signed invoice ------- was included in our recent shipment.

(A) that　　(B) any

4 Employees ------- in joining company sports teams should contact Meredith Lo by May 1.

(A) interest　　(B) interested

5 Those employees ------- in an assembly area must wear protective gear at all times.

(A) are working　　(B) working

6 *Studio Ceramics Monthly* does not accept manuscripts ------- have previously appeared in print.

(A) that　　(B) they

STEP 02

빈칸에 가장 알맞은 것을 고르세요.

7 I would like to thank Dr. Frank, ------- has agreed to deliver an address at the ceremony.

(A) anyone　　(B) whose
(C) whichever　　(D) who

8 The company's financial advisor recommended an investment ------- rose steadily in value.

(A) that　　(B) they
(C) what　　(D) when

9 The marketing department has announced a new incentive bonus program ------- will begin next week.

(A) when　　(B) such
(C) which　　(D) until

10 Employees should complete their expense reports by using the template ------- was sent out by Ms. Chu last week.

(A) whose　　(B) maybe
(C) next　　(D) that

| WORDS | 1 summarize 요약하다 profit 수익, 이득 2 offer 제공하다 3 confirm 확인하다 receipt 수령 invoice 송장, 청구서
4 join 가입하다 contact 연락하다 5 assembly 조립 protective gear 보호 장비 6 manuscript 원고 7 deliver an
address 연설을 하다 ceremony 식, 기념식 8 financial advisor 재정 고문[자문] investment 투자, 투자물 steadily
꾸준히 9 incentive bonus 장려금 10 complete 작성하다 expense 지출 template 템플릿, 견본 양식

목적격과 소유격 관계대명사

① 목적격 관계대명사 + 주어 + 동사

목적격 관계대명사는 관계사절에서 목적어 자리를 대신하므로 뒤에 목적어가 빠진 〈주어 + 동사〉 구조가 옵니다.

- Mr. Mills / confirmed / <u>the reservation</u> / and <u>he made</u> it last Friday.
  밀스 씨는 / 확인했다 / 예약을 / 그리고 그는 그것을 지난주 금요일에 했다

→ Mr. Mills / confirmed <u>the reservation</u> which[that] <u>he made</u> last Friday.
                          선행사   목적격 관계대명사 주어 동사 (목적어 없음)
  밀스 씨는 / 확인했다 / 그가 지난주 금요일에 했던 예약을

② 목적격 관계대명사의 생략

목적격 관계대명사는 단독으로 생략될 수 있습니다. 생략이 되면 선행사인 명사 뒤에 〈주어 + 동사〉가 바로 연결되어 문장 구조 파악이 어려울 수 있으므로 주의하세요.

- <u>The programmer</u> [(whom, that) <u>we met</u> at the seminar] / is very competent.
      선행사   주어 동사 (목적어 없음)

= <u>The programmer</u> [we met at the seminar] / is very competent.
  우리가 세미나에서 만난 그 프로그래머는 / 매우 유능하다

③ 소유격 관계대명사 + 명사

소유격 관계대명사는 관계사절에서 명사 앞에 소유격이 빠진 자리를 대신하므로 바로 뒤에 명사가 옵니다. 소유격 관계대명사는 선행사가 사람이나 사물일 때 모두 whose를 사용하여 that으로 대신할 수 없습니다.

- They / will introduce / <u>a new car</u> / and its design has not been revealed.
  그들은 / 소개할 것이다 / 신차를 / 그리고 그것의 디자인은 공개되지 않았다

→ They / will introduce / <u>a new car</u> (whose, ~~that~~) design has not been revealed.
                               선행사   소유격 관계대명사   명사
  그들은 / 소개할 것이다 / 디자인이 공개되지 않은 신차를

ETS 문제로 훈련하기

STEP 01

(A), (B) 중 알맞은 것을 고르세요.

1 Refunds will be given to all customers ------- orders are damaged in shipping.
(A) which (B) whose

2 The applicant ------- the professor recommended will come for an interview soon.
(A) that (B) when

3 Metropolitan Artworks is an organization ------- mission is to support public art projects.
(A) which (B) whose

4 The book ------- ordered yesterday will be delivered tomorrow morning.
(A) you (B) your

5 Akira Tsukada's novel, ------- title hasn't been finalized yet, will be released next year.
(A) which (B) whose

6 The agenda you received yesterday outlines several topics ------- plan to discuss.
(A) my (B) I

STEP 02

빈칸에 가장 알맞은 것을 고르세요.

7 Employers prefer to interview candidates ------- résumés are well written and clearly organized.
(A) that (B) than
(C) whose (D) which

8 Attached please find the notes from last week's budgeting seminar ------- you requested.
(A) then (B) that
(C) what (D) when

9 Skytown Airlines apologized to the passengers for the delays ------- experienced.
(A) they (B) their
(C) them (D) this

10 Michael Sanders and Olivia Lim, the artists ------- paintings are currently on display at the Villanueva Gallery, both attended Fenmoor University.
(A) whose (B) who
(C) their (D) they

| WORDS | 1 refund 환불(금) order 주문(품) 2 applicant 지원자, 신청자 professor 교수 recommend 추천하다, 권하다 3 organization 기관, 단체 mission 임무 4 deliver 배송하다 5 finalize 확정하다 release 출간하다, 발행하다 6 agenda 안건, 의제 outline 개요를 서술하다 7 candidate 후보자, 지원자 organized 정리된, 체계적인 8 attached 첨부된 note 메모, 노트 budgeting 예산 편성 request 요청하다 9 apologize 사과하다 delay 지연, 연착 10 on display 전시 중인

관계부사

① 관계부사의 종류

부사 역할을 하는 관계부사에는 시간을 나타내는 when, 장소를 나타내는 where, 이유를 나타내는 why, 방법을 나타내는 how가 있습니다. 어떤 관계부사를 쓸지는 문장의 전후 맥락이나 선행사를 보고 결정해야 합니다.

의미	선행사	관계부사
시간	the time, the day, the year	when
장소	the place, the building	where
이유	the reason	why
방법	(the way) *the way와 how는 함께 쓸 수 없고 둘 중 하나만 씀	how

[시간]   The airline industry / suffered losses / last year when oil prices rose sharply.
항공 업계는 / 손실을 보았다 / 유가가 급격히 상승했던 지난해에

[장소]   Many people / like a workplace where people enjoy their work.
많은 사람들은 / 사람들이 자기 일을 즐기는 직장을 좋아한다

[이유]   There are several reasons why a company needs its own Web site.
회사에 자체 웹사이트가 필요한 몇 가지 이유가 있다

[방법]   The customer / was disappointed / with how the company handled her complaint.
관계부사 how 앞에 선행사 역할을 하는 the way가 생략되었음
그 고객은 / 실망했다 / 회사가 자신의 불만을 처리하는 방식에

② 관계대명사와 관계부사의 차이점

관계대명사는 대명사를 대신하므로 관계대명사절 뒤에는 '불완전한' 절이 오지만, 관계부사는 부사를 대신하므로 관계부사절 뒤에는 '완전한' 절이 옵니다. 또, 관계부사는 대개 〈전치사 + which〉로 바꾸어 쓸 수 있습니다.

• The city / renovated / the historic building (that / where) was built 200 years ago.
주격 관계대명사   불완전한 절(주어 없음)
시는 / 보수했다 / 200년 전에 지어진 역사적인 건물을

• The conference / will take place / in the city, / (which / where) the company was founded.
관계부사   완전한 절

= The conference / will take place / in the city, / in (which / where) the company was founded.
전치사 + 관계대명사   완전한 절
콘퍼런스는 / 열릴 것인데 / 그 도시에서 / 그곳에서 그 회사가 설립되었다

ETS 문제로 **훈련하기**

(A), (B) 중 알맞은 것을 고르세요.

1 Ms. Han's goal is to establish a charity foundation in the city ------- she grew up.

(A) where   (B) when

2 June is the month ------- GW Products releases its annual research report.

(A) why   (B) when

3 Health care practitioners are required to obtain licenses from every country ------- they practice.

(A) which   (B) in which

4 The manager has the key to the storage room ------- the office supplies are kept.

(A) where   (B) why

5 Please check the boxes next to the projects on ------- you prefer to work.

(A) which   (B) where

6 All shipments arrive at the receiving dock, ------- a warehouse worker checks their tracking labels.

(A) which   (B) where

빈칸에 가장 알맞은 것을 고르세요.

7 The Starmax Hotel renovated its restaurant in 2010 ------- two more chefs were hired.

(A) that   (B) what
(C) who   (D) when

8 A group of engineers will visit Maizin, Inc., to study ------- the company produces environmentally-friendly vehicles.

(A) which   (B) what
(C) who   (D) how

9 Global corporations must be sensitive to the values of each culture in ------- they advertise.

(A) when   (B) whose
(C) where   (D) which

10 Supplementary materials are available to employees ------ would like to learn more about the design of Giraldi Photos' imaging software.

(A) when   (B) such
(C) that   (D) until

| WORDS | **1** goal 목표 establish 설립하다 charity 자선 foundation 재단 **2** release 발표하다 annual 연례의, 1년마다의 **3** health care 의료 서비스, 보건 practitioner 개업 의사 license 면허증 **4** storage room 저장고, 창고 **5** prefer 선호하다 **6** shipment 배송품, 운송품 receiving dock 하역장 warehouse (물류) 창고 tracking 추적 **7** renovate 보수하다, 수리하다 hire 채용하다 **8** environmentally-friendly 친환경적인 **9** corporation (대)기업 sensitive 민감한, 세심한 advertise 광고하다 **10** supplementary 보충의

아래 토익 필수 어휘들을 표현과 함께 익혀 보세요.

conveniently	편리하게	securely	단단히, 안전하게
properly	제대로, 적절히	thoroughly	철저히
reasonably	(가격이) 합리적으로	adversely	불리하게
gradually	점차로, 서서히	steadily	꾸준하게
positively	긍정적으로	strongly	강력하게, 단호하게
typically	전형적으로, 일반적으로	briefly	간단히; 잠시
rapidly	빨리, 급속히	slightly	약간, 조금
absolutely	절대적으로, 완전히	readily	손쉽게, 기꺼이
scarcely	거의 ~ 않다	marginally	아주 조금
anxiously	애타게	virtually	사실상

어휘 표현 익히기   위의 단어들을 외우고 아래 표현을 완성해 보세요.

1. The office is _____ located.   사무실은 **편리하게** 위치해 있다.
2. advance slowly but _____   느리지만 **꾸준하게** 나아가다
3. _____ priced items   가격이 **합리적으로** 책정된 물품들
4. rise _____   **서서히** 증가하다
5. investigate the cause _____   원인을 **철저하게** 조사하다
6. _____ explain   **간단히** 설명하다
7. be functioning _____   **제대로** 작동 중이다
8. _____ disagree with the plan   계획에 **강력하게** 반대하다
9. _____ free of charge   **완전히** 무료로
10. _____ affect the global economy   세계 경제에 **불리하게** 영향을 미치다

| ANSWERS | 1. conveniently 2. steadily 3. reasonably 4. gradually 5. thoroughly
　　　　　　　6. briefly 7. properly 8. strongly 9. absolutely 10. adversely

ETS 문제로 **훈련하기**

STEP 01

(A), (B) 중 알맞은 것을 고르세요.

1 Our marketing strategy will be -------- influenced by the results of the survey.

(A) loudly   (B) strongly

2 Decisions about vacation time are ------- made by the department head.

(A) scarcely   (B) typically

3 Production has increased ------- to keep up with growing consumer demand.

(A) approximately   (B) steadily

4 The unseasonably cold weather has ------- affected the availability of some fruits.

(A) adversely   (B) accurately

STEP 02

빈칸에 가장 알맞은 것을 고르세요.

5 There is a variety of restaurants -------- located on the same street as the convention center.

(A) conveniently   (B) marginally
(C) gradually   (D) quickly

6 The cost of a train ticket is set to increase ------- on January 1.

(A) quickly   (B) slightly
(C) urgently   (D) equally

7 The deadline for submitting shareholder proposals to Lozerin International is ------- approaching.

(A) securely   (B) rapidly
(C) carefully   (D) anxiously

8 Innovative and ------- priced Italian food draws a lively crowd at Echo Restaurant.

(A) virtually   (B) gratefully
(C) thoroughly   (D) reasonably

| WORDS | **1** marketing strategy 마케팅 전략   survey 설문 조사   **2** department head 부서장   **3** keep up with ~을 따라잡다 consumer 소비자   demand 수요   **4** unseasonably 계절에 맞지 않게   affect 영향을 미치다   availability 입수 가능성   **6** be set to ~하도록 예정되어 있다   slightly 약간, 소폭으로   **7** deadline 마감일, 마감 기한   submit 제출하다 shareholder 주주   proposal 제안(서)   approach 다가오다   **8** innovative 혁신적인   draw (마음을) 끌어들이다 crowd 사람들, 무리

ETS 실전 테스트

1 Mr. Martinelli, ------- started as a stock clerk and is now vice president of marketing, will retire in May.

(A) who
(B) that
(C) when
(D) another

2 They are renovating the lobby of the building ------- the winning photographs will be exhibited next month.

(A) how
(B) why
(C) what
(D) where

3 A free bicycle lock is available to anyone who ------- a Nakamura bike before August 1.

(A) purchase
(B) purchaser
(C) purchases
(D) purchasing

4 The teams ------- members finish the tasks by 1:30 P.M. should report to the main office to receive their next projects.

(A) its
(B) that
(C) which
(D) whose

5 Innovative Solution is an organization ------- provides technical support at reduced rates to small businesses.

(A) who
(B) where
(C) that
(D) what

6 All new employees receive training folders that ------- information about their assignments.

(A) containing
(B) contained
(C) contain
(D) contains

7 Passengers ------- wish to upgrade their economy tickets to business class may do so using the airline's Web site.

(A) who
(B) whose
(C) whoever
(D) to whom

8 Many people ------- were interviewed felt that they did not need a large car.

(A) which
(B) whom
(C) what
(D) that

9 The opening remarks by Judge Yamamoto, ------- were devoted to international trade law, were the highlight of the conference.

(A) who
(B) which
(C) what
(D) whose

10 Morris Homes has several in-house ------- who will work on this project.

(A) designing
(B) design
(C) designed
(D) designers

정답 및 해설 p.158

Questions 11-14 refer to the following article.

UNIVERSITY TO EXPAND BUSINESS COLLEGE

After two years of ------- , the Newhouse University Board of Trustees has decided to increase
               11
the number of courses offered at Newhouse Business College. The new course schedule,

------- was recently approved by the board of trustees, will take effect next September.
12

The ------- course selection is expected to increase enrollment and therefore allow Newhouse
       13
to more effectively compete with other business schools in the region.

------- . According to University President Ahmed Sabresh, attracting more evening students
  14
to Newhouse is a major objective of the university.

---

11 (A) consider
   (B) considered
   (C) consideration
   (D) considerable

12 (A) who
   (B) which
   (C) when
   (D) why

13 (A) automatic
   (B) expanded
   (C) frequent
   (D) corrected

14 (A) A new university president will be
       appointed next October.
   (B) Many of the new courses will be
       offered in the evening.
   (C) One of those contests is called "Young
       Entrepreneurs."
   (D) There is currently a surcharge for late
       registration.

| WORDS | **1** stock 재고(품) clerk 사무원, 직원 **2** renovate 개조하다, 수리하다 winning 상을 받은, 우승한 exhibit 전시하다 **3** available 입수할 수 있는 **4** task 일, 과제 main office 본사 **5** at reduced rates 할인된 요금으로 **6** folder 서류철, 폴더 assignment 과제, 업무 **7** passenger 승객 airline 항공사 **9** opening remarks 개회사 be devoted to ~에 바쳐지다 highlight 하이라이트, 압권 conference 콘퍼런스, 총회 **10** in-house 사내의 **11-14** expand 확대하다 business college 경영 대학원 Board of Trustees 이사회 increase 늘리다 approve 승인하다 take effect 효력을 발휘하다 selection 선택, 선택 가능한 것들 enrollment 등록 effectively 효과적으로 compete with ~와 경쟁하다 university president 대학 총장 objective 목표 **14** appoint 임명하다 entrepreneur 기업가 surcharge 추가 수수료 registration 등록

RC

PART 06

Part 6 기초 쌓기

UNIT 01

동사 시제 고르기

풀이전략 | 빈칸 앞뒤 문맥과 시제를 통해 정답 고르기

동사 시제 고르기 문제는 시제의 단서가 되는 시간 표현이 빈칸 문장 안에 대부분 제시되지 않기 때문에 문법 문제 중에서 난이도가 가장 높은 문제 유형 중 하나입니다. 빈칸 앞뒤 문맥과 문장의 시제를 통해 정답을 고를 수 있으며 한 문장 안에서만 해결하고자 하면 오답을 선택할 수 있습니다.

ETS 예제

Question refers to the following note.

From the Desk of the Callicoon Art Gallery

Thank you for your generous gift to the Callicoon Art Gallery. Your contribution will allow us to extend the classes we offer beyond sculpture and painting. In February, we ------- a drawing class, too. From the very first class, all materials will be supplied to students with funds from this campaign to which so many contributed. Thank you for helping us move toward our goal of providing easily accessible arts education to the Callicoon community.

Yours faithfully,
The Callicoon Art Gallery

캘리쿤 미술관의 사무실로부터

캘리쿤 미술관에 보내주신 후한 선물에 감사드립니다. 귀하의 기부로 저희가 운영하는 강좌를 조각과 회화 너머로 확대할 수 있게 될 것입니다. 2월에는 소묘 강좌도 개설할 예정입니다. 맨 첫 수업부터 모든 재료는 아주 많은 분들께서 기부해 주신 이 캠페인의 자금으로 학생들에게 제공될 것입니다. 캘리쿤 지역 사회에 쉽게 이해할 수 있는 미술 교육을 제공한다는 저희의 목표를 향해 나아가는 데 도움을 주셔서 감사합니다.

캘리쿤 미술관

(A) opening
(B) opened
(C) had opened
(D) will open

STEP 01

빈칸 앞뒤 내용 파악하기

빈칸 앞: 강좌를 조각과 회화 강좌 너머로 확대할 것이다.

빈칸 뒤: 소묘 강좌에서는 첫 수업부터 모든 재료를 제공할 것이다.

STEP 02

빈칸 앞뒤 시제 파악하기

빈칸 앞: 단순미래 시제(will allow)

빈칸 뒤: 단순미래 시제(will be supplied)

STEP 03

정답 선택하기

동사 자리에 올 수 없는 형태인 (A) opening은 우선 제외한다. 앞 문장에서 강좌를 조각과 회화 강좌 너머로 확대할 것이라고 했고, 뒤 문장에서도 소묘 강좌에서 첫 수업부터 모든 재료를 제공할 것이라고 하므로 미래 시제인 (D) will open이 정답이다.

만점 전략 1   빈칸 앞 또는 뒤에 날짜가 있는 경우 문서 작성일과 비교하기

회람 작성일

> Date: June 3
> 날짜: 6월 3일

빈칸에 들어갈 시제

A flexible work schedule (C) will be offered as of July 1.
근무 시간 자유 선택제는 7월 1일부터 실시될 예정이다.

이메일, 편지, 회람은 작성일을 제시하는 경우가 많은데, 작성일이 시제를 판단하는 단서가 될 수 있습니다. 회람 작성일이 6월 3일인데, 7월 1일을 언급하고 있으므로 미래 시제 will be offered로 표현하는 것이 적절합니다.

| 오답 | (A) was offering, (B) had offered, (D) to be offering

만점 전략 2   빈칸 앞뒤 문장의 시간 표현과 시제 흐름으로 시제를 파악하기

앞 문장 시간 표현

> We would like to schedule an interview with you during the upcoming week.
> 다음 주에 귀하와의 면접 일정을 정하고 싶습니다.

빈칸에 들어갈 시제

I (B) will be out of the office on a business trip until Tuesday afternoon.
저는 화요일 오후까지 자리를 비울 예정입니다.

빈칸 앞 문장에서 미래를 나타내는 시간 표현인 다음 주(upcoming week)가 나왔으므로 빈칸에서도 미래 시제 will be로 자리를 비울 예정이라고 표현하는 것이 적절합니다.

오답: (A) was, (C) had been, (D) being

빈칸에 들어갈 시제

Employees from across the Toronto region (D) have rated their companies.
토론토 전역에서 직원들이 그들의 회사를 평가했다.

뒤 문장 시제

> Businesses selected for the survey had to employ at least 50 people.
> 설문 조사에 선정된 업체들은 최소 50명을 고용하고 있어야 했다.

빈칸 뒤의 문장에서 설문 조사에 선정된 업체들은 최소 50명의 직원을 고용하고 있어야 했다(had to)고 과거 시제로 말하고 있으므로 설문 조사가 이미 완료된 상황임을 현재완료 시제 have rated로 표현하는 것이 적절합니다.

| 오답 | (A) will rate, (B) are rating, (C) will have been rating

Question 1 refers to the following letter.

10 February

Dear Mr. Garcia,

The Garden and Flower Society is proud to announce that we --------- our fifth Spring Garden and Houseplant Sale on Saturday, 3 May. This event takes place every year on the front lawn at Forest Park. Since you sold your lovely watercolour paintings at last year's sale, I thought you might want to join us again this year. I am attaching the necessary information and application form if you are interested in participating. We look forward to hearing from you.

Sincerely,

Sanford Sladen,
GFS Events Coordinator

(A) hold
(B) held
(C) holding
(D) will hold

Question 2 refers to the following e-mail.

Dear Mr. Jackson,

Please accept my apologies for not getting back to you sooner. I ------- to determine what happened to your order. Unfortunately, it took the shipper two days to return my phone call. I was informed that the delay was caused by a heavy snowstorm on the shipping route. As a result, your two dozen watches should be delivered by 10 February. Again, I apologize for the delay. Thank you for your business and your patience.

(A) am going to try
(B) might try
(C) am trying
(D) have been trying

| WORDS |

1 announce 발표하다 houseplant 실내용 화초, 화분 식물 lawn 잔디밭 attach 첨부하다 necessary 필요한 application 지원(서), 신청(서) participate 참여하다 look forward to -ing ~하기를 고대하다 coordinator 코디네이터, 진행자
2 accept 받아들이다 apology 사과 determine 알아내다, 결정하다 inform 알리다 cause 원인이 되다, 야기하다 snowstorm 폭설 shipping route 운송 경로 dozen 12개 patience 인내심

ETS 실전 테스트

Questions 1-4 refer to the following job listing.

Sales and Marketing Leader—Southeast Region

Daily Green Foods is hiring a new sales and marketing leader to help grow its reach in the Southeast Region. The chosen candidate will be in charge of ------- sales by promoting our products at local supermarkets. ------- . Knowledge of the brand and competing markets is therefore ------- .

1   **2**   **3**

The selected candidate is expected to achieve quarterly sales goals and expand the visibility of the Daily Green Foods brand. Our sales and marketing leader ------- our company goal of making healthy eating simple and accessible for all.
4

Please contact Amy Kipkorir at akipkorir@dgf.com for more information about the position.

---

1 (A) communicating
   (B) increasing
   (C) competing
   (D) proceeding

2 (A) We are discussing the expansion of our manufacturing facility.
   (B) Please forward your résumé, a cover letter, and three references.
   (C) The candidate will also develop our regional marketing strategy.
   (D) We are looking for a start date in January.

3 (A) desirably
   (B) desirable
   (C) desires
   (D) desire

4 (A) will support
   (B) has supported
   (C) is supporting
   (D) had supported

PART 6 | UNIT 01

| WORDS |

reach (영향을 미치는) 범위, 구역 candidate 지원자 in charge of ~을 담당하는 promote 홍보하다 knowledge 지식 competing 경쟁하는 selected 선정된 achieve 달성하다 quarterly 분기별의 visibility 가시성 accessible 접근할 수 있는
2 discuss 논의하다 expansion 확대, 확장 facility 시설 forward 보내다 reference 추천인, 추천서

정답 및 해설 p.164

191

대명사 고르기

풀이전략 | 대명사가 지칭하는 명사를 빈칸 앞 문장에서 문맥을 통해 찾기

인칭대명사의 격을 묻는 문제는 한 문장 안에서 정답을 고를 수 있습니다. 하지만 다양한 대명사가 섞여 있는 경우에는 빈칸 앞 문장에서 대명사가 대신할 수 있는 명사를 찾아야 할 수도 있습니다.

 Question refers to the following notice.

The Redistock Office Supplies Web site is currently unavailable because of maintenance. The updated site can be accessed after midnight tonight. In addition to providing enhanced security to protect your information, the online store will include **features** to make ordering from Redistock easier than ever. ------- include more user-friendly menus and product suggestions based on your order history.

Thank you for your patience during this time. The improvements should provide smoother transactions in the future.

레디스톡 사무용품 웹사이트는 현재 보수 작업으로 인해 이용이 불가능합니다. 업데이트된 사이트는 오늘 밤 자정 이후 접속 가능합니다. 여러분의 정보를 보호하기 위해 강화된 보안을 제공함과 더불어, 온라인 매장은 레디스톡에서 그 어느 때보다도 더 쉽게 주문할 수 있게 하는 기능들을 포함할 것입니다. 이는 더 사용하기 쉬운 메뉴와 귀하의 주문 이력에 기반한 상품 제안을 포함합니다.

이 기간 동안 참고 기다려주셔서 감사합니다. 이번 개선 작업으로 향후 더 순조로운 거래가 제공될 것입니다.

(A) **These**
(B) Any
(C) You
(D) Mine

STEP 01

선택지를 먼저 살펴보기

선택지의 보기는 동사 include 앞의 주어 자리에 쓰일 수 있는 대명사로 문법상 모두 가능하다.

STEP 02

빈칸 앞 명사 어휘 살펴보기

빈칸 앞: 온라인 매장은 더 쉽게 주문할 수 있는 기능들 (features)을 포함할 것이다.

STEP 03

정답 선택하기

빈칸 앞 문장에서 온라인 매장은 쉽게 주문할 수 있게 하는 기능들 (features) 이 있다고 했고, 빈칸 뒤에 더 사용하기 쉬운 메뉴들이 포함된다고 하므로 features를 대신할 수 있는 대명사 (A) These가 정답이다.

만점 전략 1   빈칸의 대명사를 지칭하는 명사를 빈칸 앞에서 문맥으로 찾기

앞 문장 키워드

We hope you will participate in a brief online
survey composed of four questions.
네 가지 질문으로 구성된 간단한 온라인 설문 조사에 참여해 주시기를 바랍니다.

빈칸에 들어갈 인칭대명사의 인칭

**Please answer (B) them
as honestly as possible.**
가능한 한 솔직하게 그것들에 답변해주십시오.

빈칸에서 답변의 대상이 되는 것은 빈칸 앞 문장에서 언급된 네 가지 질문(four questions)이므로 four
questions를 지칭하는 인칭대명사의 목적격 them이 적절합니다.

| 오답 | (A) him, (C) either one, (D) everybody

만점 전략 2   인칭대명사의 격을 묻는 문제는 한 문장 안에서 해결하기

빈칸에 들어갈 인칭대명사의 격

The owner of East End Hardware is very proud of (C) her business' vital role in the community.
이스트 엔드 하드웨어의 소유주는 지역 사회에서 자신의 업체가 하고 있는 중요한 역할에 대해 매우 자랑스러워하고 있습니다.

빈칸 뒤에 명사 business가 있으므로 명사를 수식해 줄 수 있는 소유격 인칭대명사 her가 적절합니다.

| 오답 | (A) she, (B) hers, (D) herself

만점 전략 3   주어 you가 생략된 명령문에서 재귀대명사의 인칭 구별하기

빈칸에 들어갈 재귀대명사

Please take extra care to clean up after (B) yourself while we share their space.
우리가 그들의 공간을 같이 사용하는 동안에는 뒷정리에 각별히 신경 써주십시오.

명령문은 주어가 you가 생략된 문장이므로 빈칸은 전치사 after의 목적어 자리에 2인칭을 나타내는 재귀대명사
yourself가 적절합니다. 참고로 clean up after oneself는 '~의 뒷정리를 하다'라는 의미를 가집니다.

| 오답 | (A) himself, (C) ourselves, (D) themselves

TIP 주어 자리에 오지 못하는 대명사
재귀대명사 (oneself), each other (둘이 서로), one another (셋 이상이 서로)

Question 1 refers to the following e-mail.

Dear Ms. Wu,

We have shipped the requested part for your handheld leaf blower. Please accept ------- apology for the piece that was not included in the box. We hope that this free shipment will make up for any inconvenience. The missing piece has been sent via postal express delivery. You should receive a separate e-mail with the shipment's tracking information.

We hope this resolves the matter but please let us know if there is anything we can do to improve your satisfaction.

(A) his

(B) our

(C) her

(D) their

Question 2 refers to the following announcement.

Nyveg Technology Hardware Competition

Nyveg Ventures is now accepting applications for our sixth annual Technology Hardware Competition to be held in Oslo, Norway, beginning on 1 November. We will be selecting teams from around the world who have taken new hardware projects past the idea stage and have already built a working prototype.

Applications should be submitted online by 15 September. Accepted applicants will spend one week in Oslo working on further developing ------- prototypes. Each of the accepted teams will receive funding and technical support from our partners.

(A) they

(B) them

(C) their

(D) theirs

| WORDS |

1 ship 배송하다 part 부품 handheld 휴대용의 leaf blower 낙엽 송풍기 accept 받아들이다 make up for ~을 보상하다 inconvenience 불편 missing 사라진, 빠진 via ~을 통하여 postal 우편의 separate 별도의 tracking 추적 resolve 해결하다 satisfaction 만족(도)
2 competition 경쟁, 경연 대회 application 지원(서), 신청(서) annual 해마다 일어나는, 연례의 prototype 시제품, 원형 funding 자금 지원 technical support 기술, 지원

ETS 실전 테스트

Questions 1-4 refer to the following article.

LOS ANGELES (May 1)—Online marketer Sun Settings ------- an office in downtown
San Diego last week. The newly acquired space will accommodate 45 employees who
currently work -------.
1

2

"We are not moving any departments to San Diego," said Sun Settings spokeswoman
Jacqueline Gutierrez. "We are just offering office space to employees who are
scattered throughout that city. As our customer base grows, we find that it benefits our
telecommuters, who work from home offices, to work face-to-face on occasion."

Sun Settings has experienced rapid growth since its founding seven years ago. ------- .
The company has been expanding its telecommuting program at the same time.
3

"The program has really improved how effectively our salespeople can meet the needs of
our customers," said Ms. Gutierrez. " ------- will only continue to grow."
4

1 (A) sold
(B) opened
(C) painted
(D) inspected

2 (A) quietly
(B) recently
(C) remotely
(D) efficiently

3 (A) A new CEO was hired late last year.
(B) A new marketing plan was just announced.
(C) The company specializes in home goods.
(D) Its customer base has doubled in that time.

4 (A) It
(B) Yours
(C) Myself
(D) One another

| WORDS |

acquire 취득하다 accommodate 수용하다 currently 현재 scattered 흩어져 있는 benefit 도움이 되다, 유익하다
telecommuter 재택근무자 on occasion 이따금 rapid 급속한, 빠른 founding 설립 expand 확대하다 effectively 효과적으로
3 specialize in ~을 전문으로 하다 customer base 고객층 double 두 배가 되다

정답 및 해설 p.168

PART 6 | UNIT 02

195

UNIT 03

어휘 고르기

> **풀이전략 |** 문맥의 흐름을 파악하고 지문 안에서 동의어 단서를 찾아 정답을 고르기
>
> 어휘 고르기 문제는 명사와 동사 어휘가 가장 많이 출제됩니다. 특히 명사 어휘는 관사 the, this, these와 같은 한정사와 수식어에 유의하여 지문 내에서 동의어 단서를 찾도록 해야 합니다. 동사 어휘는 목적어를 받아줄 수 있는 동사에 집중하여 문맥의 흐름을 파악하면서 풀어야 합니다.

 Question refers to the following press release.

SHANGHAI (10 January)—Xing Marketing Group has announced a new -------. Julia Salartash will be joining Xing as director of the Perth, Australia, office. Ms. Salartash has fifteen years of experience in promotional campaign design and project management. "She is an accomplished marketing leader," said Xing president Ting Yu. "Her expertise will be an asset to our company as we continue to grow the business beyond Asia." Ms. Salartash will begin her new role on 12 February.

상하이 (1월 10일)–싱 마케팅 그룹이 신임 채용자를 발표했다. 줄리아 살라타시는 호주 퍼스 사무소 이사로 싱에 합류할 예정이다. 살라타시 씨는 홍보 캠페인 기획과 프로젝트 관리에 15년의 경력을 보유하고 있다. "그녀는 뛰어난 마케팅 리더입니다." 싱 사장 팅 유가 말했다. "우리가 아시아를 넘어 사업을 계속 성장시키고 있기 때문에 그녀의 전문 지식은 우리 회사에 자산이 될 것입니다." 살라타시 씨는 2월 12일부터 새로운 역할을 시작할 예정이다.

STEP 01
빈칸 앞을 살펴보기
빈칸 앞: 수식어 a new에 유의한다.

STEP 02
빈칸 뒤 동의어 단서 찾기
빈칸 뒤: Julia Salartash가 이사(director)라는 직책으로 합류할 예정이다.

STEP 03
정답 선택하기
빈칸 앞에서 새로운 ____을 발표했다고 했으며, 빈칸 뒤에서는 새로운 직책 director가 나오므로 대신할 수 있는 명사 어휘 (D) hire(직원)가 정답이다.

(A) project 프로젝트
(B) budget 예산
(C) location 장소
(D) hire 직원

만점 전략 1   문맥의 흐름을 살피면서 정답의 단서를 찾아내기

빈칸에 들어갈 동사 어휘

The first floor break room will be entirely (A) remodeled in the second week of March.
3월 둘째 주에 1층 휴게실을 완전히 개조할 예정입니다.

뒤 문장 키워드

In preparation for the construction, please remove all of your food from the refrigerator.
공사를 준비하기 위해 냉장고에 있는 음식을 모두 치워주십시오.

빈칸 뒤 문장에서 공사(construction) 준비를 하기 위해서 냉장고의 음식을 치워달라는 말이 나오고 있으므로 1층의 휴게실을 개조할 것(remodeled)이라는 의미가 되는 것이 자연스럽습니다.

| 오답 | (B) stocked, (C) separated, (D) completed

만점 전략 2   빈칸에 들어갈 어휘의 동의어 단서를 지문 안에서 찾아내기

앞 문장 키워드

We want to know your opinion about our service.
저희 서비스에 대한 고객님의 의견을 알고 싶습니다.

빈칸에 들어갈 명사 어휘

We hope we can receive your (D) feedback within 24 hours of receiving this message.
본 메시지를 수신하신 후 24시간 이내에 저희가 고객님의 피드백을 받을 수 있기를 바랍니다.

빈칸 앞 문장에서 고객의 의견(opinion)을 알고 싶다고 했으므로 opinion의 동의어인 피드백(feedback)을 받을 수 있기를 바란다는 것이 적절합니다.

| 오답 | (A) reservation, (B) upgrade, (C) confirmation

만점 전략 3   such as / especially 앞, these 뒤의 빈칸에서는 통칭명사를 고려하기

빈칸에 들어갈 명사 어휘

Reports should detail all necessary business (B) expenses, such as transportation and lodging costs. 보고서에는 교통비와 숙박비 같은 모든 필요한 업무 경비를 상세히 기록해야 합니다.

빈칸에는 교통비와 숙박비를 통틀어 가리키는 통칭명사인 업무 경비(expenses)가 정답으로 적절합니다.

| 오답 | (A) trips, (C) purposes, (D) locations

TIP   통칭명사(통틀어 지칭하는 명사)의 예시들

구체적인 예시	통칭명사
old files, used boxes	waste materials (폐기물)
paper, toner cartridges, folders	office supplies (사무용품들)
date, venue, a list of attendees, registration fee	information (정보)

Question 1 refers to the following information.

Your Omicron Office Copier is one of the most important tools you have. Therefore, knowing how to care for your copier properly is an important part of running an efficient business. Here are four vital tips from our team of experts to keep your copier in top shape. First, use Omicron-approved ------- , especially Omicron toner cartridges. Second, be careful when loading paper. Following the instructions in the manual will ensure proper loading of the paper and prevent paper jams. Third, clean the copier regularly. Use only soft cloths and cleaning materials recommended by Omicron. Finally, if your copier is in need of repair, we advise that you select a certified professional technician. Following these tips will prolong the life of your office copier.

(A) employees
(B) supplies
(C) access
(D) power

Question 2 refers to the following notice.

Our refrigerated display case is broken. We hope to have it ------- by this weekend if not sooner. Meanwhile, all perishable items normally kept in the case are in the refrigerator in the storage room. A complete list of these products is posted below. Please inform customers of these circumstances when they enter the shop. Offer to retrieve anything that interests them, and assure them that doing so is not an inconvenience.

(A) repaired
(B) answered
(C) generated
(D) satisfied

| WORDS |

1 care for ~을 돌보다, 관리하다 properly 제대로, 적절히 run 진행하다, 운영하다 efficient 효율적인 vital 필수적인 tip 조언, 정보 expert 전문가 in top shape 최상으로 especially 특히 load 싣다, 넣다 instructions 지시 사항, 설명 ensure 보장하다, 확실히 하다 proper 적절한, 제대로 된 loading 싣기, 넣기 prevent 막다, 방지하다 paper jam 용지 걸림 recommend 추천하다, 권장하다 in need of ~을 필요로 하는 certified 자격증 있는, 공인된 prolong 연장하다
2 refrigerated 냉장한 display case 진열장 if not sooner 늦어도 perishable 상하기[썩기] 쉬운 normally 보통은, 정상적으로는 storage room 저장고, 창고 inform A of B A에게 B를 알리다 retrieve 찾아 오다

Questions 1-4 refer to the following e-mail.

To: p.swain@ulofarms.com
From: support@plastimattic.com
Date: April 28
Subject: RE: Order #908190

Dear Mr. Swain,

We are sorry to hear that the plastic sheeting you purchased is performing unsatisfactorily. Usually when customers report a fault with our products, the ties on the corners of the plastic have not been affixed correctly to the equipment. ------- 1 . From what you have described, the way the plastic was ------- 2 does not seem to be the cause. You indicated that the plastic is ripping at the seams. We have not previously encountered a problem like this.

------- 3 , we at Plastimattic, Inc., are committed to 100 percent customer satisfaction. We can issue you a full refund, or we can send replacement sheets overnight at no extra cost. Please let us know ------- 4 option you prefer.

Kind regards,
Alejandro Gonzales, Plastimattic Customer Support

---

1 (A) We found your report to be very concerning.
(B) Your order should be arriving soon.
(C) We use a proprietary formula for the plastic in our products.
(D) Perhaps you would like to purchase some accessories.

2 (A) folded
(B) shipped
(C) cleaned
(D) attached

3 (A) Similarly
(B) Thus
(C) Nevertheless
(D) Rather

4 (A) that
(B) why
(C) when
(D) which

| WORDS |

perform 성능을 보이다 unsatisfactorily 만족스럽지 못하게 fault 결함 affix 부착하다 equipment 장비 describe 설명하다 cause 원인 indicate 지적하다 rip 뜯어지다, 터지다 seam 봉합선[봉제선] previously 이전에 encounter 접하다 be committed to ~에 전념하다 satisfaction 만족 issue 지급하다 replacement 교체(품) overnight 하룻밤 사이에 at no extra cost 추가 비용 없이
1 concerning 걱정스러운 proprietary 전매 상표가 붙은 formula 공식, 방식 accessories 부대용품

접속부사 고르기

무료인강 바로가기

> **풀이전략 |** 빈칸 앞·뒤 문장의 논리적 관계를 파악하고 알맞은 접속부사 고르기
>
> 접속부사는 빈칸 앞·뒤 문장의 논리적 관계(인과, 대조, 내용 추가, 시간의 순서)를 파악해야 합니다. 또한
> 접속부사는 〈주어 + 동사 ~. _____ , 주어 + 동사 ~〉와 같은 문장 구조에서 흔히 쓰이며 접속부사 자리에
> 접속사와 전치사는 들어갈 수 없습니다.

 Question refers to the following memo.

As part of our healthy-eating initiative, I am pleased to announce that McClug, Inc., is introducing an exciting new program for employees. We have entered into an agreement with Windsor Farms to provide you with fresh, organically grown vegetables.

Those who participate will receive a box of fresh selections delivered weekly to their desks starting on June 21. -------, at harvest time beginning in August, all program participants will be invited to pick their own blackberries, blueberries, and raspberries from Windsor Farms' fields.

건강한 식생활 계획의 일환으로, 맥클러그 사에서 직원들을 위한 흥미진진한 새 프로그램을 도입하게 되었음을 발표하게 되어 기쁩니다. 우리는 여러분에게 신선한 유기농 재배 채소를 제공하기 위해 원저 농장과 계약을 체결했습니다.

참가자는 6월 21일부터 매주 자기 자리로 배달되는 선별된 신선한 채소 한 상자를 받게 될 것입니다. 덧붙여 8월에 시작되는 수확철에는 프로그램 참가자 전원이 초청을 받아 원저 농장 밭에서 직접 블랙베리, 블루베리, 라즈베리를 따게 됩니다.

(A) Meanwhile 한편
(B) Instead 대신
(C) In addition 덧붙여
(D) For instance 예를 들어

STEP 01
선택지가 접속부사인지 확인

선택지: 모두 접속부사이다.

STEP 02
빈칸 앞·뒤 논리 관계 확인

빈칸 앞: 참가자들은 신선한 채소 상자를 배달받는다.
빈칸 뒤: 참가자들은 농장에서 직접 다양한 베리들을 딸 수 있다.

STEP 03
정답 선택하기

빈칸 앞·뒤에서 모두 새로운 식생활 프로그램의 내용을 소개하고 있으므로 내용 추가를 나타내는 접속부사 (C) In addition(덧붙여)이 정답이다.

만점 전략 1   빈출 접속부사 알아두기

내용 전환	however 그러나 in contrast 대조적으로 otherwise 그렇지 않으면	on the contrary 반대로 nevertheless/nonetheless 그럼에도 불구하고 instead/alternatively 대신에	on the other hand 반면에 even so 그렇다 해도
내용 추가	in addition/besides 게다가	moreover/furthermore 더욱이	similarly 유사하게
시간 순서	then 그러고 나서 in the meantime/meanwhile 그동안	afterwards/subsequently 그 후에	
결론·결과	therefore 그러므로 consequently/as a result 결과적으로	thus 따라서	accordingly 그에 따라
강조 예시	in fact 실제로는 for example 예를 들면	indeed 사실은	specifically 구체적으로

만점 전략 2   빈칸 앞·뒤 동사의 의미에 주목하여 상관관계 파악하기

앞 문장 키워드 　　　　　　　빈칸에 들어갈 접속부사 　　　　　　　뒤 문장 키워드

> My network of gourmet food importers would be an asset for your company.
> 저의 고급 식품 수입업체 인맥은
> 귀사에 자산이 될 것입니다.

(B) In addition,
게다가

> I am dedicated to providing quality customer service.
> 저는 수준 높은 고객 서비스를 제공하는 데
> 전념하고 있습니다.

빈칸 앞 문장에서 자신의 인맥이 귀사의 자산이 될 것이라는 장점을 언급하고 있으며, 빈칸 뒤에서도 수준 높은 고객 서비스를 제공하는데 전념한다는 자신의 장점을 추가적으로 언급하고 있으므로 내용을 추가할 때 쓰이는 접속부사 (B) In addition이 적절합니다.

| 오답 | (A) Otherwise, (C) Therefore, (D) Nevertheless

만점 전략 3   접속부사 자리에 접속사나 전치사는 쓰일 수 없으므로 소거하기

앞 문장 　　　　　　　빈칸에 들어갈 접속부사 　　　　　　　뒤 문장

> Please note that payment is required upon receipt of your invoice.
> 청구서 수령 즉시 결제해야 한다는 점을
> 주의해 주십시오.

(D) However,
하지만

> Your renewal term will not begin until your current subscription cycle is completed. 갱신 기간은 현재의 구독 기간이
> 완료되기 전에는 시작되지 않을 것입니다.

빈칸은 접속부사 자리이므로 부사절 접속사인 선택지들을 소거하고 남은 접속부사 (D) However가 정답입니다.

| 오답 | (A) Unless, (B) Although, (C) After

Question 1 refers to the following e-mail.

Dear PK,

Thank you again for the wonderful job you did creating our Web site last month. We have received much positive feedback on the site from our employees and from other visitors. I am writing to inquire whether you are available to add a couple of new features to the site.

------- , we would like to include an employee directory and a section for ongoing research projects.

We look forward to working with you again. Please let us know.

Warm regards,

Krystal Galido, Site Manager

RJA Laboratories, Inc.

(A) Specifically

(B) Nevertheless

(C) Instead

(D) Similarly

Question 2 refers to the following letter.

Dear Mr. Go:

Thank you for your recent order. Although most of your items have already shipped, the Full-Spectrum Desk Lamp (model B07) is temporarily out of stock. We would be happy to substitute a similar item of your choice, or we can refund your payment for this item.

We appreciate your patience and hope to serve you in a timelier manner in the future. -------, please contact our order department at 716-555-0160 with any questions.

Carrie Weber

Director, Granger's Lighting, Inc.

(A) Instead

(B) Besides

(C) In contrast

(D) Meanwhile

| WORDS |

1 positive 긍정적인 feedback 피드백, 의견 be available to ~할 수 있다 feature 특징, 기능 employee directory 직원 명부 section 섹션, 부문 ongoing 진행 중인

2 temporarily 일시적으로 out of stock 재고가 없는, 품절된 substitute 대체하다 refund 환불하다 appreciate 감사하다 in a timely manner 적절한 때에

ETS 실전 테스트

Questions 1-4 refer to the following e-mail.

To: Amelia Le <amelia.le@restaurant154.com>
From: Oliver Hendriks <ohendriks@domaneengineering.com>
Date: June 30
Subject: Thank you

Dear Ms. Le,

On behalf of everyone at Domane Engineering, I would like to thank you for the excellent catering service ------- by your staff at our recent company awards dinner. The feedback
1
I have received from attendees has been overwhelmingly positive. ------- , many of them
2
are still raving about the delicious food and exceptional service.

We organize several company events each year, and we certainly hope to work with you at Restaurant 154 again. Incidentally, I have recommended your restaurant to an acquaintance ------- is searching for a place to hold a holiday party. ------- .
3   4
Sincerely,

Oliver Hendriks

Office Manager, Domane Engineering

1 (A) was provided
   (B) to be providing
   (C) has been providing
   (D) provided

2 (A) Otherwise
   (B) Indeed
   (C) Nonetheless
   (D) Even so

3 (A) one
   (B) herself
   (C) who
   (D) mine

4 (A) We were honored to receive the award.
   (B) Because of this, I will need to reschedule the event.
   (C) That is why we requested a change to the menu.
   (D) I expect that she will be contacting you soon.

| WORDS |

on behalf of ~을 대표하여 catering service 출장 연회 서비스 attendee 참석자 overwhelmingly 압도적으로 rave 극찬하다
exceptional 특별한 organize 주최하다 incidentally 덧붙여 말하면 acquaintance 지인, 아는 사람
4 be honored to ~하게 되어 영광이다

UNIT 05

문장 고르기

풀이전략 | **선택지나 빈칸 앞·뒤 문장의 단서 표현을 통해 알맞은 문장 고르기**

빈칸에 들어갈 문장을 고르는 문제는 파트 6에서 난이도가 가장 높은 문제 유형으로, 지문당 한 개씩
출제됩니다. 선택지에 지시어(this, these 등)나 「the(그) + 명사」가 있다면 그것이 지칭하는 명사가 빈칸 앞에
있는지를 확인하고 문맥이 자연스러우면 정답으로 선택합니다. 만약 지시어나 대명사 등의 단서만으로 정답을
찾기 어렵다면 독해를 통해 문맥을 파악해야 합니다.

 Question refers to the following article.

Mountain Heights Travel News

SPRINGFIELD (10 September)—On 4 September, Flying
Star Airways launched its new, individualized baggage-
tracking application. The new system is simple: When the
bags arrive, passengers are alerted by online notification to
the specific baggage-claim area where they are located. In
addition, the application notifies passengers when there are
delays. ------- . The free app is available for download on
most smartphones.

마운틴 하이츠 교통 정보

스프링필드(9월 10일)-9월 4일 플라잉 스타 항공은 새로운 개인별 수하물 추적
애플리케이션을 출시했다. 새로운 시스템은 간단하다: 가방이 도착하면 승객은 가방이 있는
특정 수하물 찾는 곳을 온라인 알림으로 통보받는다. 뿐만 아니라, 이 애플리케이션은 지연이
발생하면 승객에게 알려준다. 이 무료 앱은 대부분의 스마트폰에서 다운로드할 수 있다.

(A) Passengers were notified of their seat assignments.
승객들은 좌석 배정을 통보받았다.

**(B) The system will even notify passengers if their bags
will arrive on a later flight.**
심지어 이 시스템은 가방이 더 늦은 비행편으로 도착할 경우 승객에게 알려줄 것이다.

(C) Passengers are advised to make their bags easily
distinguishable.
승객들은 자신들의 가방을 쉽게 구별할 수 있도록 해야 한다.

(D) Baggage-claim carousels have been upgraded.
수하물 인수대가 개선되었다.

빈칸 앞 동사 어휘 확인하기 **STEP 01**

빈칸 앞: 수하물 지연시
애플리케이션의 알림 기능에
대해 설명하고 있다. 동사
notifies에 주목한다.

오답 소거하기 **STEP 02**

(A) 수하물 알림 기능과 관계 없는
좌석 배정 알림에 대해 언급하고
있으며, 시제 또한 과거 시제로
오답.

(C) 가방을 구별할 수 있도록 하는
것은 수하물 알림 기능과
무관하므로 오답.

(D) 수하물 인수대의 개선은 수하물
알림 기능과 무관하므로 오답.

정답 선택하기 **STEP 03**

빈칸 앞에서 애플리케이션은
수하물의 지연이 발생하면 승객에게
알려준다(notifies)고 했으므로,
빈칸에서는 강조부사 even를
사용하여 심지어 더 늦은 비행편으로
도착할 경우에도 알려줄 것이다(will
notify)라는 부연 설명이 이어지는
것이 자연스러우므로 정답은 (B)이다.

만점 전략 1 앞 문장의 주요 명사/동사 어휘를 부연 설명하는 문장에 주목하기

앞 문장 키워드

> We hope we can receive your feedback.
> 저희가 고객님의 피드백을 받을 수 있기를 바랍니다.

빈칸에 들어갈 문장

**If we do, you will receive $50
toward the cost of your next flight.**
그렇게 하시면 다음 비행 시 50달러 할인을 받으실 수 있습니다.

앞 문장에서 피드백을 줄 것을 요청했으며 빈칸에서는 그 피드백에 대한 혜택을 언급하는 것이 문맥상
자연스럽습니다.

만점 전략 2 지시어(this/that), 정관사(the), 인칭대명사(he/she, it, they), 부사(also/even), 접속부사(However)와 같은 단서 표현에 유의하기

앞 문장 키워드

> The human resources department has generously
> offered to share their break room with us.
> 인사부에서 관대하게도 인사부 휴게실을 같이 사용하자고 제안했습니다.

빈칸에 들어갈 문장

**That room is on the second
floor by the elevators.**
그 방은 2층 엘리베이터 옆에 있습니다.

빈칸 앞에서는 인사부 휴게실을 함께 사용할 수 있다는 내용이 언급되고 있으므로 빈칸에는 인사부 휴게실의
위치를 알려주는 문장이 들어가는 것이 문맥상 자연스럽습니다.

만점 전략 3 빈칸 뒤 문장의 단서 표현과 어울리는 문장을 선택하기

빈칸에 들어갈 문장

**The results are currently being
compiled.**
결과는 현재 집계 중이다.

뒤 문장 키워드

> The outcome will be a list of the top 100
> places to work in the region.
> 설문 결과는 이 지역의 상위 100대 직장의 목록이 될 것이다.

빈칸 뒤 문장 The outcome(결과)을 언급했으므로 빈칸에는 설문 조사의 응답 결과를 집계 중이라는 내용이
들어가는 것이 문맥상 적절합니다.

Question 1 refers to the following press release.

The Plantas Group, an environmental research institution based in Cardiff, Wales, has received a grant from the Green Community Foundation (GCF). The grant was awarded for a proposal submitted to GCF. The funds will be used on the energy-efficient redesign of the Plantas headquarters. ------- . Karyna Silver, Plantas' Facilities Director, will oversee the work in consultation with Frieda Schmidt of GCF.

(A) Installing LCD lighting is a common efficiency update.
(B) The upgrades include installation of a charging station for electric cars.
(C) Ms. Silver is experienced in advancing conservation measures.
(D) Energy-saving construction techniques have increased in popularity.

Question 2 refers to the following e-mail.

To All:

Next Monday, Sanjay Corporation will hold its annual Safety Day. We ask that you check all the chemicals and products in your area on Monday morning and dispose of any that have reached their expiration date. Please also discard old files, used boxes, and other office materials that cannot be recycled. ------- . With your help, this may be Sanjay Corporation's safest year yet!

(A) Special bins for these waste materials will be placed on each floor.
(B) The laboratory inspection results will be announced soon.
(C) Place this new safety equipment in the cabinets.
(D) Employees enjoyed great food and conversation at the picnic.

| WORDS |

1 institution 기관 based in ~에 근거지가 있는 grant 보조금 award 수여하다 fund 기금 energy-efficient 에너지 효율이 좋은 efficiency 효율성 advance 진행시키다 conservation 보존 measures 조치, 방안 energy-saving 에너지를 절약하는
2 hold 개최하다 annual 연례의 chemicals 화학 물질 dispose of ~을 처분하다 expiration date 유효 기간 material 재료 recycle 재활용하다 bin 큰 통, 쓰레기통 waste 폐기물 inspection 점검 result 결과 safety equipment 안전 장비 conversation 대화

정답 및 해설 p.178

ETS 실전 테스트

Questions 1-4 refer to the following memo.

To: Box Office Staff
From: G. Anders, General Director
Date: 24 November
Subject: Policy Update

I am writing to inform you of a change in the ------- policy for our classical music series,
                                              1
effective immediately. There have been many requests on the day of the concert from

patrons who prefer to sit on the aisle because there is more leg room. From now on,

we will accept such requests ------- at the time tickets are purchased. Subsequently,
                              2
audience members ------- extra space may ask for a seat in the back two rows, as
                    3
those are not usually filled. ------- . This policy should help us avoid complaints once a
                              4
performance has begun.

1 (A) refund
(B) pricing
(C) seating
(D) recording

2 (A) only
(B) less
(C) very
(D) late

3 (A) needed
(B) who need
(C) they need
(D) having needed

4 (A) Many people prefer to sit there, near
the orchestra.
(B) Saturday evening performances attract
the largest crowds.
(C) Ticket holders may not enter the
theater after the performance begins.
(D) It is further from the stage, but it is
more comfortable there.

| WORDS |

inform A of B A에게 B를 알리다 immediately 즉시, 곧바로 patron 고객 aisle (좌석·선반 사이의) 통로 leg room 발을 뻗을 수
있는 공간 from now on 지금부터 subsequently 그 뒤에, 나중에 audience 청중, 관중 row 줄, 열 avoid 피하다 complaint 불평
performance 공연, 연주

RC

PART 07

패러프레이징 1   동의어로 바꿔 쓰기

무료인강 바로가기

지문에서 사용된 단어나 구를 동일한 의미의 다른 표현으로 바꿔 쓰거나 풀어 쓰는 방식입니다.

● 예제

Rosario's Printing Services

Posters, brochures, business cards, and much more!
Save big! **The following discounts are available online to first-time customers.**

- 10 percent off any order of at least $100
- 15 percent off any order of at least $150
- 20 percent off any order of at least $200
- 25 percent off any order of at least $250

discounts
→ offer 할인
first-time customers
→ new customers
처음 이용하는 고객 ▶ 신규 고객

신규 고객만 온라인에서 할인받을 수 있다고 했으므로 정답은 **(B)**

Q. What is indicated about the offer?
(A) It is for in-store use only.
(B) It is for new customers.

왼쪽의 표현과 의미가 비슷한 것을 (A)~(C) 중 골라 선으로 연결하세요.

1. draw visitors   •   • (A) an extra fee
2. an additional charge   •   • (B) attract tourists
3. a complimentary beverage •   • (C) a free drink

박스 안의 문장과 의미가 가장 가까운 것을 고르세요.

4.

> You can watch Mr. Rau's talk on the conference Web site later.

(A) Mr. Rau's session is being rescheduled.
(B) Mr. Rau's session will soon be available online.

5.

> Manazuru Air publishes flight schedules twelve months in advance.

(A) Manazuru Air releases its flight schedules a year in advance.
(B) Manazuru Air purchases a new fleet of aircraft a year in advance.

| WORDS | brochure (광고용) 소책자, 브로슈어 business card 명함 available 이용 가능한 in advance 미리
release 발표하다 fleet (한 회사가 소유한 차량, 항공기, 선박의) 무리 aircraft 항공기

정답 및 해설 p.182

패러프레이징 2 포괄적인 개념으로 바꿔 쓰기

지문에서 사용된 단어나 구를 포괄하는 개념, 즉 더 큰 범주의 표현으로 바꿔 쓰는 방식입니다.

● 예제

CROVER and WAYFIELD ASSOCIATES

Providing reliable tax advice and accounting services for thirty-eight years

Members of our firm specialize in services for:

- **Individuals and Families**
- **Small businesses**
- **Corporations**

Reduced rates proudly offered to nonprofit organizations.

small businesses, corporations
→ companies
소규모 사업체, 대기업 ▶ 회사들

개인 및 가족, 기업 고객들을 상대로 서비스를 제공하고 있음을 알 수 있으므로 정답은 **(B)**

Q. What is stated about Crover and Wayfield Associates?
(A) They have been in operation for more than forty years.
(B) They serve both individuals and companies.

왼쪽의 표현과 의미가 비슷한 것을 (A)~(C) 중 골라 선으로 연결하세요.

1. ride the bus ●
2. cardboard, newspapers, and magazines ●
3. the region's best known painter ●

● (A) paper products
● (B) a local artist
● (C) use public transportation

박스 안의 문장과 의미가 가장 가까운 것을 고르세요.

4.
> Ms. Arnold began her professional career as a college professor.

(A) Ms. Arnold's first career was an educator.
(B) Ms. Arnold's first career was a chef.

5.
> All entrées are served with salad, coffee or tea, and fresh bread.

(A) Dessert is included with all entrées.
(B) A drink is included with all entrées.

| WORDS | reliable 믿을 수 있는 accounting 회계 specialize in ~을 전문으로 하다 corporation (대)기업, 주식회사
reduced rate 할인 요금 nonprofit organization 비영리 단체 entrée 주요리, 앙트레

패러프레이징 3   요약해서 표현하기

지문에서 사용된 구나 문장을 더 짧고 간단하게 요약하여 표현하는 방식입니다.

● 예제

Reviews	Menu	Directions

"The meals may be a bit pricey, but they are worth every cent. **With diverse items designed to impress any gourmet, I had difficulty making up my mind!** I ended up choosing a fresh and tasty salmon salad. Be aware that the parking lot is very small, so arrive early to get a spot." — Diego M.

diverse items
→ The variety
다양한 품목 ▶ 다양함

미식가에게 깊은 인상을 줄 다양한 품목이 있었다고 했으므로 정답은 (A)

Q. What did Diego M. like most about the restaurant?

(A) The variety on the menu

(B) The attractive design

왼쪽의 표현과 의미가 비슷한 것을 (A)~(C) 중 골라 선으로 연결하세요.

1. a full-time managerial position in our advertising department   •

2. a map that shows the best options for parking your vehicle.   •

3. visit Dalter's major tourist attractions   •

  • (A) go sightseeing

  • (B) advertising manager

  • (C) a parking map

박스 안의 문장과 의미가 가장 가까운 것을 고르세요.

4.
> The position requires a person who is outgoing, organized, and familiar with the Newville community.

(A) Organizational skills are mentioned as a requirement for the job.

(B) Management experience is mentioned as a requirement for the job.

5.
> The voucher, valid for any Azure Sky Airlines flight, is valued at RM800 and must be redeemed within one year.

(A) The voucher has an expiration date.   (B) The voucher is accepted by multiple airlines.

| WORDS | pricey 비싼 gourmet 미식가 outgoing 외향적인 organized 정리된, 체계적인 familiar with ~을 잘 아는 voucher 상품권, 쿠폰 valid 유효한 be valued at (가격·가치가) ~로 평가되다 redeem (상품권 등을) 상품[현금]으로 바꾸다 expiration 만료, 만기 multiple 다수의

패러프레이징 4   추론하여 바꿔 쓰기

문맥상 의미를 추론하여 의미가 통하는 다른 표현으로 바꿔 쓰는 방식입니다

● 예제

> **Rosa Gonzalez [10:16 A.M.]**
> I made reservations for us to have lunch in the lobby restaurant at noon.
>
> **Anna Losch [10:17 A.M.]**
> Good, but it's going to be a working meal. We need to go over the slides for our design presentation so we have time

working meal, go over the slides for our design presentation
→ Review a presentation
일하면서 먹는 식사, 디자인 프레젠테이션을 위한 슬라이드 검토 ▶ 프레젠테이션 검토

점심 식사를 하면서 디자인 프레젠테이션을 검토할 것임을 추론할 수 있으므로 정답은 (A)

Q. What will the group most likely do at noon?

(A) Review a presentation

(B) Attend a special session

왼쪽의 표현과 의미가 비슷한 것을 (A)~(C) 중 골라 선으로 연결하세요.

1. at any branch of Podric's Pizza •
2. be founded in 1940 •
3. be posted every few minutes •

 • (A) be in operation for many years
 • (B) The business has multiple locations.
 • (C) be updated frequently

박스 안의 문장과 의미가 가장 가까운 것을 고르세요.

4.

> Max Hinkle has critiqued almost every dining establishment in Millford.

(A) Max Hinkle is a chef.

(B) Max Hinkle is a food critic.

5.

> Construction on our new Auckland resort will be completed in eight months.

(A) A resort will open.

(B) A new service will be offered.

| WORDS | go over 검토하다, 점검하다   critique 평론을 쓰다, 비평하다   dining establishment 식당 critic 비평가, 평론가   construction 건설, 공사   complete 완료하다

UNIT 01

주제 / 목적 문제

무료인강 바로가기

글의 전반적인 내용을 묻는 주제 및 목적 문제는 가장 기본적인 질문으로, 주로 지문의 초반부에 주제나 목적이 제시되는 경우가 대부분입니다.

빈출 질문 유형

주제	What is the **main topic** of the letter?	편지의 주제는?
	What does the article **describe**?	기사에서 설명하는 것은?
	What are the writers **discussing**?	글쓴이들이 논의하고 있는 것은?
	What is the announcement **about**?	무엇에 관한 안내인가?
	What is being **advertised[announced]**?	무엇이 광고[안내]되고 있는가?
목적	What is the **purpose** of the notice[memo]?	공지[회람]의 목적은?
	Why did Ms. Nilsson **send** the e-mail?	닐슨 씨가 이메일을 보낸 이유는?
	Why was the article **written**?	기사를 작성한 이유는?

주제 / 목적 문제 정답 단서 찾기

목적	This is a reminder that the following date and time were reserved for your regular exam and cleaning:	귀하의 정기 검진과 스케일링이 다음 일시로 예약되었음을 알려 드립니다:
	Q. Why was the e-mail sent to Ms. Silva?	Q. 실바 씨에게 이메일을 보낸 이유는?
	A. To remind her of an appointment	A. 예약 사실을 상기시키기 위해
주제	We at Angelica's on Hanover invite you to enjoy fine dining in a truly historic setting.	안젤리카스 온 하노버는 실로 유서 깊은 공간에서 멋진 식사를 즐길 수 있도록 여러분을 초대합니다
	Q. What is being advertised?	Q. 무엇을 광고하고 있는가?
	A. A restaurant	A. 레스토랑
목적	I am writing to confirm your reservation of the Regency Ballroom on Wednesday, April 14, from 6:00 P.M. to 9:00 P.M.	4월 14일 수요일, 오후 6시에서 9시까지 리전시 연회장을 예약하신 것을 확인하기 위해 **편지를 씁니다**.
	Q. What is the purpose of the letter?	Q. 편지의 목적은 무엇인가?
	A. To confirm some plans	A. 몇 가지 계획 확인

주제 / 목적 문제 풀이 전략

전략 1.
제목에서 주제나 목적을 미리 파악하기

이메일(e-mail), 기사(article), 보도 자료(press release), 광고(advertisement)처럼 제목이 있는 지문은 제목에서 글의 주제나 목적을 미리 알 수 있는 경우가 많습니다.

전략 2.
지문의 서두와 후반부에 주목하기

대부분 서두에 주제나 목적이 제시되지만, 후반부에서 제안이나 요청 사항으로 목적을 나타내는 경우도 종종 있습니다.

┌─ | 풀이 전략 적용하기 | ─

To: DarGoo2@Riverguest.com
From: A.Heron@ACC.edu
Date: May 21
Subject: Cruise `전략 1. 제목에서 정답 단서 찾기`

Dear Mr. Goodman,

A few weeks ago, I went on one of your boat tours and had a great time. I enjoyed the food, especially the pasta and spring rolls.

I teach at Armont Community College, and I'd like to take a group of ecology students on a field trip. In class, we're focusing on freshwater ecosystems right now, so a Sunrise River Cruise seems like a good idea. Could you offer a discount for a group of 25 students? Also, would you be able to arrange a simple lunch? Please let me know what you can do for us.

Amanda Heron `전략 2. 지문의 후반부에 주목하기`

`글의 목적을 묻는 문제`

수신: DarGoo2@Riverguest.com
발신: A.Heron@ACC.edu
날짜 5월 21일
제목: 유람선 여행

굿맨 씨께,

몇 주 전에 보트 투어를 갔는데 무척 즐거웠습니다. 음식을 맛있게 먹었는데, 특히 파스타와 스프링롤이 맛있었어요.

저는 아르몽 지역전문대학에서 가르치고 있는데 생태학 학생들을 데리고 현장조사 여행을 가고 싶습니다. 지금 수업에서 담수 생태계를 중점으로 다루고 있으므로 선라이즈 리버 크루즈가 좋은 생각인 것 같습니다. 학생 25명으로 구성된 단체에 할인을 해주실 수 있나요? 또 간단한 점심 식사도 준비해주실 수 있을까요? 저희를 위해 어떻게 해주실 수 있는지 알려주세요.

아만다 헤론

PART 7 | UNIT 01

Q. Why did Ms. Heron send the e-mail?

(A) To provide feedback about her cruise experience
(B) To find out whether same-day reservations are allowed
(C) To offer her expertise as a tour guide
(D) **To request special arrangements for her group**

헤론 씨가 이메일을 보낸 이유는?

(A) 유람선 여행 경험에 대한 의견을 제공하려고
(B) 당일 예약이 가능한지 여부를 확인하려고
(C) 여행 가이드로서 전문 지식을 제공하려고
(D) **단체를 위해 특별한 준비를 요청하려고**

전략 1 제목이 '유람선 여행'이므로 유람선 서비스 이용 관련 내용임을 추측할 수 있습니다.
전략 2 첫 단락에서는 보트 투어 경험을 언급하고 있어서 목적을 알 수 없지만 지문 후반부에서 문의 사항과 함께 이에 대한 답변을 요청하고 있다는 것을 알 수 있습니다.
글의 목적 제목과 글의 후반부에서 단체 할인과 점심 제공에 대해 문의하고 있으므로 정답은 (D)입니다.

다음 지문을 읽고 문제를 풀어보세요.

Marcelyn Travel Agency

We have a new branch in the historic Centreville Shopping Center. Visit us at our grand opening!

Saturday, 2 October
10:00 A.M. to 4:00 P.M.
14 Elm Park Road, Johannesburg

Stop by to meet our highly qualified travel agents and find out how you can book the trip you've always wanted—at a great price. Enjoy complimentary coffee, tea, and snacks. We will also be giving away free tote bags while supplies last.

---

1   What is being advertised?

(A) A special event
(B) A free trip

What's Trending in Dublin?
By Peter O'Scanlon

1 March—The latest development venture of Craigson Properties will soon open. The apartments on 2101 Blandon Street are in some ways a first for the company, although it has similar properties in other cities. Yoshi Makino, vice president of Craigson Properties, says, "We've been waiting for the right location to become available in Dublin. This nineteenth-century building, formerly a bank, is perfect for the project." The building should be ready for occupancy next month, with a grand opening anticipated for mid-April.

---

2   What is the purpose of the article?

(A) To announce changes to a city's building codes
(B) To explain that a residential property will soon open

| WORDS |

1 branch 지점 historic 역사적인 grand opening 개장, 개점 stop by 잠깐 들르다 highly 매우, 고도로 qualified 자격을 갖춘 complimentary 무료의 supplies 공급품, 재고

2 property 부동산 similar 비슷한 formerly 이전에 occupancy 점유, 입주 anticipate 예상하다

Questions 1-2 refer to the following e-mail.

Lewistown Community Center • 1064 Blueberry Street • Lewistown, Montana 59457

April 21

Dear Valued Community Members,

The Lewistown Community Center (LCC) has decided to cancel most of its programming for the upcoming summer term. This is because of the ongoing building project we mentioned in our last letter. Although the decision was difficult, it was ultimately made to ensure the comfort and safety of students, staff, and construction workers. Outdoor programs are not affected by the building project and will still be offered.

We understand that the cancellation is an inconvenience to our community. To help you find alternative arrangements for summer programming, several organizations have agreed to partner with us and will offer discounted programming options to LCC members. We have enclosed a document with information about participating organizations and their offerings.

We hope that you enjoy your summer and come back to join us in September for regular programming in the new building. We appreciate your flexibility. You may address any questions to me at selma.ruan@lewistownncc.org.

Sincerely,

Selma Ruan

Selma Ruan, LCC Director

Enclosure

---

1. What is the purpose of the letter?

(A) To announce a building project

(B) To introduce a new director of the LCC

(C) To invite individuals to a sponsored event

(D) To provide an update about upcoming changes

2. What does Ms. Ruan say that several organizations will do?

(A) Let LCC members borrow sports equipment

(B) Provide temporary space for LCC programs

(C) Give LCC members a discount

(D) Close for the summer

| WORDS |

community 공동체, 지역 사회 cancel 취소하다 upcoming 다가오는 ongoing 진행 중인 mention 언급하다 ultimately 궁극적으로 ensure 보장하다 comfort 편안함 safety 안전 construction 건설, 공사 affect 영향을 미치다 offer 제공하다 inconvenience 불편 alternative 대체 가능한 arrangement 준비, 마련 organization 단체, 조직 partner with ~와 제휴하다 enclose 동봉하다 participating 참가하는 flexibility 융통성 address (~ 앞으로) 보내다

1 individual 개인 sponsored event 후원 행사 update 최신 정보 2 temporary 임시의

세부 사항 문제

무료인강 바로가기

세부 사항을 묻는 문제는 가장 많이 출제되는 질문 유형으로 질문 속의 인물, 장소, 시간 등이 지문에서 정답을 찾는 중요한 단서 표현이 됩니다. 할인 정보, 마감일, 요청 사항, 연락 방법이나 이유를 묻는 문제는 지문의 후반부에 제시되는 경우가 많습니다.

빈출 질문 유형

육하원칙	Who must **provide an approval**?	승인해주어야 하는 사람은?
	When will the **bus route** be available?	버스 노선을 이용할 수 있는 때는?
	Where will **a company activity** take place?	사내 활동은 어디에서 이루어지는가?
	What does **Mr. Bachman offer to do**?	바크만 씨가 하겠다고 제안하는 것은?
	Why has Mr. Qian **paid a fee**?	첸 씨가 요금을 지불한 이유는?
	How will **Ms. Meyer help** with the event?	메어 씨는 행사를 어떻게 도울 것인가?
요청사항	What does Mr. Walson **request**?	월슨 씨가 요청하는 것은?
	What are fair attendees **encouraged[asked, required/advised/instructed] to do**?	박람회 참가자들이 하도록 권장[요구/지시]되는 것은?
연락이유	According to the notice, **why** should someone **contact Mr. Rabin**?	공지에 따르면, 누군가가 라빈 씨에게 연락해야 하는 이유는?

세부 사항 문제 정답 단서 찾기

육하원칙	Parking spaces are available in the garage for a fee. Q. What feature do renters at Wellbridge Apartment Complex need to pay extra to use? A. The parking garage	주차 공간은 주차장에서 유료로 이용할 수 있습니다. Q. 웰브리지 아파트 단지의 임차인이 추가 이용료를 지불해야 하는 항목은? A. 주차장
요청사항	Please take time now to inspect your purchase to make sure the contents have arrived in good condition. Q. What does the notice ask customers to do? A. Examine the condition of an item	지금 시간을 내서 구매하신 제품을 점검하시고 내용물이 좋은 상태로 도착했는지 확인해주십시오. Q. 공지에서 고객들에게 해달라고 요청하는 것은? A. 제품 상태를 점검할 것
연락이유	If you have difficulty reading your meter, please call our customer service center immediately. Q. According to the notice, why should customers contact customer service? A. To get help reading their water meter	계량기를 읽는 데 어려움이 있는 경우, 고객 서비스 센터로 즉시 전화하십시오. Q. 공지에 따르면, 고객들이 고객 서비스에 연락해야 하는 이유는? A. 수도 계량기를 읽는 데 도움을 받으려고

세부 사항 문제 풀이 전략

전략 1.
질문 키워드 파악하기

질문에서 등장하는 고유명사(회사명, 인명, 제품명)이나 숫자(날짜, 할인율)는 정답을 찾는 중요한 단서입니다.

> ### 전략 2.
> **정답의 단서가 될 문장을 찾아 선택지와 대조하기**
>
> 질문 키워드와 관련된 내용이 언급되는 문장을 주의 깊게 읽으며 패러프레이징된 표현에 유의합니다.

| 풀이 전략 적용하기 |

Turaco

Delight Delivered in a Box

Imagine a box arriving at your front door. You open it. Inside are ...

- Easy, nutritious recipes so you don't have to worry about preparing a complicated dish
- Ingredients in pre-measured packages so nothing goes to waste
- Insulated containers so the ingredients stay fresh

투라코

상자 속에 배달되는 기쁨

현관문에 상자가 도착한다고 상상해 보세요. 그것을 열어보십시오. 안에는⋯

- 복잡한 요리를 준비할 걱정은 안 해도 되도록 쉽고, 영양가 많은 조리법
- 낭비되는 것이 없도록 미리 계량된 재료 패키지
- 재료가 신선하게 유지되도록 단열 처리된 포장

전략 2. 지문에서 문제의 단서 찾기

Sign up today; there is never a charge to enroll. Order whenever you wish; there is no minimum order. To say "welcome," we'll give you your first four orders at 20% off. In addition, we'll ship your first order with no delivery charge. Just enter the following code at turaco, net: WELCOME 14

오늘 등록하세요. 등록비는 전혀 없습니다. 원하실 때 언제든 주문하세요. 최소 주문 금액은 없습니다. "환영"하는 의미에서 처음 4차례 주문까지 20퍼센트 할인해 드립니다. 덧붙여 첫 번째 주문은 배송비가 무료입니다. turaco.net에서 코드 WELCOME14만 입력하세요.

세부 사항 묻는 문제 | **전략 1. 질문 키워드 파악하기**

Q. What special deal is offered?

(A) A new customer's first order will be delivered for free.
(B) After four full-price purchases, the next order is free.
(C) When a certain cost is reached, the order is discounted.
(D) The charge for customer enrollment has been reduced.

어떤 특가 상품이 제안되는가?

(A) 신규 고객의 첫 번째 주문은 무료로 배송된다.
(B) 정가로 4회 구매한 뒤 다음 주문은 무료다.
(C) 일정 가격에 도달하면 주문이 할인된다.
(D) 고객 등록비가 인하되었다.

전략 1 질문에서 키워드 special deal(특가 상품)을 우선 파악하고 지문에서 특가 관련된 내용이 있는 부분을 찾아 읽습니다.

전략 2 지문 후반부에서 20% 할인(20% off)이 언급되었고 첫 4차례 주문은 20% 할인되고 또 첫 주문은 배송비가 무료라고 언급하고 있습니다. with no delivery charge가 be delivered for free로 패러프레이징된 점도 주목해주세요.

세부 사항 지문 후반부에서 첫 주문은 할인과 함께 배송비가 무료라고 하므로 정답은 (A)입니다.

다음 지문을 읽고 문제를 풀어보세요.

Appliance Instructions

1. Place your dirty laundry into the drum of the appliance.

2. Adjust the dial to the appropriate cycle—light soil, heavy soil, etc.

3. Select the water temperature (cold, warm, hot) by pressing the corresponding button.

4. Add detergent to the dispenser. Also put in fabric conditioner (optional) for best results.

5. Close the door securely and press the START button.

---

1 According to the instructions, how can users get the best results?

(A) By adjusting the dial to a specific setting

(B) By using an additional product with the detergent

January 6

By Janelie Rivers, Metro Styles Shop

I purchased the Tateno Turbo after a friend recommended it to me. It is a good choice for effortlessly cleaning your residence or business. As a business owner intent on keeping a spotless salon, I find that to be vital. When I clean after my last customer, it's impossible to find even one stray hair on the floor. It is well worth the price.

There are some things that I don't like about the product. The color choices are limited, and it fails to hold a charge. The battery sometimes drains after just twenty minutes. It's not a major inconvenience, as it does not take long to charge to full power on the docking station.

---

2 What type of business does Ms. Rivers own?

(A) A hair salon

(B) An appliance store

| WORDS |

1 appliance 기기, 가전제품 adjust 조절하다, 맞추다 appropriate 적합한 temperature 온도 corresponding 해당하는 detergent 세제

2 recommend 추천하다 effortlessly 힘들이지 않고 residence 주택 intent on ~에 몰두하는 spotless 티끌 하나 없는 vital 필수적인, 아주 중요한 worth the price 제값을 하다 drain 방전되다 docking station 거치대

정답 및 해설 p.190

ETS 실전 테스트

Questions 1-2 refer to the following notice.

Pimsborough Film Festival

The fourth annual Pimsborough Film Festival celebrates filmmakers from around the region. It will take place from March 16 to March 22 at cinemas throughout the county. Members of the public are offered three pass options to choose from.

Cinema Pass: $80 general admission; $50 for students
  ✓ All access to film viewings

Social Pass: $200 general admission; $150 for students
  ✓ All access to film viewings
  ✓ Ticket to opening night reception

Backstage Pass: $300 general admission; $250 for students
  ✓ All access to film viewings
  ✓ Ticket to opening night reception
  ✓ Four exclusive "Meet the Director" sessions

---

1. How much does a Social Pass ticket cost for people who are not students?

(A) $50
(B) $200
(C) $250
(D) $300

2. What do the three pass options have in common?

(A) They allow ticket holders to meet film directors.
(B) They offer discounted prices for early purchase.
(C) They allow ticket holders to see every film.
(D) They include entry to a festival reception.

| WORDS |

annual 연례의 celebrate 기념하다 take place (행사가) 열리다 reception 축하연 exclusive 독점적인, 전용의

2 in common 공통적으로 ticket holder 티켓 소지자 entry 입장

UNIT 03

Not / True / 추론 문제

무료인강 바로가기

Not / True(사실 확인) 문제는 지문 전반이나 특정 세부 사항을 묻는 문제로 선택지와 지문에 있는 단서들을 하나하나 대조하면서 풀어야 하는 문제 유형입니다. 추론 문제는 지문에서 간접적으로 언급된 문장을 근거로 정답을 유추해내는 난이도가 가장 높은 문제 유형입니다.

빈출 질문 유형

Not / True 문제	What is **true** about the company?	회사에 대해 사실인 것은?
	What is **stated** about Mr. Peck?	펙 씨에 대해 언급된 것은?
	What is **NOT indicated** about the survey?	설문 조사에 대해 알 수 없는 것은?
	What is **NOT mentioned** as a benefit of flextime?	탄력 근무제의 이점으로 언급되지 않은 것은?
추론 문제	What is **suggested** about the writers?	작가들에 대해 시사되는 것은?
	What is **implied** by the advertisement?	광고에서 암시되는 것은?
	For whom is the notice mainly **intended**?	이 공지는 주로 누구를 대상으로 하는가?
	What will **probably** be discussed at the meeting?	회의에서 무엇이 논의될 것 같은가?
	Who **most likely** is Ms. Sears?	시어스 씨는 누구일 것 같은가?

Not / True / 추론 문제 정답 단서 찾기

Not 문제	We provide on-site cooking classes, personal shopping tours, and one-on-one consultations. **Q.** What is NOT mentioned in the notice as something that Eckman Markets offers? **A.** Samples of products	저희는 현장 요리 실습과 개인 쇼핑 투어, 일대일 상담을 제공해 드립니다. **Q.** 에크먼 마켓이 제공하는 것으로 공지에 언급되지 않은 것은? **A.** 제품 견본
True 문제	My wife and I recently traveled to Solvenia. Since we were not familiar with it, ~. **Q.** What is indicated about Mr. Jennings? **A.** He had not been to Slovenia before.	아내와 저는 최근 슬로베니아로 여행을 갔습니다. 우리는 그곳을 잘 몰라서 ~. **Q.** 제닝스 씨에 관해 암시되는 것은? **A.** 슬로베니아에 가본 적이 없다.
추론 문제	We will also be giving away free tote bags while supplies last. **Q.** What is suggested in the flyer? **A.** Gifts are available in limited quantities.	또한 저희는 무료 토트백을 재고 소진 시까지 증정해 드릴 예정입니다. **Q.** 광고에 시사되는 것은? **A.** 사은품은 한정된 수량으로 받을 수 있다.

Not / True / 추론 문제 문제 풀이 전략

전략 1.
질문이나 선택지에서 키워드 파악하기

질문에 명확한 키워드가 없이 지문 전체나 특정 인물에 대해 묻는 경우에는 선택지에서 키워드를 파악해야 합니다.

전략 2.
지문에서 근거 문장을 찾기

질문의 키워드가 지문에서 한 번 언급된 경우에는 근거 문장을 찾고 정답을 고르면 됩니다. 하지만 질문의 키워드가 지문에 흩어져 있는 경우에는 선택지에 있는 키워드를 중심으로 지문에서 근거 문장을 찾아 대조해나가면서 정답을 찾아야 합니다.

| 풀이 전략 적용하기 |

To: l.auwae@polmail.co.uk
From: tsahner@osokinacafe.co.uk
Date: Tuesday, 10 February
Subject: Osokina Café

전략 2. 지문에서 근거 문장을 찾기

Dear Mr. Auwae,

I wanted to check your availability to come to Osokina Café. We need some updated pictures for our Web site. We've made significant improvements to our facility, particularly to our outside seating area. It gets great sun in the morning from when we open at 7:30 A.M. until about 9:30 A.M., so I suggest you come sometime within that time frame.

I look forward to hearing from you.

Best regards,
Talulah Sahner

수신: l.auwae@polmail.co.uk
발신: tsahner@osokinacafe.co.uk
날짜: 2월 10일 화요일
제목: 오소키나 카페

오웨이 씨께,

오소키나 카페에 와 주실 수 있는지 확인하고 싶습니다. 우리는 카페 웹사이트에 올릴 최신 사진이 몇 장 필요합니다. 우리 시설, 특히 바깥쪽 좌석 구역을 크게 개선했거든요. 우리가 문을 여는 오전 7시 반부터 9시 반경까지 내리쬐는 아침 햇살이 근사하니까 그 시간대 안에 오시는 것을 추천합니다.

연락 기다리겠습니다.

탈룰라 사너

추론 문제 / **전략 1. 질문과 선택지에서 키워드 파악하기**

Q. What is suggested about the Osokina Café?

(A) It has received positive reviews.

(B) It has been remodeled.

(C) It has opened a second location.

(D) It has changed its hours of operation.

오소키나 카페에 대해 시사되는 것은?

(A) 긍정적인 평가를 받았다.

(B) 보수 공사를 했다.

(C) 두 번째 매장을 열었다.

(D) 운영 시간을 변경했다.

전략 1   질문의 키워드 Osokina Café를 파악하고 추론 문제라는 것을 확인합니다.

전략 2   지문에서 키워드 Osokina Café가 처음에 언급되고 그 내용이 계속 이어지므로 선택지의 키워드 중심으로 지문에서 근거 문장이 있는지를 파악합니다. 근거 문장을 집중적으로 읽으면서 근거 문장의 내용과 일치하는 선택지를 고릅니다. We've made significant improvements to our facility가 It has been remodeled.로 패러프레이징된 점도 주목해주세요.

추론 문제   지문의 좌석 구역을 개선했다는 내용이 선택지에서는 보수 공사를 한 것으로 패러프레이징되었으므로 정답은 (B)입니다.

ETS 문제로 훈련하기

다음 지문을 읽고 문제를 풀어보세요.

Straudberg Water Corporation
Reading Your Water Meter

Customers of Straudberg Water Corporation can take a meter reading at any time. Doing so can help you confirm that a water bill is correct or estimate the cost of an upcoming bill. To read your meter, record the number that appears on the first day of the billing cycle—typically the first of the month. Then record the number that appears on the last day of the billing cycle. Subtracting the first number from the second will give you the number of units used. You can also take readings every day or once a week to determine the amount of water that is used for activities that require water.

---

1 What is NOT mentioned as a reason for customers to read their water meters?

(A) To make sure that a bill is accurate

(B) To know when the meter needs to be adjusted

Item#	Title	Author	Category	Quantity	Unit Price	Total
H2875	*Biodiversity in the Nicobar Islands*	Sheena Patel	4	30	$9.25	$277.50
F9150	*Iceland's Wandering Horses*	Eva Grimsdottir	4	25	$8.60	$215.00
B6442	*Mysterious Foxes*	Costas Nikolaidis	4	10	$8.20	$82.00
S7301	*Wild Animals and Their Diets*	DoDat Vu	4	50	$10.15	$507.50
Payment is due within 30 days.					**Total**	**$1,082.00**

---

2 In the invoice, category 4 most likely represents what subject?

(A) Travel

(B) Nature

| WORDS |

1 water meter 수도 계량기 confirm 확인하다 water bill 수도 요금 청구서 estimate 추산하다 upcoming 다가오는 appear 나타나다 billing cycle 청구서 발송 주기 typically 보통 subtract 빼다 determine 알아내다

2 biodiversity 생물 다양성 wandering 방랑하는 due 지불해야 하는

Questions 1-4 refer to the following online chat discussion.

Milo Tamboli (1:06 P.M.) Hi Sammy and Lily. Isn't the quarterly review meeting still happening today at 1?

Sammy Adjani (1:08 P.M.) The meeting got moved to tomorrow.

Milo Tamboli (1:09 P.M.) I must have missed that somehow.

Sammy Adjani (1:11 P.M.) Sorry about that! We discussed the change yesterday at the marketing meeting. I completely forgot you were out.

Milo Tamboli (1:13 P.M.) It's OK. I needed to check the room projector for my workshop, and I do not think it is working.

Sammy Adjani (1:14 P.M.) Are you still there now?

Milo Tamboli (1:15 P.M.) I'm just leaving.

Sammy Adjani (1:17 P.M.) If you can hold on a minute, I can come over right now and we can try to get the equipment running.

Milo Tamboli (1:18 P.M.) Sure thing.

Lily Orenson (1:40 P.M.) Sorry for the misunderstanding today, Milo! Were you able to get the projector working?

Sammy Adjani (1:45 P.M.) No. We called IT, and they will try to fix it. But let's see if there is another conference room available for tomorrow just in case?

Lily Orenson (1:48 P.M.) OK–I will check and let you know.

Sammy Adjani (1:49 P.M.) Great.

1. What is Mr. Tamboli confirming?

   (A) A repair request
   (B) A supply order
   (C) A workshop topic
   (D) A meeting time

2. What is true about Mr. Tamboli?

   (A) He manages the marketing department.
   (B) He planned a quarterly meeting.
   (C) He was absent for a meeting on the previous day.
   (D) He is Mr. Adjani and Ms. Orenson's supervisor.

3. At 1:18 P.M., what does Mr. Tamboli most likely mean when he writes, "Sure thing"?

   (A) He will wait for a coworker.
   (B) He will create an agenda.
   (C) He understands his mistake.
   (D) He is certain a workshop will be successful.

4. What will Ms. Orenson most likely do next?

   (A) Arrange for a conference call
   (B) Look for a different meeting space
   (C) Try to repair the projector
   (D) Confirm that IT has been contacted

| WORDS |

quarterly 분기별의 completely 완전히 hold on a minute 잠깐 기다리다 equipment 장비 available 이용 가능한

UNIT 04

동의어 문제

무료인강 바로가기

문장 속의 제시어의 의미를 묻는 문제 유형으로 다의어가 많이 출제됩니다. 익숙한 어휘라 하더라도 문맥 속에서 의미를 파악하고 선택해야 합니다. 이중 / 삼중 지문에서는 지문 종류를 먼저 알려주기 때문에 제시어의 위치를 확인하는 시간을 줄일 수 있습니다.

빈출 문제 유형

단일 지문	The word "adjust" in paragraph 2, line 3, is closest in meaning to	두 번째 단락 3행의 'adjust'와 의미상 가장 가까운 것은?
복수 지문	In the form, the word "Note" in paragraph 1, line 2, is closest in meaning to	양식에서 첫 번째 단락 2행의 'Note'와 의미상 가장 가까운 것은?

빈출 다의어 표현

assume	extend	serve
① 떠맡다 (= take over)	① 주다 (= offer)	① 근무하다 (= work)
② 추정하다 (= suppose)	② 연장하다 (= postpone)	② 제공하다 (= provide, offer)
perform	**decline**	**neglect**
① 완료하다 (= complete)	① 거절하다 (= refuse, reject)	① 잊다 (= forget)
② 수행하다 (= carry out)	② 감소하다 (= decrease)	② 무시하다 (= ignore)
cover	**note**	**present**
① 논의하다 (= discuss)	① 말하다 (= mention)	① 제시하다 (= display)
② 포함하다 (= include)	② 알아채다 (= realize)	② 야기하다 (= pose)
③ 처리하다 (= deal with)	③ 유념하다 (= observe)	③ 제출하다 (= submit)

빈출 동의어 표현

draw 끌다 (= attract, appeal to)	balance 잔액 (= remainder)	boom 성장 (= growth)
fit 부합하다 (= match)	concern 관심사 (= interest)	step 단계 (= phase, stage)
go 진행되다 (= proceed)	fashion 방식 (= manner)	plus 이점 (= benefit)
illustrate 보여주다 (= represent)	scale 크기 (= size)	critical 중요한 (= important)
meet 충족시키다 (= fulfil, satisfy)	space 구역 (= area)	fair 적당한 (= reasonable)
resolve 해결하다 (= settle)	terms 조건 (= conditions)	solid 빈틈없는 (= thorough)

동의어 문제 풀이 전략

전략 1.
제시어가 속한 문장의 의미를 파악하기

제시어가 위치한 문장을 지문에서 찾은 후, 문장의 의미를 알아본 다음, 문맥 속에서 제시어의 의미를 파악합니다.

>

전략 2.
문맥상 의미가 가장 알맞은 어휘 고르기

다의어는 동의어를 여러 개 제시하는 경우가 많으므로 문맥상 의미가 가장 가까운 어휘를 선택해야 합니다. 특히 동사 어휘는 목적어와의 의미를 되새기면서 동의어를 찾도록 합니다.

| 풀이 전략 적용하기 |

Local Business Recognized

DAVENPORT (January 25)—Another city business has been named one of the state's Top Ten Companies to Work For by *Argent Magazine*. Forman Furniture Company, located on Highway 17 in eastern Davenport, was ranked Number 8 on this year's list. Gary's Chocolate Factory was ranked Number 6 last year.

Argent Magazine conducts workforce surveys on an annual basis and publishes its rankings every January. Companies interested in being evaluated must submit an application that describes the company's personnel policies. The magazine then sends a survey to employees of companies that fit its criteria.

전략 1. 제시어가 속한 문장의 의미를 파악하기

동의어를 묻는 문제

지역 업체 인정받다

데번포트(1월 25일)—또 다른 시내 업체가 〈아전트 매거진〉이 선정하는 주에서 가장 일하기 좋은 10대 기업 중 하나에 이름을 올렸다. 데번포트 동부 17번 간선도로에 위치한 포먼 가구 회사는 올해 명단에서 8위에 올랐다. 지난해에는 개리즈 초콜릿 공장이 6위에 올랐다.

〈아전트 매거진〉은 해마다 직원 상대로 설문 조사를 실시하고 매년 1월 순위를 게재한다. 평가 받는데 관심이 있는 기업은 회사의 인사 정책을 설명하는 신청서를 제출해야 한다. 그러면 잡지 측에서 기준에 부합하는 기업의 직원들에게 설문지를 보낸다.

Q. The word "fit" in paragraph 2, line 6, is closest in meaning to

전략 2. 문맥상 의미가 알맞은 어휘 고르기

(A) measure
(B) prepare
(C) adjust
(D) match

2번째 단락 6행의 'fit'과 의미상 가장 가까운 것은?

(A) 측정하다
(B) 준비하다
(C) 조절하다
(D) 맞다

전략 1	'기준(criteria)에 부합하는 기업의 직원들'이라는 말이 어울리며, 제시어 'fit'은 '부합하다'라는 의미인 것을 파악합니다.
전략 2	선택지에서 '기준(criteria)'을 목적어로 취해 기준에 '부합하다'라는 의미와 가장 유사한 어휘를 고릅니다. 동사 fit은 준비하다(prepare), 조절하다(adjust)는 의미도 갖고 있으므로 유의해야 합니다.
동의어 문제	match가 '기준(criteria)'을 목적어로 취해 '기준에 맞다'라는 의미를 가지므로 정답은 (D)입니다.

다음 지문을 읽고 문제를 풀어보세요.

---

www.davencarcare.com/requestanappointment

DAVEN CAR CARE—Appointment Form

Use this form to request an appointment, and we will call you with a confirmation. Note that your requested time slot may not be available, but we will do our best to accommodate your choice or offer the closest possible alternative time. To ensure maximum availability, please make your request at least 24 hours in advance of your preferred appointment time.

Name: | James Lindemann
Phone: | 555 0107
Purpose of your visit: | Yearly inspection
Preferred appointment time: | August 12, 8:00 A.M.
Are you a repeat customer? | NO
Do you need a shuttle service? | NO

---

1   In the form, the word "Note" in paragraph 1, line 2, is closest in meaning to

(A) remind
(B) observe

Dear Benedict,

I like your idea about hiring a dietitian to work in Eckman Markets. At the weekly meeting on Thursday, I am going to propose your idea. I think it is likely that Mr. Cummings will approve your suggestion. This seems like a good time to promote something new, since we will be launching our new line of healthy foods. It makes sense to have a professional give sound advice on diets and menus to shoppers who want it. I will recommend that we begin with the Perth branch location.

---

2   In the e-mail, the word "sound" in paragraph 1, line 5, is closest in meaning to

(A) loud
(B) sensible

| WORDS |

1 confirmation 확인 time slot 시간대 accommodate 수용하다, 맞추다 alternative 대체의

2 dietitian 영양사 launch 출시하다 make sense 타당하다 professional 전문가 branch location 지점

ETS 실전 테스트

Questions 1-3 refer to the following contract.

Speaker Contract

This contract, entered into on 26 January, is between the Thaya Institute and Franck Woog, an independent contractor, for his services as Guest Speaker. Mr. Woog agrees to give his talk on the role of honey bees in cross-pollination at Goethal University's Ferland Hall from noon to 2 P.M. on 15 February.

The Thaya Institute agrees to pay Mr. Woog €600.00 for his services. Payment will be processed within 30 days of the speaking date. Additionally, Mr. Woog's travel expenses can be reimbursed up to €200.00. All travel receipts must be presented to receive reimbursement.

Mr. Woog agrees to have his talk filmed and photographed. These materials may be published online by the Thaya Institute.

Agreed by:

_Franck Woog_____   _26 January_____
Speaker   Date

_Laurine Rey_____   _26 January_____
Representative of the Thaya Institute   Date

---

1. What does the contract suggest about Mr. Woog?
   (A) He is a student at the Thaya Institute.
   (B) He will attend a lecture on January 26.
   (C) He will receive payment for a talk.
   (D) He has met Ms. Rey before.

2. The word "presented" in paragraph 2, line 4, is closest in meaning to
   (A) gifted
   (B) exposed
   (C) submitted
   (D) revealed

3. What does Mr. Woog agree to do?
   (A) Have a speech video recorded
   (B) Submit a copy of his notes
   (C) Publish an article
   (D) Take photographs of an event

| WORDS |

enter into (계약을) 체결하다 independent 독립적인 contractor 계약자 cross-pollination 교잡 수분 process 처리하다
expense 지출, 경비 reimburse 환급하다 receipt 영수증 reimbursement 환급(금)

PART 7 | UNIT 04

UNIT 05

문장 삽입 문제

문장 삽입 문제는 신문 기사, 이메일, 광고, 홈페이지 리뷰 지문에서 주로 등장합니다. 삽입문에 제시된 연결어나 지시어는 중요한 연결 고리 역할을 하며 지문 구조를 파악하여 문맥상 삽입문이 들어갈 단락을 찾는 것에도 도움이 됩니다. 대부분 지문 구조는 주제, 세부 사항, 미래 계획의 순서로 이루어집니다.

빈출 질문 유형

In which of the positions marked [1], [2], [3], and [4] does the following sentence best belong?

[1], [2], [3], [4]로 표시된 곳 중에서 다음 문장이 들어가기에 적합한 곳은?

삽입문에 제시된 연결어를 활용하기

삽입문에 however(그러나), moreover(게다가), therefore(그러므로), thus(그래서)와 같은 연결어가 있으면 앞 문장과의 논리 관계로 삽입문이 들어갈 위치를 찾을 수 있습니다.

앞 문장 키워드

The job requires loading and unloading heavy equipment on the stage. 그 일자리는 무대에서 무거운 장비를 올리고 내리는 일이 필요합니다.

삽입문

Therefore, the ideal candidate should be in good physical condition. 그러므로 이상적인 지원자는 신체가 건강해야 합니다.

삽입문에서 정답의 단서는 결론을 나타내는 연결어 Therefore이므로 앞 문장에서는 신체가 건강해야 하는 이유를 나타내는 내용이 와야 합니다. 따라서 무거운 장비를 올리고 내리는 일을 해야 한다는 문장 뒤에 오는 것이 적절합니다.

삽입문에 제시된 지시어나 대명사를 활용하기

삽입문에 this / these, he / she / it / they / them이 있으면 이러한 지시어나 대명사가 지칭하는 구체적인 명사가 언급된 문장을 찾아서 자연스럽게 이어지는지 확인합니다

앞 문장 키워드

Most notably, the hotel will have six restaurants on the property. 가장 눈에 띄는 것은 호텔 구내에 있는 6개의 식당이다.

삽입문

One of them will feature dishes by the acclaimed chef Avery Fekete. 그 중 하나는 인정받는 주방장인 에이버리 페킷의 요리를 선보일 예정이다.

삽입문에서 정답의 단서는 숫자를 나타내는 One of them이므로 지문에서 이와 관련된 숫자가 언급된 부분을 먼저 찾아야 합니다. 앞 문장에 six restaurants라는 숫자 표현이 있으므로 그 뒤에 삽입문이 들어가는 것이 적절합니다.

문장 삽입 문제 풀이 전략

전략 1.
삽입문에서 단서 표현 찾기

삽입문에서 연결어, 지시어, 대명사와 같은 단서 표현이 있는지 우선 확인합니다.

전략 2.
문맥상 적절한 단락 찾기

삽입문의 의미를 파악하고 같은 주제를 다루는 단락을 찾습니다. 빈칸 뒤에 이어지는 문장 속의 단서 표현과 내용이 잘 이어지는지 확인합니다.

| 풀이 전략 적용하기 |

My wife and I recently traveled to Slovenia. We booked the visit through Garvin Travel, and thanks to their expertise, we had an excellent trip. —[1]—. We worked with Abby Adelman from Garvin Travel to create an itinerary. She made the planning easy and provided many helpful suggestions. —[2]—. She also arranged for a tour guide, Nikola Zuber, to lead us on several excursions once we got there.

Nikola met us at the airport and drove us to our hotel in Ljubljana. Over the next three days, he took us to some of the major attractions and some of the lesser-known attractions that were just as amazing. His recommendations for where to eat and other things to do were much appreciated. —[3]—.

전략 2. 문맥상 적절한 단락 찾기

I highly recommend Garvin Travel. —[4]—. We will use them again the next time we plan a trip.

문장 삽입 문제

아내와 저는 최근 슬로베니아로 여행을 갔습니다. 우리는 가빈 여행사를 통해 방문을 예약했고 여행사의 전문성 덕분에 여행이 아주 즐거웠습니다. –[1]–. 우리는 가빈 여행사 애비 아델만 씨와 협력해 여행 일정을 짰습니다. 그녀는 계획 수립을 수월하게 해주었고 유용한 제안을 많이 해주었습니다. –[2]–. 그녀는 또한 우리가 거기 도착하면 몇 차례 여행을 안내해줄 관광 가이드 니콜라 주버도 주선해주었습니다.

니콜라 씨가 공항으로 마중을 나와서 류블랴나에 있는 호텔까지 차로 데려다 주었습니다. 이후 사흘 동안 그는 주요 관광 명소들, 그리고 덜 유명하지만 똑같이 멋진 관광지들로 우리를 데려갔습니다. 그가 먹을 장소와 다른 활동을 추천해 줘서 아주 고마웠습니다. –[3]–.

저는 가빈 여행사를 적극 추천합니다. –[4]–. 다음에 여행을 계획할 때 그곳을 다시 이용하려고 합니다.

Q. In which of the positions marked [1], [2], [3], and [4] does the following sentence best belong?

"It would have been hard to see and do so much without his help." **전략 1. 삽입문에서 단서 표현 찾기**

(A) [1]   (B) [2]

(C) [3]   (D) [4]

[1], [2], [3], [4]로 표시된 곳 중에서 다음 문장이 들어가기에 가장 적합한 곳은?

"그의 도움이 없었다면 그렇게 많은 것을 보고 하기는 힘들었을 것입니다."

(A) [1]   (B) [2]

(C) [3]   (D) [4]

전략 1	삽입문에서 정답의 단서가 되는 대명사 his를 확인하고 남자가 등장하는 문장에 주목합니다.
전략 2	his help(그의 도움)가 언급된 단락을 우선 찾아보면 첫 단락의 [1]과 [2] 앞에서는 남자 이름이 등장하지 않았으며, 마지막 단락에서도 [4]의 앞 문장은 여행사를 추천하므로 적절하지 않습니다.
문장 삽입	삽입문에서 without his help(그의 도움이 없었다면)라는 표현이 있으므로 Nikola의 도움을 설명한 문장들이 주로 언급된 둘째 단락의 마지막에 위치한 (C)가 정답입니다.

PART 7 | UNIT 05

다음 지문을 읽고 문제를 풀어보세요.

For Sale: Three 200-liter Rain Barrels

I bought these rain barrels a few years ago from an agricultural supply store, but I have since upgraded to a bigger water-collection system that works better for my number of crops.

These barrels work well and are simple to set up. I have already rinsed them out so they're ready to use immediately. —[1]—. Since their color has faded from being out in the sun, I'm selling them for $20 each. That's a great deal, considering used rain barrels of this size generally sell for about $30 – $40.

Please contact me to make arrangements for pickup. Serious inquiries only, please. —[2]—. —Marcus Tarrant, 555-0132.

---

1   In which of the positions marked [1] and [2] does the following sentence best belong?

"Just place them under a drainpipe to catch water when it rains."

(A) [1]   (B) [2]

Listening To Your Customers

Being successful in retail is more difficult than ever given the rise in online shopping. When a customer comes to your store, whether physically or online, offering high-quality service is a must, especially when that customer has a problem. —[1]—.

Customers want to feel heard, but they do not want to have to repeat their story over and over. To avoid irritation on the part of customers, staff members must be trained to listen carefully to their customers and to ask relevant questions that provide further insight into the exact nature of the problem. —[2]—. Only then should staff members start working on a resolution of the matter.

Building trust with the customer is more than half the story. Active listening can go a long way toward building and restoring that trust.

---

2   In which of the positions marked [1] and [2] does the following sentence best belong?
"Additionally, the customer should be offered an apology for the inconvenience."

(A) [1]   (B) [2]

| WORDS |

1 barrel 큰 통 agricultural 농업의 crop 작물 rinse 씻다, 헹구다 fade 바래다, 희미해지다 drainpipe 홈통, 하수관
2 retail 소매업 physically 실제로 relevant 관련 있는, 적절한 insight 통찰(력) go a long way 큰 효과가 있다 restore 회복하다

Questions 1-3 refer to the following e-mail.

E-mail

To:	Jin-Ho Ro <jro@ventnorresorts.co.nz>
From:	Cynthia Rooney <crooney@ventnorresorts.co.nz>
Subject:	Information
Date:	3 March
Attachment:	📎 Employment Launch, Jobs list

Dear Jin-Ho:

As discussed at the meeting last month, we're trying Employment Launch. — [1] —.
We've signed a 6-month contract. If we decide to continue with them, we can extend the
contract at a discounted rate. — [2] —.

The company promises to post jobs on all types of social media. For this initial venture,
we've asked them to post the currently open corporate positions. For example, I've
asked them to list the positions available in accounting, digital engineering, and
advertising. — [3] —.

Construction on our new Auckland resort will be completed in eight months, so we'll
wait before advertising for the jobs we'll need there, such as housekeeping staff, front
desk employees, and maintenance workers. — [4] —. I've attached the details about
Employment Launch and the current jobs list. Please let me know what you think.

Sincerely,

Cynthia Rooney
Human Resources Manager
Ventnor Resorts

---

1. Why did Ms. Rooney e-mail Mr. Ro?

(A) To ask him to post a job notice
(B) To discuss a product advertising
    campaign
(C) To offer him a temporary position
(D) To explain a strategy to recruit employees

2. According to the e-mail, what will most likely
happen in eight months?

(A) A resort will open.
(B) A new service will be offered.
(C) A new product will be launched.
(D) A transfer will take place.

3. In which of the positions marked [1], [2],
[3], and [4] does the following sentence
best belong?

"Employment Launch should have them all
posted across social media by tomorrow."

(A) [1]
(B) [2]
(C) [3]
(D) [4]

| **WORDS** |

contract 계약(서) extend 연장하다 discounted rate 할인된 요금 initial 최초의 venture (모험적인) 시도 currently 현재
corporate 기업의, 법인의 available 이용[채용] 가능한 accounting 회계 construction 공사, 건축 housekeeping (호텔·병원
등의) 시설 관리 maintenance 유지 관리, 정비 attach 첨부하다 current 현재의 **1** temporary 임시의 strategy 전략 **2** transfer
이전 take place 발생하다

UNIT 06

편지와 이메일

무료인강 바로가기

편지나 이메일에 자주 등장하는 표현

글의 목적	I'm writing to ~	~하기 위해 이 글을 씁니다
	I'd like to inform you that ~	~을 알려드리고자 합니다
	This is to remind you that ~	~을 다시 한 번 알려드리고자 합니다
	We'd like to offer you ~	당신에게 ~을 제공하고자 합니다
	I'm very sorry to tell you that ~	~을 알려드리게 되어 매우 유감입니다
감사	Thank you for ~ / I really appreciate that ~	~에 대해 감사드립니다
	I'm deeply grateful[thankful] for ~	~에 대해 진심으로 감사드립니다
	As a token of our appreciation[gratitude]	감사의 표시로
요청/ 요구	I would appreciate it if you ~	당신이 ~해주시면 감사하겠습니다
	Please let me know ~	~을 제게 알려주십시오
	Could you please ~	~해주시겠어요?
	You are required to submit ~ / Please submit ~	~을 제출해주십시오

주제별 어휘

주문	place an order 주문을 하다	free of charge 무료로
	out of stock 재고가 없는, 품절인	by courier 택배로
	replacement 교체물, 후임자	reimburse 환급하다
	a full refund 전액 환불	upon receipt 수령하자마자
업무	duty 업무	assign 배정하다
	disruption 중단, 지장	take on (일을) 떠맡다 (= assume)
	oversee 감독하다	reschedule 일정을 변경하다
	be in charge of ~을 담당하다	familiarize 익숙하게 하다
문서·서류	include 포함하다	electronically 컴퓨터로
	attach 첨부하다	relevant 관련 있는
	enclose 동봉하다	update 수정하다
구직	résumé 이력서	certificate 자격증, 증명서
	application form 지원서	degree 학위
	cover letter 자기소개서	candidate 지원자 (= applicant)
추천	recommend 추천하다	contribution 기여, 공헌
	demonstrate 입증하다	letter of reference 추천서 (= referral)
	capacity 능력; 수용 인원	qualified 자격을 갖춘
	asset 자산	dedicated 헌신적인
	attitude 태도	fit 적합한 사람

편지(letter)와 이메일(e-mail) 풀이 전략

- 발신자 / 수신자의 이메일 계정으로 인물 관계(사내 연락, 회사↔고객) 및 업종을 알 수 있습니다.
- 이메일 제목(Subject, Re), 글의 목적, 혜택, 요청 사항, 첨부 파일의 언급에 주의합니다.
- 발신자 / 수신자의 이름을 통해 지문에서 I / we와 you, 제3자인지를 파악합니다.

┤ 이메일 지문 흐름 학습 ├

수신인	To: krbrogan@mail.net	수신: krbrogan@mail.net
발신인	From: customerservice@barroselascc.com	발신: customerservice@barroselascc.com
	Date: September 2	날짜: 9월 2일
제목	Subject: Your online order	제목: 귀하의 온라인 주문

Dear Keenan,
키넌 씨에게,

❶ 글의 목적 Thank you for visiting our online store. **1,3**Your shopping cart contains several items that will be saved for you through September 5. —[1]—.

저희 온라인 매장을 방문해주셔서 감사합니다. **1,3**고객님의 장바구니에 몇 가지 품목이 담겨 있는데 9월 5일까지 저장됩니다.

❷ 혜택
❸ 요청 사항 If you complete your order by the date specified above, **2**you will receive ten percent off your total purchase price. Please consider completing your order now to take advantage of the savings. —[2]—.

위에 명시된 날짜까지 주문을 완료하시면 **2**총 구매가에서 10퍼센트를 할인받으시게 됩니다. 지금 주문을 완료해 절약 기회를 이용하는 것을 고려하십시오.

❹ 연락 방법 In case you couldn't finish your order because you need some help with the ordering process, contact our support team at 650-555-0083 or customerservice@barroselascc.com. —[3]—.

주문 과정에 도움이 필요해 주문을 완료하실 수 없는 경우에는 650-555-0083 또는 customerservice@barroselascc.com으로 저희 지원 팀에 연락하세요.

Thanks for shopping! —[4]—.
쇼핑에 감사드립니다!

이메일 빈출 질문 위의 전체 흐름을 잘 숙지하고 이메일에 자주 나오는 질문을 기억해두세요.

❶ 목적	**이메일을 쓴 목적은?** 제목에서 온라인 주문임을 알 수 있고 첫 단락에서 장바구니에 담긴 물품의 저장 마감일을 상기시켜주고 있습니다.	Q. What is **the purpose** of the e-mail? A. **To remind a customer of an incomplete order** 고객에게 완료되지 못한 주문을 상기시키려고
❷ 세부 사항	**고객에게 제공되는 것은?** 고객은 you로 표현되기에 you와 receive가 들어간 문장에서 정답을 찾을 수 있습니다. ten percent off가 discount로 패러프레이징된 점도 주목해주세요.	Q. What is the customer **offered**? A. **A discount** 할인
❸ 문장 삽입	**[1], [2], [3], [4]로 표시된 곳 중에서 다음 문장이 들어가기에 가장 적합한 곳은?** "저희는 그 때까지만 그 품목들을 구입하실 수 있도록 보장할 수 있습니다." 삽입문에 until that time이 있으므로 기한을 제시한 앞 문장이 중요한 단서가 될 수 있습니다.	Q. In which of the positions marked [1], [2], [3], and [4] does the following sentence best belong? "We can ensure the availability of your items only until that time." A. **[1]**

다음 지문을 읽고 문제를 풀어보세요.

To: Lana Richman <lrichman@richmanproducts.com>
From: Paul Ross <pross@nationalhouseholdcleaningproductsconv.org>
Date: January 7
Subject: Vendor assignment

Dear Ms. Richman,

This is to confirm that your company, Richman Products, is assigned to Booth 287 at the National Household Cleaning Products Convention at the Municipal Conference Center in Seattle from February 11 through February 13. Please plan to arrive on February 10 before 2:00 P.M. to set up your booth display. Conference center workers will meet exhibitors at Entrance 3 to assist with any items being brought in for display.

We look forward to your participation at this event!

Sincerely,
Paul Ross

---

1   What is the purpose of the e-mail?

(A) To provide information to an event participant
(B) To notify a company owner of a schedule change

Dear Ms. Stephenson:

We are very sorry to hear that two of the Pristine Collection plates in your recent order were cracked when you received them. We would be pleased to send you replacements.

We have enclosed a return kit for the damaged items. In it, you will find packing materials and a label addressed to us. Upon receipt of the returned items, we will send new plates free of charge.

Once again, we apologize for the inconvenience. Thank you very much for your business.

---

2   What is included with the letter?

(A) New plates   (B) A mailing label

| WORDS |

1 vendor 판매업체 assignment 배정 municipal 지자체의, 시의 exhibitor 전시회 참가자

2 cracked 금이 간 replacement 교체(물) return 반송하다; 반송 damaged 손상된 apologize for ~을 사과하다 inconvenience 불편함

                                                              정답 및 해설 p.206

Questions 1-2 refer to the following e-mail.

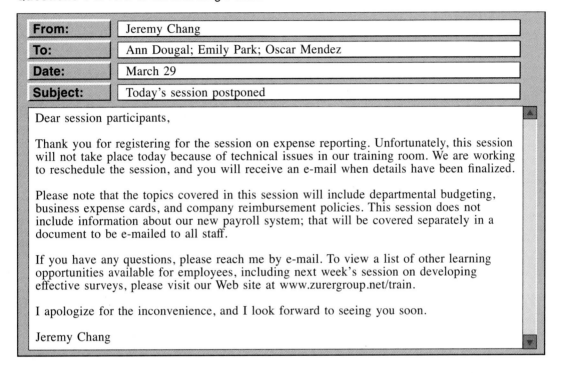

From:	Jeremy Chang
To:	Ann Dougal; Emily Park; Oscar Mendez
Date:	March 29
Subject:	Today's session postponed

Dear session participants,

Thank you for registering for the session on expense reporting. Unfortunately, this session will not take place today because of technical issues in our training room. We are working to reschedule the session, and you will receive an e-mail when details have been finalized.

Please note that the topics covered in this session will include departmental budgeting, business expense cards, and company reimbursement policies. This session does not include information about our new payroll system; that will be covered separately in a document to be e-mailed to all staff.

If you have any questions, please reach me by e-mail. To view a list of other learning opportunities available for employees, including next week's session on developing effective surveys, please visit our Web site at www.zurergroup.net/train.

I apologize for the inconvenience, and I look forward to seeing you soon.

Jeremy Chang

1. Who most likely is Mr. Chang?

(A) A finance consultant
(B) A payroll specialist
(C) A repair technician
(D) A training coordinator

2. What can staff expect to receive by e-mail?

(A) A registration form
(B) An employee-satisfaction survey
(C) A list of online learning opportunities
(D) A document about a company system

PART 7 | UNIT 06

| WORDS |

postpone 연기하다 register 등록하다 unfortunately 아쉽게도 finalize 확정하다 budgeting 예산 편성 reimbursement 환급
policy 정책, 방침 opportunity 기회 available 이용 가능한 effective 효과적인

Questions 3-5 refer to the following letter.

La Scala Properties
208 Bedford Street
Eden Terrace
Auckland 1010

1 May

Ms. Janna Fritz
300 Mount Eden Road
Mount Eden
Auckland 1024

Dear Ms. Fritz:

Thank you for being a valued client. — [1] —. I would like to inform you that according to our property agreement, your rental period comes to an end in just two months. Therefore, I have enclosed a form on which you may indicate your intentions. — [2] —. If you intend to remain at La Scala Properties, you have the option of renewing your lease for a period of six months, to 1 January, or extending the lease for one year, to 1 July of next year. — [3] —. If you intend to leave, please note that the apartment must be vacated by 30 June. Whatever your determination, please complete and return the form by 1 June. — [4] —.

Do not hesitate to contact me if you have any questions or concerns.

Robert Karam

Robert Karam
Manager, La Scala Properties

Enclosure

3. What is the purpose of the letter?

(A) To confirm receipt of a contract
(B) To issue a contract reminder
(C) To describe a new policy
(D) To request a payment extension

4. By what date should Ms. Fritz inform Mr. Karam about a decision?

(A) January 1
(B) May 1
(C) June 1
(D) July 1

5. In which of the positions marked [1], [2], [3], and [4] does the following sentence best belong?

"There are two options."

(A) [1]
(B) [2]
(C) [3]
(D) [4]

| WORDS |

property 부동산 valued 소중한 inform 알리다 agreement 계약 rental 임대 period 기간 enclose 동봉하다 form 양식 indicate 나타내다 intention 의도, 의사 intend to ~할 작정이다 option 선택 사항 renew 갱신하다 lease 임대차 계약 extend 연장하다 vacate 비우다 determination 결심, 결정 complete 작성하다 hesitate 망설이다 concern 관심사 enclosure 동봉물
3 confirm 확인하다 receipt 수령 issue 발부하다 reminder 독촉장 describe 설명하다 policy 정책 extension 연장
4 decision 결정

Questions 6-8 refer to the following e-mail.

To:	All members
From:	Jack Muir
Subject:	Policies regarding performances
Date:	January 15

Dear members of the Jack Muir Big Band,

Thanks for your excellent performance this past Saturday night! The clients enjoyed their event and praised your part in making the evening so special. That said, I feel it is necessary at this time, with so many new members, to remind you of our policies regarding performances.

The drummer, setup crew, and I must report to the performance venue one hour before the gig. All other band members must arrive no later than 30 minutes before showtime. It is unacceptable to arrive just moments before the event begins, as has happened on several recent occasions.

All members serve on the setup crew on a rotating basis. The crew roster is posted for your convenience on the band's Web site by our manager, Ann Tanner. Ms. Tanner also places all the information for each engagement—including locations, times, and dress code—on the Web site. Although our usual attire is concert black, some events are less formal, so it is important to check the Web site before each gig. The information is at jackmuirbigband.com/gigs.

Thank you!

Jack Muir, Band Leader

6. What most likely caused Mr. Muir to send the e-mail?

(A) Some clients disliked a performance.
(B) A concert was booked on very short notice.
(C) Some members arrived at an event later than expected.
(D) New members requested the information.

7. According to the e-mail, what is one of Ms. Tanner's jobs?

(A) Providing information to the band
(B) Playing drums in the band
(C) Transporting equipment to events
(D) Updating the design of a Web site

8. The word "check" in paragraph 3, line 5, is closest in meaning to

(A) mark up
(B) look at
(C) slow down
(D) pay for

| WORDS |

performance 공연 excellent 훌륭한 praise 칭찬하다 crew 작업반 report to ~에 도착을 알리다 venue (행사) 장소 gig 공연 unacceptable 용납할 수 없는 recent 최근의 occasion 경우 on a rotating basis 교대로 roster 근무자 명단 post 게시하다, 올리다 convenience 편리함, 편의 engagement 약속, 계약 including ~을 포함해 location 장소 attire 복장 formal 격식을 차린

UNIT 07

광고와 공지

무료인강 바로가기

광고나 공지에 자주 등장하는 표현

최신 정보 안내	We're pleased to announce ~	~을 알리게 되어 기쁩니다
	We have some updates on ~	~에 관한 최신 정보가 있습니다
혜택	We've enclosed a gift certificate.	저희가 상품권을 동봉했습니다.
	This discount is valid for ~	이 할인은 ~에 유효합니다
	We offer free delivery on ~	~에 대해 무료 배송을 제공합니다
	Take advantage of this ~	이런 ~을 이용하시기 바랍니다
	Only while supplies last!	재고 소진 시까지만!
요청	Please keep in mind the following ~	다음의 ~을 기억해주시기 바랍니다
	We recommend that ~	~할 것을 추천합니다
	Reserve your spot before ~	~ 전에 자리를 예약하시기 바랍니다
	Stop in to speak with ~	잠시 들르셔서 ~와 얘기를 나눠보세요
	Contact sales representative ~	판매 담당자에게 연락하세요

주제별 어휘

제품 특징	come with ~이 딸려 있다	state-of-the-art 최첨단의
	feature ~을 특징으로 하다	substantial 내구성이 있는 (= durable)
	warranty 품질 보증서	specification 사양
	guarantee 보장하다	optional 선택 사양인
서비스 특징	special occasion 특별 행사	accommodate 수용하다 (= house)
	benefit 혜택	be eligible for ~의 자격이 있다
	patron 단골, 고객	complimentary 무료의 (= free)
	personalized 개인 맞춤형의	at no extra charge 추가 요금 없이
	available 이용 가능한	in advance 미리 (= beforehand)
구인 구직	job opening 공석	required 필수적인 (= mandatory)
	responsibility 책임, 의무	job description 직무 기술서
	applicant 지원자	qualification 자격 요건
정책 규정	effective / beginning + 날짜 ~부로	alternative 대체의
	return policy 반품 정책	activate 활성화시키다, 작동시키다
행사	exhibition 전시	launch 시작하다, 출시하다
	gathering 모임	commemorate 기념하다
	advance registration 사전 등록	sign up for ~에 등록하다 (= register for)
	make arrangements 준비하다	reserve 예약하다
	host 주최하다	suspension 중단, 보류

광고(advertisement)와 공지(notice, announcement, memo) 풀이 전략

- 제목과 글의 첫 부분에서 상품명, 업종, 대상자, 글의 목적, 주제와 관련된 정보를 알 수 있습니다.
- 표나 세부 사항에서는 항목을 주요 단서로 하여 필요한 정보를 빠르게 찾아내는 것이 중요합니다.
- 글의 마지막 부분에서 마감일, 할인 정보, 제공받는 것, 연락 이유, 요청 사항 등의 내용에 주의하세요.

| 공지 지문 흐름 학습 |

❶ 업체명/ 대상

TO ALL DMC EMPLOYEES USING THE NEWBURGH HEALTH CLUB

뉴버그 헬스클럽을 이용하는 모든 DMC 전 직원들께

❷ 글의 목적

[1]Effective July 1, corporate membership rates will change. The Newburgh Health Club offers individual and family plans for weekdays only, weekends only, or for seven days a week. The new monthly rates are listed below.

[1]7월 1일부로 기업 회원 이용료가 변경됩니다. 뉴버그 헬스클럽은 개인 및 가족 프로그램을 평일 한정, 주말 한정, 또는 일주일 내내로 구분해 제공합니다. 변경된 월별 이용료는 다음과 같습니다.

❸ 세부 사항

Newburgh Health Club Membership Plan	DMC Corporate Membership	
	Individual	Family
Weekdays Only (Mon.–Fri., 6 A.M.–10 P.M.)	$22.00	$55.00
Weekends Only (Sat. and Sun., 6 A.M.–8 P.M.)	$22.00	$55.00
[2,3]**Full Membership** (Weekends 6 A.M.–8 P.M. & Weekdays 6 A.M.–10 P.M.)	$40.00	[2]$100.00
[3]**Executive Membership** (all the benefits of full membership plus the services of a nutritionist and personal trainers)	$48.00	$120.00

뉴버그 헬스클럽 회원제 프로그램	DMC 기업 회원	
	개인	가족
평일 한정(월–금, 오전 6시 –오후 10시)	22달러	55달러
주말 한정(토–일, 오전 6시 –오후 8시)	22달러	55달러
[2,3]**정회원**(주말 오전 6시– 오후 8시 & 평일 오전 6시 –오후 10시)	40달러	[2]100달러
[3]**특별 회원**(모든 정회원 혜택에 영양사와 개인 트레이너 서비스 추가)	48달러	120달러

❹ 요청 사항

DMC employees who are interested in becoming new members of the health club can pick up application forms from Ms. Donna Lin in room 701.

헬스클럽 신규 회원이 되는 데 관심이 있는 DMC 직원들은 701호실에서 도나 린 씨에게 신청서를 받으면 됩니다.

공지 빈출 질문 위의 전체 흐름을 잘 숙지하고 공지에 자주 나오는 질문을 기억해두세요.

❶ 목적

공지의 목적은?
제목에서 업체명과 대상을 제시하였으며 글의 맨 앞에서 목적이 언급되었습니다.

Q. What is the purpose of this notice?
A. To give notice of a price change at a health club
헬스클럽의 이용료 변경을 공지하기 위해

❷ 세부 사항

DMC 직원의 가족 정회원이 지불해야 할 월간 이용료는?
세부 사항에서 가족 정회원을 키워드로 정답을 찾을 수 있습니다.

Q. What is the monthly rate for full membership for the family of an employee at DMC?
A. $100 100달러

❸ 문장 삽입

특별 회원에 관해 언급된 사항은?
세부 사항에서 특별 회원을 키워드로 정답을 찾을 수 있습니다.

Q. What is stated about the executive membership?
A. It allows use of the club on weekdays and weekends.
평일과 주말에 클럽을 이용할 수 있다.

다음 지문을 읽고 문제를 풀어보세요.

April 2

Attention, Restaurants of Hazeltown!

The Hazeltown Civic Council is pleased to announce Hazeltown's Second Annual Street Festival, which will take place from May 28 through May 31. We invite you to reserve a booth during the event!

The festival will be held on the four-block area of Main Street beginning at its intersection with Chestnut Street, continuing through the intersections with Oak Street and Pine Street, and ending at Main Street's intersection with Sagamore Street.

We recommend that each restaurant limit itself to preparing four dishes. There will be a separate booth for the sale of beverages, so please do not offer them at your booth. Also, please note that the Hazeltown Jazz Trio and the Hazeltown High School Choir will be providing entertainment. Music may be played at your booth only between their performances.

---

1   For whom is the announcement intended?

(A) Residents of Hazeltown

(B) Members of the festival planning committee

Contractors and Trades Magazine

We are your monthly resource for all trades. Reach over 52,000 subscribers throughout the United States and Canada. Advertise in our publication in the coming year!

Reserve your spot before the end of December and your ad will run a second time for free during the month of your choice. Contact sales representative Eesha Bradford today at adsales@candtmag.net.

---

2   What is indicated about *Contractors and Trades Magazine*?

(A) It is offered free of charge.

(B) It is distributed internationally.

| WORDS |

1 intersection 교차로 separate 별도의 beverage 음료수 performance 공연
2 contractor 도급업자 trade (특정) 사업, 업계 resource 자원 reach 연락하다 subscriber 구독자 advertise 광고하다
publication 출판(물) reserve 예약하다 spot 자리 ad 광고 sales representative 영업 담당자

Questions 1-2 refer to the following notice.

Jonscope Corporation
Computer Fundamentals Workshop

Location: Main Floor Conference Room
Date and Time: Thursday, January 12, 10:00 A.M. to 2:00 P.M.

Take advantage of this professional development opportunity to learn about:
- Office computer basics
- Troubleshooting minor problems
- Creating and organizing files
- Word processing tips
- Using spreadsheets

Register with the Human Resources Department before January 10.

1. Who most likely will attend the workshop?

(A) Jonscope customers
(B) Jonscope retirees
(C) Jonscope employees
(D) Jonscope job applicants

2. What is indicated about the workshop?

(A) It is given once per month.
(B) It is limited to ten attendees.
(C) It will take place in the computer room.
(D) It requires advance registration.

PART 7 | UNIT 07

| WORDS |

fundamental 기초; 기초적인 take advantage of ~을 이용하다 opportunity 기회 troubleshoot (문제를) 해결하다
organize 정리하다 register 등록하다
1 retiree 퇴직자 applicant 지원자 2 limit 제한하다 attendee 참석자 advance registration 사전 등록

AEREA SYSTEMS

Job Description–Technical Writer

Aerea Systems is a growing, global company in the aviation industry and has an immediate opening for a technical writer to join its team in Canby. The ideal candidate will contribute to successful project completion by creating technical documentation packages that meet company specifications, satisfy customer requirements, and comply with government standards.

Responsibilities:
Write and review documents, including
— operator manuals
— flight crew checklists
— flight guide supplements
— equipment maintenance manuals

Salary is negotiable and commensurate with qualifications and experience.
Apply to hr@aerea.com/job code 2482.

3. What does Aerea Systems most likely manufacture?

(A) Service uniforms
(B) Travel accessories
(C) Security equipment
(D) Commercial aircraft

4. What is NOT a responsibility of the position?

(A) Editing checklists
(B) Meeting with customers
(C) Creating operator training materials
(D) Reviewing maintenance documents

| WORDS |

job description 직무 기술서 aviation 항공 contribute to ~에 기여하다 specifications 기술 설명서 comply with ~에 따르다
operator 장비 운영자 supplement 증보판 maintenance 정비 negotiable 협상 가능한 commensurate with ~에 상응하는

Questions 5-7 refer to the following memo.

TO: Customer service team
FROM: Harold Park, Manager
DATE: January 3
RE: Assignments

As you know, the *Seaview Times* has increased its circulation dramatically over the past year. In order to address efficiently the large volume of customer-service e-mails and telephone calls that has resulted, each member of the customer service team is being assigned one area of customer service to focus on. Below is a list of our team members and the type of calls and e-mails that will be directed to each person.

Marian Larson	Subscription renewals
Adam Foley	Subscription cancellations
Beth Brown	Delivery failures: Late, damaged, or missed newspapers
Hal Carter	Temporary suspension of delivery

We hope this will improve efficiency and allow us to continue the quality of work that we pride ourselves on.

5. What is the *Seaview Times*?
   (A) A magazine
   (B) A Web site
   (C) A newsletter
   (D) A newspaper

6. In the memo, the word "volume" in paragraph 1, line 2, is closest in meaning to
   (A) loudness
   (B) amount
   (C) book
   (D) space

7. What is indicated about the *Seaview Times*?
   (A) It has increased its number of subscribers.
   (B) It has recently hired new employees.
   (C) It will move into a larger building.
   (D) It will close for one month.

| WORDS |

circulation 판매 부수 address (문제를) 다루다 efficiently 효율적으로 assign 배정하다 direct ~로 보내다, 향하다 renewal 갱신 cancellation 취소 delivery failure 배달 오류 temporary 일시적인 suspension 중단 quality 질, 품질 pride oneself on ~을 자랑스럽게 여기다

5 newsletter 회보, 소식지 7 subscriber 구독자

UNIT 08

문자 메시지와 온라인 채팅

무료인강 바로가기

문자 메시지/온라인 채팅에 자주 등장하는 표현

대화의 목적	Can you give me an update on ~?	~의 최근 상황에 대해 알려주실래요?
	Do you have a minute to look at ~?	~을 잠시 볼 시간이 있나요?
	I want to remind you that ~	다시 한 번 말씀 드리지만 ~
	I can't find ~	~을 못 찾고 있어요
상황, 문의	How are they going?	어떻게 진행되고 있나요?
	How are things coming along with ~?	~은 어떻게 되어가고 있나요?
	Could you give me more details on ~?	~에 대해 좀 더 자세히 이야기해 주실래요?
	Let me check on that.	확인해 볼게요.
	Are you sure that ~?	~이 확실한가요?
	I head back to ~.	~로 돌아가는 중이에요.
	I'm on my way.	가는 중이에요.
	That's a great comfort.	큰 위안이 되네요.
수락, 거절	I'll let you know.	내가 알려줄게요.
	I'll give that a try.	그렇게 해볼게요.
	That definitely works.	정말 그러면 되겠어요.
	No problem.	문제 없어요.
	Not at this time.	지금은 아니에요.

주제별 어휘

일정	delay 지연	push back 연기하다 (= postpone)
	be supposed to ~하기로 되어 있다	resume 재개하다
	behind schedule 일정보다 뒤처진	call off 취소하다 (= cancel)
	reschedule 일정을 조정하다	in advance 미리, 사전에
업무 처리	process 처리하다	work order 작업 명령서
	serve 제공하다(= provide)	verify 확인하다, 입증하다
	set up 준비하다, 설치하다	final draft 최종안
	set aside 챙겨두다, 확보하다	assignment 과제, 업무
지원	misplace 잘못 두어 못 찾다	suggestion 제안
	not working 작동이 안 되다	volunteer 자원하다; 자원 봉사자
	assistance 도움, 지원	request 요청하다

- 첫 부분에서 대화의 주제나 목적이 언급되며, 상사 또는 동료와의 대화인지를 파악할 수 있습니다.
- 인칭대명사(I/my, we/our)와 호칭에서 인물 관계와 부서명을 추론할 수 있습니다.
- 문자 메시지나 온라인 채팅 지문에는 의도 파악 문제가 포함됩니다. if 조건절, 요청문, 의문문에서 의도를 묻는 문제의 단서를 찾을 수 있기에 특히 유의해야 합니다.

⎯ | 문자 메시지 지문 흐름 학습 | ⎯⎯⎯⎯⎯⎯⎯⎯⎯⎯⎯⎯⎯⎯⎯⎯⎯

❶ 대화목적

Angus Dunbar (9:59 A.M.)
Hi, team. **1**I finished installing the new office printer that was delivered yesterday.

Tobey Cahill (10:01 A.M.)
I sent a budget spreadsheet just now, but it didn't print. Am I doing something wrong?

❷ 문제점

Frances Ortiz (10:02 A.M.)
Tobey, your laptop may still be set up to send jobs to the old printer.

❸ 해결 방법

Angus Dunbar (10:03 A.M.)
2Oh, there's a chance the printer needs to be configured to handle that document type. If nothing else works, just let me know.

Tobey Cahill (10:15 A.M.)
I did need to switch to the new printer—thanks Frances. But unfortunately, **3**I'm still having trouble. Angus, I've tried everything I can do.

❹ 요청 사항

Angus Dunbar (10:16 A.M.)
3I'll be right there.

앵거스 던바 (오전 9:59)
팀원 여러분 안녕하세요. 어제 배송된 새 사무실 프린터를 설치했어요.

토비 카힐 (오전 10:01)
방금 예산 스프레드시트를 보냈는데 인쇄가 안 됐어요. 제가 뭘 잘못하고 있는 거죠?

프랜시스 오티즈 (오전 10:02)
토비, 노트북이 아직 예전 프린터로 작업을 전송하도록 설정되어 있을 수도 있어요.

앵거스 던바 (오전 10:03)
프린터가 해당 문서 유형을 처리하도록 환경 설정을 해야 할 수도 있어요. 아무리 해도 안 되면 저에게 알려주세요.

토비 카힐 (오전 10:15)
새 프린터로 전환했어야 했네요. 고마워요 프랜시스. 그런데 유감스럽게도 아직 문제가 있네요. 앵거스, 제가 할 수 있는 건 다 해 봤어요.

앵거스 던바 (오전 10:16)
바로 갈게요.

PART 7 | UNIT 08

문자 메시지 빈출 질문   위의 전체 흐름을 잘 숙지하고 문자 메시지에 자주 나오는 질문을 기억해두세요.

❶ 주제	**글쓴이들이 주로 논의하는 것은?** 대화 첫 부분에서 주제가 언급되었습니다.	Q. What are the writers **mainly discussing?** A. A piece of office equipment 사무실 장비
❷ 추론	**던바 씨는 누구이겠는가?** 던바 씨의 대화 내용에서 어떤 일을 하는지를 파악하여 직업을 추론할 수 있습니다.	Q. Who most likely is **Mr. Dunbar?** A. A technology assistant 기술 지원 담당자
❸ 의도	**오전 10시 15분에 카힐 씨가 "제가 할 수 있는 건 다 해 봤어요."라고 쓸 때, 무엇을 의미하는가?** 10시 16분에 바로 가서 도와주겠다고 한 답변에서 추론할 수 있습니다.	Q. At 10:15 A.M., what does Mr. Cahill mean when he writes, "I've tried everything I can do"? A. He hopes a colleague will resolve a problem. 동료가 문제를 해결해 주었으면 한다.

다음 지문을 읽고 문제를 풀어보세요.

Asad Buule (11:51 A.M.) Hi, Dominique. This job is taking longer than we expected. There were more items to be moved than Cooper Inc.'s work order indicated. We also found some desk drawers that hadn't been emptied and an employee was still packing some legal files.

Dominique Lavaud (11:52 A.M.) Unbelievable!

Asad Buule (11:53 A.M.) Yes. I just wanted to let you know. We should be leaving here in about 30 minutes. I'll let you know when we arrive at the new location and start unloading the truck. I don't think we'll be able to take a lunch break until late today.

Dominque Lavaud (11:54 A.M.) OK. Thank you for the update.

---

1 For what type of business do Mr. Buule and Ms. Lavaud most likely work?

(A) A furniture store
(B) A moving company

Kyong Han [11:08 A.M.] Hi, Terrence and LaMonica. Did we receive the certificate from the fire safety inspector?

Terrence Lawson [11:09 A.M.] Not yet. I called the inspector's office about an hour ago and I was told to check back in two days.

Kyong Han [11:11 A.M.] Okay, could you stay on top of that, please? The branch can't open without that certificate. LaMonica, do we have the ingredients needed for the various menu items?

LaMonica Elroy [11:12 A.M.] I went over the list of ingredients myself. Every single one was in stock.

Kyong Han [11:14 A.M.] That's a great comfort.

---

2 At 11:14 A.M., what does Ms. Han most likely mean when she writes, "That's a great comfort"?

(A) She is happy with the various menu options.
(B) She is pleased that all ingredients are available.

| WORDS |

1 work order 작업 주문서 empty 비우다 unload 짐을 부리다

2 certificate 증명서, 검사증 inspector 검사관 stay on top of ~의 상황을 항상 파악하다 ingredient 재료 in stock 재고가 있는

Questions 1-2 refer to the following text-message chain.

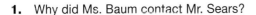

> **Juliana Baum (9:12 A.M.)**
> Hi, Marcus. Is the marketing team up to speed on the planning for next week's virtual presentation?
>
> **Marcus Sears (9:13 A.M.)**
> Actually, I'd like to meet once more to discuss it, if that's not a bother.
>
> **Juliana Baum (9:14 A.M.)**
> Not at all.
>
> **Marcus Sears (9:16 A.M.)**
> Could we meet on Tuesday at 11 A.M.?
>
> **Juliana Baum (9:17 A.M.)**
> Let me check my calendar.
>
> **Marcus Sears (9:18 A.M.)**
> Oh, you know what? Could we move it to 1 P.M. instead? I have another meeting at 11 A.M.
>
> **Juliana Baum (9:20 A.M.)**
> Even better. My schedule is free most of the afternoon.
>
> **Marcus Sears (9:21 A.M.)**
> Perfect! I'll send out the calendar invitation to the rest of the team.

PART 7 | UNIT 08

1. Why did Ms. Baum contact Mr. Sears?

   (A) To request a planning update
   (B) To reschedule an upcoming meeting
   (C) To cancel a company gathering
   (D) To share a virtual presentation

2. At 9:20 A.M., what does Ms. Baum most likely mean when she writes, "Even better"?

   (A) Two hours is enough time to finish a project.
   (B) She will be happy to clear her schedule.
   (C) An afternoon meeting is preferable.
   (D) A team should share a calendar.

| WORDS |

up to speed on ~에 대한 최신 정보를 알고 있는 virtual 가상의 actually 사실은 bother 성가심 invitation 초대(장) rest 나머지
1 upcoming 곧 있을 gathering 모임 share 공유하다 **2** clear 비우다 preferable 선호하는

Questions 3-4 refer to the following text-message chain.

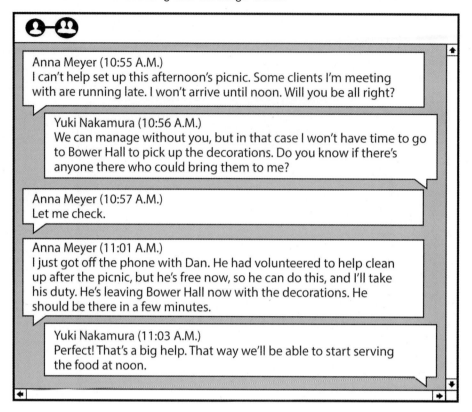

Anna Meyer (10:55 A.M.)
I can't help set up this afternoon's picnic. Some clients I'm meeting with are running late. I won't arrive until noon. Will you be all right?

Yuki Nakamura (10:56 A.M.)
We can manage without you, but in that case I won't have time to go to Bower Hall to pick up the decorations. Do you know if there's anyone there who could bring them to me?

Anna Meyer (10:57 A.M.)
Let me check.

Anna Meyer (11:01 A.M.)
I just got off the phone with Dan. He had volunteered to help clean up after the picnic, but he's free now, so he can do this, and I'll take his duty. He's leaving Bower Hall now with the decorations. He should be there in a few minutes.

Yuki Nakamura (11:03 A.M.)
Perfect! That's a big help. That way we'll be able to start serving the food at noon.

3. At 10:57 A.M., what does Ms. Meyer indicate she will do when she writes, "Let me check"?

(A) Talk to a colleague
(B) Look for the decorations
(C) Confer with the clients
(D) Verify her arrival time

4. How will Ms. Meyer help with the event?

(A) By inviting guests
(B) By preparing food
(C) By hanging decorations
(D) By assisting with cleanup

| WORDS |

set up 준비하다, 설치하다 run late 늦어지다 decoration 장식물 get off the phone 전화를 끊다 volunteer 자원하다
3 confer 상의하다 verify 확인하다, 입증하다 4 assist 돕다 cleanup 청소, 정화

Questions 5-8 refer to the following online chat discussion.

Ken Martin (3:09 P.M.)	My team and I are trying to work with the new Colormaz Graphics computer program, but the directions for its use seem minimal. Some of us are true beginners. Where do we start? Is there a more in-depth user's manual?
Susan Ahmadi (3:12 P.M.)	When Colormaz developed this program, they purposely kept the directions for use very basic. The company wants to encourage users to explore the program in their own unique way to allow for more design innovation.
Beatrice Yeager (3:15 P.M.)	That's my understanding, too. They've created a community around this product. A good place for you to start is by checking out some of the projects that other users have posted. Just look for the Colormaz user forum online.
Ken Martin (3:19 P.M.)	That sounds great. I'll look there now.
Beatrice Yeager (3:20 P.M.)	As my team members work with the program, I've been encouraging them to post their projects and notes to the forum as well.
Susan Ahmadi (3:22 P.M.)	And in a few weeks we will schedule a department meeting where our teams will be asked to share what they've learned.
Ken Martin (3:22 P.M.)	Thank you both.

5. What most likely is Mr. Martin's job?

(A) Software developer
(B) Technical writer
(C) Graphic designer
(D) Computer salesperson

6. What is suggested about the participants in the chat discussion?

(A) They are members of separate teams.
(B) They work for Colormaz.
(C) They are training new employees.
(D) They are looking for new computer programs.

7. At 3:19 P.M., what does Mr. Martin most likely mean when he writes, "I'll look there now"?

(A) He will consult the user's manual.
(B) He will check inside his desk.
(C) He will visit a Web site.
(D) He will go to a community center.

8. What will Mr. Martin's team members most likely be asked to do?

(A) Explain how they use the Colormaz Graphics program
(B) Create a user forum for clients
(C) Send a report to Ms. Ahmadi
(D) Compile a list of questions for a meeting

| WORDS |

in-depth 상세한 purposely 고의로 encourage 장려하다 unique 독특한

5 developer 개발자 6 separate 별개의 7 consult 참조하다 8 create 만들다, 형성하다 compile 취합하다

UNIT 09

기사와 안내문

무료인강 바로가기

기사 / 안내문에 자주 등장하는 표현

새로운 소식, 계획 공지	회사명 + announced that ~	~라고 발표하였다
	도시/회사명 + plans to ~	~할 계획이다
	도시/회사명 + will host / is opening	~을 개최할 것이다
조언 표현	We suggest that ~	~하신 것을 제안합니다
	Please follow these steps ~	다음 절차들을 따라주세요
인용, 결과 발표	According to the company spokesperson, ~	회사 대변인에 따르면
	" ~, " remarked/said Mr. Walters.	~라고 월터 씨는 말했다
	A recent survey found that ~	최근의 설문 조사는 ~라는 것을 밝혔다

주제별 어휘

기업·경영	expand 확장하다	focus on ~에 주력하다
	acquire 인수하다 (= take over)	take over 떠맡다 (= assume)
	relocate 이전하다 (= move)	headquartered[based] in ~에 본사를 둔
	invest 투자하다	headquarters 본사, 본부 (= main office)
	restructure 구조조정하다	spokesperson 대변인
	revenue 수익, 매출	lucrative 수익성 있는 (= profitable)
	market share 시장 점유율	competitive 경쟁력 있는
	competitor 경쟁자, 경쟁업체	merger and acquisition 합병과 인수
	company executive 기업 임원	takeover (기업) 인수
	founder 설립자	step down 물러나다
	upturn 경기 호전	downsize 인원을 줄이다
관광지·건축	landmark 주요 지형지물	refurbish 재단장하다
	proximity 인접, 근접	transform 변형시키다
	restoration 복구, 복원	convert 전환하다
	architect 건축가	adjacent 인접한
도로 교통	boulevard 대로	motorist 운전자 (= driver)
	improvement 개선	pedestrian 보행자
	intersection 교차로	ridership (교통수단의) 이용자 수
	traffic congestion[jam] 교통 체증	city official 시 공무원
문화 예술	renowned 유명한 (= famed, noted)	debut 데뷔; 데뷔하다, 첫 출연하다
	respected 존경받는	author 작가 (= writer)
	recognized 인정받는	director 감독
	reputation 평판, 명성	playwright 극작가
	distinctive 특유한, 특이한	celebrity 유명인사

- 주제와 대상을 묻는 문제는 제목과 글의 초반부에서 정답을 찾을 수 있습니다.
- 인용문이나 특정 인물과 관련하여 문제가 제시되기에 등장 인물의 이름에 주목해야 합니다.

기사 지문 흐름 학습

❶ 제목	**GMK To Be Restructured**		**GMK 구조조정 추진**
❷ 주제	SYDNEY (15 July)—G. M. Kramer (GMK) announced today that [1]its board of directors has approved a restructuring plan. The move will reduce the company's debts, which have grown steadily as competitors have moved into the market.		시드니 (7월 15일)–G. M. 크레이머(GMK)는 오늘 이사회가 구조조정 계획을 승인했다고 발표했다. 이번 조치로 경쟁사들이 시장에 진입하면서 꾸준히 증가해온 그 회사의 부채가 줄어들 것이다.
❸ 세부 내용	The plan involves selling off the company's furniture and electronics divisions, which have been challenged by the rise of online retailers. [2]The company plans to focus instead on its apparel lines, which generate most of the company's revenue.		이 계획에는 온라인 소매업체들의 부상으로 어려움을 겪어 온 회사의 가구와 전자제품 사업부 매각이 포함된다. 회사는 대신 수익의 대부분을 차지하고 있는 의류 제품군에 주력할 계획이다.
❹ 특정 인물	GMK's restructuring plan will be overseen by the company's current vice president of finance, Soo-Mi Chong. In September, [3]Ms. Chong will take over as CEO, replacing Overton Ferebee, who is retiring after leading the company for a decade.		GMK의 구조조정 계획은 정수미 현 재무 담당 부사장이 감독할 예정이다. 9월에 정 씨는 CEO직을 맡아 10년 동안 회사를 이끈 후에 은퇴하는 오버튼 페레비를 대신할 것이다.
❺ 현 상황	GMK currently operates 50 stores in Australia and more than 30 stores overseas.		GMK는 현재 호주에 50개, 해외에 30개 이상의 매장을 운영하고 있다.

기사 빈출 질문 위의 전체 흐름을 잘 숙지하고 기사에 자주 나오는 질문을 기억해두세요.

❶ 주제	기사에 따르면, GMK는 무엇을 할 계획인가? 제목과 글의 맨 앞부분에서 announced today that 이하 내용에 주로 나와 있습니다.		Q. According to the article, what does GMK plan to do? A. Reduce its current debt 부채 절감
❷ 세부 사항	GMK에 많은 수익을 내주는 품목은 무엇인가? 세부 내용에서 수익(revenue)을 언급한 항목에 유의합니다. apparel lines가 Shirts and dresses로 패러프레이징된 점도 주목해주세요.		Q. What items generate considerable income for GMK? A. Shirts and dresses 셔츠와 원피스
❸ 추론	정 씨에 대해 알 수 있는 것은? Ms. Chong이 등장하는 단락에서 정답을 찾습니다.		Q. What is suggested about Ms. Chong? A. She will take on new responsibilities. 새로운 책임을 맡게 될 것이다.

다음 지문을 읽고 문제를 풀어보세요.

Best Practices for Guest Satisfaction: Introduction

This is a guide to equipping and maintaining guest rooms in a manner that results in a high level of guest satisfaction. The information is organized into four sections.

Section One: Effective heating, cooling, and ventilation systems; regulation of room temperature
Section Two: Furnishing rooms for comfort and attractiveness
Section Three: Appearance and care of towels, bed linens, and window coverings
Section Four: Equipping rooms with appliances and technology

---

1 For whom is the guide most likely written?

(A) Tourists   (B) Hotel managers

Singing Duo Soon to Launch Athletic-Wear Clothing Line

AUCKLAND (22 August)—Martino Johnson and Emily Taylor, who make up the popular singing duo Fall Wind, have announced they are creating an eco-friendly line of athletic clothing. —[1]—. Known as Martily, the moderately priced tops, bottoms, and socks will be made of organic cotton and recycled polyester.

"A lot of the earth-friendly athletic apparel that's out there is too expensive," Ms. Taylor explained. "People who don't have a lot of money to spend want to do their part to help the planet, too."

The women's line will be sold exclusively at Sydney Sports stores across the nation and is expected to hit the shelves in early November. —[2]—.

---

2 In which of the positions marked [1] and [2] does the following sentence best belong?

"The men's line will not be available until next March."

(A) [1]   (B) [2]

| WORDS |

1 practice 관행, 관례 satisfaction 만족 equip 장비를 갖추다 maintain 유지하다 manner 방식 result in ~한 결과를 낳다 organize 구성[조직]하다 section 항, 절 effective 효과적인 ventilation 환기 regulation 조절, 조정 temperature 온도 furnish (가구를) 비치하다 appearance 외관 care 관리 appliance 전자 기기

2 eco-friendly 친환경적인 organic 유기농의 recycled 재생의 athletic apparel 운동복 planet 행성, 지구 exclusively 독점적으로 hit the shelf (서점, 가게 등에) 나오다

Questions 1-2 refer to the following information.

www.davencarcare.com/faqs

DAVEN CAR CARE—Frequently Asked Questions

What services do you provide?
We perform maintenance checks and mechanical and electric repairs on all makes of vehicle.

Do you offer any special deals?
We currently offer $10 coupons in exchange for reviews posted on our website. Testimonials from satisfied customers are our most important way of attracting new customers.

What incentives are extended to first-time customers?
New customers receive a complimentary oil change the first time they come for a maintenance check or any major repair.

Can I bring my own parts?
Yes. However, please be aware that shopping for your own parts may cost you more in the long run. You might choose low-quality parts that will not stand the test of time. Any parts you purchase on your own will most likely not be covered by warranty. In contrast, we use only certified, warranty-covered parts that are durable yet lower priced than those of our competitors.

Do you offer a shuttle while my car is being serviced?
Yes. Drop off your vehicle, and we will be happy to drive you home or to work and to pick you up again when your vehicle is ready.

1. What can customers do to receive discounts?

(A) Leave customer feedback online
(B) Present a repeat-customer card
(C) Purchase a parts warranty
(D) Refer new customers

2. What is NOT mentioned as a benefit of using parts provided by Daven Car Care?

(A) The parts last a long time.
(B) The parts may be less expensive.
(C) The parts are covered by a warranty.
(D) The parts are familiar to the mechanics.

| WORDS |

maintenance 정비 repair 수리 attract 끌어들이다 complimentary 무료의 in the long run 결국 stand 견디다
purchase 구매하다 warranty 품질 보증 certified 공인된 competitor 경쟁업체
1 repeat-customer 재방문 고객, 단골 refer 추천하다 **2** be familiar to ~에 익숙하다 mechanic 정비공

Questions 3-5 refer to the following article.

K.L.P. to Invest in Robotics

BUSAN (May 3) — Houston-based toy company K.L.P. announced Monday that it plans to invest $20 million in robotic technology in South Korea for use in all of its factories over the next two years.

Industry analysts believe K.L.P. is attempting to remain competitive with rival firms, most of which have adopted new manufacturing techniques. Such techniques have dramatically increased factory output, and K.L.P.'s executives indicated they are ready to try them as well.

"We have researched other companies, and we are confident that this investment will ultimately boost our annual revenue to $200 million within five years," explained K.L.P.'s Hana Ryu.

In recent years, K.L.P.'s revenues have hovered around the $160 million mark compared to its top two competitors, which posted earnings of around $180 million and $170 million last year.

Ryu indicated that K.L.P. is considering other ways to increase profits, such as relocating their headquarters to a more efficient building, but they are certain that this overseas investment will be lucrative.

3. What is suggested about K.L.P. in comparison to its competitors?
(A) Its technology is outdated.
(B) It recently opened a new factory.
(C) Its products are more innovative.
(D) It is hiring new employees at a faster pace.

4. Who most likely is Ms. Ryu?
(A) A computer analyst
(B) A business journalist
(C) A company executive
(D) A professor of robotics

5. About how much did K.L.P. earn last year?
(A) $160 million
(B) $170 million
(C) $180 million
(D) $200 million

| WORDS |

invest 투자하다 analyst 분석가 attempt 시도하다 competitive 경쟁력 있는 firm 회사 adopt 도입하다, 채택하다 manufacturing 제조 dramatically 극적으로 increase 늘리다, 증가시키다 output 생산고, 산출량 executive 임원, 중역 indicate 밝히다, 표시하다 confident 확신하는, 자신하는 investment 투자 ultimately 결국, 궁극에는 boost 늘리다, 끌어올리다 annual 연례의 revenue 수익 recent 최근의 hover 맴돌다 compared to ~와 비교하여 competitor 경쟁자, 경쟁업체 earning 수익, 소득 profit 이익, 수익 relocate 이전하다 headquarters 본사, 본부 efficient 효율적인 lucrative 수익성 있는

Questions 6-9 refer to the following article.

SAN DIEGO (June 1)—Windle Brothers Party Supplies (WBPS) announced today that it is acquiring Denver-based Grable's Costumes. — [1] —.

Long recognized as a reliable source of costumes for all occasions within the United States, Grable's Costumes made a successful move into East Asia last year, quickly capturing a sizeable portion of the costume market. — [2] —. WBPS has long been planning a move beyond the North American market, and the acquisition of Grable's Costumes is part of that strategy.

"Grable's has a physical presence in the Asian market with stores in major cities. It also has brand recognition," said WBPS CEO Maya Anderson. — [3] —. "Our goal is to capitalize on that success. All those Grable's stores in Asia will carry not just costumes, but Windle Brothers' entire array of party supplies as well. "

Grable's Costumes' current president, Charles Grable, will be named executive vice president. — [4] —. He will report directly to Ms. Anderson.

"This is a win for everybody," said Mr. Grable. "Although Grable's has had some success in the East Asian market, WBPS is a much larger organization with more resources, so there's no limit for our costume sales now."

Founded in Denver 26 years ago, Grable's Costumes has 22 stores in major markets in the United States, along with its four stores in China, three in Japan, and three in Korea. Headquartered in San Diego for all of its 43 years of operation, WBPS has 93 stores in the United States and Canada.

6. What is the subject of the article?

(A) A recent trend in costume design

(B) The retirement of a popular CEO

(C) A company's takeover of another company

(D) Changing conditions in the export market

7. What did WBPS find most attractive about Grable's Costumes?

(A) It carries unusual sizes.

(B) It is headquartered in Denver.

(C) It makes costumes for all occasions.

(D) It already has stores in Asian countries.

8. What is indicated about WBPS?

(A) It wants to increase its online sales.

(B) Its founder is the current CEO.

(C) It sells party supplies in Canada.

(D) It is not as old as Grable's Costumes.

9. In which of the positions marked [1], [2], [3], and [4] does the following sentence best belong?

"Details are still being negotiated, but the deal is expected to be finalized by November."

(A) [1]

(B) [2]

(C) [3]

(D) [4]

| WORDS |

acquire 인수하다 recognized 인식된, 인정받은 reliable 신뢰할 만한 source 공급원 costume 의상 occasion (특별한) 경우, 때 capture 점유하다 sizeable 상당히 큰 portion 부분, 1인분 acquisition 인수 strategy 전략 physical presence 물리적 존재감 capitalize on ~을 활용하다 an array of 다양하게 구비된 found 설립하다 along with ~와 함께 headquartered in ~에 본사를 둔 **6** takeover 인수 export 수출 **7** carry 취급하다 **9** negotiate 협상하다 deal 거래 finalize 마무리하다

UNIT 10

양식 및 기타 지문

무료인강 바로가기

양식이나 기타 지문에 자주 등장하는 표현

초대장	You're cordially invited to ~	~에 정중히 초대합니다
	We invite all who ~	~한 사람들을 초대합니다
	Please join us for ~	~에 참석해주세요
	This is an invitation-only event.	초대자 전용 행사입니다.
	Please bring this invitation with you.	본 초대장을 가져오십시오.
	Limited seating, please arrive early.	좌석이 한정되어 있으니 일찍 도착하시기 바랍니다.
일정표	The schedule can be accessed at ~	일정표는 ~에서 이용할 수 있습니다
	Please find the schedule for ~	~의 일정표를 보시기 바랍니다
설문지, 양식	Complete and submit this form to ~	본 양식을 작성해 ~에 제출해주세요
	Fill out the form below and send it to ~	아래의 양식을 작성해 ~로 보내주세요
	We would appreciate your feedback.	의견에 감사 드립니다.
	Please rate the following on a scale of ~	~의 척도로 다음 사항을 평가해주세요.

주제별 어휘

송장 영수증	description 설명	receipt 영수증
	unit price 단가 (= price per unit)	approval date 승인 일자
	quantity 수량	recipient 수신자, 수령자
	itemized total 항목별 총액	expedited shipping 빠른 배송
청구·결제	deposit 보증금	back-order 이월 주문하다
	balance 잔액	overdue 기한이 지난
	include 포함하다	billing address 청구 주소
	advance purchase 사전 구매	shipping address 배송지 주소
설문	fill in the blanks 빈칸을 채우다	preference 선호, 기호
	survey 설문 조사	comments 의견
	questionnaire 설문지	feedback 피드백
초대장	celebrate 축하하다	be open to ~에게 공개되다
	in honor of ~을 기념하여	fund-raising campaign 모금 캠페인
	limited 한정된	proceeds 수익금
	RSVP 회신 바람	banquet 연회
여행	itinerary 여행 일정표	advance notice 사전 통보
	available 이용 가능한	departure 출발
	vacation 휴가	souvenir 기념품

| 이용 후기 지문 흐름 학습 |

❶ 만족도 ★ ★ ★ ★ ☆   ★ ★ ★ ★ ☆

❷ 구매 정보   I just purchased the Nodori Floor Sweeper for my home. This portable floor sweeper is the best. [1,3]It is compact and lightweight. —[1]—.

❸ 장점   I love that it fits anywhere–in closets of any size or even on a hook behind a door. I can use the sweeper on my hardwood floors, my tile floors, and my thick carpets. —[2]—. It has a long handle, so I do not have to bend or stretch to use it. Plus, since it is wireless, it has no cords or cables and does not have to be plugged into an outlet. As an added bonus, it took only a few minutes to assemble.

❹ 단점   For the record, however, it does not replace a standard vacuum for tough jobs. —[3]—. [2]You

❺ 결론   will still need your regular vacuum cleaner for deep cleaning. However, for everyday floor-cleaning jobs and touch-up jobs, I highly recommend the simple, efficient Nodori Floor Sweeper. —[4]—.

Maura Angulo, September 13

얼마 전에 노도리 바닥 청소기를 집에서 쓰려고 구입했습니다. 이 휴대용 바닥 청소기는 최고입니다. [1,3]작고 가볍습니다. –[1]–. 어떤 크기의 벽장이든 혹은 문 뒤의 걸이든 아무데나 수납이 되는 게 마음에 듭니다. 딱딱한 나무 바닥과 타일 바닥, 두꺼운 카펫에서 청소기를 사용할 수 있습니다. –[2]–. 손잡이가 길어서 청소기를 사용하려고 몸을 구부리거나 뻗을 필요가 없습니다. 게다가 무선이라서 코드나 케이블이 없고 콘센트에 꽂을 필요도 없습니다. 추가 보너스로, 조립하는 데 몇 분밖에 걸리지 않았습니다.

하지만 분명히 말하는데 이 제품은 까다로운 작업에는 표준 진공청소기를 대체하지 못합니다. –[3]–. [2]꼼꼼한 청소에는 여전히 일반 진공청소기가 필요할 겁니다. 그래도 일상적인 바닥 청소와 간단한 작업에는 간편하고 효율적인 노도리 바닥 청소기를 적극 추천합니다. –[4]–.

9월 13일, 마우라 앙굴로

PART 7 | UNIT 10

이용 후기 빈출 질문   위의 전체 흐름을 잘 숙지하고 후기에 자주 나오는 질문을 기억해두세요.

❶ Not/True	**노도리 바닥 청소기의 이점으로 언급되지 않은 것은?** 글의 첫 부분 구매 정보에 이어진 긍정적인 표현에서 오답을 소거하면서 정답을 찾아야 합니다.	Q. What is NOT a stated benefit of the Nodori Floor Sweeper? A. Its affordability 적당한 가격
❷ 세부 사항	**앙굴로 씨는 무엇을 추천하는가?** 마지막 단락에서 청소 작업의 난이도에 따라 다른 청소기를 사용하라고 추천하고 있습니다.	Q. What does Ms. Angulo recommend? A. Using two cleaning appliances 청소기 2대 사용하기
❸ 문장 삽입	**[1], [2], [3], [4]로 표시된 곳 중에서 다음 문장이 들어가기에 가장 적합한 곳은?** "그래서 방에서 방으로 쉽게 옮길 수 있습니다." 쉽게 옮길 수 있는 이유를 언급한 앞 문장을 찾는 것이 중요합니다.	Q. In which of the positions marked [1], [2], [3], and [4] does the following sentence best belong? "Thus, I can easily move it from room to room." A. [1]

ETS 문제로 **훈련하기**

다음 지문을 읽고 문제를 풀어보세요.

Hazeltown's Second Annual Street Festival
Booth Registration Form

Please return this form by April 15 to Charlotte Fernandes at 43 Willow Street, Hazeltown.

Restaurant Name   *Hazeltown Bistro*

Location Request   *The corner of Main Street and Chestnut Street*

Dates Attending   *May 28–31*

Form Received (to be completed by Ms. Fernandes)   *April 13*

---

1 By what date must the registration form be returned?

(A) April 15
(B) May 31

The Bilbridge Arts Institute (BAI)
Fall Course Schedule

Photography Basics (6:00 P.M. to 8:00 P.M.) Mondays in September	**Ceramics I** (6:00 P.M. to 8:00 P.M.) Fridays in October
Ceramics II (5:00 P.M. to 8:00 P.M.) Tuesdays in November	**Painting** (6:30 P.M. to 8:30 P.M.) Thursdays in December

Visit www.bai.edu/classes for a detailed description of topics covered. For those classes that require students to purchase supplies, a supply list is included with the description.

Registration accepted online and in person. Course fee: $125 for residents of Algonville; $140 for nonresidents.

---

2 What do all of the BAI's classes have in common?

(A) They begin at the same time.
(B) They cost less for Algonville residents

| WORDS |

1 registration 등록 form 양식, 서식

2 ceramics 도예, 도자기류 description 묘사, 설명 registration 등록, 신청 in person 직접, 몸소 resident 주민, 거주민

260   정답 및 해설 p.238

Questions 1-2 refer to the following chart.

Krastek Medical Center					
Nursing Staff Weekday Schedule: March 15–March 19					
Please contact your nursing supervisor, Ms. Gresham, with any questions.					
Name	**Monday March 15**	**Tuesday March 16**	**Wednesday March 17**	**Thursday March 18**	**Friday March 19**
1st FLOOR STAFF					
Cornelio Alvarez	Vacation	Vacation	9 A.M.–8 P.M.	9 A.M.–9 P.M.	10 A.M.–8 P.M.
Maryann Dietz	7 A.M.–3 P.M.	9 A.M.–5 P.M.	9 A.M.–5 P.M.	Vacation	Vacation
Honoka Kita	6 A.M.–2 P.M.	6 A.M.–1 P.M.	6 A.M.–4 P.M.	UNSCHEDULED	6 A.M.–6 P.M.
Rumaysa Gowda	1 P.M.–8 P.M.	UNSCHEDULED	1 P.M.–1 A.M.	1 P.M.–1 A.M.	UNSCHEDULED
2nd FLOOR STAFF					
Ashleigh Morrison	6 A.M.–3 P.M.	6 A.M.–3 P.M.	6 A.M.–6 P.M.	6 A.M.–3 P.M.	Vacation
Taiki Saito	7 A.M.–7 P.M.	7 A.M.–1 P.M.	3 P.M.–9 P.M.	7 A.M.–7 P.M.	3 P.M.–10 P.M.
Tim Whitmore	2 P.M.–11 P.M.	1 P.M.–11 P.M.	4 P.M.–11 P.M.	UNSCHEDULED	4 P.M.–11 P.M.
Ping Yan	9 A.M.–9 P.M.	9 A.M.–9 P.M.	9 A.M.–9 P.M.	UNSCHEDULED	UNSCHEDULED

1. What is true about the nursing staff members on the schedule?

(A) All work on the first floor.

(B) All report to Ms. Gresham.

(C) All work until 5:00 A.M. or later.

(D) All will miss a day of work this week.

2. Who will begin vacation on March 18?

(A) Cornelio Alvarez

(B) Maryann Dietz

(C) Ashleigh Morrison

(D) Ping Yan

| WORDS |

medical 의료의 nursing 간호직 contact 연락하다 supervisor 감독관, 상사 vacation 휴가

Questions 3-5 refer to the following invitation.

The Council for International Business Success (CIBS) presents
"Understanding International Partners"

Date and time: Wednesday, 26 June, 3:00 P.M.–4:00 P.M. British Summer Time
Location: The Board Room in Hargrove House, London (limited seating, please arrive early)
Live video stream: Dial-in numbers with pass codes will be provided on the day of the event.

Please join us for our next presentation, which will feature Mr. Kenji Umehara, president of Binkwa Shipping International, and Ms. Maria Tivoli, CEO of Scarpa Software Company. Mr. Umehara and Ms. Tivoli will share information about their vibrant and evolving markets. They will give attendees an insider's understanding of opportunities and challenges, competitive environments, and cultural norms and will pass along tips for working with partners and customers. The presentation will be held live in our London bureau and broadcast by live stream for CIBS members and businesses in other locations. A replay will be available for those unable to attend the live meeting.

To succeed in every market, it is important to have a global mind-set and a respect for local markets. We hope you will make every effort to join us.

---

3. What is the purpose of the presentation?

(A) To discuss updating international shipping requirements
(B) To explain a new video streaming technology
(C) To help members develop international business skills
(D) To give CIBS employees new conference-call pass codes

4. What is suggested about CIBS?

(A) It was founded as part of Scarpa Software Company.
(B) It is a financial partner of Binkwa Shipping International.
(C) Its headquarters have been moved to London.
(D) Its members work in a variety of industries.

5. How can participants get a seat at Hargrove House?

(A) By arriving before 3:00 P.M.
(B) By registering online
(C) By purchasing a ticket
(D) By showing a membership card at the door

| WORDS |

council 위원회 pass code 암호 vibrant 활기찬 evolving 진화하는 attendee 참석자 competitive 경쟁적인 norm 기준, 규범
pass along 전달하다, 널리 알리다 bureau 사무실 replay 다시 보기 mind-set 사고 방식 respect 존중 make every effort 모든 노력을 하다

Questions 6-9 refer to the following form.

We at Fehring International appreciate your trust in us as your relocation experts. We would like to know more about your experience, as we always strive to improve our services. Please help us by completing this form and returning it to us in the enclosed envelope. Your answers will be kept confidential.

First Name: <u>Nadia</u> Family Name: <u>Siddiqui</u>

Origin: <u>London, England</u> Destination: <u>Kuala Lumpur, Malaysia</u>

Rate the services you used from 1=not satisfied to 5=extremely satisfied. NA=not applicable.

Packing personal belongings	1	2	3	4	⑤	NA
Moving	1	②	3	4	5	NA
Vehicle shipping	1	2	3	4	5	ⓃⒶ
Relocation support	1	2	3	④	5	NA

Please explain your ratings in the box below.

I am grateful for your team's effort to give me a positive relocation experience when I moved to Kuala Lumpur for my new work assignment. My furniture and clothing arrived in good condition. The care you took packing and labeling all of our belongings made settling into our new home much easier. The welcome packet of information on local shops and schools was a thoughtful touch.

I was disappointed that it took longer than promised to receive our possessions, although I know you did what you could to make this move as smooth as possible. I plan to use your services again when my assignment in Malaysia comes to an end in four years and we move to our next location.

6. What is the purpose of the form?

(A) To apply for a refund
(B) To improve customer service
(C) To gather stories to use in advertisements
(D) To request relocation services

7. According to the form, why did Ms. Siddiqui move to Kuala Lumpur?

(A) To join her relatives
(B) To attend a university
(C) To enjoy life in an international city
(D) To begin a new job assignment

8. What does Ms. Siddiqui indicate on the form?

(A) She did not use all of the company's services.
(B) She decided not to ship her furniture to Malaysia.
(C) She needed more time than expected to identify items.
(D) She was pleased with all of the services she used.

9. According to the form, what will Ms. Siddiqui probably do in four years?

(A) Find a new employer
(B) Retire from the company
(C) Buy a house in Kuala Lumpur
(D) Hire Fehring International

| WORDS |

appreciate 고마워하다 trust 신뢰, 믿음 relocation 이주 strive to ~하고자 노력하다 enclosed 동봉된 envelope 봉투
confidential 기밀의 assignment 임무 possession 소유(물)

PART 7 | UNIT 10

UNIT 11

이중 지문

무료인강 바로가기

출제 유형

- 시험에서 이중 지문은 2세트가 출제되며 한 세트당 5문제씩 총 10문제가 출제됩니다.
- 이중 지문에서 연계 질문은 1-2개가 출제됩니다.
- 두 지문에 동시에 단서가 있는 연계 질문이 반드시 출제되므로 내용의 연관성을 생각해야 합니다.

연계 지문 예시

아래 두 개의 지문의 내용을 보며 연계 질문이 어떻게 출제되는지 살펴봅시다.

지문 1 언론 보도	지문 2 이메일
MVA 사의 부사장이 첫 해외 지점을 돕기 위해 오클랜드로 이주했다.	언론 보도에 따르면, MVA의 첫 해외 지점이 당신(잭슨 씨)이 사는 도시이다

질문 잭슨 씨가 거주하고 있는 도시는? (지문 2에서 단서, 지문 1에서 정답을 찾는 연계 문제)
정답 오클랜드

이중 지문 풀이 전략

전략 1 **두 지문의 연관 관계 파악하기**

글의 제목, 수신자/발신자 정보에서 두 지문이 서로 왜 쓰였는지를 대략적으로 파악합니다.

전략 2 **질문 키워드 파악하기**

질문에 숫자나 인명과 지명 등이 있을 경우 지문에서 해당 단어가 쓰인 부분을 중심으로 살펴봅니다.

전략 3 **연계 문제 단서 찾기**

연계 문제의 단서는 대부분 애매모호하게 표현됩니다. 두 지문에서 내용이 중복되는 경우에 어떤
내용이 관련이 있는지 표시하며 문제를 풉니다. 특히 첫 지문의 마지막 단락에 등장하는 마감일,
조건부 할인, 연락 담당자, 부서명, 요청 사항이 연계 문제로 이어지는 경우가 많습니다.

| 풀이 전략 적용하기 |

전략 1. 두 지문 연관 관계 파악하기

Question refers to the following letter and e-mail.

FINE FABRIC MARKET

15 November

Mr. Sanz:

Our digital catalog will be available at the beginning of December. Until then, here are a few highlights of our exclusive new products (swatches are enclosed):

"Climb" (Item 462): The finest polished cotton; blue and yellow.
"Morning" (Item 517): Silk damask; white and brown.
"Circles" (Item 614): Linen; violet, beige, and green.
"Phases" (Item 628): Wool; gold and midnight blue.

As a bonus to our valued customers, we are currently offering a 15 percent discount on orders of any particular fabric over 20 meters.

Sincerely,

Kentaro Manabe, Sales Director

전략 3. 연계 문제 단서 찾기

To: kmanabe@FFMt.com
From: msanz@vestigia.cl
Date: 20 November
Subject: Today's order

Dear Mr. Manabe:

I wish to confirm my order of 12 meters of "Climb," Item 462, and 26 meters of "Morning," Item 517. As I mentioned, we are considering a third fabric, "Phases," which would look very nice on a popular model of our occasional chairs. The sample swatch that you sent is rather small. If possible, please forward a larger sample of this product to us so that we may make a determination of the fabric's suitability.

Regards,

Manuel Sanz

파인 패브릭 마켓

11월 15일

산츠 씨께:

디지털 카탈로그는 12월 초부터 이용하실 수 있습니다. 그때까지 저희가 독점 판매하는 주요 신제품을 소개합니다(견본 동봉).

"상승" (품번 462): 최고급 유광 면직물; 파란색과 노란색.
"아침" (품번 517): 실크 다마스크; 흰색과 갈색.
"원" (품번 614): 리넨; 보라색, 베이지색, 녹색.
"주기" (품번 628): 양모; 금색과 암청색.

소중한 고객님들께 드리는 보너스로, 현재 모든 특정 원단을 20미터 이상 주문하시면 15퍼센트 할인해 드리고 있습니다.

마나베 켄타로, 영업부장

수신: kmanabe@FFMt.com
발신: msanz@vestigia.cl
날짜: 11월 20일
제목: 오늘 주문

마나베 씨께:

품번 462 "상승" 12미터, 품번 517 "아침" 26미터 주문을 확정하고자 합니다. 앞서 언급했듯이, 저희는 세 번째 원단인 "주기"를 고려하고 있습니다. 이 원단은 인기 있는 예비 의자 모델에 아주 잘 어울릴 듯합니다. 보내 주신 견본 천은 조금 작습니다. 가능하다면 저희가 천의 적합성을 결정할 수 있도록 이 제품의 더 큰 견본을 보내 주시기 바랍니다.

마누엘 산츠

PART 7 | UNIT 11

Q. For which fabric will Mr. Sanz receive a discount?

(A) Climb
(B) Morning
(C) Circles
(D) Phases

전략 2. 질문 키워드 파악하기

산츠 씨는 어떤 원단을 할인 받을 것인가?

(A) 상승
(B) 아침
(C) 원
(D) 주기

전략 1 두 개의 지문을 훑어보면 발신자/수신자가 주문과 관련하여 주고 받은 내용이라는 것을 알 수 있습니다.

전략 2 질문에서 산츠 씨가 어떤 원단을 할인 받을 것인지는 첫 지문 마지막 단락에서 단서(모든 특정 원단을 20미터 이상 주문하면 15퍼센트 할인 제공)를 찾아야 합니다.

전략 3 두 번째 지문에서 Morning (Item 517) 26미터 주문을 확정했다고 했으므로 정답은 (B) Morning입니다.

265

1. [e-mail/memo]

To: Amina Noorani <anoorani@lightcast.ca>
From: Lucy Godfrey <lgodfrey@bedgeburys.ca>
Subject: Information
Date: 6 January

Dear Ms. Noorani:

I am pleased to verify the details of your part-time position at our Bedgeburys store on Garden Street in Hamilton. As a part-time employee, you are not eligible for our benefits package, but you do receive a 20 percent employee discount on all of your Bedgeburys purchases.

Training begins at 8:00 A.M. on 16 January. Please report to the human resources office on the lower level, just past men's and women's shoes.

Sincerely,
Lucy Godfrey
Human Resources Manager

MEMO

To: All employees
From: Alan Moya
Subject: Important information
Date: 4 November

I am pleased to announce our sales associates of the year. As you know, employees must meet certain qualifications to be nominated, among which is that they must be full-time employees for at least six months.

Please join me in congratulating Bennett Selwyn (Electronics), Li Pan (Jewelry), and Amina Noorani (Women's Clothing). All three will join honorees from other Bedgeburys stores at a banquet in Toronto next month.

What is suggested about Ms. Noorani?

(A) She will be moving to Toronto next year.
(B) She became eligible for an employee benefits package.

| WORDS |

verify 확인해주다 eligible for ~에 자격이 되는 benefits package 복리후생 제도, 복지 혜택 level 층
associate 사원 qualifications 자격 nominate 지명하다 congratulate 축하하다 honoree 수상자 banquet 연회

  정답 및 해설 p.246

Jenkins Market Reveals New Brand Name

DUBLIN (15 February)—Jenkins Market today announced the launch of its new line of store-brand products. Called "White Moon," the line will feature frozen, canned, and packaged foods. These include frozen fruits and vegetables, canned soups, and pastas. The line will not include beverages or candy. All Jenkins Market locations will carry White Moon products starting at the end of this month.

Jenkins Market has 40 stores throughout Ireland and will soon be expanding into England, beginning in Leeds. Other stores are planned for Liverpool and Manchester.

Jenkins Market
Grand opening!

21 April, 7:00 A.M.–9:00 P.M.
47 Post Road, Leeds

Ribbon cutting at 10:00 A.M.

Complimentary coffee and cake until 3:00 P.M.

Shoppers can spin our prize wheel to win T-shirts, hats, and umbrellas.

The first 100 shoppers will receive a £50 gift card!

Enter our contest: correctly guess how many people attend our grand opening event and win a bag overflowing with groceries!

What is most likely true about the event on April 21?

(A) It will be held on a different date than originally planned.
(B) It will take place at the first Jenkins Market store in England.

| WORDS |

reveal 드러내다, 공개하다 launch 출시 location 영업장 carry 취급하다 expand 확장하다
spin 돌리다 overflow 넘치다

Questions 1-5 refer to the following e-mails.

From:	onlineorders@scottishwoollens.com
To:	Marie Nykvist <mnykvist@euromail.com>
Date:	30 November
Subject:	Order Confirmation

Thank you for shopping at Scottish Woollens! Here are your order details:

Order Number: 3645   **Order Date:** 29 November

Billing address: **Shipping address:**
Marie Nykvist   Same as billing address
Vogulund Gate 23
4534 Harstad
Norway

Payment Method: Credit card *********3490

Item	Quantity	Unit Price (€)	Charges (€)
Glasgow Designers women's sweater	1	132.00	132.00
Shetland Farm women's cap	2	60.00	120.00
Shetland Farm women's gloves	1	33.00	33.00
Glasgow Designers women's scarf	1	21.00	21.00
VAT			65.20
Shipping			(no charge)
		Order Total:	**€371.20**

From:	support@scottishwoollens.com
Date:	2 December
To:	Marie Nykvist <mnykvist@euromail.com>
Re:	Change to order 3645

Dear Ms. Nykvist,

In response to your inquiry, let me reassure you that customers often neglect to indicate a separate "ship to" address when they order gifts for others in addition to purchasing items for themselves. If we receive notice of the problem before the orders ship, we are happy to correct it. In your case, we were able to separate the orders in time, and the Glasgow Designers sweater was shipped to Farsund this morning. Your sister should receive the package by 11 December.

Best regards,

Roberta MacDonald, Customer Representative
Scottish Woollens
Aberdeen, Scotland

1. When did Ms. Nykvist make her online purchase?

    (A) On November 29
    (B) On November 30
    (C) On December 2
    (D) On December 11

2. What is suggested about Scottish Woollens?

    (A) It sells bedding as well as clothing.
    (B) It offers free shipping on some orders.
    (C) It has a flexible return policy.
    (D) It is under new management.

3. How much did Ms. Nykvist pay for a gift purchase?

    (A) €21
    (B) €33
    (C) €120
    (D) €132

4. In the second e-mail, the word "neglect" in paragraph 1, line 1, is closest in meaning to

    (A) forget
    (B) arrange
    (C) ignore
    (D) believe

5. Where does Ms. Nykvist's sister most likely live?

    (A) In Harstad
    (B) In Farsund
    (C) In Glasgow
    (D) In Aberdeen

| WORDS |

quantity 수량 unit price 단가 in response to ~에 답하여 reassure 거듭 확인하다 neglect to ~하는 것을 소홀히 하다 separate 별도의 correct 바로잡다

2 flexible 유연한 management 경영진

UNIT 12

삼중 지문

무료인강 바로가기

출제 유형

- 시험에서 삼중 연계 지문은 3세트가 출제되며 한 세트당 5문제씩 총 15문제가 출제됩니다.
- 삼중 연계 지문에서 연계 질문은 2개씩 출제됩니다.

연계 지문 예시

아래 세 개의 지문의 내용을 보면서 연계 질문이 어떻게 출제되는지 살펴봅시다.

지문 1 공지		지문 2 이메일		지문 3 편지
신문사 뉴스 팀에서 저널리즘 인턴을 구함. 집필 분야의 학력 또는 전문 경력은 필수. 지원 신청서 제출 마감일: 5월 15일	**+**	제나위 씨의 인턴 지원 신청서 제출. 지원서 제출일: 5월 17일	**+**	자란스키 교수의 추천서. 제나위 씨를 지난 2년간 가르침.

질문 1 제나위 씨의 신청서는 어떤 문제가 있겠는가? (지문 1 + 지문 2 연계)
정답 마감일 이후에 제출되었다.
질문 2 자란스키 씨의 전문 분야는 무엇일 것 같은가? (지문 1 + 지문 3 연계)
정답 저널리즘

삼중 지문 풀이 전략

전략 1 세 지문의 연관 관계 파악하기
지문 유형을 우선 살펴본 다음 지문의 제목으로 세 지문이 왜 쓰였는지를 대략적으로 파악합니다.

전략 2 질문 키워드 파악하기
문제에서 요구하는 사항에 맞춰 지문을 읽습니다. 예를 들어 문제에 숫자나 인명과 지명 등이 있을 경우 지문에서 해당 단어가 쓰인 부분을 중심으로 살펴봅니다.

전략 3 연계 문제 단서 찾기
삼중 지문에는 반드시 연계 문제가 출제되므로 각 지문에서 서로 관련성이 있는 두 지문을 찾습니다. 두 지문의 자세한 내용을 읽을 때 관련이 있는 내용에 표시를 하면서 문제를 풉니다.

Question refers to the following e-mails and coupon.

To: Esmeralda Gill <egill@bountifulinbulkgrains.com>
From: Taylor Peck <tpeck@peckprovisions.com>
Date: November 19
Subject: Available products

Dear Ms. Gill,
Thank you for sending my last bulk order. The quality of your bulgur wheat and pearl barley is the best I have ever seen. (중략)

Recently, my customers have been asking about red rice. Do you sell that? I didn't see it listed on your Web site.

Sincerely, Taylor Peck
Owner, Peck Provisions

수신: 에스메랄다 길 〈egill@bountifulinbulkgrains.com〉
발신: 테일러 펙 〈tpeck@peckprovisions.com〉
날짜: 11월 19일
제목: 입수 가능 제품

길 씨께,
지난번에 대량 주문했던 물품을 보내주셔서 감사합니다. 당신의 벌거 밀과 통보리의 품질은 제가 본 것 중 최고입니다.

최근에, 제 고객들이 홍미에 대해 문의하고 있습니다. 그것을 판매하시나요? 당신의 웹사이트 목록에 그것이 있는 것을 보지 못했습니다.

테일러 펙
펙 프로비전스 업주

To: Taylor Peck <tpeck@peckprovisions.com>
From: Esmeralda Gill <egill@bountifulinbulkgrains.com>
Date: November 20
Subject: RE: Available products

Dear Mr. Peck,
Thank you for writing and for your positive feedback about our products. Please note that we do carry **the grain you asked about.** It is listed on our Web site in the specialties tab. (중략)

Regards,
Esmeralda Gill
General Manager, Bountiful in Bulk Grains

수신: 테일러 펙 〈tpeck@peckprovisions.com〉
발신: 에스메랄다 길 〈egill@bountifulinbulkgrains.com〉
날짜: 11월 20일
제목: RE: 입수 가능 제품

펙 씨께,
이메일을 보내주시고 저희 제품에 대해 긍정적인 피드백을 주셔서 감사합니다. 문의하신 곡물을 취급하고 있음을 유의해주십시오. 저희 웹사이트의 특산품 탭에 있는 목록에 들어가 있습니다.

에스메랄다 길
바운티풀 인 벌크 그레인즈 총괄 관리자

Peck Provisions

Featuring natural whole grains, homemade baked goods, locally grown fresh fruits and vegetables, and more

Coupon good for:
• One complimentary Bountiful Brownie (while supplies last)
• 20 percent discount on teff, red rice, and all vitamins and supplements
Expires December 15

펙 프로비전스

천연 통곡물, 집에서 만든 제빵 제품, 지역에서 재배한 신선한 과일과 채소 등을 주로 취급

쿠폰 적용 대상:
• 무료 바운티풀 브라우니 1개 (재고가 남아 있는 동안)
• 테프, 홍미, 모든 비타민 및 보충제 20% 할인
12월 15일 종료

Q. According to Ms. Gill, what product is listed in the specialties tab of the Web site?

(A) Bulgur wheat
(B) Pearl barley
(C) Red rice
(D) Organic quinoa

길 씨에 따르면, 웹사이트의 특산품 탭에는 어떤 제품이 나열되어 있는가?

(A) 벌거 밀
(B) 통보리
(C) 홍미
(D) 유기농 퀴노아

전략 1 세 개의 지문을 순서대로 제목과 수신자/발신자를 훑어보면 Peck Provisions의 사장이 입수 가능한 제품에 대해 문의한 이메일과 답장으로 받은 이메일 그리고 Peck Provisions가 발행한 쿠폰임을 알 수 있습니다.

전략 2 질문에서 길 씨의 이메일을 먼저 언급하기 때문에 두 번째 지문에서 단서를 찾아야 합니다.

전략 3 두 번째 지문에서 '당신이 문의한 곡물이 웹사이트의 특산품 탭의 목록에 들어가 있다'고 하므로 문의한 곡물이 무엇인지 첫 번째 지문에서 찾아야 합니다. 첫 번째 지문 마지막 부분에서 문의한 곡물은 홍미이므로 정답은 (C)입니다.

1 [e-mails/Web page]

From: Svetlana Ridic
To: Marcello Rossillo
Subject: Design notes
Date: February 19

Dear Marcello,

I'd like to deal with a few issues as we make modifications to the CR 465. Note that updated government emissions regulations for motorcycles come out this week, so the design will need to address any changes that are new. Also, bikes that are more than two years old seem to have trouble with fading paint.

The design phase must be completed by June 8. The deadline is firm this time around—manufacturing does not want to face the same time and budget issues it had to deal with last year.

The market is healthy for this type of bike, and this is a great opportunity for Roadwell Motorcycles to strengthen our reputation. As with previous CR 465 models, we will continue to focus on creating quality products rather than on beating our competitors' prices.

Thanks, Svetlana

From: Marcello Rossillo
To: Svetlana Ridic
Subject: Design notes
Date: February 20

Dear Svetlana,

We received advance notice of the regulations yesterday. We are also looking at using a new product with UV protection to keep it looking shiny. I'll get back to you with my views on manufacturing costs; I don't expect the design changes to have a radical impact.

Best, Marcello

---

http://www.goroadreviews.com
Mini-review: Roadwell CR 465
★★★★

The newest model of this attractive bike debuted from Roadwell Motorcycles in October. This bike has a slightly different feel from last year's machine, probably because it weighs in at 10 kilograms heavier. Roadwell has designed several new options for the bike's trim and its handlebar, and the bike is available in a greater variety of colors. Pricing is comparable to last year's model.

By Tom333

What is most likely true about the newest model of the CR 465 ?

(A) It performs best in wet conditions.

(B) It costs more than competitors' products.

| WORDS |

modification 수정 strengthen 강화하다 reputation 명성, 평판 previous 이전의, 과거의 beat 이기다, 물리치다
advance 미리 하는 protection 보호, 방지 radical 급진적인 impact 영향 attractive 매력적인 debut 첫선을 보이다
slightly 약간, 조금 weigh 무게가 나가다 trim (손잡이·핸들 등의) 장식 a variety of 다양한 comparable 비슷한

La Chapelle

1655 Castlerock Dr. • Billings, MT 59101 • Phone: (406) 555-0193 • www.lachapelle.com

La Chapelle, located in the heart of the city of Billings, Montana, is the perfect venue for private parties, workshops, photography sessions, corporate events, and various other functions.

Rates are $95/hour for events lasting two hours, $85/hour for events lasting four hours, and $75/hour for events lasting five hours or more.

Cancellations must be made in writing and must be received no later than three weeks before the scheduled function. Cancellations received after this cutoff time will result in a charge equal to the full amount of the scheduled service. For reservations and additional terms and conditions, visit www.lachapelle.com.

---

www.lachapelle.com/reservation_form
La Chapelle: Reservation Form

Your Name:	Amy Blanchard
Company Name:	Murray Public Relations
E-mail:	ablanchard@murraypr.com
Phone Number:	406 555-0165
Date/Time of Event:	January 14, 12:00 P.M.—5:00 P.M. (five hours)
Type of Event:	Annual awards ceremony and luncheon
Number of Attendees:	26

Dear Ms. Blanchard:

We are pleased to host Murray Public Relations on January 14. Regarding your queries, I would recommend Silverwood Café for your catering needs. It is one of our business partners and it has a wide assortment of food items at reasonable prices. As for technology equipment, our space has wireless Internet connectivity, an interactive whiteboard, and a digital projector.

Please let me know if you need any further assistance.

Sincerely,

Maggie Hanlon, Events Coordinator, La Chapelle

How much will Murray Public Relations be charged per hour?

(A) $ 75

(B) $ 85

| WORDS |

venue (행사) 장소 function 행사 rate 요금 cancellation 취소 equal to ~와 동일한 full amount 전액
terms and conditions 계약 조건 attendee 참석자 a wide assortment of 광범위한 구색의 assistance 도움

Questions 1-5 refer to the following e-mails and table.

From:	David Levine
To:	All AFIN Employees
Date:	Wednesday, June 3, 3:47 P.M.
Subject:	Internship Orientation Program

Dear Colleagues,

From Monday, July 20, through Friday, August 28, Aidos Footwear Industries (AFIN) will be hosting its Summer Internship Program for the twelfth consecutive year. To inform the interns about our day-to-day operations and what is expected of them, a series of orientation sessions will be held on the first day.

Employees are needed to help facilitate those sessions. Two employees are needed for each session, one of whom will be the main facilitator. Only those who have previously participated in an internship orientation session will be eligible to assume that role.

If you are interested in participating in this event, find the "Internship Orientation Program" spreadsheet on the shared drive and sign up by Friday, June 12, for one or more activities listed. It is expected that each team will meet at least once between June 15 and the July 17 deadline to discuss the organization of their session.

Thank you for your cooperation.

Sincerely,

David Levine
Internship Program Director, Aidos Footwear Industries

Aidos Footwear Industries (AFIN) Intern Orientation Program Monday, July 20			
Sessions	**Time**	**Main Facilitator**	**Assistant Facilitator**
Registration and breakfast	8:15 A.M. – 9:00 A.M.	Farid Hassannejad	Iwona Kubiak
Welcome and introductions	9:00 A.M. – 9:30 A.M.	Tanya Sipe	Andrew Collingwood
Introduction to AFIN	9:30 A.M. – 10:00 A.M.	Cliff Oriolowo	Pierce Tobin
Internship rules and regulations	10:00 A.M. – 10:30 A.M.	Karishma Ramkalawan	Darnell Ganaway
Laptop distribution and setup	10:30 A.M. – noon	Kristen Boden	Sakura Arakaki
Lunch break	Noon – 1:00 P.M.		
Office and campus tour	1:00 P.M. – 2:00 P.M.	Karishma Ramkalawan	Pierce Tobin
Obtain access badge	2:00 P.M. – 3:00 P.M.		
Question and answer session	3:00 P.M. – 3:45 P.M.	Martin Kersey	Cliff Oriowolo
Adjourn	3:45 P.M.		

From:	Pierce Tobin
To:	Karishma Ramkalawan
Cc:	Shimon Adelstein
Date:	Thursday, July 16, 9:51 A.M.
Subject:	Schedule conflict

Dear Karishma,

I regret to have to inform you that I will no longer be able to assist you with Monday's internship orientation session. My department manager has just scheduled an urgent meeting about a project that I am in charge of. Unfortunately, the start time of the meeting coincides with that of the orientation session, and postponing the meeting is not an option.

However, my office mate, Shimon Adelstein, has graciously offered to take over my responsibilities as assistant session facilitator. I will brief him later today about the particulars. He will contact you afterwards to see if you may have any additional information for him.

My sincere apologies for the short notice. Good luck with the session.

Pierce Tobin

1. What is the purpose of the first e-mail?

(A) To introduce a company initiative
(B) To invite employees to take on a task
(C) To announce an extension of a deadline
(D) To emphasize the importance of teamwork

2. By what date should teams finalize their session?

(A) June 12
(B) June 14
(C) July 17
(D) July 20

3. Who has previously participated in an internship orientation session?

(A) Ms. Kubiak
(B) Ms. Sipe
(C) Mr. Collingwood
(D) Mr. Ganaway

4. What session will Mr. Adelstein help with?

(A) Introduction to AFIN
(B) Internship rules and regulations
(C) Office and campus tour
(D) Question and answer session

5. According to the second e-mail, why is Mr. Tobin changing his plans?

(A) He urgently needs to complete an assignment.
(B) He has to attend an important project meeting.
(C) His manager withdrew the permission given earlier.
(D) His manager wants him to assist with a different session.

| WORDS |

consecutive 연속되는 facilitate 수월하게 만들다 facilitator 조력자 previously 이전에 eligible to ~할 자격이 되는 assume 맡다
urgent 긴급한 coincide 일치하다 postpone 연기하다 graciously 고맙게도 take over 넘겨받다 short notice 촉박한 통지

ETS
FINAL
TEST

ETS
실전
모의고사

READING TEST

In the Reading test, you will read a variety of texts and answer several different types of reading comprehension questions. The entire Reading test will last 75 minutes. There are three parts, and directions are given for each part. You are encouraged to answer as many questions as possible within the time allowed.

You must mark your answers on the separate answer sheet. Do not write your answers in your test book.

PART 5

Directions: A word or phrase is missing in each of the sentences below. Four answer choices are given below each sentence. Select the best answer to complete the sentence. Then mark the letter (A), (B), (C), or (D) on your answer sheet.

101. Any queries regarding advertising should be sent ------- to the marketing department.

(A) direction
(B) directly
(C) directs
(D) directing

102. Please remove food from the refrigerator each Friday ------- keep the lunchroom clean.

(A) and
(B) thus
(C) rather
(D) instead

103. Jabanna Cosmetics provides products to celebrities who mention the brand in ------- social media posts.

(A) them
(B) they
(C) their
(D) themselves

104. Customers must present the weekly coupon to the cashier in order to receive the 15 percent -------.

(A) work
(B) discount
(C) detail
(D) schedule

105. Reducing downtown parking fees is expected to increase ------- business revenues by at least 25 percent.

(A) local
(B) locally
(C) localities
(D) localize

106. Mr. Goff agreed to finish installing the customer's carpet ------- one week.

(A) within
(B) beyond
(C) behind
(D) through

107. Auto Parts Ltd. encourages its employees to offer ------- for improving the production process.

(A) suggesting
(B) suggest
(C) suggestive
(D) suggestions

108. Samad Industries will ------- confirm its hiring plans for commercial warehouse positions.

(A) very
(B) soon
(C) ever
(D) unevenly

109. The Bartleby Sweets Company ------- introduced a line of naturally sweetened products.

(A) recent
(B) more recent
(C) recently
(D) most recent

110. Many new office buildings have ------- electricity costs because they are equipped with solar panels.

(A) close
(B) gradual
(C) lower
(D) dense

111. Employees and their managers must complete all annual reviews ------- March 2.

(A) also
(B) prior to
(C) first
(D) as well as

112. Mr. Miguel is hoping for a ------- and usually offers to take on extra duties.

(A) perception
(B) condition
(C) compilation
(D) promotion

113. Mizusugi Hobby Suppliers stocks a ------- range of products for creating model airplanes.

(A) diverse
(B) diversity
(C) diversely
(D) diversify

114. ------- to the annual awards banquet will be mailed on Monday.

(A) Attractions
(B) Compliments
(C) Invitations
(D) Sentiments

115. If you ------- in attending the company picnic, please let Melissa White know by Friday.

(A) interest
(B) interests
(C) are interested
(D) were interesting

116. Employees at Papaloos Hardware were surprised ------- the shop owner sold the business.

(A) which
(B) either
(C) nor
(D) when

117. The Help Desk has resolved technical issues ------- since hiring additional team members.

(A) efficient
(B) efficiently
(C) efficiency
(D) more efficient

118. ------- there was a traffic jam on the highway, Madison missed her flight to Libreville.

(A) Until
(B) Because
(C) Whether
(D) Even if

119. The new improvements in our medical technologies will allow for a ------- of health-care costs.

(A) reduce
(B) reduced
(C) reduces
(D) reduction

120. In general, theatergoers loved the movie's fast pace but found its story line too -------.

(A) assorted
(B) predictable
(C) mutual
(D) reluctant

Go on to the next page

121. Since she ------- the company very early on, Ms. Elliott was able to experience all stages of its development.

(A) joins
(B) joined
(C) has joined
(D) will join

122. After months of difficult negotiations, Essane Ltd.'s acquisition of Channing Perfumery was ------- completed yesterday.

(A) finally
(B) repeatedly
(C) knowingly
(D) strongly

123. Linville Market will celebrate its opening on May 1 ------- offering 10 percent off all purchases.

(A) where
(B) although
(C) by
(D) for

124. The Stockler Group ------- numerous sporting events, including the Shishi Marathon.

(A) happens
(B) becomes
(C) cooperates
(D) sponsors

125. The software includes a video ------- provides instructions for customizing documents.

(A) who
(B) this
(C) that
(D) what

126. The workshop focused on ------- strategies for increasing sales in a variety of businesses.

(A) each
(B) fascinated
(C) willing
(D) common

127. Niagara Space Ventures will send an ------- satellite to Jupiter within the next five years.

(A) explore
(B) explored
(C) explores
(D) exploratory

128. ------- the end of the training session, participants will be presented with a certificate of completion.

(A) Along
(B) At
(C) Except
(D) Between

129. Trelstem researchers will spend one month ------- the fuel-efficiency data and then write up the results.

(A) evaluation
(B) evaluated
(C) evaluative
(D) evaluating

130. Ryou Fujita has ------- the entire ground-floor space at 480 Shaw Boulevard to exhibit contemporary art.

(A) paid
(B) leased
(C) trained
(D) advanced

PART 6

Directions: Read the texts that follow. A word, phrase, or sentence is missing in parts of each text. Four answer choices for each question are given below the text. Select the best answer to complete the text. Then mark the letter (A), (B), (C), or (D) on your answer sheet.

Questions 131-134 refer to the following e-mail.

From: United Lamps, Inc. <customerservice@unitedlampsinc.com>
To: Shannon Cohen <scohen@britemail.com>
Date: January 31
Subject: Your order
Attachment: Mail form

Dear Ms. Cohen,

Thank you for your order from United Lamps, Inc. We will be shipping your lamps ------- and
                                                                                131.
will send a confirmation e-mail at that time.

Occasionally, items arrive at their ------- damaged. ------- . We will ------- a replacement as
                                     132.   133.   134.
soon as we receive the original items.

Thank you for your continued patronage.

Customer Service Team

---

131. (A) short
(B) shortly
(C) shorter
(D) shortest

132. (A) estimate
(B) storage
(C) destination
(D) appointment

133. (A) If this happens, please use the attached label to return the item.
(B) Your lamps should arrive within the next week.
(C) Our lamps have won awards for outstanding craftsmanship.
(D) Shipping costs have gradually increased.

134. (A) recommend
(B) provide
(C) design
(D) purchase

Go on to the next page

To: Jin-Hee Yang <jyang@herongifts.ca>

From: Tom Vermette <tvermette@vermettehca.ca>

Date: 16 May

Subject: Installation Information

Attachment: Proposal

Dear Ms. Yang:

Thank you for trusting Vermette Heating, Cooling, and Air with your service needs. I ------- the **135.** proposal for the new air-conditioning system. Please let me know if you have any questions about ------- . You will find that this unit will function more efficiently than your current system. **136.** ------- , you should see a decrease in your monthly electric bills. ------- . It includes annual **137.** **138.** tune-ups of your system. For more information, call our office at 613-555-0164. We can answer any questions about the plan and payment options.

Sincerely,

Tom Vermette

---

135. (A) attaches
(B) attaching
(C) had attached
(D) have attached

136. (A) him
(B) it
(C) them
(D) anyone

137. (A) Nevertheless
(B) Otherwise
(C) Consequently
(D) In contrast

138. (A) You can save even more money by signing up for our maintenance plan.
(B) You may submit your payment through our online system.
(C) Many businesses in the area are upgrading their heating systems now.
(D) I read your proposal with great interest.

Mr. Adam Weisberg
37 Autumn Road
Nyack, NY 10960

June 24

Dear Mr. Weisberg,

This letter is being sent to remind you ------- it is time for your dental appointment with Dr.
                                          139.
Shuyama. During your last visit, you scheduled an appointment to have your teeth cleaned

on Tuesday, July 16, at 3:00 P.M. If you need to reschedule, please call us ------- at (845) 555-
                                                                             140.
0162.

We would like to take this opportunity to inform you about our latest giveaway campaign.

Throughout the month of July, ------- will keep a jar filled with toothbrushes on the registration
                                141.
desk. Patients are asked to guess the number of toothbrushes in the jar. Whoever comes

closest to the actual number will win a True Smile electric toothbrush valued at $135.

------- .
142.

We look forward to seeing you soon.

Shuyama Dental Associates

---

139. (A) that
    (B) how
    (C) unless
    (D) whenever

140. (A) instead
    (B) as if
    (C) nevertheless
    (D) at your convenience

141. (A) we
    (B) you
    (C) one
    (D) they

142. (A) Contact our front desk for a free
        consultation.
    (B) We recommend that you see the
        dentist twice a year.
    (C) True Smile is the best electric
        toothbrush available.
    (D) A fee of $25 will be charged for
        canceled appointments.

Go on to the next page

Questions 143-146 refer to the following passage.

Event Calendar

August 18–19

The popular Antique and Vintage Trade Show returns for its tenth consecutive year. Sponsored by the Fullman Antique Dealers Association, the show offers a chance to view private collections from around the country. ------- **143.** . The first, located in East Hall, includes collectibles such as jewelry, toys, silverware, and dishes. A second area, in South Hall, will ------- **144.** handcrafted furniture. Finally, rare books, vintage signs, and historical artifacts will be displayed in West Hall. The first day is limited to ------- **145.** association members only. Doors will be open to the public ------- **146.** August 19. All tickets must be purchased in advance on our Web site or by calling 555-0142.

---

143. (A) There are several steps to get signed up.
(B) Exhibits will be divided into three categories.
(C) The director has shared a few of her favorite memories.
(D) A number of changes have been made to the event.

144. (A) polish
(B) determine
(C) feature
(D) charge

145. (A) register
(B) registers
(C) registered
(D) registration

146. (A) about
(B) except
(C) after
(D) on

PART 7

Directions: In this part you will read a selection of texts, such as magazine and newspaper articles, e-mails, and instant messages. Each text or set of texts is followed by several questions. Select the best answer for each question and mark the letter (A), (B), (C), or (D) on your answer sheet.

Questions 147-148 refer to the following advertisement.

Mishri's, located at 1077 Cedar Avenue, is a thriving department store that has been serving the San Francisco area for more than two decades. Mishri's offers everything from work uniforms to the latest fashions, indoor and outdoor furniture, electronics, and sporting goods. We currently have an opening for an experienced sales consultant in the furniture department. The full-time position includes a competitive salary with paid holidays. Take a look online at mishris.com/jobs to learn more. Interested applicants should contact Vikas Tawde, sales manager, at 415-555-0185 to arrange an interview.

147. What is suggested about Mishri's?

(A) It recently reorganized the store layout.
(B) It has sold a variety of goods to customers for many years.
(C) It is opening a new location in another city.
(D) It plans to expand its current location.

148. Why are readers encouraged to call Mr. Tawde?

(A) To place an order
(B) To provide feedback
(C) To arrange a delivery
(D) To set up a meeting

Go on to the next page

Questions 149-150 refer to the following text-message chain.

Jamal Kirby [9:15 A.M.]
Hi, Paula. I'm working at home today. Could you please send me the Torvale Enterprises contracts and let me know when to expect them? I would like to review them as soon as possible.

Paula Lahti [9:16 A.M.]
Of course. I can have our expedited delivery service pick them up later this morning, so you should get them this afternoon. The address I have on file for you is 140 Riverside Drive.

Jamal Kirby [9:17 A.M.]
No, sorry, that is my old place. I'm now at 35 Elston Avenue, Apartment 103.

Paula Lahti [9:18 A.M.]
Got it. I'll send the documents you need there.

Jamal Kirby [9:19 A.M.]
That sounds good. Be sure to update your records, too. Thanks, Paula.

149. What is most likely true about Mr. Kirby?

(A) He is currently on a business trip.
(B) He wants to receive some documents soon.
(C) He plans to move his office.
(D) He is writing an article about Torvale Enterprises.

150. At 9:19 A.M., what does Mr. Kirby mean when he writes, "Be sure to update your records, too"?

(A) Ms. Lahti should note the new value of a property.
(B) Ms. Lahti should revise an address on file.
(C) Ms. Lahti needs to destroy a client report.
(D) Ms. Lahti must use a different delivery service.

Questions 151-152 refer to the following coupon.

A Special Offer from Spee-Dee Long-Term Parking

Present this coupon to get a 10 percent discount on our long-term parking rates!

- We're just minutes away from Kingston Airport.
- Our complimentary shuttle bus leaves on the hour to drop passengers off at their flight terminals.
- We're open 7 days a week, 24 hours a day.

Reserve your space in advance at www.spee-dee.com!
No charge if you need to cancel.

Only one coupon accepted per visit. Cannot be combined with other coupons.
Expires 31 December.

---

151. What is suggested about Spee-Dee Long-Term Parking?

(A) It is closed on holidays.
(B) It is near an airport.
(C) It does not accept reservations.
(D) It charges a cancellation fee.

152. What is true about the coupon?

(A) It is valid at other locations.
(B) It is offered to first-time customers only.
(C) It expires at the end of the year.
(D) It includes a discount on a shuttle-bus ticket.

Go on to the next page

ETS 실전 모의고사

WE MISS YOU!

All of us on the staff here at Mike's Workout Center in Taylorville miss seeing you!

If you are ready to renew your membership, we are offering one-half off the standard monthly membership rate for the next three months. This offer will expire at the end of July.

Come enjoy our regular sessions featuring dance fitness, cycling, and strength training. In addition, take time to check out our recently updated athletic boutique, featuring top-quality exercise apparel, tote bags, and more. Many boutique items are now branded with the Mike's Workout Center logo!

Contact the membership office today. We will help you keep on track with your fitness plan and do it in style!

153. For whom is the flyer written?

(A) New residents of Taylorville
(B) Exercise class instructors
(C) Current members of a fitness club
(D) Frequent customers of a boutique

154. What is suggested about Mike's Workout Center?

(A) Its branded apparel sells well.
(B) Its discount offer will no longer be available in August.
(C) It has introduced new classes recently.
(D) It has seen an increase in membership.

Fariba Khan, 28 April

Although I travel to Bartonsburg for work several times a year, this was the first time I stayed at the Lazy Lilac Inn. I normally reserve a room at a hotel next to my company's Bartonsburg location, but it was unable to accommodate the four-night visit I needed, so I opted for the Lazy Lilac Inn at the suggestion of a colleague. It was extending a special promotion when I made the reservation, and I received a discounted rate.

Overall, my stay was pleasant enough. Though the inn was farther from my company's office than my usual lodging, it was closer to the airport, which was convenient. It has an exercise room as well as a space that functions as a business center. There was also a room where I could wash a load of dirty clothes. My main qualm about the Lazy Lilac Inn was that it does not have a full-service breakfast. Though I ate most of my meals with my colleagues, it would have been nice to eat at the inn in the morning. However, it had just pastries and hot beverages available. I certainly recommend it for any of you who may take a similar trip.

---

155. For whom most likely is the blog post written?

(A) Tour companies
(B) Residents of Bartonsburg
(C) Business travelers
(D) Family vacationers

156. The word "extending" in paragraph 1, line 5, is closest in meaning to

(A) delaying
(B) stretching
(C) offering
(D) moving

157. What is mentioned as an amenity of the Lazy Lilac Inn?

(A) Laundry facilities
(B) An outdoor patio
(C) Airport limousine service
(D) An event room

Go on to the next page

MEMO

From: Fred Stiller, President, ROE Smart Solutions
To: All Staff
Subject: All-staff meeting
Date: June 4

The next all-staff meeting will be on Tuesday, June 11, at 1:00 P.M. in Conference Room A. On-site employees are expected to attend in person. Those of you working remotely will be receiving a link that, once activated, will enable you to participate in the meeting over the Internet.

As you know, earlier this year we acquired Greer Technologies and merged its management, products, and operations with our company. At the all-staff meeting, I will be focusing on some key issues stemming from this development, including changes within company management. Among other things, I will be introducing Mr. Paul Oberweis, the former director of finance at Greer Technologies and now our new chief financial officer. He will be reviewing our financial projections for the year.

If you have questions that you would like to have answered during the meeting, please submit them to Adrienne Petruso (a.petruso@roe.org) by June 10.

158. What is one item on the agenda for the June 11 meeting?

(A) A course offered to employees
(B) A managerial job opening
(C) A budgetary forecast
(D) A merger procedure

159. The word "issues" in paragraph 2, line 3, is closest in meaning to

(A) publications
(B) reasons
(C) matters
(D) titles

160. What is true about Mr. Oberweis?

(A) He wrote the memo.
(B) He purchased a company.
(C) He has developed new technologies.
(D) He has a new position.

To:	Caiaro Realty Employees
From:	Sean Patrick
Date:	January 29
Subject:	Real Estate Agent of the Year finalist

Dear Colleagues:

I am pleased to announce that our colleague, Shanice Walker, is a finalist for the Real Estate Agent of the Year award that is being presented by the California Board of Real Estate Agents. — [1] —. Ms. Walker has had an outstanding year and is very deserving of this honor. — [2] —. She has been a real estate agent for fifteen years, the last ten with Caiaro Realty. The winner will be announced at the awards banquet, which will be held on February 28 at the High Lingon Hotel from 6 p.m. to 10 p.m. — [3] —. I encourage everyone to attend and support Ms. Walker. If you do plan to attend, please e-mail my assistant, Mingzhe Zhou, to reserve your spot. Make sure to congratulate Ms. Walker when you see her. — [4] —.

Best,

Sean Patrick
President, Caiaro Realty

161. What is indicated about Ms. Walker?

(A) She just received an award.
(B) She has been a finalist for an award in the past.
(C) She recommended a colleague to become a board member.
(D) She has worked for Caiaro Realty for ten years.

162. What should someone who wants to attend the banquet do?

(A) Reply to Mr. Patrick's e-mail
(B) Visit a Web site
(C) Call the High Lingon Hotel
(D) Send an e-mail to Ms. Zhou.

163. In which of the positions marked [1], [2], [3], and [4] does the following sentence best belong?

"Caiaro Realty will be hosting several tables at the banquet."

(A) [1]
(B) [2]
(C) [3]
(D) [4]

Go on to the next page

Questions 164-167 refer to the following article.

CRESTWOOD (March 22)—A pipe on the top floor of the Crestwood Theater burst open on Wednesday morning, causing flooding that soaked the antique wood flooring and several interior walls. Nathan Therriault, a spokesperson for Gilliam Associates, which owns and operates the historic theater building, said the issue was discovered when a maintenance team arrived to perform routine cleaning. Mr. Therriault said that given the considerable damage, Gilliam Associates is already in the process of selecting a company to tackle the repairs.

"The Crestwood Theater is one of our town's treasures, so we are committed to maintaining the beauty and character of the original interior as we plan for this restoration work," Mr. Therriault said. He added that he is hopeful the theater will be able to reopen for the autumn/winter performance season.

Crestwood Theater staff are now determining whether the performances slated for the spring and summer will be postponed or canceled entirely. The theater had been seeing unprecedented levels of attendance since hiring a new artistic director who began a strong outreach campaign in the local community. Many performance dates were already sold out. Theater manager Janice Mershon warned that decisions about the performances will take some time to make and asked that ticket holders remain patient. When the schedule is finalized, the box office will contact ticket holders directly to issue new tickets or to make arrangements for full refunds, she said.

164. What is one purpose of the article?

(A) To report on changes to a building's construction schedule
(B) To present historical facts about a building
(C) To describe recent damage to a building
(D) To provide information about a building's sale

165. What has Gilliam Associates begun to do?

(A) Search for a company to do restoration work
(B) Conduct a safety inspection
(C) Find an alternate space to host performances
(D) Increase the size of the maintenance team

166. What is indicated about the Crestwood Theater?

(A) It is seeking a new artistic director.
(B) It is typically closed during the summer months.
(C) Its shows have become popular among Crestwood residents.
(D) Its ticket prices have been criticized for being too high.

167. According to the article, what are all ticket holders advised to do?

(A) Check the theater's Web site for updates
(B) E-mail the theater's management to request a refund
(C) Visit the box office to exchange their tickets
(D) Wait for a theater employee to contact them

Questions 168-171 refer to the following advertisement.

Aiyar's Cleaning Services

One way of making your office look its best is by keeping your carpeting clean and bright. —[1]—. Aiyar's Cleaning Services (ACS) is a full-service commercial carpet cleaning company. We use specialized equipment to remove dirt, dust, and stains from carpeting. We can also clean area rugs and upholstery on chairs and sofas. —[2]—. Area rugs can be cleaned either at your facility or at ours.

To avoid disruption to your employees' schedules, our technicians can work after hours, overnight, or during weekends. —[3]—. They will move office furniture as needed and return everything back to its place when cleaning is complete.

Located in Troy, ACS serves businesses within the greater metropolitan area. Visit our Web site at www.acs.com to get a price quote or to schedule an appointment. To speak with a customer service agent about special service requests, call us at 555-0101. —[4]—. New customers receive a ten percent discount on their first service.

---

168. According to the advertisement, what is one service ACS provides?

(A) Carpet repair
(B) Trash removal
(C) Window washing
(D) Furniture cleaning

169. What is mentioned about area rugs?

(A) They can be moved offsite for cleaning.
(B) They are more durable than carpeting.
(C) They are easier to clean than carpeting.
(D) They require the use of special chemical cleaners.

170. According to the advertisement, why might customers want to visit the ACS Web site?

(A) To file a complaint
(B) To find an office location
(C) To obtain a cost estimate
(D) To read customer reviews

171. In which of the positions marked [1], [2], [3], and [4] does the following sentence best belong?

"We are experienced at handling cotton, wool, and synthetic fabrics."

(A) [1]
(B) [2]
(C) [3]
(D) [4]

Go on to the next page

Questions 172-175 refer to the following online chat discussion.

 — □ X

Carlene Ramirez (11:02 A.M.)
Regina and Alfonso, I need some help this afternoon. A school group is coming at 1:00, and I just found out that Charles Toskin is out with a cold.

Regina Marcum (11:04 A.M.)
Isn't Lydia available to take them around?

Carlene Ramirez (11:07 A.M.)
No. She's away at a conference. Can one of you fill in for Charles?

Alfonso Vesga (11:08 A.M.)
Since my specialty is modern photography, I'm not sure I feel comfortable discussing Impressionist painting. Regina, you have knowledge in that field, right?

Regina Marcum (11:09 A.M.)
Actually, I deal mostly with Renaissance painting. I am familiar enough with the Impressionists, though. I could talk about them.

Carlene Ramirez (11:11 A.M.)
Looks like we've got it covered then. The group plans to eat in the café and then gather in the first-floor lobby at 1:00.

Regina Marcum (11:12 A.M.)
I'll meet them there and show them the Impressionist collection. After that, I'll bring them to the Asian sculpture exhibit for you to take over, Carlene.

Carlene Ramirez (11:14 A.M.)
Great, Regina. I'll let you get back to work. Alfonso, I'll bring the students to you around 4:00.

Alfonso Vesga (11:15 A.M.)
Sounds good, Carlene.

172. Who most likely is Ms. Ramirez?

(A) A university professor
(B) A professional photographer
(C) A museum educator
(D) A conference organizer

173. What most likely is Mr. Toskin's area of specialization?

(A) Asian sculpture
(B) Renaissance painting
(C) Impressionist painting
(D) Modern photography

174. At 11:11 A.M., what does Ms. Ramirez most likely mean when she writes, "Looks like we've got it covered then"?

(A) She understands Mr. Vesga's concern.
(B) She accepts Ms. Marcum's offer.
(C) She knows why an exhibit is closed.
(D) She plans to pay for a group's admission.

175. What will Ms. Marcum most likely do next?

(A) Call Ms. Ramirez for advice
(B) Return to her usual duties
(C) Go to the lobby to wait
(D) Eat lunch in the café

Go on to the next page

To:	Rita May
From:	Jason Woyimo
Date:	September 13, 10:20 A.M.
Subject:	Request for information

Hello Ms. May,

Could you provide me with some information, please? I just had a call from Ms. Linda Bandasack with the Kirkwood Corporation. She wants to place an order for 1,000 fine-point gel pens but is unable to reach Christopher Warren, her assigned sales representative here at Executive Stationery, Inc. I was unable to find his name in our employee database, possibly suggesting that Mr. Warren has left the company. I happened to come across an organizational chart, though, that indicates that Mr. Warren reports to you. With this in mind, and so that I can provide Ms. Bandasack with the correct information, can you confirm that Mr. Warren has left the company, and if so, which sales representative is now serving his clientele?

Thanks,

Jason Woyimo
Customer Service Specialist
Executive Stationery, Inc.

To:	linda.bandasack@kirkwoodcorp.com
From:	kgrainer@esi.com
Date:	September 13, 1:04 P.M.
Subject:	Your order

Hello Ms. Bandasack,

My name is Kenyatta Grainer, and I am a sales representative from Executive Stationery, Inc. (ESI). I understand that you have been trying to contact Mr. Warren. Please note that Mr. Warren retired from our company on September 1. I have been assigned his clients and will do my utmost to provide you with the same excellent service he provided to you.

I have been informed about your order. According to the information I have, you are looking to place the same order as last year. Can you verify that this is correct?

Please feel free to contact me by e-mail or telephone at any time. I look forward to a long, successful business relationship with you.

Sincerely,

Kenyatta Grainer
Sales Representative
Executive Stationery, Inc.
Phone: 416-555-0149
E-mail: kgrainer@esi.com

176. According to the first e-mail, what is Ms. Bandasack's problem?

(A) She cannot find ESI's organizational chart.
(B) She cannot get access to some reports.
(C) She cannot place an order online.
(D) She cannot contact a sales agent.

177. What most likely is Ms. May's role at ESI?

(A) Recruiter
(B) Sales manager
(C) Database administrator
(D) Product designer

178. What is a reason why Ms. Grainer contacted Ms. Bandasack?

(A) To introduce herself
(B) To inform her of a policy change
(C) To ask her for her contact information
(D) To thank her for being a loyal customer

179. What is suggested about Ms. Bandasack?

(A) She wanted to find an affordable supply company.
(B) She ordered 1,000 pens the previous year.
(C) She regularly met with Mr. Warren.
(D) She was contacted by Ms. May.

180. What is Ms. Bandasack asked to do?

(A) Comment on ESI's service
(B) Assign a different representative
(C) Confirm the accuracy of an order
(D) Send Mr. Warren a thank-you note

Go on to the next page

MEMO

From: Anja Biermann, CEO
To: All Stamitz Group Employees
Date: June 6
Subject: Company honored

I am pleased to announce that on June 4 the National Federation of Civil Engineers (NFCE) awarded its highest honor, the Platinum Engineering Achievement Award, to the Stamitz Group. Our success is the outcome of the hard work you have done over the last few years. I know that some of you were skeptical about our move into the business of designing apartment complexes, given our longtime reputation as designers of office buildings. This acknowledgment clearly shows the value of business diversification.

On June 30, the NFCE will be holding an awards banquet, where I will formally accept the award. Since most employees will not be able to attend that event, we will hold a reception at our headquarters on June 22. An invitation for this gathering will be sent later today. Please respond to the invitation by June 15 so that we know how many people plan to attend.

NFCE Announces Awards

By Zulfiqar Nawaz

June 10—The National Federation of Civil Engineers (NFCE) has announced the winners of its annual Engineering Achievement Awards. It bestowed its highest honor, the Platinum Award, to the Stamitz Group, which received glowing praise for its work on the Venice Tower building in downtown Kayleb City. The Stamitz Group had been expected to win the award last year for its design of the new headquarters of Helios Bank; however, the award went to MCL Contractors, a well-known architectural firm that designs department stores.

The NFCE Awards are different from other engineering awards in that their focus is not on innovation. "Our evaluation of a structure is solely based on its longevity," said NFCE president Laura Fordham. "We are keenly interested in the materials used and features added that will result in the long-term existence of an architectural work. Thus, the structures we honor are not necessarily the ones that are most eye-catching or trendy; rather, they are the ones we believe are more likely to still be standing in one hundred years' time."

181. What kind of business most likely is the Stamitz Group?

(A) An investment bank
(B) An architectural firm
(C) A department store
(D) A software engineering firm

182. In the memo, the word "acknowledgment" in paragraph 1, line 7, is closest in meaning to

(A) contract
(B) example
(C) admission
(D) recognition

183. When will an event be held at the office of the Stamitz Group?

(A) On June 4
(B) On June 15
(C) On June 22
(D) On June 30

184. What is most likely the primary use of Venice Tower?

(A) Residential
(B) Medical
(C) Governmental
(D) Cultural

185. According to the article, what does the NFCE look for in a building?

(A) Durability
(B) Profitability
(C) Stylishness
(D) Innovation

Go on to the next page

Stony Hill Museum of Art (SHMA) Yearly Membership Levels

Student Membership: For full-time students of any age with a current student identification. $30.00

Individual Membership: Includes one guest pass. $50.00

Dual Membership: For two adults living in the same household. Includes two guest passes. $70.00

Family Membership: For two adults and up to four children. Includes four guest passes and priority registration for children's summer camps. $90.00

Contributor Membership: Includes four guest passes, two museum posters, and early admission to all exhibitions. $110.00

Sustainer Membership: Includes all the benefits of the contributor membership plus complimentary single admission to over 1,000 museums in the United States. $250.00

All membership levels include unlimited admission to SHMA, invitations to members-only programs, a 10 percent discount at the Museum Shop and Café, and a free subscription to the SHMA newsletter. To purchase or renew a membership, please fill out the form at www.shma.org/membership. If you have questions, send an e-mail to the museum's member services coordinator, Jeff Hill, at jhill@shma.org or call him at 518-555-0158.

To:	Jeff Hill <jhill@shma.org>
From:	Nadia Amari <namari@thrumail.com>
Date:	December 10
Subject:	Membership

Dear Mr. Hill,

My current membership at SHMA expires at the end of the month and is set up for automatic renewal. However, I want to upgrade my dual membership to the next level, which includes priority registration for summer camps, but I am unable to do so on your Web site. I cannot figure out how to pay the additional cost for the upgrade. I called your number, and the automated system immediately transferred me to voice mail. I left a message on December 5, but my call has not been returned. Please let me know how to proceed. I want to resolve this issue before the beginning of January, when the special exhibition of Marco Stellitano's work opens.

Thank you,

Nadia Amari

To:	Nadia Amari <namari@thrumail.com>
From:	Jeff Hill <jhill@shma.org>
Date:	December 12
Subject:	RE: Membership

Dear Ms. Amari,

Thank you for contacting me regarding your membership. To upgrade to the next membership level, you will need to stop your automatic payment and then reenroll at the next level. This can be done online or over the phone with me at 518-555-0158.

Please accept my apologies for the difficulty you experienced. I was out of the office for a week, and, unfortunately, I neglected to forward my messages to another staff member. As a token of our appreciation for your understanding, we will be sending you a coffee mug that has a painting from our special exhibition opening on January 1.

Please let me know if I can be of further assistance.

Sincerely,

Jeff Hill, Member Services Coordinator
Stony Hill Museum of Art

---

186. What is included with an SHMA student membership?

(A) A museum guest pass
(B) Discounts on museum programs
(C) Unlimited museum admission
(D) A museum poster

187. How much is an SHMA membership that includes free entry to other museums?

(A) $70
(B) $90
(C) $110
(D) $250

188. What membership level does Ms. Amari want to purchase?

(A) Individual
(B) Family
(C) Contributor
(D) Sustainer

189. According to the second e-mail, what did Mr. Hill forget to do?

(A) Have a coworker receive his messages
(B) Inform colleagues about his absence
(C) Stop Ms. Amari's automatic renewal
(D) Send a membership card to Ms. Amari

190. What is suggested about the coffee mug that Ms. Amari will receive?

(A) It is sold in the Museum Shop.
(B) It is being discontinued.
(C) It features a work by Mr. Stellitano.
(D) It holds more coffee than most mugs.

Go on to the next page

Magazine Changes Chief

NEW YORK (January 21)—It has just been announced that Rina Talbot will assume the editorial leadership of *Financial Age Magazine*. Her predecessor, Finn Cobb, made the announcement at a press conference this morning.

"I have full confidence that Ms. Talbot will continue to deliver the quality reporting on world financial markets that has made *Financial Age Magazine* as respected as it is today," Mr. Cobb said.

Ms. Talbot is no newcomer to the magazine. In fact, she started there 22 years ago as a staff writer, filing numerous financial news stories from Asia. Later she was named to head the magazine's European bureau.

Kosuke Higa, chair of ASBI Media, which owns the magazine, said that he is sad to see Mr. Cobb leave. "For 25 years, Mr. Cobb has led the magazine to major success," Mr. Higa said. "However, I have complete confidence in Ms. Talbot's ability to build on his very successful record."

To:	Finn Cobb
From:	Kosuke Higa
Subject:	Your career
Date:	January 22

Dear Mr. Cobb,

We both know where *Financial Age Magazine* was 25 years ago and where it is today. You led the publication through some very challenging periods, and I am proud to have witnessed your success. And now you are retiring. I know that at first you were hesitant about the person selected to assume your role, so I was pleased to learn that you fully support this choice. This is deeply appreciated.

Soon you will be receiving an invitation to a celebration in honor of your work. We haven't informed the rest of the company yet, but I thought it appropriate for me to let you know in advance of the announcement. In addition to inviting current employees and colleagues, we will also have a very special guest as the keynote speaker: your first supervisor at the magazine and the person who held this position before I did! It will be quite a night.

Yours,

Kosuke Higa

```
You are cordially invited to
a celebration in honor of

Finn Cobb

Keynote speaker: Thomas Jean-Pierre

Date: Friday, February 12
Time: 7:00 P.M. to 10:00 P.M.

Place: Morvyn Manor, 787 Manor Drive

Confirm your attendance by sending an e-mail to
feb12rsvp@morvynmanor.com by February 5.
```

191. What does the article state about Ms. Talbot?

(A) She has written many articles for a magazine.
(B) She is responsible for issuing press releases.
(C) She will soon head a magazine's European office.
(D) She arrived late to a news conference.

192. What is the purpose of the e-mail?

(A) To get advice on career development
(B) To respond to a question about an article
(C) To describe a change in business strategy
(D) To offer congratulations to an employee

193. In the e-mail, what does Mr. Higa note as one of Mr. Cobb's achievements?

(A) Hiring a number of successful editors
(B) Guiding a magazine through difficult times
(C) Expanding *Financial Age Magazine* to cover the global market
(D) Writing quality articles about Asian financial markets

194. What made Mr. Cobb doubtful initially?

(A) The appointment of Ms. Talbot
(B) The choice of a place for a celebration
(C) The rapid growth of a magazine
(D) The plans for a new publication

195. What can be inferred about Mr. Jean-Pierre?

(A) He organized a press conference.
(B) He has worked for *Financial Age Magazine*.
(C) He was hired by Mr. Higa 25 years ago.
(D) He works at Morvyn Manor.

Go on to the next page ➡

https://www.continuousgrowth.com.au

Continuous Growth offers training for aspiring agricultural specialists who want to explore the latest technological advances in the field.

We offer four online prerecorded video modules, each led by a guest expert. The topics covered are as follows:

- Creative Water Catchment Systems, with Samir Wadekar
- Advanced Soil Health Strategies, with Garth Martin
- Tree Care, with Jessica Chin
- Animal Systems, with Dawn Brown

Modules can be purchased individually for $150 each. Access to any courses purchased is good for two years.

Additionally, we offer a comprehensive and intensive programme consisting of 80 total hours of instruction. The four online modules described above make up the core of the intensive programme curriculum. But also included are multiple in-person workshops at our training centre where attendees will participate in hands-on projects. In addition, students will be responsible for reading key selections from research journals. Enrollment in the two-month programme is capped at fifteen students and costs $1200. Certificates are awarded to students upon successful completion of the programme.

To:	Intensive Programme Students
From:	Darlene Stein
Date:	22 October
Subject:	Apprenticeship

Students,

I am sure you are busy working on your final projects, but I wanted to take a moment to pass on to you some important information. Our expert trainer who specializes in water collection systems is looking to hire two apprentices at his agricultural engineering firm. Those interested should let me know.

Also, all those seeking employment should read the latest article on the Australia Eco-Farming Web site that explains how to effectively market yourself to agricultural-industry employers.

Best,

Darlene Stein

Congratulations on completing all 80 hours of our intensive programme. Please take a moment to comment about your experience.

Name: Jack Nguyen

I enjoyed everything about these courses. The workshops were incredibly helpful, and I had a wonderful time getting to know the other students. I suggest that students be shown examples of farms that have actually implemented some of the techniques presented in the readings. That is the only thing that I felt was lacking. Overall, the tuition was money well spent, and I would recommend it to anyone interested in the agricultural field.

196. What does the Web page indicate about the intensive program?

(A) It requires students to publish research.
(B) It takes about two years to complete.
(C) There is an established class-size limit.
(D) Students must take a comprehensive written examination.

197. Who is hiring apprentices?

(A) Mr. Wadekar
(B) Mr. Martin
(C) Ms. Chin
(D) Ms. Brown

198. According to the e-mail, why should people visit the Australia Eco-Farming Web site?

(A) To read training-program reviews
(B) To find resources for completing projects
(C) To learn more about available courses
(D) To take advantage of career-related advice

199. What is most likely true about Mr. Nguyen?

(A) He viewed all four online modules.
(B) He gardens as a hobby.
(C) He recently accepted a new position.
(D) He still has coursework to finish to earn a certificate.

200. What does Mr. Nguyen want Continuous Growth to do?

(A) Provide hands-on workshops instead of online modules
(B) Show how some methods are being used in the real world
(C) Reduce the cost of the program
(D) Offer courses for those wanting to work in a different field of study

Stop! This is the end of the test. If you finish before time is called, you may go back to Parts 5, 6, and 7 and check your work.

ANSWER SHEET

Final Test

응시일자 : 20   년   월   일

수험번호

성명	한글
	한자
	영자

LISTENING (Part I ~ IV)

READING (Part V ~ VII)

토익 정기시험 기출입문서 RC

정답 및 해설

주어와 동사 ETS 문제로 훈련하기 STEP 1

교재 p.29

1 (A)	2 (B)	3 (B)	4 (B)	5 (A)	6 (A)

1

Jarwin Pharmaceuticals / (requires) / participants / to meet certain eligibility criteria.
자원 제약은　　　　　　　요구한다　　참여자들이　　　　특정 자격 기준을 충족하도록
　　　　　　　　　　　　↳ 주어 뒤 동사 자리

(A) requires 요구하다　　　　　　　　(B) requirement 요구, 필요

번역 자원 제약은 참여자들이 특정 자격 기준을 충족하도록 요구한다.

2

(All profits) / will be donated / to the public library.
모든 수익은　　기부될 것이다　　　공공도서관에
　　　　　　↳ 명사 주어, 동사는 주어가 될 수 없음

(A) profited 이득을 얻었다　　　　　(B) profits 이익, 수익

번역 모든 수익은 공공도서관에 기부될 것이다.

3

Your letter / (will be) sent / to our customer service department.
귀하의 편지는　전달될 것입니다　저희 고객 서비스 부서로
　　　　　　↳ 조동사 + 동사원형

(A) sends　　　　　　　　　　　　(B) be sent

번역 귀하의 편지는 저희 고객 서비스 부서로 전달될 것입니다.

4

(Walking) / is a form of exercise / that has been recommended / by doctors.
걷기는　　　운동 방식이다　　　　추천되어 온　　　　　　　의사들에 의해
　　　↳ 주어 역할을 하는 동명사

(A) Walks　　　　　　　　　　　(B) Walking

번역 걷기는 의사들이 추천해 온 운동 방식이다.

5

A service engineer / (repairs) / the broken copy machine / in the lobby.
서비스 기사는　　　　　수리하고 있다 고장 난 복사기를　　　　로비에 있는
　　　　　　　　　　↳ 주어 뒤 동사 자리

(A) repairs　　　　　　　　　(B) repairing

번역 서비스 기사는 로비에 있는 고장 난 복사기를 수리한다.

6

When you (want) / to access your account, / please type your password.
원할 때는　　　　계정에 접속하기를　　　　비밀번호를 입력하세요
　　　↳ 시간 부사절의 동사 자리, 〈동사원형 + -ing〉는 동사 자리에 쓸 수 없음

(A) want　　　　　　　　　　(B) wanting

번역 계정에 접속하기를 원할 때는 비밀번호를 입력하세요.

7 (A)	8 (D)	9 (A)	10 (C)

7

Weather forecasters / (predicted) / that heavy rain would come / to this region.
기상 캐스터는　　　　　　　예보했다　　　　폭우가 내릴 것이라고　　　　이 지역에
　　　　　　　　　　　　　 ↳ 주어 뒤 동사 자리

(A) predicted 예보하다　(B) predictably 예상대로　(C) predictable 예측 가능한　(D) prediction 예측

해설 **주어 + 동사:** 빈칸은 주어 Weather forecasters 뒤에 나오는 동사 자리이므로, 과거 시제 동사 (A) predicted가 정답입니다. 부사 (B) predictably(예상대로), 형용사 (C) predictable(예측 가능한), 명사 (D) prediction(예측)은 동사 자리에 들어갈 수 없습니다.

번역 기상 캐스터는 이 지역에 폭우가 내릴 것이라고 예보했다.

8

(Correspondence from *Megavision Monthly*) / may sometimes include / special offers / from
월간 메가비전의 홍보전단은　　　　　　　　　　 때때로 포함할 수 있다　　　특별 제안을　　　 제 3자의
　　　　　　　　　 ↳ 문장의 주어

third parties.

(A) Correspond　　　　　　　　　　(B) Corresponds

(C) Corresponded　　　　　　　　　(D) Correspondence

해설 **주어로 쓰이는 명사 선택:** 빈칸 뒤 from *Megavision Monthly*와 결합하여 주어 역할을 할 수 있는 명사가 필요합니다. 따라서 정답은 명사인 (D) Correspondence입니다.

번역 월간 메가비전의 홍보전단은 제3자의 특별 제안이 때때로 포함될 수 있다.

9

The White Fountain Inn / (will accept) / reservations / only for parties of six people or more.
화이트 파운튼 인은　　　　 받을 것이다　　예약을　　　　 6인 이상 단체만
　　　　　　　　　　　　　　　　 ↳ 주어 뒤 동사 자리

(A) accept　　　　　　　　　　　(B) accepts

(C) accepting　　　　　　　　　(D) accepted

해설 **조동사 + 동사원형:** 빈칸 앞에 조동사 will이 있습니다. 조동사 뒤에는 항상 동사원형을 써야 하므로 (A) accept가 정답입니다.

번역 화이트 파운튼 인은 6인 이상 단체 예약만 받는다.

10

The variety of athletic equipment) / at Ready-Set-Go Sporting Goods / is impressive.
다양한 운동 장비가　　　　　　　　 레디-셋-고우 스포츠 용품의　　　　 인상적이다
　　　　　　　 ↳ 문장의 주어

(A) various 다양한　　　　　　　　(B) vary 서로 다르다

(C) variety 여러 가지　　　　　　　(D) varied 다양한

해설 **주어로 쓰이는 명사 선택:** 빈칸 뒤 of athletic equipment와 결합하여 주어 역할을 할 수 있는 명사가 필요합니다. 따라서 정답은 명사인 (C) variety입니다

번역 레디-셋-고우 스포츠 용품의 다양한 운동 장비가 인상적이다.

1 (B)	2 (B)	3 (B)	4 (A)	5 (A)	6 (A)

1

Mr. Sharma predicts / that Clearfoto's latest camera will be a ⟨great success⟩ / in the retail
샤르마 씨는 예측한다   클리어포토의 최신 카메라가 큰 성공을 거둘 것임을   소매 시장에서

marketplace.
→ 주격 보어(명사)

(A) succeed 성공하다   (B) success 성공

번역   샤르마 씨는 클리어포토의 최신 카메라가 소매 시장에서 큰 성공을 거둘 것이라고 예측한다.

2

The president of Cuddly Toys, Inc., / has announced / ⟨plans⟩ / to expand the company's
커들리 장난감 주식회사의 사장은   발표했다   계획을   회사의 생산 시설을 확장할

production facility.
→ 동사 has announced의 목적어

(A) will plan 계획할 것이다   (B) plans 계획

번역   커들리 장난감 주식회사의 사장은 회사의 생산 시설을 확장할 계획을 발표했다.

3

The agreement / becomes / ⟨effective⟩ / once both parties have signed the documents.
계약이   ~된다   발효되는   일단 양측이 서류에 서명하면
→ 주격 보어(형용사)

(A) effectively 효과적으로   (B) effective 발효되는

번역   일단 양측이 서류에 서명하면 계약이 발효된다.

4

The survey / asked / respondents / whether they enjoy ⟨taking⟩ a walk / in the morning.
그 설문 조사는   물었다   응답자들에게   그들이 산책을 즐기는지   아침에

(A) taking   (B) took
→ 동사 enjoy는 동명사를 목적어로 취함

번역   그 설문 조사는 응답자들에게 그들이 아침에 산책을 즐기는지 물었다.

5

The new software / has made / the design team / ⟨more productive⟩.
새로운 소프트웨어는   만들었다   디자인 팀을   더 생산적으로
→ 목적격 보어

(A) productive 생산적인   (B) productively 생산적으로

번역   새로운 소프트웨어는 디자인 팀을 더 생산적으로 만들었다.

6

Wang and Associates / will be interviewing / ⟨applicants⟩ for the managerial position / next week.
왕앤어소시에이츠는   인터뷰할 예정이다   관리직 지원자를   다음 주에

(A) applicants 지원자들   (B) apply 지원하다
→ 동사 will be interviewing의 목적어

번역   왕앤어소시에이츠는 다음 주에 관리직 지원자를 인터뷰할 예정이다.

7 (C)	8 (A)	9 (D)	10 (D)

7

Please send / (submissions) / for the logo design contest / to Alicia Chang / in the communications
보내주세요   제출물을   로고 디자인 콘테스트를 위한   앨리샤 창에게   커뮤니케이션 부서의

department.
→ 동사 send의 목적어

(A) submitting 제출하기   (B) submitted 제출했다

(C) submissions 제출물   (D) submissible 제출될 수 있는

해설 목적어로 쓰이는 명사: 빈칸 앞 동사 send의 목적어 역할을 하는 명사 자리입니다. (A) submitting과 (C) submissions 중에서 빈칸 뒤 전치사구(for the ~ contest)의 수식을 받는 명사인 (C) submissions가 정답입니다.

번역 로고 디자인 콘테스트를 위한 제출물은 커뮤니케이션 부서의 앨리샤 창에게 보내주세요.

8

It is (necessary) / to make hotel reservations / at least three weeks / in advance.
~해야 한다   호텔 예약을 하다   적어도 3주   전에
→ 주격 보어(형용사)

(A) necessary 필요한   (B) necessarily 필연적으로

(C) necessitate 필요하게 만들다   (D) necessity 필요, 필수품

해설 보어로 쓰이는 형용사: 빈칸 앞 be동사 is의 주격 보어 자리로, 주어 It을 보충 설명하는 말이 필요합니다. 따라서 형용사 (A) necessary(필요한)가 정답입니다. 참고로 It은 가주어로, 진짜 주어는 뒤에 나오는 to부정사 구문(to make ~ in advance)입니다.

번역 적어도 3주 전에 호텔 예약을 해야 한다.

9

Mr. Gallos / renewed / (the registration) / on the company automobile / one week before it expired.
갈로스 씨는   갱신했다   등록을   회사 자동차의   만료 1주일 전에

(A) to register   (B) registered
                        → 동사 renewed의 목적어

(C) register   (D) registration

해설 목적어로 쓰이는 명사: 빈칸 앞 정관사 the와 함께 동사 renewed의 목적어 역할을 할 수 있는 명사가 필요합니다. 따라서 정답은 명사인 (D) registration입니다.

번역 갈로스 씨는 만료 1주일 전에 회사 자동차의 등록을 갱신했다.

10

The Fornsworth Transportation Council / will look over / the amended fee structure / to make
폰스워스 교통위원회는   검토할 것이다   개정된 요금구조를   확인하기 위해

sure / the changes are (reasonable).
변경 사항이 타당한지
→ 주격 보어

(A) reason 이유; 추리하다   (B) reasonably 합리적으로

(C) reasoning 추리, 추론   (D) reasonable 타당한

해설 보어로 쓰이는 형용사: 빈칸은 be동사 are의 주격 보어 자리로, 주어 the changes를 보충 설명합니다. 문맥상 '변경 사항이 타당하다'라는 의미가 자연스러우므로, (D) reasonable(타당한)이 정답입니다.

번역 폰스워스 교통위원회는 변경 사항이 타당한지 확인하기 위해 개정된 요금구조를 검토할 것이다.

1 (A)	2 (B)	3 (B)	4 (A)	5 (A)	6 (A)

1

WRX Express / successfully opened / three new rail lines / last year.
WRX 익스프레스는   성공적으로 개통했다   3개의 신규 철도 노선을   작년에
→ 동사 opened를 수식하는 부사

(A) successfully 성공적으로   (B) success 성공

번역 WRX 익스프레스는 작년에 3개의 신규 철도 노선을 성공적으로 개통했다.

2

Belton's shipbuilding industry / provides / a sizable market / for local steel manufacturers.
벨턴의 조선 산업은   제공한다   상당한 규모의 시장을   현지 철강 제조업체들에게
→ 명사 market을 수식하는 형용사

(A) size 규모, 크기   (B) sizable 상당한 규모의

번역 벨턴의 조선 산업은 현지 철강 제조업체들에게 상당한 규모의 시장을 제공한다.

3

Temperatures / are consistently warm / in Dulang City, / even in winter.
기온은   한결같이 따뜻하다   두랑 시에서   겨울에도
→ 형용사 warm을 수식하는 부사

(A) consists 이루어져 있다   (B) consistently 한결같이, 지속적으로

번역 두랑 시의 기온은 겨울에도 한결같이 따뜻하다.

4

Owing to rising fuel prices, / Fleetstand Trucking / plans / to restructure some of its divisions.
연료 가격의 상승으로   플릿스탠드 트럭킹은   계획이다   몇몇 부서를 구조조정할 것을
→ 문장 전체를 수식하는 전치사구

(A) Owing to ~ 때문에   (B) Even if ~이라고 할지라도

번역 연료 가격의 상승으로, 플릿스탠드 트럭킹은 몇몇 부서를 구조 조정할 계획이다.

5

Hamilton City traffic information / is readily accessible / online.
해밀턴 시 교통 정보는   손쉽게 접근할 수 있다   온라인상으로

(A) readily 손쉽게   (B) ready 준비된
→ 형용사 accessible 수식

번역 해밀턴 시 교통 정보는 온라인상으로 손쉽게 접근할 수 있다.

6

The best-selling item / in Ronie Fashion's new line / is a reversible sweatshirt.
가장 많이 팔리는 품목은   로니 패션의 신제품군에서   양면으로 입을 수 있는 스웨터 셔츠이다

(A) reversible 양면으로 입을 수 있는   (B) reverses 뒤바꾸다
→ 명사 sweatshirt를 수식하는 형용사

번역 로니 패션의 신제품군에서 가장 많이 팔리는 품목은 양면으로 입을 수 있는 스웨터 셔츠다.

7 (C)	8 (B)	9 (B)	10 (A)

7

The Transit Association / operates / an (extensive) network / of bus routes / between Clifton and
트랜싯 어소시에이션은   운영한다   광범위한 네트워크를   버스 노선의   클리프턴과 로빌 사이의
⌐→ 형용사
Lawville.

(A) extend 연장하다   (B) extends 연장하다

(C) extensive 광범위한   (D) extensively 광범위하게

해설 형용사 + 명사: 빈칸 뒤 명사 network를 수식하는 형용사 자리이므로 (C) extensive(광범위한)가 정답입니다.

번역 트랜싯 어소시에이션은 클리프턴과 로빌 사이의 광범위한 버스 노선 네트워크를 운영한다.

8

The dental office remodel / was delayed / (because the flooring was back-ordered .)
치과 리모델링이   지연되었다   바닥재가 주문이 밀려 있었기 때문에
⌐→ 부사절

(A) whether ~인지 아닌지   (B) because ~ 때문에

(C) as well as ~뿐만 아니라 …도   (D) with reference to ~와 관련하여

해설 접속사 + 주어 + 동사: 빈칸 뒤의 절(the flooring was back-ordered)을 이끄는 접속사 자리이므로 접속사 (B) because가
정답입니다. 구전치사 (D) with reference to(~와 관련하여)는 뒤에는 명사(구)가 옵니다.

번역 바닥재의 주문이 밀려 있어서 치과 리모델링이 지연되었다.

9

The Springlea Times / recently published / a list of area doctors / who (actively) keep blogs.
〈스프링리 타임즈〉는   최근 발표했다   지역 의사들의 명단을   블로그를 활발하게 운영하는
⌐→ 부사

(A) activating 활성화시키기   (B) actively 활발하게

(C) active 활발한   (D) activate 활성화시키다

해설 부사 자리 (동사 수식): 빈칸은 동사 keep을 수식하는 자리이므로, 부사 (B) actively가 정답입니다.

번역 〈스프링리 타임즈〉는 최근 블로그를 활발하게 운영하는 지역 의사들의 명단을 발표했다.

10

Krowip employees / must submit / their time sheets / (by the end of the day today).
크로윕 직원들은   제출해야 한다   근무시간 기록표를   오늘 퇴근 전까지
⌐→ 전치사구

(A) by   (B) or

(C) then   (D) to

해설 전치사 + 명사구: 빈칸 뒤 명사구 the end of the day today를 목적어로 취하는 전치사 자리로, 문맥상 '오늘 퇴근 전까지'라는 의미가
자연스럽습니다. 따라서 전치사 (A) by가 정답입니다.

번역 크로윕 직원들은 오늘 퇴근 전까지 근무시간 기록표를 제출해야 한다.

1 (A)	**2** (B)	**3** (B)	**4** (A)

1

The board of directors / will vote on (the plan / to) merge with Fray Publishing.
이사회는   계획에 투표할 것이다   프레이 출판사와 합병하는
                                                              ↳ ~하는 계획

(A) plan 계획   (B) summary 요약, 개요

번역 이사회는 프레이 출판사와의 합병 계획에 대해 투표할 것이다.

2

As a (safety precaution), / all employees / must wear / goggles / in the experiment room.
안전 예방책으로   모든 직원들은   써야 한다   보안경을   실험실에서
     ↳ 안전 예방책

(A) specialty 특가품, 특색   (B) precaution 예방책

번역 안전 예방책으로 모든 직원들은 실험실에서 보안경을 써야 한다.

3

Mr. Yost / has decided / to rent an apartment / (for the duration of) his stay / in Manchester.
요스트 씨는   결정했다   아파트를 임차하는 것을   체류하는 기간 동안   맨체스터에
                                                              ↳ ~ 기간 중

(A) collection 수집품, 소장품   (B) duration 기간

번역 요스트 씨는 맨체스터에 체류하는 기간 동안 아파트를 임차하기로 결정했다.

4

The company / (has a reputation / for) producing stoves / of the highest quality.
그 회사는   유명하다   가스레인지를 생산하는 것으로   최고 품질의
          ↳ ~로 유명하다

(A) reputation 명성, 평판   (B) perception 지각, 자각

번역 그 회사는 최고 품질의 가스레인지를 생산하는 것으로 유명하다.

| 5 (C) | 6 (D) | 7 (A) | 8 (D) |

5

The (membership application) / should include / a letter / explaining your reasons / for wanting to
회원 신청서는   포함해야 한다   편지를   이유를 설명하는   우리 단체에
                    └→ 회원 신청서는

join us.
가입하고자 하는

(A) guideline 지침   (B) inventory 재고

(C) application 신청(서)   (D) committee 위원회

해설 application 신청(서): 빈칸 앞 명사 membership과 어울려 쓰이는 명사를 선택해야 합니다. 문맥상 가입 이유를 설명하는 편지가
포함되어야 하는 것은 '회원 신청서'임을 알 수 있으므로, (C) application이 정답입니다.

번역 회원 신청서는 우리 단체에 가입하고자 하는 이유를 설명하는 편지를 포함해야 한다.

6

(Damaged merchandise) / must be documented / and returned / to the warehouse / immediately.
손상된 상품은   서류에 기록되어야 한다   그리고 돌려보내져야 한다 / 창고로   즉시
             └→ 손상된 상품

(A) information 정보   (B) establishments 기관, 시설

(C) services 서비스   (D) merchandise 상품

해설 merchandise 상품: 빈칸에는 damaged(손상된)와 어울리는 명사가 들어가야 합니다. 문맥상 서류에 기록된 후에 창고로 즉시
돌려보내져야 하는 것은 '손상된 상품'임을 알 수 있으므로, (D) merchandise가 정답입니다.

번역 손상된 상품은 즉시 서류에 기록되고 창고로 돌려보내져야 한다.

7

(Advance registration) / is required / for all technical staff / who wish / to attend the conference.
사전 등록이   필수이다   모든 기술진들에게   ~하고 싶은   회의에 참석하다
           └→ 사전 등록

(A) registration 등록   (B) influence 영향

(C) operation 운영   (D) significance 중요성

해설 advance registration 사전 등록: 빈칸 앞의 Advance(사전의)와 어울려 쓰이는 명사를 선택해야 합니다. 문맥상 참석하고자 하는
사람들에게 요구되는 것은 '사전 등록'일 수 있으므로, (A) registration이 정답입니다.

번역 회의에 참석하고 싶은 모든 기술진들은 사전 등록이 필수이다.

8

In his new role, / Mr. Oh / will be responsible / (for ensuring the quality) / of all products.
자신의 새 역할에서   오 씨는   책임지게 될 것이나   품질 보장에 대해   보는 제품의
                                                        └→ 품질을 보장하기

(A) procedure 절차   (B) layer 층, 켜

(C) accessory 부대용품   (D) quality 품질

해설 quality 품질: 빈칸은 동명사 ensuring의 목적어 역할을 하는 명사 자리로, 빈칸 뒤 전치사구 of all products의 수식을 받습니다.
문맥상 '모든 제품의 품질을 보장하는 것'이라는 의미가 자연스러우므로, (D) quality가 정답입니다.

번역 자신의 새 역할에서, 오 씨는 모든 제품의 품질 보장에 대해 책임지게 될 것이다.

1 (C)	**2** (B)	**3** (A)	**4** (B)	**5** (D)

1

The Evonton Library / has / (a digital collection) / of more than 1,500 business journals and
에번톤 도서관은   소장하고 있다   디지털 컬렉션을   1,500개 이상의 비즈니스 저널과 정기 간행물의

periodicals.
└→ 전자판

(A) collects   (B) collecting   (C) collection   (D) collected

> **해설**   **목적어 자리:** 빈칸은 동사 has의 목적어 자리이므로 빈칸에는 명사 (C) collection(컬렉션, ~판)이 들어가야 합니다. (B) collecting (채집)도 명사이지만, '디지털 채집'이라는 의미로 문맥상 어울리지 않습니다.

> **번역**   에번톤 도서관은 1,500개 이상의 비즈니스 저널과 정기 간행물의 전자판을 소장하고 있다.

2

Upon entering the building, / please (register) / at the front desk.
건물 안으로 들어가자마자   등록하세요   프런트에서
                                             └→ 주어가 생략된 명령문의 형태

(A) registration   (B) register   (C) registering   (D) registered

> **해설**   **동사원형으로 시작하는 명령문:** 빈칸은 주어 you가 생략된 명령문의 동사원형 자리이므로, 동사원형 (B) register(등록하다)가 정답입니다.

> **번역**   건물 안으로 들어가자마자 프런트에서 등록하세요.

3

Research / suggests / that Termal, / a popular allergy medicine, / (may induce) / sleep.
연구는   제안한다   터말이   인기 있는 알레르기 치료제인   유발할 수 있다는 것을 / 수면을
                                                    └→ that절의 동사 자리

(A) induce   (B) induced   (C) inducing   (D) will induce

> **해설**   **조동사 + 동사원형:** 빈칸 앞에 조동사가 있으므로 동사원형인 (A) induce(유도하다)가 정답입니다.

> **번역**   연구에 따르면 인기 있는 알레르기 치료제인 터말이 수면을 유발할 수 있다고 한다.

4

It is / the (intention) of Hyde-Cooper, Inc., / to continue / providing / the highest level of customer
~이다   하이드-쿠퍼 주식회사의 의도   지속하는 것이   제공하는 것을   최고 수준의 고객 만족을

satisfaction.
           └→ 보어로 쓰인 명사

(A) intentional 의도적인   (B) intention 의도   (C) intend 의도하다   (D) intended 의도하는

> **해설**   **보어 자리:** 빈칸은 동사 is의 보어 명사 자리이므로, 명사 (B) intention(의도)이 정답입니다.

> **번역**   하이드-쿠퍼 주식회사의 의도는 최고 수준의 고객 만족을 지속적으로 제공하는 것이다.

5

The range of research studies / presented / on the first day / of the conference / was / very
조사 연구들의 범위가   발표된   첫째 날에   회의의   ~였다   매우

(impressive).
인상적인
   └→ 보어로 쓰인 형용사

(A) impressed 감동받은   (B) impress 감명을 주다   (C) impressively 인상 깊게   (D) impressive 인상적인

> **해설**   **보어 자리:** 빈칸은 was의 주격 보어 자리로, 주어 The range of research studies를 보충 설명합니다. 문맥상 '조사 연구들의 범위가 매우 인상적이었다'라는 의미가 자연스러우므로, (D) impressive(인상적인)가 정답입니다. '감동받은'이라는 의미의 (A) impressed는 사람을 의미하는 명사를 보충 설명합니다.

> **번역**   회의의 첫째 날에 발표된 조사 연구들의 범위가 매우 인상적이었다.

6 (D)	7 (C)	8 (B)	9 (D)	10 (D)

6

Advances / in medical technology / have allowed / doctors / to diagnose illnesses / with greater
발전은　　　의학 기술의　　　　　　　　허락했다　　　의사들이　　　병을 진단하도록　　　더 정확하게
　　　　　→ 문장의 주어

accuracy.

(A) Advanced　(B) Advancing　(C) Advancement　(D) Advances

해설　**주어 자리:** 빈칸 뒤의 in medical technology와 결합하여 have allowed의 주어 역할을 할 수 있는 (복수) 명사가 필요합니다. 따라서 정답은 명사인 (D) Advances입니다.

번역　의학 기술의 발전으로 의사들은 더 정확하게 병을 진단할 수 있게 되었다.

7

As the audience expectantly waited / for the actor / to appear onstage, / he surprised / them / by
관객들이 기대하면서 기다리고 있을 때　　　　　　　배우가　　　무대에 등장하기를　　　그가 놀라게 했다　　관객을
　　　　　　　　　→ 동사 waited를 수식하는 부사

marching down the aisle.
통로를 걸어 내려옴으로써

(A) expectant 기대하는　(B) expect 기대하다　(C) expectantly 기대하여　(D) expectation 기대

해설　**동사를 수식하는 부사:** 빈칸은 동사구인 waited for를 수식하는 부사 자리입니다. 따라서 부사 (C) expectantly(기대하여)가 정답입니다.

번역　관객들이 배우가 무대에 등장하기를 기대하면서 기다리는데, 그가 통로를 걸어 내려와 관객을 놀라게 했다.

8

To secure / the floorboards / to the porch framing, / use / large decking screws / spaced at 12-
단단히 고정시키려면　마룻장을　　　　　현관 틀에　　　　박으세요　목재용 큰 나사못을　　12인치 간격을 두고

inch intervals.　　　　　　　　　　　→ 명령문의 동사 형태

(A) to use　(B) use　(C) useful　(D) using

해설　**동사원형으로 시작하는 명령문:** 빈칸 앞 to부정사 구문(To secure ~ the porch framing)은 문장 전체를 수식하는 부사 역할을 하며, 빈칸은 주어 you가 생략된 명령문의 동사원형 자리입니다. 따라서 동사원형 (B) use가 정답입니다.

번역　현관 틀에 마룻장을 단단히 고정시키려면, 12인치씩 간격을 두고 목재용 큰 나사못을 박으세요.

9

The new printer / greatly reduced / the amount of waste / produced by the accounting
새 프린터는　　　　크게 줄였다　　　폐기물 양을　　　　회계부에서 발생하는
　　　　　　　→ 동사 reduced를 수식하는 부사

department.

(A) great　(B) greater　(C) greatest　(D) greatly

해설　**동사를 수식하는 부사:** 빈칸은 동사 reduced를 수식하는 부사 자리입니다. 따라서 부사 (D) greatly(크게, 대단히)가 정답입니다.

번역　새 프린터로 회계부에서 발생하는 폐기물 양이 크게 줄었다.

10

In its advertisements, / Filmore Furniture / emphasizes / the strength and reliability / of its products.
광고에서　　　　　　　필모어 퍼니처는　　　강조한다　　내구력과 신뢰성을　　　　　자사 제품의
　　　　　　　　　　　　　　　　　　　　　　　　　　　　　　　　　→ 신뢰성

(A) rely 의지[의존]하다　(B) reliable 신뢰할 수 있는　(C) reliably 신뢰할 수 있게　(D) reliability 신뢰성, 신뢰도

해설　**목적어 자리:** 빈칸은 the strength와 함께 '강조하다'라는 의미의 동사 emphasizes의 목적어 역할을 하므로, 빈칸에는 제품의 강점을 나타내는 명사가 들어가야 합니다. 따라서 '신뢰성'이라는 의미의 명사 (D) reliability가 정답입니다.

번역　광고에서 필모어 퍼니처는 제품의 내구력과 신뢰성을 강조한다.

| 11 (C) | 12 (A) | 13 (D) | 14 (B) |

Questions 11-14 refer to the following e-mail.

To: Alexa Kyros

From: Ronald Bergsma

Subject: February Conference

Date: November 15

Attachment: Contract

Alexa:

Because I will be on vacation, / you will be the contact person / for the
제가 휴가 중일 예정이라   당신이 연락 담당자가 될 것입니다   통상 회의를 위한

trade conference / that will be held here at the Teanon Hotel, / February
이곳 티논 호텔에서 열릴   2월 5~10일에

5–10. I want to make sure / that you have the **11.** information beforehand.
확실히 하고 싶습니다   그 전에 당신이 정보를 받아 보시도록

The conference chair / is Pari Kumar. I will send her an e-mail /
회의 의장은   패리 쿠마르 씨입니다   제가 그녀에게 이메일을 보낼 겁니다

↗ 부사적 용법의 to부정사

12. (to introduce) you. The conference is a large one, / requiring the use of
당신을 소개하기 위해   이번 회의는 큰 회의입니다   그랜드 불룸의 이용을 필요로 하는

the Grand Ballroom. Ms. Kumar will give you / the final count of attendees /
쿠마르 씨가 당신에게 보내줄 것입니다   최종 참석자 수를

in early January. After that, / you can **13.** (coordinate) with the catering
1월 초에   그 이후   당신은 연회부서와 조율할 수 있을 겁니다
↘ 조동사 뒤 동사원형

department / regarding the menus and number of meals.
메뉴 및 식사의 수와 관련하여

I am attaching the contract / for you to review. **14.** I suggest / we meet in
계약서를 첨부해 드립니다   검토하실 수 있도록   제안 드립니다   다음 주에 직접

person next week / to go over it together.
만나서   함께 검토하기 위하여

Ron Bergsma

Event Manager

11-14 이메일

수신: 알렉사 카이로스
발신: 로날드 벌즈마
제목: 2월 회의
날짜: 11월 15일
첨부: 계약서

알렉사:

제가 휴가 중일 예정이라, 당신이 이곳 티논 호텔에서 2월 5~10일에 열릴 통상 회의를 위한 연락 담당자가 될 것입니다. 그 전에 정보를 받아 보시도록 하고자 합니다. 회의 의장은 패리 쿠마르 씨입니다. 제가 당신을 소개하기 위해 그녀에게 이메일을 보낼 겁니다. 이번 회의는 그랜드 불룸의 이용을 필요로 하는 큰 회의입니다. 쿠마르 씨가 1월 초에 최종 참석자 수를 당신에게 보내 줄 것입니다. 그 이후, 당신은 메뉴 및 식사의 수와 관련하여 연회부서와 조율할 수 있을 겁니다.

검토하실 수 있도록 계약서를 첨부해 드립니다. 다음 주에 직접 만나 함께 검토할 것을 제안 드립니다.

론 벌즈마
이벤트 매니저

11

(A) payment
(B) issue
(C) information
(D) service

(A) 지불
(B) 주제, 쟁점
(C) 정보
(D) 서비스

> 해설 **어휘 문제:** 빈칸 앞 문장 Because I will be ~ trade conference에서 이메일 수신자 you가 통상 회의를 위한 연락 담당자가 될 것이라고 했습니다. 빈칸을 포함해서 '정보를 받아 보게 하고자 한다'라는 의미가 문맥상 자연스러우므로, (C) information이 정답입니다.

12

(A) to introduce
(B) introduction
(C) will introduce
(D) introductory

> 해설 **부사 역할을 하는 to부정사:** 빈칸 뒤 you는 빈칸의 목적어 역할을 하는 명사입니다. 빈칸을 포함한 구문은 앞에 나오는 문장을 수식하여 '당신을 소개하기 위해, 이메일을 보낸다'라는 의미를 나타내는 것이 문맥상 자연스럽습니다. 따라서 목적어를 취하면서 부사 역할을 하는 to부정사 (A) to introduce가 정답입니다.

13

(A) coordinating
(B) coordinator
(C) coordinates
(D) coordinate

> 해설 **조동사 + 동사원형:** 빈칸 앞에 조동사 can이 있습니다. 조동사 뒤에는 항상 동사원형을 써야 하므로 (D) coordinate이 정답입니다.

14

(A) This was the list of the electronic equipment that Ms. Kumar sent.
(B) I suggest we meet in person next week to go over it together.
(C) The same conference last year had about 350 attendees.
(D) Please be aware that my e-mail address has changed.

(A) 이것은 쿠마르 씨가 보낸 전자 장비 목록이었습니다.
(B) 다음 주에 직접 만나 함께 검토할 것을 제안 드립니다.
(C) 작년의 같은 회의에는 약 350명이 참석했습니다.
(D) 제 이메일 주소가 변경되었음을 알아두십시오.

> 해설 **문장 고르기:** 빈칸 앞에 검토할 계약서를 첨부한다는 내용이 있으므로 계약서 검토와 관련된 내용이 들어가는 것이 문맥상 자연스러우며, 선택지 (B)의 go over it together가 그 계약서를 검토하는 것을 의미하므로 정답은 (B)입니다

명사의 쓰임과 위치 ETS 문제로 훈련하기 STEP 1

교재 p.41

1 (A)	2 (B)	3 (A)	4 (A)	5 (B)	6 (A)

1

Preparations / for the fund-raiser / normally / begin / in February.
준비는   모금 행사를 위한   보통   시작된다   2월에
↳ 문장의 주어로 쓰인 명사

(A) Preparations 준비   (B) Prepare 준비하다

번역 모금 행사를 위한 준비는 보통 2월에 시작된다.

2

Sales of compact cars / have surpassed / industry analysts' predictions.
소형차 판매량이   넘어섰다   산업 분석가들의 예측을
↳ 소유격 analysts'의 수식을 받는 명사

(A) predicted 예상되는   (B) predictions 예측

번역 소형차 판매량이 산업 분석가들의 예측을 넘어섰다.

3

In accordance with their contract, / Keller Automotive Company / charges / rental fees / on an
계약에 따라   켈러 자동차 회사는   부과한다   사용료를   시간당으로
↳ 전치사 In의 목적어 역할을 하는 명사
hourly basis.

(A) accordance 일치, 조화   (B) accordingly 그에 맞춰

번역 계약에 따라 켈러 자동차 회사는 시간당 사용료를 부과한다.

4

To order / replacement parts / for broken machines, / please contact / the manufacturer.
주문하려면   교체 부품을   고장 난 기계를 위한   연락해 주십시오   제조사에
                                          정관사 뒤에 위치하며, 동사 contact의 목적어 역할을 하는 명사 자리
(A) manufacturer 제조사   (B) manufactured 제작된

번역 고장 난 기계를 위한 교체 부품을 주문하려면 제조사에 연락해 주십시오.

5

This / is a reminder / that all employees should submit / telephone service work orders.
이것은   다시 한 번 알려주는 것이다 / 모든 직원이 제출해야 한다는 것을   전화 서비스 작업 주문서를
                                          ↳ 관사 뒤 보어 역할을 하는 명사 자리
(A) remind 상기시키다   (B) reminder 상기시키는 것

번역 모든 직원이 전화 서비스 작업 주문서를 제출해야 한다는 것을 다시 한 번 알려 드립니다.

6

The hotel cost / included / shuttle service / to the airport, / making it an excellent value.
호텔 비용은   포함했다   셔틀 서비스를   공항까지의   그래서 가성비가 뛰어나게 만들었다
                                                            형용사 excellent의 수식을 받는 명사
(A) value 가치   (B) valuable 가치 있는

번역 호텔 비용에는 공항까지의 셔틀 서비스가 포함되어 있어 가성비가 뛰어났다.

7 (A)	8 (A)	9 (B)	10 (C)

7   The Museum of Natural History / will be closed / for six months / for a complete (renovation).
자연사 박물관은   휴관될 것이다   6개월간   전면적인 개조 공사를 위해
                                                         형용사의 수식을 받는 명사 ←

(A) renovation   (B) renovate

(C) renovated   (D) renovates

> **해설** a(n) + 형용사 + 명사: 빈칸 앞에 a와 형용사 complete(전면적인, 완전한)이 있으므로 빈칸에는 명사 (A) renovation(개조 공사)이 들어가야 합니다.
>
> **번역** 자연사 박물관은 전면적인 개조 공사를 위해 6개월간 휴관할 것이다.

8   You / may adjust / the (brightness) of your monitor / so the image on the screen / is suitable / for
당신은   조절할 수 있습니다 모니터의 밝기를   화면의 이미지가 ~하도록   적합하다   보기에
                            → 동사의 목적어

viewing.

(A) brightness 밝기   (B) brighter 더 밝은

(C) brighten 밝아지다   (D) bright 밝은

> **해설** 동사 + 명사: 빈칸은 동사 adjust 뒤에서 목적어 역할을 하는 명사 자리이므로 정답은 명사인 (A) brightness입니다.
>
> **번역** 화면의 이미지를 보기에 적합하도록 모니터의 밝기를 조절할 수 있습니다.

9   Basic (qualifications) / for the editor position / include / a journalism degree / and knowledge of
기본 자격 요건   편집자 자리를 위한   포함한다   언론학 학위   그리고 출판 소프트웨어에
                     → 형용사의 수식을 받는 명사

publishing software.
대한 이해

(A) qualifying   (B) qualifications 자격, 자격 요건

(C) qualifies   (D) qualify 자격을 주다

> **해설** 형용사 + 명사: 빈칸 앞 형용사 Basic의 수식을 받는 명사 자리이므로, 명사 (B) qualifications(자격, 자격 요건)가 정답입니다. 동명사 (A) qualifying은 부사가 수식합니다.
>
> **번역** 편집자 자리를 위한 기본 자격 요건 중에는 언론학 학위와 출판 소프트웨어에 대한 이해가 포함된다.

10   After five years in (operation), / Empress Chemical / plans to expand / by opening a second site.
5년간의 영업 이후에   엠프레스 케미컬은   확장할 계획이다   두 번째 지점을 열어
               → 전치사 in의 목적어 역할을 하는 명사

(A) operate 운용하다, 영업하다   (B) operated 작동되는

(C) operation 영업, 운영   (D) operational 운영상의

> **해설** 전치사 + 명사: 빈칸 앞 전치사 in의 목적어 역할을 하는 명사 자리이므로, 명사 (C) operation(영업, 운영)이 정답입니다.
>
> **번역** 5년간 영업한 후에, 엠프레스 케미컬은 두 번째 지점을 열어 사업을 확장할 계획이다.

1 (A)	2 (B)	3 (A)	4 (A)	5 (B)	6 (A)

1

Retail sales / in apparel / declined / in August / after a significant ⌐increase⌐ / in July.
소매 판매는   의류에서   감소했다   8월에   크게 증가한 후   7월에
↳ 관사 a 뒤에 쓰인 단수 가산 명사

(A) increase   (B) increases

번역 의류의 소매 판매는 7월에 크게 증가한 후 8월에 감소했다.

2

The library / will accept / donations of used ⌐equipment⌐ / by March 31.
그 도서관은   받을 것이다   중고 용품의 기증을   3월 31일까지
↳ 빈칸 앞에 관사가 없으므로 불가산 명사가 쓰임

(A) computer 컴퓨터   (B) equipment 장비, 용품

번역 그 도서관에서는 3월 31일까지 중고 용품의 기증을 받는다.

3

Obtaining ⌐certification⌐ / to be a medical assistant / usually / requires / a high school diploma.
자격을 얻는 것은   의료 보조원이 되는   일반적으로   필요하다   고등학교 졸업장이
↳ 빈칸 앞에 관사가 없으므로 불가산 명사가 쓰임

(A) certification 증명, 증명서 (교부)   (B) certificate 자격증, 증서

번역 의료 보조원이 되는 자격을 얻으려면 일반적으로 고등학교 졸업장 취득이 필요하다.

4

Markon Airway passengers / can claim / lost ⌐baggage⌐ / at the airline counter.
마콘 항공의 승객들은   요청할 수 있다   분실된 짐을   항공사 카운터에서
↳ 빈칸 앞에 관사가 없으므로 불가산 명사가 쓰임

(A) baggage 짐, 수화물   (B) suitcase 여행 가방

번역 마콘 항공의 승객들은 항공사 카운터에서 분실된 짐을 요청할 수 있다.

5

Discount ⌐tickets⌐ / for the jazz concert / are available / in Ms. Klein's office.
할인 표는   재즈 음악회를 위한   구할 수 있다   클라인 씨의 사무실에서
↳ 빈칸 뒤에 복수 동사 are가 왔으므로 복수 명사가 쓰임

(A) ticket   (B) tickets

번역 재즈 음악회 할인 표를 클라인 씨의 사무실에서 구할 수 있다.

6

⌐Competition⌐ / in the automotive industry / is expected / to increase / in the years ahead.
경쟁은   자동차 업계의   예상된다   증가할 것으로   향후 몇 년 간
↳ 빈칸 앞에 관사가 없고 뒤에 단수 동사 is가 쓰였으므로 불가산 명사가 옴

(A) Competition 경쟁   (B) Competitor 경쟁업체

번역 자동차 업계의 경쟁은 향후 몇 년 간 증가할 것으로 예상된다.

| 7 (A) | 8 (D) | 9 (A) | 10 (A) |

7

As stated / in our memo, / equipment / should not be used / for non-work-related (purposes).
언급된 바와 같이 / 메모에서　　　장비는　　　사용될 수 없다　　　업무와 관련이 없는 용도로
→ 복수 가산 명사

(A) purposes
(B) purpose 목적, 용도
(C) purposely 고의로, 일부러
(D) purposeful 목적이 있는

해설　단수 가산 명사와 복수 가산 명사 구분: 빈칸 앞 형용사 non-work-related의 수식을 받는 명사 자리이므로, 명사 (A) purposes와 (B) purpose가 들어갈 수 있습니다. 형용사 non-work-related 앞에 관사 a(n), the가 없으므로, 복수 가산 명사 (A) purposes(목적, 용도)가 정답입니다.

번역　메모에서 언급된 바와 같이, 장비는 업무와 관련이 없는 용도로 사용될 수 없다.

8

Han Airport / is seeking / an experienced air-traffic controller / for long-term (employment).
한 공항은　　　찾고 있다　　　경력직 항공 교통 관제사를　　　장기간 고용으로
→ 불가산 명사

(A) employer 고용주
(B) employed 취업하고 있는
(C) employs 고용하다
(D) employment 고용

해설　가산 명사와 불가산 명사 구분: long-term(장기간의)이라는 형용사 뒤에 올 수 있는 것은 명사이므로 (A) employer와 (D) employment가 정답 후보인데, 빈칸 앞에 a(n), the가 없는 것으로 보아 불가산 명사 (D) employment(고용, 근무)가 정답입니다.

번역　한 공항은 장기간 근무할 경력직 항공 교통 관제사를 찾고 있다.

9

Candidates / must demonstrate / a high (level) of expertise / in international policy.
지원자는　　　보여주어야 한다　　　높은 수준의 전문 지식을　　　국제 정책 분야에서

(A) level
(B) levels
→ 관사 a가 함께 쓰인 단수 가산 명사
(C) leveling
(D) leveled

해설　수량 표현에 맞는 명사 선택: 빈칸 앞에 단수 가산 명사와 함께 쓰이는 부정관사 a가 있으므로, 단수 가산 명사 (A) level(수준)이 정답입니다.

번역　지원자는 국제 정책 분야에서 높은 수준의 전문 지식을 보여주어야 한다.

10

Beth's Bazaar / has received / (compliments) / from customers / on the beautiful displays / in the
베스 바자는　　　받고 있다　　　찬사를　　　고객들로부터　　　아름다운 진열로
store window.
상점 진열창의
→ 복수 가산 명사

(A) compliments
(B) compliment 칭찬, 찬사
(C) complimented
(D) complimentary 칭찬하는

해설　단수 가산 명사와 복수 가산 명사 구분: 빈칸 앞 동사 has received의 목적어 역할을 하는 명사 자리이므로, 명사 (A) compliments와 (B) compliment가 들어갈 수 있습니다. 빈칸 앞에 관사 a(n), the가 없으므로, 복수 가산 명사 (A) compliments(칭찬)가 정답입니다.

번역　베스 바자는 상점 진열창의 아름다운 진열로 고객들로부터 찬사를 받고 있다.

● 명사 앞에 쓰이는 수량 표현 ETS 문제로 훈련하기 STEP 1

1 (B)	2 (B)	3 (A)	4 (A)	5 (A)	6 (B)

1

Ms. Dalton / will face / (many challenges) / in her new position.
달턴 씨는　　직면하게 될 것이다 / 많은 도전을　　　새 직책에서
　　　　　　　　　　　　　　　　　　　　→ many + 복수 가산 명사

(A) challenge　　　　　　　　　　(B) challenges

> **번역** 달턴 씨는 새 직책에서 많은 도전에 직면하게 될 것이다.

2

The new car / will consume / less fuel / while emitting / (fewer pollutants).
신형 자동차는　　소비할 것이다　　더 적은 연료를　배출하는 한편　　더 적은 오염 물질을
　　　　　　　　　　　　　　　　　　　　　　　　　　　→ fewer + 복수 가산 명사

(A) pollutant　　　　　　　　　　(B) pollutants

> **번역** 신형 자동차는 연료를 더 적게 소비하는 한편, 오염 물질을 더 적게 배출할 것이다.

3

Despite some earlier (confusion) / regarding the opening date, / we / will be ready / by October 1.
초기에 일부 혼선이 있었지만　　　　개장일과 관련하여　　　　우리는 / 준비될 것이다　　10월 1일까지
　　　　　　　　→ 한정사 some과 같이 쓰이는 불가산 명사

(A) confusion 혼란　　　　　　　　(B) confuse 혼란시키다

> **번역** 개장일과 관련하여 초기에 일부 혼선이 있었지만, 우리는 10월 1일까지 준비될 것이다.

4

(All employees) / should attend / the safety training meeting.
모든 직원은　　　　　참석해야 한다　　안전 교육 모임에

(A) All　→ All + 복수 가산 명사　　(B) Every

> **번역** 모든 직원은 안전 교육 모임에 참석해야 한다.

5

(Each applicant) / must have / a valid driver's license.
각 지원자는　　　　소지하고 있어야 한다 / 유효한 운전 면허증을
　　　　　→ Each + 단수 가산 명사

(A) applicant　　　　　　　　　　(B) applicants

> **번역** 각 지원자는 유효한 운전 면허증을 소지하고 있어야 한다.

6

Laforn Transit's drivers / have (little influence) / on policies / affecting fare increases.
라폰 트랜짓의 운전기사들은　　영향력이 거의 없다　　방침에　　요금 인상에 영향을 미치는

(A) few　　　　　　　　　　(B) little　→ little + 불가산 명사

> **번역** 라폰 트랜짓의 운전기사들은 요금 인상에 영향을 미치는 방침에 영향력이 거의 없다.

| 7 (C) | 8 (B) | 9 (B) | 10 (B) |

7 The new restaurant / has generated / much (excitement) / because of the reputation of its chef.
새로 생긴 레스토랑은   불러일으켰다   많은 흥미를   셰프의 명성 때문에
→ 불가산 명사

(A) many   (B) few

(C) much   (D) little

해설 **much + 불가산 명사:** 빈칸 뒤의 excitement는 불가산 명사이므로 정답이 될 수 있는 것은 (C) much와 (D) little입니다. 내용을 보면 새로 생긴 레스토랑이 많은 흥미를 불러일으키고 있다고 해야 자연스러우므로, 정답은 (C) much입니다.

번역 새로 생긴 레스토랑은 셰프의 명성 때문에 많은 흥미를 불러일으켰다.

8 (Several) recent tests / provide / proof / that the XK1Ultra motorcycle is quieter / than its
최근 수차례의 시험은   제공한다 증거를 XK1울트라 오토바이가 더 조용하다는 것을   경쟁 제품들보다
→ 뒤에 복수 가산 명사가 옴
competitors.

(A) test   (B) tests

(C) testing   (D) tested

해설 **several + 복수 가산 명사:** 빈칸은 문장의 주어에 해당하는 명사 자리로 형용사인 several과 recent의 수식을 받고 있습니다. several 다음에는 복수 가산 명사가 와야 하므로 정답은 (B) tests입니다.

번역 최근 수차례의 시험에서는 XK1울트라 오토바이가 경쟁 제품들보다 더 조용하다는 증거를 제공한다.

9 In order to ensure / a timely response, / please include / your account number / on all
확실히 하기 위해   시기 적절한 대응을   넣어주세요   귀하의 계정 번호를   모든 서신에
(correspondence).
→ 한정사 all의 수식을 받는 불가산 명사

(A) are corresponding   (B) correspondence 서신

(C) corresponds   (D) correspond 서신을 주고 받다

해설 **all + 불가산 명사:** 빈칸 앞에 한정사 all이 있으므로 빈칸에는 명사가 들어가야 합니다. all 뒤에는 복수 가산 명사, 불가산 명사 모두 올 수 있습니다. 따라서 정답은 불가산 명사인 (B) correspondence(서신)입니다.

번역 확실히 시기 적절하게 대응할 수 있도록 하기 위해, 모든 서신에 귀하의 계정 번호를 넣어주세요.

10 Any (employee) / interested in participating / in the seminar / should contact / Dan Bezel.
직원은 누구나   참가하는 것에 관심이 있는   세미나에   연락하면 된다   댄 베젤에게
→ 단수 가산 명사

(A) Both   (B) Any

(C) Few   (D) All

해설 **any(어떤) + 단수 가산 명사:** 빈칸 뒤에 단수 가산 명사 employee가 있으므로, 단수 가산 명사와 함께 쓰일 수 있는 한정사 (B) Any(어떤)가 정답입니다. Any가 '약간'이라는 의미로 쓰일 경우에는 복수 가산 명사 또는 불가산 명사와 함께 쓰이지만, any가 '어떤'이라는 의미로 쓰일 경우에는 단수 가산 명사, 복수 가산 명사, 불가산 명사 모두와 함께 쓰일 수 있습니다. (A) Both, (C) Few, (D) All 뒤에는 복수 가산 명사가 나와야 하므로, 오답입니다

번역 세미나 참가에 관심이 있는 직원은 누구나 댄 베젤에게 연락하면 된다.

1 (A)	**2** (A)	**3** (B)	**4** (B)

1

The ability / to gain / the (confidence) of your clients / is essential / in a sales job.
능력은   얻는   고객들의 신뢰를   필수적이다   영업직에서
                                 → 신뢰

(A) confidence 신뢰, 확신   (B) liability 책임, 부담

번역 고객들의 신뢰를 얻는 능력은 영업직에서 필수적이다.

2

The cafeteria / in the Rowles Building / serves / a variety of sandwiches.
구내식당은   라울즈 건물의   제공한다   다양한 종류의 샌드위치를

(A) variety 다양성   (B) type 종류   → 다양한

번역 라울즈 건물의 구내식당에서는 다양한 종류의 샌드위치를 제공한다.

3

The (itinerary) for Mr. Ogawa's trip / includes / stops / in London and Paris.
오가와 씨의 여행 일정은   포함한다   체류를   런던과 파리에서의
               → 여행 일정

(A) position 자리, 위치   (B) itinerary 여행 일정

번역 오가와 씨의 여행 일정 중에는 런던과 파리에서의 체류가 포함되어 있다.

4

The (audience) / should turn off / mobile phones / for the duration / of the concert.
청중들은   꺼야 한다   휴대 전화를   기간 동안   연주회의
     → 청중, 관중

(A) residence 거주, 주택   (B) audience 청중, 관중

번역 청중들은 연주회 내내 휴대 전화를 꺼야 한다.

5 (A)	6 (B)	7 (C)	8 (B)

5

Toynik Stores' profits / have decreased recently, / so the chain / is ⟨under pressure⟩ / to cut costs.
토이닉 스토어즈의 수익이   최근 감소했다   그래서 그 체인이   압박을 받고 있다   비용 삭감의
                                                        ↳ 압박을 받는

(A) pressure 압박, 압력   (B) burden 부담, 짐

(C) weight 무게   (D) load 짐

해설 under pressure 압박을 받는: 빈칸 앞 전치사 under와 어울려 쓰이면서 문맥상 의미가 적절한 명사를 선택해야 합니다. 따라서 (A) pressure가 정답입니다.

번역 토이닉 스토어즈의 수익이 최근 감소해서 그 체인은 비용 삭감의 압박을 받고 있다.

6

Your résumé / shows / excellent ⟨qualifications⟩, / and we / would like to arrange / a time /
귀하의 이력서가   보여준다   훌륭한 자격 요건을   그래서 우리는   정하고 싶다   시간을
                                              ↳ 자격 요건

for an interview.
면접을 위한

(A) recognition 인식; 인정   (B) qualifications 자격 (요건), 자질

(C) scheduling 일정 관리   (D) invitation 초대, 초청

해설 qualifications 자격 요건: 이력서에서 보여줄 수 있는 내용은 지원자의 자격 요건입니다. 따라서 문맥상 (B) qualifications가 정답입니다.

번역 귀하가 이력서상 훌륭한 자격 요건을 갖추고 있어서, 우리는 면접 시간을 정하고 싶습니다.

7

Henry Allen / will deliver a presentation / on his ⟨invention⟩ / of a new manufacturing process.
헨리 앨런은   발표할 것이다   자신의 개발에 관해   새로운 제작 공정의
                                              ↳ 발명, 개발

(A) sequence 연속, 순서   (B) decision 결정

(C) invention 개발, 발명(품)   (D) situation 상황

해설 invention 발명, 개발: 빈칸은 뒤의 전치사구 of a new manufacturing process의 수식을 받는 자리로, '새로운 제작 공정 개발에 관한 발표'라는 의미가 자연스러우므로, (C) invention이 정답입니다.

번역 헨리 앨런은 자신의 새로운 제작 공정 개발에 관해 발표할 것이다.

8

The community housing authority / gives / limited ⟨financial assistance⟩ / to first-time home buyers.
지역 주택 당국은   해준다   제한적인 재정 지원을   생애 최초 주택 구매자에게
                                              ↳ 재정 지원

(A) division 분할   (B) assistance 도움, 지원

(C) statement 성명(서)   (D) association 협회, 연계

해설 financial assistance 재정 지원: 동사 gives의 목적어 역할을 하는 명사 자리로, 빈칸 앞의 형용사 financial의 수식을 받습니다. 문맥상 '재정 지원을 해주다'라는 의미가 자연스러우므로, (B) assistance가 정답입니다.

번역 지역 주택 당국에서는 생애 최초 주택 구매자에게 제한적인 재정 지원을 해준다.

1 (D)	2 (B)	3 (B)	4 (D)	5 (A)

1

The (extension) / of the deadline / allowed / the Tobin Group / to finish / its proposal / on time.
연장이   마감일의   가능하게 했다 / 토빈 그룹이   마치는 것을   제안서를   제시간에
   → 주어 역할을 하는 명사

(A) extended 길어진   (B) extend 연장하다   (C) extendable 늘일 수 있는   (D) extension 연장

해설 the + 명사: 빈칸 앞의 정관사 The와 함께 동사 allowed의 주어 역할을 하므로, 빈칸에는 명사가 들어가야 합니다. 따라서 명사 (D) extension(연장)이 정답입니다.

번역 마감일 연장으로 토빈 그룹은 제안서를 제시간에 마칠 수 있었다.

2

Valgor Corporation / has adopted / innovative marketing (approaches) / for its latest products.
발고어사는   채택했다   혁신적인 마케팅 접근 방식을   자사의 최신 제품을 위해
                           → 앞에 관사가 없으므로 복수 가산 명사가 쓰임

(A) approach   (B) approaches   (C) approached   (D) approaching

해설 단수 가산 명사와 복수 가산 명사 구분: 빈칸 앞의 명사 marketing과 짝을 이루어 동사 has adopted의 목적어 역할을 하는 명사 자리입니다. 형용사 innovative 앞에 a(n), the 등이 없으므로, 단수 가산 명사는 정답이 될 수 없습니다. 복수 가산 명사 (B) approaches가 정답입니다.

번역 발고어사는 자사의 최신 제품을 위해 혁신적인 마케팅 접근 방식을 채택했다.

3

Visitors / to Farnhem Garden / will be delighted / to discover / an incredible (variety) / of annual
방문자들은   파른햄 가든의   즐거워할 것이다   발견하고   굉장히 다양한   일년생
                           형용사 수식을 받는 명사 (a variety of 다양한)

flowering plants.
꽃식물들을

(A) varied   (B) variety   (C) varies   (D) vary

해설 a(n) + 형용사 + 명사: 빈칸은 부정관사 an과 형용사 incredible 뒤에 나오는 명사 자리이므로, (B) variety가 정답입니다.

번역 파른햄 가든 방문자들은 굉장히 다양한 일년생 꽃식물들을 발견하고 즐거워할 것이다.

4

Given the (durability) of certain fashion trends, / Ms. Zheng / believes / we will be able to sell some
특정 패션 트렌드의 지속성을 감안할 때   쳉 씨는   믿는다   우리가 과잉재고의 일부를
     → Given의 목적어 역할을 하는 명사

of our overstock / next summer.
팔 수 있을 것임을   내년 여름에

(A) durable 튼튼한   (B) durably 튼튼하게   (C) more durable 더 튼튼한   (D) durability 지속성, 내구성

해설 the + 명사: 빈칸 앞의 정관사 the와 함께 쓰여 Given의 목적어 역할을 하므로, 빈칸에는 명사가 들어가야 합니다. 따라서 (D) durability(지속성, 내구성)이 정답입니다.

번역 특정 패션 트렌드의 지속성을 감안할 때, 쳉 씨는 우리가 내년 여름에 과잉재고의 일부를 팔 수 있을 것이라고 믿는다.

5

(Every) informational packet / will include / the conference schedule / as well as local hotel
모든 안내 자료집은   포함할 것이다   회의 일정을   지역 호텔 정보는 물론
     → 뒤에 단수 명사만 옴

information.

(A) Every   (B) Few   (C) Whole   (D) Many

해설 every + 단수 가산 명사: 빈칸 뒤에 단수 가산 명사 packet이 있으므로, 단수 가산 명사와 함께 쓰이는 (A) Every가 정답입니다. (B) Few와 (D) Many는 복수 가산 명사와 함께 쓰이므로 오답입니다. 형용사 (C) Whole은 앞에 관사가 있어야 단수 가산 명사를 수식할 수 있으며, 주로 〈the + whole + 명사〉의 형태로 쓰입니다.

번역 모든 안내 자료집에는 지역 호텔 정보는 물론 회의 일정이 포함될 것이다.

ETS 실전 테스트

교재 p.48

6 (C)	7 (A)	8 (B)	9 (A)	10 (A)

6

According to Ms. Lee's (calculations), / 150 square meters of hardwood flooring / are needed /
리 씨의 추산에 따르면   150제곱미터의 경재 마룻바닥재가   필요하다

to complete the project.   → 소유격 뒤의 명사
그 프로젝트를 완성하는 데

(A) calculate   (B) calculated   (C) calculations   (D) calculates

해설 **소유격 + 명사:** 빈칸 앞에 소유격 Ms. Lee's가 있으므로, 명사 (C) calculations(추산, 계산)가 정답입니다. Mr Lee's calculations는
앞의 전치사구 According to의 목적어 역할을 합니다.

번역 리 씨의 추산에 따르면, 그 프로젝트를 완성하는 데 150제곱미터의 경재 마룻바닥재가 필요하다.

7

If you are interested / in the (position) of Chief Managing Editor, / submit / your cover letter and
만약 당신이 관심이 있다면   편집장 직책에   제출하세요   자기소개서와 이력서를

résumé / no later than Friday.   → 전치사 in의 목적어 역할을 하는 명사
            늦어도 금요일까지는

(A) position   (B) positioning   (C) positioned   (D) positions

해설 **the + 명사:** 빈칸 앞의 정관사 the와 함께 전치사 in의 목적어 역할을 하므로, 빈칸에는 명사가 들어가야 합니다. 따라서 명사 (A)
position(직책)이 정답입니다. 동명사 (B) positioning도 전치사의 목적어 역할을 할 수 있지만 '위치 선정에'라는 의미로 문맥상
어울리지 않습니다.

번역 편집장 직책에 관심이 있으시면, 늦어도 금요일까지는 자기소개서와 이력서를 제출하세요.

8

Contact / the IT department / if any software (complications) arise / during the online meeting.
문의하십시오   IT 부서에   소프트웨어 문제가 발생하면   온라인 회의 중에
                                                    → if절의 주어 역할을 하는 명사

(A) complicated 복잡한   (B) complications 문제들   (C) complicate 복잡하게 만들다   (D) complicates

해설 **any + 셀 수 있는 복수 명사:** any 뒤에는 셀 수 있는 복수 명사나 셀 수 없는 명사가 올 수 있습니다. complication은 '문제'라는
의미로 셀 수 있는 명사이므로, (B) complications가 정답입니다.

번역 온라인 회의 중에 소프트웨어 문제가 발생할 경우 IT 부서에 문의하십시오.

9

Geraldo Guiterez / has just been appointed / to a prestigious position in (management) / at
제랄도 기테레스는   얼마 전에 임명되었다   고위 경영직에
                                                            불가산 명사 ←
Cardero Advertising.
카데로 광고사에서

(A) management 관리, 경영(진)   (B) manager 관리자   (C) managing 관리하기   (D) manages 관리하다, 간신히 해내다

해설 **가산 명사와 불가산 명사 구분:** 빈칸 앞 전치사 in의 목적어 역할을 하는 명사 자리이므로, 명사 (A) management와 (B) manager가
들어갈 수 있습니다. 빈칸 앞에 a(n), the 등이 없으므로, 불가산 명사 (A) management가 정답입니다. 동명사 (C) managing도
전치사의 목적어 역할을 할 수 있지만, '관리함에 있어서'라는 의미로 문맥상 어울리지 않습니다.

번역 제랄도 기테레스는 얼마 전에 카데로 광고사에서 고위 경영직에 임명되었다.

10

Ms. Gleason / does not have / the (authority) / to hire new employees, / but her recommendations /
글리슨 씨는   갖고 있지 않다   권한을   신입사원을 채용할   그러나 그녀의 추천은
                                    └→ 정관사 뒤에 쓰인 명사

are highly valued.
매우 중요하다

(A) authority 권한   (B) authorize 권한을 부여하다   (C) authored 저술된   (D) author 작가

해설 비슷한 명사의 의미 구별: 빈칸 앞의 정관사 the와 함께 동사 have의 목적어 역할을 하므로, 빈칸에는 명사가 들어가야 합니다. '채용할
권한'이라는 내용이 문맥상 적절하므로, '권한'이라는 뜻의 명사 (A)가 정답입니다.

번역 글리슨 씨는 신입사원을 채용할 권한이 없지만, 그녀의 추천은 매우 중시된다.

ETS 실전 테스트

11 (C)	**12** (A)	**13** (D)	**14** (B)

Questions 11-14 refer to the following memo.

To: First Shift Employees

From: Santosh Gulati

Date: April 13

Subject: Revised shift times

Next month, / West Side Grocery will begin / selling bread and pastries
다음 달   웨스트 사이드 식료품점은 시작할 것입니다   레이포드 베이커리의 빵과 페이스트리를

from Rayford's Bakery. **11.** Their products sell very well / in this region.
판매하기를   그들의 제품은 매우 잘 팔립니다   이 지역에서

Our customers have frequently requested / that we carry these items.
우리 고객들은 자주 요청해 왔습니다   이 상품들을 취급해 달라고

The only time slot / they have available in their daily delivery route /
유일한 시간대는   그들이 매일 배송 경로에서 할애할 수 있는

is 6:00 A.M. **12.** Accordingly, / starting May 1, / the first shift will begin at
오전 6시입니다   따라서   5월 1일부터   첫 근무조는 오전 5시 30분에 근무를

5:30 A.M. / instead of 5:45 A.M. Employees must be ready / to greet the
시작합니다   오전 5시 45분이 아니라 직원들은 준비가 되어 있어야 합니다   기사를 맞이하고

driver and accept the delivery. This will leave enough time / to **13.** display
배송품을 받을   이렇게 하면 시간이 충분할 겁니다   제빵 제품들을

the baked goods and open the store / at the usual time.
진열하고 매장을 열 수 있는   평소 시간대로

Thank you for your **14.** (cooperation).
협조해 주셔서 감사합니다
                      └→ 소유격 your 뒤의 명사

Santosh Gulati, Manager

11-14 메모

수신: 첫 근무조 직원
발신: 산토시 굴라티
날짜: 4월 13일
제목: 근무 시간 변경

다음 달, 웨스트 사이드 식료품점은 레이포드 베이커리의 빵과 페이스트리를 판매하기 시작할 것입니다. 그들의 제품은 이 지역에서 매우 잘 팔립니다. 우리 고객들은 이 상품을 취급해 달라고 자주 요청해 왔습니다.

그들이 매일 배송 경로에서 할애할 수 있는 유일한 시간대는 오전 6시입니다. 따라서 5월 1일부터 첫 근무조는 오전 5시 45분이 아니라 오전 5시 30분부터 시작될 것입니다. 직원들은 기사를 맞이하고 배송품을 받을 준비가 되어 있어야 합니다. 이렇게 하면 제빵 제품들을 진열하고 평소 시간대로 매장을 열 수 있는 시간이 충분할 것입니다.

협조해 주셔서 감사합니다.

산토시 굴라티 관리자

11 (A) Please contact your manager immediately.

(B) They are meeting the targets they have set.

(C) Their products sell very well in this region.

(D) It is important to arrive on time.

(A) 관리자에게 즉시 연락하십시오.

(B) 그들은 설정한 목표를 달성하고 있습니다.

(C) 그들의 제품은 이 지역에서 매우 잘 팔립니다.

(D) 제시간에 도착하는 것이 중요합니다.

해설 문장 고르기: 빈칸 앞에는 레이포드 베이커리의 빵과 페이스트리 판매 개시를, 빈칸 뒤에는 이 상품을 취급해 달라는 고객의 요청이 언급되었습니다. 따라서 빈칸에도 이 빵과 페이스트리와 관련된 내용이 들어가는 것이 문맥상 자연스러우며, 선택지 (C)의 Their products가 판매 개시를 하는 빵과 페이스트리를 의미하므로 정답은 (C)입니다.

12 (A) Accordingly

(B) Likewise

(C) As usual

(D) Since then

(A) 따라서

(B) 마찬가지로

(C) 평상시와 같이

(D) 그 이후로

해설 어휘 문제: 빈칸 앞 문장 The only time ~ is 6:00 A.M.에서 배송 시간을 언급했습니다. 빈칸 뒤 starting May 1, ~ instead of 5:45 A.M.에서 근무 시간의 변경을 언급했으므로, 앞과 뒤 내용의 인과관계를 나타내는 접속부사 (A) Accordingly(따라서, 그런 이유로)가 정답입니다.

13 (A) test

(B) make

(C) cool

(D) display

(A) 시험하다

(B) 만들다

(C) 식히다

(D) 진열하다

해설 어휘 문제: 빈칸 앞 문장 Employees must be ready to greet the driver and accept the delivery.에서 배송품을 받을 준비를 언급했습니다. 빈칸을 포함하여 '제빵 제품들(배송품)을 진열할 충분한 시간'이라는 의미가 문맥상 자연스러우므로, (D) display가 정답입니다.

14 (A) cooperative

(B) cooperation

(C) cooperated

(D) cooperate

해설 명사 자리 (전치사의 목적어): 빈칸 앞에 소유격 your가 있으므로, 명사 (B) cooperation이 정답입니다. your cooperation은 앞의 전치사 for의 목적어 역할을 합니다.

PART 5 | Unit 03 대명사

● 인칭대명사 ETS 문제로 훈련하기 STEP 1

교재 p.53

1 (A)	**2** (B)	**3** (B)	**4** (A)	**5** (B)	**6** (B)

1

Mr. Martinez / will be available / to sign / copies of (his) new book.
마르티네즈 씨는   시간이 있을 것이다   사인할   자신의 새 책들에
⤷ 소유격 + 명사

(A) his   (B) he

번역 마르티네즈 씨는 자신의 새 책들에 사인할 시간이 있을 것이다.

2

Mr. Randall / asked / us / to fix / the broken fence / (by ourselves).
랜달 씨는   요청했다   우리에게 / 수리하라고 / 망가진 울타리를   우리 힘으로
⤷ by + 재귀대명사

(A) our own   (B) ourselves

번역 랜달 씨는 망가진 울타리를 (도움을 받지 않고) 우리 힘으로 수리하라고 요청했다.

3

New hires / must fill out / all employee paperwork / by the end of (their) first week.
신입사원들은   작성해야 한다   입사 서류를 전부   첫 주 안에
소유격 ←

(A) them   (B) their

번역 신입사원들은 근무 첫 주 안에 입사 서류를 전부 작성해야 한다.

4

Ms. Williams / has given / (us) / a detailed construction schedule.
윌리엄스 씨는   주었다   우리에게 / 상세한 공사 일정을
⤷ 목적격

(A) us   (B) our

번역 윌리엄스 씨는 우리에게 상세한 공사 일정을 주었다.

5

Employees / should verify / the calculations / (themselves).
직원들은   확인해야 한다   계산을   직접
⤷ 재귀대명사

(A) their   (B) themselves

번역 직원들은 계산을 직접 확인해야 한다.

6

Mr. Erikson / has submitted / his sales report, / but Ms. Wyman / has not yet submitted / (hers).
에릭슨 씨는   제출했다   판매 보고서를   그러나 와이먼 씨는   아직 제출하지 않았다   그녀의 것을
소유대명사 ←

(A) her   (B) hers

번역 에릭슨 씨는 판매 보고서를 제출했지만 와이먼 씨는 아직 자신의 보고서를 제출하지 않았다.

| 7 (D) | 8 (C) | 9 (C) | 10 (C) |

7

Ms. Kim / will oversee / operations, / and all group leaders / will report / back to (her).
김 씨가   감독할 것이다   작업을   그리고 모든 그룹 리더들이   보고할 것이다   그녀에게
↳ 목적격

(A) she   (B) herself
(C) hers   (D) her

[해설] 인칭대명사의 격 선택: 빈칸 앞 전치사 to의 목적어 역할을 하는 자리로, 앞에 있는 주어 Ms. Kim을 대신합니다. 따라서 목적격 인칭대명사 (D) her가 정답입니다. 재귀대명사 (B) herself는 절 내의 주어인 all group leaders와 일치하지 않으므로 오답입니다.

[번역] 김 씨가 작업을 감독할 것이고, 모든 그룹 리더들이 그녀에게 보고할 것이다.

8

All Dokgo Design employees / should update / (their) timesheets / daily.
독고 디자인사 전 직원들은   갱신해야 합니다   근무시간 기록표를   매일
↳ 소유격

(A) theirs   (B) them
(C) their   (D) they

[해설] 인칭대명사의 격 선택: 빈칸 뒤에 명사 timesheets가 있으므로, 명사를 한정하는 소유격 인칭대명사 (C) their가 정답입니다.

[번역] 독고 디자인사 전 직원들은 근무시간 기록표를 매일 갱신해야 합니다.

9

As an account manager, / (you) / need to ensure / that Ms. Han receives your budget reports.
고객 관리자로서   당신은   반드시 ~해야 합니다   한 씨가 당신의 예산안을 받도록
주격 ←

(A) yours   (B) your
(C) you   (D) yourself

[해설] 인칭대명사의 격 선택: 빈칸은 동사 need의 주어 역할을 하는 자리이므로, 주격 인칭대명사 (C) you가 정답입니다.

[번역] 고객 관리자로서, 당신이 작성한 예산안을 한 씨가 반드시 받도록 해야 합니다.

10

Mr. Roberts / took / Ms. Taylor's portfolio / because he mistakenly thought it was (his).
로버츠 씨는   가져갔다   테일러 씨의 포트폴리오를   실수로 그것이 자신의 것이라고 생각했기 때문에
소유대명사 ←

(A) him   (B) himself
(C) his   (D) he

[해설] 인칭대명사의 격 선택: 빈칸 앞 be동사 was의 보어 역할을 하는 자리로, 사물 주어 it과 동격 관계를 이룹니다. 문맥상 '그의 것(Mr. Roberts' portfolio)'이라는 의미가 자연스러우므로, 소유대명사 (C) his가 정답입니다.

[번역] 로버츠 씨는 테일러 씨의 포트폴리오를 자신의 것으로 착각해서 가져갔다.

1 (A)	2 (B)	3 (B)	4 (B)	5 (A)	6 (B)

1

(This mechanic) / has worked / at Mr. Kim's Auto Shop / for years.
이 정비사는 　　　　일해 왔다　　김 씨의 자동차 정비소에서　　수년간
→ This + 단수 명사
(A) This　　　　　　　　　(B) These

번역　이 정비사는 김 씨의 자동차 정비소에서 수년간 일해 왔다.

2

FQX Tech's customer service / is better / than (that) / of Applebaum Tech.
FQX 테크의 고객 서비스는　　더 낫다　　고객 서비스보다 / 애플바움 테크의
(A) this　　　　　　　　　(B) that
→ = customer service

번역　FQX 테크의 고객 서비스는 애플바움 테크의 고객 서비스보다 낫다.

3

Although Mia Cheung is new to the sales team, / her skillful presentations / seemed like
미아 정은 영업팀의 신입 사원이지만　　　그녀의 능숙한 프레젠테이션은
(those) of an experienced salesperson.
경험이 풍부한 영업사원의 프레젠테이션처럼 보였다
→ = presentations
(A) these　　　　　　　　(B) those

번역　미아 정은 영업팀 신입사원이지만 그녀의 능숙한 프레젠테이션은 경험이 풍부한 영업사원의 프레젠테이션처럼 보였다.

4

Only (those) / with valid photo identification / may enter / the building.
~한 사람들만　　사진이 부착된 유효 신분증을 가진　　들어갈 수 있다　　건물 안으로
→ '~한 사람들'이라는 뜻의 지시대명사
(A) this　　　　　　　　　(B) those

번역　사진이 부착된 유효 신분증을 가진 사람들만 건물 안으로 들어갈 수 있다.

5

(Those employees) / affected / by the plan / should watch / the online presentation.
직원들은　　영향을 받는　계획안에　지켜봐야 한다　온라인 발표를
→ Those + 복수 명사
(A) Those　　　　　　　　(B) Which

번역　그 계획안에 영향을 받는 직원들은 온라인 발표를 지켜봐야 한다.

6

(Those) / who are planning / to move to a new house / need to consider / hidden costs / such as
~한 사람들은 / 계획하는　　새 집으로 이사를　　고려해야 한다　보이지 않는 비용을　보험과 같은
→ 관계사절 who ~ to a new house의 수식을 받는 지시대명사
insurance.
(A) They　　　　　　　　(B) Those

번역　새 집으로 이사를 계획하는 사람들은 보험과 같은 보이지 않는 비용을 고려해야 한다.

| 7 (B) | 8 (D) | 9 (C) | 10 (A) |

7

Since Ms. Rahman has withdrawn her application, / (these) analysts / will be interviewed /
라만 씨가 지원을 철회했기 때문에　　　　　　　이 애널리스트들이　　　　면접을 치를 것이다
　　　　　　　　　　　　　　　　　　　　　　　　　　→ 복수 명사를 수식하는 지시형용사

for the position.
그 자리를 놓고

(A) they　　　　　　　　　　　(B) these
(C) this　　　　　　　　　　　 (D) that

해설　these + 복수 명사: 빈칸은 명사 앞에 있으므로 지시형용사가 들어갈 자리입니다. 지시형용사로 쓰이는 (B) these, (C) this, (D) that 중에서 복수 명사인 analysts 앞에 올 수 있는 것은 (B) these입니다.

번역　라만 씨가 지원을 철회했기 때문에 이 애널리스트들이 그 자리를 놓고 면접을 치를 것이다.

8

The screen / of the latest computer / is 15 percent larger / than (that) / of the previous model.
화면은　　　최신 컴퓨터의　　　　　15퍼센트 더 크다　　　화면보다　　 이전 모델의
　　　　　　　　　　　　　　　　　　　　　　　　　　　　　　　→ = the screen

(A) which　　　　　　　　　　　(B) those
(C) whose　　　　　　　　　　　(D) that

해설　지시대명사 선택: 비교 대상이 되는 명사의 반복을 피하기 위해서 지시대명사를 사용하는데, 단수형은 that, 복수형은 those를 씁니다. 빈칸에 들어갈 지시대명사가 받는 것이 단수형인 The screen이므로 정답은 (D) that입니다.

번역　최신 컴퓨터의 화면은 이전 모델의 화면보다 15퍼센트 더 크다.

9

(Those) / who have not received the form / should report / to the registration desk.
~한 사람들은 / 양식을 받지 못한　　　　　　　알려야 합니다　　　접수 창구에
　　→ '~한 사람들'이라는 뜻의 지시대명사

(A) These　　　　　　　　　　　(B) This
(C) Those　　　　　　　　　　　(D) That

해설　지시대명사 선택: 빈칸은 주격 관계대명사 who가 이끄는 절(who ~ the form)의 수식을 받는 자리로, '양식을 받지 못한 사람들'이라는 의미를 나타냅니다. 따라서 '사람들'이라는 의미를 나타내는 지시대명사 (C) Those가 정답입니다.

번역　양식을 받지 못한 사람들은 접수 창구에 알려아 합니다.

10

This year's revenue figures / are remarkably similar / to (those) / of the preceding four years.
올해 수익은　　　　　　　　놀라울 만큼 비슷하다　　　수익과　　 지난 4년 간의
　　　　　　　　　　　　　　　　　　　　　　　　　→ = revenue figures

(A) those　　　　　　　　　　　(B) that
(C) them　　　　　　　　　　　 (D) this

해설　지시대명사 선택: 빈칸은 앞에 나온 revenue figures라는 복수 명사를 대신하여 사용된 지시대명사 자리로, (A) those가 정답입니다.

번역　올해 수익은 지난 4년 간의 수익과 놀라울 만큼 비슷하다.

1 (A)	2 (B)	3 (A)	4 (A)	5 (A)	6 (B)

1

Irena Laboratory / decided / to hire / (both of the technical analysts).
이리나 연구소는　　　결정했다　고용하기로　그 기술 분석가 둘 다를
　　　　　　　　　　　　　　　　　　　　　　　↘ both of the + 가산 명사 복수

(A) both　　　　　　　　　　　(B) much

> **번역**　이리나 연구소는 그 기술 분석가 둘 다를 고용하기로 결정했다.

2

(Several of the passengers) / on flight 246 / missed / connecting flights / in Dublin.
승객 중 일부가　　　　　　246 항공편의　　놓쳤다　연결 항공편을　　더블린에서
　　↘ Several of the + 가산 명사 복수

(A) Everybody　　　　　　　　(B) Several

> **번역**　246 항공편의 승객 중 일부가 더블린에서 연결 항공편을 놓쳤다.

3

(Some of our employees) / in guest services / will arrange / the meeting rooms / for the seminar.
우리 직원 몇 명이　　　　　고객 서비스 담당　준비할 것이다　회의실을　　　세미나를 위해
　　↘ Some of + 가산 명사 복수

(A) Some　　　　　　　　　　(B) Much

> **번역**　우리 고객 서비스 담당 직원 몇 명이 세미나를 위해 회의실을 준비할 것이다.

4

(Most of the new employees) / were able to attend the orientation.
신입 직원들 대부분이　　　　오리엔테이션에 참석할 수 있었다
　　↘ Most of the + 가산 명사 복수

(A) Most　　　　　　　　　　(B) Other

> **번역**　신입 직원들 대부분이 오리엔테이션에 참석할 수 있었다.

5

Of the three parking garage plans, / two / are unacceptable, / while (the other) / is possible.
세 개의 주차장 설계도 중에서　　두 개는 / 받아들일 수 없다　반면 나머지 하나는　가능하다
　　　　　　　　　　　　　　　　　　　　(특정 범위의) '나머지 하나'의 의미 ↙

(A) the other　　　　　　　　(B) other

> **번역**　세 개의 주차장 설계도 중에서 두 개는 받아들일 수 없고 나머지 하나는 가능하다.

6

(One of the musicians) / in the group / attended / Japler School of the Arts.
뮤지션 중 한 명이　　　　그룹의　　다녔다　제이플러 예술 학교에
　　↘ One of the + 가산 명사 복수

(A) The one　　　　　　　　(B) One

> **번역**　그룹의 뮤지션 중 한 명이 제이플러 예술 학교에 다녔다.

7 (D)	**8** (C)	**9** (A)	**10** (D)

7

Customers / can visit / the Web site / to find / reviews of some of Yantar Manufacturing
고객은　　　방문할 수 있다 / 웹사이트를　　찾기 위해　Yantar Manufacturing 회사의 가장 인기있는 몇몇 제품에 대한

Company's most popular products.
몇몇 후기를　　　　　↳ some of + 복수 명사

(A) so　　　　　　　　　　　(B) such
(C) ones　　　　　　　　　　(D) some

해설　알맞은 부정대명사 선택: 빈칸은 〈부정대명사 + of + 가산 명사 복수〉 구조에서 부정대명사가 들어갈 자리임을 알 수 있습니다. 빈칸 뒤 of Yantar ~ popular products와 함께 '몇몇 제품'이라는 의미가 가장 적절하므로 정답은 (D) some(몇몇)입니다.

번역　고객은 Yantar Manufacturing 회사의 가장 인기있는 몇몇 제품에 대한 후기를 찾기 위해 웹사이트를 방문할 수 있다.

8

Cency Apparel / has / one of the most loyal customer bases / in the fashion industry.
센시 의류는　　　가지고 있다 / 가장 충실한 고객층 중 하나를　　　　패션 업계에서
　　　　　　　　　　　　↳ one of the + 가산 명사 복수

(A) instead　　　　　　　　(B) still
(C) one　　　　　　　　　　(D) those

해설　알맞은 부정대명사 선택: 빈칸 앞 동사 has의 목적어 역할을 하는 자리로, 빈칸 뒤 전치사구 of the most loyal customer bases의 수식을 받습니다. 문맥상 '가장 충실한 고객층 중 하나'라는 의미가 자연스러우므로, 부정대명사 (C) one이 정답입니다.

번역　센시 의류는 패션 업계에서 가장 충실한 고객층 중 하나를 가지고 있다.

9

As they trained together, / the athletes / challenged / one another, / and the team / became
함께 훈련하면서　　　　선수들은　　도전했다　서로에게　　　그래서 그 팀은　　더 강하게 되었다

stronger / overall.
　　　전반적으로　　　　　　　↳ '서로'의 의미

(A) one another　　　　　　(B) each
(C) its own　　　　　　　　(D) other

해설　알맞은 부정대명사 선택: 빈칸은 동사 challenged의 목적어 역할을 하는 명사 자리로, 문맥상 '서로에게 도전했다'라는 의미가 자연스러우므로, 대명사 (A) one another(서로)가 정답입니다.

번역　함께 훈련하면서 선수들은 서로에게 도전했고, 그래서 팀은 전반적으로 더 강해졌다.

10

Although many tourists plan a day / at the local history museum, / some / simply want / to go
많은 관광객들이 하루를 보낼 것을 계획하지만　　그 지역의 역사 박물관에서　　몇몇은　　그저 원한다

shopping.
쇼핑을 가는 것을　　　　　　　　　　↳ '몇몇'의 의미

(A) another　　　　　　　　(B) anyone
(C) other　　　　　　　　　(D) some

해설　알맞은 부정대명사 선택: 빈칸 뒤 동사 want의 주어 역할을 하는 자리입니다. 문맥상 '몇몇은 쇼핑을 가고 싶어한다'라는 의미가 자연스러우므로, 부정대명사 (D) some이 정답입니다. (A) another와 (B) anyone은 단수 동사와 함께 사용됩니다.

번역　많은 관광객들이 그 지역의 역사 박물관에서 하루를 보낼 것을 계획하지만 몇몇은 그저 쇼핑을 가고 싶어한다.

1 (A)	2 (B)	3 (A)	4 (B)

1

Big Fields, Ltd., / is committed / to the (conservation / of natural resources).
빅 필즈사는 　　전념한다 　　보존에 　　천연자원의
　　　　　　　　　　　　　　　　　→ 천연자원의 보존

(A) conservation 보존　　　　(B) suggestion 제안

번역 빅 필즈사는 천연자원 보존에 전념한다.

2

Milgrove Township / continues / to experience / a 4 percent annual (population increase).
밀그로브 군구는 　지속하고 있다 　경험하는 것을 　연간 4퍼센트의 인구 증가를
　　　　　　　　　　　　　　　　　→ 인구 증가

(A) expense 비용　　　　(B) increase 증가

번역 밀그로브 군구는 연간 4퍼센트의 인구 증가를 계속 경험하고 있다.

3

All participants / at the seminar / are asked / to complete the (evaluation form).
모든 참가자들은 　세미나의 　요청받는다 　평가서를 작성하라고
　　　　　　　　　　　　　　　→ 평가서

(A) form 서식, 양식　　　　(B) claim 주장

번역 세미나의 모든 참가자들은 평가서를 작성하라는 요청을 받는다.

4

I / am attaching / a copy of my résumé / for your (consideration).
저는 / 첨부합니다 　제 이력서 한 부를 　귀사의 검토를 위해
　　　　　　　　　　　　　　　→ 검토, 고려

(A) explanation 설명　　　　(B) consideration 검토, 고려, 심사숙고

번역 귀사의 검토를 위해 제 이력서 한 부를 첨부합니다.

5 (B)	6 (A)	7 (B)	8 (A)

5

The prices / listed in the Silesian Sun Tour catalog / are effective / until (further notice).
가격들은   실레지안 선 투어 카탈로그에 표시된   유효하다   추후 공지가 있을 때까지
                                                                                              → 추후 공지

(A) mark 표시   (B) notice 공지
(C) ability 능력   (D) attention 주의

[해설] until further notice 추후 공지가 있을 때까지: 빈칸 앞에 있는 전치사 until, 형용사 further와 의미상 가장 잘 어울리는 명사를
선택해야 합니다. 따라서 명사 (B) notice가 정답입니다.

[번역] 실레지안 선 투어 카탈로그에 표시된 가격들은 추후 공지가 있기 전까지는 유효하다.

6

The bank / has introduced / a variety of / banking products / (to meet the demands) / of its
그 은행은   출시했다   다양한   은행 상품을   요구에 부응하기 위해서   고객들의
                                                                                → 요구에 부응하다
customers.

(A) demands 수요, 요구   (B) rewards 보상, 보답
(C) duties 의무   (D) advantages 장점

[해설] demand 수요, 요구: 은행에서 다양한 은행 상품을 출시한 것은 고객들의 '수요'나 '요구'가 있었기 때문일 것입니다. '수요를
충족시키다, 요구에 부응하다'라는 의미의 숙어 meet the demands를 완성하는 (A) demands가 정답입니다.

[번역] 그 은행은 고객들의 요구에 부응하기 위해서 다양한 은행 상품을 출시했다.

7

The department / has been (under the supervision of) Jane Harden / for the past three years.
그 부서는   제인 하덴 씨의 관리하에 있다   지난 3년 동안
                                        → ~의 관리하에

(A) attendance 참석   (B) supervision 관리, 감독
(C) sight 시야   (D) provision 공급

[해설] under the supervision of ~의 관리하에: 빈칸 앞 전치사 under와 어울려 쓰이는 명사를 선택해야 합니다. 빈칸 뒤 전치사구 of
Jane Harden의 수식을 받아 '제인 하덴 씨의 감독하에'라는 의미가 문맥상 자연스러우므로, (B) supervision이 정답입니다.

[번역] 그 부서는 지난 3년 동안 제인 하덴 씨의 관리하에 있다.

8

All factory employees / should follow / (standard procedures) / when operating / heavy machinery.
모든 공장 직원들은   따라야 한다   표준 절차를   조작할 때   중장비를
                                              → 표준 설차

(A) procedures 절차   (B) developments 발달
(C) categories 범주   (D) qualifications 자격

[해설] standard procedures 표준 절차: 빈칸 앞의 standard와 함께 동사 should follow의 목적어 역할을 하는 명사 자리입니다. 문맥상
'표준 절차를 따라야 한다'라는 의미가 자연스러우므로, (A) procedures가 정답입니다.

[번역] 모든 공장 직원들은 중장비를 조작할 때 표준 절차를 따라야 한다.

1 (A)	2 (B)	3 (A)	4 (D)	5 (B)

1

Ms. Pamu / has scheduled / a meeting / with (her) chief financial officer, Mr. Chambers.
파무 씨는　　일정을 짰다　　회의를　　그녀의 재무 담당 이사인 챔버스 씨와
→ 뒤의 명사를 수식하는 소유격

(A) her　(B) she　(C) herself　(D) hers

해설　**소유격 + 명사**: 빈칸 뒤에 명사 chief financial officer(재무 담당 이사)가 있으므로, 소유격 (A) her가 정답입니다. her chief financial officer는 앞의 전치사 with의 목적어 역할을 합니다.

번역　파무 씨는 그녀의 재무 담당 이사인 챔버스 씨와 회의 일정을 잡았다.

2

A weekly rail pass / is the most economical option / for commuters, / but (others / are) available.
주간 열차 패스가　　가장 경제적인 선택이다　　통근자들에게　　그러나 다른 것들도 / 이용할 수 있다
→ others + 복수 동사

(A) other　(B) others　(C) the other　(D) another

해설　**알맞은 부정대명사 선택**: 복수 동사 are의 주어 역할을 하는 자리이므로, 부정대명사 (B) others가 정답입니다. (A) other는 형용사이므로 주어가 될 수 없고, (C) the other, (D) another는 be동사 are와 수 일치하지 않으므로, 오답입니다.

번역　주간 열차 패스가 통근자들에게 가장 경제적인 선택이지만 다른 것들도 이용할 수 있다.

3

Due to unusually high demand, / (some of our lawn supplies) / need to be restocked.
대단히 높은 수요 때문에　　우리 잔디 관리 용품 중 몇 품목의 재고는　　다시 채워야 한다
→ some of + 가산 명사 복수

(A) some　(B) something　(C) other　(D) each other

해설　**알맞은 부정대명사 선택**: 빈칸은 동사 need의 주어 역할을 하는 자리로, 빈칸 뒤 전치사구 of our lawn supplies의 수식을 받습니다. 문맥상 '잔디 관리 장비 중 일부'라는 의미가 자연스러우므로, 부정대명사 (A) some이 정답입니다.

번역　대단히 높은 수요 때문에, 우리 잔디 관리 용품 중 몇 품목의 재고를 다시 채워야 한다.

4

Although employee participation in community-service projects / is strictly voluntary, / (all) / are
직원들의 지역사회 봉사 프로젝트 참여는 전적으로　　　　　　　자발적이지만　　모두
'모두'의 의미 ←

encouraged / to join in.
장려된다　　동참하도록

(A) everything　(B) nowhere　(C) theirs　(D) all

해설　**알맞은 부정대명사 선택**: 빈칸은 동사 are의 주어 역할을 하는 자리입니다. 문맥상 '모두 동참하도록 독려한다'라는 의미가 자연스러우므로, 부정대명사 (D) all이 정답입니다.

번역　직원들의 지역사회 봉사 프로젝트 참여는 전적으로 자진해서 하는 것이지만, 모두 동참하도록 장려된다.

5

Ms. Chan / worked / on the budget summary / (by herself) / until Ms. Sumardi was free /
챈 씨는　　작업했다　　예산안 개요를　　혼자서　　수마르디 씨가 시간이 날 때까지

to help.
도와줄
→ by + 재귀대명사

(A) her　(B) herself　(C) she　(D) hers

해설　**by oneself 혼자서, 스스로**: 빈칸 앞 전치사 by의 목적어 역할을 하는 자리로, 전치사 by와 함께 '혼자서'라는 의미를 나타낼 수 있는 재귀대명사 (B) herself가 정답입니다.

번역　챈 씨는 수마르디 씨가 도와줄 시간이 날 때까지 혼자서 예산안 개요를 작업했다.

6 (B)	**7** (D)	**8** (C)	**9** (A)	**10** (C)

6

The Rowleigh Company / has once again increased / (its) quarterly profits.
로울리 사는   다시 한 번 늘렸다   분기 수익을

                                                        └→ 뒤의 명사를 수식하는 소유격

(A) itself   (B) its   (C) it   (D) us

해설 소유격 + 명사: 빈칸 뒤에 명사 quarterly profits(분기 수익)가 있으므로, 소유격 (B) its가 정답입니다. its quarterly profits는 앞의 동사 has ~ increased의 목적어 역할을 합니다.

번역 로울리 사는 다시 한 번 분기 수익을 늘렸다.

7

In order to finish / the candidate interviews, / Ms. Asaki / believes / that (she) will need to stay in
끝마치기 위해서   지원자 면접을   아사키 씨는   생각한다   자신이 뉴욕에 하루 더 머물러야 할 것이라고

New York another day.   └→ 주격

(A) her   (B) hers   (C) herself   (D) she

해설 인칭대명사의 격 선택: 빈칸은 동사 will need to stay의 주어 역할을 하는 자리이므로, Ms. Asaki를 대신하는 주격 인칭대명사 (D) she가 정답입니다. 〈소유격 + 명사〉를 대신하는 소유대명사 (B) hers는 '그녀의 것이 머무르다'라는 의미가 되어 문맥상 부자연스럽습니다.

번역 지원자 면접을 끝마치기 위해서, 아사키 씨는 자신이 뉴욕에 하루 더 머물러야 할 것이라고 생각한다.

8

Ms. Lu's administrative assistant / will mail / a copy of the annual report / to (those) / who cannot
루 씨의 행정 비서가   발송할 것이다 / 연간 보고서 한 부를   사람들에게   참석할 수 없는

attend / the meeting.   └→ '~한 사람들'의 의미
        회의에

(A) them   (B) this   (C) those   (D) then

해설 '사람들'을 뜻하는 those: 빈칸 앞 전치사 to의 목적어 역할을 하는 자리로, 주격 관계대명사 who가 이끄는 절(who ~ the meeting)의 수식을 받습니다. 문맥상 '회의에 참석할 수 없는 사람들'이라는 의미가 자연스러우므로, 지시대명사 (C) those가 정답입니다. 목적격 인칭대명사 (A) them은 앞에 언급된 특정인들을 대신하므로, 적절하지 않습니다.

번역 루 씨의 행정 비서가 회의에 참석할 수 없는 사람들에게 연간 보고서 한 부를 발송할 것이다.

9

(These are) the accounts / that need to be updated / by Matt Jepsen / in the Sales Department.
이것들은 장부들이다   업데이트되어야 할   매트 젭슨에 의해   영업부의
     └→ These + 복수 동사

(A) These   (B) Something   (C) Another   (D) More

해설 지시대명사 선택: 빈칸은 복수 동사 are의 주어 역할을 하는 자리이므로, 지시대명사 (A) These가 정답입니다. (B) Something, (C) Another는 be동사 are와 수가 일치하지 않고 (D) More는 단독으로 주어 역할을 할 수 없으므로 오답입니다.

번역 이것들은 영업부의 매트 젭슨에 의해 업데이트되어야 할 장부들이다.

10

Brookton Furnishings / has transformed / (itself) / into a competitive company / through an
브룩톤 퍼니싱즈는　　　　　변모시켰다　　　스스로를　경쟁력 있는 기업으로　　　　공격적인 마케팅 캠페인을 통해

aggressive marketing campaign.
　　　　　　　　　　　　　　　　→ 주어(Brookton Furnishings)와 동일한 대상을 지칭하는 재귀대명사

(A) it　(B) its　(C) itself　(D) its own

해설 인칭대명사의 격 선택: 빈칸 앞 동사구 has transformed의 목적어 역할을 하는 자리로, 앞의 주어 Brookton Furnishings를 지칭합니다. 목적어가 주어와 같은 사람이나 사물을 지칭할 때, 목적어 자리에 재귀대명사가 오므로 재귀대명사 (C) itself가 정답입니다.

번역 브룩톤 퍼니싱즈는 공격적인 마케팅 캠페인을 통해 경쟁력 있는 기업으로 변모했다.

ETS 실전 테스트

11 (A)　　　　　**12** (D)　　　　　**13** (C)　　　　　**14** (D)

Questions 11-14 refer to the following memo.

Date: September 14

To: Henderson Store 195

From: Alex Sitton

Re: Final days at Henderson

Hello Henderson 195 staff. It is with a heavy heart / that I announce /
헨더슨 195 직원 여러분 안녕하세요　마음이 무겁네요　　　알리게 돼

that I will be leaving the store later this month. 11. (My) final day / will be
이번 달 말에 매장을 떠난다는 것을　　　　　　　제 마지막 날은　　9월 30일입니다
　　　　　　　　　　　　　　　　　　　　　　→ 뒤의 명사를 수식하는 소유격

September 30. I have decided / to take a position as general manager /
　　　　　　　　　저는 결정했습니다　　총지배인 직을 맡기로

at the Henderson Store in Plains City.
플레인즈 시에 있는 헨더슨 스토어에서

I have thoroughly enjoyed my time / as your manager here / at store 195.
아주 즐겁게 지냈어요　　　　　　　여기 매니저로 근무하면서　　195호 매장에서

The opportunity in Plains City, / 12. (however), / was one / I could not pass up.
플레인즈 시에서 일할 기회는　　　　　하지만　　~것이었어요　놓칠 수 없는
　　　　　　　　　　　　　　→ '하지만'의 의미

Emily Linares from store 196 / will take over as your general manager /
196호 매장 에밀리 리나레스가　　　　여러분의 총괄 매니저를 맡을 겁니다

beginning on October 1. Emily will be a great fit / for this store. 13. She
10월 1일부터　　　　　　에밀리는 딱 맞는 적임자일 겁니다　이 매장에　　　　그녀는

looks forward / to joining the team here.
고대하고 있어요　　여기 팀에 합류하기를

Thank you for a fantastic experience / 14. (throughout) the past few years.
멋진 경험을 선사해 주셔서 감사해요　　지난 몇 년 동안 쭉
　　　　　　　　　　　　　　　　　→ '~ 동안 쭉'의 의미

I will miss seeing you all.
여러분 모두 보고 싶을 거예요

11-14 회람

날짜: 9월 14일
수신: 헨더슨 스토어 195
발신: 알렉스 시튼
Re: 헨더슨에서 보내는 마지막 날들

헨더슨 195 직원 여러분 안녕하세요. 이번 달 말에 제가 매장을 떠난다고 알리게 되어 마음이 무겁네요. 제 마지막 근무일은 9월 30일입니다. 저는 플레인즈 시에 있는 헨더슨 스토어에서 총지배인 직을 맡기로 결정했습니다.

195호 매장에서 매니저로 근무하면서 아주 즐겁게 지냈어요. 하지만 플레인즈 시에서 일할 기회는 놓칠 수 없는 것이었어요.

196호 매장 에밀리 리나레스가 10월 1일부터 여러분의 총괄 매니저를 맡을 겁니다. 에밀리는 이 매장에 딱 맞는 적임자일 겁니다. 그녀는 여기 팀에 합류하기를 고대하고 있어요.

지난 몇 년 동안 쭉 멋진 경험을 선사해주셔서 감사해요. 여러분 모두 보고 싶을 거예요.

11 (A) My

(B) Her

(C) Our

(D) Their

해설 알맞은 인칭대명사 선택: 빈칸 앞 문장에서 사직을 알리게 되어 마음이 무겁다고 언급했습니다. 문맥상 '제 마지막 근무일은 9월 30일'이라는 의미가 자연스러우므로, 1인칭 소유격 형용사 (A) My가 정답입니다.

---

12 (A) therefore

(B) for example

(C) comparatively

(D) however

(A) 그러므로

(B) 예를 들어

(C) 비교적

(D) 하지만

해설 알맞은 접속부사 선택: 빈칸 앞 문장에서 이곳 매니저로 근무하면서 즐거웠다고 언급했으나, 빈칸을 포함한 뒤 문장에서는 플레인즈 시에서 일할 기회는 놓칠 수 없었다고 했습니다. 따라서 역접의 의미를 나타내는 접속부사 (D) however가 정답입니다.

---

13 (A) Actually, I was born in Plains City.

(B) Call me if you have any additional questions.

(C) She looks forward to joining the team here.

(D) You may have heard this news already.

(A) 사실, 저는 플레인즈 시에서 태어났어요.

(B) 추가 문의 사항이 있으면 전화 주세요.

(C) 그녀는 여기 팀에 합류하기를 고대하고 있어요

(D) 여러분은 이미 이 소식을 들었을지도 모르겠네요.

해설 문장 고르기: 빈칸 앞 문장 Emily will be a great fit for this store.에서 에밀리가 이 매장의 적임자일 것이라고 언급했습니다. 따라서 빈칸에는 에밀리와 관련된 내용이 들어가는 것이 문맥상 자연스러우며, 선택지 (C)의 She가 에밀리를 가리키므로 정답은 (C)입니다.

---

14 (A) except

(B) despite

(C) besides

(D) throughout

(A) ~을 제외하고

(B) ~에도 불구하고

(C) ~ 외에

(D) ~ 동안 쭉

해설 알맞은 전치사 선택: 빈칸 뒤 명사구 the past few years를 목적어로 취하는 전치사 자리로, 문맥상 '지난 몇 년 동안 쭉'이라는 의미가 되어야 자연스럽습니다. 따라서 전치사 (D) throughout이 정답입니다.

● **형용사와 부사의 쓰임** ETS 문제로 훈련하기 STEP 1 교재 p.65

1 (A)	**2** (B)	**3** (A)	**4** (B)	**5** (B)	**6** (B)

1
The redecorated lobby / will feature / (comfortable) chairs.
새로 장식된 로비는   놓을 것이다   편안한 의자들을
                                                  → 뒤 명사 chairs를 수식하는 형용사
(A) comfortable 편안한   (B) comfortably 편안하게

번역 새로 장식된 로비에는 편안한 의자들을 놓을 것이다.

2
The cinema / is (conveniently) located / near a major shopping district.
그 극장은   편리하게 위치해 있다   주요 상업지구 근처에
                                         → 형용사[분사] located를 수식하는 부사
(A) convenience 편리   (B) conveniently 편리하게

번역 그 극장은 주요 상업지구 근처에 편리하게 위치하고 있다.

3
(Fortunately), / our sales / have increased / for the past three months.
다행히도   우리의 매출이   증가했다   지난 3개월 동안
      → 뒤 문장을 수식하는 부사
(A) Fortunately 다행히도   (B) Fortunate 운이 좋은

번역 다행히도 우리의 매출이 지난 3개월 동안 증가했다.

4
The display of Mexican crafts / will remain (open) / for a limited time only.
멕시코 공예품 전시는   계속 열릴 것이다   한정된 시간 동안만
                                               → 주격 보어(형용사)
(A) openly 공공연하게, 솔직히   (B) open 열린, 연

번역 멕시코 공예품 전시는 한정된 시간 동안만 열릴 것이다.

5
The banquet facility / is the (ideal) venue / for business luncheons.
그 연회 시설은   이상적인 장소이다   업무용 오찬을 위한
                                          → 뒤 명사 venue를 수식하는 형용사
(A) idealize 이상화하다   (B) ideal 이상적인

번역 그 연회 시설은 업무용 오찬을 위한 이상적인 장소이다.

6
This special offer / is available / (exclusively) to employees of Moriyama Association.
이 특별 할인은   이용할 수 있다   모리야마 어소시에이션 직원만
                                          → 전치사구(to ~ Association)를 수식하는 부사
(A) exclusionary 배제하기 위한   (B) exclusively 독점적으로, 오로지

번역 이 특별 할인은 모리야마 어소시에이션 직원만 이용할 수 있다.

7 (A)	**8** (C)	**9** (D)	**10** (B)

PART 5 | UNIT 04

7

When studies are (complete), / Deni Contracting Group / will make a bid / on the project.
연구가 완료되면   보어   데니 컨트랙팅 그룹은   입찰할 것이다   그 프로젝트에

(A) complete 완결한, 완전한   (B) completion 완료, 완성

(C) completeness 완성도   (D) completely 완전히, 전적으로

해설 보어로 쓰이는 형용사: 빈칸은 are의 주격 보어 자리로, 주어 studies를 보충 설명합니다. 따라서 형용사인 (A) complete(완전한)이 정답입니다. 명사가 주격 보어로 나오는 경우에는 주어와 동격 관계를 이루는데, 명사 (B) completion과 (C) completeness는 주어 studies와 동격 관계를 이루지 않으므로, 오답입니다.

번역 연구가 완료되면, 데니 컨트랙팅 그룹은 그 프로젝트에 입찰할 것이다.

8

Training / will enable / employees / to respond (appropriately) / to customer service concerns.
교육은   가능하게 할 것이다 / 직원들이   적절히 대응하는 것을   고객 서비스 관심사에
                                   to respond 수식

(A) appropriate 적절한   (B) more appropriate 더 적절한

(C) appropriately 적절하게   (D) appropriateness 적절함

해설 to부정사구를 수식하는 부사: 빈칸은 to부정사구인 to respond를 수식하는 부사 자리로, '적절히'라는 의미의 부사 (C) appropriately가 정답입니다.

번역 교육은 직원들이 고객 서비스 관심사에 적절히 대응할 수 있게 해 줄 것이다.

9

Affirmatis, Inc., / (intentionally) made / the scope of the research / broad / during its initial stage.
어퍼머티스 사는   의도적으로 만들었다   연구 범위를   넓게   초기 단계에서
                             동사 made 수식

(A) intend 의도하다   (B) intention 의도

(C) intentional 의도적인   (D) intentionally 의도적으로

해설 동사를 수식하는 부사: 빈칸은 5형식 동사 made를 수식하는 부사 자리이므로, 부사 (D) intentionally(의도적으로)가 정답입니다.

번역 어퍼머티스 사는 초기 단계에서 의도적으로 연구 범위를 넓게 만들었다.

10

New employees / may find / themselves / (dependent) / on their coworkers / for advice.
신입 직원들은   발견할 수도 있다 / 자신들을   의존하는   동료 직원들에게   조언을 위해
                           보어

(A) dependence 의존   (B) dependent 의존하는

(C) dependently 의존적으로   (D) depend 의존하다, 의지하다

해설 보어로 쓰이는 형용사: 빈칸은 동사 find의 목적어 역할을 하는 themselves를 보충 설명하는 목적격 보어 자리이므로, 형용사 (B) dependent(의존하는)가 정답입니다. 명사가 목적격 보어로 나오는 경우에는 목적어와 동격 관계를 이루는데, 명사 (A) dependence는 목적어 themselves와 동격 관계를 이루지 않습니다.

번역 신입 직원들은 조언을 위해 동료 직원들에게 의존하는 자신을 발견할 수도 있다.

1 (A)	2 (A)	3 (B)	4 (B)	5 (B)	6 (B)

1

Customer service employees / should be (respectful) / to customers.
고객 서비스 직원들은 　　　　　　 예의 바르게 대해야 한다 　　　고객들에게
　　　　　　　　　　　　　　　　　　　　　　　　　→ 예의 바른

(A) respectful 예의 바른　　　　　　　(B) respective 각자의, 각각의

번역 고객 서비스 직원들은 고객들에게 예의 바르게 대해야 한다.

2

Mr. Robinson's flight / from Kuala Lumpur / was delayed / for (more than) three hours.
로빈슨 씨의 비행기는　　쿠알라룸푸르에서 출발하는　　지연되었다　　3시간 이상
　　　　　　　　　　　　　　　　　　　　　　　　　　　　　→ 숫자를 수식하는 부사

(A) more than ~이상　　　　　　　(B) still 아직, 그런데도

번역 쿠알라룸푸르에서 출발하는 로빈슨 씨의 비행기는 3시간 이상 지연되었다.

3

Mr. Himura / has been (deeply) involved / in the development / of Visetrix wireless headsets.
히무라 씨가　　깊이 관여해 왔다　　　　　개발에　　　　바이스트릭스 무선 헤드셋의
　　　　　　　　　　→ 깊이, 크게

(A) deep (물리적으로) 깊게　　　(B) deeply 깊이, 크게

번역 히무라 씨가 바이스트릭스 무선 헤드셋 개발에 깊이 관여해 왔다.

4

All passengers / should be / (considerate) of others / by speaking softly / when talking on mobile
모든 승객은　　~해야 합니다　다른 사람들을 배려하는　　작게 말함으로써　　휴대 전화로 통화할 때
　　　　　　　　　　　　　　　　　→ 배려하는
phones.

(A) considerable 상당한, 많은　　　(B) considerate 배려하는, 사려 깊은

번역 모든 승객은 휴대 전화로 통화할 때 작게 말함으로써 다른 사람들을 배려해야 합니다.

5

Most managers / (closely) examine / applicants' educational backgrounds.
대부분의 관리자들은　면밀히 검토한다　　지원자들의 학력을
　　　　　　　　　　→ 면밀히

(A) close 가까이, 바싹　　　　　(B) closely 면밀히

번역 대부분의 관리자들은 지원자들의 학력을 면밀히 검토한다.

6

(Lately) / Ms. Lacombe / has been working / overtime / to meet the deadline.
최근　　라콤브 씨는　　일하고 있다　　초과근무를　마감일을 맞추기 위해
　　　　　　→ 최근에

(A) Late 늦은; 늦게　　　　　(B) Lately 최근에

번역 최근 라콤브씨는 마감일을 맞추기 위해 야근을 하고 있다.

7 (A)	8 (A)	9 (C)	10 (A)

7

We / expect / there will be (approximately) 250 people attending the convention.
우리는 예상한다　　컨벤션에 참석하는 사람들이 대략 250명쯤 있을 것으로

→ 숫자 250 수식

(A) approximately 대략　　　　　　(B) approximate 가까워지다; 가까운

(C) approximation 근사치　　　　(D) approximated 비슷한, 근사치의

해설　숫자를 수식하는 부사: 빈칸 뒤 250을 수식하는 부사 자리로, '대략'이라는 의미의 부사 (A) approximately가 정답입니다.

번역　우리는 컨벤션에 참석하는 사람들이 대략 250명쯤 될 것으로 예상한다.

8

Kananga Electric's project / to develop / solar-powered home appliances / has been (successful).
카낭가 일렉트릭의 프로젝트는　　개발하려는　　태양열로 작동되는 가전제품을　　성공적으로 진행되어 왔다

성공적인 ←

(A) successful 성공적인　　　　(B) successive 연속적인

(C) success 성공　　　　　　　(D) succeed 성공하다

해설　비슷한 형용사의 의미 구별: be동사의 현재완료형인 has been 뒤에 빈칸이 있으므로 주격 보어 역할을 할 수 있는 형용사가 필요합니다. 프로젝트가 성공적이었다는 내용이 문맥상 적절하므로, '성공적인'이라는 뜻의 형용사 (A) successful이 정답입니다.

번역　태양열로 작동되는 가전제품을 개발하려는 카낭가 일렉트릭의 프로젝트는 성공적으로 진행되어 왔다.

9

Penter Electronics' newest machines / require (hardly) / any additional equipment.
펜터 일렉트로닉스의 최신 기계들은　　　　거의 필요하지 않다　어떠한 추가 장비도

→ 거의 ~않다

(A) hardest 가장 단단한　　　　(B) harder 더 단단한

(C) hardly 거의 ~ 않다　　　　(D) hard 단단한; 열심히

해설　부정 부사: 문맥상 '어떠한 추가 장비도 거의 필요하지 않다'라는 의미가 자연스러우므로, (C) hardly(거의 ~ 않다)가 정답입니다. 부사 (D) hard는 '열심히'라는 의미이므로, 적절하지 않습니다.

번역　펜터 일렉트로닉스의 최신 기계들은 어떠한 추가 장비도 거의 필요하지 않다.

10

Ms. Falconi / is (largely) responsible / for the increase / in sales of team uniforms.
팔코니 씨는　　주로 책임이 있다　　　　증대에　　　팀 유니폼 판매의

→ 형용사 responsible 수식

(A) largely 주로, 크게　　　　(R) largest 가장 큰

(C) larger 더 큰　　　　　　　(D) large 큰

해설　형용사를 수식하는 부사: 빈칸 뒤 형용사 responsible을 수식하는 부사 자리이므로, (A) largely(주로, 크게)가 정답입니다. 부사는 문장 구조상 생략이 가능하므로, 빈칸이 없어도 완전한 문장이 된다면 부사 자리입니다.

번역　팔코니 씨는 팀 유니폼 판매 증대를 주로 책임지고 있다.

1 (A)	**2** (A)	**3** (A)	**4** (B)

1

On average, / Mr. Jarvela / takes / two business trips / a month.
평균적으로   자벨라 씨는   간다   두 번 출장을   한 달에
  └→ 평균적으로
(A) average 평균   (B) norm 규준, 기준

번역 평균적으로 자벨라 씨는 한 달에 두 번 출장을 간다.

2

Dr. Cha / has been one of the most respected researchers / in her field.
차 박사는   가장 훌륭한 연구자들 중 한 명이다   자신의 분야에서
                                                              └→ 분야
(A) field 분야   (B) account 계정, 계좌

번역 차 박사는 자신의 분야에서 가장 훌륭한 연구자들 중 한 명이다.

3

The engineering team / has not yet finalized / all the details of the design.
기술팀은   아직 마무리하지 못했다   설계의 모든 세부 사항을
                                                              └→ 세부 사항
(A) details 세부 사항   (B) policies 정책, 방침

번역 기술팀은 설계의 모든 세부 사항을 아직 마무리하지 못했다.

4

New tenants / have no obligation / to pay / for any damage / before moving in.
새 세입자들은   의무가 없다   배상할   훼손에 대해   입주하기 전에
              └→ 의무가 없다
(A) promise 약속   (B) obligation 의무

번역 새 세입자들은 입주하기 전에 발생한 훼손에 대해 배상할 의무가 없다.

5 (D)	6 (D)	7 (D)	8 (A)

5

There will be (delays) / in implementing repairs / to the Chicago assembly line.
지체가 있을 것이다　　　　　　수리를 시행하는 데　　　　　　　시카고 조립 라인에

└→ 지체, 지연

(A) places 장소　　　　　　　　　　　(B) inclusions 포함

(C) oppositions 반대　　　　　　　　　(D) delays 지체

해설　delay 지체, 지연: 빈칸에는 수리를 시행함에 있어 발생할 수 있는 상황을 언급하는 명사가 들어가야 합니다. 문맥상 '수리를 시행하는 데 지체가 있다'라는 의미가 자연스러우므로, (D) delays가 정답입니다. 참고로 (C) oppositions는 '~에 반대하여'라는 의미를 나타낼 경우, ⟨in opposition to⟩의 구조로 쓰입니다.

번역　시카고 조립 라인 수리를 시행하는 데 지체가 있을 것이다.

6

The purchase of additional land / will allow / Montauk Logistics / to double / their warehouse
추가 토지의 매입은　　　　　　　　가능하게 할 것이다 / 몬턱 로지스틱스가　　　두 배로 늘리는 것을 / 창고 용량을

(capacity). → 용량, 수용 능력

(A) modification 수정　　　　　　　　(B) ability 능력

(C) qualification 자격 요건　　　　　　(D) capacity 용량

해설　capacity 용량, 수용 능력: 추가로 토지를 매입할 경우 창고의 용량이 커지게 될 수 있으므로, '용량, 수용 능력'이라는 뜻의 (D) capacity가 정답입니다.

번역　추가 토지를 매입함으로써 몬턱 로지스틱스는 창고 용량을 두 배로 늘리게 될 것이다.

7

Health-conscious parents / restrict / the (amount) of sugar / their children consume.
건강을 생각하는 부모들은　　　　　제한한다　　설탕의 양을　　　　　자녀들이 먹는

└→ 양

(A) reason 이유　　　　　　　　　　　(B) total 합계

(C) location 위치　　　　　　　　　　(D) amount 양

해설　amount 양: 빈칸은 동사 restrict의 목적어 역할을 하는 명사 자리로, 빈칸 뒤 전치사구 of sugar의 수식을 받습니다. 문맥상 '설탕의 양을 제한한다'라는 의미가 자연스러우므로, (D) amount가 정답입니다.

번역　건강을 생각하는 부모들은 자녀들이 먹는 설탕의 양을 제한한다.

8

(For your reference), / we / have included / a copy of your purchase order / with this shipment.
참고하시라고　　　　　　　저희가 / 포함시켰습니다　　주문서 사본을　　　　　　　이 발송품에

└→ 참고하시라고

(A) reference 참고　　　　　　　　　(B) learning 학습

(C) direction 방향　　　　　　　　　(D) meaning 의미

해설　reference 참고: 빈칸에는 주문서 사본을 포함한 이유를 나타내는 명사가 들어가야 합니다. 문맥상 '참고하시라고'라는 의미가 자연스러우므로, '참고'라는 뜻의 (A) reference가 정답입니다.

번역　참고하시라고, 저희가 이 발송품에 주문서 사본을 포함시켰습니다.

1 (B)	**2** (B)	**3** (A)	**4** (C)	**5** (A)

1

Ms. Hirai and Ms. Byrd / have / (different) strategies / for conducting consumer research.
히라이 씨와 버드 씨는　　　　가지고 있다 / 다른 전략을　　　　소비자 조사를 수행하기 위한

→ 명사 strategies 수식

(A) differ 다르다　(B) different 다른　(C) difference 차이　(D) differently 다르게

해설 **명사를 수식하는 형용사:** 빈칸 뒤 명사 strategies를 수식하는 형용사 자리이므로, (B) different(다른)가 정답입니다.

번역 히라이 씨와 버드 씨는 소비자 조사를 수행하기 위한 전략이 다르다.

2

Ms. Jeong / has requested / a prompt response, / (preferably) / within the week.
정 씨는　　　　요청했다　　　　신속한 답변을　　　　되도록이면　　　이번 주 내에

→ 전치사구 within the week 수식

(A) preferable 더 좋은　(B) preferably 되도록이면　(C) preference 선호　(D) prefer 선호하다

해설 **전치사구를 수식하는 부사:** 빈칸 뒤 전치사구 within this week를 수식하는 부사 자리이므로, 부사 (B) preferably(되도록이면, 가급적이면)가 정답입니다.

번역 정 씨는 되도록이면 이번 주 내에 신속한 답변을 달라고 요청했다.

3

The area around Lake Clamonde / is (widely) accepted / to be among the country's most scenic.
클라몬드 호수 주변 지역은　　　　널리 인정받고 있다　　　이 나라에서 가장 경치가 좋은 곳 가운데 하나로

→ 과거분사 accepted를 수식

(A) widely 널리　(B) wide 넓은　(C) widen 넓히다　(D) wider 더 넓은

해설 **분사를 수식하는 부사:** 빈칸 뒤의 과거분사 accepted를 수식하는 부사 자리이므로, 부사 (A) widely(널리)가 정답입니다.

번역 클라몬드 호수 주변은 이 나라에서 가장 경치가 좋은 곳 가운데 하나로 널리 인정받고 있다.

4

Mr. Phillips / will discuss / (additional) approaches / for the promotion of our merchandise.
필립스 씨는　　　　논의할 것이다　　추가적인 접근 방식을　　　　우리 상품의 홍보를 위한

→ 명사 approaches 수식

(A) addition 추가, 부가물　(B) additions 첨가제　(C) additional 추가적인　(D) additionally 게다가

해설 **명사를 수식하는 형용사:** 동사 will discuss의 목적어 역할을 하는 명사 approaches가 빈칸 뒤에 있으므로, 빈칸에는 명사 approaches를 수식하는 형용사가 와야 합니다. 따라서 형용사 (C) additional(추가적인)이 정답입니다.

번역 필립스 씨는 우리 상품의 홍보를 위한 추가적인 접근 방식을 논의할 것이다.

5

An updated telemarketing database / could provide / a (distinct) advantage / to the firm's sales
최신 텔레마케팅 데이터베이스가　　　　줄 수도 있다　　　분명한 우위를　　　　그 회사 영업 팀에

team.

→ 명사 advantage 수식

(A) distinct 분명한, 뚜렷한　(B) distinctly 뚜렷하게　(C) distinction 차이, 뛰어남　(D) distinctively 특징적으로, 독특하게

해설 **명사를 수식하는 형용사:** 빈칸 앞의 부정관사 a와 빈칸 뒤 명사 advantage 사이에서 명사를 수식하는 형용사 자리이므로, (A) distinct(분명한, 뚜렷한)가 정답입니다.

번역 최신 텔레마케팅 데이터베이스가 그 회사 영업 팀에 분명한 우위를 줄 수도 있다.

6 (A)	**7** (C)	**8** (B)	**9** (B)	**10** (D)

6

To ensure / safe swimming conditions, / employees of ST Pool Systems / must add / chemicals /
보장하기 위해　　안전한 수영 환경을　　　　ST 풀 시스템즈의 직원들은　　　　첨가해야 한다　화학 약품을

to the pools / regularly .
수영장에　　　　정기적으로 ────> 동사 add 수식

(A) regularly 정기적으로　(B) regular 정기적인　(C) regularity 정기적임　(D) regularize 합법화하다

해설 동사를 수식하는 부사: 빈칸에는 동사 add를 수식해 줄 수 있는 부사가 필요합니다. 따라서 '정기적으로'라는 의미의 (A) regularly가
정답이 됩니다.

번역 안전한 수영 환경을 보장하기 위해 ST 풀 시스템즈의 직원들은 정기적으로 수영장에 화학 약품을 첨가해야 한다.

7

The training program / on writing / effective policies and procedures / starts / on Monday.
교육 프로그램은　　　　작성에 대한　　　효과적인 정책 및 절차의　　　　시작한다　월요일에
　　　　　　　　　　　　　　　　　　　　　　────> 명사 policies와 procedures를 수식

(A) effect 영향, 결과　(B) effects 물품, 물건　(C) effective 효과적인　(D) effectively 효과적으로

해설 형용사 + 명사: 빈칸 뒤 명사 policies와 procedures를 수식하는 형용사 자리이므로, 형용사 (C) effective(효과적인)가 정답입니다.

번역 효과적인 정책 및 절차의 작성에 대한 교육 프로그램은 월요일에 시작한다.

8

The readers' response / to the updated magazine format / has been overwhelmingly positive.
독자들의 반응은　　　　새로 바뀐 잡지 구성에 대한　　　압도적으로 긍정적이다
　　　　　　　　　　　　　　　　　　　형용사 positive 수식 ────

(A) overwhelming 압도적인　(B) overwhelmingly 압도적으로　(C) overwhelmed 압도된　(D) overwhelm 압도[제압]하다

해설 형용사를 수식하는 부사: 빈칸 뒤 형용사 positive를 수식하는 부사 자리이므로, (B) overwhelmingly(압도적으로)가 정답입니다.
부사는 문장 구조상 생략이 가능하므로, 빈칸이 없어도 완전한 문장이 된다면 부사 자리입니다.

번역 새로 바뀐 잡지 구성에 대한 독자들의 반응은 압도적으로 긍정적이다.

9

Although Ms. Gutierrez / has been working / as a trader / for only two months, / she / is highly
구티에레즈 씨는　　　　일하고 있지만　　　중개인으로　겨우 두 달째　　　그녀는　높이

regarded / by clients.
평가받고 있다　고객들에게　　　　　　높이 ────

(A) high 높은　(B) highly 높이　(C) higher 더 높은　(D) highest 가장 높은

해설 뜻을 주의해야 하는 부사: 빈칸은 과거분사인 regarded를 수식하는 부사 자리입니다. 문맥상 '대단하게 평가받고 있다'라는 의미가
자연스러우므로, 부사 (B) highly(높이, 크게)가 정답입니다. (A) high 또한 부사로 쓰일 수 있지만, '(물리적으로) 높이, 높은 곳에'라는
의미이므로 적절하지 않습니다.

번역 구티에레즈 씨는 중개인으로 일한 지 두 달밖에 안됐지만 고객들에게 높이 평가받고 있다.

10

Ms. Wang / works cooperatively / with city officials / to ensure / that her neighborhood is served
왕 씨는　　　협력하여 일하고 있다　　　시 공무원들과　　　확실히 할 수 있도록 / 지역 주민들이 잘 서비스 받는 것을

well.　　　　　　　　　────> 동사 works 수식
좋게

(A) cooperate 협력하다　(B) cooperated 협력된　(C) cooperative 협력하는　(D) cooperatively 협력하여

해설 동사를 수식하는 부사: 빈칸 앞의 동사 works를 수식하는 부사 자리이므로 (D) cooperatively(협력하여)가 정답입니다.

번역 왕 씨는 지역 주민들이 좋은 서비스를 받을 수 있도록 시 공무원들과 협력하여 일하고 있다.

Questions 11-14 refer to the following e-mail.

To: Abdul James <ajames@gesondcellular.com>
From: Rebecca Quinn <rquinn@vhobitech.com>
Subject: Thank you for the interview
Date: November 14

Dear Mr. James,

Thank you again for taking the time / to speak to me / about the office
시간을 내 주셔서 다시 한 번 감사드립니다   제게 말씀해 주셔서   사무장 자리에 대해

manager position. I would like / to provide you with a professional
~하고 싶습니다   직장 추천인을 알려드리고

reference. **11.** You can speak with Erin Gover, / my team lead at Vhobi
에린 고버 씨와 이야기하시면 됩니다   포비테크에서 제 팀장이었던

Tech. We have worked together / for five years. In particular, / she
우리는 함께 일했습니다   5년 동안   특히   그녀는

supervised my **12.** (extensive) work / during Vhobi Tech's move. She can
저의 방대한 작업을 감독했습니다   포비테크가 전진하는 동안   의견을 주실 겁니다
→ 뒤 명사 work 수식

comment / knowledgeably / on my **13.** performance. Please let me know /
잘 알고   제 실적에 대해   알려주시기 바랍니다

if you have any other questions / or would like me to send you any further
다른 문의 사항이 있거나   제가 추가 정보를 당신에게 보내기를 원한다(면)

information. I hope my résumé demonstrates / how **14.** seriously I have
제 이력서가 보여줬으면 합니다   제가 얼마나 진지하게 직장생활에

pursued a career / in this industry. I look forward / to hearing from you.
정진했는지   이 업계에서   기다리겠습니다   당신의 연락을

Sincerely,

Rebecca Quinn

11-14 이메일

수신: 압둘 제임스 〈ajames@gesondcellular.com〉
발신: 레베카 퀸 〈rquinn@vhobi-tech.com〉
제목: 면접 감사합니다
날짜: 11월 14일

제임스 씨께,

시간을 내서 사무장 자리에 대해 말씀해 주셔서 다시 한 번 감사드립니다. 직장 추천인을 알려드리고 싶습니다. 포비테크에서 제 팀장이었던 에린 고버 씨와 이야기하시면 됩니다. 우리는 5년 동안 함께 일했습니다. 특히 고버 씨는 포비테크가 전진하는 동안 저의 방대한 작업을 감독했습니다. 제 실적에 대해 잘 아시므로 의견을 주실 겁니다. 다른 문의 사항이 있거나 추가 정보를 보내야 하면 알려주시기 바랍니다. 제가 이 업계에서 얼마나 진지하게 직장생활에 정진했는지 제 이력서가 보여줬으면 합니다. 연락 기다리겠습니다.

레베카 퀸

11 (A) I do not have any names to give you right now.

    (B) I would like to learn more about the pending merger with Mobi Denwa.

    (C) You can speak with Erin Gover, my team lead at Vhobi Tech.

    (D) I can be reached by e-mail or by phone.

(A) 지금 당장은 드릴 이름이 없습니다.

(B) 임박한 모비 덴와와의 합병 건에 대해 좀 더 알고 싶습니다.

(C) 포비테크에서 제 팀장이었던 에린 고버 씨와 이야기하시면 됩니다.

(D) 제게 이메일이나 전화로 연락하시면 됩니다.

> **해설** 문장 고르기: 빈칸 앞 문장 I would like to provide you with a professional reference.에서 직장 추천인을 언급했습니다. 따라서 빈칸에는 이 추천인과 관련된 내용이 이어지는 것이 문맥상 자연스러우므로, 정답은 (C)입니다.

12 (A) extend

    (B) extensive

    (C) extending

    (D) extends

(A) 확대하다

(B) 방대한

(C) 확대

(D) 확대하다

> **해설** 형용사 + 명사: 빈칸 앞에 소유격 대명사 my가 있고 빈칸 뒤에 명사 work가 있으므로, 형용사 (B) extensive(방대한)가 정답입니다.

13 (A) display

    (B) agenda

    (C) operation

    (D) performance

(A) 전시

(B) 안건

(C) 운영

(D) 실적

> **해설** 어휘 문제: 빈칸 앞 문장 she supervised my extensive work에서 방대한 작업을 감독한 사람을 언급했습니다. 문맥상 이는 (업무) 실적을 잘 안다는 것으로 볼 수 있으므로, (D) performance가 정답입니다.

14 (A) seriously

    (B) consequently

    (C) cautiously

    (D) firmly

(A) 진지하게

(B) 결과로

(C) 중하게

(D) 확고하게

> **해설** 어휘 문제: 빈칸 앞 문장 Please let me ~ further information.에서 문의 사항이나 보내야 할 추가 정보를 알려 달라고 했습니다. 따라서 빈칸을 포함한 부분은 '얼마나 진지하게 직장생활에 정진했는지'라는 의미가 문맥상 자연스러우므로, (A) seriously가 정답입니다.

원급 비교와 비교급 비교 ETS 문제로 훈련하기 STEP 1

교재 p.75

1 (A)	**2** (A)	**3** (B)	**4** (B)	**5** (B)	**6** (B)

1

Bonus payments / will be smaller / than they were / last year.
성과금 지불액은   더 적을 것이다   그랬던 것보다   작년에

(A) smaller   (B) small
→ 비교급 (형용사) + than

번역 성과금 지불액은 지난해보다 더 적을 것이다.

2

The renovated break room / is as spacious as the cafeteria / on the tenth floor.
개조한 휴게실은   구내식당만큼 넓다   10층에 있는

(A) spacious 넓은   (B) space 공간
→ as + 원급 (형용사) + as

번역 개조한 휴게실은 10층에 있는 구내식당만큼 넓다.

3

The Slenderline mobile phone / is smaller / than other models.
슬렌더라인 휴대폰은   더 작다   다른 모델보다

(A) at   (B) than
→ 비교급 (형용사) + than

번역 슬렌더라인 휴대폰은 다른 모델보다 더 작다.

4

Employees / should feel free / to consult the on-site physician / as often as needed.
직원들은   자유롭게 ~해야 한다   사내 의사의 진찰을 받다   필요할 때는 언제든

(A) than   (B) as
→ as + 원급 (부사) + as

번역 직원들은 필요할 때는 언제든 자유롭게 사내 의사의 진찰을 받아야 한다.

5

The Piazza Bridge / is even wider / than the bridge / over the Lucca River.
피아차 다리는   훨씬 더 넓다   다리보다   루카 강 위의

(A) more   (B) even
→ 비교급(wider) 강조 부사

번역 피아차 다리는 루카 강 위의 다리보다 훨씬 더 넓다.

6

According to Coville Deli, / orange juice / sells / just as well as coffee / in the morning.
코빌 델리에 따르면   오렌지 주스가   팔린다 커피만큼이나 잘   아침에

(A) more than   (B) just as
→ as + 원급 (부사) + as

번역 코빌 델리에 따르면, 아침에 오렌지 주스가 커피만큼이나 잘 팔린다고 한다.

7 (C)	8 (A)	9 (B)	10 (D)

7

We / believe / that a job applicant's work history / is (as important / as) his or her education.
우리는 생각합니다　구직자의 근무 경력이　　　　　　　　　　중요하다고　　　학력만큼

(A) like   (B) much
(C) as   (D) less

↳ as + 원급 + as

해설 as + 원급 + as: 빈칸 뒤에 형용사와 as가 나오고 문맥상 '~만큼 중요하다'라는 의미가 적절하므로, as ~ as의 구문이 필요합니다. 따라서 (C) as가 정답입니다.

번역 우리는 구직자의 근무 경력이 학력만큼 중요하다고 생각합니다.

8

Winblaze running shoes / are not quite (as light / as) comparably priced brands.
윈블레이즈 운동화는　　　　　　가볍지 않다　　　비슷한 가격의 다른 브랜드의 운동화만큼

(A) light 가벼운   (B) lightly 가볍게 ↳ as + 원급 + as
(C) lightest 가장 가벼운   (D) lightness 가벼움

해설 as + 원급 + as: 빈칸 앞과 뒤에 as가 있는 것으로 보아 '~만큼 …한'이라는 의미의 〈as + 형용사 + as〉 원급 구문임을 알 수 있습니다. 따라서 정답은 원급 형용사 형태인 (A) light입니다.

번역 윈블레이즈 운동화는 비슷한 가격의 다른 브랜드의 운동화만큼 가볍지 않다.

9

Even though (lighter / than) forecast, / rain / caused / the tennis tournament / to be delayed / by
더 약하기는 했지만　　일기예보보다　　비가　야기했다　테니스 경기가　　　　지연되는 것을　　한 시간

an hour. ↳ 비교급 + than

(A) light   (B) lighter
(C) lightly   (D) lightest

해설 비교급 선택: 빈칸 뒤에 than이 있으므로 비교급 표현이 필요함을 알 수 있으므로 비교급 형용사 형태인 (B) lighter가 정답입니다.

번역 일기예보보다는 약했지만, 비로 인해 테니스 경기가 한 시간 지연되었다.

10

Our European markets / have grown (considerably) stronger / since the company's launch.
당사의 유럽 시장은　　　상당히 더 견고해졌다　　　회사 창립 이후

(A) consideration 고려   (B) considerate 사려 깊은 ↳ 비교급 형용사 stronger 수식
(C) considerable 상당한   (D) considerably 상당히

해설 비교급 강조 부사: 빈칸은 비교급 형용사 형태인 stronger를 수식하는 부사 자리이므로, 부사 (D) considerably(상당히)가 정답입니다.

번역 당사의 유럽 시장은 회사 창립 이후 상당히 더 견고해졌다.

1 (B)	2 (A)	3 (A)	4 (A)	5 (A)	6 (A)

1

Attendance figures / at this year's environmental summit / were (the highest) / on record.
참석자 수는   올해 환경 정상회담의   최고였다   공식적으로
↳ the + 최상급

(A) higher   (B) highest

번역 올해 환경 정상회담 참석자 수는 공식적으로 최고였다.

2

The route of the new high-speed train / will provide / (ready) access / to the resort towns.
새로운 고속 열차의 노선은   제공할 것이다   편리한 접근을   휴양 도시로
↳ 명사 access를 수식하는 형용사

(A) ready   (B) readiest

번역 새로운 고속 열차의 노선은 휴양 도시로의 편리한 접근을 제공할 것이다.

3

Applications / for the accounting position / must be received / (no later than) April 19.
지원서는   회계직을 위한   접수되어야 합니다   늦어도 4월 19일까지는
↳ 늦어도 ~까지는

(A) later   (B) further

번역 회계직 지원서는 늦어도 4월 19일까지는 접수되어야 합니다.

4

Our support staff / receives / (the same salary increase / as) the managerial group.
우리의 지원 인력은   받는다   동일한 급여 인상을   관리자 집단과
↳ the same + 명사 + as

(A) same   (B) as

번역 우리의 지원 인력은 관리자 집단과 동일한 급여 인상을 받는다.

5

A recent customer poll / suggests / that Heirloom Seating / is (the more durable / of the two) sofa
최근 실시된 고객 의견 조사는   시사한다   에얼룸 시팅이   더 내구성이 있다는 것을   두 소파 브랜드 중에서
brands.   the + 비교급 + of the two ←

(A) more durable   (B) most durable

번역 최근 실시된 고객 의견 조사는 두 소파 브랜드 중에서 에얼룸 시팅이 더 내구성이 있다는 것을 시사한다.

6

(Of all the candidates), / Mr. Wang / appears to be (the most promising).
모든 지원자들 중에서   왕 씨가   가장 유망해 보인다
↳ the + 최상급 + of + 복수 명사: ~ 중에서 가장 …한

(A) most   (B) much

번역 모든 지원자들 중에서 왕 씨가 가장 유망해 보인다.

50

7 (B)	8 (C)	9 (B)	10 (B)

7

Our accessory packages / offer / telephone customers / (the widest) selection / of carrying cases /
저희 액세서리 패키지는   제공합니다 / 전화 사용 고객들에게   가장 다양한 선택을   휴대용 케이스의

and covers / in the marketplace.
그리고 커버의   시장에서   └→ the + 최상급

(A) wider   (B) widest

(C) more widely   (D) most widely

해설 최상급 선택: 빈칸 뒤 명사 selection을 수식하는 형용사 자리이므로, 빈칸에는 형용사의 비교급 (A) wider와 최상급 (B) widest가 들어갈 수 있습니다. 빈칸 뒤에 범위를 나타내는 전치사구 in the marketplace가 있으므로, '시장에서 가장 다양한 휴대용 케이스와 커버'라는 의미가 문맥상 자연스럽습니다. 따라서 최상급 (B) widest가 정답입니다.

번역 저희 액세서리 패키지는 전화 사용 고객들에게 시장에서 선택 가능한 가장 다양한 휴대용 케이스와 커버를 제공합니다.

8

The X200's crisp images / prove / that it is the most (highly) advanced digital camera / on the
X200의 선명한 이미지는   입증한다   그것이 최첨단 디지털 카메라라는 것을   시장에서

market.
                       └→ 고도로, 대단히

(A) high   (B) higher

(C) highly   (D) highest

해설 뜻을 주의해야 하는 부사: 빈칸 뒤의 형용사 advanced를 수식해 줄 부사가 필요한데, 빈칸 앞의 the most와 함께 '가장 많이 발전된'이라는 의미가 적절하므로, (C) highly(고도로, 대단히)가 정답입니다. (A) high도 부사로 쓸 수 있지만 '높게'라는 의미이므로 문맥에 어울리지 않습니다.

번역 X200은 선명한 이미지로 시장에서 최고로 발전된 디지털 카메라임을 입증한다.

9

Developing work schedules / that are both effective and fair / is (one of the toughest challenges) /
작업 일정을 개발하는 것은   효과적이고 공정한   가장 어려운 도전 중 하나이다

faced by managers.
관리자가 직면한   one of the + 최상급 + 복수 명사 ←

(A) challenge   (B) challenges

(C) challenging   (D) challenged

해설 비교 구문 관용표현: ⟨one of the + 최상급 + 복수 명사⟩의 형태이므로, 복수 가산 명사 (B) challenges(도전들)가 정답입니다.

번역 효과적이고 공정한 작업 일정을 개발하는 것은 관리자가 직면한 가장 어려운 도전 중 하나이다.

10

Mr. Yamaguchi / wants / to order / (the brightest) possible lamps / for all employee offices.
야마구치 씨는   원한다   주문하기를   가능한 가장 밝은 램프를   모든 직원 사무실에 설치할
                                     └→ the + 최상급

(A) bright 밝은   (B) brightest 가장 밝은

(C) brightens 밝게 하다   (D) brightness 밝음, 빛남

해설 최상급 선택: 빈칸 뒤 형용사 possible과 함께 명사 lamps를 수식하는 형용사 자리이므로, 빈칸에는 형용사의 원급 (A) bright와 최상급 (B) brightest가 들어갈 수 있습니다. 빈칸 앞에 정관사 the가 있고 '가능한 가장 밝은 램프'라는 의미가 자연스러우므로 최상급 형용사인 (B) brightest가 정답입니다.

번역 야마구치 씨는 모든 직원 사무실에 설치할 가장 밝은 램프를 주문하고 싶어 한다.

1 (B)	**2** (A)	**3** (B)	**4** (A)

1

Our Web site / informs / you / about all (related materials) and costs.
저희 웹사이트는　　알려드립니다　여러분에게 / 모든 관련 자재와 비용에 관해
　　　　　　　　　　　　　　　　　　　　　　　　　└→ 관련 자재

(A) shapes 모양　　　　　　　　　　　(B) materials 자재, 재료

번역　저희 웹사이트에서 모든 관련 자재와 비용에 관해 알려드립니다.

2

Ms. Idassi / needed / to take care of (personal matters) / before returning / to the office.
이다시 씨는　　필요가 있었다 / 개인적인 일들을 처리할　　　　돌아가기 전에　　　사무실로
　　　　　　　　　　　　　　　　　　　　└→ 개인적인 일들

(A) matters 문제, 일　　　　　(B) conclusions 결론

번역　이다시 씨는 사무실로 돌아가기 전에 개인적인 일들을 처리할 필요가 있었다.

3

Click, Inc., / has announced / that its (profits) / have risen 16 percent / in the last six months.
클릭사는　　　발표했다　　　　자사의 수익이　　16퍼센트 상승했다고　　　지난 6개월간
　　　　　　　　　　　　　　　　　└→ 수익, 이익

(A) employees 직원, 고용인　　　(B) profits 수익, 이익

번역　클릭사는 지난 6개월간 자사의 수익이 16퍼센트 상승했다고 발표했다.

4

Due to unexpected (system failures), / the workshop / is postponed / until next month.
예상치 못한 시스템 장애 때문에　　　　　　워크숍이　　　연기되었다　　　다음 달까지
　　　　　　　　　└→ 시스템 장애

(A) failures 장애, 고장　　　　　(B) components 요소, 부품

번역　예상치 못한 시스템 장애 때문에 워크숍이 다음 달까지 연기되었다.

5 (A)	6 (B)	7 (D)	8 (B)

5

Mr. Blondell / tried / to protect his family / from (media attention) / during his run for the National
블론델 씨는　　애썼다　　자신의 가족을 보호하려고　　언론의 관심으로부터　　　　국회의원에 출마한 기간 동안

Assembly.
　　　　　　　　　　　　　　　　　　　　　→ 언론의 관심

(A) attention 관심, 주목　　　　　　　(B) payment 지불

(C) possibility 가능성　　　　　　　　(D) registration 등록

> 해설　media attention 언론의 관심(주목): 빈칸 앞 명사 media와 결합하여 전치사 from의 목적어 역할을 하는 명사 자리로, 빈칸을 포함한 전치사구는 protect를 수식합니다. 문맥상 '언론의 관심으로부터 가족을 보호하려고 애썼다'라는 의미가 자연스러우므로, (A) attention이 정답입니다.

> 번역　블론델 씨는 국회의원에 출마한 기간 동안 언론의 관심으로부터 자신의 가족을 보호하려고 애썼다.

6

Musicflux / will reduce / its (fees) / for access to its digital music files / by 20 percent.
뮤직플럭스는　　인하할 것이다　　요금을　　디지털 음악 파일 이용에 대한　　　　20퍼센트만큼

(A) entrance 입장, 입구　　　　　　(B) fees 요금
　　　　　　　　　　　　　　　　　　　　→ 요금

(C) earnings 수입　　　　　　　　　(D) decision 결정

> 해설　fee 요금: 빈칸 앞 동사 will reduce의 목적어 역할을 하는 명사 자리로, 빈칸 뒤 전치사구(for access ~ music files)의 수식을 받습니다. 문맥상 '음악 파일 이용에 대한 요금'이라는 의미가 자연스러우므로, (B) fees가 정답입니다.

> 번역　뮤직플럭스는 디지털 음악 파일 이용 요금을 20퍼센트 인하할 것이다.

7

The (site) / for the proposed complex / is at the intersection / of Gaskins Road and Patterson
부지는　　　제안된 복합 단지의　　~가 만나는 지점에 있다　　개스킨스로와 패터슨가의

Avenue.
　　→ 부지

(A) belief 믿음　　　　　　　　　　(B) advancement 발전

(C) travel 여행　　　　　　　　　　(D) site 부지

> 해설　site 부지: 빈칸은 동사 is의 주어 역할을 하는 명사 자리로, 위치를 나타내는 전치사구 at the intersection이 빈칸을 수식합니다. 따라서 빈칸에는 장소와 관련된 명사가 들어가는 것이 적절하므로, '부지'라는 의미의 (D) site가 정답입니다.

> 번역　제안된 복합 단지의 부지는 개스킨스로와 패터슨가가 만나는 지점에 있다.

8

Advance Limited / is involved / in the (manufacture, sale, and distribution) / of its products.
어드밴스사는　　담당한다　　제조, 판매와 유통에　　　　　　　　자사 제품들의

(A) solution 해결　　　　　　　　(B) distribution 유통
　　　　　　　　　　　　　　　　　　　→ 제조, 판매, 유통

(C) exception 예외　　　　　　　　(D) repetition 반복

> 해설　distribution 유통: 빈칸은 접속사 and로 연결된 명사 manufacture, sale과 함께 전치사구 of its products의 수식을 받습니다. 문맥상 '제품의 제조, 판매, 유통'이라는 의미가 자연스러우므로, 정답은 (B) distribution입니다.

> 번역　어드밴스사는 자사 그 제품들의 제조, 판매, 유통에 담당한다.

1 (C)	2 (B)	3 (C)	4 (B)	5 (B)

1

In your search for an architect, / you / could not hope / to find / a (more accurate) designer / (than)
건축가를 구할 때　　　　　　당신은　바랄 수 없을 것입니다　찾는 것을　더 정확한 설계자를

Ms. Lopez.
로페즈 씨보다 더　　　　　　　　　　　　　　　　비교급 형용사 + 명사 + than, ~보다 …한 명사 ←

(A) more accurately　(B) most accurately　(C) more accurate　(D) most accurate

> **해설** 비교급 선택: 빈칸 뒤에 than이 있으므로 비교급 표현이 필요함을 알 수 있는데, 비교의 대상인 designer를 수식해야 하므로 비교급은 부사가 아닌 형용사 형태인 (C) more accurate이 정답입니다.

> **번역** 건축가를 구할 때, 로페즈 씨보다 더 정확한 설계자를 찾는 것을 바랄 수 없을 것입니다.

2

Less expensive laundry detergents / can be just (as effective / as) the more expensive products.
덜 비싼 세탁용 세제가　　　　　　　　더 비싼 제품만큼 효과적일 수 있다

(A) more　(B) as　(C) very　(D) much　　　　　　→ as + 원급 + as

> **해설** 원급 비교 구문: 빈칸 뒤에 형용사 effective와 as가 있는 것으로 보아 '~만큼 …한'이라는 의미의 〈as + 형용사 + as〉 원급 구문임을 알 수 있습니다. 따라서 정답은 (B) as입니다.

> **번역** 덜 비싼 세탁용 세제가 더 비싼 제품만큼이나 효과적일 수 있다.

3

Red Badge / has been gaining / market share / and is now Talo Security's (strongest) competitor.
레드 배지는　　늘려 나가고 있다　시장 점유율을　그래서 지금은 탈로 시큐리티의 가장 강력한 경쟁사이다
　　　　　　　　　　　　　　　　　　　　명사 competitor를 수식하는 최상급 형용사 ←

(A) strongly　(B) strength　(C) strongest　(D) most strongly

> **해설** 최상급 선택: 빈칸에는 명사 competitor(경쟁사)를 수식하는 형용사가 들어가야 하는데, 보기 중 형용사는 최상급 형태인 strongest밖에 없으므로 (C) strongest가 정답입니다.

> **번역** 레드 배지는 시장 점유율을 늘려 나가고 있으며 그래서 지금은 탈로 시큐리티의 가장 강력한 경쟁사이다.

4

Reimbursements / will be paid / (as quickly as) possible / after all forms have been received.
환급금은　　　　　　지불될 것이다　가능한 한 빨리　　　　서류가 모두 접수된 이후에
　　　　　　　　　　　　　　　　　　→ as + 부사 + as

(A) quick　(B) quickly　(C) quicker　(D) quickest

> **해설** as + 형용사[부사] + as: as와 as 사이에 형용사가 들어갈지 부사가 들어갈지 선택하는 방법은 as가 없다고 생각하고 문장 구조를 살펴보는 것입니다. 여기에서는 동사 will be paid를 수식하는 부사가 필요하므로 (B) quickly가 정답입니다.

> **번역** 환급금은 서류가 모두 접수된 후에 가능한 한 빨리 지급될 것이다.

5

Edwards Plumbing / earned / (the highest) ratings / for customer satisfaction / in this year's Best
에드워즈 플러밍은　　얻었다　최고 평점을　　　고객 만족도 항목에　　　올해의 '최우수 업체'

Businesses survey.
설문 조사에서　　　　　　→ the + 최상급 형용사, 뒤 명사 ratings 수식

(A) higher　(B) highest　(C) more highly　(D) most highly

> **해설** 최상급 선택: 빈칸 앞의 정관사 the와 함께 뒤의 명사 ratings를 수식해 줄 수 있는 것은 최상급 형용사인 (B) highest입니다. 빈칸 뒤 범위를 나타내는 전치사구 in this year's Best Businesses survey가 빈칸에 최상급이 필요하다는 것을 뒷받침해 주고 있습니다.

> **번역** 에드워즈 플러밍은 올해의 '최우수 업체' 설문 조사의 고객 만족도 항목에 최고 평점을 얻었다.

6 (A)	7 (C)	8 (B)	9 (B)	10 (B)

6

Plastic / is now a (much) more versatile construction material / than it was in the past.
플라스틱은   이제 훨씬 더 다양하게 쓰이는 건축 자재이다   과거에 그랬던 것보다
                                        → 뒤에 비교급 형용사 more versatile 강조

(A) much   (B) so   (C) very   (D) really

해설 비교급 강조 표현 much: 빈칸 뒤에 비교급 형용사 more versatile이 있으므로, 빈칸에는 비교급을 강조하는 부사가 들어가야 합니다. 따라서 비교급을 강조하여 '훨씬'이라는 의미를 나타내는 (A) much가 정답입니다.

번역 이제 플라스틱은 과거에 그랬던 것보다 훨씬 더 다양하게 쓰이는 건축 자재이다.

7

Sky Miles Airlines / canceled / (more flights / than) any other North American airline / in July.
스카이 마일즈 항공은   취소했다   더 많은 항공편을   다른 어떤 북미 항공사보다도   7월에
                                            → 비교급 + than

(A) as   (B) while   (C) than   (D) whether

해설 비교급 구문 관용표현: 빈칸 앞에 비교급 표현 more flights가 있으므로 (C) than이 정답입니다. 참고로 비교급 관용표현 〈비교급 + than any other + 명사〉는 '어떤 다른 ~보다 더 …한'이라는 의미로 최상급을 나타냅니다.

번역 스카이 마일즈 항공은 7월에 다른 어떤 북미 항공사보다도 더 많은 항공편을 취소했다.

8

The general contractor / expects / Mountain Office Park / to be ready for occupancy / (no later than)
시공사는   예상한다   마운틴 오피스 파크가   입주 준비가 될 것으로   늦어도 다음 달까지는
next month.   늦어도 ~까지 ←

(A) late   (B) later   (C) latest   (D) lately

해설 비교급 구문 관용표현: 빈칸은 형용사 ready를 수식하는 부사 자리로, 빈칸 뒤 than과 어울리는 비교급 부사가 들어가야 합니다. 따라서 비교급 (B) later가 정답입니다. 〈no later than + 시간〉은 '늦어도 ~까지'라는 관용표현으로 묶어서 기억하세요.

번역 시공사는 마운틴 오피스 파크가 늦어도 다음 달까지는 입주 준비가 될 것으로 예상한다.

9

Sorin's Lakeview Grill / is the largest restaurant (ever) to be built / along the shores of Lake
소린즈 레이크뷰 그릴은   지금까지 세워진 가장 큰 식당이다   스웬슨 호숫가를 따라
Swensen.   → 비교급이나 최상급 뒤에 쓰여 그 의미를 강조

(A) usually   (B) ever   (C) always   (D) constantly

해설 최상급 + ever: 빈칸 앞에 최상급인 the largest restaurant가 있으므로 '지금까지 세워진'이라는 범위 표현을 완성하는 (B) ever가 정답입니다.

번역 소린즈 레이크뷰 그릴은 스웬슨 호숫가를 따라 지금까지 세워진 가장 큰 식당이다.

10

Researchers / are working / on a new material / that will be twice (as durable / as) ordinary
연구원들은   연구하고 있다   새로운 물질을   내구성이 2배가 될   일반 콘크리트보다
concrete.   → as + 형용사 + as

(A) durably 튼튼하게   (B) durable 내구성이 있는   (C) durability 내구성   (D) durableness 튼튼함

해설 as + 형용사[부사] + as: as와 as 사이에는 형용사 또는 부사의 원급이 들어갈 수 있습니다. 원급인 (A) durably와 (B) durable이 가능한데, 여기서는 be동사의 보어 역할을 할 수 있는 형용사가 필요하므로, (B) durable이 정답입니다.

번역 연구원들은 일반 콘크리트보다 내구성이 2배가 될 새로운 물질을 연구하고 있다.

| 11 (A) | 12 (C) | 13 (C) | 14 (D) |

Questions 11-14 refer to the following notice.

At Mitiwa Publishing House, / we are always looking for / the next best-
미티와 출판사에서는 　　　　　　　항상 찾고 있습니다 　　　　독자를 위한

seller for our readers. To encourage more submissions, / we have recently
차세대 베스트셀러를 　　　　더 많은 투고를 장려하기 위해 　　　당사는 최근 변경했습니다

changed / our online manuscript submission process / to be 11. easier /
　　　　　　온라인 원고 제출 과정을 　　　　　　　　　더 쉽게

for writers. This new system / also / allows our editors 12. to read / and
작가들을 위해 　이 새로운 시스템은 　　또한 　편집자가 읽을 수 있게 합니다 　　　그리고
　　　　　　　　　　　　　　　　　allow + 목적어 + to 동사원형

provide constructive feedback / on your work / more quickly. If you are
건설적인 의견을 제공하게 합니다 　　　여러분의 작품에 대해　더 신속하게 　만약 여러분이

ultimately given a contract, / you will be assigned an editor / to help publish
최종 계약을 맺게 되면 　　　　편집자를 배정받게 됩니다 　　　　　출판 및 홍보를 도울

and promote / your new 13. book.
　　　　　당신 신간의

If you have any questions / about using the updated system, / please
질문이 있으시면 　　　　새로 바뀐 시스템을 이용하는 것과 관련해 　　　업무지원센터로

e-mail the help desk / at help@mitiwaph.org. 14. You will receive a
이메일을 보내세요 　　help@mitiwaph.org로 　　　　답변을 받으실 수 있습니다

response / within three days.
　　　사흘 이내에

11-14 공지

미티와 출판사에서는 항상 독자를 위한 차세대 베스트셀러를 찾고 있습니다. 더 많은 투고를 장려하기 위해, 당사는 최근 작가들을 위해 온라인 원고 제출 과정을 더 쉽게 변경했습니다. 또한 이 새로운 시스템을 통해 편집자는 여러분의 작품을 더 신속하게 읽고 건설적인 의견을 제공할 수 있습니다. 만약 여러분이 최종 계약을 맺게 되면, 신간 출판 및 홍보를 도울 편집자를 배정받게 됩니다.

새로 바뀐 시스템을 이용하는 데 질문이 있으시면 업무지원센더 help@mitiwaph.org로 이메일을 보내세요. 사흘 이내에 답변을 받으실 수 있습니다.

11 (A) easier

(B) braver

(C) sharper

(D) broader

(A) 더 쉬운

(B) 더 용감한

(C) 더 날카로운

(D) 더 넓은

> **해설** 어휘 문제: 빈칸 앞 To encourage more submissions에서 원고 제출을 더 독려하기 위한 목적을 제시했습니다. '작가들을 위해 제출 과정을 더 쉽게'라는 의미가 문맥상 자연스러우므로, (A) easier가 정답입니다.

---

12 (A) reading

(B) read

(C) to read

(D) have read

> **해설** 목적격 보어(to부정사): 빈칸은 동사 allows의 목적어 our editors의 행동을 보충 설명하는 목적격 보어 자리입니다. '허용하다'라는 의미의 동사 allow는 to부정사를 목적격 보어로 취하므로, (C) to read가 정답입니다. 〈allow + 목적어 + to 동사원형(목적격 보어)〉의 구조로 묶어서 기억하세요.

---

13 (A) music

(B) site

(C) book

(D) show

(A) 음악

(B) 사이트, 위치, 현장

(C) 책, 서적

(D) 쇼, 공연물

> **해설** 어휘 문제: 빈칸 앞의 형용사 new의 수식을 받는 명사 자리입니다. 문맥상 '신간 서적의 출판 및 홍보'라는 의미가 자연스러우므로 (C) book이 정답입니다.

---

14 (A) Mitiwa has an excellent reputation for publishing.

(B) Our editing staff members have a lot of experience.

(C) Our template was developed to increase our efficiency.

(D) You will receive a response within three days.

(A) 미티와는 출판계에서 평판이 아주 좋습니다.

(B) 저희 편집부 직원들은 경험이 많습니다.

(C) 저희 템플릿은 효율성을 높이기 위해 개발되었습니다.

(D) 사흘 이내에 답변을 받으실 수 있습니다.

> **해설** 문장 고르기: 빈칸 앞 문장 If you ~ at help@mitiwaph.org에서 질문이 있으면 이메일을 보낼 것을 요청했습니다. 따라서 빈칸에는 이메일에 대한 답변을 언급하는 것이 문맥상 자연스러우므로 정답은 (D)입니다.

동사의 형태 ETS 문제로 훈련하기 STEP 1

교재 p.85

1 (B)	2 (B)	3 (A)	4 (A)	5 (A)	6 (B)

1

The Darlingstone Hotel / (is offering) / a complimentary breakfast / to all of its guests.
달링스톤 호텔은   제공하고 있다   무료 아침 식사를   모든 투숙객에게
                                 → be + 현재분사: 진행·능동의 의미

(A) offered   (B) offering

> **번역** 달링스톤 호텔은 모든 투숙객에게 아침 식사를 무료로 제공하고 있다.

2

Adion Airlines / (cannot guarantee) / that all flights depart / on time.
아디온 항공사는   보장할 수 없습니다   모든 항공기가 출발하는 것을   정시에
                         → 조동사 + 동사원형

(A) guarantees   (B) guarantee

> **번역** 아디온 항공사에서는 모든 항공기의 정시 출발을 보장할 수 없습니다.

3

The Desorbo Company / will (be introducing) / its new leather boots / in the fall catalog.
데소보 사는   선보일 것이다   새 가죽 부츠를   가을 카탈로그에서
                         → be + 현재분사: 진행·능동의 의미

(A) introducing   (B) introduced

> **번역** 데소보 사는 가을 카탈로그에서 새 가죽 부츠를 선보일 것이다.

4

The information / should (be written) / carefully / in the space / provided.
정보는   작성되어야 한다   주의 깊게   공간에   주어진
                         → be + 과거분사: 수동의 의미

(A) written   (B) wrote

> **번역** 정보는 주어진 공간에 주의 깊게 작성되어야 한다.

5

The workers / (have replaced) / the batteries / in the fire alarm system.
작업자들이   교체했다   건전지를   화재 경보 시스템의
                         → have + 과거분사: 완료의 의미

(A) replaced   (B) replacing

> **번역** 작업자들이 화재 경보 시스템의 건전지를 교체했다.

6

A survey technician / (finished) / mapping the property lines / at 10 Mulberry Drive / last Monday.
측량 기술자는   마쳤다   대지 경계선 측량하기를   10 멀베리 드라이브의   지난주 월요일에
                       → 동사 자리, last Monday라는 과거 시점에 일어난 일을 나타내는 과거 시제

(A) finishing   (B) finished

> **번역** 측량 기술자는 지난주 월요일에 10 멀베리 드라이브의 대지 경계선 측량하기를 마쳤다.

PART 5 | UNIT 06

7 (A)	8 (B)	9 (D)	10 (D)

7

Our company / must establish / contacts / quickly / to build new trade relationships.
우리 회사는 　　쌓아야 한다 　　인맥을 　　신속히 　　새로운 거래 관계를 구축하기 위해
　　　　　　　　　　　　　　　　　　→ 조동사 + 동사원형

(A) establish

(B) establishing

(C) to establish

(D) establishes

해설 **조동사 + 동사원형:** 빈칸 앞에 조동사 must가 있습니다. 조동사 뒤에는 항상 동사원형을 써야 하므로 (A) establish가 정답입니다.

번역 우리 회사는 새로운 거래 관계를 구축하기 위해 신속히 인맥을 쌓아야 한다.

8

The holiday travel brochures / arrived / by registered mail / this morning.
휴가 여행 안내 소책자가 　　도착했다 　　등기 우편으로 　　오늘 아침에
　　　　　　　　　　　　　　→ 문장의 동사 자리

(A) arriving

(B) arrived

(C) arrival

(D) to arrive

해설 **주어 + 동사:** 빈칸은 주어 The holiday travel brochures 뒤에 나오는 동사 자리이고 과거 시점인 this morning이 있으므로, 과거시제 동사 (B) arrived가 정답입니다. 동명사 (A) arriving과 to부정사 (D) to arrive는 동사 자리에 들어갈 수 없고, (C) arrival은 명사이므로 적절하지 않습니다.

번역 휴가 여행 안내 소책자가 오늘 아침에 등기 우편으로 도착했다.

9

Café Rouge's manager / is continually striving / to improve the dessert menu.
카페 루즈의 매니저는 　　계속 노력하고 있다 　　디저트 메뉴를 개선하기 위해

(A) have strived

(B) strive
　　　　　　　→ be + 현재분사: 진행의 의미

(C) been striving

(D) striving

해설 **be + 현재분사(진행의 의미):** 앞에 is가 있으므로, '~하고 있다'는 진행의 의미인 〈be + 현재분사〉 구조가 되어야 합니다. 따라서 정답은 (D) striving입니다.

번역 카페 루즈의 매니저는 디저트 메뉴를 개선하기 위해 계속 노력하고 있다.

10

Please consult / the owner's manual / before using your Kivi Craft oven / for the first time.
참고하세요 　　사용자 설명서를 　　키비 크래프트 오븐을 사용하기 전에 　　처음으로
　　　　　　　　　　　　　　　　→ 주어가 생략된 명령문의 동사 형태

(A) consulting

(B) consulted

(C) consults

(D) consult

해설 **동사원형으로 시작하는 명령문:** 빈칸은 주어 you가 생략된 명령문의 동사원형 자리이므로, 동사원형 (D) consult(참고하다)가 정답입니다.

번역 키비 크래프트 오븐을 처음 사용하기 전에 사용자 설명서를 참고하세요.

1 (B)	2 (B)	3 (A)	4 (B)	5 (B)	6 (A)

1

Our updated Web site / now / (allows) / users / to upload images and audio files.
우리 최신 웹사이트는   이제   가능하게 한다 / 사용자들이 / 이미지와 오디오 파일을 올리는 것을
                                        └→ 문장의 동사 자리, 주어가 Our updated Web site로 단수이므로 단수 동사가 옴
(A) allowing   (B) allows

번역   이제 사용자들은 우리 최신 웹사이트에 이미지와 오디오 파일을 올릴 수 있다.

2

Sending a letter of thanks / after a job interview / (is) highly recommended.
감사 편지를 보내는 것은   취업 면접 후에   강력하게 추천된다
                                        └→ 동명사 주어(단수 취급) + 단수 동사
(A) are   (B) is

번역   취업 면접 후에 감사 편지를 보내는 것은 강력하게 추천된다.

3

The documents / in the filing cabinet / (need) to be organized / alphabetically.
서류들은   파일 보관함의   정리되어야 한다   알파벳순으로
                                        └→ 복수 주어 + 복수 동사
(A) need   (B) needs

번역   파일 보관함의 서류들은 알파벳순으로 정리되어야 한다.

4

Our research (results) / were published / in the July issue of *Breakthrough*.
우리 연구 결과는   실렸다   〈브레이크스루〉 7월호에
                  └→ 복수 주어 + 복수 동사
(A) result   (B) results

번역   우리 연구 결과는 〈브레이크스루〉 7월 호에 실렸다.

5

The sales figures of the Gamma Company / (were reported) / in many newspapers.
감마사의 매출액은   보도되었다   많은 신문에
                                        └→ 복수 주어 + 복수 동사
(A) was reported   (B) were reported

번역   감마사의 매출액은 많은 신문에 보도되었다.

6

What the survey results show / (is) that tourism to Jeju Island has significantly increased.
설문 조사 결과가 보여주는 것은   제주도 관광업이 크게 성장했다는 것이다
                                  └→ 단수 주어(what 명사절)
(A) is   (B) are

번역   설문 조사 결과가 보여주는 것은 제주도 관광업이 크게 성장했다는 점이다.

7 (A)	8 (A)	9 (A)	10 (C)

7

Salary (increases) / are determined / after performance reviews / by area managers.
급여 인상은   결정된다   인사 고과 후에   지역 관리자들에 의한
         └→ 복수 주어 + 복수 동사

(A) increases   (B) increasing

(C) increase   (D) increasingly

해설 〈복수 주어 + 복수 동사〉의 수 일치: 빈칸 뒤에 be동사의 복수형 are가 있으나, 빈칸 앞 Salary는 are와 수 일치하지 않습니다. 따라서 빈칸에 are와 수 일치하는 명사의 복수형이 들어가야 하므로, (A) increases(증가, 인상)가 정답입니다.

번역 급여 인상은 지역 관리자들에 의한 인사 고과 후에 결정된다.

8

The approved (design) / for the new city park / features / flower gardens, benches, / and a picnic
승인된 디자인은   새로운 도시 공원의   포함한다   꽃 정원, 벤치   그리고 피크닉 공간을

area.   └→ 단수 주어 + 단수 동사

(A) design   (B) designs

(C) designed   (D) designers

해설 〈단수 주어 + 단수 동사〉의 수 일치: 빈칸은 단수형 동사 features의 주어 자리이므로, 단수 명사 (A) design이 정답입니다. 형용사 (C) designed(계획적인, 고의의)는 주어 자리에 들어갈 수 없습니다.

번역 승인된 새로운 도시 공원의 설계에는 꽃 정원, 벤치 및 피크닉 공간이 포함되어 있다.

9

Event organizers / (anticipate) / an increase / in the number of vendors / at this year's art festival.
행사 주최자들은   예상한다   증가를   노점상 수의   올해 예술 축제에서
               └→ 복수 주어 + 복수 동사

(A) anticipate   (B) anticipates

(C) anticipating   (D) to anticipate

해설 〈복수 주어 + 복수 동사〉의 수 일치: 빈칸은 주어 Event organizers 뒤에 나오는 동사 자리입니다. 주어가 복수형이므로, 빈칸에도 수 일치하는 동사의 복수형이 들어가야 합니다. 따라서 (A) anticipate(예상하다, 기대하다)가 정답입니다. 동명사 / 현재분사 (C) anticipating과 to부정사 (D) to anticipate는 동사 자리에 들어갈 수 없습니다.

번역 행사 주최자들은 올해 예술 축제에서 노점상 수가 증가할 것으로 예상한다.

10

The final installment / in the popular mystery series / (was) due to arrive / in stores / yesterday.
마지막 권이   인기있는 미스터리 시리즈의   도착할 예정이었다   매장에   어제
                                              └→ 단수 주어, yesterday가 있으므로 과거 시제를 사용

(A) is   (B) are

(C) was   (D) were

해설 〈단수 주어 + 단수 동사〉의 수 일치: 빈칸은 주어 The final installment 뒤에 나오는 동사 자리로, 빈칸 앞 전치사구(in ~ series)는 installment를 수식합니다. 따라서 빈칸에는 단수 주어인 The final installment와 수 일치하는 동사의 단수형이 들어가야 합니다. (A) is와 (B) was 둘 다 be동사의 단수형이지만 문장 마지막에 과거 시제에 쓰이는 부사 yesterday가 있으므로 (C) was가 정답입니다.

번역 인기있는 미스터리 시리즈의 마지막 권이 어제 매장에 도착할 예정이었다.

1 (B)	2 (A)	3 (B)	4 (B)	5 (A)	6 (A)

1

Every security camera / installed in the laboratories / (records) / 24 hours a day.
모든 보안 카메라는   실험실들에 설치된   녹화한다   하루 24시간
↳ 단수 주어 + 단수 동사

(A) record　　　　　(B) records

번역 실험실들에 설치된 모든 보안 카메라는 하루 24시간 녹화한다.

2

All of the (applicants) / for the laboratory technician position / possess / the necessary training.
모든 지원자는   실험실 기술자 직책에 대한   받는다   필요한 교육을
↳ 복수 주어 + 복수 동사

(A) applicants　　　　　(B) application

번역 실험실 기술자 직책에 대한 모든 지원자는 필요한 교육을 받는다.

3

Roughly half of the employees / at Century Photo Labs / (commute) to work / by bus.
직원들의 거의 반 정도가   센추리 현상소의   출근한다   버스로
↳ half of the + 복수 명사 + 복수 동사

(A) commutes　　　　　(B) commute

번역 센추리 현상소 직원들의 거의 반 정도가 버스로 출근한다.

4

A number of vehicles / (are) parked / illegally / despite the city's strict regulations.
많은 차량들이   주차되어 있다   불법으로   시의 엄격한 규제에도 불구하고
↳ A number of + 복수 명사 + 복수 동사

(A) is　　　　　(B) are

번역 시의 엄격한 규제에도 불구하고 많은 차량들이 불법 주차되어 있다.

5

The number of smartphone users / (is) expected / to increase / by 30% / this year.
스마트폰 이용자 수가   예상된다   증가할 것으로   30퍼센트   올해에
↳ The number of + 복수 명사 + 단수 주어

(A) is　　　　　(B) are

번역 스마트폰 이용자 수가 올해 30퍼센트 증가할 것으로 예상된다.

6

(All) vendors / are required / to register with the receptionist / when entering the building.
모든 판매상들은   요구된다   접수 담당자에게 등록하도록   건물에 들어갈 때
↳ 복수 주어 + 복수 동사

(A) All　　　　　(B) Each

번역 모든 판매상들은 건물에 들어갈 때 접수 담당자에게 등록해야 한다.

PART 5 | UNIT 06

| **7** (C) | **8** (C) | **9** (C) | **10** (D) |

7

The number of toy manufacturers / has remained steady / nationwide, / except in the board-
장난감 제조업체의 수는 　　　　　계속 일정한 상태이다　　전국적으로　　보드게임 분야를 제외하고는

game sector.
→ The number of + 복수 명사 + 단수 동사

(A) manufacture

(B) manufactured

(C) manufacturers

(D) manufacturing

해설 〈the number of + 복수 명사 + 단수 동사〉: the number of(~의 수)와 결합할 수 있는 복수 명사를 선택해야 합니다. 따라서 복수
명사 (C) manufacturers가 정답입니다.

번역 보드게임 분야를 제외하고는 장난감 제조업체의 수는 전국적으로 계속 일정한 상태이다.

8

One possible conclusion / is that bigger projects receive more funding / and are therefore more
한 가지 가능한 결론은　　　　더 큰 프로젝트가 더 많은 자금을 받고　　　　　따라서 더 성공적이라는 것이다

successful.
→ 단수 주어 + 단수 동사

(A) conclusive 결정적인

(B) conclude 결론을 내리다

(C) conclusion 결론, 결말

(D) concluding 결론 내리기

해설 주어로 쓰이는 명사 (단수): 빈칸 앞의 One possible과 함께 is의 주어 역할을 하는 단수 명사 자리이므로, (C) conclusion이
정답입니다. (A) conclusive와 (B) conclude는 각각 형용사와 동사이므로 주어가 될 수 없고, 동명사 (D) concluding은 one과 같이
사용할 수 없으므로 오답입니다.

번역 한 가지 가능한 결론은 더 큰 프로젝트가 더 많은 자금을 지원받고 따라서 더 성공적이라는 것이다.

9

Because of the economic upturn, / most of the business leaders / hope / to make a big profit.
경기 호전 때문에　　　　　　　기업주들 대부분이　　　　　바란다　　큰 수익을 내기를

(A) hoping

(B) hopes

(C) hope

(D) to hope
→ most of the + 복수 명사 + 복수 동사

해설 most of the + 복수 명사 + 복수 동사: 주어 자리에 〈most of the + 명사〉가 있을 경우 명사의 단, 복수에 따라 동사의 수가
결정됩니다. the business leaders가 복수 명사이므로 복수 동사인 (C) hope가 정답입니다.

번역 경기 호전 때문에 기업주들 대부분이 큰 수익을 내기를 바란다.

10

According to the policy, / each team member / receives / an annual performance review.
방침에 따르면　　　　　　각 팀원은　　　　받는다　　연례 인사 고과를

(A) receive

(B) to receive
→ each + 단수 명사 + 단수 동사

(C) have received

(D) receives

해설 each + 단수 명사 + 단수 동사: 주어가 each team member로 단수 명사이므로 빈칸에는 단수 동사가 와야 합니다. 따라서 정답은 (D)
receives입니다.

번역 방침에 따르면, 각 팀원은 연례 인사 고과를 받는다.

1 (B)	**2** (A)	**3** (B)	**4** (B)

1

Construction costs for the tunnel / are expected / to ⬚exceed⬚ $300 million.
터널 건설 비용이　　　　　　　　예상된다　　　　3억 달러를 초과할 것으로

(A) excel 뛰어나다　　　　　　　(B) exceed 초과하다　　⌐→ 초과하다

> **번역** 　터널 건설 비용이 3억 달러를 초과할 것으로 예상된다.

2

The mayor / will ⬚address⬚ / the issue of road improvement / in today's speech.
시장은　　　　다룰 것이다　　　　도로 개선 문제를　　　　　오늘 연설에서
　　　　　　　　　　　　　└→ 다루다, 연설하다

(A) address 다루다, 연설하다　　　　(B) educate 교육하다

> **번역** 　시장은 오늘 연설에서 도로 개선 문제에 대해 다룰 것이다.

3

Emone Motor / has not ⬚experienced⬚ / any delays / in production / this quarter.
에몬 자동차 회사는　　겪지 않았다　　　어떠한 지연도　　생산에서　　이번 분기에
　　　　　　└→ 겪다, 경험하다

(A) submitted 제출하다　　　　　　(B) experienced 겪다, 경험하다

> **번역** 　에몬 자동차 회사는 이번 분기에 어떠한 생산 지연도 겪지 않았다.

4

Ms. Gupta / wishes / to ⬚modify⬚ / the terms of her employment contract.
굽타 씨는　　희망한다　　수정하기를　　자신의 고용계약서 조항들을
　　　　　　　　　　　　　　　　　　　　　└→ 수정하다, 변경하다

(A) respond 응답하다, 대답하다　　　(B) modify 수정하다, 변경하다

> **번역** 　굽타 씨는 자신의 고용계약서 조항들을 수정하기를 희망한다.

| 5 (C) | 6 (B) | 7 (A) | 8 (A) |

5

Most public telephones / in France and Italy / only (accept telephone cards), / which are for sale /
대부분의 공중전화는   프랑스와 이탈리아의   전화 카드만 받는다(전화 카드로만 사용할 수 있다) / 그것들은 판매된다

at post offices.
우체국에서   ↳ 전화 카드로 사용하다

(A) include 포함하다   (B) import 수입하다

(C) accept 받다, 수락하다   (D) enter 들어가다

해설 accept 받다, 수락하다: 빈칸 뒤의 목적어인 명사구 telephone cards와 어울리는 동사를 선택해야 합니다. 문맥상 '전화 카드를
받는다'라는 의미가 자연스러우므로 (C) accept가 정답입니다.

번역 프랑스와 이탈리아의 대부분의 공중전화는 우체국에서 판매하는 전화 카드가 있어야 사용할 수 있다.

6

The new laser printer / arrived / yesterday, / but it has not been (installed) yet, / so please continue /
새로운 레이저 프린터가   도착했다   어제   그러나 그것은 아직 설치되지 않았다   그러니 계속 ~해주세요

using the old one.
기존의 것을 사용하는 것을   ↳ 설치하다

(A) conducted 행하다   (B) installed 설치하다

(C) admitted 인정하다   (D) posted 게시하다

해설 install 설치하다: 빈칸 앞 be동사의 과거분사 been과 함께 수동의 의미를 나타내는 과거분사 자리입니다. 주어 it은 앞 절의 주어 The
new laser printer를 대신하는 인칭대명사입니다. 문맥상 '새 레이저 프린터가 아직 설치되지 않았다'라는 의미가 자연스러우므로, (B)
installed가 정답입니다.

번역 새로운 레이저 프린터가 어제 도착했지만, 아직 설치되지는 않았으니 기존 프린터를 계속 사용해 주세요.

7

It is important / that all members of the project team (attend / tomorrow's meeting).
중요하다   프로젝트 팀의 모든 구성원이 참석하는 것이   내일 회의에
                                                                        ↳ 내일 회의에 참석하다

(A) attend 참석하다   (B) belong 속하다

(C) commit 저지르다   (D) arrive 도착하다

해설 attend 참석하다: 빈칸 뒤 명사구 tomorrow's meeting을 목적어로 취해 가장 잘 어울리는 동사를 선택해야 합니다. 문맥상 '내일
회의에 참석하다'라는 의미가 자연스러우므로 (A) attend가 정답입니다.

번역 프로젝트 팀의 모든 구성원이 내일 회의에 참석하는 것이 중요하다.

8

All visitors / must sign in / with the receptionist / and (obtain) / a visitor's identification tag.
모든 방문자는   서명하고 들어가야 한다 / 접수 담당자에게   그리고 받아야 한다 / 방문자 이름표를

(A) obtain 획득하다   (B) define 정의하다   ↳ 획득하다, 얻다

(C) recall 상기하다   (D) inquire 문의하다

해설 obtain 획득하다, 얻다: 빈칸 뒤 명사구 a visitor's identification tag을 목적어로 취하는 타동사 자리입니다. 문맥상 접수 담당자에게
서명하고 들어간 후에 '방문자 이름표를 받는다'라는 내용이 이어지는 것이 자연스러우므로, (A) obtain이 정답입니다.

번역 모든 방문자는 접수 담당자에게 서명하고 들어가서 방문자 이름표를 받아야 한다.

1 (B)	**2** (B)	**3** (A)	**4** (D)	**5** (B)

1

The current system / (allows) / users / to access their online banking accounts / by entering a
현 시스템은   허용한다   사용자들이 /   온라인 뱅킹 계좌에 접속하는 것을   비밀번호를 입력해

password.
               → 단수 주어 + 단수 동사

(A) allowed   (B) allows   (C) allow   (D) allowing

> **해설** 현재 상태를 나타내는 현재 시제: 빈칸 앞에 현재의 시점을 나타내는 current가 있고 주어가 The current system으로 3인칭
> 단수이므로, 단수 동사인 (B) allows가 정답입니다.
>
> **번역** 현 시스템은 사용자들이 비밀번호를 입력해 온라인 뱅킹 계좌에 접속하도록 허용한다.

2

Ms. Chiodo, / our chief financial officer, / is pleased / that (annual profits) have been rising / steadily.
치오두 씨는   우리의 최고재무관리자인   기뻐한다   연간 수익이 늘고 있어서   꾸준히
                                            → 복수 주어 + 복수 동사

(A) profit   (B) profits   (C) profitable   (D) profiting

> **해설** 〈복수 주어 + 복수 동사〉의 수 일치: 빈칸은 복수형 동사 have been rising의 주어 자리이므로, 복수 명사 (B) profits가 정답입니다.
> 형용사 (C) profitable(수익성 있는)은 주어 자리에 들어갈 수 없고, 현재분사 / 동명사 (D) profiting이 주어인 경우에는 동사의
> 단수형이 뒤에 나와야 합니다.
>
> **번역** 우리의 최고재무관리자인 치오두 씨는 연간 수익이 꾸준히 늘고 있어서 기뻐하고 있다.

3

The lightweight trailer / by Tow-Well Manufacturing / (can accommodate) / almost any kind of
경량 트레일러는   토우웰 매뉴팩처링의   실을 수 있다   거의 온갖 종류의 소형 보트를

small boat.
                      → 조동사 + 동사원형

(A) accommodate   (B) to accommodate   (C) accommodates   (D) accommodating

> **해설** 조동사 + 동사원형: 빈칸 앞에 조동사가 있으므로 동사원형인 (A) accommodate(수용하다)가 정답입니다.
>
> **번역** 토우웰 매뉴팩처링에서 생산한 경량 트레일러에는 거의 온갖 종류의 소형 보트를 실을 수 있다.

4

Weathervane LLC, / a research firm based in Denton, / (helps) / clients / understand consumer
웨더베인 LLC는   덴턴에 기반을 둔 연구회사인   돕는다   고객들을   소비자 동향을 이해하도록

trends / in the region.
      그 지역의   → 단수 주어 + 단수 동사

(A) helpful   (B) to help   (C) helping   (D) helps

> **해설** 주어 + 동사: 빈칸은 명사구 a research ~ Denton의 수식을 받는 주어 Weathervane LLC 뒤에 나오는 동사 자리이므로 동사 (D)
> helps가 정답입니다. 형용사 (A) helpful, to부정사 (B) to help, 현재분사 / 동명사 (C) helping은 동사 자리에 들어갈 수 없습니다.
>
> **번역** 덴턴에 기반을 둔 연구 회사인 웨더베인 LLC는 고객들이 지역 소비자 동향을 이해하도록 돕는다.

5

The time / needed / to acquire all of the necessary materials / (depends) on several factors.
시간은   필요한   필요한 모든 자료들을 입수하는 데   몇 가지 요인에 달려 있다
                                             → 단수 주어 + 단수 동사

(A) depend   (B) depends   (C) depending   (D) to depend

> **해설** 〈단수 주어 + 단수 동사〉의 수 일치: 빈칸은 주어 The time 뒤에 나오는 동사 자리로, 빈칸 앞 과거분사 구문(needed ~ materials)은
> time을 수식합니다. 따라서 빈칸에는 단수 주어인 The time과 수 일치하는 동사의 단수형이 들어가야 하므로, (B) depends
> (의존하다)가 정답입니다. 현재분사 / 동명사 (C) depending과 to부정사 (D) to depend는 동사 자리에 들어갈 수 없습니다.
>
> **번역** 필요한 모든 자료들을 입수하는 데 필요한 시간은 몇 가지 요인에 달려 있다.

ETS 실전 테스트

교재 p. 92

6 (D) **7** (B) **8** (B) **9** (B) **10** (D)

6

Any questions or concerns / about the revised meeting schedule / should be directed / to Ms.
질문이나 관심사는　　　　　　　변경된 회의 시간에 대한　　　　　　보내져야 한다　　　　　　리 씨에게
→ 주어(보내져야 하는 대상) + [수식어] + 동사

Lee.

(A) direction (B) director (C) directs (D) directed

해설 주어 + [수식어] + 동사: Any questions or concerns가 주어, about the revised meeting schedule은 주어를 수식하는
전치사구, should be ____가 동사인 문장입니다. 문맥상 주어가 Any questions or concerns가 보내져야 하는 대상이므로, 수동의
의미를 지닌 과거분사 (D) directed가 정답입니다.

번역 변경된 회의 시간에 대한 질문이나 관심사는 리 씨에게 보내야 한다.

7

Palor Corporation's annual operating costs / at the Fukui plant / have remained steady.
팔러 코퍼레이션의 연간 운영비가　　　　　　후쿠이 공장에서의　　　　계속 일정한 상태이다
문장의 동사 자리(복수 주어 + 복수 동사) ←

(A) is remaining (B) have remained (C) to remain (D) remaining

해설 〈복수 주어 + 복수 동사〉의 수 일치: 빈칸은 Palor Corporation's annual operating costs의 뒤에 나오는 동사 자리로, 수 일치하는
동사의 복수형이 들어가야 하므로, (B) have remained가 정답입니다.

번역 팔러 코퍼레이션의 후쿠이 공장 연간 운영비가 계속 일정한 상태이다.

8

The number of transport companies / competing for government contracts / has decreased /
운송 회사의 수가　　　　　　　　정부 계약을 따기 위해 경쟁하는　　　　줄어들었다
→ 단수 주어 + 단수 동사

sharply.
급격히

(A) have (B) has (C) having (D) to have

해설 〈단수 주어 + 단수 동사〉의 수 일치: 주어는 The number이고 of ~ contracts는 주어를 수식하는 전치사구입니다. 따라서 단수 주어에
어울리는 단수 조동사 (B) has가 정답입니다.

번역 정부 계약을 따기 위해 경쟁하는 운송 회사의 수가 급격히 줄어들었다.

9

Last year's restructuring / of the Anyang Industries plant / has resulted in enhanced worker
지난해 구조조정은　　　　　　　안양 산업 공장의　　　　　　결과적으로 근로자 안전이 강화되었다
→ 단수 주어 + 단수 동사

safety.

(A) to result (B) has resulted (C) result (D) resulting

해설 〈단수 주어 + 단수 동사〉의 수 일치: 주어는 of ~ plant의 수식을 받는 Last year's restructuring입니다. 따라서 단수 주어에 어울리는
동사의 단수형 (B) has resulted가 정답입니다.

번역 지난해 안양 산업 공장의 구조조정은 결과적으로 근로자 안전이 강화되었다.

10

The employees at Topso Lumber / are expected / to wear company uniforms and identification
토프소 럼버의 직원들은   요구받는다   회사 유니폼과 사원증을 착용하기를
                                                              └→ 복수 주어 + 복수 동사

badges / at all times.
          항상

(A) expecting   (B) expects   (C) to be expecting   (D) are expected

해설   《복수 주어 + 복수 동사》의 수 일치: 빈칸은 주어 The employees 뒤에 나오는 동사 자리로, 빈칸 앞 전치사구 at Topso Lumber는
       주어를 수식합니다. 따라서 빈칸에는 복수 주어인 The employees와 수 일치하는 동사의 복수형이 들어가야 하므로, (D) are
       expected가 정답입니다.

번역   토프소 럼버의 직원들은 항상 회사 유니폼과 사원증을 착용하기를 요구받는다.

ETS 실전 테스트

11 (A)	**12** (B)	**13** (A)	**14** (B)

Questions 11-14 refer to the following advertisement.

11-14 광고

Jiffy Fleet Office Supply
지피 플릿 사무용품

지피 플릿 사무용품

As improved technology / makes online shopping easier than ever, /
향상된 기술이 ~함에 따라   온라인 쇼핑을 그 어느 때보다 쉽게 하다

consumers generally 11. expect / purchases / to arrive quickly and reliably.
소비자들은 일반적으로 예상합니다   구매품이   빠르고 확실하게 도착하리라고
    └→ 주어, 예상하는 주체 └→ 동사

For more than 25 years, / Jiffy Fleet Office Supply / has been providing
25년이 넘도록   지피 플릿 사무용품은   적시에 서비스를 제공해 왔습니다

timely service / to help / your business operations / run 12. smoothly.
                도울 수 있도록 / 귀사의 사업 운영이   원활하게 돌아가도록

Furthermore, / smart office managers know / that maintaining a stock of
게다가   현명한 사무 관리자들은 알고 있습니다   필수 비품의 재고 유지가 중요하다는 것을

essential supplies is important. It is what keeps your team 13. productive.
                              그것이 바로 팀의 생산성을 유지시켜 주는 일입니다

From desk chairs and whiteboards / to business cards and printer paper, /
책상 의자와 화이트보드에서부터   명함, 프린터 용지까지

we / have / you / covered. 14. We also carry / a full range of computer
저희가 / ~해 드립니다 / 당신이 / 준비되도록   저희는 또한 취급하고 있습니다 / 모든 종류의 컴퓨터 부속품을

accessories. Discover more / at jiffyfleetoffice.com.
              좀 더 알아보세요   Jiffyfleetoffice.com에서

향상된 기술로 온라인 쇼핑이 그 어
느 때보다 쉬워지면서, 소비자들은
일반적으로 구매품이 빠르고 확실
하게 도착하리라고 예상합니다. 25
년이 넘도록 지피 플릿 사무용품은
귀사가 원활하게 운영될 수 있도록
적시에 서비스를 제공해 왔습니다.
게다가, 현명한 사무실 관리자들은
필수 비품의 재고 유지가 중요하다
는 것을 알고 있습니다. 그것이 바
로 팀의 생산성을 유지시켜 주는 일
이니까요. 책상 의자와 화이트보드
에서부터 명함, 프린터 용지까지 저
희가 준비해 드립니다. 저희는 모든
종류의 컴퓨터 부속품 또한 취급하
고 있습니다. Jiffyfleetoffice.com
에서 좀 더 알아보세요!

11 (A) expect

(B) expecting

(C) expectations

(D) are expected

> 해설 **동사 자리:** 빈칸은 주어 consumers 뒤에 나오는 동사 자리입니다. 빈칸을 수식하는 부사 generally는 보통 현재 시제와 함께 쓰이는 부사이며 As가 이끄는 종속절의 시제도 현재이므로, 주절의 동사도 현재 시제인 (A) expect가 정답입니다. 현재분사 / 동명사 (B) expecting과 명사 (C) expectations는 동사 역할을 할 수 없으며, 수동태 현재 (D) are expected는 빈칸 뒤에 목적어 purchases가 있으므로 오답입니다.

12 (A) largely

(B) smoothly

(C) eagerly

(D) notably

(A) 주로, 대체로

(B) 원활하게

(C) 열심히

(D) 현저히

> 해설 **어휘 문제:** 빈칸은 동사 run을 수식하는 부사 자리입니다. 문맥상 '원활하게 운영되다'라는 의미가 자연스러우므로, (B) smoothly가 정답입니다.

13 (A) productive

(B) attractive

(C) original

(D) exclusive

(A) 생산적인

(B) 마음을 끄는

(C) 원래의

(D) 독점적인

> 해설 **어휘 문제:** 빈칸 앞 문장 maintaining a stock of essential supplies is important에서 필수 비품 재고 유지의 중요성을 언급했습니다. 따라서 빈칸을 포함한 부분은 '팀의 생산성 유지'라는 의미가 문맥상 자연스러우므로, (A) productive가 정답입니다.

14 (A) Our desk chairs are designed for your comfort.

(B) We also carry a full range of computer accessories.

(C) Prices for printer paper have gone up recently.

(D) Overnight delivery requests will incur an additional fee.

(A) 저희 책상 의자는 고객님의 편안함을 위해 설계되었습니다.

(B) 저희는 모든 종류의 컴퓨터 부속품 또한 취급하고 있습니다.

(C) 최근에 프린터 용지의 가격이 올랐습니다.

(D) 익일 배송 요청 시 추가 요금이 발생하게 됩니다.

> 해설 **문장 고르기:** 빈칸 앞에서 각종 사무실 용품을 제공한다며 책상, 의자, 화이트보드, 프린터 용지 등을 나열했습니다. 따라서 빈칸에도 사무실 용품에 관련된 내용이 들어가는 것이 문맥상 자연스러우며, 선택지 (B)의 computer accessories가 사무실 용품에 해당하므로 정답은 (D)입니다.

● 단순 시제와 진행 시제 **ETS 문제로 훈련하기 STEP 1**   교재 p. 97

1 (B)	**2** (A)	**3** (A)	**4** (B)	**5** (B)	**6** (A)

1

Mr. Hirose / (worked) / at First Street Financial / five years ago.
히로세 씨는   일했다   퍼스트 스트리트 파이낸셜에서   5년 전에
             └→ 과거 시점을 나타내는 과거 시제

(A) works   (B) worked

> **번역** 히로세 씨는 5년 전에 퍼스트 스트리트 파이낸셜에서 일했다.

2

The factory president / (will retire) / sometime / during the next three years.
그 공장장은   은퇴할 것이다   언젠가는   향후 3년 내에
            └→ 미래 시점을 나타내는 과거 시제

(A) will retire   (B) retires

> **번역** 그 공장장은 향후 3년 내에 언젠가는 은퇴할 것이다.

3

At 9 P.M. last night, / Mr. Holbroke / (was talking) / to his client / on the phone.
어젯밤 9시에   홀브로크 씨는   통화를 하고 있었다   의뢰인과   전화로
                   └→ 과거 시섬(At 9 P.M. last night)의 동작 진행을 나타내는 시제

(A) was talking   (B) is talking

> **번역** 홀브로크 씨는 어젯밤 9시에 의뢰인과 전화 통화를 하고 있었다.

4

Cartford Museum / opens / at 9 A.M. / and (closes) / at 5 P.M. / on weekdays.
카트포드 박물관은   개관한다   오전 9시에   그리고 오후 5시에 폐관한다   평일에

(A) closed   (B) closes
                   └→ 일반적인 사실을 나타내는 현재 시제

> **번역** 평일에 카트포드 박물관은 오전 9시에 개관해서 오후 5시에 폐관한다.

5

The visitors / (will be touring) / our production facilities / at 10 A.M. tomorrow.
방문객들은   둘러보고 있을 것이다   우리의 생산 설비를   내일 오전 10시에
                └→ 미래 시점(at 10 A.M. tomorrow)의 동작 진행을 나타내는 시제
(A) were   (B) will be

> **번역** 방문객들은 내일 오전 10시에 우리의 생산 설비를 둘러보고 있을 것이다.

6

Aviaty Airlines / (will be offering) / free snacks / on all of its flights / starting next January.
에이비에티 항공은   제공할 것이다   무료 스낵을   모든 항공편에서   내년 1월부터
                └→ 미래 시점(starting next January)의 동작 진행을 나타내는 시제
(A) will be offering   (B) are offered

> **번역** 에이비에티 항공은 내년 1월부터 모든 항공편에서 무료 스낵을 제공할 것이다.

7 (D)	8 (D)	9 (C)	10 (B)

7

Mei Watanabe / often / anticipates / changes in consumer behavior / with surprising accuracy.
메이 와타나베 씨는   자주, 흔히   예측한다   소비자 행동의 변화를   놀라울 정도로 정확하게
              → 현재 시제와 자주 쓰이는 부사

(A) very   (B) early

(C) fast   (D) often

> **해설** 현재 시제와 함께 쓰는 말: 동사가 현재 시제(anticipates)이고 '종종 정확하게 예측하다'라는 의미가 자연스러우므로, 반복되는 정도(빈도)를 나타내는 부사 (D) often이 정답입니다.
>
> **번역** 메이 와타나베 씨는 자주 소비자 행동의 변화를 놀라울 정도로 정확하게 예측한다.

8

Next month / the employee cafeteria / will be closing / at 2:00.
다음 달에는   직원 구내식당이   문을 닫을 예정이다   2시에
                                → 미래진행 시제

(A) was   (B) are

(C) has been   (D) will be

> **해설** 미래 시점과 어울리는 미래 시제: 미래 시점을 나타내는 Next month(다음 달)로 보아 미래 시제가 되어야 하므로, (D) will be가 정답입니다.
>
> **번역** 다음 달에는 직원 구내식당이 2시에 문을 닫을 예정이다.

9

Mr. Melniczak / will distribute / the minutes of this afternoon's client meeting / before the end of
멜닉자크 씨가   배포할 예정입니다   오늘 오후에 있었던 고객 회의의 회의록을   퇴근 전에

the day.
                  → 미래 시점

(A) distribute   (B) to be distributed

(C) will distribute   (D) has been distributing

> **해설** 미래 시점과 어울리는 미래 시제: 문장 마지막에 미래 시점을 나타내는 before the end of the day(오늘 퇴근 전에)가 있으므로 미래 시제가 와야 합니다. 따라서 정답은 (C) will distribute입니다.
>
> **번역** 멜닉자크 씨가 오늘 오후에 있었던 고객 회의의 회의록을 퇴근 전에 배포할 예정입니다.

10

Ms. Diaz / created / a template / last year / that can be reused / for the new database project.
디아즈 씨는   개발했다   템플릿을   작년에   재사용될 수 있는   새 데이터베이스 프로젝트를 위해
                  → 과거 시제

(A) create   (B) created

(C) has created   (D) will create

> **해설** 과거 시점과 어울리는 과거 시제: 빈칸은 주어 Ms. Diaz 뒤에 나오는 동사 자리입니다. 과거 시점을 나타내는 부사구 last year가 있으므로, 과거 시제 동사 (B) created가 정답입니다.
>
> **번역** 디아즈 씨는 작년에 새 데이터베이스 프로젝트를 위해 재사용 가능한 템플릿을 개발했다.

1 (B)	2 (B)	3 (B)	4 (A)	5 (A)	6 (B)

1

The warehouse / (has been used) / to store Yetla Fertilizer / since 1999.
그 물류 창고는　　사용되어 왔다　　예틀라 비료를 보관하는 데　　1999년 이래로
→ since(~이래로)와 어울리는 현재완료

(A) was　　　　(B) has been

번역 그 물류 창고는 1999년 이래로 예틀라 비료를 보관하는 데 사용되어 왔다.

2

The 10:17 A.M. train / (had) already (left) / before Mr. Abaki's team arrived / at the station.
오전 10시 17분 기차는　이미 떠났다　　아바키 씨의 팀이 도착하기 전에　　역에
→ 과거 시점(arrived) 이전의 동작을 나타내는 과거완료

(A) has　　　　(B) had

번역 아바키 씨의 팀이 역에 도착하기 전에 오전 10시 17분 기차는 이미 떠났다.

3

The manufacturer / (has extended) / the warranty / on its latest camera models / by twelve
그 제조업체는　기간을 연장했다　품질 보증　자사의 최신 카메라 제품에 대해　12개월만큼
months.
→ 완료의 의미를 나타내는 현재완료

(A) extend　　　　(B) has extended

번역 그 제조업체는 자사의 최신 카메라 제품에 대해 품질 보증 기간을 12개월 연장했다.

4

Feltlove Charity / (will have raised) / enough money / to build a library / by the end of the year.
펠트러브 자선 단체는　모금할 것이다　충분한 비용을　도서관을 건립할　연말까지
→ 미래 시점의 동작 완료를 나타내는 미래완료

(A) will have raised　　　　(B) have raised

번역 펠트러브 자선 단체는 연말까지 도서관을 건립할 비용을 충분히 모금할 것이다.

5

Several Tiger Gym health clubs / (have opened) / recently / in the city center.
타이거 짐 헬스클럽 여러 곳이　문을 열었다　최근에　시내 중심지에
→ recently(최근에)와 어울리는 현재완료

(A) have opened　　　　(B) will have opened

번역 최근 타이거 짐 헬스클럽 여러 곳이 시내 중심지에 문을 열었다.

6

Ms. Jameson / (has already begun) / working on resolving the problems / with the client.
제임슨 씨는　이미 시작했다　문제들을 해결하기 위한 노력을　그 고객과의
→ already(이미, 벌써)와 어울리는 현재완료

(A) quick　　　　(B) already

번역 제임슨 씨는 그 고객과의 문제들을 해결하기 위한 노력을 이미 시작했다.

7 (B)	**8** (D)	**9** (D)	**10** (B)

7

For the last fifteen years, / Matlock, Inc., / (has ranked) / among the nation's leading toy
지난 15년간　　　　　　　매트락사는　　　　자리 잡아 왔다　　　전국 최고의 장난감 제조업체 중의 하나로

manufacturers.
　　　　　　　　　　　　　　　　　　→ 현재완료

(A) rank　　　　　　　　　　　　　　(B) ranked

(C) ranking　　　　　　　　　　　　(D) ranks

> **해설**　〈for + 기간〉과 어울리는 현재완료: 〈for + 기간〉의 형태인 부사구 For the last fifteen years는 현재완료 시제와 어울리므로, 현재완료 시제 has ranked를 완성하는 (B) ranked가 정답입니다.

> **번역**　지난 15년간 매트락사는 전국 최고의 장난감 제조업체 중의 하나로 자리 잡아 왔다.

8

By the time the technicians discovered / the computer problem, / several files / (had disappeared).
기사들이 발견했을 때는　　　　　　　　　컴퓨터의 문제를　　　　몇 개 파일이　　　사라지고 없었다
　　　　　　　　　　　　　　　　　　　　　과거 시점(discovered) 이전의 동작을 나타내는 과거완료 ←

(A) are disappearing　　　　　　　　(B) will have disappeared

(C) disappear　　　　　　　　　　　(D) had disappeared

> **해설**　과거 시점 이전의 동작을 나타내는 과거완료: By the time으로 시작하는 부사절에 동사의 과거형(discovered)이 왔고, 빈칸에는 '발견하기 전에 이미 사라졌다'라는 과거 이전의 동작을 나타내는 과거완료 시제(had p.p.)가 들어가는 것이 문맥상 자연스러우므로, (D) had disappeared가 정답입니다.

> **번역**　기사들이 컴퓨터의 문제를 발견했을 때는 몇 개 파일이 사라지고 없었다.

9

Because the warranty (has expired) / already, / the store / is not obligated / to replace the product.
품질 보증 기간이 만료되었기 때문에　　　　이미　　　매장은　　　의무가 없다　　　그 제품을 교환해 줄
　　　　　　　　　　　　　　→ 현재완료

(A) is expiring　　　　　　　　　　(B) will expire

(C) expires　　　　　　　　　　　(D) has expired

> **해설**　already와 어울리는 현재완료: 빈칸 뒤의 부사 already(이미, 벌써)는 과거나 현재완료 시제와 어울리므로 현재완료 시제인 (D) has expired가 정답입니다.

> **번역**　품질 보증 기간이 이미 만료되어서 매장에서는 그 제품을 교환해 줄 의무기 없디.

10

Arten Publishing / (has experienced) / an average annual growth of 7 percent / since it went
아르텐 출판사는　　　　경험했다　　　　7퍼센트의 연 평균 성장률을　　　　　　　상상한 이후로
　　　　　　　　　　　　　　　→ 현재완료

public / twenty years ago.
　　　　20년 전에

(A) experiences　　　　　　　　　(B) has experienced

(C) will experience　　　　　　　(D) experiencing

> **해설**　since(~한 이래로)와 어울리는 현재완료: since it went public twenty years ago가 문제 해결의 단서입니다. since는 '~ 이래로'라는 의미로 과거부터 현재까지의 시간을 나타내므로, 현재완료 시제와 어울립니다. 따라서 (B) has experienced가 정답입니다.

> **번역**　아르텐 출판사는 20년 전에 상장한 이후로 7퍼센트의 연 평균 성장률을 경험했다.

1 (A)	**2** (B)	**3** (A)	**4** (A)

1

These chemicals / are hazardous / and should be (handled) / with care.
이 화학 약품들은　　　　　위험하다　　　　그래서 취급되어야 한다　　　　조심스럽게
　　　　　　　　　　　　　　　　　　　　　　　　　　　　　　　　　→ 다루다, 취급하다

(A) handled 다루다, 처리하다　　　　　(B) dislocated 위치를 바꾸다, 옮겨놓다

번역　이 화학 약품들은 위험해서 조심스럽게 취급되어야 한다.

2

The new botanic garden / will (attract) / tourists / during the summer.
새로운 식물원은　　　　　끌어모을 것이다　　관광객들을　　여름 동안
　　　　　　　　　　　　　　　　　　　　　　　　　→ 끌어들이다, 유치하다

(A) appeal 간청하다, 애원하다　　　　　(B) attract 끌어들이다, 유치하다

번역　새로운 식물원은 여름에 관광객들을 끌어 모을 것이다.

3

The shipping department / (loaded) / products / onto twenty trucks / this morning.
배송부는　　　　　실었다　　제품을　　트럭 20대에　　　오늘 아침에
　　　　　　　　　　　　　　→ 싣다, 적재하다

(A) loaded 싣다, 적재하다　　　　　(B) served 제공하다

번역　배송부에서는 오늘 아침 트럭 20대에 제품을 실었다.

4

For security reasons, / only authorized personnel / are (permitted) / to use this room.
보안상의 이유로　　　　인가받은 직원들만이　　　　　허락된다　　　이 방을 사용하도록
　　　　　　　　　　　　　　　　　　　　　　　　　　　→ 허락하다

(A) permitted 허락하다　　　　　(B) written 쓰다

번역　보안상의 이유로, 인가받은 직원들만이 이 방을 사용하도록 허락된다.

PART 5 | UNIT 07

5 (A)	6 (D)	7 (D)	8 (D)

5

Michael Keller, / president of Teekman Financial, / (appeared) / on a special broadcast of *The*
마이클 켈러가　　틱맨 금융의 사장인　　　　　출연했다　　프랜시스 팅 쇼의 특별 방송에

Frances Ting Show.
→ 출연하다

(A) appeared 출연하다　　　　　(B) seemed ~인 것 같다

(C) approved 승인하다, 찬성하다　(D) numbered 번호를 매기다

해설　appear 출연하다: 빈칸 뒤 전치사구 on a ~ Ting Show와 어울리는 동사 자리입니다. 문맥상 '특별 방송에 나타났다(출연했다)'라는 내용이 이어지는 것이 자연스러우므로, (A) appeared가 정답입니다.

번역　틱맨 금융의 사장인 마이클 켈러가 프랜시스 팅 쇼의 특별 방송에 출연했다.

6

The new projections show / that we will need to (reduce) / next year's production / by 15 percent.
새로운 전망은 보여준다　　우리가 줄일 필요가 있다　　내년 생산량을　　15퍼센트만큼

(A) decline 거절하다　　　　(B) consume 소비하다　→ 줄이다

(C) arise 발생하다, 일어나다　(D) reduce 줄이다

해설　reduce 줄이다: 빈칸 뒤에 next year's production이 있는데 문맥상 '생산량을 줄이다'가 자연스러우므로, (D) reduce가 정답입니다.

번역　새로운 전망은 우리가 내년 생산량을 15퍼센트 줄일 필요가 있을 것임을 보여준다.

7

All construction materials / will be (delivered) / to the loading dock / at the rear of the building.
모든 건축 자재는　　　　배달될 것이다　　하역장으로　　건물 뒤쪽의
→ 배달하다

(A) produced 생산하다　　　(B) assembled 조립하다

(C) equipped 장비를 갖추다　(D) delivered 배달하다, 배송하다

해설　deliver 배달하다: 빈칸 뒤에 to the loading dock이 있는데 문맥상 '하역장으로 배달되다'가 자연스럽습니다. 따라서 '배달하다'라는 의미의 (D) delivered가 정답입니다.

번역　모든 건축 자재는 건물 뒤쪽의 하역장으로 배달될 것이다.

8

Because of poor weather conditions, / the outdoor concert / has been (postponed) / until next
악천후로 인해　　　　　야외 콘서트는　　연기되었다　　다음 주까지

week.
미루다, 연기하다 ←

(A) expected 기대하다　　(B) scheduled 일정을 잡다

(C) continued 지속하다　(D) postponed 미루다, 연기하다

해설　postpone 미루다, 연기하다: 빈칸 앞 has been과 함께 현재완료 시제를 이루는 과거분사 자리입니다. Because of poor weather conditions를 통해 야외 콘서트가 연기되었음을 알 수 있으므로, '연기하다'라는 의미의 (D) postponed가 정답입니다.

번역　악천후로 인해 야외 콘서트는 다음 주까지 연기되었다.

1 (D)	**2** (A)	**3** (A)	**4** (C)	**5** (B)

1

Businesses on Ellory Avenue / (closed) / early yesterday / to allow / work crews / to repave the
엘로리 가에 있는 상점들은   문을 닫았다   어제 일찍   허용하기 위해 작업반들이   거리를 재포장하는 것을

street.
       └→ 과거 시제

(A) are closed   (B) to close   (C) closing   (D) closed

해설   **과거 시점과 어울리는 과거 시제:** 빈칸 뒤에 yesterday라는 과거 시점을 나타내는 부사가 있으므로 동사의 과거형인 (D) closed가
정답입니다.

번역   엘로리 가에 있는 상점들은 작업반들이 거리를 재포장할 수 있도록 어제 일찍 문을 닫았다.

2

MO Hardware / (is offering) / free flashlights / to the first 50 customers / during its grand opening /
MO 하드웨어는   제공할 것이다   무료 손전등을   선착순 50명의 고객들에게   개점 행사 때

next Friday.   └→ 가까운 미래를 나타내는 현재진행 시제
다음 주 금요일

(A) is offering   (B) having offered   (C) was offered   (D) to offer

해설   **미래를 나타내는 현재진행 시제:** 문장 맨 뒤에 next Friday가 있으므로 미래를 이야기하고 있지만, 선택지에 미래 시제가 없으므로,
가까운 미래를 표현할 때 자주 사용되는 현재진행형을 쓰면 됩니다. 따라서 정답은 (A) is offering입니다.

번역   MO 하드웨어는 다음 주 금요일 개점 행사 때 선착순 50명의 고객들에게 손전등을 무료로 제공할 것이다.

3

Ms. Choi / described / the proposed project / while she (was having) a lunch meeting / with the
최 씨는   설명했다   제안된 프로젝트를   그녀가 점심 식사 미팅을 하는 동안   새 고객들과 함께

new clients.   └→ 과거진행 시제

(A) was having   (B) having   (C) has   (D) will have

해설   **과거 시점의 동작 진행을 나타내는 과거진행형:** 빈칸은 접속사 while(~ 동안)이 이끄는 부사절 안에서 동사 자리이며, 주절의
동사 described를 통해 과거의 일임을 알 수 있습니다. 따라서 빈칸에는 '점심 미팅을 하고 있던 동안'이라는 과거진행의 의미가
자연스러우므로, (A) was having이 정답입니다. (B) having은 단독으로 동사 자리에 들어갈 수 없습니다.

번역   최 씨는 새 고객들과 점심 미팅을 하면서 제안된 프로젝트를 설명했다.

4

Last year / the quality control team / (implemented) / several new policies / designed / to improve
작년에   품질 관리팀은   실행했다   몇 가지 새로운 정책을   고안된   효율성 개선을 위해
                                     └→ 과거 시제

efficiency.

(A) implementation   (B) implements   (C) implemented   (D) implementing

해설   **과거 시점과 어울리는 과거 시제:** 빈칸은 주어인 the quality control team의 뒤에 나오는 동사 자리입니다. 문장 맨 앞에 과거 시점을
나타내는 부사구 Last year가 있으므로 과거 시제 동사 (C) implemented가 정답입니다.

번역   품질 관리팀은 작년에 효율성 개선을 위해 고안된 몇 가지 새로운 정책을 실행했다.

5

Effective next Monday, / Ms. Garcia / (will be) responsible / for keeping track of staff vacation time.
다음 주 월요일부터   가르시아 씨가   책임지게 될 것이다   직원들 휴가 기간 관리를
                                 └→ 미래 시제

(A) was   (B) will be   (C) to be   (D) had been

해설   **미래 시점과 어울리는 미래 시제:** 빈칸은 주어 Ms. García 뒤에 나오는 동사 자리이고 문장 앞에 미래 시점을 나타내는 next
Monday가 있으므로, 미래 시제 동사 (B) will be가 정답입니다. to부정사 (C) to be는 동사 자리에 들어갈 수 없습니다.

번역   다음 주 월요일부터, 가르시아 씨가 직원들 휴가 기간 관리를 책임지게 될 것이다.

6 (D)	7 (B)	8 (B)	9 (A)	10 (D)

6

Dr. Suzuki / arrived for the ceremony / on time / even though her train (had left) / twenty minutes
스즈키 박사는　　예식에 도착했다　　　　제시간에　　기차가 출발했음에도 불구하고　　　　　20분 늦게

late.
　　　　　　　　　　　　　　　　　　　과거 시점(arrived) 이전의 동작을 나타내는 과거완료 ↙

(A) is leaving　　(B) will leave　　(C) to leave　　(D) had left

해설 과거 시점 이전의 동작을 나타내는 과거완료: 주절의 시제가 과거(arrived)로, 기차가 20분 늦게 출발한 것이 Suzuki 박사가 식장에 도착한 것보다 먼저 일어난 일이므로 과거완료 시제(hap p.p.)가 되어야 합니다. 따라서 (D) had left가 정답입니다.

번역 스즈키 박사는 기차가 20분 늦게 출발했는데도 불구하고 예식에 제시간에 도착했다.

7

With advance notice, / the restaurant / is (currently) able to accommodate / parties of ten or more.
사전 통보가 있으면　　　그 식당은　　　현재 수용할 수 있다　　　　　　　10명이 넘는 일행을
　　　　　　　　　　　　　　　　　　　　→ 현재의 일임을 나타내는 표현

(A) ahead　　(B) currently　　(C) enough　　(D) before

해설 현재 시제와 어울리는 시간 표현: 빈칸은 뒤의 형용사 able을 수식하는 부사 자리로, 시제가 현재(is)이므로 '현재 수용할 수 있다'라는 의미가 문맥상 자연스러우므로, '현재'라는 의미의 부사 (B) currently가 정답입니다.

번역 사전 통보가 있으면 그 식당은 현재 10명이 넘는 일행을 수용할 수 있다.

8

Seeking new sources of income, / many regional orchards / (have begun) / catering to tourists /
새로운 수입원을 찾으면서　　　　　　많은 지역 과수원들이　　　시작했다　　관광객들에게 음식을 제공하기

in the last few years.
지난 몇 년 동안　　　　　　　　　　　　　　→ 현재 완료

(A) will begin　　(B) have begun　　(C) will have begun　　(D) to begin

해설 〈in + 기간〉과 어울리는 현재완료: 〈in + 기간〉의 형태인 부사구 in the last few years는 현재완료 시제와 어울리므로, 현재완료 시제 (B) have begun이 정답입니다.

번역 새로운 수입원을 찾으면서 많은 지역 과수원들이 지난 몇 년 동안 관광객들에게 음식을 제공하기 시작했다.

9

The lights / suddenly / went out / while the audience (was watching) / a musical performance / of
불이　　　갑자기　　나갔다　　관객들이 관람하고 있던 중에　　　　뮤지컬 공연을

Man of La Mancha.
〈맨 오브 라만차〉의　　　　　　　　　　→ 과거진행 시제

(A) was watching　　(B) is watching　　(C) watches　　(D) will watch

해설 과거 시점의 동작 진행을 나타내는 과거진행형: 갑자기 불이 나갔다(went out)는 과거 시점을 나타내고, 바로 그 시점에 관객들은 뮤지컬을 보고 있던 중이었으므로, 과거진행형인 (A) was watching이 정답입니다.

번역 관객들이 〈맨 오브 라만차〉 뮤지컬 공연을 관람하는 중에 갑자기 불이 나갔다.

10

After Noriko Tamaguchi `had mastered` / the skills for her job, / her manager / asked / her /
노리코 다마구치가 숙달한 후에   자신의 직무 기술을   그녀의 관리자는   요청했다   그녀에게

to help / train / new employees.   ⌐ 과거 시점(asked) 이전의 동작을 나타내는 과거완료
도와 달라고   교육하는 것을 / 신입사원들을

(A) is mastering   (B) has mastered   (C) masters   (D) had mastered

해설   과거 시점 이전의 동작을 나타내는 과거완료: 주절의 시제가 과거(asked)인데 'Noriko Tamaguchi가 기술을 숙달한 후에 관리자가 도움을 요청했다'라고 하는 것이 자연스러우므로, 빈칸에는 과거 이전의 동작을 나타내는 과거완료 시제 (D) had mastered가 정답입니다.

번역   노리코 다마구치가 자신의 직무 기술을 숙달하고 나자, 그녀의 관리자는 신입사원 교육을 도와 달라고 그녀에게 요청했다.

ETS 실전 테스트   교재 p. 103

11 (B)   **12** (A)   **13** (C)   **14** (D)

Questions 11-14 refer to the following article.

TEMA, GHANA (10 April)—Ghana Aluminium Company (GAC) / is pleased /
테마, 가나 (4월 10일)   가나 알루미늄 회사(GAC)는   기뻐한다

to announce the appointment of Madhu Quaye / as chief operating officer
마드후 쿠아예를 임명한다고 발표하게 되어   모잠비크 사업부의 최고 운영 책임자로

of its Mozambique division / effective 1 July. His 30 years of experience in
         7월 1일부로   업계에서 30년간 쌓은 쿠아예 씨의 경력이

the **11.** industry / made him / the obvious choice for the position, /
       그를 만들었다   그 자리에 확실한 선택으로

according to company spokesperson Gladys Ayambe. Mr. Quaye /
글래디스 아얌베 회사 대변인에 따르면   쿠아예 씨는

graduated with a master of science degree in mining engineering / from the
광산 공학 석사 학위를 취득했다   ⌐ 과거의 일임을 나타내는 과거 시제

National University of Ghana. He then **12.** `began` his career / as a process
가나 국립대학교에서   그 후 그는 경력을 시작했다   공정 설계

design engineer / at Accra Mining Industries (AMI). Two decades ago, /
엔지니어로   애크라 마이닝 인더스트리즈(AMI)에서   20년 전

he left AMI / for GAC. **13.** Most recently, / he has served / as GAC's vice
그는 AMI를 떠났다 / GAC로 오기 위해   가장 최근에는   그는 근무했다   GAC의 개발 사업부

president of development. In Mozambique, / Mr. Quaye will oversee day-
부사장으로   모잠비크에서   쿠아예 씨는 일상 업무를 관리할 것이다

to-day operations / at Maputo Aluminium, Inc., / over **14.** `which` GAC has
       마푸토 알루미늄 주식회사의   GAC가 지배적 지분을 획득한

acquired a controlling interest.   앞에 있는 명사 Maputo Aluminium,
                 Inc.를 부연 설명하는 관계사절을 이끄는 목적격 관계대명사

11-14 기사

테마, 가나 (4월 10일)-가나 알루미늄 회사(GAC)는 7월 1일부로 모잠비크 사업부의 최고 운영 책임자로 마드후 쿠아예를 임명한다고 발표하게 되어 기뻐한다. 글래디스 아얌베 회사 대변인에 따르면 업계에서 30년간 쌓은 쿠아예 씨의 경력으로 그를 그 자리에 확실하게 선택하게 되었다고 한다. 쿠아예 씨는 가나 국립대학교에서 광산 공학 석사 학위를 취득했다. 그 후 그는 애크라 마이닝 인더스트리즈(AMI)의 공정 설계 엔지니어로 자신의 경력을 시작했다. 20년 전 그는 GAC로 오기 위해 AMI를 떠났다. 가장 최근에는 GAC의 개발 사업부 부사장으로 일했다. 모잠비크에서 쿠아예 씨는 GAC가 지배적 지분을 획득한 마푸토 알루미늄 주식회사의 일상 업무를 관리할 것이다.

11
(A) license
(B) industry
(C) outset
(D) program

(A) 면허(증)
(B) 업계
(C) 시초
(D) 프로그램

> **해설** 어휘 문제: 빈칸은 전치사 in의 목적어 역할을 하는 명사 자리로, 빈칸을 포함한 전치사구(in the ~)는 앞에 있는 명사구 His 30 years of experience를 수식합니다. 문맥상 '업계에서 30년간 쌓은 경력'이라는 의미가 자연스러우므로, (B) industry가 정답입니다.

12
(A) began
(B) had begun
(C) was beginning
(D) will begin

> **해설** 과거 시점과 어울리는 과거 시제: 빈칸은 주어 He 뒤에 나오는 동사 자리입니다. 빈칸을 수식하는 부사 then과 함께 빈칸 앞뒤 문장의 동사 graduated와 left에서 과거의 경력을 순서대로 나열하고 있음을 알 수 있으므로, 과거 시제 동사 (A) began이 정답입니다. 과거완료 시제 동사 (B) had begun은 뒤에 나오는 과거 시제 동사 left의 대과거는 될 수 있지만, 앞에 있는 과거 시제 동사 graduated와는 시간 순서상 연결되지 않으므로 오답입니다. 과거진행 시제 동사 (C) was beginning은 과거 당시 동작의 강조를 나타내므로, 경력을 나열하는 앞뒤 과거 시제 동사와 일관성을 이루지 않습니다.

13
(A) The company also has a division in Guinea.
(B) He developed an interest in mining at a young age.
(C) Most recently, he has served as GAC's vice president of development.
(D) The downsizing came after reports of huge financial losses.

(A) 그 회사는 또한 기니에 사업부를 두고 있다.
(B) 그는 어린 나이에 광업에 관심을 갖게 되었다.
(C) 가장 최근에는 GAC의 개발 사업부 부사장으로 일했다.
(D) 엄청난 재정 손실이 보고된 후에 규모 축소가 이루어졌다.

> **해설** 문장 고르기: 빈칸 앞 문장 Two decades ago, he left AMI for GAC.에서 20년 전 이직한 사실을, 빈칸 뒤 문장 In Mozambique, Mr. Quaye will oversee day-to-day operations에서 새로운 곳에서 앞으로 맡을 업무를 언급했습니다. 따라서 빈칸에는 20년 전부터 최근까지의 경력과 관련된 내용이 들어가는 것이 문맥상 자연스러우므로 정답은 (C)입니다.

14
(A) when
(B) that
(C) what
(D) which

> **해설** 전치사 + 관계대명사: 빈칸 뒤의 절(GAC has acquired a controlling interest)을 이끄는 관계사 자리로, 앞의 전치사 over의 목적어 역할도 합니다. 빈칸을 포함한 절(over ~ interest)은 앞에 있는 사물 명사 Maputo Aluminium, Inc.를 부연 설명하므로, 관계사절을 이끄는 관계대명사 (D) which가 정답입니다. 목적격 관계대명사 (B) that은 전치사의 목적어 역할을 할 수 없고, (C) what이 이끄는 절은 명사 역할을 하므로 오답입니다.

능동태와 수동태의 구분 ETS 문제로 훈련하기 STEP 1

교재 p. 107

1 (A)	2 (B)	3 (A)	4 (A)	5 (A)	6 (B)

1

Jindo Industrial / opened / a $15 million addition / to its Singapore factory / last week.
진도 인더스트리얼은　개설했다　천오백만 달러짜리 증축 시설을　싱가포르 공장의　지난주에
→ '개설한' 주체

(A) opened　　　　　　　　　　(B) was opened

번역 진도 인더스트리얼은 지난주 천오백만 달러짜리 싱가포르 공장 증축 시설을 개설했다.

2

The Phaliya Hotel / is located / in the Bangkok business district.
팔리야 호텔은　위치해 있다　방콕의 상업 지구에
→ '위치되어진' 대상

(A) locating　　　　　　　　　　(B) located

번역 팔리야 호텔은 방콕의 상업 지구에 위치해 있다.

3

Companies / can always develop / better marketing strategies.
회사들은　항상 개발할 수 있다　더 나은 마케팅 전략들을
→ '개발하는' 주체

(A) develop　　　　　　　　　　(B) be developed

번역 회사들은 항상 더 나은 마케팅 전략들을 개발할 수 있다.

4

The use of flash photography / is prohibited / in this building.
플래시를 터뜨리는 사진 촬영은　금지됩니다　이 건물에서
→ '금지되는' 대상

(A) prohibited　　　　　　　　　　(B) prohibiting

번역 이 건물에서 플래시를 터뜨리는 사진 촬영은 금지됩니다.

5

An increase / in competition / last year / has caused / a significant drop / in sales.
심화는　경쟁의　지난해　야기했다　커다란 감소를　매출에서
→ '야기한' 주체

(A) has caused　　　　　　　　　　(B) is caused

번역 지난해 경쟁 심화로 매출이 크게 감소했다.

6

The computer training guidelines / were revised / by Rita Chen and Deborah Woo.
컴퓨터 교육 지침은　수정되었다　리타 첸과 데보라 우에 의해
→ '수정된' 대상

(A) revising　　　　　　　　　　(B) revised

번역 컴퓨터 교육 지침은 리타 첸과 데보라 우에 의해 수정되었다.

7 (D)	8 (C)	9 (C)	10 (B)

7

(The career fair) / will be held / on July 2 / in the Human Resources building.
취업 박람회가　　　　　열릴 것이다　　　7월 2일에　　　인사부 건물에서

(A) holds　　　　↳ '열리는' 대상　　　(B) holding
(C) hold　　　　　　　　　　　　　　　(D) held

[해설] 능동태와 수동태 구별: 주어 The career fair가 '개최하다'라는 의미의 동사 hold의 주체인지 대상인지를 먼저 파악해야 합니다. 문맥상 취업 박람회는 '개최되는' 대상이므로, be동사와 결합하여 수동태를 만드는 과거분사 (D) held가 정답입니다. 동사 (A) holds와 (C) hold는 be동사 뒤에 올 수 없습니다.

[번역] 7월 2일 인사부 건물에서 취업 박람회가 열릴 것이다.

8

(The committee) / unanimously selected / Anuja Ganguli's *To the Mountain* / as the Book of the Year.
위원회는　　　　　만장일치로 선정했다　　　아누자 강굴리의 〈산으로〉를　　　　　'올해의 책'으로

(A) select　　　　↳ '선정한' 주체　　　(B) selecting
(C) selected　　　　　　　　　　　　(D) was selected

[해설] 능동태와 수동태 구별: 빈칸은 주어 The committee 뒤에 나오는 동사 자리로, 빈칸 뒤 명사구 Anuja Ganguli's *To the Mountain*을 목적어로 취합니다. 위원회는 '올해의 책'을 선정했던 주체이므로, 능동의 의미를 나타내는 과거 시제 동사 (C) selected가 정답입니다.

[번역] 위원회는 만장일치로 아누자 강굴리의 〈산으로〉를 '올해의 책'으로 선정했다.

9

(Your belongings) / should be kept safe / at all times / when you travel / around the tourist
소지품은　　　　　　안전하게 보관돼야 한다　　　항상　　　당신이 여행할 때는　　　관광 명소들을

attractions.　↳ '보관되는' 대상

(A) keep　　　　　　　　　　(B) kept
(C) be kept　　　　　　　　　(D) be keeping

[해설] 동사원형 선택 / 능동태와 수동태 구별: 빈칸 앞에 조동사 should가 있으므로 빈칸에는 동사원형이 와야 합니다. 또한 주어 Your belongings는 안전하게 '보관되는' 대상이므로 수동태 동사형인 (C) be kept가 정답입니다.

[번역] 관광 명소들을 여행할 때는 항상 소지품을 안전하게 보관해야 한다.

10

Please visit / Klara Cosmetics / on Bauer Street / while the (East Avenue location) is being
방문하십시오　　　클라라 코스메틱스를　　　바우어 가에 있는　　　이스트 애비뉴 점이 보수되고 있는 동안
　　　　　　　　　　　　　　　　　　　　　　　　　　　　　　　↳ '보수되는' 대상

renovated.

(A) renovates　　　　　　　　(B) renovated
(C) renovating　　　　　　　　(D) renovations

[해설] 능동태와 수동태 구별: 주어 the East Avenue location이 동사 renovate의 주체인지 대상인지를 먼저 파악해야 합니다. 문맥상 이스트 애비뉴 점은 '보수되는' 대상이므로, be동사 is being과 결합하여 수동태를 만드는 과거분사 (B) renovated가 정답입니다.

[번역] 이스트 애비뉴 점이 보수되는 동안 바우어 가에 있는 클라라 코스메틱스를 방문하십시오.

1 (A)	2 (A)	3 (B)	4 (A)	5 (B)	6 (A)

1

Skin ages / fast / if it (is exposed / to) the sun / too much.
피부는 노화한다　빠르게　그것이 노출된다면　햇빛에　지나치게 많이
(A) to　　　　(B) with
↳ ~에 노출되다

번역 햇빛에 지나치게 많이 노출되면 피부는 빠르게 노화한다.

2

Momoko Masaoka's paintings of the sea / (are inspired / by) her childhood / in the Matsushima
모모코 마사오카의 바다 그림들은　영감을 받았다　유년시절에서　마쓰시마 지역에서 보낸
region.　　↳ ~에 영감 받다
(A) by　　　　(B) to

번역 모모코 마사오카의 바다 그림들은 마쓰시마 지역에서 보낸 유년시절에서 영감을 받았다.

3

One of the most promising candidates / (was associated / with) the company's competitors.
가장 유망한 지원자들 중 한 명이　연관이 있다　회사의 경쟁 업체와
(A) embarrassed 당혹한　　(B) associated 관련된　↳ ~와 관련이 있다

번역 가장 유망한 지원자들 중 한 명이 회사의 경쟁 업체와 연관이 있었다.

4

The marketing department / (is) somewhat (related / to) the advertising department.
마케팅부는　어느 정도 연관이 있다　광고부와
(A) to　　　　(B) by　↳ ~와 연관이 있다

번역 마케팅부는 광고부와 어느 정도 연관이 있다.

5

Employees / (were surprised / at) the board's decision / to make / Ms. Vasilev / the new vice
직원들은　놀랐다　이사회의 결정에　임명한　바실레브 씨를　신임 부사장으로
president.　↳ ~에 놀라다
(A) surprising　　(B) surprised

번역 직원들은 바실레브 씨를 신임 부회장에 임명한 이사회의 결정에 놀랐다.

6

All orders / placed online / will be (shipped) / from our Santa Cruz warehouse / within 24 hours.
모든 제품은　온라인으로 주문된　발송된다　우리 산타 크루즈 물류 창고에서　24시간 이내에
(A) shipped 배송하다　　(B) arrived 도착하다　↳ 배송하다

번역 온라인으로 주문한 모든 제품은 우리 산타 크루즈 물류 창고에서 24시간 이내에 발송될 것이다.

| 7 (B) | 8 (B) | 9 (C) | 10 (B) |

7

Ms. Drake / (was satisfied / with) the service / the subcontractor provided / for Ormsby Industries.
드레이크 씨는　　만족했다　　　　서비스에　　　　　하도급 업체가 제공한　　　　옴스비 인더스트리즈에
→ ~에 만족하다

(A) satisfies　　　　　　　　　(B) was satisfied
(C) will satisfy　　　　　　　(D) satisfied

해설　수동태 구문: be satisfied with는 '~에 만족하다'라는 의미이므로 (B)가 정답입니다.

번역　드레이크 씨는 하도급 업체에서 옴스비 인더스트리즈에 제공한 서비스에 만족했다.

8

Highvale Restaurant / (is committed / to) using only the freshest ingredients / in all of its dishes.
하이베일 레스토랑은　　전력을 다하고 있습니다 / 가장 신선한 재료만을 사용하는 것을　　　모든 요리에
→ 뒤의 명사를 수식하는 소유격

(A) commit　　　　　　　　　(B) committed
(C) to commit　　　　　　　(D) committing

해설　by 이외의 전치사를 쓰는 수동태 표현: be committed to는 '~에 헌신[전념]하다'라는 의미이므로, (B) committed가 정답입니다.

번역　하이베일 레스토랑은 모든 요리에 가장 신선한 재료만을 사용하고자 전력을 다하고 있습니다.

9

The board of directors' meeting / (is scheduled / for) the first Monday of every month.
이사회 회의는　　　　　　　예정되어 있다　매달 첫째 주 월요일로
→ ~로 예정되어 있다

(A) schedule　　　　　　　　(B) schedules
(C) scheduled　　　　　　　(D) scheduling

해설　수동태 구문: 주어 The board of directors' meeting이 '예정하다'라는 의미의 동사 schedule의 주체인지 대상인지를 먼저 파악해야 합니다. 문맥상 이사회 회의는 '예정되는' 대상이므로, be동사와 결합하여 수동태를 만드는 과거분사 (C) scheduled가 정답입니다. 동사 (A) schedule과 (B) schedules는 be동사 뒤에 나올 수 없습니다.

번역　이사회 회의는 매달 첫째 주 월요일로 예정되어 있다.

10

The newly renovated laboratory / (is equipped / with) state-of-the-art research equipment.
새로 개조한 연구실은　　　갖추어져 있다　최첨단 연구 장비가
→ ~을 갖추고 있다

(A) by　　　　　　　　　　　(B) with
(C) in　　　　　　　　　　　(D) to

해설　by 이외이 전치사를 쓰는 수동배 표현: be equipped with는 '~을 갖추고 있다'라는 의미이므로, (B) with가 정답입니다.

번역　새로 개조한 연구실에는 최첨단 연구 장비가 구비되어 있다.

1 (A)	**2** (B)	**3** (A)	**4** (A)

1

All employees / are required / to complete / annual evaluations / every December.
전 직원은　　　　 요구되다　　　 작성하도록　　　 연간 평가서를　　　　 매년 12월에
　　　　　　　　　　　　　　　　　　　　　　　→ 작성하다

(A) complete 작성하다　　　　　　　　　(B) agree 동의하다

번역 　전 직원은 매년 12월에 연간 평가서를 작성해야 한다.

2

The accountants / have been authorized / to access our databases.
그 회계사들은　　　　　 허가받았다　　　　　 우리 데이터베이스에 접속하도록
　　　　　　　　　　　　　　　　　　　　　　　　　　　　→ 접속하다, 접근하다

(A) solve 풀다, 해결하다　　　　　　　　(B) access 접속하다, 접근하다

번역 　그 회계사들은 우리 데이터베이스에 접속하도록 허가받았다.

3

It will be difficult / to enforce the safety regulations / without effective monitoring.
어려울 것이다　　　　 안전 규정을 시행하는 것은　　　　　　　　 효과적인 감시 없이
　　　　　　　　　　　→ 시행하다, 강요하다

(A) enforce 시행하다, 강요하다　　　　(B) imply 암시하다, 시사하다

번역 　효과적인 감시 없이 안전 규정을 시행하는 것은 어려울 것이다.

4

Markos Industries / is pleased / to report / a 10 percent rise / in quarterly earnings.
마코즈 인더스트리즈는　　 기쁩니다　 알리게 되어　　 10퍼센트 증가를　　　　 분기별 수익에서
　　　　　　　　　　　　　　　　　　　　　→ 보고하다, 알리다

(A) report 보고하다, 알리다　　　　　　(B) advise 조언하다

번역 　마코즈 인더스트리즈는 분기별 수익이 10퍼센트 증가했음을 알리게 되어 기쁩니다.

5 (A)	6 (D)	7 (D)	8 (A)

5 Companies / often collaborate / with their contractors / to find solutions / to shared concerns.
기업들은   자주 협력한다   계약 업체와   (그 결과) 해결책을 찾기 위하여 / 공통의 관심사에 대한
                    └→ ~와 협력하다

(A) collaborate 협력하다   (B) evaluate 평가하다

(C) conduct 수행하다   (D) support 지지[지원]하다

해설 collaborate 협력하다: 빈칸 뒤의 with their contractors가 문제 해결의 단서입니다. 동사 collaborate는 전치사 with와 결합해 '~와 협력하다'라는 의미로 쓰입니다. 빈칸에 collaborate를 넣어 보면 '계약업체와 협력하여 해결책을 찾기 위하여'라는 의미가 되어 문맥이 자연스러우므로 정답은 (A) collaborate입니다.

번역 기업들은 공통의 관심사에 대한 해결책을 찾기 위하여 계약 업체와 자주 협력한다.

6 Nova Appliances / guarantees / that all of its washing machines are free / of mechanical defects.
노바 어플라이언시즈는   보증합니다   자사의 모든 세탁기에는 없다는 것을   기계적인 결함이
               └→ 보증하다, 보장하다

(A) prevents 막다, 예방하다   (B) organizes 조직하다

(C) controls 통제하다   (D) guarantees 보증하다

해설 guarantee 보증하다, 보장하다: 빈칸 뒤 명사절(that all ~ free of mechanical defects)을 목적어로 취하는 동사 자리입니다. 문맥상 '기계적인 결함이 없음을 보증한다'라는 내용이 자연스러우므로, (D) guarantees가 정답입니다.

번역 노바 어플라이언시즈는 자사의 모든 세탁기에 기계적인 결함이 없음을 보증합니다.

7 The popular television series *On the Fences* / features / a very talented cast.
인기 있는 텔레비전 시리즈 〈온 더 펜시즈〉는   포함한다   매우 재능 있는 출연자들을
                        └→ 특별히 포함하다, 특징으로 하다

(A) applies 신청하다   (B) senses 감지하다

(C) marks 표시하다   (D) features 특별히 포함하다

해설 feature 특별히 포함하다, 특징으로 하다: 빈칸 뒤 명사구 a very talented cast를 목적어로 취하는 동사 자리입니다. 문맥상 '재능 있는 출연자들이 등장한다(특별히 포함하다)'라는 의미가 자연스러우므로, (D) features가 정답입니다.

번역 인기 있는 텔레비전 시리즈 〈온 더 펜시즈〉에는 매우 재능 있는 출연자들이 등장한다.

8 The Rogers family of retail stores / is seeking / experienced managers / for several northeast locations.
로저스 소매점 가족은   구하고 있습니다   경력직 관리자들을   북동부의 몇몇 매장에서 일할
                        └→ 구하다, 찾다

(A) seeking 구하다   (B) looking 보다

(C) entering 들어가다   (D) inquiring 물어보다

해설 seek 구하다, 찾다: 빈칸 뒤 명사구 experienced managers를 목적어로 취하는 타동사 자리입니다. 문맥상 '경력직 관리자들을 구하고 있다'라는 의미가 자연스러우므로, 타동사의 현재분사형 (A) seeking이 정답입니다. 자동사 (B) looking은 전치사 for와 결합하여 '~을 찾다'라는 의미를 나타냅니다.

번역 로저스 소매점 가족은 북동부의 몇몇 매장에서 일할 경력직 관리자들을 구하고 있습니다.

1 (C)	**2** (A)	**3** (D)	**4** (B)	**5** (A)

1

Payment / on the latest shipment / is due / and must be received / within five days.
대금이   최근의 배송에 대한   결제일이 되었습니다 / 그래서 납부되어야 합니다 / 5일 이내에
↳ '납부되는' 대상

(A) to receive   (B) receive   (C) be received   (D) received

해설   동사원형 선택 / 능동태와 수동태 구별: 빈칸 앞에 조동사 must가 있으므로, 빈칸에는 동사원형이 들어가야 합니다. 문맥상 주어 Payment(지불)는 '납부되는' 대상이므로, (C) be received가 정답입니다.

번역   최근의 배송에 대한 대금의 결제일이 되었으며 5일 이내에 납부되어야 합니다.

2

The new lighting fixtures / arrived / this morning / and will be installed / tomorrow afternoon.
새로운 조명 기구들이   도착했다   오늘 아침에   그리고 설치될 것이다   내일 오후에
↳ '설치되는' 대상

(A) installed   (B) installing   (C) installment   (D) installation

해설   능동태와 수동태 구별: 주어 The new lighting fixtures가 '설치하다'라는 의미의 동사 install의 주체인지 대상인지를 먼저 파악해야 합니다. 문맥상 조명 기구는 '설치되는' 대상이므로, be동사와 결합하여 수동태를 만드는 과거분사 (A) installed가 정답입니다. 명사 (C) installment(할부)와 (D) installation(설치)은 be동사 뒤에서 주격 보어로 쓰일 수 있지만, 문맥상 주어와 동격 관계를 이루지 않으므로 오답입니다.

번역   새로운 조명 기구들이 오늘 아침에 도착했고 내일 오후에 설치될 것이다.

3

If you correspond / with the company president / regarding this matter, / a copy of your letter /
귀하가 서신을 주고받는다면   그 회사 사장과   이 문제에 관해   귀하의 편지 사본이

should be sent / to his secretary / as well.
보내져야 할 것입니다   그의 비서에게도   역시
            '보내지는' 대상 ←

(A) send   (B) sent   (C) to send   (D) be sent

해설   동사원형 선택 / 능동태와 수동태 구별: 빈칸 앞에 조동사 should가 있으므로, 빈칸에는 동사원형이 들어가야 합니다. 문맥상 주어 a copy of your letter는 '보내지는' 대상이므로, 수동의 의미를 나타내는 동사원형 (D) be sent가 정답입니다.

번역   귀하가 이 문제에 관해 그 회사 사장과 서신을 주고받는다면, 귀하의 편지 사본이 그의 비서에게도 보내져야 할 것입니다.

4

Fluctuations / in the price of corn / usually can be tied / to changes / in the region's weather.
(급격한) 변동은   옥수수 가격의   일반적으로 관계가 있을 수 있다 변화와   지역 날씨의
↳ '관계되는' 대상

(A) tied   (B) can be tied   (C) will have tied   (D) are able to tie

해설   능동태와 수동태 구별: 주어 Fluctuations는 '관계가 되는' 대상이므로 수동태 동사형인 (B) can be tied가 정답입니다.

번역   옥수수 가격의 변동은 일반적으로 지역 날씨의 변화와 관계가 있을 수 있다.

5

The new advertisement / has been customized / to reflect / your company's image.
새 광고는   맞춤 제작되었습니다   반영할 수 있도록 / 귀사의 이미지를
↳ '맞춤 제작되는' 대상

(A) customized   (B) customize   (C) customizing   (D) customizes

해설   능동태와 수동태 구별: 주어 The new advertisement는 맞춤 제작되는 대상이므로 수동태를 만드는 (A) customized가 정답입니다.

번역   새 광고는 귀사의 이미지를 반영할 수 있도록 맞춤 제작되었습니다.

6 (B)	7 (C)	8 (A)	9 (D)	10 (C)

6

Kinghorn Publicity Press / (is known / for) creating advertisements / that leave a strong
킹혼 퍼블리시티 프레스는   알려져 있다   광고 제작으로   강한 인상을 남기는

impression / on viewers.   ↳ ~로 알려져 있다
                시청자에게

(A) will know   (B) is known   (C) to know   (D) has known

해설 수동태 구문: be known for는 '~로 알려져 있다'라는 의미이므로 (B) is known이 정답입니다.

번역 킹혼 퍼블리시티 프레스는 시청자에게 강한 인상을 주는 광고 제작으로 알려져 있다.

7

Nearly half / of the Scortflex Corporation's (distribution centers) / are situated / in major coastal cities.
거의 절반은   스코트플렉스 사의 유통 센터들의   ↳ '위치되어지는' 대상   위치해 있다   주요 해안 도시에

(A) are situating   (B) situate   (C) are situated   (D) situates

해설 능동태와 수동태 구별: 주어 distribution centers가 '위치시키다'라는 의미의 동사 situate의 주체인지 대상인지를 먼저 파악해야
합니다. 문맥상 유통 센터는 '위치되어지는' 대상이므로, 수동태 동사형인 (C) are situated가 정답입니다.

번역 스코트플렉스 사의 유통 센터들의 거의 절반은 주요 해안 도시에 위치해 있다.

8

Last week, / (senior managers) at Alameda Hardware / were instructed / to begin / a review of
지난주에   알라메다 철물의 선임 관리자들은   지시받았다   시작하라고   안전 절차에 대한 검토를

safety procedures.   ↳ '지시를 받는' 대상

(A) were instructed   (B) instructed   (C) instructing   (D) will instruct

해설 능동태와 수동태 구별: 전치사구 at Alameda Hardware의 수식을 받는 주어 senior managers는 검토에 착수하라는 '지시를 받는'
대상이므로 수동태 동사형인 (A) were instructed가 정답입니다.

번역 지난주에 알라메다 철물의 선임 관리자들은 안전 절차에 대한 검토에 착수하라고 지시받았다.

9

(An exhibition) of Andrea Lenin's paintings / is being held / in the Noya Gallery.
안드레아 레닌의 회화 전시회가   열리고 있다   노야 미술관에서
    ↳ '열리는' 대상

(A) holds   (B) has held   (C) is holding   (D) is being held

해설 능동태와 수동태 구별: 빈칸은 주어 An exhibition 뒤에 나오는 동사 자리입니다. 문맥상 전시회는 '열리는' 대상이므로, 수동의 의미를
나타내는 (D) is being held가 정답입니다. (A) holds, (B) has held, (C) is holding은 모두 능동의 의미를 나타내는 동사입니다.

번역 안드레아 레닌의 회화 전시회가 노야 미술관에서 열리고 있다.

10

(The delegation) / will depart / from the embassy / at 9 A.M. / and will be accompanied / to the
대표단은   출발 예정이다   대사관에서   오전 9시에   그리고 동행될 것이다   공항까지
                                        ↳ '동행 되는' 대상

airport / by the Minister of Sports.
            체육부 장관에 의해

(A) will accompany   (B) accompanied   (C) will be accompanied   (D) being accompanied

해설 능동태와 수동태 구별: 빈칸은 주어 The delegation의 동사 자리로, 대표단은 장관에 의해 공항까지 '동반되는' 대상이며, 빈칸 뒤의 by
the Minister of Sports(by + 행위자)로 보아, 수동의 의미를 나타내는 미래 시제 동사 (C) will be accompanied가 정답입니다.

번역 대표단은 오전 9시에 대사관에서 출발 예정이며, 체육부 장관이 공항까지 동행할 것이다.

Questions 11-14 refer to the following letter.

June 30

Peter Mazzie
14 Wyndmoor Court, Apartment A
Edinburgh, EH5 2TU

Dear Mr. Mazzie:

Your subscription / to *Financial News Weekly* / will expire / on October 30.
귀하의 정기 구독이 〈주간 파이낸셜 뉴스〉에 대한 만료될 예정입니다 / 10월 30일에

That's still four months away, / but if you **11.** renew / before July 21, /
그것은 아직 4개월이 남아 있습니다 그러나 만약 갱신하신다면 7월 21일까지
조건절에서 미래 시제를 대신하는 현재 시제

we will add / one extra month / to your subscription. All you have to do /
저희는 연장해 드립니다 / 추가 한 달을 구독 기간에 귀하가 하실 일은

is complete and return / the enclosed card. You do not need to enclose
작성하고 반송하는 것 뿐입니다 동봉된 카드를 귀하는 구독료를 동봉하실 필요가 없습니다

your **12.** payment / at this time. We / will send / you / an invoice, / and you /
이번에는 저희가 / 보내 드릴 것입니다 / 귀하에게 / 송장을 그리고 귀하는

can send / your money / later. **13.** So / mail / the card / today. You / will not
보내 주시면 됩니다 / 대금을 나중에 그러니 / 보내주십시오 / 카드를 오늘 귀하는 놓치지 않을

miss / a **14.** single copy of *Financial News Weekly*, / and you / will receive /
것입니다 / 단 한 부의 〈주간 파이낸셜 뉴스〉도 그리고 귀하는 받아볼 수 있습니다

an extra month / for free!
한 달을 추가로 무료로

Sincerely,

Sharon Oakman
Circulation Manager

6월 30일

피터 마지
14 윈드무어 코트 아파트 A동
에딘버러, EH5 2TU

마지 씨께:

귀하의 〈주간 파이낸셜 뉴스〉 정기 구독이 10월 30일에 만료될 예정입니다. 아직 4개월이 남았지만, 7월 21일까지 구독을 갱신하시면 구독 기간을 한 달 연장해 드립니다. 귀하께서는 동봉된 카드를 작성해 반송해 주시기만 하면 됩니다. 이번에는 구독료를 동봉하실 필요가 없습니다. 저희가 송장을 보내 드릴 것이며, 귀하께서는 나중에 대금을 보내 주시면 됩니다. 그러니 오늘 카드를 보내 주십시오. 단 한 부의 〈주간 파이낸셜 뉴스〉도 놓치지 않을 뿐더러 무료로 한 달을 더 받아볼 수 있습니다!

섀런 오크먼
판매 부장

11 (A) renew

(B) renewing

(C) had renewed

(D) will be renewed

> **해설** 미래 시제를 대신하는 현재 시제: 이 문장은 '귀하가 구독을 갱신한다면'이라는 조건을 제시하고 있으므로, 조건절을 포함한 문장입니다. 조건절에서는 현재 시제가 미래 시제를 대신하므로 정답은 (A) renew(갱신하다)입니다.

---

12 (A) rent

(B) bill

(C) résumé

(D) payment

(A) 집세

(B) 계산서

(C) 이력서

(D) 대금

> **해설** 명사 어휘 문제: 이 지문은 독자에게 잡지의 구독 갱신을 권유하는 편지이므로, '구독료'는 지금 보낼 필요가 없다는 내용이 가장 자연스럽습니다. 따라서 정답은 (D) payment입니다.

---

13 (A) Carry the card at all times.

(B) So mail the card today.

(C) We have charged your credit card.

(D) Your next copy will arrive shortly.

(A) 항상 카드를 휴대해 주십시오.

(B) 그러니 오늘 카드를 보내 주십시오.

(C) 귀하의 신용카드로 청구했습니다.

(D) 다음 호 잡지가 곧 도착할 것입니다.

> **해설** 문장 고르기: 구독을 갱신하려면 동봉된 카드를 반송하면 된다는 내용과 함께, 결제 방법이 앞에서 설명되고 있습니다. 이 편지의 목적은 구독을 연장시키는 데 있으므로, 앞서 언급한 그 카드를 오늘 보내 달라는 내용인 (B)가 빈칸에 들어가는 것이 자연스럽습니다.

---

14 (A) single

(B) recognized

(C) treatable

(D) lonely

(A) 하나의

(B) 인정된

(C) 치료할 수 있는

(D) 외로운

> **해설** 어휘 문제: 서적·잡지·신문 등과 같은 출판물의 '1부, 1권'을 뜻하는 copy를 적절하게 수식하는 형용사를 찾아야 합니다. (A) single은 '하나의'라는 의미로 빈칸 앞의 부정관사 a를 더욱 강조하여 '단 하나의'라는 표현이 되므로 정답입니다.

● to부정사의 쓰임 ETS 문제로 훈련하기 STEP 1

교재 p.117

1 (A)	2 (B)	3 (B)	4 (B)	5 (B)	6 (B)

1

The team / is doing / everything possible / (to meet) the deadline.
팀은　　　　　~하고 있다　　가능한 모든 일을　　　　　　　마감일을 맞추기 위해서

(A) meet

(B) meeting
→ to부정사의 형태: to + 동사원형

번역 팀에서는 마감일을 맞추기 위해서 가능한 모든 일을 하고 있다.

2

One of your tasks / as a computer programmer / is (to update) our Web site.
당신의 직무 중 하나는　　컴퓨터 프로그래머로서　　　　　우리 웹사이트를 업데이트하는 것이다

(A) updates

(B) to update
→ 보어 역할을 하는 to부정사

번역 컴퓨터 프로그래머로서 당신의 직무 중 하나는 우리 웹사이트를 업데이트하는 것이다.

3

Travelers / should call / the airline / (to confirm) their flights / 24 hours before departure.
여행자는　　전화해야 한다　항공사에　　항공편 확인을 위해　　　　출발 24시간 전에

(A) for

(B) to
→ 동사 call을 수식하는 to부정사

번역 여행자는 출발 24시간 전에 항공편 확인을 위해 항공사에 전화해야 한다.

4

The team / (decided / to cancel) the project / because of budget constraints.
그 팀은　　　　결정했다　　프로젝트를 취소하기로　　　　예산의 제약으로 인해
→ decide: to부정사를 목적어로 취하는 동사

(A) cancel

(B) to cancel

번역 그 팀은 예산의 제약으로 인해 프로젝트를 취소하기로 결정했다.

5

It is effective / (to circulate) a meeting agenda / to the attendees / in advance.
효율적이다　　회의 안건을 돌리는 것이　　　　　　　회의 참석자들에게　　사전에
→ 진주어로 사용되는 to부정사

(A) circulated

(B) to circulate

번역 회의 참석자들에게 사전에 회의 안건을 돌리는 것이 효율적이다.

6

Mr. Woo / (declined / to comment) on rumors / that he is planning to retire.
우 씨는　　　　거절했다　　소문에 대해 논평하는 것을　　자신이 은퇴할 계획 중이라는
→ decline: to부정사를 목적어로 취하는 동사

(A) commenting

(B) comment

번역 우 씨는 자신이 은퇴할 계획이라는 소문에 대해 논평하는 것을 거절했다.

PART 5 | UNIT 09

7 (D)	8 (A)	9 (A)	10 (D)

7

The Benson Investment Group / plans / to purchase stock / in more than 300 companies /
벤슨 인베스트먼트 그룹은   계획이다   주식을 매입할   300개 이상의 회사에서
                                                  → to부정사의 형태: to + 동사원형

worldwide.
전 세계적으로

(A) purchased   (B) purchases

(C) purchasing   (D) purchase

해설 to부정사의 형태: plan은 '계획하다'라는 의미의 타동사이므로 〈to + _____〉이 plan의 목적어 역할을 하고 있음을 알 수 있습니다. 명사 역할을 하는 to부정사는 to 뒤에 동사원형이 들어가므로 정답은 (D) purchase(구입[매입]하다)입니다.

번역 벤슨 인베스트먼트 그룹은 전 세계 300개 이상의 회사 주식을 매입할 계획이다.

8

To build fine furniture, / Mr. Taylor / uses / special wood / that is not available / in stores.
좋은 가구를 만들기 위해   테일러 씨는   사용한다   특별한 목재를   구할 수 없는   상점에서
       → 문장을 수식하는 to부정사

(A) To build   (B) Build

(C) Built   (D) Has built

해설 문장을 수식하는 to부정사: 빈칸 뒤 fine furniture는 빈칸의 목적어 역할을 하는 명사구입니다. _____ the furniture는 뒤에 나오는 문장을 수식하여 '좋은 가구를 만들기 위해 ~을 사용한다'라는 의미를 나타내는 것이 문맥상 자연스럽습니다. 따라서 목적어를 취하면서 부사 역할을 하는 to부정사 (A) To build가 정답입니다.

번역 좋은 가구를 만들기 위해 테일러 씨는 상점에서 구할 수 없는 특별한 목재를 사용한다.

9

In an effort / to improve sales, / we have sent / a questionnaire / to previous customers.
노력의 일환으로   매출 증대를 위한   우리는 보냈다   설문지를   예전 고객들에게
                                  → 앞 명사 an effort를 수식하는 to부정사

(A) to improve   (B) improved

(C) has improved   (D) improving

해설 명사를 수식하는 to부정사: 빈칸 뒤 sales는 빈칸의 목적어 역할을 하는 명사이므로 목적어를 취하면서 형용사 역할을 하는 to부정사 (A) to improve가 정답입니다. 참고로 〈in an effort to + 동사원형〉은 '~하려는 노력의 일환으로'라는 의미의 관용표현입니다.

번역 매출 증대를 위한 노력의 일환으로, 우리는 예전 고객들에게 설문지를 보냈다.

10

In order to attract / more tourists, / the Henly Museum / is offering / free admission / in July.
유치하기 위해   더 많은 관광객을   헨리 박물관은   제공하고 있다   무료 입장을   7월에
       → in order to + 동사원형: ~하기 위해서

(A) attraction   (B) attracting

(C) attractive   (D) attract

해설 〈in order to + 동사원형〉 구문: '~하기 위해서'라는 목적을 나타내는 to부정사 관용표현인 〈in order to + 동사원형〉을 완성하는 문제입니다. 따라서 정답은 동사원형인 (D) attract입니다.

번역 더 많은 관광객을 유치하기 위해 헨리 박물관은 7월에 무료 입장을 제공하고 있다.

1 (B)	2 (B)	3 (B)	4 (A)	5 (B)	6 (A)

1

Ms. Pieraccini / has nearly (finished / editing) the budget report.
피에라치니 씨는   거의 끝냈다   예산 보고서를 편집하는 것을
                                   → finish: 동명사를 목적어로 취하는 동사
(A) to edit   (B) editing

번역 피에라치니 씨는 예산 보고서 편집을 거의 끝냈다.

2

(Introducing) yourself / to the audience / is the first step of your presentation.
자신을 소개하는 것이   청중들에게   프레젠테이션의 첫 번째 단계이다
        → 주어 역할을 하는 동명사
(A) Introduction   (B) Introducing

번역 청중들에게 자신을 소개하는 것이 프레젠테이션의 첫 번째 단계다.

3

The train company / has decided / to reduce fares / as a way / of (attracting) customers.
그 철도 회사는   결정했다   요금을 인하하기로   방법으로   손님들을 끌어들이는
(A) attraction   (B) attracting   → 전치사의 목적어 역할을 하는 동명사

번역 그 철도 회사는 손님들을 끌어들이는 방법으로 요금을 인하하기로 결정했다.

4

The dieticians / (recommend / eating) a well-balanced breakfast / daily.
영양사들은   권한다   균형 잡힌 아침 식사를 하는 것을   매일
                → recommend: 동명사를 목적어로 취하는 동사
(A) eating   (B) eaten

번역 영양사들은 매일 균형 잡힌 아침 식사를 하라고 권한다.

5

Our new method / of (producing) rubber for tires / is still being tested / in the lab.
우리 회사의 새로운 방법이   타이어용 고무를 생산하는   아직 시험 중이다   연구실에서
                        → 전치사의 목적어 역할을 하는 동명사
(A) to produce   (B) producing

번역 타이어용 고무를 생산하는 우리 회사의 새로운 방법이 연구실에서 아직 시험 중이다.

6

Forty hours of training / in machine operation / is a (requirement) / for new product assemblers.
40시간의 교육은   기계 작동에 대한   필수 사항이다   신제품 조립 기술자에게
(A) requirement   (B) requiring   → 부정관사 a 뒤에 위치하며, 보어로 쓰인 명사

번역 기계 작동에 대한 40시간의 교육은 신제품 조립 기술자에게 필수 사항이다.

| 7 (C) | 8 (A) | 9 (D) | 10 (D) |

7

For many years / the local government / has (considered / designating) / Red Valley / as a
다년간　　　　　　지방 정부는　　　　고려해 왔다　　　지정하는 것을　　레드 계곡을　　야생 공원으로

wilderness park.
　　　　　　　　　　　　동사 consider의 목적어 역할을 하는 동명사 ←

(A) designate 지정하다　　　　　(B) designates 지정하다

(C) designating 지정하는 것　　　(D) designation 지정, 지명

해설　consider + 동명사: 빈칸에는 Red Valley를 목적어로 취하는 동시에 has considered의 목적어가 될 수 있는 문장 성분이 와야
합니다. consider(고려하다)는 동명사를 목적어로 취하므로 (C) designating이 정답입니다.

번역　다년간 지방 정부는 레드 계곡을 야생 공원으로 지정하는 것을 고려해 왔다.

8

After (carefully) interviewing / a number of applicants, / we / are pleased / to offer / you /
신중하게 인터뷰한 후　　　　　　　　많은 지원자를　　　　　우리는/ 기쁩니다　　제공할 수 있게 되어 / 귀하에게

a position.　↘ 동명사 interviewing을 수식하는 부사
일자리를

(A) carefully　　　　　(B) to care

(C) careful　　　　　　(D) most careful

해설　동명사를 수식하는 부사: 빈칸은 동명사 interviewing을 수식하는 자리이므로, 부사 (A) carefully가 정답입니다. 명사는
수식하지만, 동명사는 동사적 성질을 지니고 있어 부사가 수식합니다.

번역　많은 지원자를 신중하게 인터뷰한 후, 우리가 귀하에게 일자리를 제공할 수 있게 되어 기쁩니다.

9

Because of his success / in (organizing) the merger, / Mr. Rivera / was promoted / to vice
그의 성공으로 인해　　　　　　합병을 조직하는 데 있어　　리베라 씨는　　승진되었다　　부사장으로

president.　　　　　↘ 전치사의 목적어 역할을 하는 동명사

(A) organize 조직하다　　　　(B) organization 조직, 단체

(C) organizer 조직자, 창시자　(D) organizing 조직하기

해설　전치사의 목적어 역할을 하는 동명사: 빈칸은 전치사의 목적어 역할을 하는 동시에 the merger를 목적어로 취할 수 있는 동명사 (D)
organizing이 정답입니다. 빈칸 뒤에 the merger가 있으므로 명사인 (B) organization과 (C) organizer는 정답이 될 수 없습니다.

번역　리베라 씨는 합병을 성공적으로 해냈기 때문에 부회장으로 승진되었다.

10

(In appreciation / for) her years of service, / the company / threw / Ms. Parida / a retirement party.
감사로　　　　　장기 근속에 대한　　　　회사는　　열어 주었다 / 패리다 씨에게　은퇴 기념 파티를
　　　　　↘ ~에 감사하여

(A) appreciating 감사하기　　　(B) appreciative 고마워하는

(C) appreciate 고마워하다, 진가를 알아보다　(D) appreciation 감사, 감탄, 감상

해설　전치사 + 명사(전치사의 목적어 역할): 빈칸은 전치사 in의 목적어 자리이므로 명사 역할을 할 수 있는 동명사 (A) appreciating, 명사
(D) appreciation이 정답 후보입니다. 주로 타동사로 쓰이는 appreciate는 뒤에 목적어가 필요하므로 동명사인 (A) appreciating은
정답이 될 수 없습니다. 따라서 정답은 명사인 (D) appreciation입니다.

번역　회사는 장기 근속에 대한 감사로 패리다 씨에게 은퇴 기념 파티를 열어 주었다.

1 (B)	2 (B)	3 (B)	4 (A)	5 (B)	6 (A)

1

Ms. Park / has (asked / her assistant / to type) the report / tomorrow.
박 씨는   요청했다   자신의 비서에게   보고서를 타이핑해 달라고   내일

                             → ask + 목적어 + to 동사원형

(A) will type   (B) to type

번역   박 씨는 자신의 비서에게 내일 보고서를 타이핑해 달라고 요청했다.

2

The newspaper's circulation department / (is committed / to providing) excellent service.
신문사 판매국은   전념한다   훌륭한 서비스를 제공하는 데

(A) provided   (B) providing   → be committed to + 동명사: ~하는 것에 전념하다

번역   신문사 판매국은 훌륭한 서비스를 제공하는 데 전념한다.

3

The corporate charter / (requires / its executives / to act) / in the best interest of the company.
기업 설립 강령은   요구한다   중역들에게   행동하도록   최대한 회사를 위해

                             → require + 목적어 + to 동사원형

(A) acting   (B) to act

번역   기업 설립 강령에서는 중역들에게 최대한 회사를 위해 행동하도록 요구한다.

4

The shipment / is (too big to load) / into our delivery van.
그 배송품은   너무 커서 실을 수 없다   우리 배달 트럭에

                         → too + 형용사 / 부사 + to 동사원형: 너무 ~해서 …할 수 없는

(A) too   (B) very

번역   그 배송품은 너무 커서 우리 배달 트럭에 실을 수 없다.

5

Mr. Saito / (is used to giving) presentations / to international clients.
사이토 씨는   발표하는 데 익숙하다   해외 고객들에게

                  → be used to + 동명사: ~하는 것에 익숙하다

(A) give   (B) giving

번역   사이토 씨는 해외 고객들에게 발표하는 데 익숙하다.

6

Guests / are asked / to register / at the front desk / (upon entering) the main lobby.
방문객들은   요청을 받는다   등록하라고   프런트 데스크에서   중앙 로비에 들어서자마자

(A) upon   (B) in order to   → upon[on] + 동명사: ~하자마자

번역   방문객들은 중앙 로비에 들어서자마자 프런트 데스크에서 등록하라는 요청을 받는다.

PART 5 | UNIT 09

| **7** (C) | **8** (B) | **9** (D) | **10** (D) |

7

Mail carriers / are encouraged / (to wear) comfortable shoes / while on duty.
우편 배달원들은   권장받는다   편안한 신발을 신도록   근무 중에
↳ 동사 encourage의 보어 역할을 하는 to부정사

(A) wearing   (B) wore

(C) wear   (D) worn

> **해설** to부정사의 형태: 〈encourage + mail carriers(목적어) + to 동사원형(목적격 보어)〉의 능동태가 수동태로 전환된 문장이므로, 빈칸에 동사원형이 들어가야 합니다. 따라서 (C) wear가 정답입니다. to부정사의 to와 전치사 to를 혼동하지 않도록 주의해야 합니다.

> **번역** 우편 배달원들은 근무 중에 편안한 신발을 신도록 권장받는다.

8

You / are invited / (to attend) / the third annual conference / for digital sound engineers.
귀하는 초대되었습니다 참석하도록   제3차 연례 회의에   디지털 사운드 엔지니어들을 위한
↳ 동사 invite의 보어 역할을 하는 to부정사

(A) attending   (B) to attend

(C) attend   (D) attended

> **해설** 목적격 보어 역할을 하는 to부정사: 〈invite + you(목적어) + to 동사원형(목적격 보어)〉의 능동태가 〈You + are invited + to 동사원형〉의 수동태로 전환된 문장이므로, 빈칸에는 to부정사가 들어가야 합니다. 따라서 (B) to attend가 정답입니다.

> **번역** 귀하는 디지털 사운드 엔지니어들을 위한 제3차 연례 회의에 참석하도록 초대되었습니다.

9

The president / stated / that he was (looking forward / to beginning) work / on the construction
사장은   말했다   그는 고대하고 있다고   작업에 착수하기를   건설 프로젝트의

project.   ↳ look forward to + 동명사: ~하기를 고대하다
작업에

(A) begin   (B) began

(C) begins   (D) beginning

> **해설** look forward to + 명사 / 동명사: look forward to(~을 고대하다) 뒤에는 명사나 동명사가 올 수 있습니다. 따라서 동명사 (D) beginning이 정답입니다.

> **번역** 사장은 건설 프로젝트 작업에 착수하기를 고대하고 있다고 말했다.

10

All advertising / at the National Textile Convention / is subject to (approval) / by the board of
모든 광고는   전국 직물 협의회의   승인을 받아야 한다   이사회의

directors.   전치사 to의 목적어이자, 뒤에 목적어가 없으므로 명사가 와야 함

(A) approve 찬성하다, 승인하다   (B) approvingly 찬성하여

(C) approving 승인하기   (D) approval 찬성, 승인

> **해설** be subject to + 명사 / 동명사: be subject to(~을 받아야 한다) 뒤에는 명사나 동명사가 와야 하므로 (C) approving과 (D) approval이 정답으로 가능합니다. (C) approving이 정답이 되기 위해서는 뒤에 목적어가 필요하므로 정답은 (D) approval입니다.

> **번역** 전국 직물 협의회에서 이루어지는 모든 광고는 이사회의 승인을 받아야 한다.

1 (A)	**2** (B)	**3** (B)	**4** (A)

1

Highway 140 / is not accessible / by Exit 2A / due to road construction.
140번 간선 도로는   접근이 가능하지 않다   출구 2A를 통해   도로 공사 때문에
→ 접근 가능한

(A) accessible 접근 가능한   (B) possible 가능한

번역   도로 공사 때문에 출구 2A를 통해 140번 간선 도로로 나갈 수 없다.

2

A valid identification card / is required / before entering the plant.
유효한 신분증이   필요하다   공장에 들어가기 전에
→ 유효한, 타당한

(A) severe 극심한, 심각한   (B) valid 유효한

번역   공장에 들어가려면 유효한 신분증이 필요하다.

3

Waldman Graphics / will increase / its workforce / by 15 percent / in the upcoming year.
월드먼 그래픽스는   늘릴 것이다   인력을   15퍼센트만큼   다음 해에
→ 곧 있을, 다가오는

(A) previous 이전의, 예전의   (B) upcoming 곧 있을, 다가오는

번역   월드먼 그래픽스는 다음 해에 인력을 15퍼센트 늘릴 것이다.

4

Versatility and flexibility / are essential / to getting / a good entry-level job.
다재다능함과 융통성이   필수적이다   얻는 데 있어   괜찮은 말단직을
→ 필수적인, 극히 중요한

(A) essential 필수적인   (B) initial 처음의, 초기의

번역   괜찮은 말단직을 얻는 데 있어 다재다능함과 융통성이 필수적이다.

| 5 (A) | 6 (C) | 7 (D) | 8 (D) |

5

The monitor / was damaged / in shipping / because the packaging was not (adequate).
모니터가   파손되었다   배송 과정에서   포장이 적절하지 않기 때문에
                                                              → 적절한

(A) adequate 충분한, 적절한   (B) likely ~할 것 같은, 가능성 있는

(C) intended 의도된, 계획된   (D) expected 예상된, 기대된

해설 adequate 충분한, 적절한: 배송 중 모니터가 파손된 것은 포장이 '적절하지' 않기 때문일 것이므로, '충분한, 적절한'이라는 의미의 (A) adequate이 정답입니다.

번역 포장이 적절하지 않기 때문에 배송 과정에서 모니터가 파손되었다.

6

Until the central heating can be repaired, / portable heaters / will be used / as a (temporary)
중앙 난방 장치가 수리될 수 있을 때까지   휴대용 난방기가   사용될 것이다   임시 조치로
measure.   임시의, 잠정적인 ←

(A) brief 간단한, 짧은   (B) summary 요약한

(C) temporary 임시의, 잠정적인   (D) perishable 상하기 쉬운

해설 temporary 임시의: '임시 조치'라는 의미가 문맥상 적합하므로, '임시의'를 뜻하는 (C) temporary가 정답입니다.

번역 중앙 난방 장치가 수리될 수 있을 때까지 임시 조치로 휴대용 난방기가 사용될 것이다.

7

The managerial position / would offer / (additional) flexibility / in scheduling / and a higher salary.
관리직은   제공할 것이다   추가적인 유연성을   일정 관리에 있어   그리고 더 높은 급여를
                                    → 추가의, 추가적인

(A) fixed 고정된   (B) multiple 다수의

(C) hopeful 희망하는   (D) additional 추가의

해설 additional 추가의, 추가적인: 빈칸 뒤 명사 flexibility를 수식하는 형용사 자리로, 전치사구 in scheduling 또한 명사 flexibility를 수식합니다. 문맥상 '일정 관리에 있어 추가적인 유연성'이라는 의미가 자연스러우므로, (D) additional이 정답입니다.

번역 관리직은 일정 관리에 있어 추가적인 유연성과 더 높은 급여를 제공할 것이다.

8

Mr. Yoo / (was responsible / for) the successful completion / of the downtown hotel renovation
유 씨는   책임지고 있었다   성공적인 완수를   시내 호텔 보수 공사 계획의
project.   → be responsible for: ~에 책임이 있다

(A) probable 개연성 있는   (B) trusting 신뢰하는

(C) powerful 강력한   (D) responsible 책임지는

해설 be responsible for ~에 책임이 있다: 빈칸 뒤 전치사 for와 함께 사용되면서, 주어 Mr. Yoo를 보충 설명하는 형용사를 선택해야 합니다. '성공적인 완수에 책임이 있었다'라는 의미가 문맥상 자연스러우므로, (D) responsible이 정답입니다.

번역 유 씨는 시내 호텔 보수 공사 계획의 성공적인 완수를 책임지고 있었다.

1

Dental patients / are advised / to return to our office / every six months / for a checkup.
치과 환자들은   권유받는다   우리 병원을 다시 찾아줄 것을   6개월마다   검진을 위해
                                        → 동사 advise의 보어 역할을 하는 to부정사

(A) return   (B) returns   (C) returned   (D) returning

> **해설** **to부정사의 형태:** 〈advise + dental patients(목적어) + to 동사원형 (목적격 보어)〉의 능동태가 〈Dental patients + are
> advised + to 동사원형〉의 수동태로 전환된 문장이므로, 빈칸에는 동사원형이 들어가야 합니다. 따라서 (A) return이 정답입니다.

> **번역** 치과 환자들은 검진을 위해 6개월마다 우리 병원을 다시 찾아줄 것을 권유받는다.

2

They / delayed / cleaning the offices / so that the meeting could continue / without disturbance.
그들은   미뤘다   사무실을 청소하는 것을   회의가 계속될 수 있도록   방해 없이
                     → 동사 delay는 동명사를 목적어로 취함

(A) clean   (B) cleaned   (C) to clean   (D) cleaning

> **해설** **delay + 동명사:** 빈칸 앞의 동사 delay(미루다)는 동명사를 목적어로 취합니다. 따라서 동명사 (D) cleaning이 정답입니다.

> **번역** 그들은 방해 없이 회의가 계속될 수 있도록 사무실 청소를 미뤘다.

3

After inspecting the tire / on Ms. Hoven's rental car, / the mechanic / advised / her / to replace it.
타이어를 점검한 후   호벤 씨의 렌터카의   정비사는   권했다   그녀에게 / 그것을 교체하라고
  → 전치사의 목적어 역할을 하는 동명사

(A) inspected 점검했다   (B) inspection 점검, 검사   (C) inspecting 점검하기   (D) inspects 점검하다

> **해설** **전치사의 목적어 역할을 하는 동명사:** 빈칸은 전치사 After의 목적어 역할을 하는 자리이므로, 명사 (B) inspection(점검, 검사)과
> 동명사 (C) inspecting(점검[검사]하기)이 빈칸에 들어갈 수 있습니다. 하지만 뒤에 빈칸의 목적어 역할을 하는 명사구 the tire가
> 있으므로, 목적어를 취할 수 있는 동명사 (C) inspecting이 정답입니다.

> **번역** 호벤 씨의 렌터카 타이어를 점검한 후, 정비사는 그녀에게 타이어 교체를 권했다.

4

Stow University / offers / online programs / to help mid-level managers / who wish to advance /
스토대학교는   제공한다   온라인 프로그램을   중간급 관리자를 돕기 위한   승진하기를 바라는
                                                              동사 wish의 목적어 역할을 하는 to부정사 ←

in their careers.
직장에서

(A) advance 승진하다, 전진하다   (B) advancement 발전, 진보

(C) advances 전진; 전진하다, 출세하다   (D) advancing 전진하기, 출세하기

> **해설** **동사의 목적어로 쓰이는 to부정사:** wish는 '바라다'라는 의미의 타동사이므로 〈to + _____〉이 wish의 목적어 역할을 하고 있음을 알
> 수 있습니다. 명사 역할을 하는 to부정사는 to 뒤에 동사원형이 들어가므로 (A) advance가 정답입니다.

> **번역** 스토대학교는 직장에서 승진하기를 바라는 중간급 관리자를 돕기 위한 온라인 프로그램을 제공한다.

5

The Internet / has made it easier / for vehicle buyers / to search for banks / that offer the best
인터넷은   더 쉽게 만들었다   차량 구입자들이   은행을 검색하는 것을   가장 좋은 대출을 제공하는

loans.
                                        → 진목적어 역할을 하는 to부정사

(A) to search   (B) search   (C) have searched   (D) searches

> **해설** **진목적어로 사용되는 to부정사:** it은 가목적어 역할을 하고 있으며, 빈칸에는 진목적어 역할을 할 수 있는 to부정사가 들어가야 하므로,
> 정답은 (A) to search입니다. for vehicle buyers는 to부정사의 의미상의 주어입니다.

> **번역** 인터넷은 차량 구입자들이 가장 좋은 대출 상품을 제공하는 은행을 검색하는 것을 더 쉽게 만들었다.

ETS 실전 테스트

교재 p.124

6 (B)	**7** (A)	**8** (A)	**9** (A)	**10** (A)

6

Ms. Peng / called / this morning / ⟨to inform⟩ / Mr. Torres / of the latest changes / to plans for the
펭 씨가　　전화했다　오늘 아침에　　알려주기 위해　토레스 씨에게　　최근 변동 사항을　　　　　지네온 프로젝트 계획안의

Gineon project.
　　　　　　　　　　　　　　　→ 동사 called를 수식하는 부사 역할을 하는 to부정사

(A) will inform　(B) to inform　(C) was informing　(D) has been informed

해설 부사 역할을 하는 to부정사: 문장에 동사 called가 있으므로 동사인 (A), (C), (D)는 빈칸에 들어갈 수 없습니다. 문맥상 '토레스 씨에게 알려주기 위해서 전화했다'가 자연스러우므로 부사 역할을 하는 to부정사 (B) to inform이 정답입니다.

번역 오늘 아침에 펭 씨가 토레스 씨에게 지네온 프로젝트 계획안의 최근 변동 사항을 알려주기 위해 전화했다.

7

Syna Corporation's earnings / were not ⟨impressive enough / to attract⟩ more investors.
시나사의 수익은　　　　　　　　충분히 인상적이지 않았다　　　　더 많은 투자자들을 끌어들일 만큼

(A) enough　(B) fully　(C) quite　(D) rather
　　　　　　　　　　　　　　　→ 형용사 + enough + to 동사원형: ~할 만큼 충분히 …한

해설 형용사(부사) + enough + to부정사: 빈칸은 to부정사 구문(to attract more investors)과 함께 형용사 impressive를 수식하는 부사 자리입니다. 문맥상 '더 많은 투자자를 끌어들일 만큼 충분히 인상적인'이라는 의미가 자연스러우므로, (A) enough가 정답입니다.

번역 시나사의 수익은 더 많은 투자자들을 끌어들일 만큼 충분히 인상적이지 않았다.

8

The entire sales team / must meet / the annual target / ⟨in order to qualify⟩ / for performance
전 영업 팀이　　　　　달성해야 한다　연간 목표를　　　자격을 얻기 위해서는　　실적 보너스에 대한

bonuses.
　　　　　　　　　　　　　　　　　　　　→ in order to 동사원형: ~하기 위해서

(A) in order to ~하기 위해서　(B) instead of ~ 대신에　(C) even if 비록 ~일지라도　(D) so that ~하도록

해설 ⟨in order to 동사원형⟩ 구문: 빈칸 뒤 동사원형 qualify와 결합하여 '자격을 얻기 위해서'라는 의미를 나타내는 것이 문맥상 자연스러우므로, (A) in order to가 정답입니다. 전치사구 (B) instead of 뒤에는 동명사가, 접속사 (C) even if와 (D) so that 뒤에는 주어와 동사로 이루어진 완전한 절이 와야 하므로 오답입니다.

번역 실적 보너스 자격을 얻기 위해서는 전 영업 팀이 연간 목표를 달성해야 한다.

9

Combro Electronics, Inc., / made the decision / ⟨to suspend⟩ / production of their latest mobile
콤브로 일렉트로닉스 주식회사는　　결정을 했다　　중단하는　　최신형 휴대전화의 생산을

phone / due to design flaws.
　　설계 결함으로 인해　　　　　→ 앞 명사 decision을 수식하는 형용사 역할을 하는 to부정사

(A) suspend　(B) suspended　(C) suspends　(D) suspending

해설 형용사 역할을 하는 to부정사: 빈칸 뒤 production은 빈칸의 목적어 역할을 하는 명사이므로 목적어를 취하면서 형용사 역할을 하는 to부정사가 적합합니다. 형용사 역할을 하는 to부정사는 to 뒤에 동사원형이 들어가므로 (A) suspend가 정답입니다.

번역 콤브로 일렉트로닉스 주식회사는 설계 결함으로 인해 최신형 휴대전화의 생산을 중단하기로 결정했다.

10

Youth Networking / is a nonprofit organization / that ⟨is committed / to arranging⟩ part-time job
유스 네트워킹은　　　비영리 단체이다　　　　　전념하는　　　시간제 일자리 기회를 마련해 주는 데

opportunities / for students.
　　　　　학생들에게　　　　　　→ be committed to + 동명사: ~하는 것에 전념하다

(A) arranging　(B) arrangement　(C) arrangements　(D) arranges

ETS 실전 테스트

교재 p. 125

| **11** (A) | **12** (C) | **13** (B) | **14** (D) |

Questions 11-14 refer to the following article.

11-14 기사

New Fusion Restaurant / Headed for 47th Street in Omaha Park
새로운 퓨전 식당이   오마하 파크 지역의 47번가로 온다

새로운 퓨전 식당이 오마하 파크 지역의 47번가로 온다

neighborhood

Veteran chef Ned Sheehan / is bringing fusion food / to Omaha Park.
베테랑 주방장 네드 쉬한이   퓨전 음식을 들여온다   오마하 파크로

베테랑 주방장 네드 쉬한이 오마하 파크로 퓨전 음식을 들여온다. "동네 주민들은 대담하고 혁신적인 식당을 즐기려면 시내로 나가야 한다고 말하죠." 그는 말했다. "하지만 저는 가까운 곳에 창의적인 식사 장소를 만들어드리고 싶었습니다."

"Neighborhood residents say / that they have to go downtown / to enjoy
동네 주민들은 말하죠   시내로 나가야 한다고   대담하고

bold, innovative eateries," / he said. **11.** But I want / them / to have creative
혁신적인 식당을 즐기려면   그는 말했다   하지만 저는 하고 싶습니다 / 그들이 / 창의적인

dining options / nearby.
식사 장소를 갖도록   가까운 곳에

Sheehan, / a former chef at the downtown restaurant Carlotti's Café, /
쉬한은   시내에 있는 식당인 카를로티즈 카페의 주방장이었던

시내에 있는 식당인 카를로티즈 카페의 주방장이었던 쉬한은 늦가을에 47번가 13 웨스트에 디오즈 피쩨리아가 있던 자리에 퓨전 잇츠를 개업할 예정이다.

(expects **12.** to open) Fusion Eats / at the old site of Dio's Pizzeria, 13 West
퓨전 잇츠를 개업할 예정이다   47번가 13 웨스트에 디오즈 피쩨리아가 있던 자리에
⟶ expect + to 동사원형: ~할 것으로 예상하다

47th Street, / in late autumn.
                늦가을에

"I've already prepared / more than 30 **13.** recipes / for Fusion Eats," /
벌써 준비했습니다   30가지 이상의 조리법을   퓨전 잇츠를 위한

"벌써 퓨전 잇츠를 위한 조리법을 30가지 이상 준비했습니다." 쉬한은 말했다. "그것들은 모두 친숙한 식재료와 이국적인 식재료를 섞은 것을 특징으로 하지요." 메뉴 품목에는 오리고기 카레, 새우 만두, 버섯 파이가 포함될 것이다. 오마하 파크 토박이인 쉬한은 47번가에 면한 가게 자리를 고르기 전에 20곳의 다른 식당 후보지를 평가했다고 말했다.

Sheehan said. "They all feature / a mix of familiar and exotic ingredients."
쉬한은 말했다.   그것들은 모두 특징으로 합니다 / 친숙한 식재료와 이국적인 식재료를 섞은 것을

Menu items / will include / duck curry, shrimp dumplings, and mushroom
메뉴 품목들은   포함할 것이다   오리고기 카레, 새우 만두, 그리고 버섯 파이를

pies. Sheehan, an Omaha Park native, said / he evaluated 20 other
오마하 파크 토박이인 쉬한은 말했다   20곳의 다른 후보지를 평가했다고

potential **14.** locations / for the restaurant / before choosing the 47th Street
                식당을 위한   47번가에 면한 가게 자리를 고르기 전에

storefront.

11
(A) But I want them to have creative dining options nearby.

(B) As a result, there is less traffic in the downtown area.

(C) I was surprised because I have never lived in Omaha Park.

(D) In fact, few people will attend those cooking classes.

(A) 하지만 저는 가까운 곳에 창의적인 식사 장소를 만들어드리고 싶었습니다.

(B) 그 결과 시내 중심부의 교통량이 감소했습니다.

(C) 저는 오마하 파크에 살아본 적이 없어서 놀랐습니다.

(D) 사실 그 요리 교실에 참석할 사람은 거의 없을 겁니다.

해설 문장 고르기: 빈칸 앞 문장에서, 동네 주민들은 '대담하고 혁신적인 식당을 즐기려면 시내로 나가야 한다고 말한다고 했으므로, 자신은 가까운 곳에 창의적인 식사 장소를 만들어 주고 싶었다'고 말하는 내용이 이어지는 것이 자연스러우므로 (A)가 정답입니다.

12
(A) opened

(B) to be opened

(C) to open

(D) being open

해설 expect to부정사: expect to 동사원형은 '~할 것으로 예상하다'라는 의미로, (B) to be opened와 (C) to open이 정답 후보입니다. 그런데 이 문장의 주어인 Sheehan이 '능동적으로' 개업을 하는 것이므로 수동의 의미를 갖는 (B)는 오답이 되며 (C) to open이 정답입니다.

13
(A) bowls

(B) recipes

(C) instructions

(D) personnel

(A) 그릇

(B) 조리법

(C) 사용 설명서

(D) 인원

해설 어휘 문제: 빈칸 다음의 문장에서 그것들은 친숙한 식재료와 이국적인 식재료를 섞은 것이라고 했으므로 (B) recipes가 정답입니다.

14
(A) renovations

(B) investors

(C) managers

(D) locations

(A) 보수

(B) 투자자

(C) 관리자

(D) 장소

해설 어휘 문제: '47번가에 면한 가게 자리를 고르기까지 20곳의 다른 가능성 있는 ~을 평가했다'는 문맥이므로 빈칸 뒤의 storefront를 대신할 수 있는 (D) locations가 정답입니다.

현재분사와 과거분사 ETS 문제로 훈련하기 STEP 1

교재 p.129

1 (A)	2 (A)	3 (A)	4 (B)	5 (A)	6 (B)

1

The deposit / is not refundable / if a (confirmed) reservation is canceled.
보증금은　　　　　환불해 드리지 않습니다　　　확정된 예약을 취소하면
　　　　　　　　　　　　　　　　　　　　　└→ 형용사 역할을 하는 분사

(A) confirmed 확정된　　　　　　　　(B) confirmation 확인

번역 확정된 예약을 취소하는 경우 보증금은 환불해 드리지 않습니다.

2

Please place / your payment / in the (enclosed) envelope / and mail it / by April 20.
넣어 주세요　　대금을　　　　동봉된 봉투에　　　　　　그리고 그것을 우편으로 발송해주세요 / 4월 20일까지
　　　　　　　　　　　　　　└→ 수동적 의미의 과거분사

(A) enclosed　　　　　　　　　　(B) enclosing

번역 대금을 동봉된 봉투에 넣어서 4월 20일까지 우편으로 발송해 주세요.

3

Research / has shown / that consumers prefer / (personalized) advertisements / over those
연구는　　보여주었다　　소비자들이 선호한다는 것을　　개별 맞춤된 광고를　　　　　일반 대중을

aimed at the general public.
겨냥한 광고보다　　　　　　　　　　　　　└→ 수동적 의미의 과거분사

(A) personalized　　　　　　　　(B) personalizing

번역 연구에 따르면 소비자들은 일반 대중을 겨냥한 광고보다 개별 맞춤형 광고를 선호한다.

4

Adequate storage space / is important / to companies / (producing) large quantities of materials.
충분한 저장 공간은　　　　중요하다　　기업에게　　　자재를 대량 생산하는

(A) produced　　　　　　　　　　(B) producing
　　　　　　　　　　　　　　　　　　　　└→ 능동적 의미의 현재분사

번역 충분한 저장 공간은 자재를 대량 생산하는 기업에게 중요하다.

5

Mr. Nam / is an excellent employee / and completes work / (assigned) to him / quickly and
남 씨는　　우수한 직원이다　　　그리고 업무를 완수한다　　자신에게 할당된　　　신속하고 철저하게

thoroughly.
　　　　　　　　　└→ 수동적 의미의 과거분사

(A) assigned　　　　　　　　　　(B) assigning

번역 남 씨는 우수한 직원이며 자신에게 할당된 업무를 신속하고 철저하게 완수한다.

6

Next week, / the candidates / will be on television / (introducing) their ideas.
다음 주에　　후보자들이　　　텔레비전에 나올 것이다　　자신들의 생각을 발표하며

(A) introduced　　　　　　　　　(B) introducing
　　　　　　　　　　　　　　　　　　　　└→ 능동적 의미의 현재분사

번역 다음 주에 후보자들이 텔레비전에 나와 자신들의 생각을 발표할 것이다.

7 (B)	**8** (D)	**9** (D)	**10** (A)

7

Notify / our office / if you cannot open / the (attached) workshop schedule.
알려주세요 / 사무실에　　만약 당신이 열 수 없다면　첨부된 워크숍 일정을
　　　　　　　　　　　　　　　　　　　　　　　　→ 수동적 의미의 과거분사

(A) attach　　　　　　　　　　(B) attached
(C) attaching　　　　　　　　　(D) attachment

해설　현재분사와 과거분사 구별: 빈칸은 명사구 workshop schedule을 앞에서 수식하는 형용사 자리입니다. 문맥상 '첨부된 워크숍 일정'이라는 수동의 의미가 자연스러우므로, 과거분사 (B) attached가 정답입니다.

번역　첨부된 워크숍 일정을 열 수 없는 경우 사무실에 알려주세요.

8

It is imperative / that all employees attend / the annual sales meeting / (scheduled) for March 21.
필수적이다　　전 직원이 참석하는 것이　　연례 영업 회의에　　3월 21일로 예정된
　　　　　　　　　　　　　　　　　　　　　　　　　　→ 형용사 역할을 하는 분사

(A) has been scheduled　　　　(B) schedules
(C) will schedule　　　　　　　(D) scheduled

해설　형용사 역할을 하는 분사: 빈칸은 명사구 the annual sales meeting을 뒤에서 수식하는 형용사 자리로, 문맥상 '3월 21일로 예정된'이라는 의미가 자연스러우므로, 과거분사 (D) scheduled가 정답입니다. that절에 동사 attend가 있으므로 동사인 (A), (B), (C)는 빈칸에 들어갈 수 없습니다.

번역　3월 21일로 예정된 연례 영업 회의에 전 직원이 반드시 참석해야 한다.

9

The pamphlets / were redesigned / to include photographs / of the hotel's (updated) interior design.
팸플릿은　　다시 디자인되었다　　사진들이 포함되도록　　호텔의 최신 실내 디자인의
　　　　　　　　　　　　　　　　　　　　　　　　　　　→ 수동적 의미의 과거분사

(A) updating　　　　　　　　　(B) update
(C) updates　　　　　　　　　　(D) updated

해설　현재분사와 과거분사 구별: 빈칸은 명사구 interior design을 앞에서 수식하는 형용사[분사] 자리로, interior design은 update의 대상이므로 수동 의미의 과거분사 (D) updated(새로 바뀐, 최신의)가 정답입니다.

번역　팸플릿은 호텔의 최신 실내 디자인 사진들이 포함되도록 다시 디자인되었다.

10

A banquet / (celebrating) the appointment of the new president / was held / yesterday / at the
연회가　　신임 사장의 임명을 축하하는　　　　　　　　열렸다　　어제　　애스턴
Aston Hotel.　　→ 능동적 의미의 현재분사
호텔에서

(A) celebrating　　　　　　　　(B) celebration
(C) celebrates　　　　　　　　　(D) celebrated

해설　현재분사와 과거분사 구별: 연회(banquet)가 축하를 받는 것이 아니라 '임명을 축하하는 연회'이므로 능동의 의미를 가진 현재분사 (A) celebrating이 정답입니다.

번역　신임 사장의 임명을 축하하기 위한 연회가 어제 애스턴 호텔에서 열렸다.

1 (B)	2 (A)	3 (B)	4 (B)	5 (B)	6 (B)

1

The speech / made a (lasting) impression / on participants / at the banquet.
그 연설은　　　오랜 감명을 주었다　　　　　　　참석자들에게　　　연회의
　　　　　　　　　　　→ lasting 오래 지속하는

(A) lasted　　　　　　　　　　　(B) lasting

번역　그 연설은 연회 참석자들에게 오랜 감명을 주었다.

2

The sales representative / is (disappointed) / in the negative feedback / from his customers.
그 영업 직원은　　　　　　　실망하고 있다　　　　부정적인 의견에　　　　　고객들로부터의
　　　　　　　　　　　　　　　　　　　　　　　　→ 감정을 느끼는 사람 명사와 결합하는 과거분사

(A) disappointed 실망한, 낙담한　　(B) disappointing 실망스러운

번역　그 영업 직원은 고객들의 부정적인 의견에 실망하고 있다.

3

New construction, / including additions / to (existing) buildings, / requires / the acquisition of a
새로운 건축은　　　　　증축을 포함하여　　　기존 건물에 대한　　　　　필요하다　　허가 취득이

permit.
　　　　　　　　　　　　　　　　　　→ 기존의, 현재 사용되는

(A) existed　　　　　　　　　　　(B) existing

번역　기존 건물의 증축을 포함하여 새로운 건축을 하려면 허가 취득이 필요하다.

4

La Cantina Han / offers / the most (surprising) dining experience / in the city.
라 칸티나 한은　　　선사한다　 가장 놀라운 식사 경험을　　　　　　　그 도시에서
　　　　　　　　　　　　　　　　　　　　→ 감정을 일으키는 사물 명사와 결합하는 현재분사

(A) surprised 놀란　　　　　　　(B) surprising 놀라운

번역　라 칸티나 한은 그 도시에서 가장 놀라운 식사 경험을 선사한다.

5

Some students / have complained / that Physics 301 is too (demanding) / for them.
몇몇 학생들은　　　불평했다　　　301 물리학이 너무 힘들다고　　　　　자신들에게
　　　　　　　　　　　　　　　　　　　　　　　→ 힘든, 부담이 큰

(A) demanded　　　　　　　　　(B) demanding

번역　몇몇 학생들은 301 물리학이 자신들에게 너무 힘들다고 불평했다.

6

If you are (interested) / in attending tomorrow's workshop, / please let your supervisor know.
관심이 있다면　　　　　　내일 열리는 워크숍에 참석하는 데　　　　상사에게 알려주세요
　　　　　　　　　　　　　　　　　　　　　　　→ 감정을 느끼는 사람 명사와 결합하는 과거분사
(A) interesting 재미있는, 흥미로운　　(B) interested 관심 있어 하는

번역　내일 열리는 워크숍에 참석하는 데 관심 있는 사람은 상사에게 알려주세요.

7 (D)	**8** (D)	**9** (D)	**10** (C)

7

Fan Musica / is one of the (leading) international journals / on classical music.
〈팬 무지카〉는   가장 앞서가는 세계적인 잡지 중 하나이다   고전 음악에 대한
→ 형용사 역할을 하는 분사

(A) led   (B) leads
(C) leader   (D) leading

해설 **형용사 역할을 하는 분사:** 빈칸 뒤 명사구 international journals를 수식하는 형용사 자리입니다. 따라서 '앞서가는, 선두의, 주요한'이라는 의미의 형용사로 사용되는 현재분사 (D) leading이 정답입니다.

번역 〈팬 무지카〉는 가장 앞서가는 세계적인 고전 음악 잡지 중 하나이다.

8

Inoue and Hisakawa Ltd. / is seeking / (qualified) applicants / for a legal assistant position.
이노우 앤드 히사카와 주식회사는   찾고 있다   자격을 갖춘 지원자를   법률 비서 자리에
→ 형용사 역할을 하는 분사

(A) qualify   (B) qualification
(C) qualifies   (D) qualified

해설 **형용사 역할을 하는 분사:** 빈칸은 명사 applicants를 앞에서 수식하는 형용사 자리입니다. 따라서 형용사 역할을 하는 분사 (D) qualified가 정답입니다.

번역 이노우 앤드 히사카와 주식회사는 법률 비서 자리에 자격을 갖춘 지원자를 찾고 있다.

9

The city's rigid building codes / have become too (frustrating) / for Mr. Cooper / to accommodate.
시의 엄격한 건축 규정은   너무 실망스러워졌다   쿠퍼 씨가   수용하기에는
→ 감정을 일으키는 사물 명사와 결합하는 현재분사

(A) frustrated 좌절감을 느끼는   (B) frustration 좌절감, 불만
(C) frustrate 좌절감을 주다   (D) frustrating 불만스러운, 좌절감을 주는

해설 **감정을 나타내는 분사:** 주어인 The city's rigid building codes가 실망감을 주는 주체이므로 능동의 의미를 갖는 현재분사 (D) frustrating이 정답입니다. 수동의 의미를 갖는 (A) frustrated(실망을 느끼는)는 주어가 사람일 때 사용합니다.

번역 시의 엄격한 건축 규정은 쿠퍼 씨가 수용할 수 없을 정도로 너무 실망스러워졌다.

10

Many consumers / think / that the instructions for assembling furniture are overly (complicated).
많은 소비자들은   생각한다   가구 조립을 위한 설명서가 너무 복잡하다고
형용사 역할을 하는 분사 ←

(A) complicates   (B) complicate
(C) complicated   (D) complication

해설 **형용사 역할을 하는 분사:** 빈칸은 주어 instructions를 보충 설명하는 주격 보어 자리로, 문맥상 '설명서가 복잡하다'라는 의미가 자연스럽습니다. 따라서 형용사 역할을 하는 과거분사 (C) complicated가 정답입니다. (D) complication(문제, 합병증)은 주어 instructions와 동격 관계를 이루지 않으므로 빈칸에 들어갈 수 없습니다.

번역 많은 소비자들은 가구 조립 설명서가 너무 복잡하다고 생각한다.

1 (B)	2 (A)	3 (B)	4 (A)	5 (A)	6 (B)

1

(Conducting a survey) / last month, / the polling firm / visited / every resident / in town.
설문 조사를 실시하면서   지난달   여론 조사 업체는   방문했다   모든 주민을   시의
→ = As the polling firm was conducting a survey (동시 상황)

(A) Conducted   (B) Conducting

[번역] 지난달 설문 조사를 실시하면서, 여론 조사 업체는 시의 모든 주민을 방문했다.

2

(Written / in plain language), / the magazine / is easy / to read.
쓰여 있어서 쉬운 말로   그 잡지는   편하다 읽기에
→ = Because the magazine is written in plain language (이유)

(A) Written   (B) Writing

[번역] 그 잡지는 쉬운 말로 쓰여 있어서 읽기 편하다.

3

(Constructed / three decades ago), / the exhibition hall / needs / to be renovated.
건설되어서   30년 전에   그 전시회장은   필요가 있다 / 보수할
→ = Because the exhibition hall was constructed three decades ago (이유)

(A) Constructing   (B) Constructed

[번역] 그 전시회장은 30년 전에 건설되어서 보수할 필요가 있다.

4

(Reviewing the draft of the contract), / Mr. Kelvin / found / some errors / in it.
계약서 초안을 살펴보다가   켈빈 씨는   발견했다 몇 군데 오류를   그 안에서
→ = When Mr. Kelvin reviewed the draft of the contract (시간)

(A) Reviewing   (B) Reviewed

[번역] 켈빈 씨는 계약서 초안을 살펴보다가 몇 군데 오류를 발견했다.

5

(When negotiating / your salary), / it is important / to consider regional pay scales.
협상 시   급여를   중요하다   지역별 급여 체계를 고려하는 것이
→ = When you negotiate your salary (시간)

(A) negotiating   (B) negotiation

[번역] 급여 협상 시 지역별 급여 체계를 고려하는 것이 중요하다.

6

Stormy weather / led to / power outages / last night, / (leaving some residents without electricity.)
폭풍우 치는 날씨는 일으켰다 정전을   어젯밤   그래서 일부 주민들을 전기 없는 상태가 되게 했다
= and stormy weather left some residents without electricity (연속 상황) ←

(A) leaves   (B) leaving

[번역] 폭풍우 치는 날씨는 어젯밤 정전을 일으켰고, 일부 주민들을 전기 없이 지내게 만들었다.

7 (B)	8 (A)	9 (A)	10 (C)

7

Located / in proximity to the airport, / the Tominski Hotel / is an ideal choice / for business
위치해 있어서　공항 근처에　　　　　　　토민스키 호텔은　　　　이상적인 선택이다　　비즈니스 여행객들에게

travelers.　　　　　→ = Because the Tominski Hotel is located in proximity ~ (이유)

(A) Locating　　　　　　　　　　　(B) Located

(C) Locates　　　　　　　　　　　(D) Locate

해설 분사구문: 콤마 뒤에 완전한 구조의 절이 왔으므로 콤마 앞부분은 수식어구 역할을 한다는 것을 알 수 있습니다. 문장의 주어인 the Tominski Hotel과 빈칸에 들어갈 분사와의 의미상 관계를 따져볼 때 토민스키 호텔이 공항 근처에 '위치된' 상태이므로, 과거분사 (B) Located가 정답입니다.

번역 공항 근처에 위치해 있어서, 토민스키 호텔은 비즈니스 여행객들에게 이상적인 선택이다.

8

The stock market / rose again / yesterday, / continuing / a weeklong trend.
주식 시장이　　　　다시 상승했다　어제　　　그래서 지속했다　한 주간의 추세를
　　　　　　　　　= and the stock market continued a weeklong trend (연속 상황) ←

(A) continuing　　　　　　　　　　(B) continual

(C) continues　　　　　　　　　　(D) continually

해설 분사구문: 콤마 앞에 완전한 구조의 절이 왔으므로 콤마 뒷부분은 수식어구 역할을 한다는 것을 알 수 있으며, '한 주간의 추세를 지속하다'라는 의미가 자연스럽습니다. 따라서 명사구 a weeklong trend를 목적어로 취하면서 분사구문을 이끄는 (A) continuing이 정답입니다.

번역 주식 시장이 어제 다시 상승하면서, 한 주간의 추세를 지속했다.

9

The company / earned / 150 million euros, / allowing it to fund / its planned expansion.
그 회사는　　　벌어들였다　1억 5천만 유로를　그래서 회사가 자금을 조달하는 것을 가능하게 했다 / 예정된 확장에

(A) allowing　　　　　　　　　　(B) allows　　　= and this(앞 절 전체) allowed it to fund ~ (결과) ←

(C) allowance　　　　　　　　　　(D) allowably

해설 분사구문: 콤마 앞에 완전한 구조의 절이 왔으므로 콤마 뒷부분은 수식어구 역할을 한다는 것을 알 수 있으며, '예정된 확장 사업에 자금을 조달할 수 있게 하다'라는 의미가 자연스럽습니다. 따라서 빈칸은 it을 목적어로 취하면서 분사구문을 이끄는 (A) allowing이 정답입니다.

번역 그 회사는 1억 5천만 유로를 벌어들여, 예정된 확장에 자금을 조달할 수 있게 되었다.

10

As noted / in the agreement, / the maintenance staff / will respond / to all service requests /
언급된 바와 같이 / 계약서에　　　　　유지 보수 직원은　　　　　응답할 것이다　모든 서비스 요청에
　　　　　　　　→ 접속사 + 분사

within 48 hours.
48시간 이내에

(A) notes　　　　　　　　　　　(B) note

(C) noted　　　　　　　　　　　(D) noting

해설 접속사 + 분사구문: 문맥상 '계약서에 명시된 대로'라는 의미가 자연스러우므로 '명시된, 언급된'이라는 수동 형태인 (C) noted가 정답입니다. 접속사 as뒤에 it is가 생략된 형태입니다.

번역 계약서에 언급된 바와 같이 유지 보수 직원은 48시간 이내에 모든 서비스 요청에 응답할 것이다.

| 1 (A) | 2 (B) | 3 (A) | 4 (B) |

1

The agency / can help / young businesses / identify / (potential) customers.
그 대행사는　　도움을 줄 수 있다 / 신생 업체들이　　찾아내는 데　잠재 고객들을
→ 잠재적인, 가능성 있는

(A) potential 잠재적인　　　　(B) improved 향상된, 개선된

번역 그 대행사는 신생 업체들이 잠재 고객들을 찾아내는 데 도움을 줄 수 있다.

2

If you experience a problem / with this product, / take / it / to any (authorized) service center.
만약 문제를 겪는다면　　　　　이 제품에　　　　　가져가세요 / 그것을 / 어느 공인된 서비스 센터에든

(A) sufficient 충분한　　　　(B) authorized 공인된
→ 공인된

번역 이 제품에 문제가 생기면, 그것을 어느 공인 서비스 센터에든 가져가세요.

3

Good Health Hospital / has offered / (comprehensive) services of health care.
굿 헬스 병원은　　　　제공해 왔다　　종합적인 건강 관리 서비스를
→ 종합적인, 광범위한

(A) comprehensive 종합적인, 광범위한　　(B) unaccustomed 익숙하지 않은

번역 굿 헬스 병원은 종합적인 건강 관리 서비스를 제공해 왔다.

4

Since many people want / to attend the show, / extra buses / will be made (available) / to the
많은 사람들이 원하기 때문에　　그 쇼에 참석하기를　　추가 버스편이　　이용 가능하게 될 것이다　　대중에게

public.
→ 이용 가능한

(A) frequent 자주, 빈번한　　　　(B) available 이용 가능한

번역 많은 사람들이 그 쇼에 참석하고 싶어 하기 때문에, 대중이 추가 버스편을 이용할 수 있도록 할 것이다.

| 5 (A) | 6 (A) | 7 (B) | 8 (A) |

5 Documents of a (confidential) nature / should be stored / in locked file cabinets / at all times.
기밀 성격의 서류들은 → 기밀의 보관되어야 한다 자물쇠로 잠긴 서류 캐비닛에 항상

(A) confidential 기밀의 　　　　　(B) limited 제한적인
(C) former 예전의 　　　　　(D) mandatory 의무적인

해설 confidential 기밀의: 빈칸 뒤 명사 nature(성질)를 수식하는 형용사 자리로, 빈칸을 포함한 전치사구 〈of a 빈칸 nature〉가 명사 Documents를 수식합니다. 문맥상 보관을 철저히 해야 하는 것은 기밀 성격의 서류로 볼 수 있으므로, '기밀의'라는 의미의 형용사 (A) confidential이 정답입니다.

번역 기밀 성격의 서류들은 항상 자물쇠로 잠긴 서류 캐비닛에 보관되어야 한다.

6 Ongoing training / can be the (key) element / in maintaining / a productive workforce.
지속적인 훈련이 핵심 요소일 수 있다 → 핵심인 유지하는 데 있어서 생산성 높은 노동력을

(A) key 핵심적인 　　　　　(B) handy 유용한
(C) marginal 미미한 　　　　　(D) complete 완전한

해설 key 핵심적인: 빈칸은 '요소'라는 의미의 명사 element를 수식하는 형용사 자리로, 〈빈칸 + element〉는 주어 Ongoing training과 동격 관계를 이룹니다. 문맥상 '지속적인 훈련이 핵심 요소이다'라는 의미가 자연스러우므로, '핵심적인'이라는 의미의 형용사 (A) key가 정답입니다.

번역 지속적인 훈련이 생산성 높은 노동력을 유지하는 데 있어서 핵심 요소일 수 있다.

7 Our latest product brochure / had to be reprinted / to correct / several (minor) errors.
우리 최신 제품 안내 책자는 재인쇄를 해야 했다 바로잡기 위해 몇몇 사소한 오류를 → 사소한

(A) overdue 기한이 지난 　　　　　(B) minor 사소한
(C) reliable 믿을 만한 　　　　　(D) rapid 급속한

해설 minor 사소한: 빈칸 뒤 명사 errors와 가장 잘 어울리는 형용사를 선택해야 합니다. 문맥상 '사소한 실수'라는 의미가 자연스러우므로, (B) minor가 정답입니다.

번역 우리 최신 제품 안내 책자는 몇몇 사소한 오류를 바로잡기 위해 재인쇄를 해야 했다

8 Jefferies Electronics / has enjoyed / (steady) sales / since the start of this fiscal year.
제프리스 전자는 즐기고 있다 꾸준한 매출을 → 꾸준한 이번 회계 연도 시작 이래로

(A) steady 꾸준한 　　　　　(B) detailed 상세한
(C) renewable 재생 가능한 　　　　　(D) complete 완전한

해설 steady 꾸준한: 빈칸 뒤 명사 sales를 수식하는 형용사 자리로, 문맥상 '꾸준한 매출을 올리고 있다'라는 의미가 자연스러우므로, (A) steady가 정답입니다.

번역 제프리스 전자는 올 회계 연도 시작 이래로 꾸준한 매출을 올리고 있다.

1 (C)	**2** (C)	**3** (C)	**4** (C)	**5** (D)

1

Since storage space is (limited), / all employees / are asked / to discard unwanted items.
저장 공간이 제한되어 있기 때문에 　　　모든 직원들은 　　　요청을 받는다 　　　필요 없는 물품을 버리라는
→ 형용사 역할을 하는 분사

(A) limit 제한; 제한하다　 (B) limitingly 제한적으로　 (C) limited 제한된　 (D) limitations 제약

> 해설 **형용사 역할을 하는 분사:** 빈칸은 주어 storage space를 보충 설명하는 주격 보어 자리로, 문맥상 '저장 공간이 제한되어 있다'라는 의미가 자연스럽습니다. 따라서 형용사 역할을 하는 과거분사 (C) limited가 정답입니다. 명사 (A) limit(한계, 한도)와 (D) limitations(제약)는 주어 storage space와 동격 관계를 이루지 않으므로 빈칸에 들어갈 수 없습니다.

> 번역 저장 공간이 제한되어 있기 때문에, 모든 직원들은 필요 없는 물품을 버리라는 요청을 받는다.

2

(Revised) employment contracts / will be distributed / at the end of the month.
개정된 고용 계약서는 　　　배포될 예정입니다 　　　월말에
→ 수동적 의미의 과거분사

(A) Revising　 (B) Revision　 (C) Revised　 (D) Revise

> 해설 **현재분사와 과거분사 구별:** 빈칸은 명사구인 employment contracts(고용 계약서) 앞에서 명사를 수식하는 형용사 자리이므로 형용사 역할을 할 수 있는 현재분사 (A) Revising, 과거분사 (C) Revised가 정답 후보입니다. employment contracts(고용 계약서)는 사람에 의해 '개정되는' 대상이므로 수동의 의미를 나타내는 과거분사 (C) Revised가 정답입니다.

> 번역 개정된 고용 계약서는 월말에 배포될 예정입니다.

3

Frontier University / is seeking / (interested) individuals / to participate / in a survey.
프론티어 대학교는 　　찾고 있다 　　관심 있는 사람들을 　　참여하는 데 　　설문 조사에
→ 감정을 느끼는 사람 명사와 결합하는 과거분사

(A) interest　 (B) interests　 (C) interested　 (D) interestingly

> 해설 **감정을 느끼는 사람 명사와 결합하는 과거분사:** 감정을 나타내는 동사의 분사의 경우, 수식하는 명사(주로 사물)가 감정을 일으킬 때는 현재분사를, 수식하는 명사(주로 사람)가 감정을 느낄 때는 과거분사를 씁니다. 여기서는 빈칸 뒤에 individuals(사람)가 왔으므로 과거분사인 (C) interested가 정답입니다.

> 번역 프론티어 대학교는 설문 조사에 참여하고 싶은 사람들을 찾고 있다.

4

Working so many hours of overtime / to meet the deadline / has left / the design staff / feeling
너무 많은 시간을 초과근무하는 것이 　　　마감기한을 맞추기 위해 　　　~ 되게 했다 　　디자인 팀 직원들을 　　지치게
(exhausted). → 감정을 느끼는 사람 명사와 결합하는 과거분사

(A) exhaust 기진맥진하게 만들다　 (B) exhausting 진을 빼는　 (C) exhausted 기진맥진한　 (D) exhaustive 철저한

> 해설 **현재분사와 과거분사 구별:** 감정을 나타내는 현재분사는 주로 사물 명사와 어울리며, 과거분사는 주로 사람 명사와 어울립니다. feeling은 사람 명사인 the design staff의 목적격 보어이므로 과거분사인 (C) exhausted가 정답입니다.

> 번역 마감기한을 맞추기 위해 초과근무를 너무 많이 하는 바람에 디자인 팀 직원들은 지친 상태가 되게 했다.

5

Any person (involved) / in a legal case / is advised / to consult a lawyer.
연루된 사람은 누구나 　　소송에 　　권유받는다 　　변호사와 상담하라고
→ 수동적 의미의 과거분사

(A) involving　 (B) involves　 (C) involve　 (D) involved

> 해설 **현재분사와 과거분사 구별:** 빈칸은 명사구 Any person을 뒤에서 수식하는 형용사 자리로, 빈칸 뒤 전치사구 in a legal case의 수식을 받습니다. 문맥상 '소송에 연루된 사람은 누구나'라는 수동의 의미가 자연스러우므로, 과거분사 (D) involved가 정답입니다.

> 번역 소송에 연루된 사람은 누구나 변호사와 상담하라고 권유받는다.

| 6 (B) | 7 (A) | 8 (A) | 9 (B) | 10 (A) |

6

A trip to Robin Island / will leave / visitors / quite (excited) / about its beauty.
로빈 아일랜드 여행은　　　　　～ 상태가 되게 할 것이다 / 방문객들을 / 무척 흥분하게　그곳의 아름다움에
　　　　　　　　　　　　　　　　　　　　　　　　　　　　　　→ 감정을 느끼는 사람 명사와 결합하는 과거분사

(A) exciting 신나는　(B) excited 흥분한　(C) excite 흥분시키다　(D) excitement 흥분, 신남

해설 현재분사와 과거분사 구별: 빈칸은 동사 will leave의 목적어 visitors를 보충 설명하는 목적격 보어 자리이므로, 형용사 역할을 하는 현재분사 (A) exciting과 과거분사 (B) excited가 빈칸에 들어갈 수 있습니다. 사람 명사 visitors는 감정을 느끼는 수동적 입장이므로 과거분사 (B) excited가 정답입니다. 명사 (D) excitement는 visitors와 동격이 될 수 없으므로, 목적격 보어 자리에 올 수 없습니다.

번역 로빈 아일랜드 여행은 방문객들이 그곳의 아름다움에 무척 흥분하게 만들 것이다.

7

Chin Industrial Supply / is a (leading) distributor / of auto parts / internationally.
친 인더스트리얼 서플라이는　　　손꼽히는 판매 회사이다　　　자동차 부품의　　　세계적으로
　　　　　　　　　　　　　　　　→ 형용사 역할을 하는 분사

(A) leading 선도적인　(B) leader 지도자, 대표　(C) leads 이끌다, 안내하다　(D) leadership 지도력, 통솔력

해설 동사(lead)에 -ing를 붙여 만든 형용사: 빈칸 앞 부정관사 a와 빈칸 뒤 명사 distributor 사이에서 명사를 수식하는 형용사 자리이므로 (A) leading(손꼽히는, 선도적인)이 정답입니다.

번역 친 인더스트리얼 서플라이는 세계적으로 손꼽히는 자동차 부품 판매 회사이다.

8

(When removing) the lamp / from the carton, / slide it out / by the base / and avoid pulling / on the
램프를 꺼낼 때　　　　　　　　상자에서　　　밀어서 빼세요　밑면을　　　　그리고 잡아당기지 마십시오　전기 코드를
　　　　　　　　→ 접속사 + 분사

electric cord. → 접속사 + 분사

(A) removing　(B) removes　(C) removed　(D) remove

해설 분사구문: 콤마 뒤에 완전한 구조의 절이 왔으므로 콤마 앞부분은 수식어구 역할을 한다는 것을 알 수 있습니다. 문장의 생략된 주어인 you가 '램프를 꺼내는' 주체이므로 능동의 의미인 현재분사 (A) removing이 정답입니다. 시간, 이유, 조건을 나타내는 분사구문에서 접속사가 생략되지 않기도 합니다.

번역 상자에서 램프를 꺼낼 때, 밑면을 밀어서 빼내고 전기 코드를 잡아당기지 마십시오.

9

Submit / the deposit / within the (allotted) time frame / to avoid / losing the reservation.
내주십시오 /　보증금을　　배정된 시간 내에　　　　　　막기 위해　　예약을 놓치는 것을
　　　　　　　　　　　　　　　→ 수동적 의미의 과거분사

(A) allot　(B) allotted　(C) allotting　(D) allotments

해설 현재분사와 과거분사 구별: 빈칸은 명사구 time frame을 앞에서 수식하는 형용사[분사] 자리로, time frame은 배정되는 대상이므로 과거분사 (B) allotted(배정된)가 정답입니다.

번역 예약을 놓치지 않기 위해 배정된 시간 내에 보증금을 내주십시오.

10

(Opened just six months ago), / Fin's Grill / has become / one of the most popular restaurants / in
불과 6개월 전에 개업한　　　　　　　핀즈 그릴은　　되었다　　　　가장 인기 있는 레스토랑 중 하나가
　　　　　　　　→ 분사구문

Delton.
델턴에서

(A) Opened　(B) To open　(C) Been opened　(D) Had been opening

해설 분사구문: 콤마 뒤에 완전한 구조의 절이 왔으므로 콤마 앞 부분은 수식어구 역할을 한다는 것을 알 수 있습니다. 분사구문의 Being opened에서 Being이 생략된 형태인 과거분사 (A) Opened가 정답이며 (B) To open은 '개업하기 위해'라는 의미로, 문맥상 적절하지 않습니다.

번역 불과 6개월 전에 개업했지만 핀즈 그릴은 델턴에서 가장 인기 있는 레스토랑 중 하나가 되었다.

11 (A)	**12** (B)	**13** (C)	**14** (D)

Questions 11-14 refer to the following article.

11-14 기사

Packaging and Transferring Flammable Liquids
인화성 액체 포장 및 운송

인화성 액체 포장 및 운송

All vehicles and containers / that transport flammable liquids / must be
모든 차량과 컨테이너는   인화성 액체를 운송하는   명확하게

인화성 액체를 운송하는 모든 차량과 컨테이너는 명확하게 식별되어야 합니다. 라벨의 구체적인 요건은 이 문서의 6페이지에서 확인할 수 있습니다.

clearly identified. Specific requirements for the 11. labels / can be found /
식별되어야 합니다   라벨의 구체적인 요건은   확인될 수 있습니다

on page 6 of this document.
이 문서의 6페이지에서

As a general rule, / red diamond-shaped stickers with white text / should
일반적으로   적색의 다이아몬드 모양 스티커에 백색 글자가   사용되어야

일반적으로 적색의 다이아몬드 모양 스티커에 백색 글자를 사용해야 합니다. 세부 사항은 지역에 따라 다를 수 있다는 점 유의하십시오. 본인 지역의 정확한 요건을 확실히 알지 못한다면, 항상 국가 교통국에 직접 연락하십시오.

be used. Please note / that details may vary / from region to region. If you
합니다   유의하십시오   세부 사항은 다를 수 있다는 것을   지역에 따라   확실히

are 12. unsure / of the exact requirements / for your area, / always contact /
알지 못한다면   정확한 요건을   본인 지역의   항상 연락하십시오

the National Transportation Bureau / directly.
국가 교통국에   직접

While the sender must supply the correct stickers / for each container /
발송자는 맞는 스티커를 제공해야 하지만   각 컨테이너에

발송자는 운송되는 각 컨테이너에 맞는 스티커를 제공해야 하지만, 스티커를 적절하게 컨테이너에 부착하는 것을 확실히 하는 것은 수송회사의 책임입니다. 인화성 액체를 운반하는 차량에는 다른 운전자가 쉽게 볼 수 있는 플래카드도 부착해야 합니다. 어떤 경우에도 예외는 있을 수 없습니다.

→ 형용사 역할을 하는 분사

13. (being transported), / it is the carrier's responsibility / to make sure /
운송되는   수송회사의 책임입니다   확실하게 하는 것은

they are properly affixed to the containers. Vehicles / carrying flammable
스티커가 적절하게 컨테이너에 부착되는 것을   차량은   인화성 액체를 운반하는

liquids / must also display a placard / that is readily visible to other drivers.
플래카드도 부착해야 합니다   다른 운전자가 쉽게 볼 수 있는

No exceptions / are to be made / under any circumstances.
예외는   없습니다   어떤 경우에도

11 (A) labels
    (B) studies
    (C) catalogs
    (D) transactions

(A) 라벨
(B) 연구
(C) 상품 목록
(D) 거래

해설 어휘 문제: 앞 문장에서 '명확하게 식별되어야 한다(must be clearly identified)'라는 표현이 나옵니다. 따라서 식별용 표시인 '라벨'에 관한 내용이 이어지는 것이 자연스러우므로 정답은 (A) labels입니다.

12 (A) unheard
    (B) unsure
    (C) independent
    (D) incapable

(A) 들어보지 않은
(B) 확신하지 못하는
(C) 독립된
(D) 할 수 없는

해설 어휘 문제: 빈칸 뒤 주절에 '교통국에 연락하라(contact the National Transportation Bureau)'는 내용이 나옵니다. 따라서 빈칸이 있는 if절(종속절)과 주절이 자연스럽게 연결되려면 '확실히 알지 못하면 교통국에 연락하라'는 내용이 되어야 하므로 정답은 (B) unsure입니다.

13 (A) transports
    (B) transporting
    (C) being transported
    (D) having been transported

해설 형용사 역할을 하는 분사: 빈칸이 들어 있는 문장에 동사 must supply가 있으므로 (A) transports는 정답에서 제외됩니다. 빈칸은 앞에 있는 container를 수식하는 어구이므로 each container 뒤에 관계대명사가 생략되어 있음을 알 수 있습니다. 주격 관계대명사와 be동사는 함께 생략할 수 있으므로 빈칸 앞에 that is가 생략된 형태인 (C) being transported가 정답입니다. 컨테이너는 운송되는 대상으로 수동태가 되어야 하므로 (B) transporting은 정답이 될 수 없습니다.

14 (A) There are several possibilities for parking.
    (B) It has been placed there for your convenience.
    (C) This is an option when the loading area is occupied.
    (D) No exceptions are to be made under any circumstances.

(A) 주차에는 몇 가지 가능한 사항이 있습니다.
(B) 그것은 여러분의 편의를 위해 그곳에 배치되었습니다.
(C) 이는 적재 구역에 화물이 있을 때의 방안입니다.
(D) 어떤 경우에도 예외는 있을 수 없습니다.

해설 문장 고르기: 빈칸 앞 문장들에서 인화성 액체를 취급하는 발송자와 운송 회사의 책임을 언급하고 있습니다. 따라서 빈칸에는 규정에 예외가 없다고 언급하는 것이 내용 전개 면에서 자연스러우므로 정답은 (D)입니다.

시간을 나타내는 전치사 ETS 문제로 훈련하기 STEP 1

교재 p.141

1 (B)	**2** (B)	**3** (B)	**4** (A)	**5** (A)	**6** (A)

1

Judith Cooke / has been working / in the sales department / since 1999 .
주디스 쿡은　　　　　근무해 왔다　　　　　영업부에서　　　　　　　　1999년부터
→ since + 과거 시점: ~부터

(A) on　　　　　　　　　　　　　(B) since

번역　주디스 쿡은 1999년부터 영업부에서 근무해 왔다.

2

Updates to the database / are scheduled / to begin / after 5:00 P.M.
데이터베이스 업데이트는　　　　예정이다　　　시작될　　오후 5시 이후에
→ after + 시각: ~ 이후에

(A) against　　　　　　　　　　(B) after

번역　데이터베이스 업데이트는 오후 5시 이후에 시작될 예정이다.

3

Lecro Industries' customers / may request / refunds / within thirty days of purchase .
레크로 인더스트리스의 고객은　요청할 수 있다　환불을　구매 후 30일 이내에

(A) by　　　　　　　　　　　　(B) within
within + 기간: ~ 이내에

번역　레크로 인더스트리즈의 고객은 구매 후 30일 이내에 환불을 요청할 수 있다.

4

The security badge / needs to be activated / before tomorrow.
보안 신분증은　　　　　활성화되어야 한다　　　　내일 전까지
→ ~ 전에 (시점)

(A) before　　　　　　　　　　(B) on

번역　보안 신분증은 내일 전까지 활성화되어야 한다.

5

All branches / will be closing / at 4 P.M. / on Friday / because of the holiday.
모든 지점들이　　문을 닫을 것이다　오후 4시에　금요일에는　　공휴일 때문에
→ on + 요일: ~에

(A) on　　　　　　　　　　　　(B) at

번역　공휴일 때문에 금요일에는 오후 4시에 모든 지점들이 문을 닫을 것이다.

6

At the Highbridge Tech Symposium, / refreshments / are served / throughout the day / in the
하이브리지 테크 학술회에서는　　　　　　　다과가　　　제공된다　　하루 종일　　　　　　로비에서
→ ~ 동안 쭉, 내내

lobby.

(A) throughout　　　　　　　　(B) within

번역　하이브리지 테크 학술회에서는 로비에서 하루 종일 다과가 제공된다.

| 7 (A) | 8 (A) | 9 (B) | 10 (D) |

7

Williamstown Borough Bikes / is open / on weekdays / from 10 A.M. to 5 P.M.
윌리엄스타운 버러 바이크스는   문을 연다   평일에   오전 10시부터 오후 5시까지

(A) from   (B) since   from A to B: A부터 B까지 ←
(C) by   (D) until

해설 알맞은 시간 전치사 선택: 빈칸 뒤에 10 A.M. to 5 P.M.이라는 시간 표현이 있습니다. 문맥상 '오전 10시부터 오후 5시까지'라는 의미가 자연스러우므로, '~부터'라는 뜻의 전치사 (A) from이 정답입니다.

번역 윌리엄스타운 버러 바이크스는 평일 오전 10시부터 오후 5시까지 문을 연다.

8

The construction / on Highway 12 / is expected / to continue / until next month.
공사는   12번 고속도로의   예상된다   계속될 것으로   다음 달까지

(A) until   (B) across   ↳ ~까지
(C) down   (D) onto

해설 알맞은 시간 전치사 선택: 빈칸 뒤 시간 표현 next month를 목적어로 취하면서, 앞의 to부정사의 동사원형 continue를 수식하는 전치사 자리입니다. 문맥상 '다음 달까지 계속되다'라는 의미가 자연스러우므로, '~까지'라는 뜻의 (A) until이 정답입니다.

번역 12번 고속도로 공사는 다음 달까지 계속될 것으로 예상된다.

9

Mr. Desai / has been president of Southern Horizons Bank / for over ten years.
데사이 씨는   서던 호라이즌스 은행의 은행장이다   10년이 넘는 기간 동안

(A) in   (B) for   ↳ ~ 동안
(C) up   (D) from

해설 알맞은 시간 전치사 선택: 빈칸 뒤에 over ten years(10년 이상)이라는 기간 표현이 있습니다. 문맥상 '10년 이상 동안'이라는 의미가 자연스러우므로, '~ 동안'이라는 의미의 전치사 (B) for가 정답입니다.

번역 데사이 씨는 10년이 넘게 서던 호라이즌스 은행의 은행장을 맡고 있다.

10

All departments / must submit / statistical reports / by 4:00 P.M. / on Monday.
모든 부서는   제출해야 한다   통계 보고서를   오후 4시까지   월요일

(A) beside   (B) to   ↳ ~까지
(C) between   (D) by

해설 알맞은 시간 전치사 선택: 빈칸 뒤 시간 표현 4:00 P.M.을 목적어로 취하면서, 앞의 동사 must submit을 수식하는 전치사 자리입니다. 문맥상 '오후 4시까지 제출해야 한다'라는 의미가 자연스러우므로, '~까지'라는 뜻의 전치사 (D) by가 정답입니다.

번역 모든 부서는 월요일 오후 4시까지 통계 보고서를 제출해야 한다.

1 (A)	**2** (A)	**3** (A)	**4** (B)	**5** (B)	**6** (B)

1

Randy / will be doing / a product demonstration / (at) the convention.
랜디는　　할 예정이다　　　제품 시연회를　　　　컨벤션에서
　　　　　　　　　　　　　　　　　　　　　　　　└→ ~에서 (장소)

(A) at　　　　　　　　　　　　　(B) across

번역 랜디는 컨벤션에서 제품 시연회를 할 예정이다.

2

The maintenance supplies / are kept / in Room 132, / (next to) the security desk.
유지 보수용 자재는　　　보관되어 있다　132호실에　　　보안 창구 옆에 있는
　　　　　　　　　　　　　　　　　　　　　　　　　　└→ ~ 옆에

(A) next to　　　　　　　　　　(B) among

번역 유지 보수용 자재는 보안 창구 옆에 있는 132호실에 보관되어 있다.

3

Rail service / (between Montreal and New York) / was suspended / due to heavy snowfall.
철도 서비스가　　몬트리올과 뉴욕 간　　　　　　중단되었다　　　폭설로 인해
　　　　　　　　　　　　　　　　　└→ between A and B: A와 B 사이에

(A) between　　　　　　　　　　(B) against

번역 몬트리올과 뉴욕 간 철도 서비스가 폭설로 인해 중단되었다.

4

Dr. Kim's office / is located / (on) the tenth floor of the building.
김 박사의 사무실은　　위치해 있다　그 건물 10층에
　　　　　　　　　　　　　　　└→ ~ 위에 (표면에 접촉)

(A) of　　　　　　　　　　　　(B) on

번역 김 박사의 사무실은 그 건물 10층에 위치해 있다.

5

The new store / will be located / somewhere / (along) the south coast.
새 매장은　　　위치할 것이다　　어딘가에　　남부 해안을 따라
　　　　　　　　　　　　　　　　　　　　└→ ~을 따라

(A) among　　　　　　　　　　(B) along

번역 새 매장은 남부 해안을 따라 어딘가에 위치할 것이다.

6

The area's harbor / contains / the second-largest port / (in) Europe.
이 지역의 항만은　　　가지고 있다　두 번째로 큰 항구를　　유럽에서
　　　　　　　　　　　　　　　　　　　　　　　　　└→ ~에서 (지역·공간)

(A) under　　　　　　　　　　(B) in

번역 이 지역의 항만에는 유럽에서 두 번째로 큰 항구가 있다.

| 7 (D) | 8 (D) | 9 (D) | 10 (C) |

7

Guests / can find / additional linens and towels / (in) the closet.
손님들은　　찾을 수 있다　　추가 침대 시트와 수건을　　　옷장 안에서
　　　　　　　　　　　　　　　　　　　　　　　　　↳ ~안에

(A) with　　　　　　　　　　　　　(B) across
(C) for　　　　　　　　　　　　　　(D) in

해설　알맞은 장소 전치사 선택: 빈칸 뒤 명사구 the closet을 목적어로 취하는 전치사 자리입니다. 빈칸 앞의 명사 linens and towels는 문맥상 closet 안에 있는 물건으로 볼 수 있으므로, '~ 안에'라는 의미의 전치사 (D) in이 정답입니다.

번역　손님들은 옷장 안에서 추가 침대 시트와 수건을 찾을 수 있다.

8

The 502 bus / travels / (through) the city, / stopping / at Broad Street and the Medical Center.
502번 버스는　　지나간다　도심을│관통해　　　　(그리고) 정차한다 브로드 가와 메디컬 센터에
　　　　　　　　　　　　　　　↳ ~을 관통해, ~을 통과해

(A) between　　　　　　　　　　　(B) with
(C) next　　　　　　　　　　　　　(D) through

해설　알맞은 장소 전치사 선택: 빈칸 뒤 명사구 the city를 목적어로 취하는 전치사 자리로, 빈칸을 포함한 전치사구는 동사 travels를 수식합니다. 문맥상 '도심을 관통해 다니다'라는 의미가 자연스러우므로, '~을 관통해, ~을 통과해'라는 의미의 전치사 (D) through가 정답입니다.

번역　502번 버스는 도심을 관통해 지나가면서, 브로드 가와 메디컬 센터에 정차한다.

9

The tourism office / is / (near) the convention center, / across from the hotel district.
관광 안내소는　　있다 /│컨벤션 센터 근처에　　　　호텔 지구 건너편
　　　　　　　　　　↳ ~ 근처에

(A) throughout　　　　　　　　　(B) against
(C) next　　　　　　　　　　　　(D) near

해설　알맞은 장소 전치사 선택: 빈칸 뒤 명사구 the convention center를 목적어로 취하는 전치사 자리로, 문맥상 The tourism office와 the convention center의 위치 관계를 나타내고 있으므로, '~ 근처에'라는 의미의 전치사 (D) near가 정답입니다.

번역　관광 안내소는 호텔 지구 건너편, 컨벤션 센터 근처에 있다.

10

Ginnis Co. / plans / to hold seminars / to promote better communication / (among) its staff.
지니스사는　　계획이다 세미나를 열　　　더 나은 의사소통을 촉진하기 위해　　　직원들│사이의
　　　　　　　　　　　　　　　　　　　　　　　　　　　　　　　　↳ ~ 사이에

(A) under　　　　　　　　　　　(B) past
(C) among　　　　　　　　　　　(D) behind

해설　알맞은 의미의 전치사 선택: 빈칸 뒤 명사구 its staff를 목적어로 취하는 전치사 자리로, 문맥상 '직원들 사이의 더 나은 의사소통을 촉진하다'라는 의미가 자연스러우므로, '~ 사이에'라는 의미의 (C) among이 정답입니다.

번역　지니스사는 직원들 사이의 더 나은 의사소통을 촉진하기 위해 세미나를 열 계획이다.

1 (A)	2 (B)	3 (B)	4 (B)	5 (A)	6 (A)

1

(Unlike) Le Deux cookware, / Weir cookware / is dishwasher safe.
르 두 조리 기구와는 달리   위어 조리 기구는   식기세척기에 사용할 수 있다
└→ ~와 달리 (대조)

(A) Unlike   (B) Without

[번역] 르 두 조리 기구와는 달리, 위어 조리 기구는 식기세척기에 사용할 수 있다.

2

The conference site / in Lanesville / is easily accessible / (by) car or train.
그 회의 장소는   레인즈빌에 있는   쉽게 갈 수 있다   자동차나 기차로

(A) in   (B) by
                                    └→ ~을 타고 (교통수단)

[번역] 레인즈빌에 있는 그 회의 장소는 자동차나 기차로 쉽게 갈 수 있다.

3

At Pizza Delight, / we / want / to provide our customers / (with) the best service possible.
피자 딜라이트에서   저희는 / 원합니다 / 고객들께 제공하기를   가능한 최상의 서비스를
                    동반, 소지 / provide A with B(A에게 B를 제공하다) ←

(A) from   (B) with

[번역] 피자 딜라이트에서는 고객들께 가능한 한 최상의 서비스를 제공하고 싶습니다.

4

Ms. Nelson / was hired / to lead the company / (through) an organizational restructuring.
넬슨 씨는   고용되었다   회사를 이끌어 가도록   조직 개편을 통해

(A) above   (B) through
                                    └→ ~을 통해 (수단)

[번역] 넬슨 씨는 조직 개편을 통해 회사를 이끌어 갈 사람으로 고용되었다.

5

(Following) the speech, / there is / a question and answer session.
연설 후에   있습니다   질의응답 시간이
        └→ ~ 후에

(A) Following   (B) As

[번역] 연설 후에 질의응답 시간이 있습니다.

6

(In spite of) bad weather, / the event organizers / didn't cancel / the outdoor charity event / last
악천후에도 불구하고   행사 주최측은   취소하지 않았다   야외 자선 행사를   지난밤에

night. └→ ~에도 불구하고 (= Despite)

(A) In spite of   (B) Instead of

[번역] 악천후에도 불구하고 행사 주최측은 지난밤 야외 자선 행사를 취소하지 않았다.

| 7 (B) | 8 (A) | 9 (D) | 10 (D) |

7

Beginning on May 1, / Jasper Clothing / will operate / (as) an online-only retailer.
5월 1일부터　　　　　　　　　재스퍼 클로딩은　　　운영될 것이다　　온라인 전용 소매점으로
　　　　　　　　　　　　　　　　　　　　　　　　　　　　　　　　　　　　└─→ ~로(서)

(A) into　　　　　　　　　　　　　　　(B) as
(C) since　　　　　　　　　　　　　　 (D) during

해설 **알맞은 의미의 전치사 선택**: 빈칸 뒤 명사구 an online-only retailer를 목적어로 취하는 전치사 자리입니다. 빈칸을 포함한 전치사구가 주어인 Jasper Clothing의 업종을 나타내고 있으므로, '~로(서)'라는 의미의 전치사 (B) as가 정답입니다. 전치사 (C) since 뒤에는 과거 시점 명사가, 전치사 (D) during 뒤에는 기간 명사가 나와야 합니다.

번역 5월 1일부터 재스퍼 클로딩은 온라인 전용 소매점으로 운영될 것이다.

8

KSD's Web site / conveniently lists / the prices of goods and details / (about) shipping options.
KSD의 웹사이트는　　　보기 쉽게 나열한다　　　상품 가격과 세부 사항을　　　　배송 옵션에 대한
　　　　　　　　　　　　　　　　　　　　　　　　　　　　　　　　　　　└─→ ~에 대한

(A) about　　　　　　　　　　　　　　(B) along
(C) until　　　　　　　　　　　　　　 (D) into

해설 **알맞은 의미의 전치사 선택**: 빈칸은 뒤 명사구 shipping options를 목적어로 취하는 전치사 자리입니다. 문맥상 '배송 옵션에 대한 세부 사항'이라는 의미가 자연스러우므로, '~에 대한'이라는 의미의 (A) about이 정답입니다.

번역 KSD의 웹사이트는 상품 가격과 배송 옵션에 대한 세부 사항을 보기 쉽게 나열한다.

9

(Following) the completion / of 30 days of employment, / employees / are entitled / to paid vacation.
완료한 후에　　　　　　　　　　30일 근무를　　　　　직원은　　　자격이 주어진다　유급 휴가를 받을
　　└─→ ~ 후에

(A) Follow　　　　　　　　　　　　　(B) Follows
(C) Followed　　　　　　　　　　　　(D) Following

해설 **전치사 + 명사구**: 빈칸 뒤 명사구 the completion을 목적어로 취하는 전치사 자리이므로 전치사 (D) Following(~ 후에)이 정답입니다.

번역 30일 근무를 완료한 후에 직원은 유급 휴가를 받을 자격이 주어진다.

10

You / may not reproduce / the photographic material / (without) the written permission / of the
당신은　　복제할 수 없다　　　　사진 자료를　　　　　　서면 허가 없이는　　　　　　　저작권 소유자의

copyright owner.
　　　　　　　　　　　　　　　　　└─→ ~ 없이

(A) into　　　　　　　　　　　　　　(B) until
(C) among　　　　　　　　　　　　　(D) without

해설 **알맞은 의미의 전치사 선택**: 빈칸 뒤 명사구 the written permission을 목적어로 취하는 전치사 자리입니다. 문맥상 '저작권 소유자의 서면 허가 없이'라는 뜻이 되어야 하므로 (D) without(~ 없이)이 정답입니다.

번역 저작권 소유자의 서면 허가 없이는 사진 자료를 복제할 수 없다.

1 (A)	2 (A)	3 (A)	4 (B)

1

In the event of rain, / the outdoor concert / will be rescheduled.
우천 시   야외 콘서트는   일정이 변경될 것이다
      → ~할 경우에는

(A) of   (B) with

번역 우천 시 야외 콘서트 일정이 변경될 것이다.

2

Additional details / pertaining to the workshop / will be sent / to all team members.
추가 세부 사항은   워크숍과 관련된   전송될 것이다   모든 팀원에게
                                        → ~에 관계된[속하는]

(A) pertaining to ~에 관계된[속하는]   (B) in spite of ~에도 불구하고

번역 워크숍과 관련된 추가 세부 사항은 모든 팀원에게 전송될 것이다.

3

The magazine / selected / Appler / as the best agency / in terms of customer loyalty.
그 잡지는   선정했다   애플러를   최고의 대행사로   고객 충성도 면에서

(A) in   (B) without   → ~ 면에서, ~에 관해서는

번역 그 잡지는 고객 충성도 면에서 애플러를 최고의 대행사로 선정했다.

4

Article submissions / must be submitted / one week prior to publication.
투고 기사는   제출되어야 한다   발행 1주일 전에
                               → ~ 이전에, ~에 앞서

(A) before   (B) prior

번역 투고 기사는 발행 1주일 전에 제출되어야 한다.

5 (B)	6 (A)	7 (A)	8 (B)

5

Gessen Contractors / guarantees / customers / top-quality handiwork / on every job, / (regardless)
게센 콘트랙터즈는   보장한다   고객에게   최고 품질의 작업을   모든 일에서   얼마나 작든지

of how small.
상관없이   ~와 상관없이 ←

(A) in case (~의) 경우에   (B) regardless 상관 없이

(C) whether ~인지 아닌지   (D) rather than ~보다는

> **해설** regardless of ~와 상관없이: 빈칸 뒤 of와 함께 how small을 목적어로 취하는 전치사 자리로, 문맥상 '얼마나 작든지 상관없이'라는 의미가 자연스럽습니다. 따라서 (B) regardless가 정답입니다.

> **번역** 게센 콘트랙터즈는 얼마나 작든지 상관없이 모든 일에서 고객에게 최고 품질의 작업을 보장한다.

6

In the event of rain, / the reception / will be held / in the main banquet hall / (instead of) the garden.
비가 올 경우   환영 연회는   열릴 것입니다   중앙 연회장에서   정원 대신
                                                         ~ 대신

(A) instead of ~ 대신   (B) because ~ 때문에

(C) despite ~에도 불구하고   (D) when ~할 때

> **해설** instead of ~ 대신: 빈칸 뒤 the garden을 목적어로 취하는 전치사 자리입니다. the main banquet hall이 비가 올 경우에 환영 연회가 개최될 곳이므로, 〈빈칸 + the garden〉은 '정원이 아닌'이라는 의미가 문맥상 자연스럽습니다. 따라서 '~ 대신'이라는 의미의 전치사구 (A) instead of가 정답입니다.

> **번역** 비가 올 경우, 환영 연회는 정원이 아닌 중앙 연회장에서 열릴 것입니다.

7

(According to) a report / in the *Financial News*, / Han Bank / posted / a net profit of $9.5 million /
보도에 따르면   〈파이낸셜 뉴스〉의   한 은행은   발표했다   950만 달러의 순이익을
           ~에 따르면

for the second half of the year.
올해 하반기의

(A) According to ~에 따르면   (B) Nevertheless 그럼에도 불구하고

(C) Even though 비록 ~일지라도   (D) As if 마치 ~인 것처럼

> **해설** according to ~에 따르면: 빈칸 뒤 명사구 a report를 목적어로 취하는 전치사 자리로, 문맥상 '보도에 따르면'이라는 의미가 자연스럽습니다. 따라서 전치사구 (A) According to가 정답입니다. 접속부사 (B) Nevertheless와 접속사 (C) Even though, (D) As if는 명사를 목적어로 취할 수 없습니다.

> **번역** 〈파이낸셜 뉴스〉의 보도에 따르면, 한 은행은 950만 달러의 올해 하반기 순이익을 발표했다.

8

I am writing / (on) behalf of Mr. Johnson / to inform / you / of the change in the date / of our
제가 이 글을 씁니다 / 존슨 씨를 대신하여   알려 드리고자   귀께   날짜가 변경되었음을   곧 있을
                 ~을 대신하여

upcoming conference.
콘퍼런스의

(A) for   (B) on

(C) to   (D) at

> **해설** on behalf of ~을 대신하여: 문맥상 '제가 존슨 씨를 대신하여 알려 드립니다'라는 의미가 자연스럽고 빈칸 뒤에 behalf of가 있으므로 '~을 대신하여'라는 의미를 완성할 수 있는 (B) on이 정답입니다.

> **번역** 제가 존슨 씨를 대신하여 귀께 곧 있을 콘퍼런스의 날짜가 변경되었음을 알려 드리고자 이 글을 씁니다.

1 (C)	**2** (C)	**3** (D)	**4** (B)	**5** (B)

1

The Southeast Accounting Conference / will be held / (at) the Valmor Convention Center.
남동부 회계 컨퍼런스는 　　　　　　　　열릴 것이다 　　　발모르 컨벤션 센터에서

└→ ~에서 (장소)

(A) with　(B) for　(C) at　(D) from

해설　**알맞은 장소 전치사 선택:** 빈칸 뒤 명사구 the Valmor Convention Center를 목적어로 취하는 전치사 자리입니다. 문장의 주어 The Southeast Accounting Conference는 문맥상 the Valmor Convention Center라는 장소에서 개최되는 것이므로 '~에서'라는 의미의 장소 전치사 (C) at이 정답입니다.

번역　남동부 회계 컨퍼런스는 발모르 컨벤션 센터에서 열릴 것이다.

2

We / recommend / that you keep the original store receipt / (as) proof of purchase.
우리는 　권장합니다 　　당신이 원본 매장 영수증을 보관하는 것을 　　　구입 증거로서

└→ ~로(서)

(A) off　(B) except　(C) as　(D) through

해설　**알맞은 의미의 전치사 선택:** 빈칸 뒤 명사구 proof of purchase를 목적어로 취하는 전치사 자리입니다. 문맥상 '구입 증거로서 영수증을 보관하다'가 자연스러우므로 정답은 (C) as입니다.

번역　구입 증거로 원본 매장 영수증을 보관해두실 것을 권장합니다.

3

Ms. Murata / requests / that this month's sales totals be submitted / (by) the end of the day.
뮤라타 씨는 　요청한다 　이달의 총 판매액이 제출될 것을 　　　　　　퇴근 전까지

└→ ~까지

(A) within　(B) if　(C) that　(D) by

해설　**알맞은 전치사 선택:** 빈칸 뒤 시점 표현 the end of the day를 목적어로 취하면서, 앞의 동사 be submitted를 수식하는 전치사 자리입니다. 문맥상 '퇴근 전까지 제출되다'라는 의미가 자연스러우므로, '~까지'라는 뜻의 전치사 (D) by가 정답입니다.

번역　뮤라타 씨는 퇴근 전까지 이달의 총 판매액을 제출할 것을 요청한다.

4

(Despite) a recent drop / in sales, / the Talvidia laptop / remains the most popular one / on the
최근 감소에도 불구하고 　　　매출에서의 　탈비디아 노트북은 　　　여전히 가장 인기 있는 노트북이다 　　　시장에서

market. └→ ~에도 불구하고

(A) Due to ~ 덕분에　(B) Despite ~에도 불구하고　(C) Not only ~뿐만 아니라　(D) Although 비록 ~이지만

해설　**알맞은 전치사 선택:** 문맥상 '최근 매출 감소에도 불구하고'라는 뜻이 되어야 하므로 양보의 의미를 가진 (B) Despite(~에도 불구하고)가 정답입니다. despite는 in spite of와 바꿔 쓸 수 있습니다. 접속사 (D) Although 뒤에는 절이 와야 합니다.

번역　최근 매출이 감소했음에도 불구하고 탈비디아 노트북은 여전히 시장에서 가장 인기 있는 노트북이다.

5

The Vehicle Licensing Agency / sends / notices / to all commercial truck drivers / 90 days (prior to)
차량 면허 기관은 　　　　　　　보낸다 　통지문을 　모든 상업용 트럭 운전자에게 　　　　　면허 만료일 90일 전에

└→ ~이전에

their license expiration date.

(A) due to ~ 때문에　(B) prior to ~ 이전에　(C) far from ~와는 거리가 먼, 전혀 ~이 아닌　(D) outside of ~의 밖에

해설　**알맞은 구전치사 선택:** 문맥상 '면허 만료일 90일 전에'라는 의미가 자연스럽습니다. 따라서 전치사구 (B) prior to가 정답입니다.

번역　차량 면허 기관은 면허 만료일 90일 전에 모든 상업용 트럭 운전자에게 통지문을 보낸다.

---

6 (D)	7 (C)	8 (C)	9 (A)	10 (D)

6

Customer service / responded / very quickly / to our complaint / (about) the fish tank / that was
고객 서비스부는   대응했다   아주 신속하게   우리의 항의에   어항에 대한   깨진

broken / during shipment.
       배송 중에   → ~에 대한

(A) to   (B) from   (C) within   (D) about

해설 알맞은 전치사 선택: 빈칸 뒤 명사구 the fish tank를 목적어로 취하는 전치사 자리입니다. 문맥상 '어항에 대한 우리의 항의'라는 뜻이 되어야 하므로 '~에 대한'이라는 의미를 가진 전치사 (D) about이 정답입니다. 전치사 (C) within 뒤에는 기간 명사나 위치 명사가 나와야 합니다.

번역 고객 서비스부는 배송 중 깨진 어항에 대한 우리의 항의에 아주 신속하게 대응했다.

7

To request a transfer / to another department / (within) the company, / employees / should
이동을 요청하려면   다른 부서로   사내에서   직원들은   연락해야 한다

contact / Mr. Castillo / in the human resources office. → ~ 안에, ~ 내부에서
      카스틸로 씨에게   인사과의

(A) among ~ 사이에   (B) whereas ~에 반해   (C) within ~ 안에, ~ 내부에서   (D) since ~ 이후로

해설 알맞은 의미의 전치사 선택: 빈칸 뒤 명사구 the company를 목적어로 취하는 전치사 자리로, 빈칸을 포함한 전치사구는 명사구 another department를 수식합니다. 문맥상 '회사 내 다른 부서'라는 의미가 자연스러우므로, 전치사 (C) within이 정답입니다. (B) whereas(~에 반해)는 접속사로, 명사(구)를 목적어로 취하지 않습니다. 전치사 (A) among(~ 사이에) 뒤에는 복수의 의미를 나타내는 명사가, 전치사 (D) since(~ 이후로) 뒤에는 과거 시점의 명사가 나와야 합니다.

번역 사내의 다른 부서로 이동을 요청하려면, 직원들은 인사과의 카스틸로 씨에게 연락해야 한다.

8

The prime minister's speech / will be broadcast live / (across) the nation / this evening.
총리의 연설은   생방송으로 중계된다   전국에   오늘 저녁
                                       → ~ 전체에 걸쳐

(A) opposite ~ 건너편에   (B) regarding ~에 관하여   (C) across ~ 전체에 걸쳐   (D) after ~ 후에

해설 알맞은 전치사 선택: 빈칸 뒤 the nation을 목적어로 취하는 전치사 자리입니다. the nation이 The prime minister's speech가 생중계되는 범위를 나타내도록 해야 하므로 '전국에 걸쳐'라는 의미가 문맥상 자연스럽습니다. 따라서 '~ 전체에 걸쳐'라는 의미의 전치사 (C) across가 정답입니다.

번역 총리의 연설은 오늘 저녁 전국에 생방송으로 중계된다.

9

On our Web site, / online shoppers / can find / information / on our new products / (with) ease.
우리 웹사이트에서   온라인 쇼핑객들은   찾을 수 있다   정보를   신제품에 대한   쉽게
                                                    → 쉽게

(A) with   (B) to   (C) for   (D) from

해설 with ease 쉽게 (=easily): 문맥상 '쉽게 정보를 찾을 수 있다'라는 내용이 자연스럽습니다. with ease가 '쉽게(easily)'라는 뜻이므로 (A) with가 정답입니다.

번역 우리 웹사이트에서 온라인 쇼핑객들은 신제품에 대한 정보를 쉽게 찾을 수 있다.

10

Claire Smith / will be out of the office / until next Tuesday / (because of) her attendance / at a
클레어 스미스는   사무실 밖에 있을 것이다   다음주 화요일까지   참석으로 인해   ~ 때문에

corporate retreat / in Los Angeles.
사내 수련회에   로스앤젤레스에서 있을

(A) as well as 게다가   (B) moreover 게다가, 더욱이   (C) since ~이기 때문에   (D) because of ~ 때문에

해설 알맞은 전치사 선택: 빈칸 뒤 명사구 her attendance를 목적어로 취하는 전치사 자리로, 빈칸 앞의 내용 will be out of the office의 이유가 이어져야 자연스럽습니다. 따라서 정답은 '~ 때문에'라는 의미의 전치사 (D) because of입니다. 부사 (B) moreover와 이유를 나타내는 접속사 (C) since는 명사를 목적어로 취할 수 없습니다.

번역 클레어 스미스는 로스앤젤레스에서 있을 사내 수련회 참석으로 인해 다음주 화요일까지 사무실을 비울 예정이다.

ETS 실전 테스트

11 (C)	**12** (D)	**13** (A)	**14** (B)

Questions 11-14 refer to the following article.

Automobile Sales on the Rise
자동차 판매 오름세

The Commerce Board / predicts / that by the year's end / national
상공 회의소는   예측한다   올해 말까지   전국 자동차 판매가

automobile sales will have reached 910,000 units. This figure / is 15 percent
91만대에 이를 것이라고   이 수치는   15퍼센트

higher / than the **11.** previous year's number / and is just short / of the all-
더 높다   지난해 수량보다   그리고 다소 못 미친다   사상 최고치에는

time high / of three years ago. The Board attributes these gains to several
              3년 전의   상공 회의소는 이러한 증가의 원인을 몇몇 요인 때문이라고 여긴다

factors, / **12.** (including) the availability / of lower interest rates on car
          이용 가능성을 포함해   더 낮은 자동차 대출 금리의
          → ~을 포함하여: 뒤에 명사구를 목적어로 취한 전치사

loans. In contrast to the general demand / for automobiles, / the market for
        일반적인 수요와는 대조적으로   자동차에 대한   미니밴 시장은

minivans / has shown little to no **13.** growth / these past five years / despite
              성장세를 거의 또는 전혀 보이지 않았다   지난 5년 동안

intensive advertising efforts. **14.** It is even expected / that some models will
집중적인 광고 노력에도 불구하고   심지어 예상된다   일부 모델은 교체되지 않을 것으로

not be renewed / next year.
                      내년에

11-14 기사

자동차 판매 오름세

상공 회의소는 올해 말까지 전국 자동차 판매가 91만 대에 이를 것으로 예측한다. 이 수치는 지난해 수량보다 15퍼센트 더 높으며, 3년 전 사상 최고치에는 다소 못 미친다. 상공 회의소는 이러한 증가의 원인을 더 낮은 자동차 대출 금리의 이용 가능성을 포함해 몇몇 요인 때문이라고 여긴다. 자동차에 대한 일반적인 수요와는 대조적으로, 미니밴 시장은 집중적인 광고 노력에도 불구하고 지난 5년 동안 성장세를 거의 또는 전혀 보이지 않았다. 심지어 일부 모델은 내년에 교체되지 않을 것으로 예상된다.

11 (A) following   (A) 다음의

(B) current   (B) 현재의

(C) previous   (C) 이전의

(D) final   (D) 마지막의

> **해설** 어휘 문제: 올해의 자동차 판매량이 15퍼센트 더 높다고 언급했으므로, 빈칸에는 비교 대상을 나타내는 표현이 들어가는 것이 문맥상 자연스럽습니다. 따라서 year's number를 수식해 '지난해의 수량'이라는 의미를 나타내는 형용사 (C) previous가 정답입니다.

12 (A) include

(B) includes

(C) included

(D) including

> **해설** 전치사 + 명사구: 빈칸 앞에 완전한 구조의 절이 왔고, 빈칸 뒤 명사구 the availability of lower interest rates on car loans는 빈칸의 목적어 역할을 하므로 전치사인 (D) including이 정답입니다.

13 (A) growth   (A) 성장

(B) competition   (B) 경쟁, 대회

(C) value   (C) 가치

(D) interruption   (D) 중단, 방해

> **해설** 어휘 문제: 빈칸은 동사 has shown의 목적어 역할을 하는 명사 자리로, 부정적 의미의 little to no가 빈칸을 수식합니다. 전치사구 despite intensive advertising efforts를 통해 집중적인 광고를 했음에도 긍정적인 변화를 거의 보여 주지 못했음을 알 수 있으므로 '성장'이라는 의미의 명사 (A) growth가 정답입니다.

14 (A) Another factor is the changes in consumer preferences.   (A) 또 다른 요인은 소비자 선호도의 변화이다.

(B) It is even expected that some models will not be renewed next year.   (B) 심지어 일부 모델은 내년에 교체되지 않을 것으로 예상된다.

(C) The success of the advertisements took the Board by surprise.   (C) 그 광고의 성공은 상공 회의소를 놀라게 했다.

(D) Consumers prefer minivans because of their utility.   (D) 소비자들은 유용성 때문에 미니밴을 선호한다.

> **해설** 문장 고르기: 빈칸 앞 문장에서 집중적인 광고에도 불구하고 미니밴 시장이 성장하지 못했다는 문제점을 언급했습니다. 따라서 빈칸에는 그 문제점이 미니밴 생산에 미치는 부정적인 영향과 관련된 내용이 들어가는 것이 문맥상 자연스러우므로 정답은 (B)입니다.

PART 5 | Unit 12 등위접속사와 명사절 접속사

● 등위접속사와 상관접속사 ETS 문제로 훈련하기 STEP 1

교재 p.153

1 (B)	**2** (B)	**3** (A)	**4** (A)	**5** (B)	**6** (B)

1

Heavy rain or snow / is expected / to affect the region / today.
폭우 또는 폭설이   예상된다   그 지역에 영향을 미칠 것으로   오늘
└→ 또는

(A) because   (B) or

> **번역**   오늘 그 지역에 폭우 또는 폭설이 영향을 미칠 것으로 예상된다.

2

Ms. Noguchi's flight / was delayed, / but she / arrived / in time / to attend the meeting.
노구치 씨가 탄 비행기가   지연되었다   그러나 그녀는   도착했다   제때에   회의에 참석했다
└→ 그러나

(A) both   (B) but

> **번역**   노구치 씨가 탄 비행기가 지연되었지만 그녀는 제때에 도착해 회의에 참석했다.

3

The town of Monkark / has / both natural beauty and attractive architecture.
몬카크 마을은   가지고 있다 / 자연의 아름다움과 매력적인 건축물 모두를
└→ 상관접속사 both A and B

(A) both   (B) either

> **번역**   몬카크 마을은 자연의 아름다움과 매력적인 건축물 모두를 가지고 있다.

4

The company / will raise / prices / and lower / discounts / on January 1.
그 회사는   인상할 예정이다 / 가격을   그리고 줄일 예정이다 / 할인폭을   1월 1일에
└→ 그리고

(A) and   (B) again

> **번역**   그 회사는 1월 1일에 가격을 인상하고 할인폭을 줄일 예정이다.

5

Rava Metals / became / not only a profitable business / but also a multinational corporation.
라바 메탈즈는   되었다   수익성 좋은 사업체만이 아니라   다국적 기업도
└→ not only A but also B: A뿐만 아니라 B도

(A) as well as   (B) not only

> **번역**   라바 메탈즈는 수익성 좋은 사업체만이 아니라 다국적 기업도 되었다.

6

Payment / is accepted / either at the time of purchase / or upon delivery / of the merchandise.
대금은   받습니다   구매 시나   배달 시에   상품의
└→ 상관접속사 either A or B

(A) and   (B) or

> **번역**   대금은 상품의 구매 시나 배달 시에 받습니다.

7 (B)	**8** (B)	**9** (D)	**10** (A)

7

(Neither) the president (nor) his press advisor was available / for comment.
사장도 그의 언론 자문도 시간이 없었다　　　　　　　　　　　　　　　　　논평을 할
　　　　　　　　　　　　　　　　　　　　　　→ neither A nor B: A도 B도 아닌

(A) either　　　　　　　　　　　　　(B) nor

(C) and　　　　　　　　　　　　　　(D) but

해설　상관접속사 neither A nor B: 빈칸 앞에 Neither가 있으므로, 상관접속사 neither A nor B가 쓰였음을 알 수 있습니다. 따라서 the president와 his press advisor를 연결하는 (B) nor가 정답입니다.

번역　사장도 그의 언론 자문도 논평을 해줄 시간이 없었다.

8

Thanks to the chemists' hard work (and) dedication, / the product development stage / has been
화학자들의 노고와 헌신 덕분에　　　　　　　　　　　　제품 개발 단계가　　　　　　　　　성공적으로

successfully completed.
끝났다　　　　　　　　→ 같은 품사를 연결하는 등위접속사

(A) dedicated 헌신적인　　　　　　　(B) dedication 전념, 헌신

(C) dedicating 헌신하는 것　　　　　(D) dedicates 바치다, 전념하다

해설　등위접속사 and: 빈칸 앞에 같은 품사를 연결하는 등위접속사 and가 있습니다. 따라서 명사구인 the chemists' hard work와 같은 품사인 명사 (B) dedication(헌신)이 정답입니다. 동명사 (C) dedicating도 명사 역할을 하지만 문맥상 '헌신하는 것'은 자연스럽지 않으므로 오답입니다.

번역　화학자들의 노고와 헌신 덕분에 제품 개발 단계가 성공적으로 끝났다.

9

Tickets to the art museum / can be purchased / (either) online (or) by phone.
미술관 입장권은　　　　　　　　　구입될 수 있다　　　　　온라인이나 전화상으로
　　　　　　　　　　　　　　　　　　　　　　　　　　　　→ either A or B: A이거나 B인

(A) but　　　　　　　　　　　　　　(B) yet

(C) and　　　　　　　　　　　　　　(D) or

해설　상관접속사 either A or B: 빈칸 앞에 있는 either를 통해 상관접속사 either A or B가 쓰였음을 알 수 있습니다. 따라서 online과 by phone을 연결하는 (D) or가 정답입니다.

번역　미술관 입장권은 온라인이나 전화상으로 구입할 수 있다.

10

The survey / can help / a company / to identify potential customers / (as well as) analyze its
그 설문 조사는　도움을 줄 수 있다 / 회사가　잠재 고객들을 찾아내는 데　　　경쟁사를 분석하는 것은 물론

competitors.
　　　　　　　　B as well as A: A뿐만 아니라 B도 ←

(A) as well as ~은 물론　　　　　　(B) instead 대신에

(C) while ~하는 동안　　　　　　　(D) for example 예를 들어

해설　상관접속사 B as well as A: 빈칸 앞의 to identify potential customers와 빈칸 뒤의 (to) analyze its competitors를 연결하는 접속사 자리입니다. 문맥상 '경쟁사를 분석하는 것뿐만 아니라 잠재 고객들을 찾아내는 것에도'라는 의미가 자연스러우므로, (A) as well as가 정답입니다.

번역　그 설문 조사는 회사가 경쟁사를 분석하는 것은 물론 잠재 고객들을 찾아내는 데도 도움을 줄 수 있다.

1 (B)	**2** (B)	**3** (B)	**4** (A)	**5** (A)	**6** (B)

1

We / ask / (that) you please refrain / from bringing food / inside the museum.
저희는 요청합니다 / 여러분이 삼가주실 것을   음식물을 가져오는 것을   박물관 안으로
                                                  → 명사절 접속사 that ~라는 것

(A) unless   (B) that

번역 박물관 안으로 음식물을 가져오는 것을 삼가주실 것을 여러분께 요청합니다.

2

The commission / concluded / (that) funding is needed / to repair the dam.
위원회는   결론지었다   재정 지원이 필요하다고   댐을 수리하기 위해
                                  → 명사절 접속사 that ~라는 것

(A) if   (B) that

번역 위원회는 댐을 수리하기 위해 재정 지원이 필요하다고 결론지었다.

3

When asked (whether) she will retire soon, / Ms. Johannsen / said / that she will never stop
곧 은퇴할 것인지 여부를 묻는 질문을 받자   요한센 씨는   말했다   자신이 결코 일을 그만두지 않을 것임을

working.   → 명사절 접속사 whether ~인지 아닌지

(A) while   (B) whether

번역 곧 은퇴할 것인지 여부를 묻는 질문을 받자, 요한센 씨는 자신이 결코 일을 그만두지 않을 것이라고 말했다.

4

Gladsock employees / do not know / (if) they will receive / a bonus / this year.
글래드삭 직원들은   알지 못한다   자신들이 받을 것인지 아닌지   상여금을   올해
                                  → 명사절 접속사 if ~인지 아닌지

(A) if   (B) what

번역 글래드삭 직원들은 자신들이 올해 상여금을 받을지 여부를 알지 못한다.

5

(That) the business model will attract / new clients / is assumed.
그 사업 모델이 끌어들일 것으로   새로운 고객들을   추정된다
        → 명사절 접속사 that ~라는 것

(A) That   (B) If

번역 그 사업 모델이 새로운 고객들을 끌어들일 것으로 추정된다.

6

There is disagreement / about (whether) the prototype will be ready / in time for the conference.
이견이 있다   시제품이 준비될 것인지 아닌지에 대해   콘퍼런스 때에
                                  → 명사절 접속사 whether, 전치사의 목적어로 if절은 쓰이지 않음

(A) if   (B) whether

번역 시제품이 콘퍼런스 때에 맞춰 준비될 것인지 여부에 대해 이견이 있다.

7 (D)	**8** (C)	**9** (A)	**10** (C)

7

One frequent complaint / air travelers make / is (that) the overhead compartments are too small.
자주 하는 한 가지 불평은　　비행기 여행객들이 하는　　머리 위 짐칸이 너무 작다는 것이다

(A) then　　　　　　　　　　　　(B) to　　　　　　　　　　→ 명사절 접속사 that

(C) whether　　　　　　　　　　　(D) that

해설　명사절 접속사 that ~라는 것: One frequent complaint (air travelers make)가 문장의 주어이고, 빈칸 이하는 동사 is의 보어 역할을 하는 명사절인데 문맥상 '짐칸이 너무 작다는 것이다'가 자연스러우므로 (D) that이 정답입니다.

번역　비행기 여행객들이 자주 하는 한 가지 불평은 머리 위 짐칸이 너무 작다는 것이다.

8

Chef Alice Grissom / says / she must decide / (whether to open) an additional restaurant / in
앨리스 그리솜 주방장은　　말한다　　자신이 결정해야 한다고　　레스토랑을 추가로 개업할지

Strasbourg / (or) to remain / only in Colmar.　　→ whether A(to부정사) or B(to부정사): A할지 B할지
스트라스부르그에　　아니면 남아 있을지를 / 콜마르에만

(A) for　　　　　　　　　　　　　(B) if

(C) whether　　　　　　　　　　　(D) over

해설　명사절 접속사 〈whether + to부정사〉: 빈칸 뒤에 온 to부정사 to open이 문제 해결의 단서입니다. 보통 접속사 뒤에는 주어와 동사를 갖춘 절이 오지만, whether는 뒤에는 to부정사가 올 수도 있습니다. 〈whether + to부정사〉는 '~할지 말지'의 의미로 불확실한 상황을 나타냅니다. 따라서 정답은 (C) whether입니다. (B) if도 비슷한 뜻이지만 to부정사와 결합할 수 없으므로 정답이 될 수 없습니다.

번역　앨리스 그리솜 주방장은 스트라스부르그에 레스토랑을 추가로 개업할지, 아니면 콜마르에만 남아 있을지를 자신이 결정해야 한다고 말한다.

9

Before using this product / for the first time, / ensure (that) you read / the instructions / carefully.
이 제품을 사용하기 전에　　　　　처음으로　　　　반드시 읽으십시오　　　설명서를　　　주의 깊게

(A) that　　　　　　　　　　　　(B) how　　　　　　→ 명사절 접속사 that

(C) what　　　　　　　　　　　　(D) them

해설　명사절 접속사 that ~라는 것: 주절은 you가 생략된 명령문으로 빈칸 이하는 동사 ensure의 목적어 역할을 하는 명사절입니다. 문맥상 '설명서를 주의 깊게 읽는 것'이라는 의미가 자연스러우므로 (A) that이 정답입니다.

번역　이 제품을 처음 사용하기 전에 반드시 설명서를 주의 깊게 읽으십시오.

10

Mr. Nam / inspects / the landscaping work / to determine / (whether) it conforms / to company
남 씨는　　점검한다　　조경 작업을　　　　결정하기 위해　　그것이 부합하는지 아닌지를　　회사 기준에

standards.　　　　　　　　　　　　　　　　　→ 명사절 접속사 whether

(A) because　　　　　　　　　　　(B) so

(C) whether　　　　　　　　　　　(D) while

해설　명사절 접속사 whether ~인지 아닌지: 빈칸 뒤에 〈주어(it) + 동사(conforms)〉의 완전한 절이 있으므로, 빈칸에는 접속사가 들어가야 하는데 빈칸이 이끄는 절은 to determine의 목적어 역할을 하므로, 명사절 접속사 (C) whether가 정답입니다.

번역　남 씨는 조경 작업이 회사 기준에 부합하는지의 여부를 결정하기 위해 그것을 점검한다.

1 (B)	**2** (A)	**3** (B)	**4** (A)	**5** (A)	**6** (B)

1

The voters / have to decide / (which) candidate has / the greater appeal.
투표자들은　　결정해야 한다　　　어느 후보가 가지고 있는지　　더 큰 매력을
　　　　　　　　　　　　　　　　　　　　　 → 어느 것이 ~하는지

(A) whom　　　　　　　　　　　(B) which

번역　투표자들은 어느 후보가 더 마음에 드는지 결정해야 한다.

2

A local magazine / asked / people / to describe / (what) their jobs involve.
한 지역 잡지는　　　요청했다　사람들에게　설명해 달라고　본인의 일에 포함되는 것이 무엇인지

(A) what　　　　　　　　　　　(B) which　　　　　　 → 무엇이 ~하는지

번역　한 지역 잡지는 사람들에게 본인의 일에 포함되는 것이 무엇인지 설명해 달라고 요청했다.

3

(What) customers would suggest to us / will be considered / seriously.
고객들이 우리에게 제안하는 것은　　　　　　고려될 것이다　　　　심각하게
　　　　　→ '~라는 것'이라는 의미의 what

(A) That　　　　　　　　　　　(B) What

번역　고객들이 우리에게 제안하는 것은 심각하게 고려될 것이다.

4

Harbor Fish Restaurant / will continue / to offer / (what) has sold well / in the past.
하버 피시 식당은　　　　　　계속할 것이다　제공하는 것을 / 판매가 잘 되었던 것을　　과거에

(A) what　　　　　　　　　　　(B) whose　　　 → '~라는 것'이라는 의미의 what

번역　하버 피시 식당은 과거에 판매가 잘 되었던 것을 계속 제공할 것이다.

5

(What) should impress passengers most / is the comfort of the seating / at Liverpool Airport.
승객들을 가장 감동시키게 될 것은　　　　　　　좌석의 편안함이다　　　　　리버풀 공항에서
　　　　　　　　　　→ '~라는 것'이라는 의미의 what

(A) What　　　　　　　　　　　(B) When

번역　리버풀 공항에서 승객들을 가장 감동시키게 될 것은 그곳에 있는 좌석의 편안함이다.

6

We / do not know / (who) will attend / the awards ceremony.
우리는 / 모른다　　　　누가 참석할 것인지　시상식에
　　　　　　　　　　　　 → 누가 ~하는지

(A) where　　　　　　　　　　　(B) who

번역　우리는 누가 시상식에 참석할 것인지 모른다.

7 (A)	**8** (C)	**9** (C)	**10** (D)

7

At the workshop, / Mr. Aryl / will explain / ⟨how⟩ you can protect / your computers / from viruses.
워크숍에서   아릴 씨가   설명할 것이다   여러분이 어떻게 보호할 수 있는지를 / 여러분의 컴퓨터를   바이러스로부터
                                              └→ 어떻게 ~하는지

(A) how   (B) who
(C) what   (D) which

> 해설 how 어떻게 ~하는지: 빈칸 앞에는 타동사 explain(설명하다)이 있으며, 빈칸 이하는 목적어 역할을 하는 절에 해당됩니다. 의미상 '여러분의 컴퓨터를 바이러스로부터 어떻게 보호할 수 있는지'가 되는 것이 자연스러우므로, (A) how가 정답입니다.

> 번역 워크숍에서 아릴 씨가 여러분의 컴퓨터를 바이러스로부터 어떻게 보호할 수 있는지를 설명할 것이다.

8

⟨What⟩ pleased the clients most / was the effective customer service / Moradon Bank provided.
고객들을 가장 기쁘게 한 것은   효과적인 고객 서비스였다   모라돈 은행이 제공한
         └→ '~라는 것'이라는 의미의 what

(A) Who   (B) That
(C) What   (D) This

> 해설 선행사를 포함하는 what: 빈칸을 포함하여 most까지가 주어 역할을 하고 있으므로, 명사절을 이끌 수 있는 접속사가 필요합니다. 그런데 빈칸 뒤에 불완전한 절이 나왔기 때문에 (C) What이 정답입니다.

> 번역 고객들을 가장 기쁘게 한 것은 모라돈 은행에서 제공한 효과적인 고객 서비스였다.

9

The employee directory / has / a section / that tells users / ⟨who⟩ can answer questions.
직원 명부는   갖고 있다 / 부분을   이용자들에게 알려주는   누가 문의 사항에 답할 수 있는지를
                                                                    └→ 누가 ~하는지

(A) if   (B) how
(C) who   (D) he

> 해설 who 누가 ~하는지: 빈칸에는 tells(알려주다)의 직접목적어인 명사절을 이끌 수 있는 접속사가 와야 합니다. '누가 질문에 대답할 수 있는지를'이라는 의미가 자연스러우므로, (C) who가 정답입니다.

> 번역 직원 명부에는 이용자들에게 누가 문의 사항에 답할 수 있는지를 알려주는 부분이 있다.

10

The product development team / cannot say / ⟨when⟩ the new line of products / will be released.
제품 개발팀은   말할 수 없다   언제 새로운 제품군이   출시될지를
                                          └→ 언제 ~하는지

(A) which   (B) who
(C) what   (D) when

> 해설 when 언제 ~하는지: 빈칸 이하는 타동사 say의 목적어 역할을 하고 문맥상 '언제 새로운 제품군이 출시될지를'이라는 의미가 되어야 하므로, (D) when이 정답입니다.

> 번역 제품 개발팀은 언제 새로운 제품군이 출시될지를 말할 수 없다.

1 (A)	2 (B)	3 (B)	4 (A)

1

The two companies / worked together / on a (highly) profitable development project.
두 회사는　　　　　함께 진행했다　　　　대단히 수익성 높은 개발 프로젝트를
→ 대단히, 매우

(A) highly 대단히, 매우　　　　(B) tightly 단단히, 꽉

번역　두 회사는 대단히 수익성 높은 개발 프로젝트를 함께 진행했다.

2

Plumville Library / (proudly) announces / the launch / of a brand-new Web site.
플럼빌 도서관은　　자랑스럽게 발표합니다　　개설을　　새로운 웹사이트의
→ 자랑스럽게

(A) extremely 극도로, 극히　　　　(B) proudly 자랑스럽게

번역　플럼빌 도서관은 새로운 웹사이트의 개설을 자랑스럽게 발표합니다.

3

The (recently) formed client advisory division / is now hiring / financial specialists.
최근에 구성된 고객 자문 부서는　　　　현재 채용하고 있다　금융 전문가들을
→ 최근에

(A) currently 현재　　　　(B) recently 최근에

번역　최근에 구성된 고객 자문 부서는 현재 금융 전문가들을 채용하고 있다.

4

The company's stock price / is (relatively) low / compared to its annual earnings.
그 회사의 주가는　　　　상대적으로 낮다　연간 수익과 비교해서
→ 상대적으로

(A) relatively 상대적으로　　　　(B) anonymously 익명으로

번역　그 회사의 주가는 연간 수익과 비교해 상대적으로 낮다.

5 (B)	**6** (C)	**7** (C)	**8** (B)

5

Emergency equipment / is tested / (frequently) / to ensure / that it is in good working condition.
비상 장비는   테스트된다   자주   확인하기 위해서 그것이 작동 상태가 양호한지
                                                    → 자주

(A) lately 최근에   (B) frequently 자주

(C) truly 정말로   (D) relatively 비교적

해설 frequently 자주: 문맥상 장비의 작동 상태가 양호한지를 확인하려면 '자주' 시험해 볼 필요가 있을 것입니다. 따라서 정답은 부사 (B) frequently입니다.

번역 비상 장비는 작동 상태가 양호한지 확인하기 위해서 자주 테스트된다.

6

Volunteers / are (urgently) needed / to prepare a large book order / for shipping / before Friday's
자원 봉사자가   시급히 필요하다   대용량 책 주문을 준비하기 위해   발송할   금요일 마감 기한 전에

deadline.   → 시급히

(A) closely 단단히, 면밀히   (B) tightly 단단히

(C) urgently 시급히   (D) exactly 정확히

해설 urgently 시급히: 문맥상 금요일 마감 전에 준비가 되려면 자원 봉사자가 '시급히' 필요할 것입니다. 따라서 정답은 부사 (C) urgently입니다.

번역 금요일 마감 기한 전에 발송할 대용량 책 주문을 준비하기 위해 자원 봉사자가 시급히 필요하다.

7

Our division leader / announced / that the new sales team will (definitely) reach / its goal for this
우리 부서 책임자는   선언했다   새 영업 팀이 틀림없이 달성할 것이라고   올해의 목표를

year.   → 틀림없이, 확실하게

(A) freely 자유롭게   (B) extremely 극도로

(C) definitely 틀림없이   (D) usually 대개

해설 definitely 틀림없이, 확실하게: 빈칸 뒤 reach its goal과 가장 잘 어울리는 부사를 선택해야 합니다. 문맥상 '올해의 목표를 틀림없이 달성하겠다'라는 의지를 밝히는 것이 자연스러우므로, (C) definitely가 정답입니다.

번역 우리 부서 책임자는 새 영업 팀이 올해의 목표를 틀림없이 달성할 것이라고 선언했다.

8

Investors / believe / that Star Mining's growth will be stronger / than (previously) expected.
투자자들은   믿는다   스타 광업의 성장세가 더 강해질 것이라고   이전에 예상되었던 것보다

(A) completely 완전히   (B) previously 이전에   → 이전에

(C) positively 긍정적으로   (D) newly 새로

해설 previously 이전에: 빈칸 뒤 과거분사 expected를 수식하는 부사 자리입니다. 미래 시제 동사 will be stronger를 통해 문맥상 과거에 했던 예상과 비교하는 문장임을 알 수 있으므로 (B) previously가 정답입니다.

번역 투자자들은 스타 광업의 성장세가 이전에 예상되었던 것보다 더 강해질 것이라고 믿는다.

1 (C)	**2** (A)	**3** (D)	**4** (C)	**5** (B)

1

(Both) Ms. Liu (and) Ms. Schultz / are attending / the international business conference /
리우 씨와 슐츠 씨 둘 다   참석할 것이다   국제 비지니스 콘퍼런스에
         → both A and B: A와 B 둘 다

in Jakarta / next week.
자카르타에서 열리는 / 다음 주에

(A) either (B) or (C) and (D) nor

해설 　상관접속사 both A and B: 빈칸 앞에 Both가 있으므로 상관접속사 both A and B가 쓰였음을 알 수 있습니다. 따라서 정답은 (C) and입니다.

번역 　리우 씨와 슐츠 씨 둘 다 다음 주에 자카르타에서 열리는 국제 비지니스 콘퍼런스에 참석할 것이다.

2

Hua Husing's achievements / were remarkable / considering / (that) he was only twenty-six /
후아 후싱 씨의 업적은   주목할 만했다   고려하면   그가 겨우 26살이었다는 것을

at the time.   → 명사절 접속사
그 당시

(A) that (B) what (C) since (D) whether

해설 　that ~라는 것: 빈칸 이하는 분사 considering의 목적어 역할을 하는 명사절인데, 문맥상 '그 당시 그가 겨우 26살이었다는 것을 고려하면'이라는 의미가 자연스러우므로 '~라는 것'을 의미하는 명사절 접속사 (A) that이 정답입니다.

번역 　그 당시 그가 겨우 26살이었다는 점을 고려하면 후아 후싱 씨의 업적은 주목할 만했다.

3

Greenlove Publishing / specializes in / books / about environmental challenges (and) successes.
그린러브 출판사는   전문으로 한다   도서를   환경적 도전 그리고 성공에 관한

(A) those (B) when (C) onto (D) and   → 등위접속사

해설 　등위접속사 and: 빈칸 앞의 environmental challenges와 빈칸 뒤의 successes를 연결하는 접속사 자리입니다. 문맥상 '환경적 도전과 성공'이라는 의미가 자연스러우므로 등위접속사 (D) and가 정답입니다.

번역 　그린러브 출판사는 환경적 도전과 성공에 관한 도서를 전문으로 한다.

4

The company's final decision / on (whether or not to hire) Ms. Johnson / depends on the result of
회사의 최종 결정은   존슨 씨를 고용할 것인지의 여부에 관한   추천인 조회 결과에 달려 있다

a reference check.   → whether + to부정사: ~할지 말지

(A) hire (B) hiring (C) to hire (D) will hire

해설 　whether + to부정사: 빈칸 앞의 접속사 whether는 전치사 on의 목적어 역할을 하므로 명사절 접속사입니다. 명사절 접속사 whether 뒤에는 〈주어 + 동사〉의 완전한 절과 to부정사가 나올 수 있는데, whether 뒤에 주어가 없으므로, (C) to hire가 정답입니다.

번역 　존슨 씨를 고용할 것인지의 여부에 관한 회사의 최종 결정은 추천인 조회 결과에 달려 있다.

5

We have been given / specific instructions / on (how) Ms. Crane wants this task to be completed.
우리는 받았다   구체적인 지시를   크레인 씨가 이 과제가 어떻게 완수되기를 원하는지에 관한

(A) who (B) how (C) that (D) whoever   → 명사절 접속사

해설 　how 어떻게 ~하는지: 빈칸 뒤에 완전한 절이 왔으므로, 명사절을 이끄는 접속사가 필요합니다. 전치사 on의 목적어 역할을 하면서, 문맥상 '이 과제가 어떻게 완수되기를 원하는지'라는 의미가 되어야 하므로, '어떻게'라는 의미의 (B) how가 정답입니다.

번역 　우리는 크레인 씨가 이 과제를 어떻게 완수하기를 원하는지에 관한 구체적인 지시를 받았다.

6 (D)	**7** (D)	**8** (D)	**9** (C)	**10** (D)

6

Primo Publishing / has not yet decided / when they will introduce / their new software's
프리모 출판사는   아직 결정하지 못했다   그들이 언제 소개할지   신제품 소프트웨어의 최신 기능을

advanced features.
                → 명사절 접속사

(A) which   (B) who   (C) what   (D) when

해설 when 언제 ~하는지: 빈칸에는 동사 has not yet decided의 목적어가 되는 명사절을 이끄는 접속사가 필요한데, 문맥상 '언제 소개할지 결정하지 못했다'가 자연스러우므로 (D) when이 정답입니다.

번역 프리모 출판사는 언제 자사의 신제품 소프트웨어의 최신 기능을 소개할지 결정하지 못했다.

7

The purpose of this survey / is to find out / whether our performance meets / customers'
이 설문 조사의 목적은   알아내는 것이다   우리의 성과가 부응하는지   고객들의 기대에

expectations.
                → 명사절 접속사

(A) neither (둘 중) 어느 것도 ~아니다   (B) whereas ~인 데 반해   (C) although 비록 ~이긴 하지만   (D) whether ~인지 아닌지

해설 whether ~인지 아닌지: 빈칸이 이끄는 절은 빈칸 앞 타동사구 find out의 목적어 역할을 하므로, 명사절 접속사 (D) whether가 정답입니다. 부사절 접속사 (B) whereas와 (C) although가 이끄는 부사절은 타동사의 목적어 역할을 할 수 없습니다.

번역 이 설문 조사의 목적은 우리의 성과가 고객들의 기대에 부응하는지 여부를 알아내는 것이다.

8

Currently, / Skypoint Fashions / does not have / any vacancies, / but the company / expects / to
현재   스카이포인트 패션즈는   갖고 있지 않다   공석을   하지만 그 회사는   기대한다

be hiring / later this year.
채용하기를   올해 말에는   → 등위접속사

(A) or   (B) once   (C) that   (D) but

해설 알맞은 접속사 선택: 빈칸 앞의 Skypoint Fashions ~ any vacancies와 빈칸 뒤의 the company ~ this year를 연결하는 접속사 자리입니다. 문맥상 '현재는 공석이 없지만 올해 말에는 채용하기를 기대한다'라는 의미가 자연스러우므로 (D) but이 정답입니다.

번역 현재 스카이포인트 패션즈에는 공석이 없지만 올해 말에는 채용하기를 기대한다.

9

Traces of both Caribbean music and traditional jazz / can be heard / in Kendra Bauden's new
카리브해 음악과 전통 재즈의 흔적이 모두   들린다   켄드라 보든의 새 음반에서

recording.
        → both A and B: A와 B 둘 다

(A) already   (B) fewer   (C) both   (D) ever

해설 상관접속사 both A and B: 빈칸 뒤에 Caribbean music과 traditional jazz를 연결하는 and가 있으므로, 상관접속사 both A and B가 쓰였음을 알 수 있습니다. 따라서 (C) both가 정답입니다.

번역 켄드라 보든의 새 음반에서 카리브해 음악과 전통 재즈의 흔적이 모두 들린다.

10

Clients / are reminded / that the law offices will be closed / on Monday / for the holiday.
의뢰인 여러분에게 / 다시 한 번 알려 드립니다 / 법률 사무소가 문을 닫는다는 것을   월요일에   공휴일이라서
                → 명사절 접속사

(A) if   (B) yet   (C) still   (D) that

해설 명사절 접속사 that ~라는 것: 빈칸 뒤에 〈주어(the law offices) + 동사(will be closed)〉의 완전한 절이 있으므로 접속사가 들어가야 하는데, 전체 문맥상 '~이라는 것을 알린다'라는 의미가 적합하므로, 명사절 접속사 (D) that이 정답입니다.

번역 법률 사무소가 공휴일이라서 월요일에 문을 닫는다는 사실을 의뢰인 여러분에게 다시 한 번 알려 드립니다.

11 (A)	12 (C)	13 (D)	14 (B)

Questions 11-14 refer to the following e-mail.

11-14 이메일

To: Bee Goh Pon
From: Passaro Dental Group
Date: 13 January
Subject: Your teeth

수신: 비 고 폰
발신: 파사로 치과 그룹
날짜: 1월 13일
제목: 당신의 치아

Dear Mr. Pon,

폰 씨께,

Your smile / is **11.** important to us. It is time / for you / to schedule an
당신의 미소는   우리에게 중요합니다   시기가 되었습니다 / 당신이   진료를 예약하실

appointment / for a checkup and cleaning. Your last **12.** visit with us /
              검진 및 치석 제거를 위한   마지막으로 저희에게 방문하신 때가

was more than fifteen months ago. At Passaro Dental Group, / we
15개월 이상 지났습니다   파사로 치과 그룹에서   저희는

recommend / **13.** (that) you get / a routine cleaning / every six months /
권해 드립니다   받으실 것을   정기적인 치석 제거를   6개월마다

→ 명사절 접속사

and an examination / every year.
그리고 검진을   매년

당신의 미소는 우리에게 중요합니다. 검진 및 치석 제거를 위한 진료를 예약하실 시기가 되었습니다. 저희를 마지막으로 방문하신 때가 15개월 이상 지났습니다. 파사로 치과 그룹은 정기적인 치석 제거는 6개월마다 그리고 검진은 매년 받으실 것을 권해 드립니다.

We look forward / to hearing from you / and serving your dental needs.
저희는 고대합니다   당신의 소식을 듣기를   그리고 치과 서비스로 모실 수 있게 되기를

14. Please contact us / if you have any questions or concerns.
저희에게 연락 주시기 바랍니다 / 문의 사항이나 관심사가 있을 경우

당신의 소식을 듣고 치과 서비스로 모실 수 있게 되기를 고대합니다. 문의 사항이나 관심사가 있을 경우 연락 주시기 바랍니다.

Sincerely,

Barbara Ong, Hygienist
Passaro Dental Group
4587 Jaunty Road, Suite B
Singapore 168938
Phone: 65 6324 0112

바바라 옹, 치위생사
파사로 치과 그룹
4587 존티 로, B호
싱가포르 168938
전화번호: 65 6324 0112

11 (A) important
   (B) polite
   (C) available
   (D) similar

   (A) 중요한
   (B) 예의 바른
   (C) 이용할 수 있는
   (D) 비슷한

   해설 **어휘 문제:** 먼저 이메일의 발신자 Passaro Dental Group과 제목 Your teeth를 확인합니다. 빈칸 뒤 문장 It is time ~ and cleaning.에서 검진과 치석 제거를 언급했으므로, 빈칸을 포함하여 '당신의 미소는 중요하다'라는 의미가 문맥상 자연스럽습니다. 따라서 정답은 (A)입니다.

12 (A) course
   (B) reunion
   (C) visit
   (D) stay

   (A) 과목, 과정
   (B) 모임, 동창회
   (C) 방문
   (D) 머무름

   해설 **어휘 문제:** 빈칸 앞의 Your last와 뒤의 with us의 수식을 받는 명사 자리입니다. 문맥상 '(치과에) 마지막 방문'이라는 의미가 자연스러우므로 정답은 (C) visit입니다.

13 (A) what
   (B) each
   (C) most
   (D) that

   해설 **명사절 접속사 that:** we가 문장의 주어이고, 빈칸 이하는 동사 recommend의 목적어 역할을 하는 명사절인데 문맥상 '당신이 6개월마다 치석 제거를 받는 것'이라는 의미가 자연스러우므로 (D) that이 정답입니다. 대명사 (B) each와 (C) most는 절을 이끌 수 없습니다.

14 (A) It has been a pleasure doing business with your firm.
   (B) Please contact us if you have any questions or concerns.
   (C) This is your final opportunity to change your mind.
   (D) We are happy to welcome new patients to our practice.

   (A) 귀사와 함께 거래할 수 있어서 즐거웠습니다.
   (B) 문의사항이나 관심사가 있을 경우 연락 주시기 바랍니다.
   (C) 이번이 마음을 바꾸실 수 있는 마지막 기회입니다.
   (D) 새로운 환자들을 저희 병원에 모시게 되어 기쁩니다.

   해설 **문장 고르기:** 빈칸 앞 문장 We look forward ~ dental needs.에서 연락과 치과 서비스 제공을 고대한다고 했습니다. 따라서 '문의 사항이나 관심사가 있을 경우 연락을 달라'는 내용이 이어지면서 이메일을 끝맺는 것이 문맥싱 자연스러우므로 정답은 (B)입니다.

🔵 시간 / 조건을 나타내는 부사절 접속사 ETS 문제로 훈련하기 STEP 1

교재 p.165

1 (A)	2 (B)	3 (B)	4 (B)	5 (B)	6 (A)

1

Please arrive / at the conference center / by 8:00 A.M. / if you are a presenter.
와 주십시오   학회장에   아침 8시까지   당신이 발표자일 경우

(A) if   (B) until
                                                        ↳ 만약 ~라면, ~일 경우에는

> **번역** 발표자일 경우, 학회장에 아침 8시까지 와주십시오.

2

As soon as the building has been inspected, / the tenants will be able to move in.
건물이 점검이 완료되자마자   세입자들은 입주할 수 있을 것이다
          ↳ ~하자마자

(A) While   (B) As soon as

> **번역** 건물이 점검 완료되는 대로 세입자들이 입주할 수 있을 것이다.

3

The new auditorium / will be opened / once the building inspection is complete.
새 강당은   개관될 것이다   건물 준공 검사가 완료되면
                                                        ↳ 일단 ~하면

(A) whether   (B) once

> **번역** 새 강당은 건물 준공 검사가 완료되면 개관할 것이다.

4

Center Financial / will consider / all applications, / provided they are received before May 15.
센터 파이낸셜은   검토할 것이다   모든 지원서를   만약 그것들이 5월 15일 전에 접수된다면
                                                                              ↳ 만약 ~한다면
(A) if not 그렇지 않다면   (B) provided 만약 ~한다면

> **번역** 센터 파이낸셜은 5월 15일 전에 접수된다면 모든 입사 지원서를 검토할 것이다.

5

Once seafood processors have cleaned the fish, / they / package / it / for sale.
해산물 가공업자들이 생선을 손질하면   그들은 / 포장한다   그것을 / 판매용으로
          ↳ 일단 ~하면
(A) Because   (B) Once

> **번역** 해산물 가공업자들이 생선을 손질하면 그것을 판매용으로 포장한다.

6

Durham Tax Partners / will be closed / for two days / while a new electrical system is installed.
더럼 택스 파트너즈는   문을 닫는다   이틀 동안   새로운 전기 시스템이 설치되는 동안
                                                                              ↳ ~하는 동안
(A) while   (B) that

> **번역** 더럼 택스 파트너즈는 새로운 전기 시스템이 설치되는 동안 이틀 간 문을 닫는다.

| 7 (B) | 8 (D) | 9 (D) | 10 (D) |

7

Mr. Gaber, / who dislikes air travel, / only attends / professional conferences / if they are held
가버 씨는　　　　비행기 여행을 싫어해서　　　　참석할 뿐이다　　직무 콘퍼런스에　　　　그것이 근처에서 열리는 경우에
만약 ~라면, ~일 경우에는 ←

nearby.

(A) or
(B) if
(C) still
(D) unless

해설 부사절 접속사 선택: 빈칸 뒤에 〈주어(they) + 동사(are held)〉가 있으므로, 빈칸에는 절을 이끌 수 있는 접속사가 들어가야 합니다. 문맥상 '근처에서 열릴 경우에 참석한다'라는 의미가 자연스러우므로 부사절 접속사 (B) if가 정답입니다.

번역 비행기 여행을 싫어하는 가버 씨는 직무 콘퍼런스가 근처에서 열릴 경우에만 참석한다.

8

As soon as you have calculated your travel expenses, / please inform / Ms. Murakami / by
당신이 여행 경비를 계산하자마자　　　　　　　　　　　　알려주세요　　무라카미 씨에게
→ ~하자마자

e-mail.
이메일로

(A) In addition to ~에 더하여
(B) As well as ~은 물론, 게다가
(C) In regard to ~에 관해서, ~에 대한
(D) As soon as ~하자마자

해설 부사절 접속사 선택: 빈칸 뒤에 〈주어(you) + 동사(have calculated)〉가 있으므로, 빈칸에는 절을 이끌 수 있는 접속사가 들어가야 하며, 접속사 (D) As soon as가 정답입니다. 전치사 (A) In addition to와 (C) In regard to 뒤에는 절이 올 수 없고 상관 접속사 (B) As well as는 문맥상 의미가 자연스럽지 않습니다.

번역 여행 경비를 계산하자마자 무라카미 씨에게 이메일로 알려주세요.

9

Customers / can write / a check / as long as they have two pieces of identification.
고객들은　　발행할 수 있다　수표를　　그들이 두 가지 신분증을 갖고 있는 한
→ ~하는 한

(A) in case of ~의 경우에
(B) providing for ~에 대비해
(C) together with ~와 함께
(D) as long as ~하는 한

해설 부사절 접속사 선택: 빈칸 뒤에 〈주어(they) + 동사(have)〉가 있으므로, 빈칸에는 절을 이끌 수 있는 접속사가 들어가야 합니다. 따라서 부사절 접속사 (D) as long as가 정답입니다.

번역 고객들은 신분증 두 가지를 가지고 있기만 하면 수표를 발행할 수 있다.

10

Personal information / will remain / confidential / unless permission is given / for it / to be
개인 정보는　　유지될 것이다　기밀로　　승인이 주어지지 않는다면　　그것이　공개되도록
→ ~이 아니라면

released.
공개되도록

(A) whether ~인지 아닌지
(B) as if 마치 ~인 것처럼
(C) except ~을 제외하고
(D) unless ~이 아니라면

해설 부사절 접속사 선택: 빈칸 뒤에 〈주어(permission) + 동사(is given)〉가 있으므로, 빈칸에는 절을 이끌 수 있는 접속사가 들어가야 합니다. 문맥상 '공개되는 것이 승인되지 않는다면 기밀로 유지될 것이다'라는 의미가 자연스러우므로 부사절 접속사 (D) unless가 정답입니다.

번역 개인 정보는 그것이 공개되어도 된다는 승인이 주어지지 않는다면 기밀로 유지될 것이다.

이유 / 대조 등을 나타내는 부사절 접속사 ETS 문제로 훈련하기 STEP 1

교재 p. 167

1 (B)	2 (B)	3 (A)	4 (A)	5 (A)	6 (B)

1

(Although) money has been budgeted / for the program, / the director / is reluctant / to proceed.
자금이 예산으로 잡혔지만 　　　　　프로그램을 위한　　　　책임자가　　　꺼린다　　　추진하기를
→ 부사절 접속사 선택

(A) Because of ~ 때문에　　　　　　(B) Although 비록 ~이지만

[번역] 프로그램을 위한 자금 예산이 세워졌음에도 불구하고, 책임자가 추진하기를 꺼리고 있다.

2

Suits / must be worn / in the office, / (while) casual dress is allowed in the workshop.
정장을　입어야 한다　사무실에서는　　워크숍에서는 편한 복장이 허용되는 반면에
→ ~인 반면 (대조)

(A) so that ~하도록　　　　　　　(B) while ~인 반면 (대조)

[번역] 워크숍에서는 편한 복장이 허용되지만 사무실에서는 정장을 입어야 한다.

3

Mr. Medina / was unable to speak with reporters / (as) his flight arrived late.
메디나 씨는　　기자들과 이야기를 할 수 없었다　　　비행기가 늦게 도착했기 때문에
→ ~이기 때문에 (이유)

(A) as ~이기 때문에 (이유)　　　(B) while ~인 반면 (대조)

[번역] 메디나 씨는 비행기가 연착하는 바람에 기자들과 이야기를 나눌 수 없었다.

4

(Since) I have changed offices, / I / wanted to update / my contact information.
제가 사무실을 바꾸었기 때문에　　제가 / 갱신하고 싶었습니다　제 연락처를
→ ~이기 때문에 (이유)

(A) Since ~이기 때문에 (이유)　　(B) After ~ 후에 (시간)

[번역] 제가 사무실을 옮겼기 때문에, 제 연락처를 갱신하고 싶었습니다.

5

Mobile phones / have become / (so) prevalent / (that) service / is available / even in remote areas.
휴대 전화가　　되었다　　매우 널리 보급되어　서비스가　　이용 가능하다　심지어 외딴 곳에서도
→ so ~ that... 매우 ~해서 …하다 (결과)

(A) so　　　　　　　　　　　(B) still

[번역] 휴대 전화가 매우 널리 보급되어서 외딴 곳에서도 서비스가 이용 가능하다.

6

Ms. Lim / will attend / the meeting / in person, / (whereas) Mr. Parker will attend remotely.
임 씨는　　참석할 것이다　회의에　　직접　　파커 씨는 원격으로 참석할 것이기 때문에
→ 부사절 접속사 선택

(A) moreover 게다가, 더욱이　　(B) whereas ~인데 반해, ~이지만

[번역] 임 씨는 회의에 직접 참석하지만, 파커 씨는 원격으로 참석할 것이다.

140

| 7 (D) | 8 (D) | 9 (D) | 10 (C) |

7

(Even though) Ms. Flores is not available / right now, / she / may be able to help / us / next week.
플로레스 씨가 시간을 낼 수 없지만   지금은   그녀는   도울 수 있을 것입니다   우리를 / 다음 주에는
    → 비록 ~이지만 (양보)

(A) Whenever ~할 때마다   (B) In order that ~하기 위해서

(C) Once 일단 ~하면   (D) Even though 비록 ~이지만

해설 부사절 접속사 선택: 콤마 앞의 부사절과 콤마 뒤의 주절이 '지금은 시간을 낼 수 없지만, 다음 주에는 우리를 도울 수 있을 것이다'라는 문맥상 서로 상반되는 내용을 나타내고 있으므로, 양보의 부사절 접속사 (D) Even though가 정답입니다.

번역 지금은 플로레스 씨가 시간을 낼 수 없지만, 다음 주에는 그녀가 우리를 도울 수 있을 것입니다.

8

Please update / your time sheets / by Friday / (so) we can process / your paycheck / in a timely
업데이트하십시오   여러분의 근무 시간표를   금요일까지   우리가 처리할 수 있도록   여러분의 급여를   제때에
                                    → so (that) ~하도록 (목적)

fashion.

(A) even   (B) also

(C) yet   (D) so

해설 부사절 접속사 선택: 빈칸 뒤에 〈주어(we) + 동사(can process)〉가 있으므로, 빈칸에는 절을 이끌 수 있는 접속사가 들어가야 합니다. 따라서 접속사 (D) so가 정답입니다. (A) even과 (B) also는 부사이고, (C) yet(그렇지만, 그런데도)은 접속사로 사용될 수 있지만 문맥상 자연스럽지 않습니다.

번역 우리가 여러분의 급여를 제때에 처리할 수 있도록 금요일까지 근무 시간표를 업데이트해주십시오.

9

Register / your new product / online / (so that) you will have access / to technical support
등록하세요   고객님의 새 제품을   온라인으로   고객님이 접속하시도록   기술 지원 정보에
                                  → ~하기 위해서 (목적)

information.

(A) rather 다소   (B) in case of ~의 경우에

(C) as to ~에 대해   (D) so that ~하도록

해설 부사절 접속사 선택: 빈칸 뒤에 〈주어(you) + 동사(will have)〉가 있으므로, 빈칸에는 절을 이끌 수 있는 접속사가 들어가야 합니다. 따라서 부사절 접속사 (D) so that이 정답입니다. (A) rather는 부사, (B) in case of와 (C) as to는 전치사입니다.

번역 기술 지원 정보에 접속하시도록 고객님의 새 제품을 온라인으로 등록하세요.

10

(Although) the meeting began late, / we were able to discuss / the entire agenda.
회의가 늦게 시작되었지만   우리는 논의할 수 있었다   모든 안건을
   → 부사절 접속사 선택

(A) Nevertheless 그럼에도 불구하고   (B) Still 여전히, 그럼에도

(C) Although 비록 ~이지만   (D) However 하지만

해설 부사절 접속사 선택: 빈칸 뒤에 〈주어(the meeting) + 동사(began)〉가 있으므로 빈칸에는 절을 이끌 수 있는 접속사가 들어가야 하므로 (C) Although가 정답입니다. (A) Nevertheless와 (B) Still은 의미는 비슷하지만 부사이며, (D) However도 '하지만'이라는 의미로 쓰일 때는 부사이므로 절을 이끌 수 없습니다.

번역 회의가 늦게 시작되었지만, 우리는 모든 안건을 논의할 수 있었다.

| 1 (B) | 2 (A) | 3 (A) | 4 (A) | 5 (A) | 6 (B) |

1

Mr. Ono / has / all the documents / that were passed out / (during) the presentation.
오노 씨는　　갖고 있다 / 서류 전부를　　　　배부된　　　　　　발표 중에
　　　　　　　　　　　　　　　　　　　　　　　　　　　→ during + 명사(구): ~ 동안

(A) while　　　　　　　　　　　(B) during

번역　오노 씨는 발표 중에 배부된 서류 전부를 갖고 있다.

2

(Despite) budget constraints, / all employees / will receive / a salary increase.
예산상의 제약에도 불구하고　　　　　　직원들은 모두　　받게 될 것이다　　임금 인상을
　　　　　→ ~에도 불구하고

(A) Despite　　　　　　　　　　(B) When

번역　예산상의 제약에도 불구하고 직원들은 모두 임금 인상을 받게 될 것이다.

3

(Until) the new product is complete, / Dr. Seong's team / will work overtime.
신제품이 완성될 때까지　　　　　　　　　　성 박사의 팀은　　　초과 근무를 할 것이다
　　　→ until + 주어 + 동사: ~할 때까지 (시간)

(A) Until　　　　　　　　　　　(B) During

번역　신제품이 완성될 때까지 성 박사의 팀은 초과 근무를 할 것이다.

4

The younger staff / look up to / Ms. Itoh / (because of) her years of experience / in the field.
젊은 직원들은　　　　　존경한다　　　이토 씨를　　그녀의 다년간의 경험 때문에　　　　　그 분야에서의
　　　　　　　　　　　　　　　　　　　　　　　　→ because of + 명사(구): ~ 때문에

(A) because of　　　　　　　　(B) because

번역　젊은 직원들은 이토 씨를 존경하는데, 이는 그녀가 그 분야에서 다년간의 경험을 갖고 있기 때문이다.

5

(Even if) sales figures are strong, / we / still expect / to see a decline in profits / for the year.
매출액이 견고하긴 하지만　　　　　　　　우리는 여전히 예상한다　　수익 하락을 보게 될 것을　　　금년에
　　　　　→ even if + 주어 + 동사: 비록 ~이긴 하지만

(A) Even if　　　　　　　　　　(B) In spite of

번역　매출액이 견고하기는 하지만, 우리는 여전히 금년에 수익 하락을 보게 될 것으로 예상하고 있다.

6

(After) Ms. Kinder finishes her graduate degree, / she / will look for / a job.
킨더 씨는 석사 학위를 마친 후에　　　　　　　　　　그녀는　구할 것이다　　일자리를
　　　→ after + 주어 + 동사: ~한 후에 (시간)

(A) Due to　　　　　　　　　　(B) After

번역　킨더 씨는 석사 학위를 마친 후에 일자리를 구할 것이다.

PART 5 | UNIT 13

7 (B)	**8** (A)	**9** (D)	**10** (B)

7

The committee meeting / was moved / (because of) a problem / with the heating system.
위원회 회의가 변경되었다 문제 때문에 난방 시스템의
→ because of + 명사(구): ~ 때문에

(A) provided that 만약 ~이라면   (B) because of ~ 때문에

(C) throughout ~ 동안 내내   (D) even though 비록 ~일지라도

해설 알맞은 의미의 구전치사 선택: 빈칸 뒤 명사구 a problem with the heating system을 목적어로 취하는 전치사 자리로, 빈칸을 포함한 전치사구는 동사구 was moved를 수식합니다. 문맥상 '난방 시스템 문제 때문에'라는 의미가 자연스러우므로, 구전치사 (B) because of가 정답입니다. 접속사 (A) provided that과 (D) even though는 명사(구)를 목적어로 취하지 않고, 전치사 (C) throughout은 문맥상 적절하지 않습니다.

번역 난방 시스템 문제 때문에 위원회 회의가 변경되었다.

8

The office / will be closing / at 3 P.M. / on Friday / (due to) the holiday weekend.
사무실은 문을 닫을 예정이다 오후 3시에 금요일 연휴가 낀 주말이라서
→ due to + 명사(구): ~ 때문에

(A) due to ~ 때문에   (B) while ~하는 동안

(C) since ~ 이래로   (D) as if 마치 ~인 것처럼

해설 부사절 접속사와 전치사 구별: 빈칸은 명사(구)를 목적어로 취하는 전치사 자리로 문맥상 '연휴가 낀 주말이기 때문에'라는 의미가 자연스러우므로, (A) due to가 정답입니다. (C) since는 '~ 이래로'라는 의미의 경우 전치사와 접속사로 쓰이지만, '~ 때문에'라는 의미의 경우 접속사로만 쓰이므로 적절하지 않습니다.

번역 연휴가 낀 주말이라서 사무실은 금요일 오후 3시에 문을 닫을 예정이다.

9

(Now that) the weather is getting cooler, / it is important / to keep / doors / shut / in order to
날씨가 점점 더 서늘해지고 있으므로 중요하다 유지하는 것이 문들을 닫힌 상태로 에너지를 절약하기 위해
→ now that + 주어 + 동사: ~이니까
conserve energy.
에너지를 절약하기 위해

(A) However 하지만   (B) Whatever ~하는 것은 무엇이든지

(C) Because of ~ 때문에   (D) Now that ~이니까

해설 부사절 접속사 선택: 빈칸 뒤에 〈주어(the weather) + 동사(is getting)〉가 있으므로, 빈칸에는 접속사가 들어가야 합니다. 문맥상 '날씨가 점점 더 서늘해지고 있으므로, ~ 문들을 닫아 두는 것이 중요하다'라는 의미가 자연스러우므로 부사절 접속사 (D) Now that이 정답입니다. (C) Because of는 전치사구로, 절을 이끌 수 없습니다.

번역 날씨가 점점 더 서늘해 지고 있으므로, 에너지를 절약하기 위해 문들을 닫아 두는 것이 중요하다.

10

(After) arriving / at the airline terminal, / Ms. Ortiz / learned / that her flight was delayed.
도착한 후에 공항 터미널에 오티즈 씨는 알았다 자신의 항공편이 지연된다는 것을
→ 뒤에 동명사 arriving을 목적어로 취한 전치사

(A) Because   (B) After

(C) Now that   (D) Even if

해설 전치사 + 동명사: (A)~(D)는 모두 접속사로 쓸 수 있는데 (B) After는 전치사로도 쓸 수 있습니다. 빈칸은 동명사 arriving을 목적어로 취하는 전치사 자리이고, '도착한 후에'라는 의미가 자연스러우므로 (B) After가 정답입니다.

번역 공항 터미널에 도착한 후에 오티즈 씨는 자신의 항공편이 지연된다는 것을 알았다.

1 (B)	**2** (A)	**3** (B)	**4** (B)

1

The elevators in the north wing / will be closed / (temporarily) / for maintenance / next week.
북쪽 동의 엘리베이터들은   폐쇄될 것이다   임시로   정비 작업을 위해   다음 주에
                                                              └→ 임시로

(A) annually 일년에 한 번, 해마다   (B) temporarily 임시로

번역 북쪽 동의 엘리베이터들은 다음 주에 정비 작업을 위해 임시 폐쇄될 것이다.

2

The number of prizes / is (strictly) limited; / only a few / will receive / the recognition.
상의 개수는   엄격히 제한되어 있어서   단지 몇 명만   받을 것이다   그 표창을
                                                  └→ 엄격히

(A) strictly 엄격히   (B) tensely 긴장하여, 팽팽히

번역 상의 개수는 엄격히 제한되어 있어서 단지 몇 명만 그 표창을 받을 것이다.

3

Ensure that all office-related expenditures are recorded / (accurately) in the database.
반드시 모든 사무 관련 비용이 기록되도록 하세요   정확히 데이터베이스에
                                                        └→ 정확히

(A) rightly 당연히, 마땅히   (B) accurately 정확히

번역 반드시 모든 사무 관련 비용이 데이터베이스에 정확히 기록되도록 하세요.

4

The new computer / has been (widely) advertised, / but demand for it / is still low.
새 컴퓨터는   널리 광고되었다   그러나 그것에 대한 수요는   여전히 낮다
                                 └→ 널리, 크게

(A) sharply 급격히   (B) widely 널리, 크게

번역 새 컴퓨터는 널리 광고되었지만 그 수요는 여전히 낮다.

| 5 (A) | 6 (B) | 7 (A) | 8 (A) |

5

The contents of the packages / are perishable / so they must be delivered / (promptly).
그 소포의 내용물은　　　　　　　　상하기 쉽다　　　따라서 그것은 배달되어야 한다　　신속히
　　　└→ 신속히

(A) promptly 신속히　　　　　　　　　　　(B) specifically 분명히, 구체적으로

(C) extensively 광범위하게　　　　　　　　(D) objectively 객관적으로

해설 promptly 신속히: 문맥상 소포의 내용물이 상하기 쉽다면 '신속하게' 배달되어야 할 것입니다. 따라서 '신속히'라는 뜻의 부사 (A) promptly가 정답입니다.

번역 그 소포의 내용물은 잘 상하므로 신속히 배달되어야 한다.

6

In order to accommodate / the dramatic increase / in traffic, / a new bridge / is needed /
수용하기 위해서　　　　　　　급격한 증가를　　　　　　교통량의　　새로운 다리가　　필요하다

(immediately).
즉시
　└→ 즉시

(A) broadly 대략　　　　　　　　　　　　(B) immediately 즉시

(C) easily 쉽게　　　　　　　　　　　　　(D) professionally 직업적으로

해설 immediately 즉시: 문맥상 갑자기 늘어난 교통량을 수용하려면 새로운 다리가 '즉시' 필요할 것입니다. 따라서 '즉시, 곧바로'라는 의미의 (B) immediately가 정답입니다.

번역 급격히 증가한 교통량을 수용하기 위해서, 새로운 다리가 즉시 필요하다.

7

Mr. Sosa, / the area manager, / visits / all the offices / under his management / (regularly).
소사 씨는　　　그 지역 담당자인　　　방문한다　모든 사무소를　　자신이 관리하는　　　　정기적으로
　　　└→ 정기적으로

(A) regularly 정기적으로　　　　　　　　(B) widely 널리

(C) recently 최근에　　　　　　　　　　　(D) brightly 밝게

해설 regularly 정기적으로: 빈칸이 수식하는 현재 시제 동사 visits와 가장 잘 어울리는 부사를 선택해야 합니다. 지역 담당자로서 '정기적으로 방문한다'라는 의미가 문맥상 자연스러우므로, '정기적으로, 규칙적으로'라는 의미의 부사 (A) regularly가 정답입니다. '최근에'라는 의미의 부사 (C) recently는 과거 또는 현재완료 시제 동사와 어울려 쓰입니다.

번역 그 지역 담당자인 소사 씨는 자신이 관리하는 모든 사무소를 정기적으로 방문한다.

8

Read / the safety procedures / (carefully) / before operating the machine / for the first time.
읽으세요　안전 절차를　　　　　　주의 깊게　　기계를 가동하기 전에　　　　　　　　처음으로
　　　　　　　　　　　　　　　　　　　　　　└→ 주의 깊게, 신중하게

(A) carefully 주의 깊게　　　　　　　　　(B) harmlessly 해롭지 않게

(C) extremely 극히　　　　　　　　　　　(D) hardly 거의 ~ 아니다

해설 carefully 주의 깊게, 신중하게: 빈칸은 명령문 Read the safety procedures를 뒤에서 수식하는 부사 자리입니다. 문맥상 '안전 절차를 주의 깊게 읽으세요'라는 의미가 자연스러우므로, (A) carefully가 정답입니다.

번역 처음으로 기계를 가동하기 전에 안전 절차를 주의 깊게 읽으세요.

1

Tourism / has flourished / in South Joree / (as) the world has learned more / about its beautiful
관광업이   번창했다   사우스 조리에서   세계가 더 많이 알게 되면서   그곳의 아름다운 해변들에 대해

beaches.
→ 부사절 접속사: ~ 때문에, ~하면서

(A) still   (B) as   (C) rather   (D) than

해설 **부사절 접속사:** 빈칸 앞뒤로 주어와 동사를 갖춘 절이 있으므로 빈칸에는 접속사가 필요합니다. 따라서 부사 또는 형용사인 (A) still, 부사인 (C) rather는 정답에서 제외됩니다. 빈칸 뒤가 주절(관광업 번창)에 대한 이유(해변의 아름다움을 세계가 알게 된 것)를 밝히고 있으므로 정답은 이유나 동시성을 나타내는 접속사인 (B) as입니다. (D) than은 '~보다, ~할 바에는 차라리'의 의미로 정답이 될 수 없습니다.

번역 세계가 그곳의 아름다운 해변들에 대해 더 많이 알게 되면서 사우스 조리에서 관광업이 번창했다.

2

The client / canceled / her order / (because) the coffee table she wanted was no longer available.
그 고객은   취소했다   주문을   그녀가 원했던 커피 테이블을 더 이상 구할 수 없었기 때문에
→ 부사절 접속사: ~ 때문에

(A) because ~이기 때문에   (B) however 그러나   (C) for example 예를 들면   (D) as a result 결과적으로

해설 **부사절 접속사 선택:** 빈칸 뒤에 〈주어(the coffee table ~) + 동사(was)〉의 절이 있으므로 빈칸에는 접속사가 들어가야 하는데, 문맥상 '더 이상 구할 수 없어서 취소했다'가 자연스러우므로 부사절 접속사 (A) because가 정답입니다.

번역 그 고객은 자신이 원했던 커피 테이블을 더 이상 구할 수 없어서 주문을 취소했다.

3

(After) the success of his restaurant, / chef Sook Yong / wrote / a best-selling cookbook.
레스토랑의 성공 이후,   숙용 셰프는   집필했다   베스트셀러 요리책을
→ 뒤에 명사구를 목적어로 취하는 전치사

(A) Because   (B) When   (C) After   (D) Already

해설 **전치사 + 명사구:** 빈칸 뒤 명사구 the success of his restaurant를 목적어로 취하는 전치사 자리이므로 전치사 (C) After가 정답입니다. (A) Because와 (B) When은 접속사이고, (D) Already는 부사이므로 오답입니다.

번역 레스토랑 성공 이후, 숙용 셰프는 베스트셀러 요리책을 집필했다.

4

(Before) new employees can begin working, / contracts / must be signed.
신입 직원들이 근무를 시작할 수 있기 전에,   계약서가   서명되어야 한다
→ 부사절 접속사: ~ 전에

(A) Without   (B) Before   (C) Until   (D) Except

해설 **부사절 접속사 선택:** 빈칸 뒤에 〈주어(new employees) + 동사(can begin)〉가 있으므로, 접속사가 필요한 자리입니다. '신입 직원들은 근무 시작 전에 서명하라'는 문맥이 자연스러우므로, 부사절 접속사인 (B) Before가 정답입니다.

번역 신입 직원들은 근무를 시작할 수 있기 전에 계약서에 서명해야 한다.

5

(While) admission to the violin recital is free, / we / welcome / donations of any amount.
바이올린 리사이틀 입장료는 무료이지만   우리는   환영한다   기부금은 얼마이든
→ 부사절 접속사: ~이긴 하지만

(A) Despite   (B) Except   (C) While   (D) Equally

해설 **부사절 접속사 선택:** 빈칸 뒤에 〈주어(admission to the violin recital) + 동사(is)〉가 있으므로, 접속사가 필요한 자리입니다. 따라서 부사절 접속사 (C) While이 정답입니다. (A) Despite과 (B) Except는 전치사, (D) Equally는 부사입니다.

번역 바이올린 리사이틀 입장료는 무료이지만 기부금은 얼마이든 환영한다.

ETS 실전 테스트

교재 p.172

6 (B)	7 (A)	8 (A)	9 (B)	10 (D)

6

The automobile title transfer / will not be official / (until) signed by the seller and buyer.
자동차 명의 변경은 　　　　　　　　　　공식적이 되지 않을 것이다 　　　파는 사람과 사는 사람에 의해 서명이 될 때까지
　　　　　　　　　　　　　　　　　　　　　　　　　　　　　　→ 부사절 접속사: ~ 때까지

(A) without　(B) until　(C) between　(D) against

해설 　부사절 접속사 선택: 빈칸 뒤에 과거분사 signed가 있으므로, 전치사 (A) without, (C) between, (D) against는 빈칸에 들어갈 수 없습니다. 과거분사 signed 앞에는 〈주어(it) + 동사(is)〉가 생략되어 있으므로, 부사절 접속사 (B) until이 정답입니다.

번역 　자동차 명의 변경은 파는 사람과 사는 사람에 의해 서명이 되고 나서야 공식화된다.

7

(Once) you have registered with Select Software, / you will receive / a customer identification
일단 셀렉트 소프트웨어에 등록하시면 　　　　　　　　　　　당신은 받게 될 것입니다 　고객 고유 번호를
　 → 부사절 접속사: 일단 ~하면
number.

(A) Once 일단 ~하면　(B) Soon 곧　(C) As well 또한　(D) Next 다음의

해설 　부사절 접속사 선택: 빈칸 뒤에 〈주어(you) + 동사(have registered)〉의 완전한 절이 있으므로, 빈칸에는 완전한 절을 이끌 수 있는 접속사가 들어가야 합니다. 따라서 '일단 ~하면'이라는 의미의 부사절 접속사 (A) Once가 정답입니다.

번역 　일단 셀렉트 소프트웨어에 등록하시면, 고객 고유 번호를 받게 될 것입니다.

8

Werlin Paper / will not add / a new product line / this fiscal year / (as) this would require hiring
월린 제지는 　　추가하지 않을 예정이다 / 신제품군을 　　　이번 회계 연도에 　　이것은 직원을 더 고용하는 것을 필요로 할 것이기
　　　　　　　　　　　　　　　　　　　　　　　　　　　　　　　　　　　→ 부사절 접속사: ~때문에
more staff.
때문에

(A) as　(B) which　(C) until　(D) but

해설 　부사절 접속사 선택: 빈칸 뒤에 〈주어(this) + 동사(would require)〉가 있으므로, 접속사가 필요한 자리입니다. 문맥상 빈칸 뒤에 있는 문장이 빈칸 앞에 있는 문장의 이유가 되므로, (A) as가 정답입니다.

번역 　월린 제지는 이번 회계 연도에 신제품군을 추가하지 않을 예정인데, 이렇게 하려면 직원을 더 고용하는 것이 필요하기 때문이다.

9

The museum / is closed / to the public / (while) the heating system is being renovated.
그 박물관은 　　개방되지 않는다 / 일반인에게 　　난방 설비가 보수되는 동안
　　　　　　　　　　　　　　　　　　　　　　　　→ 부사절 접속사: ~하는 동안

(A) during　(B) while　(C) after　(D) along

해설 　부사절 접속사 선택: 빈칸 뒤에 〈주어(the heating system) + 동사(is being renovated)〉가 있으므로, 빈칸에는 접속사가 들어가야 합니다. 문맥상 '난방 설비를 보수하는 동안 개방되지 않는다'라는 의미가 자연스러우므로 부사절 접속사 (B) while이 정답입니다. (C) after 또한 부사절 접속사로 쓰일 수 있지만, '~ 후에'라는 의미로 문맥상 적절하지 않습니다.

번역 　그 박물관은 난방 설비를 보수하는 동안 일반인에게 개방되지 않는다.

10

Stonefair Park / will close / early this Friday / (so that) park workers can begin / setting up the art
스톤페어 파크는 　　문을 닫을 것이다 / 이번 주 금요일에 일찍 　공원 직원들이 시작할 수 있도록 　　　예술 축제 준비를
　　　　　　　　　　　　　　　　　　　　　　　　　→ 부사절 접속사: ~하도록
festival.

(A) for example 예를 들면　(B) as if 마치 ~인 것처럼　(C) even though 비록 ~일지라도　(D) so that ~하도록

해설 　부사절 접속사 선택: 빈칸 뒤에 〈주어(park workers) + 동사(can begin)〉의 절이 있으므로, 빈칸에는 접속사가 들어가야 합니다. 문맥상 '공원 직원들이 예술 축제 준비를 시작할 수 있도록'이라는 의미가 자연스러우므로 접속사 (D) so that이 정답입니다.

번역 　스톤페어 파크는 공원 직원들이 예술 축제 준비를 시작할 수 있도록 이번 주 금요일에 일찍 문을 닫을 것이다.

| 11 (C) | 12 (B) | 13 (D) | 14 (A) |

Questions 11-14 refer to the following memo.

To: All Kirbling Sales Associates
From: Tania Chow
Date: April 15
Re: Summer sales promotion

I want to remind all of you / of the upcoming summer promotion / at our
여러분 모두에게 다시 한 번 알려드립니다   다가오는 여름 판촉에 대해   우리 매장에서의

store. To celebrate the summer 11. season, / we are offering special
여름 시즌을 기념하기 위해   우리는 특별 할인을 제공하려고 합니다

discounts / on outdoor grills, garden supplies, and patio furniture. This
                  야외용 그릴, 정원 용품과 테라스 가구에   사흘 동안

three-day promotion / 12. (will begin) on May 20. 13. (Even though) we plan /
진행되는 이번 판촉은   5월 20일에 시작됩니다   계획이지만   → 부사절 접속사
                              → 미래 시점의 일을 나타내는 미래 시제

to promote the event / with signs and newspaper advertisements, / we will
행사를 홍보할   표지판과 신문 광고로   여전히

still need / word-of-mouth advertising by you / to generate interest / among
필요합니다   여러분의 입소문 광고가   관심을 불러일으키려면   고객들

our customers. 14. Please mention the sale / to your customers / before
사이에서   세일을 언급해주세요   고객에게   고객이

they leave the store. As always, / I appreciate / your outstanding work and
매장을 떠나기 전에   언제나 그렇듯이   감사드립니다   여러분의 뛰어난 노력과 헌신에

dedication!

11-14 회람

수신: 모든 커블링 판매 직원
발신: 타니아 차우
날짜: 4월 15일
Re: 여름 판촉

다가오는 우리 매장 여름 판촉에 대해 여러분 모두에게 다시 한 번 알려드립니다. 여름 시즌을 기념하기 위해, 야외용 그릴, 정원 용품, 테라스 가구에 특별 할인을 제공하려고 합니다. 사흘 동안 진행되는 이번 판촉은 5월 20일에 시작됩니다. 표지판과 신문 광고로 행사를 홍보할 계획이지만, 고객들의 관심을 불러일으키려면 여전히 여러분의 입소문 광고가 필요합니다. 고객이 매장을 떠나기 전에 세일을 언급해주세요. 언제나 그렇듯이, 여러분의 뛰어난 노력과 헌신에 감사드립니다!

11 (A) success
(B) release
(C) season
(D) completion

(A) 성공
(B) 출시
(C) 시즌
(D) 완료

해설 어휘 문제: 빈칸 앞 명사 summer와 어울려 쓰이는 명사를 선택해야 합니다. 문맥상 야외 용품을 특가로 제공하는 이유가 '여름 시즌을 기념하기 위해서'라는 것이 문맥상 자연스러우므로, (C) season이 정답입니다.

12 (A) begin
(B) will begin
(C) began
(D) beginning

해설 미래 시점과 어울리는 미래 시제: 빈칸은 주어 This three-day promotion 뒤에 나오는 동사 자리입니다. 회람 작성일이 4월 15일인데 빈칸 뒤에 on May 20(5월 20일에)라고 되어 있으므로 미래 시제 (B) will begin이 정답입니다. 현재 시제 동사 (A) begin은 앞에 나오는 단수 주어 This three-day promotion과 수가 일치하지 않습니다.

13 (A) In summary
(B) Whether
(C) In case
(D) Even though

(A) 요약하면
(B) ~이든 아니든
(C) (~할) 경우에 대비해서
(D) 비록 ~일지라도

해설 부사절 접속사 선택: 빈칸 뒤에 〈주어(we) + 동사(plan)〉가 있으므로 접속사가 필요한 자리입니다. '표지판과 신문 광고로 행사를 홍보할 계획이지만, 여전히 여러분의 입소문 광고가 필요하다'라는 문맥이 자연스러우므로, 양보의 부사절 접속사인 (D) Even though가 정답입니다.

14 (A) Please mention the sale to your customers before they leave the store.
(B) If you are interested in sales, we are now hiring for our busy summer period.
(C) Our new patio furniture features a modern design.
(D) Prices will be increasing, so make your purchases now!

(A) 고객이 매장을 떠나기 전에 세일을 언급해주세요.
(B) 판매에 관심이 있으시다면 여름 성수기를 맞아 지금 채용을 진행하고 있습니다.
(C) 새 테라스 가구는 현대적인 디자인이 특징입니다.
(D) 가격이 오를 예정이니 지금 구매하세요!

해설 문장 고르기: 빈칸 앞에서 여러분의 입소문 광고가 필요하다고 했고, 수신인은 All Kirbling Sales Associates(모든 커블링 판매 직원)로 되어 있습니다. 따라서 빈칸에는 판매 직원들이 입소문 광고를 하는 내용이 들어가는 것이 문맥상 자연스러우며, 선택지 (A)의 mention the sale to your customers가 판매 직원들이 하는 입소문 광고에 해당하므로 정답은 (A)입니다.

주격 관계대명사 ETS 문제로 훈련하기 STEP 1

교재 p.177

1 (A)	2 (A)	3 (A)	4 (B)	5 (B)	6 (A)

1

This report / includes / (a chart / which) summarizes / the company's profits.
이 보고서는 　　포함한다　　차트를　　요약하는　　　　　　　회사 수익을
　　　　　　　　　　　　　　　　　└→ 사물 선행사(a chart) + 주격 관계대명사 which

(A) which　　　　　　　　　　　　(B) who

번역 이 보고서는 회사 수익을 요약하는 차트를 포함한다.

2

Sun Airlines / offers / special discounts / (to customers / who) fly / more than once a month.
선 항공은　　　제공한다　특별 할인을　　　고객에게　　　비행하는　　　한 달에 1회 이상
　　　　　　　　　　　　　　　　　　　　└→ 사람 선행사(customers) + 주격 관계대명사 who

(A) who　　　　　　　　　　　　(B) which

번역 선 항공은 한 달에 1회 이상 비행하는 고객에게 특별 할인을 제공한다.

3

Please confirm / receipt of (the signed invoice / that) was included / in our recent shipment.
확인해 주십시오　서명한 송장을 수령했는지　　　　포함된　　　최근 배송품에
　　　　　　　　　　　　　　　　　　└→ 사물 선행사(the signed invoice) + 주격 관계대명사 that

(A) that　　　　　　　　　　　　(B) any

번역 최근 배송품에 포함된 서명한 송장을 수령했는지 확인해 주십시오.

4

Employees / (interested) / in joining company sports teams / should contact / Meredith Lo / by May 1.
직원들은　　　관심 있는　　사내 스포츠 팀 가입에　　　　　　연락해야 한다　　메러디스 로에게　5월 1일까지
　　　　　　└→ 앞에 〈주격 관계대명사 + be동사〉 생략

(A) interest　　　　　　　　　　(B) interested

번역 사내 스포츠 팀 가입에 관심 있는 직원들은 5월 1일까지 메러디스 로에게 연락해야 한다.

5

Those employees / (working) in an assembly area / must wear / protective gear / at all times.
직원들은　　　　조립 구역에서 근무하는　　　착용해야 한다　보호 장비를　　　항상
　　　　　　　　　　　　　　　　　　　　└→ 앞에 〈주격 관계대명사 + be동사〉 생략

(A) are working　　　　　　　　(B) working

번역 조립 구역에서 근무하는 직원들은 항상 보호 장비를 착용해야 한다.

6

Studio Ceramics Monthly / does not accept / (manuscripts / that) have previously appeared /
〈월간 스튜디오 세라믹스〉는　　　받지 않습니다　　　원고를　　　이전에 나온 적이 있는
　　　　　　　　　　　　　　　　　　　　　└→ 사물 선행사(manuscripts) + 주격 관계대명사 that

in print.
출판되어

(A) that　　　　　　　　　　　　(B) they

번역 〈월간 스튜디오 세라믹스〉는 이전에 출판되어 나온 적이 있는 원고는 받지 않습니다.

7 (D)	8 (A)	9 (C)	10 (D)

7

I would like to thank (Dr. Frank, / who) has agreed / to deliver an address / at the ceremony.
프랭크 박사님에게 감사하고 싶습니다　　　승낙해주신　　　연설을 하는 것을　　　기념식에서
→ 사람 선행사(Dr. Frank) + 주격 관계대명사 who

(A) anyone　　　　　　　　(B) whose
(C) whichever　　　　　　　(D) who

해설 주격 관계대명사: 빈칸 뒤에 동사 has agreed가 있으므로, 빈칸에는 접속사가 들어가야 합니다. 빈칸이 이끄는 절은 앞에 있는 사람 명사 Dr. Frank를 수식하는 역할을 하므로 사람 명사 Dr. Frank를 대신하여 동사 has agreed의 주어 역할을 하는 주격 관계대명사 (D) who가 정답입니다.

번역 기념식에서 연설하는 것을 승낙해주신 프랭크 박사님에게 감사하고 싶습니다.

8

The company's financial advisor / recommended / (an investment / that) rose steadily / in value.
회사의 재정 고문은　　　　　추천했다　　　투자처를　　　꾸준히 상승한　　가치가
→ 사물 선행사(an investment) + 주격 관계대명사 that

(A) that　　　　　　　　(B) they
(C) what　　　　　　　　(D) when

해설 주격 관계대명사: 빈칸 뒤에 동사 rose가 있으므로, 빈칸에는 접속사가 들어가야 합니다. 빈칸이 이끄는 절은 앞에 있는 사물 명사 an investment를 수식합니다. 따라서 an investment를 대신하여 동사 rose의 주어 역할을 하는 주격 관계대명사 (A) that이 정답입니다.

번역 회사의 재정 고문은 꾸준히 가치가 상승한 투자처를 추천했다.

9

The marketing department / has announced / (a new incentive bonus program / which) will begin /
마케팅부는　　　　　　발표했다　　　새로운 장려금 프로그램을　　　　시작되는
next week.
다음 주에　　사물 선행사(a new incentive bonus program) + 주격 관계대명사 which ←

(A) when　　　　　　　　(B) such
(C) which　　　　　　　　(D) until

해설 주격 관계대명사: 빈칸 뒤에 동사가 이어지고 있고 문맥상 '다음 주에 시작되는 장려금 프로그램'이 자연스러우므로 빈칸에는 관계대명사(주격)가 필요합니다. 선행사가 사물(a new incentive bonus program)이므로 정답은 주격 관계대명사 (C) which 입니다.

번역 마케팅부에서는 다음 주에 시작되는 새로운 장려금 프로그램을 발표했다.

10

Employees / should complete / their expense reports / by using (the template / that) was sent
직원들은　　　작성해야 한다　　지출 품의서를　　　템플릿을 사용해　　　보내진
out / by Ms. Chu / last week.
추 씨에 의해　　지난주에　　사물 선행사(the template) + 주격 관계대명사 that ←

(A) whose　　　　　　　(B) maybe
(C) next　　　　　　　　(D) that

해설 주격 관계대명사: 빈칸 뒤에 동사 was sent가 있으므로, 빈칸에는 접속사가 들어가야 합니다. 빈칸이 이끄는 절은 앞에 있는 사물 명사 the template을 수식하므로 사물 명사 template을 대신하여 동사 was sent의 주어 역할을 하는 주격 관계대명사 (D) that이 정답입니다.

번역 직원들은 지난주 추 씨가 보내준 템플릿을 사용해 지출 품의서를 작성해야 한다.

● 목적격과 소유격 관계대명사 ETS 문제로 훈련하기 STEP 1

1 (B)	2 (A)	3 (B)	4 (A)	5 (B)	6 (B)

1

Refunds / will be given / to (all customers / whose) orders / are damaged / in shipping.
환불이   주어질 것이다   모든 고객에게   주문품이   파손된   배송 중에

(A) which   (B) whose
→ 사람 선행사(all customers) + 소유격 관계대명사 whose

번역 배송 중에 주문품이 파손된 모든 고객에게 환불을 해줄 것이다.

2

(The applicant / that) the professor recommended / will come / for an interview / soon.
지원자가   그 교수가 추천한   올 것이다   면접을 보러   곧
→ 사람 선행사(The applicant) + 목적격 관계대명사 that

(A) that   (B) when

번역 그 교수가 추천한 지원자가 곧 면접을 보러 올 것이다.

3

Metropolitan Artworks is (an organization / whose) mission / is to support public art projects.
메트로폴리탄 아트웍스는 단체이다   임무가   공공 미술 프로젝트를 지원하는 것인

(A) which   (B) whose
→ 사물 선행사(an organization) + 소유격 관계대명사 whose

번역 메트로폴리탄 아트웍스는 임무가 공공 미술 프로젝트를 지원하는 것이 임무인 단체이다.

4

The book / (you) ordered yesterday / will be delivered / tomorrow morning.
책은   귀하가 어제 주문한   배송될 것입니다   내일 오전에
→ 앞에 목적격 관계대명사 생략

(A) you   (B) your

번역 귀하가 어제 주문한 책은 내일 오전에 배송될 것입니다.

5

Akira Tsukada's (novel, / whose) title hasn't been finalized yet, / will be released / next year.
아키라 츠카다 씨의 소설은   제목이 아직 확정되지 않은   출간될 것이다   내년에
→ 사물 선행사(novel) + 소유격 관계대명사 whose

(A) which   (B) whose

번역 제목이 아직 확정되지 않은 아키라 츠카다 씨의 소설은 내년에 출간될 것이다.

6

The agenda / you received yesterday / outlines / several topics / (I) plan to discuss.
안건은   어제 받으신   대략적으로 보여줍니다   몇 가지 주제를   제가 논의할 계획인
→ 앞에 목적격 관계대명사 생략

(A) my   (B) I

번역 어제 받으신 안건은 제가 논의할 계획인 몇 가지 주제를 대략적으로 보여줍니다.

| 7 (C) | 8 (B) | 9 (A) | 10 (A) |

7

Employers / prefer / to interview (candidates / whose) résumés / are well written and clearly
고용주들은   선호한다   지원자들과 면접하는 것을   이력서가   잘 쓰여 있고 명확하게 정리된
└→ 사람 선행사(candidates) + 소유격 관계대명사 whose

organized.

(A) that   (B) than

(C) whose   (D) which

해설 소유격 관계대명사: 빈칸 뒤에 be동사 are가 있으므로, 빈칸에는 접속사가 들어가야 합니다. 빈칸이 이끄는 절은 명사 candidates를 뒤에서 수식하므로, 관계사절입니다. 명사 candidates와 résumés는 '지원자의 이력서'라는 소유 관계가 자연스러우므로, 소유격 관계대명사 (C) whose가 정답입니다.

번역 고용주들은 이력서가 잘 쓰여 있고 명확하게 정리된 지원자들과 면접하는 것을 선호한다.

8

Attached / please find / (the notes) / from last week's budgeting seminar / (that) you requested.
첨부하니   확인 부탁드립니다   메모를   지난주 예산 편성 세미나에서의   귀하가 요청하신
└→ 사물 선행사(the notes) + 목적격 관계대명사 that

(A) then   (B) that

(C) what   (D) when

해설 목적격 관계대명사: 빈칸 뒤에 목적어가 없는 불완전한 절이 있으므로, 빈칸에는 관계대명사가 들어가야 합니다. 빈칸이 이끄는 절은 앞에 있는 사물 명사 the notes를 수식하므로 the notes를 대신하여 동사 requested의 목적어 역할을 하는 목적격 관계대명사 (B) that이 정답입니다. 참고로 이 문장은 5형식 동사 find가 the notes ~ you requested를 목적어로 취하고 있고, 목적격 보어인 attached가 문장 앞으로 도치된 형태입니다.

번역 귀하가 요청하신 지난주 예산 편성 세미나의 메모를 첨부하니 확인 부탁드립니다.

9

Skytown Airlines / apologized to the passengers / for the delays / (they) experienced.
스카이타운 항공사는   승객들에게 사과했다   지연에 대해   그들이 겪은
└→ 앞에 목적격 관계대명사 생략

(A) they   (B) their

(C) them   (D) this

해설 목적격 관계대명사 생략: 문맥상 the delays는 빈칸 뒤 동사 experienced의 목적어이므로 delays와 빈칸 사이에 목적격 관계대명사가 생략된 구조이고 승객들(the passengers)이 지연을 겪었다는 말이므로, 주격 인칭대명사 (A) they가 정답입니다.

번역 스카이타운 항공사는 승객들에게 그들이 겪은 지연에 대해 사과했다.

10

Michael Sanders and Olivia Lim, / (the artists / whose) paintings / are currently on display / at the
마이클 샌더스와 올리비아 림은   미술가들인   자신들의 그림이   현재 전시되고 있는   빌래뉴바
└→ 사람 선행사(the artists) + 소유격 관계대명사 whose

Villanueva Gallery, / both / attended / Fenmoor University.
갤러리에   모두   다녔다   펜무어 대학교에

(A) whose   (B) who

(C) their   (D) they

해설 소유격 관계대명사: 빈칸 뒤에 be동사 are가 있으므로, 빈칸에는 접속사가 들어가야 합니다. 빈칸이 이끄는 절은 명사 the artists를 뒤에서 수식하므로, 관계사절입니다. the artists와 paintings는 '그 화가들의 그림'이라는 소유 관계가 자연스러우므로, 소유격 관계대명사 (A) whose가 정답입니다.

번역 현재 빌래뉴바 갤러리에 자신들의 그림이 전시되고 있는 미술가들인 마이클 샌더스와 올리비아 림은 모두 펜무어 대학교에 다녔다.

1 (A)	**2** (B)	**3** (B)	**4** (A)	**5** (A)	**6** (B)

1

Ms. Han's goal / is to establish a charity foundation / in (the city / where) she grew up.
한 씨의 목표는　　　자선 재단을 설립하는 것이다　　　　　　도시에　　　자신이 자란

　　　　　　　　　　　　　　　　　　　　　　　　　　　↳ 장소 선행사(the city) + where

(A) where　　　　　　　　　　　　(B) when

> **번역** 한 씨의 목표는 자신이 자란 도시에 자선 재단을 설립하는 것이다.

2

June / is (the month / when) GW Products releases / its annual research report.
6월은　　달이다　　 GW 프로덕츠가 발표하는　　　　　자사의 연간 연구 보고서를

　　　　　　　　　　　　　↳ 시간 선행사(the month) + when

(A) why　　　　　　　　　　　　(B) when

> **번역** 6월은 GW 프로덕츠가 자사의 연간 연구 보고서를 발표하는 달이다.

3

Health care practitioners / are required to obtain licenses / from every country / (in which) they
의사들은　　　　　　면허증을 취득해야 한다　　　　모든 나라에서　　　자신들이 의료 행위를 하는

practice.　　　　　　　　　　　　　　　　　　　　　관계대명사와 관계부사의 구별 ↲

(A) which　　　　　　　　　　　　(B) in which

> **번역** 의사들은 의료 행위를 하는 모든 나라에서 면허증을 취득해야 한다.

4

The manager / has / the key / to (the storage room / where) the office supplies are kept.
관리인이　　갖고 있다 열쇠를　　창고의　　　　　사무용품이 보관되어 있는

　　　　　　　　　　　　　　　　　　　↳ 장소 선행사(the storage room) + where

(A) where　　　　　　　　　　　　(B) why

> **번역** 관리인이 사무용품이 보관되어 있는 창고의 열쇠를 갖고 있다.

5

Please check / the boxes / next to the projects / (on which) you prefer to work.
체크해 주십시오　　박스에　　프로젝트 옆의　　　　여러분이 진행하고 싶은

　　　　　　　　　　　　　　　　　　　　↳ 관계대명사와 관계부사의 구별

(A) which　　　　　　　　　　　　(B) where

> **번역** 여러분이 진행하고 싶은 프로젝트 옆의 박스에 체크해 주십시오.

6

All shipments / arrive / at the receiving dock, / (where) a warehouse worker checks / their tracking
모든 운송품은　　도착한다 하역장으로　　　　그리고 그곳에서 물류 창고 담당자가 확인한다　　추적 라벨을

labels.　　　　　　　　　　　　　↳ 관계대명사와 관계부사의 구별

(A) which　　　　　　　　　　　　(B) where

> **번역** 모든 운송품은 하역장으로 도착하는데, 그곳에서 물류 창고 담당자가 추적 라벨을 확인한다.

7 (D)	8 (D)	9 (D)	10 (C)

7

The Starmax Hotel / renovated / its restaurant / in ⟨2010 / when⟩ two more chefs were hired.
스타맥스 호텔은   보수했다   그곳의 식당을   2010년에   요리사 두 명이 더 채용됐던
→ 시간 선행사(2010) + when

(A) that   (B) what

(C) who   (D) when

> 해설 시간을 나타내는 관계부사: 빈칸 앞에 시간 부사구 in 2010이 있고, 뒤에는 완전한 절이 왔습니다. 문맥상 관계부사가 들어가 '두 명의 요리사를 더 채용했을 때인 2010년에'라는 의미가 되는 것이 자연스러우므로, 정답은 관계부사 (D) when입니다.

> 번역 스타맥스 호텔은 요리사 두 명을 더 채용했던 2010년에 그곳의 식당을 보수했다.

8

A group of engineers / will visit / Maizin, Inc., / to study / ⟨how⟩ the company produces /
한 그룹의 기술자들이   방문할 것이다 마이진사를   배우기 위해   그 회사가 생산하는 방법을
→ 방법을 나타내는 관계부사

environmentally-friendly vehicles.
친환경 자동차를

(A) which   (B) what

(C) who   (D) how

> 해설 방법을 나타내는 관계부사: 빈칸 뒤에 완전한 절이 왔고 문맥상 '그 회사가 ~하는 방법'이라는 의미가 자연스러우므로, 정답은 관계부사 (D) how입니다.

> 번역 한 그룹의 기술자들이 마이진사가 친환경 자동차를 생산하는 방법을 배우기 위해 그 회사를 방문할 것이다.

9

Global corporations / must be sensitive / to the values of each culture / ⟨in which they advertise⟩.
글로벌 기업들은   세심해야 한다   각 문화의 가치관에 대해   그들이 광고 활동을 하는
앞에 사물 명사 each culture를 수식하는 관계사절 ←

(A) when   (B) whose

(C) where   (D) which

> 해설 관계대명사와 관계부사의 구별: 빈칸이 이끄는 절은 앞에 있는 each culture를 수식하는 관계사절입니다. 따라서 사물 명사 each culture를 대신하는 관계대명사 (D) which가 정답입니다. 〈전치사(in) + 관계대명사(which)〉의 형태를 관계부사 where로 바꾸어 쓸 수 있습니다.

> 번역 글로벌 기업들은 그들이 광고 활동을 하는 각 문화의 가치관에 대해 세심해야 한다.

10

Supplementary materials / are available / to employees / ⟨that⟩ would like to learn more about the
보충 자료는   이용할 수 있나   직원들이   지랄디 포토의 이미징 소프트웨어 디자인에 대해 더 배우고 싶은
→ 관계대명사와 관계부사의 구별

design of Giraldi Photos' imaging software.

(A) when   (B) such

(C) that   (D) until

> 해설 관계대명사와 관계부사의 구별: 뒤에 동사가 이어지고 있고 문맥상 '지랄디 포토의 이미징 소프트웨어 디자인에 대해 더 배우고 싶은 직원들'이 자연스러우므로 빈칸에는 관계대명사(주격)가 필요합니다. 선행사가 사람(employees)이므로 정답은 관계대명사 (C) that입니다.

> 번역 지랄디 포토의 이미징 소프트웨어 디자인에 대해 더 배우고 싶은 직원들은 보충 자료를 이용할 수 있다.

1 (B)	**2** (B)	**3** (B)	**4** (A)

1

Our marketing strategy / will be (strongly) influenced / by the results of the survey.
우리의 마케팅 전략은   크게 영향을 받을 것이다   설문 조사 결과에
→ 강하게

(A) loudly 큰 소리로   (B) strongly 강하게

번역   우리의 마케팅 전략은 설문 조사 결과에 크게 영향을 받을 것이다.

2

Decisions about vacation time / are (typically) made / by the department head.
휴가 기간에 대한 결정은   일반적으로 이루어진다   부서장에 의해
→ 일반적으로

(A) scarcely 겨우, 간신히   (B) typically 일반적으로

번역   휴가 기간에 대한 결정은 일반적으로 부서장이 내린다.

3

Production / has increased (steadily) / to keep up with / growing consumer demand.
생산량이   꾸준히 증가했다   따라잡기 위해   늘어나는 소비자 수요를
→ 꾸준히

(A) approximately 대략, 약   (B) steadily 꾸준히

번역   늘어나는 소비자 수요에 따라잡기 위해 생산량이 꾸준히 증가했다.

4

The unseasonably cold weather / has (adversely) affected / the availability of some fruits.
계절에 맞지 않게 추운 날씨가   불리하게 영향을 끼쳤다   일부 과일의 수급에
→ 불리하게

(A) adversely 불리하게   (B) accurately 정확하게

번역   계절에 맞지 않게 추운 날씨가 일부 과일의 수급에 좋지 않은 영향을 끼쳤다.

| 5 (A) | 6 (B) | 7 (B) | 8 (D) |

5

There is a variety of restaurants / conveniently located / on the same street / as the convention
다양한 음식점들이 있다　　　　　　　편리하게 위치한　　　　　　같은 거리에　　　　　컨벤션 센터와
center.
　　　　　　　　　　　　　　　　→ 편리하게, 편리한 곳에

(A) conveniently 편리하게　　　　　　(B) marginally 아주 조금

(C) gradually 점차적으로　　　　　　(D) quickly 빠르게

해설　conveniently 편리하게: 다양한 식당이 컨벤션 센터와 같은 거리에 위치해 있다면 이용하기에 '편리할' 것입니다. 따라서 빈칸 뒤의 과거분사 located를 수식하는 부사 (A) conveniently(편리하게, 편리한 곳에)가 정답입니다.

번역　컨벤션 센터와 같은 거리에 다양한 음식점들이 편리하게 위치해 있다.

6

The cost of a train ticket / is set / to increase slightly / on January 1.
기차표 가격이　　　　　　예정이다　소폭 인상될　　　　　1월 1일에
　　　　　　　　　　　　　　　　　　　→ 약간, 소폭으로

(A) quickly 빨리　　　　　　　　　(B) slightly 약간, 소폭으로

(C) urgently 긴급하게　　　　　　　(D) equally 동일하게

해설　slightly 약간, 소폭으로: 빈칸 앞 동사 increase와 가장 잘 어울리는 부사를 선택해야 합니다. 기차표 가격에 대해 예정되어 있는 것은 '소폭 인상되다'일 것이므로, '약간, 소폭으로'라는 의미의 부사 (B) slightly가 정답입니다.

번역　1월 1일에 기차표 가격이 소폭 인상될 예정이다.

7

The deadline / for submitting shareholder proposals / to Lozerin International / is rapidly
마감일이　　　　주주 제안서를 제출해야 할　　　　　　　로제린 인터내셔널에　　　빠르게 다가오고 있다
approaching.　　　　　　　　　　　　　　　　　　　　　　　　　→ 급속히, 빠르게

(A) securely 단단히　　　　　　　(B) rapidly 급속히

(C) carefully 조심스럽게　　　　　　(D) anxiously 애타게

해설　rapidly 급속히: 빈칸은 뒤의 approaching을 수식하는 부사 자리로, '마감일이 빠르게 다가오고 있다'라는 의미가 문맥상 자연스러우므로, '급속히, 빠르게'라는 의미의 부사 (B) rapidly가 정답입니다.

번역　로제린 인터내셔널에 주주 제안서를 제출해야 할 마감일이 빠르게 다가오고 있다.

8

Innovative and reasonably priced Italian food / draws / a lively crowd / at Echo Restaurant.
혁신적이면서 가격이 합리적인 이탈리아 음식이　　　　　끌어들인다　활기찬 사람들을　　에코 레스토랑에서
　　　　　　→ 합리적으로, 적절하게

(A) virtually 사실상　　　　　　　(B) gratefully 감사히

(C) thoroughly 철저히　　　　　　(D) reasonably 합리적으로

해설　reasonably 합리적으로: 빈칸 뒤 과거분사 priced와 가장 잘 어울리는 부사를 선택해야 합니다. 사람을 끄는 요인은 '가격이 적정하게 매겨진' 음식일 것이므로, '합리적으로, 적절하게'라는 의미의 부사 (D) reasonably가 정답입니다.

번역　에코 레스토랑에서 혁신적이면서 가격이 합리적인 이탈리아 음식이 활기찬 사람들을 끌어들인다.

1 (A)	**2** (D)	**3** (C)	**4** (D)	**5** (C)

1

Mr. Martinelli, / who started as a stock clerk / and is now vice president of marketing, / will retire /
마티넬리 씨는 재고 관리 사원으로 출발한 그리고 현재는 마케팅 부사장인 퇴임할 예정이다
→ 사람 선행사 + 주격 관계대명사

in May.
5월에

(A) who   (B) that   (C) when   (D) another

해설 주격 관계대명사: 빈칸이 이끄는 절은 앞에 있는 사람 명사 Mr. Martinelli를 수식하는 역할을 하므로, Mr. Martinelli를 대신하여 동사 started의 주어 역할을 하는 주격 관계대명사 (A) who가 정답입니다. 주격 관계대명사 (B) that은 콤마 뒤에 올 수 없으므로 오답입니다.

번역 재고 관리 사원으로 출발해서 현재는 마케팅 부사장인 마티넬리 씨는 5월에 퇴임할 예정이다.

2

They / are renovating / the lobby of the building / where the winning photographs will be
그들은 개조하고 있다 건물 로비를 수상작 사진들이 전시될
→ 장소 선행사 + 관계부사

exhibited / next month.
다음 달에

(A) how   (B) why   (C) what   (D) where

해설 장소를 나타내는 관계부사: 빈칸 뒤에 〈주어 + 동사〉의 완전한 절이 있고, 선행사 the lobby of the building이 장소를 나타내므로, 장소를 나타내는 관계부사 (D) where가 정답입니다.

번역 그들은 다음 달에 수상작 사진들이 전시될 건물 로비를 개조하고 있다.

3

A free bicycle lock / is available / to anyone / who purchases a Nakamura bike / before August 1.
무료 자전거 잠금 장치는 받을 수 있다 누구나 나카무라 자전거를 구입하는 8월 1일 이전에
→ 선행사 anyone에 수 일치

(A) purchase   (B) purchaser   (C) purchases   (D) purchasing

해설 관계사절의 동사 자리: 빈칸 앞에 주격 관계대명사 who가 있으므로, 빈칸에는 동사가 들어가야 합니다. 주격 관계대명사 who는 앞에 있는 단수 명사 anyone을 대신하여 빈칸의 주어 역할을 합니다. 따라서 동사의 단수형 (C) purchases가 정답입니다.

번역 8월 1일 이전에 나카무라 자전거를 구입하는 사람은 누구나 무료 자전거 잠금 장치를 받을 수 있다.

4

The teams / whose members finish / the tasks / by 1:30 P.M. / should report / to the main office /
팀은 팀원들이 마치는 과제를 오후 1시 30분까지 보고해야 한다 본사에
→ 소유격 관계대명사

to receive / their next projects.
받기 위해 다음 프로젝트를

(A) its   (B) that   (C) which   (D) whose

해설 소유격 관계대명사: 빈칸이 이끄는 절은 명사구 The teams를 뒤에서 수식하므로, 관계사절입니다. 빈칸 앞의 The teams와 빈칸 뒤 members는 '팀의 구성원'이라는 소유 관계가 문맥상 자연스러우므로, 소유격 관계대명사 (D) whose가 정답입니다.

번역 오후 1시 30분까지 팀원들이 과제를 마치는 팀은 다음 프로젝트를 받기 위해 본사에 보고해야 한다.

5

Innovative Solution / is an organization / that provides / technical support / at reduced rates /
이노베이티브 솔루션즈는 단체이다 제공하는 기술 지원을 할인된 요금으로
→ 주격 관계대명사

to small businesses.
중소기업에

(A) who   (B) where   (C) that   (D) what

해설 주격 관계대명사: 빈칸이 이끄는 절은 앞에 있는 an organization을 수식하는 역할을 하므로, an organization을 대신하여 동사 provides의 주어 역할을 하는 주격 관계대명사 (C) that이 정답입니다.

번역 이노베이티브 솔루션즈는 중소기업에 할인된 요금으로 기술 지원을 제공하는 단체이다.

PART 5 | UNIT 14

| **6** (C) | **7** (A) | **8** (D) | **9** (B) | **10** (D) |

6

All new employees / receive / training folders / that (contain) information / about their assignments.
모든 신입 사원은 　　　　　 받는다 　　교육 자료 폴더를 　　정보가 포함된 　　　　　　　　　업무에 대한
　　　　　　　　　　　　　　　　　　　　　　　　　　　　　　　→ 선행사 training folders에 수 일치

(A) containing　　(B) contained　　(C) contain　　(D) contains

> **해설** **주격 관계대명사의 동사:** 빈칸 앞에 주격 관계대명사 that이 있으므로, 빈칸에는 동사가 들어가야 합니다. 주격 관계대명사 that은 앞에 있는 복수 명사 training folders를 대신하여 빈칸의 주어 역할을 합니다. 따라서 동사의 복수형 (C) contain이 정답입니다.

> **번역** 모든 신입 사원은 업무에 대한 정보가 포함된 교육 자료 폴더를 받는다.

7

(Passengers / who) wish to upgrade / their economy tickets / to business class / may do so /
승객들은 　　업그레이드하기를 원하는 　　이코노미석 표를 　　　　　비즈니스석으로 　　그렇게 할 수 있다
　　　　　　　　　　　→ 사람 선행사 + 주격 관계대명사

using the airline's Web site.
항공사의 웹사이트를 이용해

(A) who　　(B) whose　　(C) whoever　　(D) to whom

> **해설** **주격 관계대명사:** 빈칸 뒤에 동사 wish가 있으므로 빈칸에는 접속사가 들어가야 합니다. 빈칸이 이끄는 절은 앞에 있는 Passengers를 수식하므로 사람 명사 Passengers를 대신하여 동사 wish의 주어 역할을 하는 주격 관계대명사 (A) who가 정답입니다.

> **번역** 이코노미석 표를 비즈니스석으로 업그레이드하기를 원하는 승객들은 항공사의 웹사이트를 이용해 그렇게 할 수 있다.

8

(Many people / that) were interviewed / felt / that they did not need a large car.
많은 사람들은 　　인터뷰에 응한 　　　　　　　 느꼈다 / 자신들은 큰 차가 필요하지 않다고
　　　　　　　　　　→ 사람 선행사 + 주격 관계대명사

(A) which　　(B) whom　　(C) what　　(D) that

> **해설** **주격 관계대명사:** 관계대명사절이 앞의 선행사 Many people을 수식하면서 문맥상 '인터뷰 대상이 된 많은 사람들'이라는 의미가 되어야 자연스럽습니다. 선행사가 사람이므로 주격 관계대명사 (D) that이 정답입니다.

> **번역** 인터뷰에 응한 많은 사람들은 자신들에게 큰 차가 필요하지 않다고 느꼈다.

9

(The opening remarks) / by Judge Yamamoto, / (which) were devoted / to international trade law, /
개회사가 　　　　　　　　야마모토 판사의 　　　　집중적으로 다룬 　　　국제 무역법을
　　　　　　　　　　　　　　　　　　　　　→ 사물 선행사 + 주격 관계대명사

were the highlight of the conference.
그 총회의 압권이었다

(A) who　　(B) which　　(C) what　　(D) whose

> **해설** **주격 관계대명사 선택:** 빈칸 뒤의 were devoted to international trade law는 앞의 주어를 수식하는 관계사절입니다. 동사가 복수형 were인 것으로 보아 관계사절이 수식하는 것은 Judge Yamamoto가 아니라 The opening remarks임을 알 수 있습니다. 따라서 사물 선행사를 대신하는 관계대명사 (B) which가 정답입니다.

> **번역** 국제 무역법을 집중적으로 다룬 야마모토 판사의 개회사가 그 총회의 압권이었다.

10

Morris Homes / has / several in-house (designers) / who will work / on this project.
모리스 홈즈는 　　갖고 있다 / 사내 디자이너 몇 명을 　　　수행할 　　이 프로젝트를
　　　　　　　　　　　　　　　　　　　　　　→ 뒤에 관계대명사 who가 왔으므로 사람 선행사가 와야 함

(A) designing　　(B) design　　(C) designed　　(D) designers

> **해설** **관계대명사의 선행사 선택:** 빈칸 앞에 주어(Morris Homes)와 동사(has)가 있고 빈칸 뒤에 관계대명사 who가 있으므로 빈칸은 사람 선행사 자리입니다. 따라서 형용사 in-house의 수식을 받아 사람 선행사가 될 수 있는 명사 (D) designers가 정답입니다.

> **번역** 모리스 홈즈에는 이 프로젝트를 수행할 사내 디자이너가 몇 명 있다.

11 (C)	12 (B)	13 (B)	14 (B)

Questions 11-14 refer to the following article.

11-14 기사

경영 대학원을 확대하는 대학교

UNIVERSITY TO EXPAND BUSINESS COLLEGE

경영 대학을 확대하는 대학교 → 전치사 of의 목적어로 쓰인 명사

After two years of 11. (consideration), / the Newhouse University Board
2년간의 숙고 끝에   뉴하우스 대학 이사회가

of Trustees / has decided / to increase the number of courses / offered
            결정했다   강좌의 수를 늘리기로   뉴하우스

at Newhouse Business College. (The new course schedule, / 12. which)
경영 대학에서 제공되는   새로운 강의 일정은   최근
                                        → 사물 선행사 + 주격 관계대명사

was recently approved / by the board of trustees, / will take effect / next
승인되었으며   이사회에서   적용될 예정이다   다음

September.
9월부터

The 13. expanded course selection / is expected / to increase enrollment /
확대된 강좌 선택은   기대된다   등록을 늘릴 것으로

and therefore / allow Newhouse to more effectively compete / with other
그리고 그에 따라   뉴하우스를 더 효과적으로 경쟁하게 해줄 것으로   다른 경영

business schools / in the region.
대학원과   지역 내

14. Many of the new courses / will be offered / in the evening. According to
새 강좌들은 대부분   운영될 것이다   야간에   대학 총장 아흐메드

University President Ahmed Sabresh, / attracting more evening students /
사브레쉬에 따르면   야간 학생들을 더 많이 끌어모으는 것이

to Newhouse / is a major objective of the university.
뉴하우스로   이 대학교의 주요 목표이다

2년간의 숙고 끝에 뉴하우스 대학 이사회는 뉴하우스 경영 대학원에서 제공되는 강좌의 수를 늘리기로 결정했다. 새로운 강의 일정은 최근 이사회에서 승인되었으며, 다음 9월부터 적용될 예정이다.

강좌 선택의 확대로 등록을 늘리고 그에 따라 뉴하우스를 지역 내 다른 경영 대학원과 더 효과적으로 경쟁하게 해줄 것으로 기대된다.

새 강좌들은 대부분 야간에 운영될 것이다. 대학 총장 아흐메드 사브레쉬에 따르면 야간 학생들을 뉴하우스로 더 많이 끌어모으는 것이 이 대학교의 주요 목표이다.

11 (A) consider

(B) considered

(C) consideration

(D) considerable

(A) 사려하다, 여기다

(B) 깊이 생각한, 존경받는

(C) 사려, 숙고

(D) 상당한, 많은

> 해설 **전치사의 목적어:** 빈칸은 전치사 of의 목적어 자리이므로 명사인 (C) consideration이 정답입니다.

---

12 (A) who

(B) which

(C) when

(D) why

> 해설 **주격 관계대명사:** 빈칸부터 the board of trustees까지가 The new course schedule에 대한 부가 설명을 하는 관계대명사절인데 선행사인 The new course schedule이 사물이며, 관계사절의 주어 역할을 할 주격 관계대명사가 필요하므로 정답은 (B) which입니다.

---

13 (A) automatic

(B) expanded

(C) frequent

(D) corrected

(A) 자동의

(B) 확대된

(C) 잦은, 빈번한

(D) 수정한

> 해설 **어휘 문제:** 대학교의 이사회에서 '경영 대학 강좌의 수를 늘리기로 했다'는 내용이 첫 단락에서 언급되었습니다. 따라서 '확대된 강좌 선택'이라는 문맥을 완성하는 (B) expanded가 빈칸에 가장 적절합니다.

---

14 (A) A new university president will be appointed next October.

(B) Many of the new courses will be offered in the evening.

(C) One of those contests is called "Young Entrepreneurs."

(D) There is currently a surcharge for late registration.

(A) 새 대학 총장이 다음 10월에 임명될 예정이다.

(B) 새 강좌들은 대부분 야간에 운영될 것이다.

(C) 그러한 경진 대회 중 하나의 명칭은 "청년 기업가"다.

(D) 늦은 등록에는 현재 추가 수수료가 있다.

> 해설 **문장 고르기:** '더 많은 야간 학생들을 끌어들이는 것을 목표로 하고 있다'는 내용이 빈칸 뒤에 이어지고 있습니다. 따라서 빈칸에서는 '새 강좌들이 야간에 제공될 것'이라는 야간 학습과 관련된 (B)의 내용이 언급되는 것이 자연스럽습니다.

ETS 문제로 훈련하기

교재 p. 190

Q1 (D)　　　　　　　　　**Q2** (D)

Q1

10 February

Dear Mr. Garcia,

The Garden and Flower Society / is proud to announce / that we will
원예 화훼 협회는　　　　　　　　발표하게 되어 자랑스럽습니다　　개최할 것을

hold / our fifth Spring Garden and Houseplant Sale / on Saturday,
　　　제5회 봄 정원 및 실내용 화초 세일 행사를　　　　　5월 3일 토요일에

3 May). This event takes place / every year / on the front lawn at
　　　이 행사는 열립니다　　　　매년　　　포레스트 공원 앞 잔디밭에서
　　→ 미래 시점

Forest Park. Since you sold / your lovely watercolour paintings /
　　　귀하께서는 판매하셨기 때문에　　아름다운 수채화를

at last year's sale, / I thought / you might want to join us again / this
작년 세일 때　　　　생각했습니다　다시 저희와 함께하기를 원하실 것이라고　　　올해

year. I am attaching / the necessary information and application
　　　　첨부합니다　　　　필요한 자료와 신청서를

form / if you are interested / in participating. We look forward / to
　　관심이 있으시다면　　　참여하는 데　　　기다리겠습니다

hearing from you.
귀하로부터 연락을

Sincerely,

Sanford Sladen,
GFS Events Coordinator

2월 10일

가르시아 씨께,

원예 화훼 협회는 5월 3일 토요일에 제5회 봄 정원 및 실내용 화초 세일 판매 행사를 연다는 것을 발표하게 되어 자랑스럽습니다. 이 행사는 매년 포레스트 공원 앞 잔디밭에서 열립니다. 귀하께서는 작년 세일 때 아름다운 수채화를 판매하셨기 때문에 올해도 함께하기를 원하실 것으로 생각했습니다. 참여하는 데 관심이 있으시다면 필요한 자료와 신청서를 첨부합니다. 연락 기다리겠습니다.

샌포드 슬레이든
GFS 행사 코디네이터

(A) hold
(B) held
(C) holding
(D) will hold

[해설] **시제 문제 (미래):** 편지 작성일은 2월 10일인데 행사일은 5월 3일이이므로 미래 시제인 (D) will hold가 정답입니다. (A) hold, (B) held는 시제 면에서 적절하지 않고 (C) holding은 동사 자리에 올 수 없으므로 정답이 될 수 없습니다.

Q2

Dear Mr. Jackson,

Please accept my apologies / for not getting back to you / sooner.
사과를 받아주십시오 　　　　　　　회신해 드리지 못한 점에 대한 　　　더 일찍

I (have been trying) / to determine / what happened to your order.
저는 노력했습니다 　　　　알아내기 위해 　　귀하의 주문에 무슨 일이 있었는지
　　→ 과거부터 현재까지 노력해 왔다는 의미의 현재완료진행 시제

Unfortunately, / it took the shipper two days / to return my phone
유감스럽게도 　　　배송 업체가 이틀이 걸렸습니다 　　　　　제 전화에 회신하는 데

call. I was informed / that the delay was caused / by a heavy
　　　　저는 통보받았습니다 　　지연이 발생했다는 사실을 　　　폭설로 인해

snowstorm / on the shipping route. As a result, / your two dozen
　　　　　운송 경로상의 　　　　　결과적으로 　　　귀하의 24개의 시계가

watches / should be delivered / by 10 February. Again, / I apologize
배송될 것입니다 　　2월 10일까지 　　다시 한 번 　지연에 대해

for the delay. Thank you / for your business and your patience.
사과를 드립니다 　감사드립니다 　저희와 거래해주시고 참고 기다려주신 것에 대해

잭슨 씨께,

더 일찍 회신해 드리지 못한 점 사과드립니다. 저는 귀하의 주문에 무슨 일이 있었는지 알아내기 위해 노력했습니다. 유감스럽게도, 배송 업체가 제 전화에 회신하는 데 이틀이 걸렸습니다. 저는 운송 경로상의 폭설로 인해 지연이 발생했다는 사실을 통보받았습니다. 결과적으로, 귀하의 24개의 시계가 2월 10일까지 배송될 것입니다. 다시 한 번, 지연에 대해 사과를 드립니다. 저희와 거래해주시고 참고 기다려주신 것에 대해 감사드립니다.

(A) am going to try

(B) might try

(C) am trying

(D) have been trying

해설 시제 문제 (현재완료진행): 첫 문장을 통해 과거에 문의한 것에 대해 지금 회신하는 내용임을 알 수 있습니다. 따라서 문의를 받은 과거 시점부터 현재까지 상황 파악을 위해 노력해 왔다는 현재완료진행 시제(have been -ing)가 문맥상 적절하므로, (D) have been trying이 정답입니다. 현재진행 시제인 (C) am trying은 현재 노력 중이라는 의미가 되어 아직 상황 파악을 하지 못한 상태에서 쓸 수 있는 시제입니다.

1 (B)	**2** (C)	**3** (B)	**4** (A)

Questions 1-4 refer to the following job listing.

1-4 구인 광고

Sales and Marketing Leader—Southeast Region
영업 및 마케팅 리더 – 남동부 지역

영업 및 마케팅 리더 – 남동부 지역

Daily Green Foods / is hiring a new sales and marketing leader / to help
데일리 그린 푸즈는   새로운 영업 및 마케팅 리더를 채용합니다   사업 범위를

grow its reach / in the Southeast Region. The chosen candidate will be
넓히는 것을 도울   남동부 지역에서   선정된 지원자는 매출을 높이는 일을 담당하게

in charge of 1. increasing sales / by promoting our products / at local
됩니다   우리 제품을 홍보하여   현지 슈퍼마켓에서

supermarkets. 2. The candidate / will also develop / our regional marketing
지원자는   또한 개발할 것입니다   지역 마케팅 전략을

strategy. Knowledge of the brand and competing markets / is therefore
브랜드와 경쟁 시장에 대한 지식이   그래서 있으면 좋습니다

3. (desirable).
↳ 보어 역할을 하는 형용사

The selected candidate / is expected / to achieve quarterly sales goals /
선정된 지원자는   기대됩니다   분기별 매출 목표를 달성할 것으로

and expand the visibility of the Daily Green Foods brand. Our sales and
그리고 그린 푸드 브랜드의 가시성을 높일 것으로   당사의 영업 및 마케팅

marketing leader / 4. (will support) our company goal / of making healthy
리더는   당사의 목표에 협력할 것입니다   건강한 식사를 만든다는
↳ 미래 시점의 일을 나타내는 미래 시제

eating / simple and accessible for all.
간단하고 모두가 이용하기 쉽게

Please contact Amy Kipkorir / at akipkorir@dgf.com / for more information
에이미 킵커러에게 연락하십시오   akipkorir@dgf.com의   직책에 대한 자세한 정보를

about the position.
원하시면

데일리 그린 푸즈는 남동부 지역의 사업 범위 확대를 도울 새로운 영업 및 마케팅 리더를 채용합니다. 선정된 지원자는 현지 슈퍼마켓에서 우리 제품을 홍보하여 매출을 높이는 일을 담당하게 됩니다. 지원자는 또한 지역 마케팅 전략을 개발할 것입니다. 따라서 브랜드와 경쟁 시장에 대한 지식이 있으면 좋습니다.

선정된 지원자는 분기별 매출 목표를 달성하고 데일리 그린 푸즈 브랜드의 가시성을 높일 것으로 기대됩니다. 당사의 영업 및 마케팅 리더는 건강한 식사를 간단하고 모두가 이용하기 쉽게 만든다는 당사의 목표에 협력할 것입니다.

직책에 대한 자세한 정보를 원하시면 akipkorir@dgf.com의 에이미 킵커러에게 연락하십시오.

1
(A) communicating
(B) increasing
(C) competing
(D) proceeding

(A) 전달하는
(B) 늘리는
(C) 경쟁하는
(D) 진행되는

해설   **어휘 고르기:** 빈칸 뒤의 sales를 목적어로 취해 가장 자연스럽게 의미가 통하는 동명사를 골라야 합니다. 빈칸 앞 문장에서 새로운 영업 및 마케팅 리더 채용을 언급했습니다. 문맥상 이 직책 지원자는 매출을 높이는 책임이 있을 것으로 볼 수 있으므로, (B) increasing이 정답입니다.

2
(A) We are discussing the expansion of our manufacturing facility.
(B) Please forward your résumé, a cover letter, and three references.
(C) The candidate will also develop our regional marketing strategy.
(D) We are looking for a start date in January.

(A) 우리는 제조 시설의 확장에 대해 논의하고 있습니다.
(B) 이력서, 자기소개서, 추천서 3장을 보내주십시오.
(C) 지원자는 또한 지역 마케팅 전략을 개발할 것입니다.
(D) 우리는 1월 중으로 시작 날짜를 찾고 있습니다.

해설   **문장 고르기:** 빈칸 앞 문장 The chosen candidate will be in charge of increasing sales by promoting our products at local supermarkets.에서 지원자가 담당할 업무를 언급했습니다. 따라서 빈칸에도 담당할 업무와 관련된 내용이 이어지는 것이 문맥상 자연스러우므로, 정답은 (C)입니다.

3
(A) desirably
(B) desirable
(C) desires
(D) desire

(A) 바람직하게
(B) 바람직한
(C) 바라다
(D) 바람

해설   **형용사 자리:** 보어가 필요한 동사인 is와 부사 therefore 뒤에 빈칸이 있으므로 빈칸에는 보어 역할을 하면서 부사의 수식을 받을 수 있는 형용사가 필요합니다. 따라서 정답은 (B) desirable입니다.

4
(A) will support
(B) has supported
(C) is supporting
(D) had supported

해설   **시제 문제 (미래):** 빈칸 앞 문장 The selected candidate ~ Daily Green Foods brand.에 미래를 의미하는 is expected to가 있으므로, 미래 시제 동사 (A) will support가 정답입니다. 현재진행 시제인 (C) is supporting도 미래를 나타낼 수 있지만 영업 및 마케팅 리더들의 협력에 대한 의지를 표현할 수 없고, 단순히 가까운 미래만을 나타내는 상황에서 쓰는 시제입니다.

ETS 문제로 훈련하기
교재 p.194

Q1 (B)　　　　　　　　**Q2** (C)

Q1

Dear Ms. Wu,

We have shipped the requested part / for your handheld leaf blower.
저희가 요청하신 부품을 발송했습니다　　　　　귀하의 휴대용 낙엽 송풍기에 대해

→ 소유격 인칭대명사
Please accept (our) apology / for the piece / that was not included /
저희의 사과를 받아주십시오　　　　해당 부품에 대한　　들어 있지 않았던

in the box. We hope / that this free shipment will make up for any
상자에　　바랍니다　　이 무료 배송이 불편을 끼쳐드린 데 대한 보상이 되기를

inconvenience. The missing piece / has been sent / via postal
　　　　빠진 부품은　　　　발송되었습니다　　특급 우편으로

express delivery. You should receive / a separate e-mail / with the
　　　　받으실 겁니다　　　별도의 이메일을　　발송물의

shipment's tracking information.
추적 정보가 담긴

We hope / this resolves the matter, / but please let us know / if there
바랍니다　　이것으로 문제가 해결되기를　　하지만 알려주시기 바랍니다　　일이 있다면

is anything / we can do / to improve your satisfaction.
　　　　저희가 할 수 있는　고객님의 만족도를 높이기 위해

우 씨께,

귀하의 휴대용 낙엽 송풍기에 대해 요청하신 부품을 발송했습니다. 상자에 들어 있지 않았던 해당 부품에 대한 저희의 사과를 받아주십시오. 이 무료 배송이 불편을 끼쳐드린 데 대한 보상이 되기를 바랍니다. 빠진 부품은 특급 우편으로 발송되었습니다. 발송물의 추적 정보가 담긴 별도의 이메일을 받으실 겁니다.

이것으로 문제가 해결되기를 바라며, 고객님의 만족도를 높이기 위해 저희가 할 수 있는 일이 있다면 알려주시기 바랍니다.

(A) his
(B) our
(C) her
(D) their

해설 **인칭대명사 (소유격):** 지문은 We가 Ms. Wu에게 사과를 하는 내용입니다. 문맥상 '저희의 사과를 받아 달라'는 의미가 자연스러우므로, 빈칸에 들어갈 소유격 인칭대명사는 (B) our입니다.

Q2

Nyveg Technology Hardware Competition
나이벡 테크놀로지 하드웨어 경연 대회

Nyveg Ventures / is now accepting applications / for our sixth
나이벡 벤처스는   지금 참가 신청서를 받고 있습니다   제6회

annual Technology Hardware Competition / to be held in Oslo,
연례 테크놀로지 하드웨어 경연 대회의   노르웨이 오슬로에서 열리는

Norway, / beginning on 1 November. We will be selecting teams /
11월 1일부터   우리는 팀들을 선정할 것입니다

from around the world / who have taken new hardware projects /
전 세계에서   새로운 하드웨어 프로젝트를 진전시킨

past the idea stage / and have already built a working prototype.
아이디어 단계를 너머로   그래서 작동하는 시제품을 이미 제작한

Applications / should be submitted online / by 15 September.
신청서는   온라인으로 제출되어야 합니다   9월 15일까지

Accepted applicants / will spend one week in Oslo / working on
합격한 신청자는   오슬로에서 1주일을 보낼 것입니다   시제품을

further developing (their) prototypes. Each of the accepted teams /
더 발전시키는 작업을 하면서   합격한 팀은 모두
                        └→ 소유격 인칭대명사

will receive / funding and technical support / from our partners.
받게 됩니다   자금 및 기술 지원을   당사의 협력 업체로부터

나이벡 테크놀로지 하드웨어 경연 대회

나이벡 벤처스는 11월 1일부터 노르웨이 오슬로에서 열리는 제6회 연례 테크놀로지 하드웨어 경연 대회 참가 신청서를 지금 받고 있습니다. 우리는 전 세계에서 새로운 하드웨어 프로젝트를 아이디어 단계 너머로 진전시켜 작동하는 시제품을 이미 제작한 팀들을 선정할 것입니다.

신청서는 9월 15일까지 온라인으로 제출해야 합니다. 합격한 신청자는 오슬로에서 1주일을 보내면서 시제품을 더 발전시키는 작업을 하게 됩니다. 합격한 팀은 모두 당사의 협력 업체로부터 자금 및 기술 지원을 받게 됩니다.

(A) they

(B) them

(C) their

(D) theirs

해설 인칭대명사 (소유격): 빈칸 뒤에 명사 prototypes가 있으므로 명사를 수식해줄 수 있는 소유격 인칭대명사를 써야 합니다. 따라서 소유격인 (C) their가 정답입니다.

1 (B)	**2** (C)	**3** (D)	**4** (A)

Questions 1-4 refer to the following article.

1-4 기사

LOS ANGELES (May 1)—Online marketer Sun Settings / **1.** opened an
로스앤젤레스(5월 1일)   온라인 마케팅업체 선 세팅스가   샌디에이고 시내에

office in downtown San Diego / last week. The newly acquired space /
사무실을 열었다   지난주에   새로 확보한 공간은

will accommodate 45 employees / who currently work **2.** remotely.
직원 45명을 수용할 예정이다   현재 원격 근무 중인

"We are not moving / any departments / to San Diego," / said Sun Settings
우린 옮기지 않을 겁니다   어떤 부서도   샌디에이고로   선 세팅스 대변인

spokeswoman Jacqueline Gutierrez. "We are just offering office space /
재클린 구티에레스 씨는 말했다   그냥 사무 공간을 제공하려고 합니다

to employees / who are scattered throughout that city. As our customer
직원들에게   시내 곳곳에 흩어져 있는   고객층이 커지면서

base grows, / we find / that it benefits our telecommuters, / who work from
    우리는 생각합니다 / 재택근무자에게 도움이 된다고   집에 사무공간을 꾸미고

home offices, / to work face-to-face on occasion."
근무하는   이따금 얼굴을 마주 보고 일하는 것이

Sun Settings / has experienced rapid growth / since its founding / seven
선 세팅스는   빠른 성장을 경험했다   설립 이래   7년 전

years ago. **3.** Its customer base / has doubled / in that time. The company /
    고객층은   두 배가 되었다   그 기간에   회사는

has been expanding its telecommuting program / at the same time.
재택근무 프로그램을 확대해 왔다   동시에

"The program / has really improved / how effectively our salespeople can
이 프로그램은   정말로 개선했습니다   영업사원들이 효과적으로 부응하는 방식을

meet / the needs of our customers," / said Ms. Gutierrez. "**4.** It will only
고객의 요구에   구티에레스 씨가 말했다   그것은 계속

continue to grow."
성장하기만 할 것입니다

← 앞 문장의 The program을 대신하는 대명사

로스앤젤레스 (5월 1일) – 온라인 마케팅업체 선 세팅스가 지난주 샌디에이고 시내에 사무실을 열었다. 새로 확보한 공간은 현재 원격 근무 중인 직원 45명을 수용할 예정이다.

"우리는 어떤 부서도 샌디에이고로 옮기지 않을 겁니다." 선 세팅스 대변인 재클린 구티에레스 씨는 말했다. "그냥 시내 곳곳에 흩어져 있는 직원들에게 사무 공간을 제공하려고 합니다. 고객층이 커지면서 집에 사무공간을 꾸미고 근무하는 재택근무자들에게 이따금 얼굴을 마주 보고 일하는 것이 도움이 된다고 생각합니다."

선 세팅스는 7년 전 설립 이래 빠른 성장을 경험했다. 그 기간에 고객층은 두 배가 되었다. 회사는 동시에 재택근무 프로그램도 확대해 왔다.

"이 프로그램은 영업사원들이 고객의 요구에 효과적으로 부응하는 방식을 정말로 개선했습니다." 구티에레스 씨가 말했다. "그것은 계속 성장하기만 할 것입니다."

1 (A) sold

(B) opened

(C) painted

(D) inspected

(A) 판매하다

(B) 열다

(C) 페인트칠하다

(D) 점검하다

> **해설** 어휘 고르기: 빈칸 뒤 문장 The newly acquired space will accommodate 45 employees에서 새로 확보한 공간에 대해 설명하고 있습니다. 따라서 빈칸에는 '사무실을 열었다'라는 의미가 문맥상 자연스러우므로, (B) opened가 정답입니다.

---

2 (A) quietly

(B) recently

(C) remotely

(D) efficiently

(A) 조용히

(B) 최근에

(C) 원격으로

(D) 효율적으로

> **해설** 어휘 고르기: 두 번째 단락 두 번째 문장 We are just offering ~ throughout that city.에서 시내 곳곳에 흩어져 있는 직원들을 위한 사무 공간이라고 설명하고 있습니다. 따라서 빈칸을 포함한 부분은 '원격 근무 중인 직원들을 수용할 것'이라는 의미가 문맥상 자연스러우므로, (C) remotely가 정답입니다.

---

3 (A) A new CEO was hired late last year.

(B) A new marketing plan was just announced.

(C) The company specializes in home goods.

(D) Its customer base has doubled in that time.

(A) 지난해 말에 신임 CEO가 채용되었다.

(B) 새로운 마케팅 계획이 방금 발표되었다.

(C) 그 회사는 가정용품 전문이다.

(D) 그 해당 기간에 고객층은 두 배가 되었다.

> **해설** 문장 고르기: 빈칸 앞에는 회사가 설립 이래 빠른 성장을 경험했다는 내용이 언급되었습니다. 따라서 빈칸에는 성장과 관련된 내용이 들어가는 것이 문맥상 자연스러우며, 선택지 (D)의 고객층 두 배 증가가 구체적인 성장의 내용을 의미하므로 정답은 (D)입니다.

---

4 (A) It

(B) Yours

(C) Myself

(D) One another

> **해설** 대명사: 빈칸 뒤에 동사구 will only continue가 있으므로 빈칸은 주어 자리입니다. 문맥상 계속 성장하는 것은 앞 문장의 주어인 The program이므로 (A) It이 정답입니다.

Q1 (B)   **Q2** (A)

Q1

Your Omicron Office Copier / is one of the most important tools /
귀사의 오미크론 사무용 복사기는   가장 중요한 장비 중 하나입니다

you have. Therefore, / knowing how to care for your copier properly /
귀사에 있는   그러므로   복사기를 제대로 관리하는 방법을 아는 것이

is an important part / of running an efficient business. Here are /
중요한 부분입니다   효율적인 업무를 진행하는 데 있어   여기에 있습니다

four vital tips / from our team of experts / to keep your copier in
네 가지 필수적인 도움말이   저희 전문가 팀의   복사기를 최상의 상태로 유지할 수 있는

top shape. First, / use Omicron-approved supplies, / especially
첫 번째로 / 오미크론이 승인한 용품을 사용하십시오   특히

Omicron toner cartridges. Second, / be careful / when loading
오미크론 토너 카트리지를   두 번째로   주의하십시오   용지를 넣을 때

paper. Following the instructions / in the manual / will ensure proper
지시 사항을 따르는 것이   설명서의   제대로 된 급지를 보장합니다

loading of the paper / and prevent paper jams. Third, / clean the
그리고 용지 걸림을 방지할 수 있습니다 세 번째로 복사기를 정기적으로

copier regularly. Use only soft cloths and cleaning materials /
청소하십시오   부드러운 천과 청소용품만을 사용하십시오

recommended by Omicron. Finally, / if your copier is in need
오미크론에서 추천하는   마지막으로   복사기 수리가 필요하면,

of repair, / we advise / that you select a certified professional
권합니다   자격증이 있는 전문 기술자를 선택하시기를

technician. Following these tips / will prolong / the life of your office
이런 도움말을 따르는 것이   연장할 것입니다   귀사의 사무용 복사기 수명을

copier.

귀사의 오미크론 사무용 복사기는 귀사에 있는 가장 중요한 장비 중 하나입니다. 그러므로 복사기를 제대로 관리하는 방법을 아는 것이 효율적인 업무를 진행하는 데 있어 중요한 부분입니다. 여기에 우리 전문가 팀이 전하는 복사기를 최상의 상태로 유지할 수 있는 네 가지 필수적인 도움말이 있습니다. 첫 번째로 오미크론이 승인한 용품, 특히 오미크론 토너 카트리지를 사용하십시오. 두 번째로 용지를 넣을 때 주의하십시오. 설명서의 지시 사항을 따라야 제대로 된 급지가 가능하고 용지 걸림을 방지할 수 있습니다. 세 번째로 복사기를 정기적으로 청소하십시오. 오미크론이 추천하는 부드러운 천과 청소용품을 사용하십시오. 마지막으로 복사기 수리가 필요하면, 자격증이 있는 전문 기술자를 선택하시기를 권합니다. 이런 도움말을 따르면 귀사의 사무용 복사기 수명이 연장될 것입니다.

(A) employees
(B) supplies
(C) access
(D) power

(A) 직원들
(B) 용품
(C) 접근
(D) 힘

해설 **어휘 고르기**: 빈칸 뒤 especially Omicron toner cartridges에서 특정 제품을 예로 들고 있으므로, 빈칸 앞에는 '용품'이라는 의미의 명사 (B) supplies가 정답입니다.

Q2

Our refrigerated display case / is broken. We hope / to 〔have it repaired〕 /
우리의 냉장 진열장이 　　　　　　　고장 났습니다　　우리는 바랍니다 / 그것이 수리되기를
　　　　　　　　　　　　　　　　　　　have + 목적어 + 목적격보어(과거분사): ~이 …되게 하다 ←

by this weekend / if not sooner. Meanwhile, / all perishable items /
이번 주말까지는　　　　늦어도　　　　그동안에　　　　모든 상하기 쉬운 제품은

normally kept in the case / are in the refrigerator / in the storage room.
평소 진열장에 보관되었던　　　　　냉장고에 보관합니다　　　창고 안에 있는

A complete list of these products / is posted below. Please inform
이들 제품의 전체 목록은　　　　　　　　　　　아래에 게시됩니다　　고객에게 알려주시기

customers / of these circumstances / when they enter the shop.
바랍니다　　　이런 사정에 대해　　　　　　고객이 매장에 들어오면

Offer to retrieve anything / that interests them, / and assure them /
어떤 제품이든 찾아 드리겠다고 말하십시오　　고객이 관심 있어 하는　　그리고 확신시키십시오

that doing so is not an inconvenience.
그렇게 하는 일이 번거로운 일이 아님을

우리의 냉장 진열장이 고장 났습니다. 늦어도 이번 주말까지는 수리되기를 바라고 있습니다. 그동안에 평소 진열장에 보관했던 모든 상하기 쉬운 제품은 창고 안에 있는 냉장고에 보관합니다. 이들 제품의 전체 목록을 아래에 게시합니다. 고객이 매장에 들어오면 이런 사정에 대해 알려주시기 바랍니다. 고객이 관심 있어 하는 어떤 제품이든 찾아다 드리겠다고 말하십시오. 그리고 그렇게 하는 일이 번거로운 일이 아님을 확신시키십시오.

(A) repaired　　　　　　　　　　　　　(A) 수리하다

(B) answered　　　　　　　　　　　　　(B) 답변하다

(C) generated　　　　　　　　　　　　　(C) 발생시키다

(D) satisfied　　　　　　　　　　　　　(D) 만족시키다

해설 어휘 고르기: '~되게 시키다'를 뜻하는 〈have + 목적어 + 과거분사〉의 구조입니다. 첫 문장에서 진열장이 고장 났다고 하므로 이 문장은 '수리되기를 바란다'라는 의미가 적절합니다. 따라서 (A) repaired가 정답입니다.

| **1** (A) | **2** (D) | **3** (C) | **4** (D) |

Questions 1-4 refer to the following e-mail.

To: p.swain@ulofarms.com

From: support@plastimattic.com

Date: April 28

Subject: RE: Order #908190

Dear Mr. Swain,

We are sorry to hear / that the plastic sheeting you purchased is performing
알게 되어 유감입니다   구매하신 비닐 시트의 기능이 시원찮다는 소식을

unsatisfactorily. Usually / when customers report a fault / with our products, /
일반적으로   고객분들께서 결함을 신고하실 때는   당사 제품의

the ties on the corners of the plastic / have not been affixed / correctly to
비닐 모서리의 매듭이   부착되어 있지 않습니다   장비에 제대로

the equipment. **1.** We found / your report / to be very concerning. From what
저희는 생각했습니다 / 고객님의 신고 내용이 / 매우 우려되는 것으로   고객님의 설명에

you have described, / the way the plastic was **2.** attached / does not seem
의하면   비닐이 부착된 방식이   원인은 아닌 것 같습니다

to be the cause. You indicated / that the plastic is ripping at the seams.
고객님께서 지적하셨습니다   봉제선 부분에서 비닐이 뜯어지고 있다고

We have not previously encountered / a problem like this.
저희는 전에 접한 적이 없습니다   이런 문제를

3. Nevertheless, / we at Plastimattic, Inc., are committed / to 100 percent
그렇기는 하지만   저희 플라스티마틱사는 전념하고 있습니다   100% 고객 만족에

customer satisfaction. We can issue you a full refund, / or we can send
저희는 고객님께 전액을 환불해 드릴 수 있습니다   또는 교체 상품을 익일

replacement sheets overnight / at no extra cost. Please let us know /
배송해 드릴 수 있습니다   추가 비용 없이   알려주십시오

4. (which) option you prefer.
어느 쪽이 더 좋으신지
⌐─────→ 명사절을 이끄는 의문형용사

Kind regards,

Alejandro Gonzales, Plastimattic Customer Support

1-4 이메일

수신: p.swain@ulofarms.com

발신: support@plastimattic.
com

날짜: 4월 28일

제목: RE: 주문 번호 908190

스웨인 씨께

구매하신 비닐 시트의 기능이 시원
찮다는 소식을 듣게 되어 유감입니
다. 일반적으로 고객분들께서 당사
제품의 결함을 신고하실 때는 비닐
모서리의 매듭이 장비에 제대로 부
착되어 있지 않습니다. 저희는 고객
님의 신고 내용이 매우 우려되는 것
으로 생각했습니다. 고객님의 설명
에 의하면, 비닐이 부착된 방식이
원인은 아닌 것 같습니다. 고객님
께서 봉제선 부분에서 비닐이 뜯어
지고 있다고 지적하셨습니다. 저희
는 전에 이런 문제를 접한 적이 없
습니다.

그렇기는 하지만, 저희 플라스티마
틱사는 100% 고객 만족에 전념하
고 있습니다. 저희는 고객님께 전액
을 환불해 드리거나, 추가 비용 없
이 교체 상품을 익일 배송해 드릴
수 있습니다. 어느 쪽이 더 좋으신
지 알려주십시오.

알레한드로 곤잘레스, 플라스티마틱
고객 지원

1

(A) We found your report to be very concerning.

(B) Your order should be arriving soon.

(C) We use a proprietary formula for the plastic in our products.

(D) Perhaps you would like to purchase some accessories.

(A) 저희는 고객님의 신고 내용이 매우 우려되는 것으로 생각했습니다.

(B) 주문하신 물건이 곧 도착할 예정입니다.

(C) 저희는 자사 제품의 플라스틱에 전매 특허 방식을 사용합니다.

(D) 일부 부대용품을 구입하고 싶으실 수 있습니다.

> **해설** 문장 고르기: 빈칸 앞에서 일반적인 경우의 제품 결함 신고에 대해 설명했고, 빈칸 뒤에서 이번 경우는 일반적인 결함 신고가 아니라고 언급했습니다. 따라서 빈칸에는 고객의 결함 신고가 일반적인 경우가 아니라서 우려를 표현하는 것이 자연스러운 글의 흐름이므로, 정답은 (A)입니다.

2

(A) folded

(B) shipped

(C) cleaned

(D) attached

(A) 접다

(B) 발송하다

(C) 청소하다

(D) 부착하다

> **해설** 어휘 고르기: 두 번째 문장의 the ties ~ to the equipment에서 비닐 모서리 매듭의 부착을 언급했습니다. 문맥상 빈칸을 포함하여 '비닐이 부착된 방식이 원인이 아닐 것'이라는 내용이 자연스러우므로, affixed(부착된)와 비슷한 의미인 (D) attached가 정답입니다.

3

(A) Similarly

(B) Thus

(C) Nevertheless

(D) Rather

(A) 유사하게

(B) 따라서

(C) 그렇기는 하지만

(D) 오히려

> **해설** 접속부사 고르기: 빈칸 앞 문장 We have not ~ like this.에서 이런 문제가 처음이라는 내용을, 빈칸 뒤의 we at Plastimattic, Inc., ~ customer satisfaction.에서 고객 만족에 전념하고 있다는 내용을 언급했습니다. 따라서 '그렇기는 하지만, 그럼에도 불구하고'라는 양보의 의미를 나타내는 접속부사 (C) Nevertheless가 정답입니다.

4

(A) that

(B) why

(C) when

(D) which

> **해설** 의문형용사 자리: 빈칸 뒤에 명사 및 주어(you)와 동사(prefer)가 나오므로 빈칸은 명사를 수식하면서 명사절을 이끄는 의문형용사 자리입니다. 따라서 의문형용사 (D) which가 정답입니다. 의문부사 (B) why와 (C) when은 명사를 수식할 수 없으므로 오답입니다.

ETS 문제로 훈련하기
교재 p.202

Q1 (A) **Q2** (D)

Q1

Dear PK,

Thank you again / for the wonderful job you did / creating our Web
다시 한 번 감사의 말씀드립니다 / 귀하가 하신 훌륭한 작업에 대해   저희 웹사이트를 만들면서

site / last month. We have received / much positive feedback on the
      지난달   받았습니다   사이트에 대한 많은 긍정적인 의견을

site / from our employees and from other visitors. I am writing to
      저희 직원들과 다른 방문자들로부터   문의하려고 이메일을

inquire / whether you are available / to add a couple of new features
보냅니다   해 주실 수 있는지   사이트에 몇 가지 새로운 기능을 추가하는 것을

to the site.
          ┌─→ 구체적으로 말하자면

(Specifically), / we would like to include / an employee directory /
구체적으로 말하자면   넣고 싶습니다   직원 명부를

and a section for ongoing research projects.
그리고 진행 중인 연구 프로젝트 섹션을

We look forward / to working with you again. Please let us know.
기대합니다   다시 함께 일하기를   그럼 회신 주십시오

Warm regards,

Krystal Galido, Site Manager

RJA Laboratories, Inc.

PK 씨께,

지난달 저희 웹사이트를 만들면서 귀하가 하신 훌륭한 작업에 대해 다시 한 번 감사의 말씀드립니다. 저희 직원들과 다른 방문자들로부터 사이트에 대한 많은 긍정적인 의견을 받았습니다. 사이트에 몇 가지 새로운 기능을 추가해주실 수 있는지 문의하려고 이메일을 보냅니다.

구체적으로 말하자면, 직원 명부와 진행 중인 연구 프로젝트 섹션을 넣고 싶습니다.

다시 함께 일하게 되기를 기대합니다. 그럼 회신 주십시오.

크리스탈 갈리도, 사이트 관리자
RJA 래버러토리즈

(A) Specifically

(B) Nevertheless

(C) Instead

(D) Similarly

(A) 구체적으로

(B) 그럼에도 불구하고

(C) 대신에

(D) 유사하게

해설 **접속부사 고르기**: 바로 앞 문장에서 몇 가지 새로운 기능을 추가할 수 있는지 문의한다고 했는데, 빈칸 뒤의 내용이 추가하기를 원하는 새로운 기능이므로 (A) Specifically가 빈칸에 적절합니다.

Q2

Dear Mr. Go:

Thank you / for your recent order. Although most of your items have
감사드립니다   최근 주문에 대해   주문품의 대부분은 이미 발송되었지만

already shipped, / the Full-Spectrum Desk Lamp (model B07) /
                 풀 스펙트럼 탁상용 전등(모델 B07)은

is temporarily out of stock. We would be happy to substitute /
일시적으로 품절 상태입니다   기꺼이 대체해드리겠습니다

a similar item of your choice, / or we can refund your payment for
귀하께서 선택하신 것과 유사한 제품으로   아니면 이 품목의 결제 금액을 환불해드릴 수 있습니다

this item.

We appreciate your patience / and hope to serve you / in a timelier
참고 기다려주셔서 감사드립니다   그리고 귀하를 모시고 싶습니다   앞으로 더

manner in the future. (Meanwhile), / please contact our order
시기적절하게   그동안 ┐   저희 주문 부서로 연락 주십시오
                              └→ 그동안에

department / at 716-555-0160 / with any questions.
             716-555-0160번으로   혹시 문의 사항이 있으시면

Carrie Weber

Director, Granger's Lighting, Inc.

고 씨께,

최근 주문에 대해 감사드립니다. 주문품의 대부분은 이미 발송되었지만, 풀 스펙트럼 탁상용 전등(모델 B07)은 일시적으로 품절 상태입니다. 귀하께서 선택하신 것과 유사한 제품으로 기꺼이 대체해드리거나, 해당 품목의 결제 금액을 환불해드리겠습니다.

참고 기다려주셔서 감사드리며, 앞으로 더 시기적절하게 귀하를 모시고 싶습니다. 그동안 혹시 문의 사항이 있으시면 716-555-0160번으로 저희 주문 부서로 연락 주십시오.

캐리 웨버
그레인전스 조명 이사

(A) Instead

(B) Besides

(C) In contrast

(D) Meanwhile

(A) 대신에

(B) 게다가

(C) 대조적으로

(D) 그동안에

해설 접속부사 고르기: 빈칸 앞뒤를 보면 '앞으로 고객님을 다시 모시고 싶으며, 그동안 문의 사항이 있으시면 연락 주십시오'라는 내용이므로 '그동안'이라는 뜻의 (D) Meanwhile이 정답입니다.

1 (D)	**2** (B)	**3** (C)	**4** (D)

Questions 1-4 refer to the following e-mail.

To: Amelia Le <amelia.le@restaurant154.com>

From: Oliver Hendriks <ohendriks@domaneengineering.com>

Date: June 30

Subject: Thank you

Dear Ms. Le,

앞의 명사구 the excellent catering service를 수식하는 과거분사

On behalf of everyone at Domane Engineering, / I would like to thank you /
도메인 엔지니어링 전 직원을 대표하여   감사드리고 싶습니다

for the excellent catering service / 1. (provided) by your staff / at our recent
훌륭한 출장연회 서비스에   귀사 직원들에 의해 제공된   최근 저희

company awards dinner. The feedback I have received from attendees /
회사 시상식 만찬에서   참석자들로부터 받은 의견은   → 사실, 정말로

has been overwhelmingly positive. 2. (Indeed), / many of them / are still
압도적으로 긍정적입니다   사실   많은 참석자들이   지금도 극찬하고

raving / about the delicious food and exceptional service.
있습니다   맛있는 음식과 특별한 서비스에 대해

We organize several company events / each year, / and we certainly
저희는 다양한 회사 행사들을 주최합니다   해마다   그리고 귀하와 일하기를 진심으로

hope to work with you / at Restaurant 154 / again. Incidentally, / I have
희망합니다   레스토랑 154에 있는   다시   덧붙여 말씀드리면   귀사의

recommended your restaurant / to an (acquaintance / 3. who) is searching
식당을 추천했습니다   지인에게   장소를 찾고 있는
        사람 선행사(an acquaintance) + 주격 관계대명사 who ←

for a place / to hold a holiday party. 4. I expect / that she will be contacting
    휴일 파티를 열   예상합니다   그녀가 곧 귀사에 연락하리라

you soon.

Sincerely,

Oliver Hendriks

Office Manager, Domane Engineering

1-4 이메일

수신: 아멜리아 르 <amelia.le@
restaurant154.com>

발신: 올리버 헨드릭스 <ohen-
driks@domaneengineer-
ing.com>

날짜: 6월 30일

제목: 감사합니다

르 씨께,

도메인 엔지니어링 전 직원을 대표
하여, 최근 저희 회사 시상식 만찬
에서 귀사 직원들이 제공한 훌륭한
출장연회 서비스에 감사드립니다.
참석자들로부터 받은 의견은 압도
적으로 긍정적입니다. 사실은 많은
참석자들이 맛있는 음식과 특별한
서비스에 대해 지금도 극찬하고 있
습니다.

저희는 해마다 몇 차례의 회사 행
사들을 주최하고 있으며, 레스토랑
154에 있는 귀하와 다시 일하기를
진심으로 희망합니다. 덧붙여 말씀
드리면 휴일 파티를 열 장소를 찾고
있는 지인에게 귀사의 식당을 추천
했습니다. 그녀가 곧 귀사에 연락하
리라 예상합니다.

올리버 헨드릭스
사무장, 도메인 엔지니어링

1 (A) was provided

(B) to be providing

(C) has been providing

(D) provided

> 해설 **형용사 자리 (과거분사):** 빈칸은 명사구 the excellent catering service를 뒤에서 수식하는 형용사 자리로, 문맥상 '귀사 직원들에 의해 제공된'이라는 의미가 자연스러우므로, 과거분사 (D) provided가 정답입니다. 참고로 문장에 동사구 would like to thank가 있으므로 동사인 (A)와 (C)는 빈칸에 들어갈 수 없습니다.

---

2 (A) Otherwise

(B) Indeed

(C) Nonetheless

(D) Even so

(A) 그렇지 않으면

(B) 사실은

(C) 그렇기는 하지만

(D) 그렇기는 하지만

> 해설 **접속부사 고르기:** 빈칸 앞 문장에서 시상식 만찬 참석자들의 의견이 매우 긍정적이라는 내용을, 빈칸 뒤에서 많은 참석자들이 지금도 음식과 서비스를 극찬한다는 내용을 언급했습니다. 따라서 앞뒤 비슷한 내용을 연결하며 뒤에 나오는 내용을 강조하는 접속부사 (B) Indeed가 정답입니다.

---

3 (A) one

(B) herself

(C) who

(D) mine

> 해설 **관계대명사 (주격):** 빈칸 뒤에 동사 is searching for가 있으므로, 빈칸에는 접속사가 들어가야 합니다. 빈칸이 이끄는 절은 앞에 있는 사람 명사 an acquaintance를 수식하는 역할을 하므로 사람 명사 an acquaintance를 대신하여 동사 is searching의 주어 역할을 하는 주격 관계대명사 (C) who가 정답입니다.

---

4 (A) We were honored to receive the award.

(B) Because of this, I will need to reschedule the event.

(C) That is why we requested a change to the menu.

(D) I expect that she will be contacting you soon.

(A) 상을 받게 되어 영광이었습니다.

(B) 이 때문에 행사 일정을 다시 잡아야 합니다.

(C) 이런 이유로 메뉴 변경을 요청했습니다.

(D) 그녀가 곧 귀사에 연락하리라 생각합니다.

> 해설 **문장 고르기:** 빈칸 앞 문장 I have recommended ~ a holiday party.에서 파티 장소를 찾고 있는 지인에게 르 씨의 식당을 추천했다고 언급했습니다. 따라서 빈칸에는 그 지인이 연락할 것이라는 내용이 언급되는 것이 문맥상 자연스러우므로, 정답은 (D)입니다.

Q1 (B)   **Q2** (A)

Q1

The Plantas Group, / an environmental research institution / based
플랜터스 그룹이 　　　　환경 연구 기관인 　　　　　　　　웨일스의

in Cardiff, Wales, / has received a grant from the Green Community
카디프에 근거지를 둔 　　그린 커뮤니티 재단(GCF)에서 보조금을 받았다

Foundation (GCF). The grant / was awarded for a proposal /
　　　　　　　　　　이 보조금은 　　제안서에 대해 수여되었다

submitted to GCF. The funds will be used / on the energy-efficient
GCF에 제출된 　　　이 기금은 쓰일 예정이다 　　　플랜터스 본부를 에너지 효율성이

redesign of the Plantas headquarters. The upgrades / include
높게 재설계하는 데 　　　　　　　　　　업그레이드는 　　충전소 설치를

installation of a charging station / for electric cars. Karyna Silver,
포함한다 　　　　　　　　　　　전기차를 위한 　　　플랜터스의 시설

Plantas' Facilities Director, / will oversee the work / in consultation
관리소장인 카리나 실버가 　　　　작업을 감독하게 된다 　　GCF의 프리다 슈미트와

with Frieda Schmidt of GCF.
협의해

웨일스의 카디프에 근거지를 둔 환경 연구 기관 플랜터스 그룹이 그린 커뮤니티 재단(GCF)에서 수여하는 보조금을 받았다. 이 보조금은 GCF에 제출된 제안서에 대해 수여되었다. 이 기금은 플랜터스 본부를 에너지 효율성이 높게 재설계하는 데 쓰일 예정이다. 업그레이드에는 전기차 충전소 설치가 포함된다. 플랜터스의 시설 관리소장인 카리나 실버가 GCF의 프리다 슈미트와 협의해 작업을 감독하게 될 것이다.

(A) Installing LCD lighting is a common efficiency update.
(B) The upgrades include installation of a charging station for electric cars.
(C) Ms. Silver is experienced in advancing conservation measures.
(D) Energy-saving construction techniques have increased in popularity.

(A) LCD 조명을 설치하는 것은 일반적인 효율성 개선 작업이다.
(B) 업그레이드에는 전기차 충전소 설치가 포함된다.
(C) 실버 씨는 보존 조치를 진척시키는 데 경험이 있다.
(D) 에너지를 절약하는 건설 기술이 인기를 얻고 있다.

해설 문장 고르기: 빈칸 앞 문장에서 '에너지 효율성이 높은 재설계(the energy-efficient redesign)'라는 기금의 사용처를 언급했다. 따라서 빈칸에는 '에너지 효율성이 높은 재설계'에 대한 구체적인 사례가 들어가는 것이 문맥상 자연스러우므로, 정답은 (B)입니다.

Q2

To All:

Next Monday, / Sanjay Corporation / will hold its annual Safety Day.
다음 주 월요일   산제이사는   연례 안전의 날을 지킬 것입니다

We ask / that you check all the chemicals and products in your
바랍니다   여러분의 구역에 있는 모든 화학물질과 제품을 점검하시기를

area / on Monday morning / and dispose of any / that have reached
월요일 오전에   그래서 무엇이든 처리하시기를   유효 기간에 다다른 것은

their expiration date. Please also discard / old files, used boxes, /
유효 기간에 다다른   또한 폐기하시기 바랍니다   오래된 파일, 사용한 상자

and other office materials / that cannot be recycled. Special bins for
그리고 기타 사무용품을   재활용할 수 없는   이러한 폐기물을 위한

these waste materials / will be placed on each floor. With your
특별 수거함이   각 층에 놓여질 것입니다   여러분의 도움이 있다면

help, / this may be Sanjay Corporation's safest year yet!
올해는 산제이사의 가장 안전한 한 해가 될지도 모릅니다

여러분 모두에게:

다음 주 월요일, 산제이사는 연례 안전의 날을 지킬 것입니다. 월요일 오전에 여러분의 구역에 있는 모든 화학물질과 제품을 점검하고 유효 기간에 다다른 것은 무엇이든 처리하시기 바랍니다. 아울러 오래된 파일, 사용한 상자, 기타 재활용할 수 없는 사무용품도 폐기하시기 바랍니다. 이러한 폐기물을 위한 특별 수거함이 각 층에 놓여질 것입니다. 여러분의 도움이 있다면 올해는 산제이사의 가장 안전한 한 해가 될지도 모릅니다!

(A) Special bins for these waste materials will be placed on each floor.
(B) The laboratory inspection results will be announced soon.
(C) Place this new safety equipment in the cabinets.
(D) Employees enjoyed great food and conversation at the picnic.

(A) 이러한 폐기물을 위한 특별 수거함이 각 층에 놓여질 것입니다.
(B) 연구실 점검 결과가 곧 발표될 것입니다.
(C) 이 새 안전 장비를 수납장에 넣으십시오.
(D) 직원들은 야유회에서 훌륭한 음식과 대화를 즐겼습니다.

해설 문장 고르기: 바로 앞에서 폐기해야 할 여러 가지 물품에 대해 언급했으므로, 그러한 폐기물들을 위한 특별 수거함이 놓여질 장소를 알려주는 (A)가 빈칸에 들어가는 것이 자연스럽습니다.

| 1 (C) | 2 (A) | 3 (B) | 4 (D) |

Questions 1-4 refer to the following memo.

1-4 메모

To: Box Office Staff

From: G. Anders, General Director

Date: 24 November

Subject: Policy Update

I am writing / to inform you of a change in the **1.** seating policy / for our
메일을 씁니다   좌석 정책에 대한 변경 사항을 공지하고자

classical music series, / effective immediately. There have been many
우리 클래식 음악 시리즈의   곧바로 시행될   많은 요청이 있어 왔습니다

requests / on the day of the concert / from patrons / who prefer to sit on
          음악회가 있는 날이면   고객들로부터   통로 측 좌석에 앉기를 선호하는

the aisle / because there is more leg room. From now on, / we will accept
통로 측   다리를 뻗을 공간이 더 넓기 때문에   앞으로는   이와 같은 요청을

such requests / **2.** only at the time tickets are purchased. Subsequently, /
받을 예정입니다   입장권 구매 시점에만   그 후에

audience members / **3.** who need extra space / may ask for a seat in
관객들은   추가 공간이 필요한   뒤쪽 두 줄에 있는 좌석을 요청할
                    → 사람 명사 audience members를 수식하는 주격 관계대명사절

the back two rows, / as those are not usually filled. **4.** It is further from the
수 있습니다   이곳은 평소에 채워지지 않기 때문입니다   이곳은 무대에서 더 멀리 떨어져

stage, / but it is more comfortable there. This policy / should help us avoid
있습니다 하지만 그곳이 더 안락합니다   본 정책은   우리가 불평을 피하는 데 도움이

complaints / once a performance has begun.
될 것입니다   공연이 시작된 후에

1-4 메모

수신: 매표소 직원
발신: G. 앤더스, 총괄 이사
날짜: 11월 24일
주제: 정책 변경

곧바로 시행될 우리 클래식 음악 시리즈의 좌석 정책에 대한 변경 사항을 공지하고자 메일을 드립니다. 음악회가 있는 날이면, 다리를 뻗을 공간이 더 넓기 때문에 통로 측 좌석에 앉기를 선호하는 고객들로부터 많은 요청이 있어 왔습니다. 앞으로는 이와 같은 요청은 입장권 구매 시점에만 받을 예정입니다. 그 후에 추가 공간이 필요한 관객들은 뒤쪽 두 줄에 있는 좌석을 요청할 수 있는데, 이곳은 평소에 채워지지 않기 때문입니다. 이곳은 무대에서 더 멀리 떨어져 있지만 더 안락합니다. 본 정책은 우리가 공연이 시작된 후에 불평을 피하는 데 도움이 될 것입니다.

1
(A) refund
(B) pricing
(C) seating
(D) recording

(A) 환불
(B) 가격 책정
(C) 좌석
(D) 녹음

> **해설** 어휘 고르기: 빈칸을 포함한 전치사구(in the _____ policy)는 앞의 명사 change를 수식합니다. 따라서 빈칸에는 정책 변경의 내용을 구체적으로 나타내는 명사가 들어가야 합니다. 빈칸 뒤 문장에서 고객들이 통로 쪽 좌석에 앉기를 선호한다고 언급했으므로, 문맥상 '좌석 정책'과 관련된 변경임을 알 수 있습니다. 따라서 (C) seating(좌석)이 정답입니다.

2
(A) only
(B) less
(C) very
(D) late

(A) ~만
(B) 더 적게
(C) 매우
(D) 늦게

> **해설** 어휘 고르기: 빈칸 뒤 at the time tickets are purchased를 강조하는 부사 자리입니다. 문맥상 '입장권을 구매하는 시점에만'이라는 의미가 자연스러우므로, '오직, ~만'이라는 의미의 (A) only가 정답입니다.

3
(A) needed
(B) who need
(C) they need
(D) having needed

> **해설** 주격 관계대명사 + 동사: 빈칸 뒤 명사구 extra space를 목적어로 취하면서 앞에 있는 사람 명사 audience members를 수식하는 역할을 하므로, 빈칸에는 〈주격 관계대명사 + 동사〉 구조인 (B) who need가 정답입니다. 완료형 분사 (D) having needed는 주절의 동사 may ask for보다 앞선 시제를 나타내므로, 문맥상 적절하지 않습니다.

4
(A) Many people prefer to sit there, near the orchestra.
(B) Saturday evening performances attract the largest crowds.
(C) Ticket holders may not enter the theater after the performance begins.
(D) It is further from the stage, but it is more comfortable there.

(A) 많은 사람들이 그곳, 오케스트라석 근처에 앉는 것을 선호합니다.
(B) 토요일 저녁 공연에 사람이 제일 많습니다.
(C) 티켓 소지자들이 공연이 시작된 후에는 극장에 들어갈 수 없습니다.
(D) 이곳은 무대에서 더 멀리 떨어져 있지만 더 안락합니다.

> **해설** 문장 고르기: 빈칸 앞에서 추가 공간이 필요한 관객들이 뒤쪽 두 줄에 있는 좌석을 요청할 수 있다(audience members ~ in the back two rows)는 내용이 언급되었으므로, 빈칸에는 해당 위치의 좌석에 대한 부가 설명이 이어지는 것이 적절합니다. 따라서 이곳이 무대에서 더 멀리 있지만 더 안락하다고 설명한 (D)가 들어가는 것이 문맥상 자연스럽습니다.

● **예제** 교재 p.210

Rosario's Printing Services
로사리오 인쇄 서비스
 	
Posters, brochures, business cards, and much more!
포스터, 소책자, 명함, 그리고 아주 많은 물품이 있습니다!
 	
Save big! The following discounts are available online /
왕창 절약하세요! / 온라인으로 아래와 같이 할인을 받으실 수 있습니다.
 	
to first-time customers.
처음 이용하는 고객은
 	
• 10 percent off any order of at least $100
  100달러 이상 주문 시 10% 할인
 	
• 15 percent off any order of at least $150
  150달러 이상 주문 시 15% 할인
 	
• 20 percent off any order of at least $200
  200달러 이상 주문 시 20% 할인
 	
• 25 percent off any order of at least $250
  250달러 이상 주문 시 25% 할인
	로사리오 인쇄 서비스
	
	포스터, 소책자, 명함, 그리고 아주 많은 물품이 있습니다!
	왕창 절약하세요! 처음 이용하는 고객은 온라인으로 아래와 같이 할인을 받으실 수 있습니다.
	
	• 100달러 이상 주문 시 10% 할인
	• 150달러 이상 주문 시 15% 할인
	• 200달러 이상 주문 시 20% 할인
	• 250달러 이상 주문 시 25% 할인

Q.   What is indicated about the offer? | 할인에 대해 언급된 것은?

    (A) It is for in-store use only. | (A) 매장 내 사용만 가능하다.

    (B) It is for new customers. | (B) 신규 고객을 대상으로 한다.

---

1. (B)	**2.** (A)	**3.** (C)	**4.** (B)	**5.** (A)

1.   draw visitors 방문객을 유치하다

2.   an additional charge 추가 요금

3.   a complimentary beverage 무료 음료

    (A) an extra fee 추가 요금

    (B) attract tourists 관광객을 유치하다

    (C) a free drink 무료 음료

4.   You can watch Mr. Rau's talk on the conference Web site later. | 라우 씨의 강연은 차후에 컨퍼런스 웹사이트에서 보실 수 있습니다.

    (A) Mr. Rau's session is being rescheduled. | (A) 라우 씨의 세션은 일정이 조정되고 있습니다.

    (B) Mr. Rau's session will soon be available online. | (B) 라우 씨의 세션은 곧 온라인에서 이용하실 수 있습니다.

    `Paraphrasing`   on the conference Web site → online

5.   Manazuru Air publishes flight schedules twelve months in advance. | 마나즈루 항공은 12개월 전에 운항 일정을 발표한다.

    (A) Manazuru Air releases its flight schedules a year in advance. | (A) 마나즈루 항공은 1년 앞서 운항 일정을 공개한다.

    (B) Manazuru Air purchases a new fleet of aircraft a year in advance. | (B) 마나즈루 항공은 1년 앞서 새 항공기를 구매한다.

    `Paraphrasing`   twelve months → a year

패러프레이징 2 포괄적인 개념으로 바꿔 쓰기

● **예제**

교재 p.211

CROVER and WAYFIELD ASSOCIATES
크로버 앤드 웨이필드 어소시에이츠

Providing reliable tax advice and accounting services /
신뢰할 수 있는 세무 자문 및 회계 서비스 제공

for thirty-eight years
38년간

Members of our firm / specialize in services for:
당사 회원들은   다음 분야 서비스를 전문으로 합니다.

- Individuals and Families
  개인 및 가족
- Small businesses
  소기업
- Corporations
  기업

Reduced rates proudly offered to nonprofit organizations.
비영리 단체에는 할인 요금이 제공된다는 점에 자긍심을 가지고 있습니다.

크로버 앤드 웨이필드 어소시에이츠

38년간 신뢰할 수 있는 세무 자문 및 회계 서비스 제공
당사 회원들은 다음 분야 서비스를 전문으로 합니다.

- 개인 및 가족
- 소규모 사업체
- 대기업

비영리 단체에는 할인 요금이 제공된다는 점에 자긍심을 가지고 있습니다.

Q. What is stated about Crover and Wayfield Associates?

(A) They have been in operation for more than forty years.

(B) They serve both individuals and companies.

크로버 앤드 웨이필드 어소시에이츠에 대해 언급된 것은?

(A) 40년 이상 영업을 해왔다.

(B) 개인과 회사 모두 상대한다

---

1. (C)   **2.** (A)   **3.** (B)   **4.** (A)   **5.** (B)

1. ride the bus 버스를 타다
2. cardboard, newspapers, and magazines 판지, 신문, 잡지
3. the region's best known painter 지역에서 가장 유명한 화가

(A) paper products 종이 제품
(B) a local artist 지역 예술가
(C) use public transportation
대중교통을 이용하다

4. Ms. Arnold began her professional career as a college professor.

(A) Ms. Arnold's first career was an educator.

(B) Ms. Arnold's first career was a chef.

`Paraphrasing` a college professor → an educator

아놀드 씨는 대학교수로 전문직 경력을 시작했다.

(A) 아놀드 씨의 첫 번째 경력은 교육자였다.

(B) 아놀드 씨의 첫 번째 경력은 요리사였다.

5. All entrées are served with salad, coffee or tea, and fresh bread.

(A) Dessert is included with all entrées.

(B) A drink is included with all entrées.

`Paraphrasing` coffee or tea → A drink

모든 앙트레에는 샐러드, 커피 또는 차, 신선한 빵이 함께 제공됩니다.

(A) 모든 앙트레에는 디저트가 포함됩니다.

(B) 모든 앙트레에는 음료가 포함됩니다.

PART 7 | 패러프레이징

패러프레이징 3 요약해서 표현하기

● **예제**

교재 p.212

Reviews 후기	Menu 메뉴	Directions 오시는 길

"The meals may be a bit pricey, / but they are worth every cent.
음식들이 조금 비쌀지는 모르지만   한 푼도 아깝지 않습니다

With diverse items / designed to impress any gourmet, / I had
다양한 품목들이 있어   미식가들에게 깊은 인상을 주려고 만든   결정하기가

difficulty making up my mind! I ended up choosing a fresh and
어려웠어요   저는 결국 신선하고 맛있는 연어 샐러드를 선택했죠

tasty salmon salad. Be aware / that the parking lot is very
                  유의하시고   주차장이 아주 좁다는 점을

small, / so arrive early to get a spot." — Diego M.
         자리를 잡으려면 일찍 도착하세요   디에고 M.

후기	메뉴	오시는 길

"음식들이 조금 비쌀지는 모르지만, 한 푼도 아깝지 않습니다. 미식가들에게 깊은 인상을 주려고 만든 다양한 품목들이 있어, 결정하기가 어려웠어요! 저는 결국 신선하고 맛있는 연어 샐러드를 선택했죠. 주차장이 아주 좁다는 점을 유의하시고 자리를 잡으려면 일찍 도착하세요." — 디에고 M.

Q. What did Diego M. like most about the restaurant?

(A) The variety on the menu

(B) The attractive design

디에고 M.은 레스토랑의 어떤 점을 가장 마음에 들어했는가?

(A) 메뉴의 다양함

(B) 매력적인 디자인

---

1. (B)	2. (C)	3. (A)	4. (A)	5. (A)

1. a full-time managerial position in our advertising department 우리 광고부의 정규 관리직

2. a map that shows the best options for parking your vehicle 주차를 위한 최적의 선택지를 보여주는 지도

3. visit Dalter's major tourist attractions
달터의 주요 관광명소들을 방문하다

(A) go sightseeing 관광하다

(B) advertising manager 광고부장

(C) a parking map 주차 지도

4. The position requires a person who is outgoing, organized, and familiar with the Newville community.

(A) Organizational skills are mentioned as a requirement for the job.

(B) Management experience is mentioned as a requirement for the job.

그 직위에는 외향적이고, 체계적이며, 뉴빌 공동체를 잘 아는 사람이 필요하다.

(A) 그 일자리의 요건으로 체계적인 역량이 거론된다.

(B) 그 일자리의 요건으로 경영 경험이 거론된다.

Paraphrasing outgoing, organized, and familiar with the Newville community → Organizational skills

5. The voucher, valid for any Azure Sky Airlines flight, is valued at RM800 and must be redeemed within one year.

(A) The voucher has an expiration date.

(B) The voucher is accepted by multiple airlines.

모든 아주르 스카이 항공 항공편에 유효한 그 쿠폰은 가치가 800마르크로, 1년 안에 상품으로 교환해야 한다.

(A) 쿠폰에는 만료일이 있다.

(B) 여러 항공사에서 쿠폰을 받아준다.

Paraphrasing must be redeemed within one year → has an expiration date

패러프레이징 4　추론하여 바꿔 쓰기

교재 p.213

● **예제**

Rosa Gonzalez [10:16 A.M.]
로사 곤잘레스 [오전 10시 16분]

I made reservations / for us to have lunch / in the lobby
예약했어요　　　　　　　점심 회식을 위해　　　　로비 식당으로

restaurant / at noon.
　　　　　　정오에

Anna Losch [10:17 A.M.]
안나 로쉬 [오전 10시 17분]

Good, / but it's going to be a working meal. We need to go
좋아요　　하지만 업무를 겸한 식사 자리예요.　　　　검토해야 하거든요

over / the slides for our design presentation.
　　　디자인 프레젠테이션용 슬라이드를

로사 곤잘레스 [오전 10시 16분]

점심 회식을 위해 정오에 로비 식당으로 예약했어요.

안나 로쉬 [오전 10시 17분]

좋아요, 하지만 업무 겸 식사 자리예요. 디자인 프레젠테이션용 슬라이드를 검토해야 하거든요.

Q. What will the group most likely do at noon?

(A) Review a presentation

(B) Attend a special session

이 그룹은 정오에 무엇을 할 것 같은가?

(A) 프레젠테이션 검토

(B) 특별 강연 참석

---

1. (B)	**2.** (A)	**3.** (C)	**4.** (B)	**5.** (A)

1. at any branch of Podric's Pizza
포드릭 피자 어느 지점에서나

2. be founded in 1940
1940년에 설립되다

3. be posted every few minutes
몇 분마다 게시되다

(A) be in operation for many years
오랫동안 영업하고 있다

(B) The business has multiple
locations. 그 업체는 지점이 여러 군데 있다.

(C) be updated frequently
자주 업데이트되다

4. Max Hinkle has critiqued almost every dining
establishment in Millford.

(A) Max Hinkle is a chef.

(B) Max Hinkle is a food critic.

Paraphrasing　has critiqued almost every dining establishment → a food critic

맥스 힝클은 밀포드에 있는 거의 모든 식당에 대해 논평했다.

(A) 맥스 힝클은 요리사이다.

(B) 맥스 힝클은 음식 평론가이다.

5. Construction on our new Auckland resort will be
completed in eight months.

(A) A resort will open.

(B) A new service will be offered.

Paraphrasing　will be completed in eight months → will open

새로운 오클랜드 리조트 건설이 8개월 뒤에 완료될 예정이다.

(A) 리조트가 문을 열 예정이다.

(B) 새로운 서비스가 제공될 예정이다.

Q1 (A)   **Q2** (B)

Q1

Marcelyn Travel Agengy
마셀린 여행사

We have a new branch / in the historic Centreville Shopping Center.
저희가 새 지점을 엽니다   역사적인 센트레빌 쇼핑 센터에

Visit us / at our grand opening!
방문해 주세요 / 성대한 개업식에

Saturday, 2 October
10월 2일 토요일

10:00 A.M. to 4:00 P.M.
오전 10시~오후 4시

14 Elm Park Road, Johannesburg
요하네스버그, 엘름 파크로 14

Stop by / to meet our highly qualified travel agents / and find out
들르세요   우수한 자격을 갖춘 저희 여행사 직원들을 만나보세요   그리고 여행을 예약할

how you can book the trip / you've always wanted / at a great
수 있는 방법을 알아보세요   항상 원하시던   좋은 가격대로

price. Enjoy / complimentary coffee, tea, and snacks. We will also
즐기세요   무료 커피와 차, 스낵을   또한 저희는 무료

be giving away free tote bags / while supplies last.
토트백을 나누어 드릴 예정입니다   재고 소진 시까지

마셀린 여행사

저희가 역사적인 센트레빌 쇼핑 센터에 새 지점을 엽니다. 성대한 개업식에 방문해 주세요!

10월 2일 토요일
오전 10시~오후 4시
요하네스버그, 엘름 파크로 14

들르셔서 우수한 자격을 갖춘 저희 여행사 직원들을 만나보시고 항상 원하시던 여행을 좋은 가격대에 예약할 수 있는 방법을 알아보세요. 무료 커피와 차, 스낵을 즐기세요. 또한 저희는 무료 토트백을 재고 소진 시까지 나누어 드릴 예정입니다

What is being advertised?

(A) A special event

(B) A free trip

무엇이 광고되고 있는가?

(A) 특별 행사

(B) 무료 여행

해설 주제 / 목적: 광고의 대상은 주로 지문의 초반에서 찾아야 합니다. 첫 번째 단락의 We have a new branch in the historic Centreville Shopping Center.와 Visit us at our grand opening!에서 개업식을 광고하고 있음을 알 수 있으므로 정답은 (A) A special event입니다.

Q2

What's Trending in Dublin?
더블린에서 뜨고 있는 것은?

By Peter O'Scanlon
글 피터 오스캔론

1 March— / The latest development venture of Craigson Properties /
3월 1일   크레이그슨 부동산의 최신 벤처 사업 건물이

will soon open. The apartments on 2101 Blandon Street / are
곧 문을 연다   2101 블랜던 가에 있는 아파트는   어떤

in some ways a first for the company, / although it has similar
면에서 그 회사의 첫 번째 아파트이다   비록 비슷한 부동산을 보유하고 있지만

properties / in other cities. Yoshi Makino, vice president of Craigson
다른 도시에서도   크레이그슨 부동산 부사장 요시 마키노는

Properties, / says, / "We've been waiting / for the right location /
말한다   기다리고 있었죠   적당한 부지가

to become available / in Dublin. This nineteenth-century building, /
나기를   더블린에서   이 19세기 건물은

formerly a bank, / is perfect for the project." The building should
전에 은행이었던   이 프로젝트에 안성맞춤입니다   건물은 입주 준비가 될 예정이다

be ready for occupancy / next month, / with a grand opening
다음 달에   개장할 것으로 예상된다

anticipated / for mid-April.
4월 중순에

더블린에서 뜨고 있는 것은?

글 피터 오스캔론

3월 1일 – 크레이그슨 부동산의 최신 벤처 사업 건물이 곧 문을 연다. 비록 다른 도시에서도 비슷한 부동산을 보유하고 있지만, 2101 블랜던 가에 있는 아파트는 어떤 면에서 그 회사의 첫 번째 아파트이다. 크레이그슨 부동산 부사장 요시 마키노는 말한다. "더블린에서 적당한 부지가 나기를 기다리고 있었죠. 전에 은행이었던 이 19세기 건물은 이 프로젝트에 안성맞춤입니다." 건물은 다음 달에 입주 준비가 될 예정이며, 4월 중순에 개장할 것으로 예상된다.

What is the purpose of the article?

(A) To announce changes to a city's building codes

(B) To explain that a residential property will soon open

기사의 목적은?

(A) 시의 건축 법규 변경을 발표하려고

(B) 주거용 부동산이 곧 개장한다고 설명하려고

해설 **주제 / 목적:** 첫 문장에서 크레이그슨 부동산의 최신 벤처 사업 건물이 곧 문을 연다고 했고 마지막 문장에서도 그 아파트가 4월 중순 개장할 것이라고 언급하고 있습니다. 따라서 기사의 목적은 주거용 건물이 지어진다는 것을 알리려는 것이므로 정답은 (B)입니다. 글의 목적이나 주제를 묻는 문제는 주로 서두에 단서가 나온다는 것을 알아두세요.

Paraphrasing 지문의 The latest development venture → 정답의 a residential property

1 (D)	**2** (C)

Questions 1-2 refer to the following letter.

Lewistown Community Center • 1064 Blueberry Street • Lewistown, Montana 59457

April 21

Dear Valued Community Members,

1 The Lewistown Community Center (LCC) / has decided / to cancel most
루이스타운 커뮤니티 센터(LCC)는 　　　　　 결정했습니다　 대부분의 프로그램을

of its programming / for the upcoming summer term. **This is because of**
취소하기로　　　　　 다가오는 여름 학기에　　　　　 이는 진행 중인 건설 프로젝트

the ongoing building project / we mentioned / in our last letter. **Although**
때문입니다　　　　　 우리가 언급했던　　 지난번 편지에　　 비록 어려운

the decision was difficult, / it was ultimately made / to ensure the comfort
결정이었지만　　　　 궁극적으로 내린 결정이었습니다　　 학생, 직원, 그리고 건설 근로자들의

and safety of students, staff, and construction workers. **Outdoor**
편안함과 안전을 보장하기 위해　　　　　　　　　　 실외 프로그램은

programs / are not affected by the building project / and will still be offered.
　　 건설 프로젝트의 영향을 받지 않습니다　　　　 그래서 여전히 제공될 것입니다

We understand / that the cancellation is an inconvenience / to our
알고 있습니다　 이번 취소가 불편을 드린다는 점을　　　　　 우리 커뮤니티에

community. **2** To help you find alternative arrangements / for summer
　　　　　 대체 프로그램을 찾으시는 것을 돕기 위해　　　　 여름 프로그램에 대한

programming, / several organizations / have agreed to partner with us /
　　　　　 몇몇 단체들이　　　　 우리와 제휴하기로 합의했습니다

and will offer discounted programming options / to LCC members. **We have**
그리고 할인된 프로그램 옵션을 제공할 것입니다　　　 LCC 회원들에게　　　 동봉했습니다

enclosed / a document with information / about participating organizations
　　　 정보가 담긴 문서를　　　　 참가 단체들과 그들이 제공하는 서비스에 대한

and their offerings.

We hope / that you enjoy your summer / and come back to join us in
우리는 바랍니다 / 여러분이 즐거운 여름을 보내시기를　　 그리고 9월에 돌아와 우리와 함께해주시기를

September / for regular programming / in the new building. **We appreciate**
　　　 정규 프로그램을 위해　　 새로운 건물에서 하는　　　 융통성을 발휘해

your flexibility. You may address any questions / to me / at selma.ruan
주셔서 감사합니다　 문의 사항은 보내시면 됩니다　　　 제게

@lewistowncc.org.
selma.ruan@lewistowncc.org로

1-2 편지

루이스타운 커뮤니티 센터 • 1064 블루베리가 • 루이스타운, 몬태나주 59547

4월 21일

존경하는 회원 여러분,

1 루이스타운 커뮤니티 센터(LCC)는 다가오는 여름 학기에 대부분의 프로그램을 취소하기로 결정했습니다. 이는 우리가 지난번 편지에 언급했던 진행 중인 건설 프로젝트 때문입니다. 비록 어려운 결정이었지만, 궁극적으로 학생, 직원, 그리고 건설 근로자들의 편안함과 안전을 보장하기 위해 내린 결정이었습니다. 실외 프로그램은 건설 프로젝트의 영향을 받지 않으므로 여전히 제공될 것입니다.

이번 취소가 우리 커뮤니티에 불편을 드린다는 점을 알고 있습니다. **2** 여름 프로그램에 대한 대체 프로그램을 찾으시는 것을 돕기 위해, 몇몇 단체들이 우리와 제휴하기로 합의했으며 LCC 회원들에게 할인된 프로그램 옵션을 제공할 것입니다. 참가 단체들과 그들이 제공하는 서비스에 대한 정보가 담긴 문서를 동봉했습니다.

우리는 여러분이 즐거운 여름을 보내시고 새로운 건물에서 하는 정규 프로그램을 위해 9월에 돌아와 우리와 함께해주시기를 바랍니다. 융통성을 발휘해 주셔서 감사합니다. 문의 사항은 selma.ruan@lewistowncc.org로 제게 보내시면 됩니다.

Sincerely,

Selma Ruan

Selma Ruan, LCC Director

Enclosure

셀마 루안 LCC 이사

동봉물

---

1 What is the purpose of the letter?

(A) To announce a building project

(B) To introduce a new director of the LCC

(C) To invite individuals to a sponsored event

(D) To provide an update about upcoming changes

편지의 목적은?

(A) 건축 프로젝트를 발표하려고

(B) LCC의 신임 센터장을 소개하려고

(C) 후원 행사에 사람들을 초대하려고

(D) 곧 있을 변화에 대한 최신 소식을 전하려고

> **해설** 주제 / 목적: 편지의 목적을 묻는 문제는 대개 서두에 단서가 나옵니다. 첫 번째 단락에서 여름 학기에 프로그램 대부분이 취소된다고 했으므로, 정답은 (D)입니다.
>
> **Paraphrasing** 지문의 to cancel most of its programming → 정답의 upcoming changes

---

2 What does Ms. Ruan say that several organizations will do?

(A) Let LCC members borrow sports equipment

(B) Provide temporary space for LCC programs

(C) Give LCC members a discount

(D) Close for the summer

루안 씨는 몇몇 단체들이 무엇을 할 것이라고 말하는가?

(A) LCC 회원에게 스포츠 장비를 빌리게 할 것

(B) LCC 프로그램을 위한 임시 공간을 제공할 것

(C) LCC 회원에게 할인을 제공할 것

(D) 여름에 문을 닫을 것

> **해설** 세부 사항: 루안 씨는 편지를 보낸 발신인이고 두 번째 단락의 several organizations ~ to LCC members에서 몇몇 단체가 LCC와 제휴하기로 했고 LCC 회원들에게 할인된 프로그램을 제공할 것이라고 했으므로 정답은 (C)입니다.
>
> **Paraphrasing** 지문의 offer discounted programming options to LCC members → 정답의 Give LCC members a discount

ETS 문제로 훈련하기
교재 p.220

Q1 (B)   **Q2** (A)

Q1

Appliance Instructions
가전제품 사용 설명서

1. Place your dirty laundry / into the drum of the appliance.
더러운 빨래를 넣으세요   가전제품의 드럼 속에

2. Adjust the dial / to the appropriate cycle— / light soil, heavy soil,
다이얼을 맞추세요   적합한 사이클에   가벼운 오염, 찌든 때 등

etc.

3. Select the water temperature (cold, warm, hot) / by pressing the
물 온도(차가운 물, 따뜻한 물, 뜨거운 물)를 선택하세요   해당 버튼을 눌러서

corresponding button.

4. Add detergent / to the dispenser. Also put in fabric conditioner
세제를 첨가하세요   세제 나오는 곳에   심유유연제(선택 사항)도 넣으세요

(optional) / for best results.
          최상의 결과를 얻으려면

5. Close the door securely / and press the START button.
문을 꽉 닫으세요   그리고 '시작' 버튼을 누르세요

가전제품 사용 설명서

1. 더러운 빨래를 가전제품의 드럼 속에 넣으세요.

2. 다이얼을 적합한 사이클에 맞추세요 – 가벼운 오염, 찌든 때 등.

3. 해당 버튼을 눌러 물 온도(차가운 물, 따뜻한 물, 뜨거운 물)를 선택하세요.

4. 세제 나오는 곳에 세제를 첨가하세요. 최상의 결과를 얻으려면 섬유유연제(선택 사항)도 넣으세요.

5. 문을 꽉 닫고 '시작' 버튼을 누르세요.

According to the instructions, how can users get the best results?
(A) By adjusting the dial to a specific setting
(B) By using an additional product with the detergent

설명서에 따르면 사용자가 최상의 결과를 얻을 수 있는 방법은?
(A) 다이얼을 특정 설정으로 맞추기
(B) 세제와 함께 추가 제품 사용하기

해설   세부 사항: 설명서 4번에 섬유유연제로 최상의 결과를 얻는다고 언급했으므로 (B)가 정답입니다.

Paraphrasing   지문의 put in fabric conditioner → 정답의 using an additional product

Q2

January 6

By Janelie Rivers, Metro Styles Shop
자넬리 리버스, 메트로 스타일 숍

I purchased the Tateno Turbo / after a friend recommended it to
타테노 터보를 구입했습니다   친구가 그것을 제게 추천한 뒤

me. It is a good choice / for effortlessly cleaning your residence or
        탁월한 선택입니다   힘들이지 않고 집이나 사업장을 청소하는 데

business. As a business owner / intent on keeping a spotless salon, /
        업주로서   티끌 하나 없는 미용실을 유지하는 데 몰두하는

I find that to be vital. When I clean after my last customer, / it's
저에게는 그것이 아주 중요합니다 / 마지막 고객이 떠난 뒤 청소할 때

impossible / to find even one stray hair on the floor. It is well worth
불가능합니다   바닥에서 잔머리 한 올도 찾는 것이   제값을 톡톡히 합니다.

the price.

There are some things / that I don't like about the product. The
몇 가지 것들이 있습니다   제품에 대해 마음에 들지 않는   색상 선택이

color choices are limited, / and it fails to hold a charge. The battery
제한되어 있습니다   그리고 그것은 충전을 유지하지 못합니다   배터리가 때로는

sometimes drains / after just twenty minutes. It's not a major
방전됩니다   단 20분 만에   크게 불편하지는

inconvenience, / as it does not take long / to charge to full power /
않습니다   오래 걸리지는 않으므로   완전히 충전되는 데

on the docking station.
거치대에서

1월 6일

자넬리 리버스, 메트로 스타일 숍

친구의 추천을 받은 뒤. 타테노 터
보를 구입했습니다. 힘들이지 않고
집이나 사업장을 청소하는 데 탁월
한 선택입니다. 티끌 하나 없는 미
용실을 유지하는 데 몰두하는 업주
로서 저에게는 그것이 아주 중요합
니다. 마지막 고객이 떠난 뒤 청소
할 때, 바닥에서 머리카락을 한 올
도 찾을 수 없습니다. 제 값을 톡톡
히 합니다.

제품에 대해 마음에 들지 않는 점도
몇 가지 있습니다. 색상 선택이 제
한되어 있고 충전을 유지하지 못합
니다. 배터리가 때로는 단 20분 만
에 방전됩니다. 거치대에서 완전히
충전되는 데 오래 걸리지는 않으므
로 크게 불편하지는 않습니다.

What type of business does Ms. Rivers own?

(A) A hair salon

(B) An appliance store

리버스 씨가 소유한 사업체의 종류는?

(A) 미용실

(B) 가전제품 매장

해설 세부 사항: 첫 번째 단락의 When I clean after my last customer, it's impossible to find even one stray hair on the
floor.에서 리버스 씨가 미용실을 소유하고 있다는 것을 알 수 있으므로 정답은 (A)입니다.

1 (B)	**2** (C)

Questions 1-2 refer to the following notice.

1-2 공지문

Pimsborough Film Festival
핌스버러 영화제

핌스버러 영화제

The fourth annual Pimsborough Film Festival / celebrates filmmakers / from
제4회 연례 핌스버러 영화제가   영화제작자들을 기념합니다   지역

around the region. It will take place / from March 16 to March 22 /
전체의   영화제는 열립니다   3월 16일부터 3월 22일까지

at cinemas / throughout the county. Members of the public / are offered
영화관에서   카운티 전역에 있는   일반인에게는   3가지 패스가

three pass options / to choose from.
제공됩니다   선택할 수 있는

Cinema Pass: $80 general admission; $50 for students
시네마 패스: 일반 입장료 80달러;   학생 50달러

     2✓All access to film viewings
     모든 영화 관람

1Social Pass: $200 general admission; $150 for students
소셜 패스: 일반 입장료 200달러; 학생 150달러

     2✓All access to film viewings
     모든 영화 관람

     ✓Ticket to opening night reception
     개막일 밤 축하연 티켓

Backstage Pass: $300 general admission; $250 for students
백스테이지 패스: 일반 입장료 300달러;   학생 250달러

     2✓All access to film viewings
     모든 영화 관람

     ✓Ticket to opening night reception
     개막일 밤 축하연 티켓

     ✓Four exclusive "Meet the Director" sessions
     독점 '감독과의 만남' 시간 4회

제4회 연례 핌스버러 영화제가 지역 전체의 영화제작자들을 기념합니다. 영화제는 3월 16일부터 3월 22일까지 카운티 전역에 있는 영화관에서 열립니다. 일반인에게는 선택할 수 있는 3가지 패스가 제공됩니다.

시네마 패스: 일반 입장료 80달러; 학생 50달러
     2✓모든 영화 관람

1소셜 패스: 일반 입장료 200달러; 학생 150달러
     2✓모든 영화 관람
     ✓개막일 밤 축하연 티켓

백스테이지 패스: 일반 입장료 300달러; 학생 250달러
     2✓모든 영화 관람
     ✓개막일 밤 축하연 티켓
     ✓독점 '감독과의 만남' 시간 4회

1 How much does a Social Pass ticket cost for people who are not students?

(A) $50

(B) $200

(C) $250

(D) $300

학생이 아닌 사람들의 소셜 패스 티켓은 얼마인가?

(A) 50달러

(B) 200달러

(C) 250달러

(D) 300달러

> **해설** 세부 사항: 지문 중간의 Social Pass 부분을 보면 일반 입장료는 200달러이고 학생은 150달러임을 알 수 있으므로 정답은 (B)입니다.

---

2 What do the three pass options have in common?

(A) They allow ticket holders to meet film directors.

(B) They offer discounted prices for early purchase.

(C) They allow ticket holders to see every film.

(D) They include entry to a festival reception.

세 가지 패스 옵션의 공통점은?

(A) 티켓 소지자들이 영화 감독들을 만나도록 허용한다.

(B) 조기 구매 시 할인가를 제공한다.

(C) 티켓 소지자는 모든 영화를 보도록 허용한다.

(D) 영화제 축하연 입장이 포함된다.

> **해설** 세부 사항: 세 가지 패스 설명에 All access to film viewings가 공통적으로 있다는 것을 확인할 수 있으므로 티켓 소지자는 모든 영화를 볼 수 있다는 (C)가 정답입니다.
>
> **Paraphrasing** 지문의 All access to film viewings → 정답의 see every film

ETS 문제로 훈련하기

교재 p.224

Q1 (B)   **Q2** (B)

Q1

Straudberg Water Corporation
스트라우드버그 수도 공사

Reading Your Water Meter
수도 계량기 읽기

Customers of Straudberg Water Corporation / can take a meter
스트라우드버그 수도 공사의 고객들은   계량기를 읽을 수 있습니다

reading / at any time. Doing so can help you / confirm that a water
언제든지   그렇게 하면 도움이 될 수 있습니다   수도 요금 청구서가 정확한지

bill is correct / or estimate the cost of an upcoming bill. To read
확인하거나   다음 청구서 요금을 추산하는 데   계량기를

your meter, / record the number / that appears on the first day of
읽으려면   숫자를 기록하십시오   청구 주기의 첫 날에 보이는

the billing cycle / —typically the first of the month. Then record
                보통 해당 달의 첫 날   그런 다음 숫자를

the number / that appears on the last day of the billing cycle.
기록하십시오   청구 주기의 마지막 날에 보이는

Subtracting the first number from the second / will give you the
두 번째 숫자에서 첫 번째 숫자를 빼면   사용된 단위의 수가 나올

number of units used. You can also take readings / every day or
것입니다   또한 계량기를 읽으실 수 있습니다   매일 또는 일주일에

once a week / to determine the amount of water / that is used for
한 번씩   물의 양을 알아내기 위해   활동에 사용되는

activities / that require water.
            물을 필요로 하는

스트라우드버그 수도 공사
수도 계량기 읽기

스트라우드버그 수도 공사의 고객들은 언제든지 계량기를 읽을 수 있습니다. 그렇게 하면 수도 요금 청구서가 정확한지 확인하거나 다음 청구서 요금을 추산하는 데 도움이 될 수 있습니다. 계량기를 읽으려면 청구 주기의 첫 날(보통 해당 달의 첫 날)에 보이는 숫자를 기록하십시오. 그런 다음 청구 주기의 마지막 날에 보이는 숫자를 기록하십시오. 두 번째 숫자에서 첫 번째 숫자를 빼면 사용된 단위의 수가 나올 것입니다. 물을 필요로 하는 활동에 사용되는 물의 양을 알아내기 위해 매일 또는 일주일에 한 번씩 계량기를 읽으실 수도 있습니다.

What is NOT mentioned as a reason for customers to read their

water meters?

(A) To make sure that a bill is accurate

(B) To know when the meter needs to be adjusted

고객이 수도 계량기를 읽는 이유로 언급되지 않은 것은?

(A) 청구서가 정확한지 확인하려고

(B) 언제 계량기를 조정해야 할지를 알려고

해설 Not / True: 계량기를 읽으면 수도 요금 청구서가 정확한지 확인하거나 다음 청구서 요금을 추산하는 데 도움이 될 것이라고 했으므로, (B)가 정답입니다.

Q2

Item#	Title	Author	Category	Quantity	Unit Price	Total
H2875	*Biodiversity in the Nicobar Islands*	Sheena Patel	4	30	$9.25	$277.50
F9150	*Iceland's Wandering Horses*	Eva Grimsdottir	4	25	$8.60	$215.00
B6442	*Mysterious Foxes*	Costas Nikolaidis	4	10	$8.20	$82.00
S7301	*Wild Animals and Their Diets*	DoDat Vu	4	50	$10.15	$507.50
Payment is due / within 30 days. 대금을 결제해야 한다 30일 이내에					**Total $1,082.00**	

품번#	제목	저자	분류	분량	단가	총액
H2875	〈니코바르 제도의 생물 다양성〉	시나 파텔	4번	30개	9.25달러	277.50달러
F9150	〈아이슬란드의 야생마〉	에바 그림스도티어	4번	25개	8.60달러	215.00달러
B6442	〈신비로운 여우〉	코스타스 니콜라이디스	4번	10개	8.20달러	82.00달러
S7301	〈야생 동물과 먹이〉	도닷 뷔	4번	50개	10.15달러	507.50달러
대금은 30일 이내에 결제해야 합니다.					**총액 1,082.00달러**	

In the invoice, category 4 most likely represents what subject?

(A) Travel

(B) Nature

청구서에서 4번 분류는 어떤 주제를 나타내겠는가?

(A) 여행

(B) 자연

해설 추론: 청구서에서 주문한 도서가 모두 category 4로 분류되어 있는데, 제목을 보면 생물 다양성 및 각종 동물에 관한 책들임을 알 수 있습니다. 이러한 제목들을 포함하는 주제는 자연이므로 정답은 (B)입니다.

1 (D)	2 (C)	3 (A)	4 (B)

Questions 1-4 refer to the following online chat discussion.

1-4 온라인 채팅

Milo Tamboli (1:06 P.M.) Hi Sammy and Lily. **1**Isn't the quarterly review
밀로 탐볼리 (오후 1:06) 안녕하세요, 새미 그리고 릴리 분기별 검토 회의를 하지 않나요

meeting still happening / today at 1?
오늘 1시에

밀로 탐볼리 (오후 1:06)
안녕하세요, 새미 그리고 릴리. **1**분기별 검토 회의가 여전히 오늘 1시에 열리지 않나요?

Sammy Adjani (1:08 P.M.) The meeting got moved / to tomorrow.
새미 아자니 (오후 1:08) 회의는 옮겨졌어요 내일로

새미 아자니 (오후 1:08)
그 회의는 내일로 옮겨졌어요.

Milo Tamboli (1:09 P.M.) **2**I must have missed that / somehow.
밀로 탐볼리 (오후 1:09) 그걸 못 알아들었나 보네요 어쩌다

밀로 탐볼리 (오후 1:09)
2어쩌다 그걸 못 들었나 보네요.

Sammy Adjani (1:11 P.M.) Sorry about that! **2**We discussed the change
새미 아자니 (오후 1:11) 미안해요! 어제 변경하기로 했는데

yesterday / at the marketing meeting. I completely forgot / you were out.
마케팅 회의 때 까맣게 잊었네요 당신이 없었다는 것을

새미 아자니 (오후 1:11)
미안해요! **2**어제 마케팅 회의 때 변경하기로 했는데, 당신이 없었다는 걸 까맣게 잊었네요.

Milo Tamboli (1:13 P.M.) It's OK. I needed to check the room projector /
밀로 탐볼리 (오후 1:13) 괜찮아요. 회의실 프로젝터를 확인해야 했어요

for my workshop, / and I do not think it is working.
제 워크숍 때문에 그런데 그게 작동하는 것 같지 않아요.

밀로 탐볼리 (오후 1:13)
괜찮아요. 제 워크숍 때문에 회의실 프로젝터를 확인해야 했는데, 그게 작동하는 것 같지 않아요.

Sammy Adjani (1:14 P.M.) Are you still there now?
새미 아자니 (오후 1:14) 지금 아직 거기 있나요?

새미 아자니 (오후 1:14)
지금 아직 거기 있나요?

Milo Tamboli (1:15 P.M.) I'm just leaving.
밀로 탐볼리 (오후 1:15) 막 나가는 중이에요.

밀로 탐볼리 (오후 1:15)
막 나가는 중이에요.

Sammy Adjani (1:17 P.M.) **3**If you can hold on a minute, / I can come over
새미 아자니 (오후 1:17) 잠시 기다려줄 수 있으면 제가 지금 바로 그리로

right now / and we can try to get the equipment running.
갈 수 있으니까 같이 장비가 작동되도록 해봐요

새미 아자니 (오후 1:17)
3잠시 기다려줄 수 있으면, 제가 지금 바로 그리로 갈 수 있으니까 같이 장비가 작동되도록 해봐요.

Milo Tamboli (1:18 P.M.) Sure thing.
밀로 탐볼리 (오후 1:18) 그러죠.

밀로 탐볼리 (오후 1:18)
그러죠.

Lily Orenson (1:40 P.M.) Sorry for the misunderstanding today, Milo!
릴리 오렌슨 (오후 1:40) 오늘 잘못 알고 있었던 데 대해 미안해요, 밀로!

Were you able to get the projector working?
영사기를 작동시킬 수 있었나요

릴리 오렌슨 (오후 1:40)
오늘 착오가 생기게 해서 미안해요, 밀로! 프로젝터를 작동시킬 수 있었나요?

Sammy Adjani (1:45 P.M.) No. We called IT, / and they will try to fix it.
새미 아자니 (오후 1:45) 아니요. IT에 연락했어요. 그들이 고쳐볼 거예요.

4But let's see / if there is another conference room / available for tomorrow /
그래도 알아보지요 다른 회의실이 있는지 내일 이용할 수 있는

just in case?
만일에 대비해서

새미 아자니 (오후 1:45)
아니요. IT에 연락했어요. 그들이 고칠 거예요. **4**그래도 만일에 대비해서 내일 이용할 수 있는 다른 회의실이 있는지 알아보지요.

Lily Orenson (1:48 P.M.) **4**OK — / I will check and let you know.
릴리 오렌슨 (오후 1:48) 좋아요. 제가 확인해보고 알려드릴게요.

릴리 오렌슨 (오후 1:48)
4좋아요. 제가 확인해보고 알려드릴게요.

Sammy Adjani (1:49 P.M.) Great.
새미 아자니 (오후 1:49) 좋아요.

새미 아자니 (오후 1:49)
좋아요.

1 What is Mr. Tamboli confirming?

(A) A repair request

(B) A supply order

(C) A workshop topic

(D) A meeting time

탐볼리 씨가 확인하고 있는 것은?

(A) 수리 요청

(B) 물품 주문

(C) 워크숍 주제

(D) 회의 시간

> **해설** 세부 사항: 탐볼리 씨는 오후 1시 6분 메시지 Isn't the quarterly review meeting still happening today at 1?에서 분기별 검토 회의 시간을 확인했습니다. 따라서 정답은 (D)입니다.

---

2 What is true about Mr. Tamboli?

(A) He manages the marketing department.

(B) He planned a quarterly meeting.

(C) He was absent for a meeting on the previous day.

(D) He is Mr. Adjani and Ms. Orenson's supervisor.

탐볼리 씨에 대해 사실인 것은?

(A) 마케팅 부서를 관리한다.

(B) 분기 회의를 기획했다.

(C) 전날 회의에 불참했다.

(D) 아자니 씨와 오렌슨의 상사이다.

> **해설** Not / True: 오후 1시 9분에 탐볼리 씨가 어쩌다 그걸(회의) 놓쳤다(I must ~ that somehow.)고 하자 바로 이어 오후 1시 11분에 아자니 씨가 어제 회의에서 변경하기로 했다(We discussed ~ marketing meeting.)며 탐볼리 씨가 없었다는 걸 잊었다(I completely forgot you were out.)고 했습니다. 따라서 탐볼리 씨는 어제 회의에 불참했다는 것을 알 수 있으므로 정답은 (C)입니다.

---

3 At 1:18 P.M., what does Mr. Tamboli most likely mean when he writes, "Sure thing"?

(A) He will wait for a coworker.

(B) He will create an agenda.

(C) He understands his mistake.

(D) He is certain a workshop will be successful.

오후 1시 18분에 탐볼리 씨가 "그러죠"라고 쓴 의미는 무엇이겠는가?

(A) 동료 직원을 기다릴 것이다.

(B) 안건을 만들 것이다.

(C) 자신의 실수를 이해한다.

(D) 워크숍이 성공할 것이라고 확신한다.

> **해설** 의도 파악: 오후 1시 17분 아자니 씨가 기다려주면 자기가 갈 수 있으니 장비 작동을 함께해보자(If you can ~ equipment running.)라고 한 말에 대한 대답입니다. 따라서 아자니 씨를 기다리겠다는 의미로 한 말이므로 정답은 (A)입니다.
>
> **Paraphrasing** 지문의 hold on → 정답의 wait

PART 7 | UNIT 03

---

4 What will Ms. Orenson most likely do next?

(A) Arrange for a conference call

(B) Look for a different meeting space

(C) Try to repair the projector

(D) Confirm that IT has been contacted

오렌슨 씨는 다음에 무엇을 할 것 같은가?

(A) 전화 회의를 준비한다.

(B) 다른 회의 공간을 찾아본다.

(C) 프로젝터를 고치려고 노력한다.

(D) IT에 연락되었는지를 확인한다.

> **해설** 추론: 오후 1시 45분 아자니 씨의 메시지 let's see if there is another conference room available for tomorrow에서 다른 회의실이 있는지 알아보자고 하자 1시 48분에 오렌슨 씨가 OK—I will check and let you know.라고 응답했습니다. 즉, 다른 회의실을 찾아보겠다는 의미이므로 정답은 (B)입니다.
>
> **Paraphrasing** 지문의 another conference room → 정답의 a different meeting space

ETS 문제로 훈련하기

교재 p.228

Q1 (B)　　　　　　　　　**Q2** (B)

Q1

www.davencarcare.com/requestanappointment

DAVEN CAR CARE—Appointment Form
데이븐 차량 관리 – 예약 양식

Use this form / to request an appointment, / and we will call you
이 양식을 사용하세요　예약 요청을 하기 위해　　　　　　전화로 확인해 드립니다

with a confirmation. Note / that your requested time slot may not
　　　　　　유의하세요　요청한 시간대가 이용 불가능할 수도 있다는 점을

be available, / but we will do our best / to accommodate your
　　　　하지만 최선을 다하겠습니다　　고객님이 선택한 시간에 맞추거나

choice / or offer the closest possible alternative time. To ensure
　　　가능한 가장 가까운 대체 시간을 제공하도록　　　　　　이용하실 수 있는

maximum availability, / please make your request / at least 24 hours
가능성을 최대한 보장하려면　　　요청하시기 바랍니다　　　최소 24시간 전에

in advance / of your preferred appointment time.
　　　　선호하는 예약 시간의

Name: James Lindemann	
이름: 제임스 린데만	

Phone: 555 0107
전화:　555 0107

Purpose of your visit: Yearly inspection
방문 목적:　　　　　　연간 점검

Preferred appointment time: August 12, 8:00 A.M.
선호하는 예약 시간:　　　　　8월 12일 오전 8:00

Are you a repeat customer? NO
재방문 고객이신가요?　　　아니요

Do you need a shuttle service? NO
셔틀 서비스가 필요하신가요?　　아니요

데이븐 차량 관리 – 예약 양식

이 양식을 사용해 예약을 요청하시면 전화로 확인해 드립니다. 요청한 시간대가 이용이 불가능할 수도 있다는 점을 유의하십시오. 하지만 고객님이 선택한 시간에 맞추거나 가능한 가장 가까운 대체 시간을 제공하도록 최선을 다하겠습니다. 이용 가능성을 최대한 보장하려면 선호하는 예약 시간 최소 24시간 전에 요청하시기 바랍니다.

이름: 제임스 린데만

전화: 555 0107

방문 목적: 연례 점검

선호하는 예약 시간:
8월 12일 오전 8:00

재방문 고객이신가요? 아니요

셔틀 서비스가 필요하신가요?
아니요

In the form, the word "Note" in paragraph 1, line 2, is closest in meaning to

(A) remind

(B) observe

양식에서 첫 번째 단락 2행의 'Note'와 의미상 가장 가까운 것은?

(A) 상기시키다

(B) 주의하다

해설 동의어 찾기: note의 기본 뜻은 '주목하다, 주의하다'입니다. 지문의 Note that your requested time slot may not be available.에서는 요청한 시간대가 이용 불가능할 수도 있다는 것을 유의하라고 했으므로 '주시하다, 주의하다'라는 의미의 (B) observe가 정답입니다.

Q2

Dear Benedict,

I like your idea / about hiring a dietitian / to work in Eckman Markets.
당신의 아이디어가 마음에 듭니다 / 영양사를 채용하는 것에 대한 / 에크만 마켓에서 일할

At the weekly meeting on Thursday, / I am going to propose your
목요일 주간 회의에서   당신의 아이디어를 제안하겠습니다

idea. I think / it is likely that Mr. Cummings will approve your
생각합니다 / 커밍스 씨가 당신의 제안을 승인할 것으로

suggestion. This seems like a good time / to promote something
지금이 좋은 시기인 것 같습니다   무언가 새로운 것을 추진할

new, / since we will be launching our new line of healthy foods.
우리가 건강식품 신제품군을 출시할 예정이기 때문에

It makes sense / to have a professional give sound advice / on diets
일리가 있습니다   전문가가 적절한 조언을 제공하게 한다는 것은   식습관과

and menus / to shoppers / who want it. I will recommend / that we
메뉴에 대한   쇼핑객에게   그것을 원하는   나는 추천할 예정입니다   우리가 퍼스

begin with the Perth branch location.
지점부터 시작하도록

베네딕트 씨께,

에크만 마켓에서 일할 영양사를 채용하자는 당신의 아이디어가 마음에 듭니다. 목요일 주간 회의에서 당신의 아이디어를 제안하겠습니다. 커밍스 씨가 당신의 제안을 승인할 것으로 생각합니다. 우리가 건강 식품 신제품군을 출시할 예정이기 때문에 지금이 무언가 새로운 것을 추진할 좋은 시기인 것 같습니다. 식습관과 메뉴에 대해 전문가가 믿을 만한 조언을 원하는 쇼핑객에게 제공하게 한다는 것은 일리가 있습니다. 나는 우리가 퍼스 지점부터 시작하도록 추천할 예정입니다.

In the e-mail, the word "sound" in paragraph 1, line 5, is closest in meaning to

(A) loud

(B) sensible

이메일 첫 번째 단락 5행의 단어 'sound'와 의미상 가장 가까운 것은?

(A) 시끄러운

(B) 합리적인

> **해설** 동의어 찾기: give sound advice on diets and menus에서 sound는 '믿을 만한, 타당한'이라는 의미이므로 정답은 '분별있는, 합리적인'이라는 의미의 (B) sensible입니다.

1 (C)	2 (C)	3 (A)

Questions 1-3 refer to the following contract.

1-3 기타 양식 (계약서)

Speaker Contract
강사 계약

강사 계약

This contract, / entered into on 26 January, / is between the Thaya Institute
본 계약은　　　　1월 26일에 체결된　　　　　　　타야 연구소와 독립 계약자인 프랭크 욱 사이에

and Franck Woog, an independent contractor, / for his services as Guest
(체결되었다)　　　　　　　　　　　　초청 강사로서 그의 용역을 위해

Speaker. **1**Mr. Woog / agrees to give his talk / on the role of honey bees / in
욱 씨는　　　강연하기로 동의한다　　　　꿀벌의 역할에 관해

cross-polination at Goethal University's Ferland Hall / from noon to 2 P.M. /
교잡 수분에 있어 고설 대학교 퍼랜드 홀에서　　　　　　오후 12시에서 2시까지

on 15 February.
2월 15일

본 계약은 1월 26일에 타야 연구소와 독립 계약자인 프랭크 욱 사이에 체결되었으며 초청 강사로서 그의 용역에 관한 것이다. **1**욱 씨는 2월 15일 오후 12시에서 2시까지 고설 대학교 퍼랜드 홀에서 교잡 수분에 있어 꿀벌의 역할에 관해 강연하기로 동의한다.

1The Thaya Institute agrees / to pay Mr. Woog €600.00 for his services.
타야 연구소는 동의한다　　　　　　욱 씨에게 그의 용역에 대해 600유로를 지불하기로

Payment will be processed / within 30 days of the speaking date.
지불은 처리될 것이다　　　　　　강연 날짜로부터 30일 이내에

Additionally, / Mr. Woog's travel expenses can be reimbursed / up to
또한　　　　　　욱 씨의 여행 경비는 환급될 수 있다　　　　　　최대

€200.00. All travel receipts must be **2**presented / to receive reimbursement.
200유로까지 모든 여행 영수증을 제출해야 한다　　　　변상을 받기 위해서는

1타야 연구소는 욱 씨에게 그의 용역에 대해 600유로를 지불하기로 동의한다. 지불은 강연 날짜로부터 30일 이내에 처리될 것이다. 또한, 욱 씨의 여행 경비는 최대 200유로로까지 환급될 수 있다. 환급을 받기 위해서는 모든 여행 영수증을 **2**제출해야 한다.

3Mr. Woog agrees / to have his talk filmed and photographed. These
욱 씨는 동의한다　　　자신의 강연을 동영상과 사진으로 촬영하는 것에　　　이 자료들은

materials / may be published online / by the Thaya Institute.
　　　　온라인에 게재될 것이다　　　타야 연구소에 의해

3욱 씨는 자신의 강연을 동영상과 사진으로 촬영하는 것에 동의한다. 이 자료들은 타야 연구소에 의해 온라인에 게재될 것이다.

Agreed by: 계약 당사자:

Franck Woog 프랭크 욱	26 January 1월 26일
Speaker 강사	Date 날짜
Laurine Rey 로린 레이	26 January 1월 26일
Representative of the Thaya Institute 타야 연구소 대표	Date 날짜

계약 당사자:

프랭크 욱	1월 26일
강사	날짜
로린 레이	1월 26일
타야 연구소 대표	날짜

1 What does the contract suggest about Mr. Woog?

(A) He is a student at the Thaya Institute.

(B) He will attend a lecture on January 26.

(C) He will receive payment for a talk.

(D) He has met Ms. Rey before.

계약서에서 욱 씨에 대해 암시하는 것은?

(A) 타야 연구소의 학생이다.

(B) 1월 26일에 강의에 참석할 것이다.

(C) 강연에 대해 보수를 받을 것이다.

(D) 레이 씨를 전에 만난 적이 있다.

해설 추론 / 암시: 첫 번째 단락 후반부에서 욱 씨는 강연을 하는 것에 동의했고 두 번째 단락에서 타야 연구소가 욱 씨에게 그의 용역에 대한 돈을 지불할 것이라고 했습니다. 따라서 욱 씨가 보수를 받고 강연을 할 것이라는 것을 알 수 있으므로 정답은 (C)입니다.

Paraphrasing 지문의 his services → 정답의 a talk

---

2 The word "presented" in paragraph 2, line 4, is closest in meaning to

(A) gifted

(B) exposed

(C) submitted

(D) revealed

두 번째 단락 4행의 단어 'presented'와 의미상 가장 가까운 것은?

(A) 재능 있는

(B) 노출된

(C) 제출된

(D) 밝혀진

해설 동의어 찾기: All travel receipts must be presented에서 present는 동사로 '제시하다, 제출하다'라는 의미이므로, '제출하다'라는 의미의 submit의 과거분사인 (C) submitted가 정답입니다.

---

3 What does Mr. Woog agree to do?

(A) Have a speech video recorded

(B) Submit a copy of his notes

(C) Publish an article

(D) Take photographs of an event

욱 씨는 무엇을 하기로 동의하는가?

(A) 강연 동영상을 녹화하는 것

(B) 그의 노트 사본을 제출하는 것

(C) 기사를 게재하는 것

(D) 행사의 사진을 찍는 것

해설 세부 사항: 마지막 단락의 Mr. Woog agrees to have his talk filmed and photographed.에서 욱 씨가 동의한 것은 그의 강연을 녹화하고 촬영하는 것임을 알 수 있습니다. 따라서 정답은 (A)입니다.

Paraphrasing 지문의 have his talk filmed → 정답의 Have a speech video recorded

ETS 문제로 훈련하기

교재 p.232

Q1 (A)   **Q2** (B)

For Sale: Three 200-liter Rain Barrels
판매: 200리터짜리 빗물통 3개

I bought these rain barrels / a few years ago / from an agricultural supply
이 빗물통들을 구입했습니다   몇 년 전에   농업용품점에서

store, / but I have since upgraded to a bigger water-collection system /
          하지만 그 이후로 용량이 더 큰 용수 수집 시스템으로 업그레이드했습니다

that works better for my number of crops.
제가 기르는 여러 작물에 더 효과적인

These barrels work well / and are simple to set up. I have already rinsed
이 통들은 물을 잘 받습니다   그리고 설치하기도 간편합니다   제가 이미 통을 깨끗이 씻어

them out / so they're ready to use immediately. Just place them under a
두었습니다   따라서 즉시 사용할 준비가 되어 있습니다   홈통 밑에 두기만 하세요

drainpipe / to catch water / when it rains. Since their color has faded /
          물을 받도록   비가 올 때   색상이 바랬으므로

from being out / in the sun, / I'm selling them / for $20 each. That's a great
실외에 두어   햇빛에   그것들을 판매합니다   한 개 20달러에   정말 괜찮은 금액입니다

deal, / considering used rain barrels of this size generally sell for about
          이 정도 크기의 중고 빗물통이 대체로 약 30−40달러에 판매된다는 점을 감안하면

$30 – $40.

Please contact me / to make arrangements for pickup. Serious inquiries
저에게 연락 주세요   물건을 가져가실 일정을 잡으시려면   정말 관심 있는 분만 문의

only, please.
부탁드립니다

—Marcus Tarrant, 555-0132.
마커스 타런트, 555-0132.

판매: 200리터짜리 빗물통 3개

몇 년 전 농업용품점에서 이 빗물통들을 구입했지만, 그 이후로 제가 기르는 여러 작물에 더 효과적인 용량이 더 큰 용수 수집 시스템으로 업그레이드했습니다.

이 통들은 물을 잘 받고 설치하기도 간편합니다. 제가 이미 통을 깨끗이 씻어 두었으므로 즉시 사용할 준비가 되어 있습니다. 홈통 밑에 두기만 하면 비가 올 때 물을 받을 수 있습니다. 실외에 두어 햇빛에 색상이 바랬으므로 한 개 20달러에 판매합니다. 이 정도 크기의 중고 빗물통이 대체로 30~40달러에 판매된다는 점을 감안하면 정말 괜찮은 금액입니다.

물건을 가져가실 일정을 잡으시려면 저에게 연락 주세요. 정말 관심 있는 분만 문의 부탁드립니다.

– 마커스 타런트, 555-0132.

---

1 In which of the positions marked [1] and [2] does the following sentence best belong?

"Just place them under a drainpipe to catch water when it rains."

(A) [1]

(B) [2]

[1], [2]로 표시된 곳 중에서 다음 문장이 들어가기에 가장 적합한 곳은?

"홈통 밑에 두기만 하면 비가 올 때 물을 받을 수 있습니다."

(A) [1]

(B) [2]

> **해설** 문장 삽입: '홈통 밑에 두기만 하면 비가 올 때 물을 받을 수 있다'라는 말이 들어가야 하므로, 이 통들은 물을 잘 받고 즉시 사용 가능하다고 소개하는 문장들 다음에 이어지는 [1]에 들어가는 것이 가장 적절합니다.

Listening To Your Customers
고객에게 귀 기울이기

Being successful in retail / is more difficult than ever / given the rise
소매업에서 성공하기가   어느 때보다 어렵다   온라인 쇼핑이 증가하고

in online shopping. When a customer comes to your store, / whether
있음을 감안할 때   고객이 매장으로 오면   실물 매장이든

physically or online, / offering high-quality service is a must, / especially
온라인 매장이든   고품질 서비스 제공이 필수다   특히 그

when that customer has a problem.
고객에게 문제가 있을 때는 더욱 그렇다

Customers want to feel heard, / but they do not want to have to repeat
고객은 자신의 이야기를 들어주었으면 한다   하지만 이야기를 반복해야 되는 상황은 원하지 않는다

their story / over and over. To avoid irritation on the part of customers, /
                 거듭해서   고객이 짜증 내는 상황을 피하려면

staff members must be trained / to listen carefully to their customers / and
직원들은 훈련 받아야 한다   고객의 말을 주의 깊게 듣도록   그리고

to ask relevant questions / that provide further insight into the exact nature
적절한 질문을 하도록   문제의 정확한 본질에 대한 더 깊은 통찰을 제공하는

of the problem. Additionally, / the customer should be offered an apology /
                 게다가   고객은 사과를 받아야 한다

for the inconvenience. Only then / should staff members start / working on
불편함에 대해   그런 다음에야   직원들은 시작해야 한다   문제 해결에

a resolution of the matter.
노력하기를

Building trust with the customer / is more than half the story. Active
고객과 신뢰 구축이   문제 해결의 절반 이상을 차지한다   적극적인 청취가

listening can go a long way / toward building and restoring that trust.
큰 효과가 있을 수 있다   그러한 신뢰를 구축하고 회복하는 데

고객에게 귀 기울이기

온라인 쇼핑이 증가하고 있음을 감안할 때 소매업에서 성공하기가 어느 때보다 어렵다. 실물 매장이든 온라인 매장이든 고객이 오면 고품질 서비스 제공이 필수다. 특히 그 고객에게 문제가 있을 때는 더욱 그렇다.

고객은 자신의 이야기를 들어주었으면 하지만 거듭해서 반복해야 되는 상황은 원하지 않는다. 고객이 짜증 내는 상황을 피하려면 직원들은 고객의 말을 주의 깊게 듣고 문제의 정확한 본질에 대한 더 깊은 통찰을 제공하는 적절한 질문을 하도록 훈련 받아야 한다. 게다가 고객은 불편함에 대해 사과를 받아야 한다. 직원들은 그런 다음에야 문제 해결에 나서야 한다.

고객과 신뢰 구축이 문제 해결의 절반 이상을 차지한다. 적극적인 청취가 그러한 신뢰를 구축하고 회복하는 데 큰 효과가 있을 수 있다.

PART 7 | UNIT 05

---

2 In which of the positions marked [1] and [2] does the following

sentence best belong?

"Additionally, the customer should be offered an apology for the

inconvenience."

(A) [1]

(B) [2]

[1], [2]로 표시된 곳 중에서 다음 문장이 들어가기에 가장 적합한 곳은?

"게다가 고객은 불편함에 대해 사과를 받아야 한다."

(A) [1]

(B) [2]

해설 문장 삽입: 제시된 문장에서 정답의 단서는 접속부사 Additionally와 명사 inconvenience이므로 이 두 단서와 관련된 부분을 지문에서 찾아야 합니다. [2] 앞의 to listen carefully to their customers and to ask relevant questions에 더하여 사과를 받는 것이 접속부사 Additionally를 사용할 수 있는 근거가 되고 further insight into the exact nature of the problem에서 the problem이 의미상 inconvenience와 관련되므로 [2]에 제시된 문장이 들어가는 것이 가장 적절합니다.

1 (D)	2 (A)	3 (C)

Questions 1-3 refer to the following e-mail.

To: Jin-Ho Ro <jro@ventnorresorts.co.nz>
From: Cynthia Rooney <crooney@ventnorresorts.co.nz>
Subject: Information
Date: 3 March
Attachment: 📎 Employment Launch, Jobs list

Dear Jin-Ho:

As discussed at the meeting last month, / we're trying Employment
지난달 회의에서 논의한 대로   우리는 임플로이먼트 론치사를 이용해 볼 것입니다

Launch. We've signed a 6-month contract. If we decide to continue with
우리는 6개월 계약을 했습니다   계속 진행하기로 결정하면

them, / we can extend the contract / at a discounted rate.
계약을 연장할 수 있습니다   할인된 금액으로

1The company promises to post jobs / on all types of social media. **For this**
그 회사는 채용 공고를 올리겠다고 약속합니다   모든 종류의 소셜 미디어에   첫 시도로

initial venture, / we've asked them / to post the currently open corporate
그들에게 요청했습니다   현재 공석인 회사 일자리를 올려달라고

positions. **3**For example, / I've asked them to list the positions / available
예를 들어   일자리를 목록에 포함해 달라고 요청했습니다   회계, 디지털

in accounting, digital engineering, and advertising. **Employment Launch /**
엔지니어링, 광고 분야의 채용 가능한   임플로이먼트 론치사는

should have them all posted across social media / by tomorrow.
그것들을 모두 소셜 미디어에 올려 놓을 것입니다   내일까지

2Construction on our new Auckland resort / will be completed / in eight
우리가 신축 중인 오클랜드 리조트 공사는   완료될 예정입니다   8개월 후에

months, / so we'll wait before advertising for the jobs / we'll need there, /
그러므로 일자리를 광고하기 전에 기다려야 합니다   그곳에 필요한

such as housekeeping staff, front desk employees, and maintenance
시설 관리 직원, 프런트 직원, 정비 직원 등

workers. I've attached the details / about Employment Launch and the
세부 사항을 첨부했습니다   임플로이먼트 론치사와 현재 일자리 목록에 관해

current jobs list. Please let me know / what you think.
알려 주세요   어떻게 생각하시는지

Sincerely,

Cynthia Rooney
Human Resources Manager
Ventnor Resorts

수신: 노진호 <jro@ventnorresorts.co.nz>
발신: 신시아 루니 <crooney@ventnorresorts.co.nz>
제목: 정보
날짜: 3월 3일
첨부: 📎 임플로이먼트 론치, 일자리 목록

진호 씨께:

지난달 회의에서 논의한 대로, 우리는 임플로이먼트 론치사를 이용해 볼 것입니다. 6개월 계약을 했습니다. 그들과 계속 진행하기로 결정하면 할인된 금액으로 계약을 연장할 수 있습니다.

1그 회사는 모든 종류의 소셜 미디어에 채용 공고를 올리겠다고 약속합니다. 첫 시도로 그들에게 현재 공석인 회사 일자리를 올려 달라고 요청했습니다. **3**예를 들어, 회계, 디지털 엔지니어링, 광고 분야의 채용 가능한 일자리를 목록에 넣어 달라고 요청했습니다. 임플로이먼트 론치사는 내일까지 그것들을 모두 소셜 미디어에 올려 놓을 것입니다.

2우리가 신축 중인 오클랜드 리조트 공사는 8개월 후에 완료될 예정이므로, 시설 관리 직원, 프런트 직원, 정비 직원 등 그곳에 필요한 일자리를 광고하기 전에 기다려야 합니다. 임플로이먼트 론치사와 현재 일자리 목록에 관한 세부 사항을 첨부했습니다. 어떻게 생각하시는지 알려 주세요.

신시아 루니
인사 담당자
벤트너 리조트

1 Why did Ms. Rooney e-mail Mr. Ro?

(A) To ask him to post a job notice

(B) To discuss a product advertising campaign

(C) To offer him a temporary position

(D) To explain a strategy to recruit employees

루니 씨가 노 씨에게 이메일을 보낸 이유는?

(A) 채용 공고

(B) 제품 광고 캠페인에 대해 논의하려고

(C) 임시직을 제안하려고

(D) 직원 모집 전략을 설명하려고

> **해설** 주제 / 목적: 두 번째 단락 첫 번째 문장에서 계약한 회사가 소셜 미디어에 채용 공고를 올려주기로 했다(The company promises to post jobs on all types of social media.)고 했고 이후 채용 관련 내용이 계속 이어지므로 정답은 (D)입니다.

> **Paraphrasing** 지문의 post jobs → 정답의 recruit employees

---

2 According to the e-mail, what will most likely happen in eight months?

(A) A resort will open.

(B) A new service will be offered.

(C) A new product will be launched.

(D) A transfer will take place.

이메일에 따르면 8개월 후에 무슨 일이 있겠는가?

(A) 리조트가 개장할 것이다.

(B) 신규 서비스를 제공할 것이다.

(C) 신제품이 출시될 것이다.

(D) 이전이 있을 것이다.

> **해설** 세부 사항: 세 번째 단락 첫 번째 문장에서 신축 중인 오클랜드 리조트 공사가 8개월 후에 완공된다고 했으므로 정답은 (A)입니다.

---

3 In which of the positions marked [1], [2], [3], and [4] does the following sentence best belong?

"Employment Launch should have them all posted across social media by tomorrow."

(A) [1]

(B) [2]

(C) [3]

(D) [4]

[1], [2], [3], [4]로 표시된 곳 중에서 다음 문장이 들어가기에 가장 적합한 곳은?

"임플로이먼트 론치사는 내일까지 그것들을 모두 소셜 미디어에 올려 놓을 것입니다."

(A) [1]

(B) [2]

(C) [3]

(D) [4]

> **해설** 문장 삽입: 제시문의 them의 문제 해결의 단서가 됩니다. 제시문 앞에는 them을 구체적으로 설명하는 내용이 나와야 합니다. 따라서 회계, 디지털 엔지니어링, 광고 분야의 채용 가능한 일자리를 목록에 넣어 달라고 요청했다고 말하는 문장 다음에 이어지는 [3]에 들어가는 것이 가장 적절합니다.

ETS 문제로 훈련하기

교재 p.236

Q1 (A)   **Q2** (B)

To: Lana Richman <lrichman@richmanproducts.com>

From: Paul Ross <pross@nationalhouseholdcleaningproductsconv.org>

Date: January 7

Subject: Vendor assignment

Dear Ms. Richman,

This is to confirm / that your company, Richman Products, / is assigned to
이것은 확인해 드리기 위한 것입니다 / 귀사 리치먼 프로덕츠가   287번 부스에

Booth 287 / at the National Household Cleaning Products Convention /
배정되었음   전국 가정용 청소 제품 컨벤션에서

at the Municipal Conference Center / in Seattle / from February 11 through
시립 콘퍼런스 센터에서 열리는   시애틀의   2월 11일부터 2월 13일까지

February 13. Please plan to arrive on February 10 / before 2:00 P.M. / to set
            2월 10일에 도착하도록 계획하십시오   오후 2시 전에   부스

up your booth display. Conference center workers / will meet exhibitors at
전시를 준비하시려면   콘퍼런스 센터 직원들은   3번 입구에서 전시회 참가자들을

Entrance 3 / to assist with any items being brought in / for display.
만날 것입니다   그리고 모든 물품 반입을 도울 것입니다   전시를 위한

We look forward to your participation / at this event!
귀사의 참가를 고대합니다   이번 행사에

Sincerely,

Paul Ross

수신: 라나 리치먼 〈lrichman@ richmanproducts.com〉

발신: 폴 로스 〈pross@nationalh ouseholdcleaningproduc tsconv.org〉

날짜: 1월 7일

제목: 판매업체 배정

리치먼 씨께,

2월 11일부터 2월 13일까지 시애 틀 시립 콘퍼런스 센터에서 열리는 전국 가정용 청소 제품 컨벤션에서 귀사 리치먼 프로덕츠가 287번 부 스에 배정되었음을 확인해 드리기 위해 메일을 보냅니다. 부스 전시를 준비하시려면 2월 10일 오후 2시 전에 도착하도록 계획하십시오. 콘 퍼런스 센터 직원들은 3번 입구에서 전시회 참가자들을 만나 전시를 위 한 모든 물품 반입을 도울 것입니다.

이번 행사에 귀사의 참가를 고대합 니다!

폴 로스

---

1   What is the purpose of the e-mail?

(A) To provide information to an event participant

(B) To notify a company owner of a schedule change

이메일의 목적은?

(A) 행사 참가자에게 정보를 제공하려고

(B) 회사 소유주에게 일정 변경을 통지하려고

해설 주제 / 목적: 제목과 첫 문장을 통해 지문의 목적이 컨벤션 참가 회사에게 부스 배정 세부 사항을 알리려는 것임을 알 수 있으므로 정답은 (A)입니다.

Dear Ms. Stephenson:

We are very sorry to hear / that two of the Pristine Collection plates in
소식을 듣게 되어 대단히 유감입니다   고객님께서 최근 주문하신 프리스틴 컬렉션 접시 중 두 개가

your recent order / were cracked / when you received them. We would be
금이 가 있었다는   수령 당시   저희는 기꺼이

pleased / to send you replacements.
고객님께 교체 상품을 보내 드리겠습니다

We have enclosed a return kit / for the damaged items. In it, / you will
반송용 키트를 동봉합니다   손상된 물품을 넣을   그 안에   포장 재료가

find packing materials / and a label addressed to us. Upon receipt of the
보일 것입니다   그리고 저희 쪽 주소가 적힌 라벨이   반송된 물품을 수령하는 즉시

returned items, / we will send new plates / free of charge.
새 접시들을 보내 드리겠습니다   무료로

Once again, / we apologize for the inconvenience. Thank you very much
다시 한 번   불편을 드린 데 대해 사과 드립니다   거래해 주셔서 대단히 감사합니다

for your business.

스티븐슨 씨께:

고객님께서 최근 주문하신 프리스틴 컬렉션 접시 중 두 개가 수령 당시 금이 가 있었다는 소식을 듣게 되어 대단히 유감입니다. 저희는 기꺼이 고객님께 교체 상품을 보내 드리겠습니다.

손상된 물품을 넣을 반송용 키트를 동봉합니다. 그 안에 포장 재료와 저희 쪽 주소가 적힌 라벨이 보일 것입니다. 반송된 물품을 수령하는 즉시, 새 접시들을 무료로 보내 드리겠습니다.

다시 한 번, 불편을 드린 데 대해 사과 드립니다. 거래해 주셔서 대단히 감사합니다.

---

2 What is included with the letter?

(A) New plates

(B) A mailing label

편지와 함께 들어 있는 것은?

(A) 새 접시들

(B) 주소 라벨

해설   세부 사항: We have enclosed a return kit과 In it, you will find packing materials and a label addressed to us.에서 동봉된 반송용 키트 안에 주소 라벨이 들어 있음을 알 수 있으므로 정답은 (B)입니다.

Paraphrasing   지문의 have enclosed → 질문의 is included with the letter

1 (D)	**2** (D)	**3** (B)	**4** (C)	**5** (B)	**6** (C)	**7** (A)	**8** (B)

Questions 1-2 refer to the following e-mail.

From: Jeremy Chang

To: Ann Dougal; Emily Park; Oscar Mendez

Date: March 29

Subject: Today's session postponed

Dear session participants,

Thank you for registering / for the session on expense reporting.
등록해 주셔서 감사합니다   지출 보고에 관한 세션에

Unfortunately, / ¹this session will not take place today / because of
아쉽게도   이 세션은 오늘 열리지 않습니다   기술적인 문제가

technical issues / in our training room. We are working to reschedule the
있어   교육실에   우리는 세션 일정을 다시 잡기 위해 노력하고 있습니다

session, / and you will receive an e-mail / when details have been finalized.
          그리고 이메일을 받으실 겁니다   세부 사항이 확정되면

Please note / that the topics covered in this session / will include /
유념해주세요   이 세션에서 다루는 주제로는   포함된다는 것을

departmental budgeting, business expense cards, and company
부서 예산 편성, 업무 경비 카드 및 회사 환급 정책이

reimbursement policies. ²This session does not include information / about
이 세션에 정보는 포함되지 않습니다   새로운

our new payroll system; / that will be covered separately in a document /
급여 시스템에 대한   이는 문서에서 별도로 다루겠습니다

to be e-mailed to all staff.
전 직원에게 이메일로 발송되는

If you have any questions, / please reach me by e-mail. To view a list of
궁금하신 점이 있으면   이메일로 제게 연락하세요   다른 학습 기회 목록을 보려면

other learning opportunities / available for employees, / including next
          직원들이 이용할 수 있는   효과적인 설문 조사

week's session on developing effective surveys, / please visit our Web site
개발에 대한 다음 주 세션을 비롯해   우리 웹사이트

at www.zurergroup.net/train.
www.zurergroup.net/train을 방문하세요

I apologize for the inconvenience, / and I look forward to seeing you soon.
불편을 드려 사과 드립니다   그리고 곧 만나 뵙기를 고대합니다

Jeremy Chang

1-2 이메일

발신: 제레미 창

수신: 앤 두걸; 에밀리 박; 오스카 멘데즈

날짜: 3월 29일

제목: 오늘 세션 연기됨

세션 참가자 여러분께,

지출 보고에 관한 세션에 등록해 주셔서 감사합니다. ¹아쉽게도 교육실에 기술적인 문제가 있어 이 세션은 오늘 열리지 않습니다. 우리는 세션 일정을 다시 잡기 위해 노력하고 있으며, 세부 사항이 확정되면 이메일을 받으실 겁니다.

이 세션에서 다루는 주제로는 부서 예산 편성, 업무 경비 카드 및 회사 환급 정책이 포함됩니다. ²이 세션에 새로운 급여 시스템에 대한 정보는 포함되지 않습니다. 이는 전 직원에게 이메일로 발송되는 문서에서 별도로 다루겠습니다.

궁금하신 점이 있으면 이메일로 제게 연락하세요. 효과적인 설문 조사 개발에 대한 다음 주 세션을 비롯해 직원들이 이용할 수 있는 다른 학습 기회 목록을 보려면 우리 웹사이트 www.zurergroup.net/train을 방문하세요.

불편을 드려 사과 드립니다. 그리고 곧 만나 뵙기를 고대합니다.

제레미 창

1 Who most likely is Mr. Chang?

(A) A finance consultant

(B) A payroll specialist

(C) A repair technician

(D) A training coordinator

창 씨는 누구이겠는가?

(A) 재무 컨설턴트

(B) 급여 전문가

(C) 수리 기술자

(D) 교육 진행 담당자

해설　추론: 창 씨는 이메일의 발신자입니다. 제목과 첫 번째 단락의 두 번째 문장에서 교육실의 기술적인 문제로 오늘 세션이 열리지 않는다고 알리는 것으로 보아 창 씨는 교육 진행 담당자임을 알 수 있으므로 정답은 (D)입니다

---

2 What can staff expect to receive by e-mail?

(A) A registration form

(B) An employee-satisfaction survey

(C) A list of online learning opportunities

(D) A document about a company system

직원이 이메일로 받기를 기대할 수 있는 것은?

(A) 등록 양식

(B) 직원 만족도 설문 조사

(C) 온라인 학습 기회 목록

(D) 회사 시스템에 관한 문서

해설　세부 사항: 두 번째 단락의 두 번째 문장에서 새로운 급여 시스템에 대한 정보는 전 직원에게 이메일로 발송되는 문서에서 다루겠다고 했으므로 정답은 (D)입니다.

Paraphrasing　지문의 our new payroll system → 정답의 a company system

Questions 3-5 refer to the following letter.

La Scala Properties
208 Bedford Street
Eden Terrace
Auckland 1010

1 May

Ms. Janna Fritz
300 Mount Eden Road
Mount Eden
Auckland 1024

Dear Ms. Fritz:

Thank you / for being a valued client. [3]I would like to inform you / that
감사합니다   소중한 고객이 되어 주셔서   알려드립니다

according to our property agreement, / your rental period comes to an
임대 계약에 따르면   고객님의 임대 기간이 종료됨을

end / in just two months. Therefore, / I have enclosed a form / on which
두 달만 지나면   따라서   양식을 동봉했습니다   고객님의 의사를

you may indicate your intentions. **There are two options.** [5]If you intend to
표시할 수 있는   두 가지 선택 사항이 있습니다   라 스칼라 아파트에

remain at La Scala Properties, / you have the option of renewing your
계속 거주하시기 원하시면   임대차 계약을 갱신하시는 방안이 있습니다

lease / for a period of six months, to 1 January, / or extending the lease for
1월 1일까지 6개월간   또는 내년 7월 1일까지 1년간 계약을

one year, to 1 July of next year. If you intend to leave, / please note /
연장하시는   나가실 작정이라면   유념해주십시오

that the apartment must be vacated / by 30 June. [4]Whatever your
아파트를 비워 주셔야 한다는 점을   6월 30일까지   어떤 결정을 내리시든

determination, / please complete and return the form / by 1 June.
이 양식을 작성해서 반송해주십시오   6월 1일까지

Do not hesitate to contact me / if you have any questions or concerns.
망설이지 마시고 연락하십시오   질문이나 용건이 있으시면

Robert Karam
Robert Karam
Manager, La Scala Properties

Enclosure

3-5 편지

라 스칼라 부동산
베드포드가 208
이든 테라스
오클랜드 1010

5월 1일

재나 프리츠 씨
마운트 이든로 300
마운트 이든
오클랜드 1024

프리츠 씨께:

소중한 고객이 되어주셔서 감사합니다. [3]임대 계약에 따르면 두 달만 지나면 고객님의 임대 기간이 종료됨을 알려드립니다. 따라서 고객님의 의사를 표시할 수 있는 양식을 동봉했습니다. **두 가지 선택 사항이 있습니다.** [5]라 스칼라 아파트에 계속 거주하시기 원하시면 1월 1일까지 6개월간 임대차 계약을 갱신하시거나, 내년 7월 1일까지 1년간 계약을 연장하시는 방안이 있습니다. 나가실 작정이라면 아파트를 6월 30일까지 비워주셔야 한다는 점을 유념해 주십시오. [4]어떤 결정을 내리시든, 6월 1일까지 이 양식을 작성해서 반송해주십시오.

질문이나 용건이 있으시면 망설이지 마시고 연락하십시오.

로버트 카람
라 스칼라 아파트 관리자

동봉물

3 What is the purpose of the letter?

(A) To confirm receipt of a contract

(B) To issue a contract reminder

(C) To describe a new policy

(D) To request a payment extension

편지의 목적은?

(A) 계약서의 수령을 확인하려고

(B) 계약 독촉장을 발부하려고

(C) 새로운 정책을 설명하려고

(D) 지급 연장을 요청하려고

> **해설** **주제 / 목적:** 두 번째와 세 번째 문장에서 임대 기간의 종료가 두 달 남았다고 알리면서 의사 표시를 위한 양식을 동봉했다고 했습니다. 따라서 임대 계약에 대해 상기시키고 있다는 것을 알 수 있으므로 정답은 (B)입니다.

> **Paraphrasing** 지문의 a form on which you may indicate your intentions → 정답의 a contract reminder

---

4 By what date should Ms. Fritz inform Mr. Karam about a decision?

(A) January 1

(B) May 1

(C) June 1

(D) July 1

프리츠 씨는 카람 씨에게 결정에 대해 며칠까지 알려야 하는가?

(A) 1월 1일

(B) 5월 1일

(C) 6월 1일

(D) 7월 1일

> **해설** **세부 사항:** 첫 번째 단락의 마지막 문장에서 프리츠 씨에게 의사를 결정하여 양식을 6월 1일까지 보내달라고 했으므로 정답은 (C)입니다.

---

5 In which of the positions marked [1], [2], [3], and [4] does the following sentence best belong?

"There are two options."

(A) [1]

(B) [2]

(C) [3]

(D) [4]

[1], [2], [3], [4]로 표시된 곳 중에서 다음 문장이 들어가기에 가장 적합한 곳은?

"두 가지 선택 사항이 있습니다."

(A) [1]

(B) [2]

(C) [3]

(D) [4]

> **해설** **문장 고르기:** '두 가지 선택 사항이 있다'라는 말이 들어가야 하므로, 맥락상 빈칸 뒤에 선택 사항에 대한 설명이 있어야 할 것입니다. [2] 뒤의 문장을 보면 아파트 임대 계약 갱신과 계약 종료라는 두 가지 선택 사항에 대해 설명하고 있으므로, 제시된 문장이 [2]에 들어가는 것이 가장 적절합니다.

Questions 6-8 refer to the following e-mail.

To: All members
From: Jack Muir
Subject: Policies regarding performances
Date: January 15

Dear members of the Jack Muir Big Band,

Thanks for your excellent performance / this past Saturday night! The
여러분의 멋진 공연에 감사드립니다   지난 토요일 밤   고객들은

clients enjoyed their event / and praised your part / in making the evening
행사를 즐겼습니다   그리고 여러분의 역할을 칭찬했습니다   저녁 시간을 매우 특별하게 만드는

so special. That said, / I feel / it is necessary at this time, / with so many
데 있어   그렇기는 하지만   생각합니다 / 이번에 필요하다고   새로운 멤버들도 많고 하니

new members, / to remind you of our policies / regarding performances.
                우리의 방침을 되새겨보는 것이   공연과 관련된

The drummer, setup crew, and I / must report to the performance venue /
드럼 연주자, 설치 작업반, 그리고 저는   공연장에 도착을 알려야 합니다

one hour before the gig. ⁶All other band members / must arrive / no later
공연 한 시간 전에   다른 밴드 멤버들은   도착해야 합니다   늦어도 공연

than 30 minutes before showtime. It is unacceptable / to arrive just
시간 30분 전까지는   용납할 수 없습니다   행사 시작 직전에

moments before the event begins, / as has happened on several recent
도착하는 일은   최근 몇 차례 경우에 일어났던 것처럼

occasions.

All members serve on the setup crew / on a rotating basis. ⁷The crew
모든 멤버들은 설치 작업반 일을 합니다   교대로   여러분의 편의를

roster is posted for your convenience / on the band's Web site / by our
위해 작업반 명단을 올려 놓았습니다   밴드 웹사이트에   우리 매니저인

manager, Ann Tanner. Ms. Tanner also places all the information / for each
앤 태너 씨가   태너 씨는 또한 모든 정보를 올립니다   각 행사에

engagement—/ including locations, times, and dress code— / on the Web
대한   장소, 시간, 복장 규정을 포함해   웹사이트에

site. Although our usual attire is concert black, / some events are less
우리의 평소 옷차림은 콘서트 블랙이지만   일부 행사는 격식을 덜 차리기도 합니다

formal, / so it is important / ⁸to check the Web site before each gig. The
그래서 중요합니다   매번 공연 전에 웹사이트를 확인하는 것이   정보는

information / is at jackmuirbigband.com/gigs.
              jackmuirbigband.com/gigs에 있습니다

Thank you!
감사합니다

⁶Jack Muir, Band Leader

6 What most likely caused Mr. Muir to send the e-mail?

(A) Some clients disliked a performance.

(B) A concert was booked on very short notice.

(C) Some members arrived at an event later than expected.

(D) New members requested the information.

뮤어 씨가 이메일을 보낸 이유는?

(A) 일부 고객이 공연을 좋아하지 않았다.

(B) 콘서트가 매우 촉박하게 예약되었다.

(C) 일부 멤버들이 예상보다 늦게 행사에 도착했다.

(D) 신규 멤버들이 정보를 요청했다.

해설 주제 / 목적: 이메일의 마지막 부분에서 발신자인 뮤어 씨는 밴드의 리더임을 알 수 있습니다. 이메일의 두 번째 단락 All other band ~ before showtime.과 It is unacceptable ~ recent occasions.에서 공연 30분 전까지 도착하지 않은 멤버가 있다는 것을 지적하기 위해 이메일을 보냈음을 알 수 있으므로 정답은 (C)입니다.

---

7 According to the e-mail, what is one of Ms. Tanner's jobs?

(A) Providing information to the band

(B) Playing drums in the band

(C) Transporting equipment to events

(D) Updating the design of a Web site

이메일에 따르면, 태너 씨의 업무 중 하나는?

(A) 밴드에 정보를 제공하는 일

(B) 밴드에서 드럼을 연주하는 일

(C) 행사에 장비를 운반하는 일

(D) 웹사이트의 디자인을 업데이트하는 일

해설 세부 사항: 지문의 마지막 단락에서 Tanner 씨가 설치 작업반 명단을 포함해 모든 행사에 대한 정보를 웹사이트에 올린다고 했으므로 정답은 (A)입니다.

---

8 The word "check" in paragraph 3, line 5, is closest in meaning to

(A) mark up

(B) look at

(C) slow down

(D) pay for

세 번째 단락 5행의 'check'과 의미가 가장 가까운 단어는?

(A) 표시하다

(B) 살펴보다

(C) 늦추다

(D) 지불하다

해설 동의어 찾기: check은 지문의 to check the Web site before each gig에서 '살피다, 확인하다'라는 의미이므로 '~을 살펴보다'라는 의미이 (B) look at이 정답입니다.

ETS 문제로 훈련하기

교재 p.242

Q1 (A)   **Q2** (B)

April 2

Attention, Restaurants of Hazeltown!
헤이즐타운의 식당들에 알립니다!

The Hazeltown Civic Council is pleased / to announce Hazeltown's Second
헤이즐타운 시의회는 기쁩니다   헤이즐타운의 두 번째 연례 거리 축제를 발표하게 되어

Annual Street Festival, / which will take place / from May 28 through May
                              축제는 열릴 예정입니다   5월 28일부터 5월 31일까지

31. We invite you to reserve a booth / during the event!
    부스를 예약하실 것을 요청합니다   행사 동안

The Festival will be held / on the four-block area of Main Street /
축제는 열릴 것입니다   메인 스트리트의 4개 블록 구역에서

beginning at its intersection with Chestnut Street, / continuing through the
체스넛 스트리트와의 교차로에서 시작해   오크 스트리트와 파인 스트리트와의

intersections with Oak Street and Pine Street, / and ending at Main Street's
교차로를 지나 계속되어   사가모어 스트리트와 만나는 메인 스트리트의

intersection with Sagamore Street.
교차로에서 끝날 것입니다

We recommend / that each restaurant limit itself / to preparing four dishes.
우리는 권합니다   각 식당이 제한할 것을   음식 준비를 4가지로

There will be a separate booth / for the sale of beverages, / so please do
별도의 부스가 마련될 것입니다   음료 판매를 위해   그러니 음료를 제공하지

not offer them / at your booth. Also, / please note / that the Hazeltown Jazz
않기 바랍니다   여러분의 부스에서는   또한,   알고 계십시오   헤이즐타운 재즈 트리오와 헤이즐타운

Trio and the Hazeltown High School Choir / will be providing entertainment.
고등학교 합창단이   여흥을 제공할 예정임을

Music may be played at your booth / only between their performances.
음악은 여러분의 부스에서 틀 수 있습니다   그들의 공연들 사이에만

4월 2일

헤이즐타운의 식당들에 알립니다!

헤이즐타운 시의회는 헤이즐타운의 두 번째 연례 거리 축제를 발표하게 되어 기쁩니다. 축제는 5월 28일부터 5월 31일까지 열릴 예정입니다. 행사 동안 부스를 예약하실 것을 요청합니다.

축제는 메인 스트리트의 4개 블록 구역에서 열릴 예정이며 체스트넛 스트리트와의 교차로에서 시작해 오크 스트리트와 파인 스트리트와의 교차로를 지나 사가모어 스트리트와 만나는 메인 스트리트의 교차로에서 끝날 것입니다.

우리는 각 식당이 음식 준비를 4가지로 제한할 것을 권합니다. 음료 판매를 위해 별도의 부스가 마련될 것이므로, 여러분의 부스에서는 음료를 제공하지 않기 바랍니다. 또한, 헤이즐타운 재즈 트리오와 헤이즐타운 고등학교 합창단이 여흥을 제공할 예정임을 알고 계십시오. 음악은 그들의 공연들 사이에만 여러분의 부스에서 틀 수 있습니다.

---

1   For whom is the announcement intended?

(A) Residents of Hazeltown

(B) Members of the festival planning committee

공지는 누구를 대상으로 하는가?

(A) 헤이즐타운 주민

(B) 축제 기획 위원회 위원

> **해설** 추론: 지문의 The Hazeltown Civic Council ~ May 28 through May 31.과 We invite you ~ the event!에서 헤이즐타운에 사는 사람들을 위한 행사 공지임을 알 수 있으므로 정답은 (A)입니다.

Contractors and Trades Magazine
컨트랙터즈 앤드 트레이즈 매거진

We are your monthly resource / for all trades. Reach over 52,000
우리는 당신의 월간 자원입니다   모든 업종을 위한   52,000명이 넘는 구독자에게

subscribers / throughout the United States and Canada. Advertise in our
다가가세요   미국과 캐나다 전역의   우리 출판물에 광고하십시오

publication / in the coming year!
                내년에

Reserve your spot / before the end of December / and your ad will run /
자리를 예약하시면   12월 말 전에   여러분의 광고는 게재될 것입니다

a second time / for free / during the month of your choice. Contact sales
다시 한 번   무료로   선택하신 달에   영업 담당자 이셔

representative Eesha Bradford / today / at adsales@candtmag.net.
브래드포드에게 연락하십시오   오늘   adsales@candtmag.net으로

컨트랙터즈 앤드 트레이즈 매거진

우리는 모든 업종을 위한 당신의 월간 자원입니다. 미국과 캐나다 전역의 52,000명이 넘는 구독자에게 연락하십시오. 내년에 우리 출판물에 광고하십시오!

12월 말 전에 자리를 예약하시면 여러분의 광고는 선택하신 달에 다시 한 번 무료로 게재될 것입니다. 오늘 adsales@candtmag.net으로 영업 담당자 이셔 브래드포드에게 연락하십시오.

---

2   What is indicated about *Contractors and Trades Magazine*?

(A) It is offered free of charge.

(B) It is distributed internationally.

〈컨트랙터즈 앤드 트레이즈 매거진〉에 대해 암시된 것은?

(A) 무료로 제공된다.

(B) 국제적으로 유통된다.

해설   추론 / 암시: 첫 번째 단락 두 번째 문장에서 미국과 캐나다에 걸쳐 52,000명 이상의 잡지 구독자가 있다고 했으므로 정답은 (B)입니다.

1 (C)	**2** (D)	**3** (D)	**4** (B)	**5** (D)	**6** (B)	**7** (A)

Questions 1-2 refer to the following notice.

1-2 공지

[1]Jonscope Corporation
존스코프 사

Computer Fundamentals Workshop
컴퓨터 기초 워크숍

Location: Main Floor Conference Room
위치: 본관 회의실

Date and Time: Thursday, January 12, 10:00 A.M. to 2:00 P.M.
날짜와 시간: 1월 12일 목요일, 오전 10:00~오후 2:00

Take advantage of this professional development opportunity / to learn
이번 직무 능력 개발 기회를 이용해   배우세요:

about:

- **Office computer basics**
  사무용 컴퓨터 기초
- **Troubleshooting minor problems**
  사소한 문제 해결
- **Creating and organizing files**
  파일 생성과 정리
- **Word processing tips**
  문서 작성 요령
- **Using spreadsheets**
  스프레드시트 활용

[1,2]Register with the Human Resources Department / before January 10.
인사부에 등록하세요.   1월 10일 이전에

[1]존스코프 사

컴퓨터 기초 워크숍

위치: 본관 회의실
날짜와 시간: 1월 12일 목요일,
오전 10:00~오후 2:00

이번 직무 능력 개발 기회를 이용해
배우세요:
- 사무용 컴퓨터 기초
- 사소한 문제 해결
- 파일 생성과 정리
- 문서 작성 요령
- 스프레드시트 활용

[1,2]1월 10일 이전에 인사부에 등록
하세요.

1 Who most likely will attend the workshop?

(A) Jonscope customers

(B) Jonscope retirees

(C) Jonscope employees

(D) Jonscope job applicants

워크숍에 누가 참석하겠는가?

(A) 존스코프 고객

(B) 존스코프 퇴직자

(C) 존스코프 직원

(D) 존스코프 입사 지원자

> 해설 추론: 공지의 제목 Jonscope Corporation Computer Fundamentals Workshop에서 존스코프 회사에서 워크숍이 열린다는 것을 알 수 있고 지문의 맨 마지막 문장 Register with the Human Resources Department before January 10.에서 인사부에 등록하여 워크숍에 참석할 수 있음을 알 수 있습니다. 따라서 정답은 (C)입니다.

---

2 What is indicated about the workshop?

(A) It is given once per month.

(B) It is limited to ten attendees.

(C) It will take place in the computer room.

(D) It requires advance registration.

워크숍에 관해 암시되는 것은?

(A) 한 달에 한 번 제공된다.

(B) 참석자가 10명으로 제한되어 있다.

(C) 컴퓨터실에서 열릴 예정이다.

(D) 사전 등록이 필요하다.

> 해설 추론 / 암시: 지문의 맨 마지막 문장 Register with the Human Resources Department before January 10.에서 1월 10일 전에 등록하라고 했으므로 사전 등록이 필요하다는 것을 알 수 있습니다. 따라서 정답은 (D)입니다.

Questions 3-4 refer to the following advertisement.

3-4 광고

Aerea Systems
에어리어 시스템

Job Description – Technical Writer
직무 기술서 – 기술 문서 작가

[3]Aerea Systems is a growing, global company / in the aviation industry /
에어리어 시스템은 성장하는 글로벌 기업입니다   항공업계에서

and has an immediate opening / for a technical writer / to join its team
그리고 바로 지금 일자리가 있습니다   기술 문서 작가를 위한   캔비에 있는 팀에 합류할

in Canby. The ideal candidate / will contribute to successful project
이상적인 지원자는   프로젝트를 성공리에 완수하는 데 기여할 것입니다

completion / by creating technical documentation packages / that meet
기술 서류 패키지를 작성해   회사 기술 설명서에

company specifications, / satisfy customer requirements, / and comply with
맞고   고객 요구에 부응하며   그리고 정부 표준을 따르는

government standards.

Responsibilities:
직무:

Write and review documents, including
문서 작성 및 검토, 아래 포함

— [4C]operator manuals
장비 운영자 매뉴얼

— [4A]flight crew checklists
승무원 점검 목록

— flight guide supplements
항공 안내서 증보판

— [4D]equipment maintenance manuals
장비 정비 매뉴얼

Salary is negotiable / and commensurate with qualifications and
급여는 협상 가능합니다   그리고 자격과 경력에 상응합니다

experience. Apply to hr@aerea.com/job code 2482.
hr@aerea.com/job code 2482로 지원하세요

3-4 광고

에어리어 시스템

직무 기술서 – 기술 문서 작가

[3]에어리어 시스템은 항공업계에서 성장하는 글로벌 기업으로, 바로 지금 캔비에 있는 팀에 합류할 기술 문서 작가 일자리가 있습니다. 이상적인 지원자는 회사 기술 설명서에 맞고 고객 요구에 부응하며 정부 표준을 따르는 기술 서류 패키지를 작성해 프로젝트를 성공리에 완수하는 데 기여할 것입니다.

직무:
문서 작성 및 검토, 아래 포함
– [4C]장비 운영자 매뉴얼
– [4A]승무원 점검 목록
– 항공 안내서 보완
– [4D]장비 정비 매뉴얼

급여는 협상 가능하며 자격과 경력에 상응합니다. hr@aerea.com/job code 2482로 지원하세요.

3 What does Aerea Systems most likely manufacture?

(A) Service uniforms

(B) Travel accessories

(C) Security equipment

(D) Commercial aircraft

에어리어 시스템은 무엇을 제조하겠는가?

(A) 서비스 유니폼

(B) 여행 부대용품

(C) 보안 장비

(D) 민간 항공기

> **해설** 추론 / 암시: 첫 번째 단락의 Aerea Systems is a growing, global company in the aviation industry에서 에어리어 시스템은 항공업계에 있는 기업이라는 것을 알 수 있으므로 정답은 (D)입니다.

---

4 What is NOT a responsibility of the position?

(A) Editing checklists

(B) Meeting with customers

(C) Creating operator training materials

(D) Reviewing maintenance documents

직책의 직무가 아닌 것은?

(A) 점검 목록 편집

(B) 고객 면담

(C) 운영자 교재 작성

(D) 정비 문서 검토

> **해설** Not / True: 질문에 NOT이 있는 경우에는 각 선택지를 지문과 대조하여 사실 여부를 확인해야 합니다. 지문 중반부 Responsibilities에서 작성하고 검토해야 하는 문서들로 (A), (C), (D)는 언급했는데, 고객 면담은 없으므로, (B)가 정답입니다.

> **Paraphrasing** 지문의 operator manuals → (C)의 operator training materials
> 지문의 equipment maintenance manuals → (D)의 maintenance documents

Questions 5-7 refer to the following memo.

TO: Customer service team
FROM: Harold Park, Manager
DATE: January 3
RE: Assignments

As you know, / [7]the *Seaview Times* has increased its circulation
아시다시피   〈시뷰 타임즈〉는 급격하게 판매 부수 늘었습니다

dramatically / over the past year. [6]In order to address efficiently / the large
        지난해에   효율적으로 처리하기 위해   많은 양의 고객

volume of customer-service e-mails and telephone calls / that has
서비스 관련 이메일과 전화 통화를   그로 인한

resulted, / each member of the customer service team / is being assigned /
            고객 서비스 팀의 각 팀원에게   배정됩니다

one area of customer service to focus on. Below is a list / of our team
중점적으로 다룰 고객 서비스 분야 한 가지가   다음은 목록입니다 / 우리 팀원들의

members / and the type of calls and e-mails / that will be directed to each
        그리고 전화와 이메일 유형의   각자에게 전달될

person.

Marian Larson 마리안 라슨	Subscription renewals 정기 구독 갱신
Adam Foley 아담 폴리	Subscription cancellations 정기 구독 취소
Beth Brown 베스 브라운	[5]Delivery failures: Late, damaged, or missed newspapers 배달 오류: 지연, 손상, 또는 배달 누락
Hal Carter 핼 카터	Temporary suspension of delivery 일시적인 배달 중단

We hope / this will improve efficiency / and allow us to continue the quality
바랍니다   이것이 업무 효율성을 높이기를   그리고 우리가 업무의 질을 지속 가능하게 해주기를

of work / that we pride ourselves on.
         긍지를 갖고 있는

5-7 회람

수신: 고객 서비스 팀
발신: 해롤드 박, 매니저
날짜: 1월 3일
주제: 과제

아시다시피, [7]〈시뷰 타임즈〉는 지난해에 급격하게 판매 부수가 늘었습니다. [6]그로 인한 많은 양의 고객 서비스 관련 이메일과 전화 통화를 효율적으로 처리하기 위해 고객 서비스 팀의 각 팀원에게 중점적으로 다룰 고객 서비스 분야 한 가지가 할당됩니다. 다음은 우리 팀원들과 각자에게 전달될 전화와 이메일 유형의 목록입니다.

마리안 라슨	정기 구독 갱신
아담 폴리	정기 구독 취소
베스 브라운	[5]배달 오류: 지연, 손상, 또는 배달 누락
핼 카터	일시적인 배달 중단

이것이 업무 효율성을 높이고, 우리가 긍지를 갖고 있는 업무의 질을 지속 가능하게 해주기를 바랍니다.

5 What is the *Seaview Times*?

(A) A magazine

(B) A Web site

(C) A newsletter

(D) A newspaper

〈시뷰 타임스〉는 무엇인가?

(A) 잡지

(B) 웹사이트

(C) 회보

(D) 신문

> **해설** 추론 / 암시: 회람의 담당자 설명 부분 중 Delivery failures: Late, damaged, or missed newspapers에서 〈시뷰 타임스〉가 신문임을 알 수 있으므로, 정답은 (D)입니다.

---

6 In the memo, the word "volume" in paragraph 1, line 2, is closest in meaning to

(A) loudness

(B) amount

(C) book

(D) space

회람의 첫 번째 단락 2행의 단어 'volume'과 의미상 가장 가까운 것은?

(A) 소란스러움

(B) 양

(C) 책

(D) 공간

> **해설** 동의어 찾기: 해당 문장의 In order to address efficiently the large volume of customer-service e-mails는 '많은 양의 고객 서비스 관련 이메일을 효율적으로 처리하기 위해'라는 의미이므로, 여기서 volume은 '양'이라는 뜻이 자연스럽습니다. 따라서 정답은 (B) amount입니다.

---

7 What is indicated about the *Seaview Times*?

(A) It has increased its number of subscribers.

(B) It has recently hired new employees.

(C) It will move into a larger building.

(D) It will close for one month.

〈시뷰 타임즈〉에 대해 언급된 것은?

(A) 구독자 수가 늘었다.

(B) 최근에 신입 사원들을 채용했다.

(C) 더 큰 건물로 이전할 것이다.

(D) 한 달간 문을 닫을 것이다.

> **해설** Not / True: 선택지에 언급된 내용을 하나씩 확인해 봅니다. 회람의 첫 번째 단락 the *Seaview Times* has increased its circulation dramatically에서 판매 부수가 급격히 늘었다고 언급했으므로 정답은 (A)입니다.

> **Paraphrasing** 지문의 circulation → 정답의 number of subscribers

ETS 문제로 **훈련하기**

교재 p.248

Q1 (B)   **Q2** (B)

Asad Buule (11:51 A.M.) Hi, Dominique. This job is taking longer / than
아사드 뷰레 (오전 11:51   안녕, 도미니크   이번 일이 더 오래 걸리네요   우리

we expected. There were more items to be moved / than Cooper Inc.'s
예상보다   옮겨야 할 물건이 더 많았어요   쿠퍼 사의 작업 주문서에

work order indicated. We also found some desk drawers / that hadn't been
표시된 것보다   책상 서랍들도 있었어요   비우지 않은

emptied / and an employee was still packing some legal files.
            그리고 직원 하나는 아직도 법률 관련 서류철을 싸고 있어요

Dominique Lavaud (11:52 A.M.) Unbelievable!
도미니크 라보 (오전 11:52   믿을 수가 없네요!

Asad Buule (11:53 A.M.) Yes. I just wanted to let you know. We should be
아사드 불레 (오전 11:53)   그렇죠. 그냥 알려드리고 싶었어요.   우리는 여기서 떠날

leaving here / in about 30 minutes. I'll let you know / when we arrive at the
거예요   30분쯤 뒤에   알려드릴게요   새 장소에 도착해서 트럭에서

new location and start unloading the truck. I don't think we'll be able to
짐을 부리기 시작할 때   우리가 점심은 먹을 수 없을 것 같네요

take a lunch break / until late today.
            오늘 늦게까지는

Dominque Lavaud (11:54 A.M.) OK. Thank you for the update.
도미니크 라보 (오전 11:54)   알겠어요. 상황을 알려줘 고마워요.

아사드 불레 (오전 11:51)
안녕, 도미니크. 이번 일이 우리 예상보다 오래 더 걸리네요. 쿠퍼 사의 작업주문서에 표시된 것보다 옮겨야 할 물건이 더 많았어요. 비우지 않은 책상 서랍들도 있었고 직원 하나는 아직도 법률 관련 서류철을 싸고 있어요.

도미니크 라보 (오전 11:52)
믿을 수가 없네요!

아사드 뷰레 (오전 11:53)
그렇죠. 그냥 알려드리고 싶었어요. 우리는 30분쯤 뒤에 여기서 떠날 거예요. 새 장소에 도착해서 트럭에서 짐을 부리기 시작할 때 알려드릴게요. 점심은 오늘 늦게나 먹을 수 있을 것 같아요.

도미니크 라보 (오전 11:54)
알겠어요. 상황을 알려줘 고마워요.

---

1 For what type of business do Mr. Buule and Ms. Lavaud most likely work?

(A) A furniture store

(B) A moving company

불레 씨와 라보 씨는 어떤 업종에서 일하겠는가?

(A) 가구점

(B) 이사 업체

해설 추론 / 암시: 불레 씨는 오전 11시 51분 메시지 There were more items ~ order indicated.에서 옮겨야 할 물건이 더 많았다고 했고 라보 씨는 오전 11시 52분에 믿을 수 없다고 반응했습니다. 이를 통해 불레 씨와 라보 씨가 이사 업체에서 일하는 사람들임을 유추할 수 있으므로 정답은 (B)입니다.

Kyong Han [11:08 A.M.] Hi, Terrence and LaMonica. Did we receive the
한 경 [오전 11:08]   안녕, 테렌스, 라모니카.   검사증 받았나요

certificate / from the fire safety inspector?
            소방 안전 검사원에게

Terrence Lawson [11:09 A.M.] Not yet. I called the inspector's office
테렌스 로슨 [오전 11:09]   아니, 아직이요. / 1시간쯤 전에 검사원에게 전화했어요

about an hour ago / and I was told to check back / in two days.
                  그리고 다시 확인하라네요   이틀 뒤에

Kyong Han [11:11 A.M.] Okay, / could you stay on top of that, please?
한 경 [오전 11:11]   알겠어요.   계속 상황을 파악해주시겠어요?

The branch can't open / without that certificate. LaMonica, / do we have
지점을 열 수가 없어요   그 검사증이 없으면   라모니카,   우리에게 재료가 있나요

the ingredients / needed for the various menu items?
                  다양한 메뉴 품목에 필요한

LaMonica Elroy [11:12 A.M.] I went over the list of ingredients myself.
라모니카 엘로이 [오전 11:12]   제가 직접 재료 목록을 점검했어요.

Every single one / was in stock.
하나도 빠짐없이   재고가 있었어요

Kyong Han [11:14 A.M.] That's a great comfort.
한 경 [오전 11:14]   그거 정말 안심이 되네요.

한 경 [오전 11:08]
안녕, 테렌스, 라모니카. 소방 안전
검사관에게 검사증 받았나요?

테렌스 로슨 [오전 11:09]
아니, 아직이요. 1시간쯤 전에 검사
관실에 전화했는데 이틀 뒤에 다시
확인하라네요.

한 경 [오전 11:11]
알겠어요. 계속 상황을 파악해주시
겠어요? 그 검사증이 없으면 지점
을 열 수가 없어요. 라모니카, 우리
에게 다양한 메뉴 품목에 필요한 재
료가 있나요?

라모니카 엘로이 [오전 11:12]
제가 직접 재료 목록을 점검했어요.
하나도 빠짐없이 재고가 있었어요.

한 경 [오전 11:14]
그거 정말 안심이 되네요.

2   At 11:14 A.M., what does Ms. Han most likely mean when she writes,   오전 11시 14분에 한 씨가 "그거 정말
    "That's a great comfort"?   안심이 되네요"라고 쓸 때 의도하는 것은?
    (A) She is happy with the various menu options.   (A) 다양한 메뉴 선택에 만족한다.
    (B) She is pleased that all ingredients are available.   (B) 모든 재료를 이용할 수 있어 기쁘다.

해설 **의도 파악:** 한 씨가 오전 11시 11분에 do we have the ingredients needed for the various menu items?라고 물어보자
      엘로이 씨가 오전 11시 12분에 Every single one was in stock.이라고 답했고 바로 이어 오전 11시 14분에 That's a great
      comfort.라고 응답했습니다. 즉, 모든 재료를 이용할 수 있어 기쁘다는 의미이므로 정답은 (B)입니다.

1 (A)	2 (C)	3 (A)	4 (D)	5 (C)	6 (A)	7 (C)	8 (A)

Questions 1-2 refer to the following text-message chain.

1-2 문자 메시지

Juliana Baum (9:12 A.M.) Hi, Marcus. **1**Is the marketing team up to
줄리아나 바움 (오전 9시 12분)   안녕하세요, 마커스. 마케팅 팀은 잘 알고 있나요

speed / on the planning for next week's virtual presentation?
다음 주 가상 프레젠테이션을 위한 계획 수립에 대해

줄리아나 바움 (오전 9시 12분)
안녕하세요, 마커스. **1**마케팅 팀은 다음 주 가상 프레젠테이션을 위한 계획 수립에 대해 잘 알고 있나요?

Marcus Sears (9:13 A.M.) Actually, / I'd like to meet once more to discuss
마커스 시어스 (오전 9시 13분)   사실은   한 번 더 만나 그 이야기를 하고 싶어요

it, / if that's not a bother.
방해가 되지 않는다면

마커스 시어스 (오전 9시 13분)
사실은, 방해가 되지 않는다면 한 번 더 만나 그 이야기를 하고 싶어요.

Juliana Baum (9:14 A.M.) Not at all.
줄리아나 바움 (오전 9시 14분)   전혀요.

줄리아나 바움 (오전 9시 14분)
전혀요.

Marcus Sears (9:16 A.M.) Could we meet / on Tuesday at 11 A.M.?
마커스 시어스 (오전 9시 16분)   우리가 만날 수 있을까요   화요일 오전 11시에

마커스 시어스 (오전 9시 16분)
화요일 오전 11시에 만날 수 있을까요?

Juliana Baum (9:17 A.M.) Let me check my calendar.
줄리아나 바움 (오전 9시 17분)   제 일정표를 확인해 볼게요.

줄리아나 바움 (오전 9시 17분)
제 일정표를 확인해 볼게요.

Marcus Sears (9:18 A.M.) Oh, you know what? **2**Could we move it to
마커스 시어스 (오전 9시 18분)   아, 있잖아요   오후 1시로 그것을 옮길 수 있을까요

1 P.M. / instead? I have another meeting / at 11 A.M.
대신   다른 회의가 있네요   오전 11시에

마커스 시어스 (오전 9시 18분)
아, 있잖아요. **2**대신 오후 1시로 시간을 옮길 수 있을까요? 오전 11시에 다른 회의가 있네요.

Juliana Baum (9:20 A.M.) Even better. My schedule is free / most of the
줄리아나 바움 (오전 9시 20분)   훨씬 더 좋아요.   제 일정은 비어 있거든요   오후에는 대부분

afternoon.

줄리아나 바움 (오전 9시 20분)
훨씬 더 좋아요. 제 일정은 오후에는 대부분 비어 있거든요.

Marcus Sears (9:21 A.M.) Perfect! I'll send out the calendar invitation /
마커스 시어스 (오전 9시 21분)   완벽해요   일정 초대장을 보낼게요

to the rest of the team.
나머지 팀원들에게

마커스 시어스 (오전 9시 21분)
완벽해요! 나머지 팀원들에게 일정 초대장을 보낼게요.

---

1 Why did Ms. Baum contact Mr. Sears?

(A) To request a planning update

(B) To reschedule an upcoming meeting

(C) To cancel a company gathering

(D) To share a virtual presentation

바움 씨가 시어스 씨에게 연락한 이유는?

(A) 계획 수립에 대한 상황 보고를 요청하려고

(B) 곧 있을 회의 일정을 변경하려고

(C) 회사 모임을 취소하려고

(D) 가상 프레젠테이션을 공유하려고

> **해설** 세부 사항: 바움 씨의 오전 9시 12분 메시지 Is the marketing team up to speed on the planning for next week's virtual presentation?에서 시어스 씨에게 가상 프레젠테이션을 위한 계획 수정 상황에 대해 묻고 있으므로 정답은 (A)입니다.

---

2 At 9:20 A.M., what does Ms. Baum most likely mean when she writes, "Even better"?

(A) Two hours is enough time to finish a project.

(B) She will be happy to clear her schedule.

(C) An afternoon meeting is preferable.

(D) A team should share a calendar.

오전 9시 20분에 바움 씨가 "훨씬 더 좋아요"라고 적은 의도는 무엇인가?

(A) 프로젝트를 끝내는 데 두 시간이면 충분하다.

(B) 기꺼이 일정을 비울 것이다.

(C) 오후 회의가 더 좋다.

(D) 팀은 일정을 공유해야 한다.

> **해설** 의도 파악: 시어스 씨의 오전 9시 18분 메시지 Could we move it to 1 P.M. instead? I have another meeting at 11 A.M.에 대해 바움 씨가 '훨씬 더 좋아요(Even better.)'라며 오후 회의가 더 좋다는 의미로 메시지를 보냈으므로 정답은 (C)입니다.

Questions 3-4 refer to the following text-message chain.

Anna Meyer (10:55 A.M.) I can't help set up this afternoon's picnic. Some
안나 마이어 (오전 10:55)   오늘 오후 야유회 준비를 도울 수 없겠어요.   제가

clients I'm meeting with / are running late. I won't arrive until noon. Will you
만나는 고객 몇 분이   늦어져서요   정오에니 도착할 수 있어요.

be all right?
괜찮으시겠어요?

Yuki Nakamura (10:56 A.M.) We can manage without you, / ³but in that
유키 나카무라 (오전 10:56)   당신 없이 우리끼리 할 수 있어요   그런데 그렇게

case / I won't have time / to go to Bower Hall to pick up the decorations.
되면   제가 시간이 없게 돼요   장식물을 가지러 바우어 홀에 갈

Do you know if there's anyone there / who could bring them to me?
혹시 거기에 사람이 있을까요   제게 그것들을 가져다 줄

Anna Meyer (10:57 A.M.) Let me check.
안나 마이어 (오전 10:57)   확인해 볼게요.

Anna Meyer (11:01 A.M.) I just got off the phone / with Dan. ⁴He had
안나 마이어 (오전 11:01)   방금 통화했어요   댄과   그가 야유회

volunteered to help clean up after the picnic, / but he's free now, / so he
끝나고 청소를 돕기로 자원했었거든요   그런데 그가 지금 시간이 있어요 / 그래서

can do this, / and I'll take his duty. He's leaving Bower Hall now / with the
이 일을 할 수 있어요 / 그리고 제가 그가 하기로 한 일을 할 거예요 / 그가 지금 바우어 홀을 출발하고 있어요 / 장식물을

decorations. He should be there / in a few minutes.
가지고   거기로 갈 거예요   몇 분 안에

Yuki Nakamura (11:03 A.M.) Perfect! That's a big help. That way / we'll be
유키 나카무라 (오전 11:03)   완벽해요!   큰 도움이 되었어요.   그렇게 하면   우리는

able to start serving the food / at noon.
음식을 제공하기 시작할 수 있을 거예요   정오에

안나 마이어 (오전 10:55)
오늘 오후 야유회 준비를 도울 수 없겠어요. 제가 만나는 고객 몇 분이 늦어져서요. 정오에나 도착할 수 있어요. 괜찮으시겠어요?

유키 나카무라 (오전 10:56)
당신 없이 우리끼리 어떻게든 할 수는 있지만 ³그렇게 되면, 제가 장식물을 가지러 바우어 홀에 갈 시간이 없게 돼요. 혹시 거기에 제게 그것들을 가져다줄 사람이 있을까요?

안나 마이어 (오전 10:57)
확인해 볼게요.

안나 마이어 (오전 11:01)
댄과 방금 통화했어요. ⁴그가 야유회 끝나고 청소를 돕기로 자원했었거든요. 그런데 그가 지금 시간이 있어서 이 일을 하고, 제가 그가 하기로 한 일을 할 거예요. 그가 지금 장식물을 가지고 바우어 홀을 출발하고 있어요. 몇 분 안에 거기로 갈 거예요.

유키 나카무라 (오전 11:03)
완벽해요! 큰 도움이 되었어요. 그렇게 하면 우리는 정오에 음식을 제공하기 시작할 수 있을 거예요

226

3 At 10:57 A.M., what does Ms. Meyer indicate she will do when she writes, "Let me check"?

(A) Talk to a colleague

(B) Look for the decorations

(C) Confer with the clients

(D) Verify her arrival time

오전 10시 57분에 마이어 씨가 "확인해 볼게요"라고 쓴 의도는 무엇이겠는가?

(A) 직장 동료와 이야기한다

(B) 장식물을 찾아본다

(C) 고객과 협의한다

(D) 자신의 도착 시간을 확인한다

해설 의도 파악: 나카무라 씨는 오전 10시 56분 메시지 but in that ~ pick up the decorations.와 Do you know ~ them to me?에서 장식물을 자기 대신 가져다 줄 사람이 있는지를 물었고, 이에 마이어 씨가 '확인해 볼게요(Let me check.)'라고 응답했습니다. 즉, 나카무라 씨 대신 그 일을 해줄 사람을 알아보겠다는 의미이므로 정답은 (A)입니다.

---

4 How will Ms. Meyer help with the event?

(A) By inviting guests

(B) By preparing food

(C) By hanging decorations

(D) By assisting with cleanup

마이어 씨는 어떻게 행사를 도울 것인가?

(A) 손님을 초청해서

(B) 음식을 준비해서

(C) 장식물을 매달아서

(D) 청소를 도와서

해설 세부 사항: 마이어 씨가 오전 11시 01분에 He had volunteered ~ I'll take his duty.에서 야유회 끝나고 청소를 돕기로 한 댄의 일을 자신이 하겠다고 했습니다. 즉 마이어 씨가 청소를 돕는다는 의미이므로 정답은 (D)입니다.

Paraphrasing 지문의 take his duty → 정답의 assisting with cleanup

Questions 5-8 refer to the following online chat discussion.

5-8 온라인 채팅

Ken Martin (3:09 P.M.) [5,6]My team and I are trying / to work with the new
켄 마틴 (오후 3:09)　　　　　　　저와 팀은 시도하고 있어요　　　　새로운 컬러마즈 그래픽스 컴퓨터

Colormaz Graphics computer program, / but the directions for its use /
프로그램으로 작업하려고　　　　　　　　　　　그런데 사용법 설명이

seem minimal. Some of us are true beginners. Where do we start? Is there
너무 적은 것 같아요.　　우리들 중 몇 명은 진짜 초보거든요.　　　어디서 시작해야 할까요?　　더 상세한

a more in-depth user's manual?
사용자 매뉴얼이 있나요?

Susan Ahmadi (3:12 P.M.) When Colormaz developed this program, /
수잔 아마디 (오후 3:12)　　　　　컬러마즈가 이 프로그램을 개발할 때

they purposely kept the directions for use very basic. The company wants
일부러 사용법 설명을 아주 기본적인 상태로 유지했어요　　　　　　　　　그 회사는 이용자들에게

to encourage users / to explore the program in their own unique way /
장려하기를 원하거든요.　　　자신만의 독특한 방식으로 프로그램을 탐색하도록

to allow for more design innovation.
디자인 혁신을 염두에 두고

Beatrice Yeager (3:15 P.M.) That's my understanding, too. They've created
비어트리스 예거 (오후 3:15)　　　　　저도 그렇게 이해하고 있어요.　　　　사람들이 커뮤니티를

a community / around this product. A good place for you to start is by
만들었어요　　　　이 제품에 관한　　　　　처음에는 프로젝트 몇 개를 확인해보는 것부터 하는 게

checking out some of the projects / that other users have posted. [7]Just
좋을 거예요　　　　　　　　다른 이용자들이 올린　　　　　그냥

look for the Colormaz user forum / online.
컬러마즈 이용자 포럼을 살펴보세요　　　온라인에서

Ken Martin (3:19 P.M.) That sounds great. I'll look there now.
켄 마틴 (오후 3:19)　　　　그거 좋은데요.　　　　지금 그곳을 살펴볼게요.

Beatrice Yeager (3:20 P.M.) [6]As my team members work with the
비어트리스 예거 (오후 3:20)　　　　우리 팀원들이 그 프로그램으로 일하고 있어서

program, / I've been encouraging them / to post their projects and notes to
저는 팀원들에게 장려하고 있어요　　　　포럼에 자신의 프로젝트와 메모도 올리라고

the forum as well.

Susan Ahmadi (3:22 P.M.) [8]And in a few weeks / we will schedule a
수잔 아마디 (오후 3:22)　　　　　그리고 몇 주 뒤에　　　　우리는 부서 회의 일정을 잡을 거예요

department meeting / where our teams will be asked to share / what
우리 팀들이 공유하도록 요청받는　　　　　　　　　그들이 익힌 것을

they've learned.

Ken Martin (3:22 P.M.) Thank you both.
켄 마틴 (오후 3:22)　　　두 분 다 고마워요.

5-8 온라인 채팅

켄 마틴 (오후 3:09)

5,6저와 팀은 새로운 컬러마즈 그래픽스 컴퓨터 프로그램으로 작업하려고 시도하고 있어요. 그런데 사용법 설명이 너무 적은 것 같아요. 우리들 중 몇 명은 진짜 초보거든요. 어디서 시작해야 할까요? 더 상세한 사용자 매뉴얼이 있나요?

수잔 아마디 (오후 3:12)

컬러마즈가 이 프로그램을 개발할 때 일부러 사용법 설명을 아주 기본적인 것만 했어요. 그 회사는 디자인 혁신을 염두에 두고 이용자들이 자신만의 독특한 방식으로 프로그램을 탐색하도록 장려하기를 원하거든요.

비어트리스 예거 (오후 3:15)

저도 그렇게 이해하고 있어요. 사람들이 이 제품에 관한 커뮤니티를 만들었어요. 처음에는 다른 사용자들이 올린 프로젝트 몇 개를 확인해보는 것부터 하는 게 좋을 거예요. 7그냥 온라인에서 컬러마즈 사용자 포럼을 찾아보세요.

켄 마틴 (오후 3:19)

그거 좋은데요. 지금 그곳을 살펴볼게요.

비어트리스 예거 (오후 3:20)

6우리 팀원들이 그 프로그램으로 일하고 있어서 저는 팀원들에게 자신의 포럼에 프로젝트와 메모도 올리라고 장려하고 있어요.

수잔 아마디 (오후 3:22)

8그리고 몇 주 뒤에 우리는 부서 회의 일정을 잡아서 그때 우리 팀들에게 익힌 것을 공유하도록 요청할 거예요.

켄 마틴 (오후 3:22)

두 분 다 고마워요.

5 What most likely is Mr. Martin's job?

(A) Software developer

(B) Technical writer

(C) Graphic designer

(D) Computer salesperson

마틴 씨의 직업은 무엇이겠는가?

(A) 소프트웨어 개발자

(B) 기술 문서 작가

(C) 그래픽 디자이너

(D) 컴퓨터 판매원

> **해설** 추론 / 암시: 마틴 씨는 오후 3시 09분 메시지(My team and I are trying ~ computer program)에서 새로운 그래픽 프로그램을 사용하여 작업을 하려 한다고 했습니다. 이를 통해 마틴 씨가 그래픽 디자이너임을 유추할 수 있으므로 정답은 (C)입니다.

---

6 What is suggested about the participants in the chat discussion?

(A) They are members of separate teams.

(B) They work for Colormaz.

(C) They are training new employees.

(D) They are looking for new computer programs.

채팅 참가자에 관해 시사되는 것은?

(A) 별개의 팀에 속한 팀원들이다.

(B) 컬러마즈에서 일한다.

(C) 신입 사원을 교육하고 있다.

(D) 새로운 컴퓨터 프로그램을 찾고 있다.

> **해설** 추론 / 암시: 마틴 씨의 오후 3시 09분 메시지(My team and I are trying ~ computer program)와 예거 씨의 오후 3시 20분 메시지(As my team members work with the program)를 통해 채팅 참가자들이 각자 다른 팀에 속해 있다는 것을 유추할 수 있으므로 정답은 (A)입니다.

---

7 At 3:19 P.M., what does Mr. Martin most likely mean when he writes, "I'll look there now"?

(A) He will consult the user's manual.

(B) He will check inside his desk.

(C) He will visit a Web site.

(D) He will go to a community center.

오후 3시 19분에 마틴 씨가 "지금 그곳을 살펴볼게요"라고 쓸 때 의도하는 것은?

(A) 사용 설명서를 참조할 것이다.

(B) 책상 안을 확인할 것이다.

(C) 웹사이트를 방문할 것이다.

(D) 커뮤니티 센터에 갈 것이다.

> **해설** 의도 파악: 예거 씨는 오후 3시 15분 메시지(Just look for the Colormaz user forum online.)에서 온라인의 이용자 포럼을 찾아보라고 제안했습니다. 이에 대해 마틴 씨가 '지금 그곳을 살펴볼게요(I'll look there now.)'라며 웹사이트를 방문하겠다는 의미로 메시지를 보냈으므로 정답은 (C)입니다.

> **Paraphrasing** 지문의 look there → 정답의 visit a Web site

---

8 What will Mr. Martin's team members most likely be asked to do?

(A) Explain how they use the Colormaz Graphics program

(B) Create a user forum for clients

(C) Send a report to Ms. Ahmadi

(D) Compile a list of questions for a meeting

마틴 씨의 팀원들이 하도록 요청받게 될 일은?

(A) 컬러마즈 그래픽스 프로그램을 어떻게 사용하고 있는지 설명하기

(B) 고객을 위한 이용자 포럼 만들기

(C) 아마디 씨에게 보고서 보내기

(D) 회의에서 할 질문 목록 취합하기

> **해설** 세부 사항: 아마디 씨의 오후 3시 22분 메시지 And in a few weeks ~ what they've learned.에서 마틴 씨의 팀원들을 포함해 컬러마즈 그래픽스 프로그램을 사용하는 모든 팀원들이 사용법에 대해 회의에서 발표하게 될 것임을 짐작할 수 있으므로 정답은 (A)입니다.

> **Paraphrasing** 지문의 to share what they've learned → 정답의 Explain how they use the Colormaz Graphics program

ETS 문제로 훈련하기

교재 p.254

Q1 (B)   **Q2** (B)

Best Practices for Guest Satisfaction: Introduction
고객 만족을 위한 최선의 관행: 서론

This is a guide / to equipping and maintaining guest rooms / in a manner /
이 글은 안내서입니다   객실을 구비하고 유지하기 위한   방법으로

that results in a high level of guest satisfaction. **The information is**
높은 수준의 고객 만족을 도출할 수 있는   본 자료는 구성되어 있습니다

organized / into four sections.
             4개 항으로

Section One: Effective heating, cooling, and ventilation systems; regulation
1항   효과적인 난방, 냉방, 환기 시스템과 객실 온도 조절

       of room temperature

Section Two: Furnishing rooms for comfort and attractiveness
2항   편안함과 매력을 느끼게 하는 객실의 가구 비치

Section Three: Appearance and care of towels, bed linens, and window
3항   수건, 침대보, 창문 덮개의 외관 및 관리

        coverings

Section Four: Equipping rooms with appliances and technology
4항   객실에 전자 기기와 장비 설치하기

고객 만족을 위한 최선의 관행: 서론

이 글은 높은 수준의 고객 만족을 도출할 수 있는 방법으로 객실을 구비하고 유지하기 위한 안내서입니다. 본 자료는 4개 항으로 구성되어 있습니다.

1항: 효과적인 난방, 냉방, 환기 시스템과 객실 온도 조절

2항: 편안함과 매력을 느끼게 하는 객실의 가구 비치

3항: 수건, 침대보, 창문 덮개의 외관 및 관리

4항: 객실에 전자기기와 장비 설치하기

---

1 For whom is the guide most likely written?

(A) Tourists

(B) Hotel managers

안내서는 누구를 위해 작성된 것 같은가?

(A) 관광객

(B) 호텔 지배인

> **해설** 추론 / 암시: 지문의 제목 Best Practices for Guest Satisfaction과 This is a guide ~ guest satisfaction.에서 객실의 시설 관리와 유지를 책임지는 호텔 직원을 위한 안내서임을 알 수 있으므로 정답은 (B)입니다.

Singing Duo Soon to Launch Athletic-Wear Clothing Line
2인조 가수 곧 운동복 제품군 출시

2인조 가수 곧 운동복 제품군 출시

AUCKLAND (22 August)—Martino Johnson and Emily Taylor, / who make
오클랜드 (8월 22일)　　　　　마르티노 존슨과 에밀리 테일러가　　　　　인기 2인조 가수

up the popular singing duo Fall Wind, / have announced / they are creating
폴 윈드의 구성원인　　　　　　　　　발표했다　　　　친환경 운동복 제품군을

an eco-friendly line of athletic clothing. Known as Martily, / the moderately
만든다고　　　　　　　　　　　　상표명은 마틸리로　　　저렴한 가격대의 상의,

priced tops, bottoms, and socks / will be made of organic cotton and
하의, 그리고 양말이　　　　　　유기농 면과 재생 폴리에스터로 만들어질 것이다

recycled polyester.

"A lot of the earth-friendly athletic apparel / that's out there / is too
"많은 지구 친화적인 운동복들은　　　　　　시중에 나와 있는　　　너무

expensive," / Ms. Taylor explained. "People who don't have a lot of money
비쌉니다."라고　　테일러 씨는 설명했다　　"쓸 돈이 많지 않은 사람들은

to spend / want to do their part / to help the planet, / too."
자신의 역할을 하기를 원합니다　　지구를 돕기 위해　　역시"

The women's line will be sold exclusively / at Sydney Sports stores /
여성복 제품군은 독점 판매된다　　　　　　　　시드니 스포츠 매장에서

across the nation / and is expected to hit the shelves / in early November.
전국의　　　　　　　그리고 매장에 선보일 예정이다　　　　11월 초에

The men's line / will not be available until next March.
남성복 제품군은　　　내년 3월에나 만나볼 수 있을 것이다

오클랜드 (8월 22일) – 인기 2인조 가수 폴 윈드의 구성원인 마르티노 존슨과 에밀리 테일러가 친환경 운동복 제품군을 만든다고 발표했다. 상표명은 마틸리로, 저렴한 가격의 상의, 하의, 그리고 양말이 유기농 면과 재생 폴리에스터로 만들어질 것이다.

"시중에 나와 있는 많은 지구 친화적인 운동복들은 너무 비쌉니다." 라고 테일러 씨는 설명했다. "쓸 돈이 많지 않은 사람들도 지구를 돕기 위해 자신의 역할을 하기를 원합니다."

여성복 라인은 전국의 시드니 스포츠 매장에서 독점 판매되며 11월 초에 매장에 선보일 예정이다. 남성복 제품군은 내년 3월에나 만나볼 수 있을 것이다.

2　In which of the positions marked [1] and [2] does the following sentence best belong?

"The men's line will not be available until next March."

(A) [1]

(B) [2]

[1], [2]로 표시된 곳 중에서 다음 문장이 들어가기에 가장 적합한 곳은?

"남성복 제품군은 내년 3월에나 만나볼 수 있을 것이다."

(A) [1]

(B) [2]

> **해설**　문장 삽입: '남성복 제품군은 내년 3월에나 만나볼 수 있을 것이다'라는 말이 들어가야 하므로, 맥락상 빈칸 앞에 다른 특정 제품군 판매 개시와 관련된 내용이 나와야 합니다. 따라서 여성복 제품군은 11월 초에 판매를 시작할 예정이라고 말하는 문장 다음에 이어지는 [2]에 들어가는 것이 가장 적절합니다.

| **1** (A) | **2** (D) | **3** (A) | **4** (C) | **5** (A) | **6** (C) | **7** (D) | **8** (C) | **9** (A) |

Questions 1-2 refer to the following information.

1-2 정보

www.davencarcare.com/faqs

DAVEN CAR CARE – Frequently Asked Questions
데이븐 차량 관리　　　　　자주 묻는 질문

데이븐 차량 관리 – 자주 묻는 질문

What services do you provide?
어떤 서비스를 제공하나요?

어떤 서비스를 제공하나요?

We perform / maintenance checks and mechanical and electric repairs /
시행합니다　　　정비 점검, 기계 및 전기 수리를

모든 제조사의 차량에 대한 정비 점검, 기계 및 전기 수리를 시행합니다.

on all makes of vehicle.
모든 제조사의 차량에 대해

Do you offer any special deals?
특가를 제공하나요

특가를 제공하나요?

[1]We currently offer $10 coupons / in exchange for reviews posted on our
현재 10달러 쿠폰을 제공합니다　　　웹사이트에 이용 후기를 올리면

[1]현재 웹사이트에 이용 후기를 올리면 10달러 쿠폰을 제공합니다. 만족하신 고객의 추천 글은 저희가 신규 고객을 끌어들이는 가장 중요한 방법입니다.

website. Testimonials from satisfied customers / are our most important
만족하신 고객의 추천 글은　　　　　저희의 가장 중요한 방법입니다

way / of attracting new customers.
신규 고객을 끌어들이는

What incentives are extended / to first-time customers?
어떤 인센티브를 주나요　　　　　처음 방문하는 고객에게

처음 방문하는 고객에게 어떤 인센티브를 주나요?

New customers receive a complimentary oil change / the first time they
신규 고객은 무료로 오일 교환을 받습니다　　　　　처음 오실 때

신규 고객은 정비 점검이나 주요 부품 수리를 받으러 처음 오실 때 무료로 오일 교환을 받습니다.

come / for a maintenance check or any major repair.
정비 점검이나 주요 부품 수리를 받으러

Can I bring my own parts?
직접 부품을 가져 가도 되나요

직접 부품을 가져 가도 되나요?

Yes. However, / please be aware / that shopping for your own parts / may
됩니다 하지만　　　아시기 바랍니다　　　여러분이 직접 부품을 사면　　　비용이

됩니다. 하지만 여러분이 직접 부품을 사면 결국 비용이 더 들 수도 있다는 점을 아시기 바랍니다. 시간이 지날수록 마모되는 품질 낮은 부품을 선택하실 수도 있습니다. 직접 구입하신 부품은 품질 보증 적용 대상이 안 될 확률이 높습니다. 반대로, 당사는 공인된 [2C]품질 보증 적용 부품만 사용합니다. 이 부품들은 경쟁업체의 부품들보다 [2A]내구성이 좋지만 [2B]가격은 더 쌉니다.

cost you more / in the long run. You might choose low-quality parts / that
더 들 수도 있다는 점을　결국　　　품질 낮은 부품을 선택하실 수도 있습니다　　시간이

will not stand the test of time. Any parts you purchase on your own / will
지날수록 마모되는　　　　직접 구입하신 부품은

most likely not be covered by warranty. In contrast, / we use only certified,
품질 보증 적용 대상이 안 될 확률이 높습니다　　　반대로　　　당사는 공인된 품질 보증 적용 부품만

[2C]warranty-covered [2A]parts / that are durable yet [2B]lower priced / than
사용합니다　　　　　이 부품들은 내구성이 좋지만 가격은 더 쌉니다　　　경쟁업체의

those of our competitors.
부품들보다

Do you offer a shuttle / while my car is being serviced?
셔틀을 제공하나요   제 차가 정비 받는 동안

Yes. Drop off your vehicle, / and we will be happy to drive you home or to
예.   차량을 두고 가시면   기꺼이 댁이나 직장까지 차로 모시며

work / and to pick you up again / when your vehicle is ready.
         다시 모시러 갑니다   차량이 준비되면

> 제 차가 정비를 받는 동안 셔틀을 제공하나요?
> 예. 차량을 두고 가시면 기꺼이 댁이나 직장까지 차로 모시며 차량이 준비되면 다시 모시러 갑니다.

---

1   What can customers do to receive discounts?

(A) Leave customer feedback online

(B) Present a repeat-customer card

(C) Purchase a parts warranty

(D) Refer new customers

> 할인을 받으려면 고객이 할 수 있는 일은?
> (A) 고객 의견을 온라인에 남기기
> (B) 재방문 고객 카드 제시하기
> (C) 부품 품질 보증서 구입하기
> (D) 신규 고객 추천하기

해설   세부 사항: 지문 초반부 *Do you offer any special deals?*란에서 웹사이트에 이용 후기를 올리면 10달러 쿠폰을 제공한다(We currently offer $10 coupons in exchange for reviews posted on our website.)고 했으므로 정답은 (A)입니다.

Paraphrasing   지문의 reviews posted on our website → 정답의 Leave customer feedback online

---

2   What is NOT mentioned as a benefit of using parts provided by Daven Car Care?

(A) The parts last a long time.

(B) The parts may be less expensive.

(C) The parts are covered by a warranty.

(D) The parts are familiar to the mechanics.

> 데이븐 차량 관리에서 제공하는 부품 사용 시의 이점으로 언급되지 않은 것은?
> (A) 부품이 오래 간다.
> (B) 부품 가격이 더 저렴할 수 있다.
> (C) 부품에 품질 보증이 적용된다.
> (D) 부품이 정비사에게 익숙하다.

해설   Not / True: 질문에 NOT이 있는 경우에는 각 선택지를 지문과 대조하여 사실 여부를 확인해야 합니다. 지문의 *Can I bring my own parts?*란에서 후반부를 보면 (A)는 parts that are durable에서, (B)는 lower priced에서, (C)는 warranty-covered parts에서 확인할 수 있습니다. 따라서 정답은 (D)입니다.

Questions 3-5 refer to the following article.

3-5 기사

K.L.P. to Invest in Robotics
K.L.P. 로봇에 투자한다

K.L.P. 로봇에 투자한다

BUSAN (May 3)—Houston-based toy company K.L.P. announced / Monday /
부산 (5월 3일) 휴스턴에 본사를 둔 완구 회사인 K.L.P.는 발표했다 월요일에

that it plans to invest $20 million / in robotic technology / in South Korea /
2천만 달러를 투자할 계획이라고 로봇 기술에 대한민국의

for use in all of its factories / over the next two years.
모든 공장에서 사용할 향후 2년간

[3]Industry analysts believe / K.L.P. is attempting to remain competitive with
기업 분석가들은 생각한다 K.L.P.가 경쟁업체들에게 뒤처지지 않기 위해 시도하고 있다고

rival firms, / most of which have adopted new manufacturing techniques.
대다수 경쟁 업체들이 새로운 제조 기술을 도입하자

Such techniques have dramatically increased factory output, / and K.L.P.'s
이러한 기술 때문에 공장 생산량이 크게 증가했다 그리고 K.L.P.의

executives indicated / they are ready to try them as well.
임원들은 밝혔다 그들도 신기술을 시험할 준비가 되어 있다고

[4]"We have researched other companies, / and we are confident / that this
"우리는 다른 회사들을 조사해 왔습니다 그리고 확신합니다 이번 투자로

investment will ultimately boost our annual revenue to $200 million / within
연간 수익이 결국 2억 달러로 증가할 것을 5년

five years," / explained K.L.P.'s Hana Ryu.
이내에" K.L.P.의 류하나 씨가 설명했다

[5]In recent years, / K.L.P.'s revenues have hovered around the $160 million
최근 몇 년간 K.L.P.의 수익은 약 1억 6천만 달러 수준을 맴돌았다

mark / compared to its top two competitors, / which posted earnings of
상위 2개 경쟁업체에 비해 수익이 약 1억 8천만 달러와

around $180 million and $170 million / last year.
1억 7천만 달러를 기록한 지난해

Ryu indicated / that K.L.P. is considering other ways to increase profits, /
류 씨는 밝혔다 K.L.P.가 수익을 늘리기 위한 다른 방법들도 고려하고 있다고

such as relocating their headquarters to a more efficient building, / but they
본사를 더 효율적인 건물로 이전하는 방안 등 하지만

are certain / that this overseas investment will be lucrative.
확신한다고 이번 해외 투자가 수익성이 있을 것으로

부산 (5월 3일) - 휴스턴에 본사를 둔 완구 회사인 K.L.P.는 월요일 대한민국의 로봇 기술에 향후 2년간 2천만 달러를 투자하여 모든 공장에서 사용할 계획이라고 발표했다.

[3]기업 분석가들은 대다수 경쟁 업체들이 새로운 제조 기술을 도입하자 K.L.P가 이들에게 뒤처지지 않기 위해 시도하고 있다고 생각한다. 이러한 기술 때문에 공장 생산량이 크게 증가했으며, K.L.P.의 임원들은 그들도 신기술을 시험할 준비가 되어 있다고 밝혔다.

[4]"우리는 다른 회사들을 조사해 왔고, 이번 투자로 5년 이내에 연간 수익이 결국 2억 달러로 증가하리라 확신합니다." K.L.P.의 류하나 씨가 설명했다.

[5]상위 2개 경쟁업체의 수익이 지난해 약 1억 8천만 달러와 1억 7천만 달러를 기록한 데 비해 최근 몇 년간 K.L.P.의 수익은 약 1억 6천만 달러 수준을 맴돌았다.

류 씨는 본사를 더 효율적인 건물로 이전하는 방안 등 K.L.P.가 수익을 늘리기 위한 다른 방법들도 고려하고 있지만, 이번 해외 투자가 수익성이 있을 것으로 확신한다고 밝혔다.

3 What is suggested about K.L.P. in comparison to its competitors?

(A) Its technology is outdated.

(B) It recently opened a new factory.

(C) Its products are more innovative.

(D) It is hiring new employees at a faster pace.

경쟁 업체와 비교해 K.L.P.에 관해 시사되는 것은?

(A) 기술이 뒤떨어졌다.

(B) 최근 새 공장을 열었다.

(C) 제품이 더 혁신적이다.

(D) 더 빠른 속도로 신입 사원을 채용하고 있다.

해설 추론 / 암시: 두 번째 단락 첫 번째 문장에서 대다수 경쟁업체가 새로운 제조 기술(new manufacturing techniques)을 도입했고 K.L.P.가 이에 뒤처지지 않기 위해 시도한다고 했습니다. 따라서 K.L.P.는 현재 기술 면에서 뒤처져 있음을 알 수 있으므로 정답은 (A)입니다.

Paraphrasing 지문의 rival firms → 질문의 competitors

---

4 Who most likely is Ms. Ryu?

(A) A computer analyst

(B) A business journalist

(C) A company executive

(D) A professor of robotics

류 씨는 누구이겠는가?

(A) 컴퓨터 분석가

(B) 경제 전문 기자

(C) 기업 임원

(D) 로봇공학 교수

해설 추론 / 암시: 지문에 류라는 이름이 언급된 부분에서 정답의 단서를 찾아야 합니다. 세 번째 단락에서 K.L.P.'s Hana Ryu라는 이름이 등장하며 이번 투자로 K.L.P.의 연간 수익이 증가할 것(this investment will ultimately boost our annual revenue)이라고 말했습니다. 따라서 류 씨는 K.L.P.의 직원임을 알 수 있으므로 정답은 (C)입니다.

---

5 About how much did K.L.P. earn last year?

(A) $160 million

(B) $170 million

(C) $180 million

(D) $200 million

지난해 K.L.P.는 약 얼마를 벌어들였는가?

(A) 1억 6천만 달러

(B) 1억 7천만 달러

(C) 1억 8천만 달러

(D) 2억 달러

해설 세부 사항: 보기가 모두 숫자이므로 숫자가 등장하는 부분에 정답의 단서가 있습니다. 숫자가 등장하는 네 번째 단락을 보면 최근 몇 년간 K.L.P.의 수익은 1억 6천만 달러 수준이었다고 했으므로 정답은 (A)입니다. 1억 7천만 달러와 1억 8천만 달러는 각각 두 경쟁업체의 수익이므로 정답이 될 수 없습니다.

Paraphrasing 지문의 revenues → 질문의 earn
지문의 In recent years → 질문의 last year

Questions 6-9 refer to the following article.

SAN DIEGO (June 1) — [6,9]Windle Brothers Party Supplies (WBPS)
샌디에이고 (6월 1일)   윈들 브라더스 파티 용품사(WBPS)는 오늘 발표했다

announced today / that it is acquiring Denver-based Grable's Costumes.
덴버에 기반을 둔 그레이블스 코스튬즈를 인수한다고

Details are still being negotiated, / but the deal is expected to be finalized /
세부 사항은 아직 협상 중이다   그러나 거래는 마무리될 예정이다

by November.
11월까지

Long recognized / as a reliable source of costumes for all occasions /
오랫동안 인식되던   모든 행사의 믿을만한 코스튬 공급원으로

within the United States, / Grable's Costumes made a successful move
미국 내에서   그레이블스 코스튬즈는 동아시아로 성공적으로 진입했다

into East Asia / last year, / quickly capturing a sizeable portion of the
           작년에   코스튬 시장의 상당 부분을 빠르게 점유하며

costume market. WBPS has long been planning / a move beyond the North
         WBPS는 오랫동안 계획해 왔다   북미 시장 너머로의 이동을

American market, / and the acquisition of Grable's Costumes / is part of
         그리고 그레이블스 코스튬즈의 인수는   그 전략의

that strategy.
일환이다

[7]"Grable's has a physical presence / in the Asian market / with stores
"그레이블스는 물리적인 존재감을 갖고 있습니다   아시아 시장에서   주요 도시에 매장들이

in major cities. It also has brand recognition," / said WBPS CEO Maya
있어   그것은 또한 브랜드 인지도가 있습니다"라고   마야 앤더슨 WBPS 최고 경영자는

Anderson. "Our goal / is to capitalize on that success. All those Grable's
말했다   "우리의 목표는   그 성공을 활용하는 것입니다   그레이블스의 모든 아시아

stores in Asia / will carry not just costumes, / but Windle Brothers' entire
매장들은   의상뿐 아니라   윈들 브라더스의 파티 용품 전체도 취급할

array of party supplies as well."
것입니다."

Grable's Costumes' current president, / Charles Grable, / will be named
그레이블스 코스튬즈의 현 사장인   찰스 그레이블은   부사장으로 임명될

executive vice president. He will report directly / to Ms. Anderson.
예정이다   그는 직접 보고할 것이다   앤더슨 씨에게

"This is a win for everybody," / said Mr. Grable. "Although Grable's has
"이는 모두를 위한 승리입니다."라고   그레이블 씨가 말했다.   "비록 그레이블스가 어느 정도

had some success / in the East Asian market, / WBPS is a much larger
성공은 했지만   동아시아 시장에서   WBPS는 훨씬 더 큰 조직입니다

organization / with more resources, / so there's no limit for our costume
         더 많은 자원을 가진   그러니 우리 의상 판매에는 이제 한계가 없습니다."

sales now."

Founded in Denver 26 years ago, / Grable's Costumes has 22 stores /
26년 전에 덴버에 설립된   그레이블스 코스튬은 22곳의 매장을 가지고 있다

in major markets in the United States, / along with its four stores in China,
미국 내 주요 시장에   중국에 4곳, 일본에 3곳 그리고 한국에 3곳의 매장과 함께

샌디에이고 (6월 1일) – [6,9]윈들 브라더스 파티 용품사(WBPS)는 오늘 덴버에 기반을 둔 그레이블스 코스튬즈를 인수한다고 발표했다. 세부 사항은 아직 협상 중이지만 거래는 11월까지 마무리될 예정이다.

미국 내에서 모든 행사의 믿을만한 코스튬 공급원으로 오랫동안 인식되던 그레이블스 코스튬즈는 작년에 코스튬 시장의 상당 부분을 빠르게 점유하며 동아시아로 성공적으로 진입했다. WBPS는 오랫동안 북미 시장 너머로의 이동을 계획해 왔으며, 그레이블스 코스튬즈의 인수는 그 전략의 일환이다.

[7]"그레이블스는 주요 도시에 매장들이 있어 아시아 시장에서 물리적인 존재감을 갖고 있습니다. 그것은 또한 브랜드 인지도가 있습니다"라고 마야 앤더슨 WBPS 최고 경영자는 말했다. "우리의 목표는 그 성공을 활용하는 것입니다. 그레이블스의 모든 아시아 매장들은 의상뿐 아니라 윈들 브라더스의 파티 용품 전체를 취급할 것입니다."

그레이블스 코스튬즈의 현 사장인 찰스 그레이블은 부사장으로 임명될 예정이다. 그는 앤더슨 씨에게 직접 보고할 것이다.

"이는 모두를 위한 승리입니다."라고 그레이블 씨가 말했다. "비록 그레이블스가 동아시아 시장에서 어느 정도 성공은 했지만, WBPS는 더 많은 자원을 가진 훨씬 더 큰 조직입니다. 그러니 우리 의상 판매에는 이제 한계가 없습니다."

26년 전에 덴버에 설립된 그레이블스 코스튬은 미국 내 주요 시장에 22곳, 중국에 4곳, 일본에 3곳, 한

three in Japan, and three in Korea. Headquartered in San Diego / for all of
샌디에이고에 본사를 둔   43년의

its 43 years of operation, / ⁸WBPS has 93 stores in the United States and
운영 기간 내내   WBPS는 미국과 캐나다에 매장 93개를 갖고 있다

Canada.

국에 3곳의 매장을 갖고 있다. 43
년의 운영 기간 내내 샌디에이고에
본사를 둔 ⁸WBPS는 미국과 캐나
다에 매장 93개를 갖고 있다.

---

6 What is the subject of the article?

(A) A recent trend in costume design

(B) The retirement of a popular CEO

(C) A company's takeover of another company

(D) Changing conditions in the export market

기사의 주제는?

(A) 의상 디자인의 최근 경향

(B) 인기있는 최고 경영자의 은퇴

(C) 한 기업의 다른 기업 인수

(D) 수출 시장의 상황 변화

> **해설** 주제 / 목적: 지문의 첫 단락 Windle Brothers Party Supplies ~ acquiring Denver-based Grable's Costumes.에서 기업 인수를 발표한 회사에 대한 기사임을 알 수 있으므로 정답은 (C)입니다

> **Paraphrasing** 지문의 it is acquiring Denver-based Grable's Costumes → 정답의 A company's takeover of another company

---

7 What did WBPS find most attractive about Grable's Costumes?

(A) It carries unusual sizes.

(B) It is headquartered in Denver.

(C) It makes costumes for all occasions.

(D) It already has stores in Asian countries.

WBPS가 그레이블스 코스튬즈에 대해
가장 매력적이라고 생각한 것은?

(A) 흔치 않은 사이즈들을 취급한다.

(B) 덴버에 본사를 두고 있다.

(C) 모든 경우를 위한 의상을 제작한다.

(D) 아시아 국가들에 이미 매장이 있다.

> **해설** 세부 사항: 세 번째 단락에서 WBPS의 CEO는 아시아 주요 도시에 이미 그레이블스 매장이 있고 브랜드 인지도도 있기 때문에 WBPS는 그 성공을 활용할 것(to capitalize on that success)이라고 했으므로 정답은 (D)입니다.

---

8 What is indicated about WBPS?

(A) It wants to increase its online sales.

(B) Its founder is the current CEO.

(C) It sells party supplies in Canada.

(D) It is not as old as Grable's Costumes.

WBPS에 대해 명시된 것은?

(A) 온라인 판매의 증가를 원한다.

(B) 창립자가 현 최고 경영자이다.

(C) 캐나다에서 파티 용품을 판매한다.

(D) 그레이블스 코스튬즈만큼 오래되지
않았다.

> **해설** Not / True: 지문의 맨 마지막 문장에서 WBPS는 미국과 캐나다에 93개 매장이 있다(WBPS has 93 stores in the United States and Canada)고 했으므로 정답은 (C)입니다.

---

9 In which of the positions marked [1], [2], [3], and [4] does the following sentence best belong?

"Details are still being negotiated, but the deal is expected to be finalized by November."

(A) [1]   (B) [2]

(C) [3]   (D) [4]

[1], [2], [3], [4]로 표시된 곳 중에서
다음 문장이 들어가기에 가장 적합한 곳은?

"세부 사항은 아직 협상 중이지만 거래는
11월까지 마무리될 예정이다."

(A) [1]   (B)   [2]

(C) [3]   (D)   [4]

> **해설** 문장 삽입: '세부 사항은 아직 협상 중이지만 거래는 11월까지 마무리될 예정이다'라는 말이 들어가야 하므로, 맥락상 빈칸 앞에 거래 관련 내용이 나올 것입니다. 따라서 WBPS가 그레이블스 코스튬즈를 인수한다고 발표했다고 언급한 지문의 맨 첫 문장 다음에 이어지는 [1]에 들어가는 것이 가장 적절합니다.

ETS 문제로 훈련하기

교재 p.260

Q1 (A)　　　　　　　　**Q2** (B)

Hazeltown's Second Annual Street Festival
헤이즐타운의 두 번째 연례 거리 축제

Booth Registration Form
부스 신청서

Please return this form / by April 15 / to Charlotte Fernandes / at 43 Willow
이 양식을 반송하십시오　　　　4월 15일까지　　샬럿 페르난데스에게　　　　헤이즐타운 월로우

Street, Hazeltown.
스트리트 43에 있는

Restaurant Name 식당 이름	Hazeltown Bistro 헤이즐타운 비스트로
Location Request 위치 신청	The corner of Main Street and Chestnut Street 메인 스트리트와 체스넛 스트리트의 모퉁이
Dates Attending 참가 날짜	May 28-31 5월 28~31일
Form Received (to be completed by Ms. Fernandes) 양식 수령일　　　(페르난데스 씨에 의해 작성됨)	April 13 4월 13일

**헤이즐타운의 두 번째
연례 거리 축제**

부스 신청서

이 양식을 헤이즐타운 월로우 스트
리트 43에 있는 샬럿 페르난데스에
게 4월 15일까지 반송하십시오.

식당 이름 헤이즐타운 비스트로

위치 신청 메인 스트리트와 체스넛
스트리트의 모퉁이

참가 날짜 5월 28~31일

양식 수령일 (페르난데스 씨에 의
해 작성됨) 4월 13일

1　By what date must the registration form be returned?

　(A) April 15

　(B) May 31

신청서는 언제까지 반송해야 하는가?

(A) 4월 15일

(B) 5월 31일

해설 세부 사항: 지문의 Please return this form by April 15 to Charlotte Fernandes at 43 Willow Street, Hazeltown.을 통해
4월 15일까지 양식을 보내야 한다는 것을 알 수 있으므로 정답은 (A)입니다.

The Bilbridge Arts Institute (BAI)
빌브리지 예술 교육원 (BAI)

Fall Course Schedule
가을 강좌 일정

Photography Basics 사진 기초 (6:00 P.M. to 8:00 P.M.) (오후 6:00 – 오후 8:00) Mondays in September 9월 매주 월요일	**Ceramics I** 도예 I (6:00 P.M. to 8:00 P.M.) (오후 6:00 – 오후 8:00) Fridays in October 10월 매주 금요일
Ceramics II (5:00 P.M. to 8:00 P.M.) 도예 II (오후 5:00 – 오후 8:00) Tuesdays in November 11월 매주 화요일	**Painting** (6:30 P.M. to 8:30 P.M.) 회화 (오후 6:30 – 오후 8:30) Thursdays in December 12월 매주 목요일

Visit www.bai.edu/classes / for a detailed description of topics covered.
www.bai.edu/classes를 방문하세요   다루게 되는 주제에 관한 자세한 설명은

For those classes / that require students to purchase supplies, / a supply
강좌에는   수강생이 용품을 구매해야 하는   용품 목록이

list / is included with the description.
            설명에 포함되어 있습니다

Registration accepted / online and in person. Course fee: / $125 for
등록은 받습니다   온라인과 방문으로   수강료: 알곤빌 주민

residents of Algonville; / $140 for nonresidents.
125달러   비거주민 140달러

빌브리지 예술 교육원 (BAI)

가을 강좌 일정

사진 기초 (오후 6:00 – 오후 8:00) 9월 매주 월요일	도예 I (오후 6:00 – 오후 8:00) 10월 매주 금요일
도예 II (오후 5:00 – 오후 8:00) 11월 매주 화요일	회화 (오후 6:30 – 오후 8:30) 12월 매주 목요일

다루게 되는 주제에 관한 자세한 설명은 www.bai.edu/classes를 방문하세요. 수강생이 용품을 구매해야 하는 강좌에는 설명에 용품 목록이 포함되어 있습니다.

등록은 온라인과 방문으로 받습니다. 수강료: 알곤빌 주민 125달러; 비거주민 140달러.

---

2 What do all of the BAI's classes have in common?

(A) They begin at the same time.

(B) They cost less for Algonville residents.

모든 BAI 강좌의 공통점은?

(A) 같은 시간에 시작한다.

(B) 알곤빌 주민에게는 비용이 더 싸다.

해설 세부 사항: BAI 강좌 일정표 마지막에 수강료가 표시되어 있습니다. 알곤빌 주민의 경우 125달러, 비거주민의 경우 140달러이므로 정답은 (B)입니다.

1 (B)	2 (B)	3 (C)	4 (D)	5 (A)	6 (B)	7 (D)	8 (A)	9 (D)

Questions 1-2 refer to the following chart.

Krastek Medical Center
크라스텍 의료 센터

Nursing Staff Weekday Schedule: March 15-March 19
간호진 평일 일정표: 3월 15일~3월 19일

[1]Please contact your nursing supervisor, Ms. Gresham, with any questions.
문의 사항은 간호 부장 그레섬 씨에게 연락하십시오.

Name	Monday March 15	Tuesday March 16	Wednesday March 17	Thursday [2]March 18	Friday [2]March 19
1st FLOOR STAFF					
Cornelio Alvarez	Vacation	Vacation	9 A.M.-8 P.M.	9 A.M.-9 P.M.	10 A.M.-8 P.M.
[2]Maryann Dietz	7 A.M.-3 P.M.	9 A.M.-5 P.M.	9 A.M.-5 P.M.	[2]Vacation	[2]Vacation
Honoka Kita	6 A.M.-2 P.M.	6 A.M.-1 P.M.	6 A.M.-4 P.M.	UNSCHEDULED	6 A.M.-6 P.M.
Rumaysa Gowda	1 P.M.-8 P.M.	UNSCHEDULED	1 P.M.-1 A.M.	1 P.M.-1 A.M.	UNSCHEDULED
2nd FLOOR STAFF					
Ashleigh Morrison	6 A.M.-3 P.M.	6 A.M.-3 P.M.	6 A.M.-6 P.M.	6 A.M.-3 P.M.	Vacation
Taiki Saito	7 A.M.-7 P.M.	7 A.M.-1 P.M.	3 P.M.-9 P.M.	7 A.M.-7 P.M.	3 P.M.-10 P.M.
Tim Whitmore	2 P.M.-11 P.M.	1 P.M.-11 P.M.	4 P.M.-11 P.M.	UNSCHEDULED	4 P.M.-11 P.M.
Ping Yan	9 A.M.-9 P.M.	9 A.M.-9 P.M.	9 A.M.-9 P.M.	UNSCHEDULED	UNSCHEDULED

1-2 차트

크라스텍 의료 센터

간호진 평일 일정표: 3월 15일~3월 19일
[1]문의 사항은 간호 감독관 그레섬 씨에게 연락하십시오.

이름	월요일 3월 15일	화요일 3월 16일	수요일 3월 17일	목요일 [2]3월 18일	금요일 [2]3월 19일
1층 직원					
코넬리오 알바레즈	휴가	휴가	오전 9시-오후 8시	오전 9시-오후 9시	오전 10시-오후 8시
[2]매리앤 디에츠	오전 7시-오후 3시	오전 9시-오후 5시	오전 9시-오후 5시	[2]휴가	[2]휴가
호노카 키타	오전 6시-오후 2시	오전 6시-오후 1시	오전 6시-오후 4시	일정 없음	오전 6시-오후 6시
루메이사 가우다	오후 1시-오후 8시	일정 없음	오후 1시-오전 1시	오후 1시-오전 1시	일정 없음
2층 직원					
애슐리 모리슨	오전 6시-오후 3시	오전 6시-오후 3시	오전 6시-오후 6시	오전 6시-오후 3시	휴가
타이키 사이토	오전 7시-오후 7시	오전 7시-오후 1시	오후 3시-오후 9시	오전 7시-오후 7시	오후 3시-오후 10시
팀 휘트모어	오후 2시-오후 11시	오후 1시-오후 11시	오후 4시-오후 11시	일정 없음	오후 4시-오후 11시
핑 안	오전 9시-오후 9시	오전 9시-오후 9시	오전 9시-오후 9시	일정 없음	일정 없음

1 What is true about the nursing staff members on the schedule?

(A) All work on the first floor.

(B) All report to Ms. Gresham.

(C) All work until 5:00 A.M. or later.

(D) All will miss a day of work this week.

---

2 Who will begin vacation on March 18?

(A) Cornelio Alvarez

(B) Maryann Dietz

(C) Ashleigh Morrison

(D) Ping Yan

일정표에 있는 간호사들에 관해 사실인 것은?

(A) 모두 1층에서 일한다.

(B) 모두 그레셤 씨에게 보고한다.

(C) 모두 오전 5시 이후까지 일한다.

(D) 이번 주에는 모두 하루 결근할 것이다.

3월 18일부터 휴가인 사람은?

(A) 코넬리오 알바레즈

(B) 매리앤 디에츠

(C) 애슐리 모리슨

(D) 핑 얀

Questions 3-5 refer to the following invitation.

3-5 초대장

The Council for International Business Success (CIBS) presents

"[3]Understanding International Partners"
국제 비즈니스 성공 위원회(CIBS) 제공 '국외 협력사에 대한 이해'

[5]**Date and time:** Wednesday, 26 June, 3:00 P.M.– 4:00 P.M. British Summer
일시: 6월 26일 수요일 오후 3시~4시 (영국 서머타임)

Time

[5]**Location:** The Board Room in Hargrove House, London (limited seating,
장소: 런던, 하그로브 하우스의 회의실 (한정 좌석, 일찍 도착하시기 바랍니다)

please arrive early)

Live video stream: Dial-in numbers with pass codes / will be provided /
라이브 비디오 스트림: 암호와 함께 접속 번호가   제공될 예정입니다

on the day of the event.
행사 당일에

[4]Please join us for our next presentation, / which will feature / Mr. Kenji
우리의 다음 프레젠테이션에 함께 하십시오   주강사로 하는   빙콰 국제 운송의

Umehara, president of Binkwa Shipping International, / and Ms. Maria
사장인 켄지 우메하라 씨와   스카르파 소프트웨어 회사의

Tivoli, CEO of Scarpa Software Company. **Mr. Umehara and Ms. Tivoli will**
최고 경영자인 마리아 티볼리 씨를   우메하라 씨와 티볼리 씨는 정보를 공유할 것입니다

share information / about their vibrant and evolving markets. [3]They will give
공유할 것입니다   그들의 활기차며 진화하는 시장에 대한   그들은 참가자들에게

attendees / an insider's understanding / of opportunities and challenges,
전달할 것입니다   내부자의 이해를   기회와 도전, 경쟁 환경과 문화 규범에 대한

competitive environments, and cultural norms / and will pass along tips /
                                         그리고 조언해 줄 것입니다

for working with partners and customers. **The presentation will be held /**
협력사와 고객들과 함께 일하는 것에 대해   프레젠테이션은 열립니다

live in our London bureau / and broadcast by live stream / for CIBS
우리의 런던 사무실에서 라이브로   그리고 라이브 스트림으로 중계될 예정입니다   CIBS 회원 및

members and businesses / in other locations. A replay will be available /
업체들을 위해   타 지역의   다시 보기도 이용 가능합니다

for those unable to attend the live meeting.
라이브 미팅에 참여할 수 없는 사람들을 위해

To succeed in every market, / it is important / to have a global mind-set
모든 시장에서 성공하려면   중요합니다   글로벌한 사고방식과 현지 시장에 대한

and a respect for local markets. We hope / you will make every effort
존중을 갖추는 것이   바라겠습니다   최선을 다해 참석해 주시기를

to join us.
우리에게 함께해 주시기를

3-5 초대장

국제 비즈니스 성공 위원회(CIBS) 제공 '[3]국외 협력사에 대한 이해'

[5]**일시:** 6월 26일 수요일 오후 3시 ~4시 (영국 서머타임).

[5]**장소:** 런던, 하그로브 하우스의 회의실 (한정 좌석, 일찍 도착하시기 바랍니다)

라이브 비디오 스트림: 행사 당일에 암호와 함께 접속 번호가 제공될 예정입니다.

[4]빙과 국제 운송의 회장인 켄지 우메하라 씨, 스카르파 소프트웨어 회사의 최고 경영자인 마리아 티볼리 씨를 주강사로 하는 우리의 다음 프레젠테이션에 함께하십시오. 우메하라 씨와 티볼리 씨는 그들의 활기차며 진화하는 시장에 대한 정보를 공유할 것입니다. [3]그들은 참가자들에게 기회와 도전, 경쟁 환경과 문화 규범에 대한 내부자의 이해를 전달하고, 협력사와 고객들과 함께 일하는 것에 대해 조언해 줄 것입니다. 프레젠테이션은 우리의 런던 사무실에서 라이브로 열리며, 타 지역의 CIBS 회원 및 업체들을 위해 라이브 스트림으로 중계될 예정입니다. 라이브 미팅에 참여할 수 없는 사람들을 위해 다시 보기도 이용 가능합니다.

모든 시장에서 성공하려면, 현지 시장에 대한 존중과 글로벌한 사고방식을 갖추는 것이 중요합니다. 최선을 다해 참석해 주시기를 바라겠습니다.

3   What is the purpose of the presentation?

(A) To discuss updating international shipping requirements

(B) To explain a new video streaming technology

(C) To help members develop international business skills

(D) To give CIBS employees new conference-call pass codes

프레젠테이션의 목적은?

(A) 국제 운송 요건을 수정하는 것에 대해 논의하려고

(B) 비디오 스트리밍 신기술에 대해 설명하려고

(C) 회원들이 국제 비즈니스 역량을 개발하도록 도우려고

(D) CIBS 직원들에게 새로운 전화 회의 암호를 발급하려고

> **해설** 주제 / 목적: 프레젠테이션의 제목 Understanding International Partners와 두 번째 단락 They will give attendees ~ working with partners and customers.에서 프레젠테이션의 목적이 국제 비즈니스 역량 향상을 위한 도움을 제공하기 위한 것임을 알 수 있으므로 정답은 (C)입니다.

---

4   What is suggested about CIBS?

(A) It was founded as part of Scarpa Software Company.

(B) It is a financial partner of Binkwa Shipping International.

(C) Its headquarters have been moved to London.

(D) Its members work in a variety of industries.

CIBS에 대해 시사되는 것은?

(A) 스카르파 소프트웨어 회사의 일부로 설립되었다.

(B) 빙콰 국제 운송의 금융 협력사이다.

(C) 본사가 런던으로 이전했다.

(D) 회원들이 다양한 업계에서 일한다.

> **해설** 추론 / 암시: 프레젠테이션 강사가 운송회사 회장과 소프트웨어 회사의 최고 경영자인 것으로 보아 회원들이 여러 업계에 종사한다는 것을 알 수 있으므로 정답은 (D)입니다.

---

5   How can participants get a seat at Hargrove House?

(A) By arriving before 3:00 P.M.

(B) By registering online

(C) By purchasing a ticket

(D) By showing a membership card at the door

참가자들은 하그로브 하우스에 어떻게 자리를 잡을 수 있는가?

(A) 오후 3시 전에 도착함으로써

(B) 온라인으로 등록함으로써

(C) 입장권을 구입함으로써

(D) 입구에서 회원 카드를 제시함으로써

> **해설** 세부 사항: Location란에 좌석이 한정되어 있으니 하그로브 하우스에 일찍 도착하라고 되어 있고 Date and time란을 보면 오후 3시가 시작 시간이므로 정답은 (A)입니다.

> **Paraphrasing** 지문의 arrive early → 정답의 arriving before 3:00 P.M.

Questions 6-9 refer to the following form.

We at Fehring International appreciate your trust in us / as your relocation
페링 인터내셔널을 신뢰해주셔서 감사합니다   당신의 이주 전문가로

experts. ⁶We would like to know more / about your experience, / as we
우리는 더 알고자 합니다   당신의 경험에 대해   항상

always strive / to improve our services. Please help us / by completing this
노력하고 있으며   서비스 개선을 위해   도움이 되겠습니다   이 양식을 작성하시고 우리에게

form and returning it to us / in the enclosed envelop. Your answers will be
반송해 주시면   동봉된 봉투에 담아   당신의 답변은 비밀로 유지될

kept confidential.
것입니다.

First Name: Nadia   **Family Name:** Siddiqui
이름: 나디아   성: 시디퀴

Origin: London, England   **Destination:** Kuala Lumpur, Malaysia
출발지: 영국, 런던   도착지: 말레이시아, 쿠알라룸푸르

Rate the services you used from 1 = not satisfied to 5 = extremely satisfied.
당신이 이용한 서비스에 1 = 불만족부터 5 = 매우 만족까지 등급을 매겨 주십시오.

NA = not applicalbe.
NA = 해당 없음.

Packing personal belongings 개인 소지품 포장	1	2	3	4	⑤	NA
Moving 이동	1	②	3	4	5	NA
⁸**Vehicle shipping** 차량 운송	1	2	3	4	5	Ⓝ Ⓐ
Relocation support 이주 지원	1	2	3	④	5	NA

Please explain your ratings in the box below.
아래 네모 칸에 당신이 매긴 등급에 대해 설명해 주세요.

I am grateful for your team's effort / to give me a positive relocation
귀사 팀의 노력에 감사드립니다   제게 긍정적인 이주 경험을 선사하시고자 기울이신

experience / when ⁷I moved to Kuala Lumpur / for my new work
제가 쿠알라룸푸르로 이주했을 때   새로운 업무를 위해

assignment. My furniture and clothing arrived / in good condition.
제 가구와 옷이 도착했습니다   좋은 상태로

The care you took packing and labeling all of our belongings / made
우리의 모든 소지품을 포장하고 식별 표를 붙이는 데 배려가   새 집에

settling into our new home / much easier. The welcome packet of
정착하는 일을 만들었다   훨씬 더 쉽게   환영 정보 패키지는

information / on local shops and schools / was a thoughtful touch.
현지 상점 및 학교에 대한   사려 깊은 손길이었습니다

I was disappointed / that it took longer than promised / to receive our
실망스러웠습니다   약속보다 오래 걸린 점은   우리 물건들을 받는 데

possessions, / although I know you did what you could / to make this
최선을 다하셨다는 것은 알지만   이번 이주를 가능한 한

move as smooth as possible. ⁹I plan to use your services again /
순조롭게 하기 위해   귀사의 서비스를 다시 이용할 계획입니다

페링 인터내셔널을 당신의 이주 전문가로 신뢰해주셔서 감사합니다. ⁶우리는 서비스 개선을 위해 항상 노력하고 있으며, 당신의 경험에 대해 더 알고자 합니다. 이 양식을 작성하시고 동봉된 봉투에 담아 우리에게 반송해 주시면 도움이 되겠습니다. 당신의 답변은 비밀로 유지될 것입니다.

이름: 나디아   성: 시디퀴

출발지: 영국, 런던

도착지: 말레이시아, 쿠알라룸푸르

당신이 이용한 서비스에 1 = 불만족부터 5 = 매우 만족까지 등급을 매겨 주십시오. NA = 해당 없음.

개인 소지품 포장
1 2 3 4 ⑤ NA

이동   1 ② 3 4 5 NA

⁸차량 운송 1 2 3 4 5 Ⓝ Ⓐ

이주 지원 1 2 3 ④ 5 NA

아래 네모 칸에 당신이 매긴 등급에 대해 설명해 주세요.

⁷제가 새로운 업무를 위해 쿠알라룸푸르로 이주했을 때, 제게 긍정적인 이주 경험을 선사하시고자 기울이신 귀사 팀의 노력에 감사드립니다. 제 가구와 옷은 좋은 상태로 도착했습니다. 우리의 모든 소지품을 포장하고 식별 표를 붙이는데 배려해주신 덕분에 새 집에 정착하는 일이 훨씬 더 쉬웠습니다. 현지 상점 및 학교에 대한 환영 정보 패키지는 사려 깊은 손길이었습니다.

이번 이주를 가능한 한 순조롭게 최선을 다하셨다는 것은 알지만, 우리 물건들을 받는 데 약속보다 오래 걸린 점은 실망스러웠습니다. ⁹4년 후

244

when my assignment in Malayisa comes to an end / in four years /
말레이시아에서의 업무가 종료될 때   4년 후

and we move to our next location.
그리고 다음 장소로 옮길 때

말레이시아에서의 업무가 종료되고 다음 장소로 옮길 때 귀사의 서비스를 다시 이용할 계획입니다.

6 What is the purpose of the form?

(A) To apply for a refund

(B) To improve customer service

(C) To gather stories to use in advertisements

(D) To request relocation services

양식의 목적은?

(A) 환불을 신청하려고

(B) 고객 서비스를 개선하려고

(C) 광고에 사용할 사연을 모으려고

(D) 이주 서비스를 신청하려고

> **해설** 주제 / 목적: 첫 번째 단락 두 번째 문장을 통해 고객의 이용 경험을 청취해 서비스를 개선시키려는 것임을 알 수 있으며 이어서 서비스 등급 표시란과 등급 설명란도 있습니다. 따라서 정답은 (B)입니다.
>
> **Paraphrasing** 지문의 our services → 정답의 customer service

7 According to the form, why did Ms. Siddiqui move to Kuala Lumpur?

(A) To join her relatives

(B) To attend a university

(C) To enjoy life in an international city

(D) To begin a new job assignment

양식에 따르면, 시디퀴 씨가 쿠알라룸푸르로 이주한 이유는?

(A) 친척과 함께하기 위해

(B) 대학에 다니기 위해

(C) 국제 도시에서의 삶을 즐기기 위해

(D) 새 업무를 시작하기 위해

> **해설** 세부 사항: Please explain your ratings in the box below.란에서 시디퀴 씨는 새로운 업무를 위해 쿠알라룸푸르로 이주했다(I moved to Kuala Lumpur for my new work assignment)고 했으므로 정답은 (D)입니다.

8 What does Ms. Siddiqui indicate on the form?

(A) She did not use all of the company's services.

(B) She decided not to ship her furniture to Malaysia.

(C) She needed more time than expected to identify items.

(D) She was pleased with all of the services she used.

시디퀴 씨가 양식에서 명시하는 것은?

(A) 회사의 모든 서비스를 이용하지는 않았다.

(B) 말레이시아로 가구를 옮기지 않기로 결정했다.

(C) 물건들을 찾는 데 예상보다 많은 시간이 필요했다.

(D) 이용했던 모든 서비스에 만족했다.

> **해설** Not / True: 등급을 매기는 항목에서 차량 운송은 해당 없음에 표시되어 있습니다. 따라서 차량 운송 서비스는 이용하지 않았다는 것을 알 수 있으므로 정답은 (A)입니다.

9 According to the form, what will Ms. Siddiqui probably do in four years?

(A) Find a new employer

(B) Retire from the company

(C) Buy a house in Kuala Lumpur

(D) Hire Fehring International

양식에 따르면, 시디퀴 씨는 4년 후 아마도 무엇을 할 예정인가?

(A) 새 고용주를 찾는다.

(B) 회사에서 퇴직한다.

(C) 쿠알라룸푸르에 집을 산다.

(D) 페링 인터내셔널을 고용한다.

> **해설** 세부 사항: four years를 키워드로 잡고 지문에서 찾아야 합니다. 마지막 문장 I plan to use your services ~ move to our next location.에서 4년 후에 귀사의 서비스를 다시 이용하겠다고 했고 귀사는 페링 인터내셔널을 가리키는 것이므로 정답은 (D)입니다.
>
> **Paraphrasing** 지문의 use your services → 정답의 Hire Fehring International

Q1 (B)　　　　　　　**Q2** (B)

---

1. [e-mail/memo]

To: Amina Noorani <anoorani@lightcast.ca>
From: Lucy Godfrey <lgodfrey@bedgeburys.ca>
Subject: Information
Date: 6 January

Dear Ms. Noorani:

I am pleased to verify the details / of your part-time position / at our
세부 사항을 알려드리게 되어 기쁩니다　　　파트타임 직책에 대한　　　우리

Bedgeburys store / on Garden Street in Hamilton. As a part-time
베지베리스 매장의　　해밀턴의 가든 가에 있는　　　파트타임 직원으로서

employee, / you are not eligible for our benefits package, / but you do
　　당신은 당사의 복지 혜택에 대한 자격은 없습니다　　　하지만 20%의

receive a 20 percent employee discount / on all of your Bedgeburys
직원 할인을 받게 됩니다　　　　모든 베지베리스 구입품에 대해

purchases.

Training begins / at 8:00 A.M. on 16 January. Please report to the human
교육은 시작합니다　1월 16일 오전 8시에　　　인사과로 출근하시기 바랍니다

resources office / on the lower level, / just past men's and women's shoes.
　　　아래층에 있는　　　남녀 신발 코너 바로 옆에

Sincerely,
Lucy Godfrey
Human Resources Manager

---

1 [이메일 / 회람]

수신: 아미나 누라니 〈anoorani@
　　lightcast.ca〉
발신: 루시 고드프리 〈lgodfrey@
　　bedgeburys.ca〉
제목: 정보
날짜: 1월 6일

누라니 씨께:

해밀턴의 가든 가에 있는 우리 베지
베리 매장의 파트타임 직책에 대한
세부 사항을 알려드리게 되어 기쁩니
다. 파트타임 직원으로서 당신은
당사의 복지 혜택에 대한 자격은 없
지만, 모든 베지베리스 구입품에 대
해 20%의 직원 할인을 받게 됩니
다.

교육은 1월 16일 오전 8시에 시작
합니다. 아래층 남녀 신발 코너 바
로 옆에 있는 인사과로 출근하시기
바랍니다.

루시 고드프리
인사과장

MEMO

To: All employees

From: Alan Moya

Subject: Important information

Date: 4 November

수신: 전 직원

발신: 앨런 모야

제목: 중요한 정보

날짜: 11월 4일

I am pleased / to announce our sales associates of the year. As you know, /
기쁩니다　　　　　올해의 영업 사원을 발표하게 되어　　　　　　아시다시피

employees must meet certain qualifications / to be nominated, / among
직원들은 특정 자격을 갖춰야 합니다　　　　지명을 받기 위해서　　그리고 그 중

which is that they must be full-time employees / for at least six months.
하나가 정규직으로 근무해야 한다는 것입니다　　　　최소한 6개월 동안

Please join me / in congratulating Bennett Selwyn (Electronics), Li Pan
저와 함께해주세요　　　베넷 셀윈(전자 제품), 리 판(장신구), 아미나 누라니(여성복)를 축하하는 데

(Jewelry), and Amina Noorani (Women's Clothing). **All three will join**
　　　　　　　　　　　　　　　　　　　　　　이 세 사람은 모두 수상자들과 함께

honorees / from other Bedgeburys stores / at a banquet in Toronto / next
할 것입니다　　다른 베지베리스 매장의　　　　토론토에서 있을 연회에서　　　다음 달

month.

올해의 영업 사원을 발표하게 되어 기쁩니다. 아시다시피, 지명을 받기 위해서 직원들은 특정 자격을 갖춰야 하는데, 그 중 하나가 최소한 6개월 동안 정규직으로 근무해야 한다는 것입니다.

저와 함께 베넷 셀윈(전자), 리 판(장신구), 아미나 누라니(여성복)를 축하해주시기 바랍니다. 이 세 사람은 모두 다음 달 토론토에서 있을 연회에서 다른 베지베리 매장의 수상자들과 함께할 것입니다.

---

1 What is suggested about Ms. Noorani?

(A) She will be moving to Toronto next year.

(B) She became eligible for an employee benefits package.

누라니 씨에 대해 알 수 있는 것은?

(A) 내년에 토론토로 이사할 것이다.

(B) 직원 복지 혜택을 받을 자격이 생겼다.

해설 **연계:** 두 지문을 연계해서 풀어야 하는 문제입니다. 1월 6일자 수신인이 누라니인 이메일의 As a part-time ~ benefits package에서 정규직 직원만 복지 혜택을 받을 수 있음을 알 수 있습니다. 11월 4일자 회람의 employees must meet ~ at least six months와 Please join me ~ Amina Noorani (Women's Clothing).에서 6개월 이상 근무한 정규직 직원 중에 올해의 영업 사원으로 지명을 받을 수 있는데, 누라니 씨의 이름을 지명자 중에서 확인할 수 있습니다. 따라서 누라니 씨가 정규직 직원이 되어 복지 혜택을 받게 되었음을 알 수 있으므로 정답은 (B)입니다.

PART 7 | UNIT 11

2. [article/advertisement]

Jenkins Market Reveals New Brand Name
젠킨스 마켓에서 새로운 브랜드 이름을 공개한다

DUBLIN (15 February)—Jenkins Market today announced / the launch of
더블린 (2월 15일) –   젠킨스 마켓은 오늘 발표했다   자체 브랜드

its new line of store-brand products. Called "White Moon," / the line will
신제품군을 출시한다고   '화이트 문'이라고 부르는   이 제품군은

feature frozen, canned, and packaged foods. These include / frozen fruits
냉동, 통조림, 포장 식품을 선보일 예정이다   여기에는 포함된다   냉동 과일과

and vegetables, canned soups, and pastas. The line will not include /
채소, 통조림 수프, 파스타가   이 제품군에는 포함되지 않는다

beverages or candy. All Jenkins Market locations / will carry White Moon
음료나 사탕은   젠킨스 마켓 전 영업점은   화이트 문 제품을 취급할 예정이다

products / starting at the end of this month.
                이달 말부터

Jenkins Market has 40 stores / throughout Ireland / and will soon be
젠킨스 마켓은 매장 40개를 보유하고 있다   아일랜드 전역에   그리고 곧 영국으로 확장할 예정이다

expanding into England, / beginning in Leeds. Other stores are planned /
                            리즈를 시작으로   다른 매장들은 계획되어 있다

for Liverpool and Manchester.
리버풀과 맨체스터에

2 [기사 / 광고]

젠킨스 마켓에서 새로운 브랜드 이름을 공개한다

더블린 (2월 15일) – 젠킨스 마켓은 오늘 자체 브랜드 신제품군을 출시한다고 발표했다. '화이트 문'이라고 부르는 이 제품군은 냉동, 통조림, 포장 식품을 선보일 예정이다. 여기에는 냉동 과일과 채소, 통조림 수프, 파스타가 포함된다. 이 제품군에는 음료나 사탕은 포함되지 않는다. 젠킨스 마켓 전 영업점에서 이달 말부터 화이트 문 제품을 취급할 예정이다.

젠킨스 마켓은 아일랜드 전역에 매장 40개를 보유하고 있으며 곧 리즈를 시작으로 영국으로 확장할 예정이다. 다른 매장들은 리버풀과 맨체스터에 계획되어 있다.

Jenkins Market
젠킨스 마켓
Grand opening!
대개장!
21 April, 7:00 A.M.-9:00 P.M.
4월 21일, 오전 7:00 – 오후 9:00
47 Post Road, Leeds
47 포스트 로드, 리즈

Ribbon cutting at 10:00 A.M.
개점식 오전 10:00

Complimentary coffee and cake until 3:00 P.M.
무료 커피와 케이크 오후 3:00까지

Shoppers can spin our prize wheel / to win T-shirts, hats, and umbrellas.
쇼핑객 여러분은 경품 추첨 돌림판을 돌릴 수 있습니다   그리고 티셔츠, 모자, 우산을 얻을 수 있습니다

The first 100 shoppers / will receive a £50 gift card!
선착순 쇼핑객 100명은   50파운드 상품권을 받습니다

Enter our contest: correctly guess / how many people attend our grand
콘테스트에 참가하세요: 정확하게 알아맞히세요   대개장 행사에 몇 명이 참석할지

opening event / and win a bag / overflowing with groceries!
        그리고 가방을 얻으세요 식료품이 넘치게 담긴

젠킨스 마켓
대개장!

4월 21일, 오전 7:00 – 오후 9:00
47 포스트 로드, 리즈

개점식 오전 10:00
무료 커피와 케이크 오후 3:00까지

쇼핑객 여러분은 경품 추첨 돌림판을 돌려 티셔츠, 모자, 우산을 얻을 수 있습니다.
선착순 쇼핑객 100명은 50파운드 상품권을 받습니다!

콘테스트에 참가하세요: 대개장 행사에 몇 명이 참석할지 정확하게 알아맞히시고 식료품이 넘치게 담긴 가방을 얻으세요!

2 What is most likely true about the event on April 21?

(A) It will be held on a different date than originally planned.

(B) It will take place at the first Jenkins Market store in England.

4월 21일 행사에 관해 사실인 것은?

(A) 원래 계획과는 다른 날짜에 개최될 예정이다.

(B) 영국의 젠킨스 마켓 1호점에서 열릴 예정이다.

> **해설** 연계: 두 지문을 연계해서 풀어야 하는 문제입니다. 광고의 4월 21일 행사는 젠킨스 마켓이 리즈에서 매장을 여는 것을 기념하는 행사입니다. 기사의 Jenkins Market has ~ beginning in Leeds.에서 리즈 매장이 영국에 진출한 젠킨스 마켓 1호점임을 알 수 있으므로 정답은 (B)입니다.

Questions 1-5 refer to the following e-mails.

From: onlineorders@scottishwoollens.com

To: Marie Nykvist <mnykvist@euromail.com>

Date: 30 November

Subject: Order Confirmation

2Thank you for shopping / at Scottish Woollens! Here are your order details:
쇼핑해 주셔서 감사합니다   스코티시 울런즈에서   주문하신 상세 내역입니다:

Order Number: 3645
주문 번호: 3645

1Billing address:
청구 주소:

Marie Nykvist 마리 닉비스트

Vogulund Gate 23 보굴룬드 게이트 23

4534 Harstad 4534 하르스타드

Norway 노르웨이

1Order Date: 29 November
주문 날짜: 11월 29일

Shipping address:
배송지 주소:

Same as billing address
청구 주소와 동일

Payment Method: Credit card ********3490
결제 방식: 신용 카드 ********* 3490

Item	Quantity	Unit Price (€)	Charges (€)
3Glasgow Designers women's sweater	1	132.00	**3**132.00
Shetland Farm women's cap	2	60.00	120.00
Shetland Farm women's gloves	1	33.00	33.00
Glasgow Designers women's scarf	1	21.00	21.00
VAT			65.20
2Shipping			**2**(no charge)
		Order Total:	**€371.20**

1-5 [이메일 / 이메일]

발신: onlineorders@scottishwoollens.com
수신: 마리 닉비스트 〈mnykvist@euromail.com〉
날짜: 11월 30일
제목: 주문 확인

2스코티시 울런즈에서 쇼핑해 주셔서 감사합니다! 주문하신 상세 내역입니다:

주문 번호: 3645   **1**주문 날짜: 11월 29일

1청구 주소: **배송지 주소:**
마리 닉비스트   청구 주소와 동일

보굴룬드 게이트 23
4534 하르스타드
노르웨이

결제 방식: 신용 카드 ********** 3490

품목	수량	단가(유로)	요금(유로)
3글래스고 디자이너스 여성 스웨터	1	132.00	**3**132.00
셰틀랜드 팜 여성 모자	2	60.00	120.00
셰틀랜드 팜 여성 장갑	1	33.00	33.00
글래스고 디자이너스 여성 스카프	1	21.00	21.00
부가세			65.20
2배송			**2**(무료)
		주문 총계:	371.20유로

From: support@scottishwoollens.com

Date: 2 December

To: Marie Nykvist <mnykvist@euromail.com>

Re: Change to order 3645

Dear Ms. Nykvist,

In response to your inquiry, / let me reassure you / that [4]customers often
문의하신 내용에 답변 드리자면   거듭 확인해 드립니다   별도의 '배송지' 주소 표기를

neglect to indicate a separate "ship to" address / when they order gifts
소홀히 하는 경우가 많다는 점을   다른 사람을 위한 선물도 주문할 때

for others / in addition to purchasing items for themselves. If we receive
    고객이 자신을 위해 물품을 구입하는 것에 대해   저희는 문제가

notice of the problem / before the orders ship, / we are happy to correct it.
발생했다는 통지를 받으면   주문품 발송 전에   기꺼이 바로잡습니다

[3,5]In your case, / we were able to separate the orders / in time, / and the
    고객님의 경우에   주문품을 분리할 수 있었습니다   제때에   그래서

Glasgow Designers sweater was shipped to Farsund / this morning. Your
글래스고 디자이너스 스웨터는 파르순으로 배송되었습니다   오늘 아침   자매분은

sister should receive the package / by 11 December.
소포를 받을 것입니다   12월 11일까지

Best regards,

Roberta MacDonald, Customer Representative

Scottish Woollens

Aberdeen, Scotland

발신: support@scottishwool-lens.com

날짜: 12월 2일

수신: 마리 닉비스트 〈mnykvist@euromail.com〉

Re: 주문 3645 변경

닉비스트 씨께,

문의하신 내용에 답변 드리자면, 고객이 자신을 위해 물품을 구입하는 것에 더해 다른 사람을 위한 선물을 주문할 때 [4]별도의 "배송지" 주소 표기를 소홀히 하는 경우가 많다는 점 거듭 확인해 드립니다. 저희는 주문품 발송 전에 문제가 발생했다는 통지를 받으면 기꺼이 바로잡습니다. [3,5]고객님의 경우에, 제때에 주문품을 분리할 수 있었기 때문에, 글래스고 디자이너스 스웨터는 오늘 아침 파르순으로 배송되었습니다. 자매분은 12월 11일까지 소포를 받을 것입니다.

로베르타 맥도날드, 고객 담당자

스코티시 울런즈

애버딘, 스코틀랜드

---

1 When did Ms. Nykvist make her online purchase?

(A) On November 29

(B) On November 30

(C) On December 2

(D) On December 11

닉비스트 씨는 언제 온라인으로 구매했는가?

(A) 11월 29일

(B) 11월 30일

(C) 12월 2일

(D) 12월 11일

해설 **세부 사항:** 첫 번째 이메일의 Order Date와 Billing address를 통해 닉비스트 씨가 11월 29에 주문을 했다는 것을 알 수 있으므로 정답은 (A)입니다.

2 What is suggested about Scottish Woollens?

(A) It sells bedding as well as clothing.

(B) It offers free shipping on some orders.

(C) It has a flexible return policy.

(D) It is under new management.

스코티시 울런즈에 관해 시사되는 것은?

(A) 의류뿐 아니라 침구류도 판매한다.

(B) 일부 주문에 대해 무료 배송을 제공한다.

(C) 반품 정책이 유연하다.

(D) 새 경영진이 운영하고 있다.

> **해설** 추론 / 암시: 첫 번째 이메일 첫 문장에서 스코티시 울런즈에서의 물건 구매에 대해 감사(Thank you for shopping at Scottish Woollens!)를 표했고 주문내역표를 보면 배송이 무료라고 되어 있습니다. 따라서 스코티시 울런즈가 무료 배송을 제공했다는 것을 알 수 있으므로 정답은 (B)입니다.
>
> **Paraphrasing** 지문의 no charge → 정답의 free

---

3 How much did Ms. Nykvist pay for a gift purchase?

(A) €21

(B) €33

(C) €120

(D) €132

닉비스트 씨는 선물 구입에 얼마를 지불했는가?

(A) 21유로

(B) 33유로

(C) 120유로

(D) 132유로

> **해설** 연계: 두 지문을 연계해서 풀어야 하는 문제입니다. 닉비스트 씨가 수신인인 두 번째 메일의 In your case, ~ Farsund this morning.과 Your sister should ~ by 11 December.를 통해 닉비스트 씨는 자매를 위해 글래스고 디자이너스 스웨터를 구입했다는 것을 유추할 수 있습니다. 첫 번째 메일의 주문 내역을 보면 글래스고 디자이너스 스웨터는 132유로라고 되어 있으므로 정답은 (D)입니다.

---

4 In the second e-mail, the word "neglect" in paragraph 1, line 1, is closest in meaning to

(A) forget

(B) arrange

(C) ignore

(D) believe

두 번째 이메일에서, 첫 번째 단락 1행의 "neglect"와 의미상 가장 가까운 것은?

(A) 잊다

(B) 배열하다

(C) 무시하다

(D) 믿다

> **해설** 동의어 찾기: 지문의 customers often neglect to indicate a separate "ship to" address에서 neglect는 '소홀히 하다, ~하기를 잊다'라는 의미이므로 별도의 배송지 주소 표기를 종종 소홀히 한다고 했으므로 '잊다'라는 의미의 (A) forget이 정답입니다

---

5 Where does Ms. Nykvist's sister most likely live?

(A) In Harstad

(B) In Farsund

(C) In Glasgow

(D) In Aberdeen

닉비스트 씨의 자매가 어디에 살겠는가?

(A) 하르스타드

(B) 파르순

(C) 글래스고

(D) 애버딘

> **해설** 세부 사항: 두 번째 이메일 후반부에서 글래스고 디자이너스 스웨터가 파르순으로 배송되었고 자매가 소포를 받을 것이라고 했으므로 정답은 (B)입니다.

ETS 문제로 훈련하기

교재 p.272

Q1 (B)   **Q2** (A)

---

1 [e-mails/Web page]

From: Svetlana Ridic
To: Marcello Rossillo
Subject: Design notes
Date: February 19

Dear Marcello,

I'd like to deal with a few issues / as we make modifications to the CR 465.
몇 가지 문제를 처리하고자 합니다   우리가 CR 465를 수정하면서

Note / that updated government emissions regulations for motorcycles /
        개정된 정부의 오토바이에 대한 배기가스 규정이

come out / this week, / so the design will need to address any changes
발표되므로   이번 주에   디자인을 새로 변경된 모든 내용에 맞출 필요가 있습니다

that are new. Also, / bikes that are more than two years old / seem to have
        또한   2년이 넘은 오토바이는   문제가 있는 듯합니다

trouble / with fading paint.
            칠이 바래는

The design phase must be completed / by June 8. The deadline is firm /
디자인 단계는 완료되어야 합니다   6월 8일까지   마감일이 고정입니다

this time around / — manufacturing does not want to face / the same time
이번에는   제작팀은 직면하고 싶어 하지 않습니다   똑같은 시간과

and budget issues / it had to deal with last year.
예산 문제에   지난해 대처해야 했던

The market is healthy for this type of bike, / and this is a great opportunity /
이런 유형의 오토바이 시장은 건실합니다   그러므로 좋은 기회입니다

for Roadwell Motorcycles / to strengthen our reputation. As with previous
로드웰 오토바이가   평판을 공고히 할 수 있는   이전 CR 465 모델과

CR 465 models, / we will continue to focus / on creating quality products /
마찬가지로   우리는 계속 주력할 것입니다   고품질의 제품을 만드는 데

rather than on beating our competitors' prices.
경쟁사보다 가격을 낮추기보다는

Thanks, Svetlana

---

1 [이메일 / 이메일 / 웹페이지]

발신: 스베틀라나 리딕
수신: 마르첼로 로시요
제목: 디자인 관련 내용
날짜: 2월 19일

마르첼로에게,

우리가 CR 465를 수정하면서 몇 가지 문제를 처리하고자 합니다. 오토바이에 대한 정부의 배기가스 규정이 이번 주에 발표되므로 디자인을 새로 변경된 내용에 맞출 필요가 있습니다. 또한 2년이 넘은 오토바이는 칠이 바래는 문제가 있는 듯합니다.

디자인 단계는 6월 8일까지 완료되어야 합니다. 이번에는 마감일이 고정입니다. 제작팀은 지난해 대처해야 했던 똑같은 시간과 예산 문제에 직면하고 싶어 하지 않습니다.

이런 유형의 오토바이 시장은 건실하므로 로드웰 오토바이가 평판을 공고히 할 수 있는 좋은 기회입니다. 이전 CR 465 모델과 마찬가지로, 우리는 경쟁사보다 가격을 낮추기보다는 고품질의 제품을 만드는 데 계속 주력할 것입니다.

감사합니다. 스베틀라나

From: Marcello Rossillo

To: Svetlana Ridic

Subject: Design notes

Date: February 20

Dear Svetlana,

We received advance notice / of the regulations / yesterday. We are also
우리는 사전 통지를 받았습니다   규정에 관해   어제   또한 사용하는 것을

looking at using / a new product with UV protection / to keep it looking
고려하고 있습니다   자외선 차단 기능이 있는 신제품을   번쩍이는 외관을 유지하기 위해

shiny. I'll get back to you with my views / on manufacturing costs; / I don't
제 견해를 준비해 다시 연락 드리겠습니다   제조 비용에 대한   저는 예상

expect / the design changes to have a radical impact.
하지 않습니다 / 디자인 변경이 큰 영향을 미칠 것으로

Best, Marcello

---

http://www.goroadreviews.com

Mini-review: Roadwell CR 465

★★★★

The newest model of this attractive bike / debuted from Roadwell
이 멋진 오토바이 최신 모델이   로드웰 오토바이에서 첫선을 보였다

Motorcycles / in October. This bike has a slightly different feel / from last
        10월   이 오토바이는 느낌이 조금 다른데   지난해 오토바이와

year's machine, / probably because it weighs in at 10 kilograms heavier.
                아마도 무게가 10킬로그램 늘어난 때문인 듯하다

Roadwell has designed several new options / for the bike's trim and its
로드웰에서 몇 가지 새로운 옵션을 디자인했다   오토바이 트림과 핸들에

handlebar, / and the bike is available / in a greater variety of colors. Pricing
        그리고 오토바이는 이용 가능하다   더 다양한 색상으로   가격은

is comparable / to last year's model.
비슷하다   지난해 모델과

By Tom333

---

1 What is most likely true about the newest model of the CR 465 ?

(A) It performs best in wet conditions.

(B) It costs more than competitors' products.

해설 연계: 첫 번째 이메일 마지막 문장에서 이전 모델과 마찬가지로 경쟁사보다 가격을 낮추기보다는(rather than on beating our competitors' prices) 고품질 제품 제작에 주력할 것이라고 했습니다. 그리고 리뷰 마지막 문장을 보면 신모델 가격이 지난해 모델과 비슷하다(Pricing is comparable to last years' model.)고 했으므로 신모델 역시 경쟁사보다 비싸다는 것을 짐작할 수 있습니다. 따라서 정답은 (B)입니다.

발신: 마르첼로 로시요
수신: 스베틀라나 리딕
제목: 디자인 관련 내용
날짜: 2월 20일

스베틀라나에게,

우리는 어제 규정에 관해 사전 통지를 받았습니다. 또한 번쩍이는 외관을 유지하기 위해 자외선 차단 기능이 있는 신제품을 사용하는 것을 고려하고 있습니다. 제조 비용에 대한 제 견해를 준비해 다시 연락 드리겠습니다. 저는 디자인 변경이 큰 영향을 미칠 것으로 예상하지 않습니다.

마르첼로

http://www.goroadreviews.com
미니 리뷰: 로드웰 CR 465

★★★★

이 멋진 오토바이 최신 모델이 10월 로드웰 오토바이에서 첫선을 보였다. 이 오토바이는 지난해 오토바이와 느낌이 조금 다른데 아마도 무게가 10킬로그램 늘어난 때문인 듯하다. 로드웰에서 오토바이 트림과 핸들에 몇 가지 새로운 옵션을 디자인했고 오토바이는 더 다양한 색상으로 이용 가능하다. 가격은 지난해 모델과 비슷하다.

작성자 Tom333

CR 465 최신 모델에 관해 무엇이 사실이겠는가?

(A) 습한 상태에서 가장 잘 달린다.

(B) 경쟁업체 제품보다 비싸다.

La Chapelle
라 샤펠

1655 Castlerock Dr. • Billings, MT 59101 • Phone: (406) 555-0193 • www.lachapelle.com

La Chapelle, / located in the heart of the city of Billings, Montana, / is the
라 샤펠은　　　몬태나 주 빌링스 시 중심에 위치한　　　완벽한

perfect venue / for private parties, workshops, photography sessions,
장소입니다　　　사적인 파티, 워크숍, 사진 촬영, 기업 행사 등

corporate events, / and various other functions.
　　　　다양한 행사에

Rates are $95/hour / for events lasting two hours, / $85/hour / for events
요금은 시간당 95달러입니다　　2시간 지속되는 행사는　　　시간당 85달러입니다 / 4시간

lasting four hours, / and $75/hour / for events lasting five hours or more.
지속되는 행사는　　　그리고 시간당 75달러입니다 / 5시간 이상 지속되는 행사는

Cancellations must be made / in writing / and must be received / no later
취소는 해야 합니다　　　서면으로　　그리고 접수되어야 합니다　　늦어도 예정된

than three weeks before the scheduled function. Cancellations received
행사일 3주 전에　　　　　　　이 마감 시간 이후에 취소 요청이 접수되면

after this cutoff time / will result in a charge / equal to the full amount of the
　　　　요금이 부과됩니다　　　예정된 서비스의 전액과 동일한

scheduled service. For reservations and additional terms and conditions, /
　　　예약 및 추가 계약 조건은

visit www.lachapelle.com.
www.lachapelle.com을 방문하십시오

---

www.lachapelle.com/reservation_form

La Chapelle: Reservation Form
라 샤펠: 예약 양식

Your Name: Amy Blanchard
이름: 에이미 블랜처드

Company Name: Murray Public Relations
회사명: 머리 퍼블릭 릴레이션스

E-mail: ablanchard@murraypr.com
이메일: ablanchard@murraypr.com

Phone Number: 406 555-0165
전화번호: 406 555-0165

Date/Time of Event: January 14, 12:00 P.M. – 5:00 P.M. (five hours)
행사 날짜/시간: 1월 14일, 오후 12:00 – 오후 5:00 (5시간)

Type of Event: Annual awards ceremony and luncheon
행사 종류: 연례 시상식과 오찬

Number of Attendees: 26
참석자 수: 26

2 [광고 / 양식 / 이메일]

라 샤펠

1655 캐슬락 드라이브 • 빌링스, 몬태나 주 59101 • 전화: (406) 555-0193 • www.lachapelle.com

몬태나 주 빌링스 시 중심에 위치한 라 샤펠은 사적인 파티, 워크숍, 사진 촬영, 기업 행사 등 다양한 행사에 완벽한 장소입니다.

요금은 2시간 지속되는 행사는 시간당 95달러, 4시간 지속되는 행사는 시간당 85달러, 5시간 이상 지속되는 행사는 시간당 75달러입니다.

취소는 서면으로 해야 하며 늦어도 예정된 행사일 3주 전에 접수되어야 합니다. 이 마감 시간 이후에 취소 요청이 접수되면 예정된 서비스의 전액과 동일한 요금이 부과됩니다. 예약 및 추가 계약 조건은 www.lachapelle.com을 방문하십시오.

www.lachapelle.com/reservation_form

라 샤펠: 예약 양식

이름: 에이미 블랜처드

회사명: 머리 퍼블릭 릴레이션스

이메일: ablanchard@murraypr.com

전화번호: 406 555-0165

행사 날짜/시간: 1월 14일, 오후 12:00 – 오후 5:00 (5시간)

행사 종류: 연례 시상식과 오찬

참석자 수: 26명

Dear Ms. Blanchard:

We are pleased / to host Murray Public Relations / on January 14.
기쁩니다　　　　　머리 퍼블릭 릴레이션스를 모시게 되어　　　1월 14일에

Regarding your queries, / I would recommend Silverwood Café / for
문의하신 내용 관련하여　　　　실버우드 카페를 추천합니다

your catering needs. It is one of our business partners / and it has a
필요하신 음식 조달은　　　　그곳은 저희 사업 파트너 중 하나입니다　　　그리고 광범위한 음식 품목을

wide assortment of food items / at reasonable prices. As for technology
구비하고 있습니다　　　　합리적인 가격에　　　기술 장비의 경우

equipment, / our space has wireless Internet connectivity, an interactive
저희 공간에 무선 인터넷 연결, 전자 칠판이 있습니다

whiteboard, / and a digital projector.
그리고 디지털 프로젝터가

Please let me know / if you need any further assistance.
알려주십시오　　　도움이 더 필요하시면

Sincerely,

Maggie Hanlon, Events Coordinator, La Chapelle

블랜처드 씨께:

1월 14일 머리 퍼블릭 릴레이션스를 모시게 되어 기쁩니다. 문의하신 내용 관련하여, 필요하신 음식 조달은 실버우드 카페를 추천합니다. 그곳은 저희 사업 파트너 중 하나로 합리적인 가격에 광범위한 음식 품목을 구비하고 있습니다. 기술 장비의 경우, 저희 공간에 무선 인터넷 연결, 전자 칠판, 디지털 프로젝터가 있습니다.

도움이 더 필요하시면 알려주십시오.

매기 핸런, 행사 진행 코디네이터, 라 샤펠

---

2 How much will Murray Public Relations be charged per hour?

(A) $75

(B) $85

머리 퍼블릭 릴레이션스에 시간당 얼마의 요금이 부과되겠는가?

(A) 75달러

(B) 85달러

해설　연계: 광고에서 $75 / hour for events lasting five hours or more라고 했고, 양식에서 회사명이 머리 퍼블릭 릴레이션스인 것과 행사 시간이 오후 12시부터 5시까지 총 5시간인 것을 확인할 수 있습니다. 따라서 두 가지 정보를 종합하면 정답은 (A)입니다.

1 (B)　　　**2** (C)　　　**3** (B)　　　**4** (C)　　　**5** (B)

Questions 1-5 refer to the following e-mails and table.

1-5 [이메일 / 이메일 / 표]

To: David Levine

From: All AFIN Employees

Date: Wednesday, June 3, 3:47 P.M.

Subject: Internship Orientation Program

발신: 데이비드 러바인
수신: AFIN 전 직원
날짜: 6월 3일 수요일, 오후 3:47
제목: 인턴십 오리엔테이션 프로그램

Dear Colleagues,

동료 여러분께,

From Monday, July 20, through Friday, August 28, / Aidos Footwear
7월 20일 월요일부터 8월 28일 금요일까지　　　　　　　아이도스 신발 산업(AFIN)은

Industries (AFIN) / will be hosting its Summer Internship Program / for
여름 인턴십 프로그램을 개최합니다

the twelfth consecutive year. To inform the interns / about our day-to-day
12년 연속　　　　　　　　인턴 사원들에게 알리기 위해　　　일상 업무와

operations and what is expected of them, / a series of orientation sessions /
그들에게 기대하는 것들을　　　　　　　　일련의 오리엔테이션 세션이

will be held / on the first day.
열릴 예정입니다　　첫날에

7월 20일 월요일부터 8월 28일 금요일까지, 아이도스 신발 산업 (AFIN)은 12년 연속 여름 인턴직 프로그램을 개최합니다. 인턴 사원들에게 일상 업무와 그들에게 기대하는 것들을 알리기 위해, 첫날에 일련의 오리엔테이션 세션이 열릴 예정입니다.

1Employees are needed / to help facilitate those sessions. **3**Two employees /
직원들이 필요합니다　　　　이들 세션을 수월하게 진행하려면　　　직원 두 명이

are needed for each session, / one of whom will be the main facilitator.
세션마다 필요합니다　　　　　그리고 그 중 한 명이 주 조력자가 됩니다

Only those who have previously participated in an internship orientation
이전에 인턴십 오리엔테이션 세션에 참가한 사람만이

session / will be eligible to assume that role.
　　　　그 역할을 맡을 자격이 됩니다

1이들 세션을 수월하게 진행하려면 직원 여러분이 필요합니다. **3**세션마다 직원 두 명이 필요하며, 그 중 한 명이 주 조력자가 됩니다. 이전에 인턴십 오리엔테이션 세션에 참가한 사람만이 그 역할을 맡을 자격이 됩니다.

If you are interested / in participating in this event, / find the "Internship
관심이 있으시면　　　　이번 행사 참여에　　　　'인턴십 오리엔테이션 프로그램'

Orientation Program" spreadsheet / on the shared drive / and sign up by
스프레드시트를 찾으세요　　　　공유 드라이브에서　　　그리고 6월 12일

Friday, June 12, / for one or more activities listed. **2**It is expected / that
금요일까지 참가 신청을 하십시오 / 목록에 있는 하나 또는 하나 이상의 활동에　예상됩니다

each team will meet / at least once between June 15 and the July 17
각 팀이 모일 것으로　　　6월 15일부터 최종 기한인 7월 17일 사이에 최소한 한 번은

deadline / to discuss the organization of their session.
　　　　　세션 구성을 논의하기 위해

이번 행사 참여에 관심이 있으시면 공유 드라이브에서 "인턴십 오리엔테이션 프로그램" 스프레드시트를 찾아 6월 12일 금요일까지 목록에 있는 하나 또는 하나 이상의 활동에 참가 신청을 하십시오. **2**6월 15일부터 최종 기한인 7월 17일 사이에 세션 구성을 논의하기 위해 각 팀이 최소한 한 번은 모일 것으로 예상됩니다.

Thank you for your cooperation.
협조해 주셔서 감사합니다

협조해 주셔서 감사합니다.

Sincerely,

David Levine

Internship Program Director, Aidos Footwear Industries

데이비드 러바인
아이도스 신발 산업, 인턴십 프로그램 책임자

Aidos Footwear Industries (AFIN)
아이도스 신발 산업(AFIN)
Intern Orientation Program
인턴 오리엔테이션 프로그램
Monday, July 20
7월 20일 월요일

Sessions	Time	[3]Main Facilitator	Assistant Facilitator
Registration and breakfast	8:15 A.M. – 9:00 A.M.	Farid Hassannejad	Iwona Kubiak
Welcome and introductions	9:00 A.M. – 9:30 A.M.	[3]Tanya Sipe	Andrew Collingwood
Introduction to AFIN	9:30 A.M. – 10:00 A.M.	Cliff Oriolowo	Pierce Tobin
Internship rules and regulations	10:00 A.M. – 10:30 A.M.	Karishma Ramkalawan	Darnell Ganaway
Laptop distribution and setup	10:30 A.M. – noon	Kristen Boden	Sakura Arakaki
Lunch break	Noon – 1:00 P.M.		
[4]Office and campus tour	1:00 P.M. – 2:00 P.M.	Karishma Ramkalawan	[4]Pierce Tobin
Obtain access badge	2:00 P.M. – 3:00 P.M.		
Question and answer session	3:00 P.M. – 3:45 P.M.	Martin Kersey	Cliff Oriowolo
Adjourn	3:45 P.M.		

아이도스 신발 산업(AFIN)
인턴 오리엔테이션 프로그램
7월 20일 월요일

세션	시간	[3]주 조력자	보조 조력자
등록과 아침 식사	오전 8:15 – 오전 9:00	파리드 하산네자드	이보나 쿠비악
환영식과 소개	오전 9:00 – 오전 9:30	[3]타냐 사이프	앤드루 콜링우드
AFIN 소개	오전 9:30 – 오전 10:00	클리프 오리올로우	피어스 토빈
인턴십 규칙과 규정	오전 10:00 – 오전 10:30	카리슈마 람칼라완	다넬 가나웨이
노트북 배포 및 설정	오전 10:30 – 정오	크리스틴 보덴	사쿠라 아라카키
점심시간	정오 – 오후 1:00		
[4]사무실과 캠퍼스 견학	오후 1:00 – 오후 2:00	카리슈마 람칼라완	[4]피어스 토빈
출입증 수령	오후 2:00 – 오후 3:00		
질의응답 시간	오후 3:00 – 오후 3:45	마틴 커지	클리프 오리올로우
해산	오후 3:45		

From: Pierce Tobin

To: Karishma Ramkalawan

Cc: Shimon Adelstein

Date: Thursday, July 16, 9:51 A.M.

Subject: Schedule conflict

Dear Karishma,

I regret to have to inform you / that I will no longer be able to assist you /
알려드리게 되어 유감입니다   더 이상 도와드릴 수 없음을

with Monday's internship orientation session. [5]My department manager /
월요일 인턴직 오리엔테이션 세션을   부서장이

has just scheduled an urgent meeting about a project / that I am in charge
방금 프로젝트에 관한 긴급 회의를 잡았습니다   제가 맡고 있는

of. Unfortunately, / the start time of the meeting coincides with that of the
공교롭게도   회의 시작 시간이 오리엔테이션 세션 시간과 일치합니다

orientation session, / and postponing the meeting / is not an option.
그리고 회의를 연기하는 것은   불가능합니다

[4]However, / my office mate, Shimon Adelstein, / has graciously offered /
하지만   제 사무실 동료인 시몬 아델슈타인이   고맙게도 제안했습니다

to take over my responsibilities / as assistant session facilitator. I will brief
제 책임을 넘겨받겠다고   보조 세션 조력자로   오늘 나중에

him later today / about the particulars. He will contact you afterwards / to
그에게 브리핑하겠습니다 자세한 사항들에 대해   그 후에 그가 당신에게 연락할 것입니다

see if you may have any additional information for him.
당신이 그에게 줄 추가 정보가 있는지 확인하려고

My sincere apologies for the short notice. Good luck with the session.
촉박하게 알려드린 점 진심으로 사과드립니다.   세션이 잘되길 빕니다

Pierce Tobin

발신: 피어스 토빈

수신: 카리슈마 람칼라완

참조: 시몬 아델슈타인

날짜: 7월 16일 목요일 오전 9:51

제목: 일정 겹침

카리슈마 씨께,

월요일 인턴십 오리엔테이션 세션을 더 이상 도와드릴 수 없음을 알려드리게 되어 유감입니다. [5]부서장이 방금 제가 맡고 있는 프로젝트에 관해 긴급 회의를 잡았습니다. 공교롭게도 회의 시작 시간이 오리엔테이션 세션 시간과 일치하는데, 회의를 연기하는 것은 불가능합니다.

[4]하지만 제 사무실 동료인 시몬 아델슈타인이 고맙게도 보조 세션 조력자로 제 책임을 맡겠다고 제안했습니다. 오늘 나중에 그에게 자세한 사항들에 관해 브리핑하겠습니다. 그 후에 그가 당신이 알려줄 추가 정보가 있는지 확인하려고 당신에게 연락할 것입니다.

촉박하게 알려드린 점 진심으로 죄송합니다. 세션이 잘되길 빕니다.

피어스 토빈

---

1   What is the purpose of the first e-mail?

(A) To introduce a company initiative

(B) To invite employees to take on a task

(C) To announce an extension of a deadline

(D) To emphasize the importance of teamwork

첫 번째 이메일의 목적은?

(A) 회사 계획을 소개하려고

(B) 직원들에게 업무를 맡도록 권유하려고

(C) 마감 기한 연장을 알리려고

(D) 협동의 중요성을 강조하려고

해설   주제 / 목적: 첫 번째 이메일 두 번째 단락의 Employees are needed to help facilitate those sessions.에서 세션의 수월한 진행을 위해 직원들이 필요하다고 했고 이어 세부 사항을 설명하고 있습니다. 따라서 직원 중에 세션 진행을 도울 지원자를 찾기 위한 메일임을 알 수 있으므로 정답은 (B)입니다.

Paraphrasing   지문의 to help facilitate those sessions → 정답의 to take on a task

2 By what date should teams finalize their session?

(A) June 12

(B) June 14

(C) July 17

(D) July 20

팀들은 며칠까지 세션을 확정해야 하는가?
(A) 6월 12일
(B) 6월 14일
(C) 7월 17일
(D) 7월 20일

해설 세부 사항: 첫 번째 이메일의 마지막 단락 It is expected ~ organization of their session.에서 세션 구성의 최종 기한이 7월 17일임을 알 수 있으므로 정답은 (C)입니다.

Paraphrasing 지문의 deadline to discuss the organization of their session → 문제의 finalize their session

3 Who has previously participated in an internship orientation session?

(A) Ms. Kubiak

(B) Ms. Sipe

(C) Mr. Collingwood

(D) Mr. Ganaway

이전에 인턴십 오리엔테이션에 참여한 사람은?
(A) 쿠비악 씨
(B) 사이프 씨
(C) 콜링우드 씨
(D) 가나웨이 씨

해설 연계: 첫 번째 이메일 둘째 단락의 Two employees are needed ~ main facilitator.와 Only those who have ~ assume that role.을 통해 주 조력자는 이전 세션 참가 경험이 있는 사람만이 자격이 된다는 것을 알 수 있습니다. 표의 주 조력자에서 Tanya Sipe를 확인할 수 있으므로 정답은 (B)입니다.

4 What session will Mr. Adelstein help with?

(A) Introduction to AFIN

(B) Internship rules and regulations

(C) Office and campus tour

(D) Question and answer session

아델슈타인 씨는 어떤 세션을 도울 것인가?
(A) AFIN 소개
(B) 인턴십 규칙과 규정
(C) 사무실과 캠퍼스 견학
(D) 질의응답 시간

해설 연계: 발신자가 토빈 씨인 두 번째 이메일의 둘째 단락 However, my office mate, ~ as assistant session facilitator.에서 아델슈타인 씨가 토빈 씨를 대신해 보조 세션 조력자로 일을 할 것임을 알 수 있습니다. 표에서 토빈 씨가 맡은 세션은 사무실과 캠퍼스 견학임을 확인할 수 있으므로 정답은 (C)입니다.

5 According to the second e-mail, why is Mr. Tobin changing his plans?

(A) He urgently needs to complete an assignment.

(B) He has to attend an important project meeting.

(C) His manager withdrew the permission given earlier.

(D) His manager wants him to assist with a different session.

두 번째 이메일에 따르면, 투빈 씨가 계획을 바꾸는 이유는?
(A) 급하게 업무를 완료해야 한다.
(B) 중요한 프로젝트 회의에 참석해야 한다.
(C) 부서장이 앞서 해준 허가를 철회했다.
(D) 부서장이 그가 다른 세션을 돕기를 원한다.

해설 세부 사항: 두 번째 이메일의 첫 번째 단락 My department manager ~ in charge of.와 Unfortunately, the start time ~ not an option.에서 토빈 씨가 맡고 있는 프로젝트 관련 긴급 회의가 잡혔고 이 회의 시작 시간이 세션 시간과 일치한다고 알렸으므로 정답은 (B)입니다.

ETS 실전 모의고사

문항 번호	정답	문항 번호	정답	문항 번호	정답	문항 번호	정답	문항 번호	정답
101	(B)	102	(A)	103	(C)	104	(B)	105	(A)
106	(A)	107	(D)	108	(B)	109	(C)	110	(C)
111	(B)	112	(D)	113	(A)	114	(C)	115	(C)
116	(D)	117	(B)	118	(B)	119	(D)	120	(B)
121	(B)	122	(A)	123	(C)	124	(D)	125	(C)
126	(D)	127	(D)	128	(B)	129	(D)	130	(B)
131	(B)	132	(C)	133	(A)	134	(B)	135	(D)
136	(B)	137	(C)	138	(A)	139	(A)	140	(D)
141	(A)	142	(C)	143	(B)	144	(C)	145	(C)
146	(D)	147	(B)	148	(D)	149	(B)	150	(B)
151	(B)	152	(C)	153	(C)	154	(B)	155	(C)
156	(C)	157	(A)	158	(C)	159	(C)	160	(D)
161	(D)	162	(D)	163	(C)	164	(C)	165	(A)
166	(C)	167	(D)	168	(D)	169	(A)	170	(C)
171	(B)	172	(C)	173	(C)	174	(B)	175	(B)
176	(D)	177	(B)	178	(A)	179	(B)	180	(C)
181	(B)	182	(D)	183	(C)	184	(A)	185	(A)
186	(C)	187	(D)	188	(B)	189	(A)	190	(C)
191	(A)	192	(D)	193	(B)	194	(A)	195	(B)
196	(C)	197	(A)	198	(D)	199	(A)	200	(B)

101

Any queries regarding advertising should be sent directly to the marketing department.

(A) direction   (B) directly   (C) directs   (D) directing

해설 동사를 수식하는 부사: 빈칸은 동사구 be sent를 수식하는 부사 자리입니다. 따라서 부사 (B) directly(바로)가 정답입니다.

번역 광고에 관한 모든 문의는 마케팅부로 바로 보내야 합니다.

어휘 query 문의   regarding ~에 관한   directly 직접, 바로   direction 방향   direct 향하다

102

Please remove food from the refrigerator each Friday and keep the lunchroom clean.

(A) and   (B) thus   (C) rather   (D) instead

해설 등위접속사: 빈칸 앞의 remove food from the refrigerator each Friday와 빈칸 뒤의 keep the lunchroom clean을 연결하는 접속사 자리입니다. 문맥상 '냉장고에서 음식을 치워서 식당을 청결하게 유지한다'라는 의미가 자연스러우므로, (A) and가 정답입니다.

번역 매주 금요일마다 냉장고에서 음식을 치워서 식당을 청결하게 유지해주세요.

어휘 remove 치우다   refrigerator 냉장고   lunchroom 간이 식당

103

Jabanna Cosmetics provides products to celebrities who mention the brand in their social media posts.

(A) them   (B) they   (C) their   (D) themselves

해설 알맞은 인칭대명사 선택: 빈칸 뒤에 명사구 social media posts가 있으므로 명사를 한정하는 소유격 인칭대명사 (C) their가 정답입니다.

번역 자반나 코스메틱은 소셜미디어 게시글에서 자사 브랜드를 언급하는 유명 인사들에게 제품을 제공한다.

어휘 celebrity 유명 인사   mention 언급하다

104

Customers must present the weekly coupon to the cashier in order to receive the 15 percent discount.

(A) work 일, 업무   (B) discount 할인   (C) detail 세부 사항   (D) schedule 일정

해설 명사 어휘 선택: 빈칸 앞 형용사 percent의 수식을 받는 명사를 선택해야 합니다. 문맥상 제시해야 하는 쿠폰은 '15 퍼센트 할인'을 받기 위한 것임을 알 수 있으므로, (B) discount(할인)가 정답입니다.

번역 고객들은 15퍼센트 할인을 받기 위해 계산원에게 주간 쿠폰을 제시해야 한다.

어휘 present 제시하다   cashier 계산원   in order to ~하기 위해

105

Reducing downtown parking fees is expected to increase local business revenues by at least 25 percent.

(A) local   (B) locally   (C) localities   (D) localize

해설 명사를 수식하는 형용사: to부정사 to increase의 목적어 역할을 하는 명사구 business revenues가 빈칸 뒤에 있으므로, 빈칸에는 명사구 business revenues를 수식하는 형용사가 와야 합니다. 따라서 형용사 (A) local(지역의)이 정답입니다.

번역 도심 주차 요금이 인하되면 지역 업체 수익이 적어도 25퍼센트 증가할 것으로 예상된다.

어휘 reduce 인하하다   expect 예상하다   increase 증가시키다, 증가하다   revenue 수익   at least 적어도   local 지역의   locality 인근   localize 국한시키다, 지역화하다

106

Mr. Goff agreed to finish installing the customer's carpet within one week.

(A) within ~ 이내에　　(B) beyond ~ 너머　　(C) behind ~ 뒤에　　(D) through ~을 통해

해설　전치사 어휘 선택: 빈칸 뒤 명사구 one week를 목적어로 취하는 전치사 자리로, 문맥상 '일주일 이내에'라는 의미가 자연스럽습니다. 따라서 전치사 (A) within(이내에)이 정답입니다.

번역　고프 씨는 고객의 카펫 설치 작업을 일주일 안에 끝내기로 동의했다.

어휘　agree to ~하기로 동의하다　install 설치하다

107

Auto Parts Ltd. encourages its employees to offer suggestions for improving the production process.

(A) suggesting　　(B) suggest　　(C) suggestive　　(D) suggestions

해설　동사 + 명사(목적어): 빈칸은 to부정사 to offer의 목적어 역할을 하는 명사 자리로, 빈칸 뒤 전치사구 for improving the production process의 수식을 받습니다. (A) suggesting(제안하는 것)과 (D) suggestions(제안)가 들어갈 수 있습니다. 문맥상 '생산 과정을 개선하기 위한 제안을 내놓다'라는 의미가 자연스러우므로, (D) suggestions가 정답입니다.

번역　오토 파츠 사는 직원들에게 생산 공정을 개선하기 위한 제안을 내도록 장려한다.

어휘　encourage 장려하다　improve 개선하다　process 공정　suggestion 의견　suggest 제안하다　suggestive 암시하는

108

Samad Industries will soon confirm its hiring plans for commercial warehouse positions.

(A) very 매우　　(B) soon 곧　　(C) ever 언젠가　　(D) unevenly 고르지 않게

해설　부사 어휘 선택: 빈칸 뒤 confirm its hiring plans와 가장 잘 어울리는 부사를 선택해야 합니다. 문맥상 '채용 계획을 곧 확정할 것이다'라는 계획을 밝히는 것이 자연스러우므로, (B) soon이 정답입니다.

번역　사마드 산업은 상업용 물류 창고 관리직에 대한 채용 계획을 곧 확정할 예정이다.

어휘　confirm 확정하다　commercial 상업용의　warehouse (물류) 창고

109

The Bartleby Sweets Company recently introduced a line of naturally sweetened products.

(A) recent　　(B) more recent　　(C) recently　　(D) most recent

해설　동사를 수식하는 부사: 빈칸 뒤 동사 introduced를 수식하는 부사 자리이므로, 부사 (C) recently(최근에)가 정답입니다.

번역　바틀비 스위츠 사는 최근 천연적으로 단맛을 낸 제품군을 선보였다.

어휘　introduce 소개하다, 내놓다　sweetened 단맛을 낸　recent 최근의　recently 최근에

110

Many new office buildings have lower electricity costs because they are equipped with solar panels.

(A) close 가까운　　(B) gradual 점진적인　　(C) lower 더 낮은　　(D) dense 빽빽한

해설　형용사 어휘 선택: 태양 전지판을 갖추고 있기 때문에 전기 요금이 '더 낮을' 것이므로, '더 낮은'이라는 의미의 (C) lower가 정답입니다.

번역　많은 신축 사무용 건물이 태양 전지판을 갖추고 있어서 전기 요금이 더 낮다.

어휘　electricity 전기　equipped with ~을 갖춘　solar panel 태양 전지판

111

Employees and their managers must complete all annual reviews prior to March 2.

(A) also 또한　　　　(B) prior to 이전에　　　(C) first 우선　　　(D) as well as 게다가, ~에 더하여

해설　전치사 선택: 빈칸 뒤 March 2를 목적어로 취하는 전치사 자리로, 문맥상 '3월 2일 전에 완료하다'라는 의미가 자연스럽습니다. 따라서 전치사구 (B) prior to가 정답입니다. 참고로 부사 (A) also는 명사를 목적어로 취할 수 없고, 형용사 (C) first와 상관접속사 (D) as well as는 의미상 자연스럽지 않습니다.

번역　직원과 관리자는 3월 2일 이전에 모든 연례 인사 고과를 완료해야 한다.

어휘　complete 완료하다　annual 연례의　prior to ~ 이전에

112

Mr. Miguel is hoping for a promotion and usually offers to take on extra duties.

(A) perception 지각　(B) condition 상태　(C) compilation 모음집　(D) promotion 승진

해설　명사 어휘 선택: 빈칸 앞 관사 a의 수식을 받아 전치사 for의 목적어 역할을 할 수 있는 명사 자리입니다. 평소에 추가 업무를 맡는 이유는 희망하는 것이 '승진'이기 때문일 것이므로, (D) promotion(승진)이 정답입니다.

번역　미겔 씨는 승진을 희망하고 있으므로 평소에 추가 업무를 맡겠다고 제안한다.

어휘　promotion 승진　take on (일)을 맡다　duty 업무

113

Mizusugi Hobby Suppliers stocks a diverse range of products for creating model airplanes.

(A) diverse 다양한　(B) diversity 다양성　(C) diversely 다양하게　(D) diversify 다각화하다

해설　명사를 수식하는 형용사: 빈칸 앞의 부정관사 a와 빈칸 뒤 명사 range 사이에서 명사를 수식하는 형용사 자리이므로, (A) diverse(다양한)가 정답입니다.

번역　미즈스기 하비 서플라이어즈는 모형 항공기 제작을 위한 다양한 제품을 구비하고 있다.

어휘　stock (상품을) 구비하다　range 범위

114

Invitations to the annual awards banquet will be mailed on Monday.

(A) Attractions 관광 명소　(B) Compliments 칭찬　(C) Invitations 초대(장)　(D) Sentiments 정서

해설　명사 어휘 선택: 빈칸 뒤 전치사구 to the annual awards banquet의 수식을 받으면서 동사 will be mailed의 주어 역할을 할 수 있는 명사 자리로, '초대장이 발송될 것이다'라는 의미가 문맥상 자연스러우므로 (C) Invitations가 정답입니다.

번역　연례 시상식 연회 초대장은 월요일에 발송될 예정이다.

어휘　banquet 연회

115

If you are interested in attending the company picnic, please let Melissa White know by Friday.

(A) interest　　　(B) interests　　　(C) are interested　　　(D) were interesting

해설　능동태와 수동태 구별: 빈칸은 주어 you의 동사 자리로 뒤에 전치사구 in attending the company picnic이 있으므로 능동형은 올 수 없습니다. 따라서 수동형인 (C) are interested가 정답입니다. '~에 관심이 있다'라는 관용표현인 be interested in을 알면 쉽게 풀 수 있는 문제입니다.

번역　회사 야유회에 참석하는 데 관심이 있으시면 금요일까지 멜리사 화이트에게 알려주시기 바랍니다.

116

Employees at Papaloos Hardware were surprised when the shop owner sold the business.

(A) which   (B) either   (C) nor   (D) when

> **해설** 부사절 접속사: 빈칸 뒤의 절(the shop owner sold the business)을 이끄는 접속사 자리이므로 접속사 (D) when이 정답입니다. (A) which가 관계대명사로 사용될 때에는 주어나 목적어가 없는 불완전한 절을 이끕니다.

> **번역** 파팔루스 하드웨어 직원들은 매장 주인이 업체를 팔았을 때 놀랐다.

117

The Help Desk has resolved technical issues efficiently since hiring additional team members.

(A) efficient   (B) efficiently   (C) efficiency   (D) more efficient

> **해설** 동사를 수식하는 부사: 빈칸 앞 동사 has resolved를 수식하는 부사 자리이므로, (B) efficiently(효율적으로)가 정답입니다. 부사는 문장 구조상 생략이 가능하므로, 빈칸이 없어도 완전한 문장이 된다면 부사 자리입니다.

> **번역** 업무 지원 부서는 추가로 팀원을 채용한 후 기술적인 문제를 효율적으로 해결하고 있다.

> **어휘** help desk 업무 지원 부서 resolve 해결하다 issue 문제 additional 추가의 efficiently 효율적으로 efficient 효율적인 efficiency 효율(성)

118

Because there was a traffic jam on the highway, Madison missed her flight to Libreville.

(A) Until ~까지   (B) Because ~ 때문에   (C) Whether ~인지, ~이든   (D) Even if 비록 ~일지라도

> **해설** 알맞은 접속사 선택: '교통 정체 때문에 비행기를 놓쳤다'라는 문맥이 자연스러우므로, 이유를 나타내는 부사절 접속사인 (B) Because가 정답입니다.

> **번역** 고속도로에서 교통 정체가 있었기 때문에 매디슨은 리브르빌행 비행기를 놓쳤다.

> **어휘** traffic jam 교통 정체

119

The new improvements in our medical technologies will allow for a reduction of health-care costs.

(A) reduce   (B) reduced   (C) reduces   (D) reduction

> **해설** a + 명사 + 전치사: 빈칸 앞에 부정관사 a, 빈칸 뒤에 전치사 of가 있으므로 빈칸에는 명사 (D) reduction이 들어가야 합니다.

> **번역** 우리 의료 기술의 새로운 발전은 의료 비용의 절감을 가능하게 할 수도 있을 것이다.

> **어휘** improvement 개선, 향상 allow for 가능하게 하다 reduction 절감 reduce 절감하다

120

In general, theatergoers loved the movie's fast pace but found its story line too predictable.

(A) assorted 갖가지의   (B) predictable 예상 가능한   (C) mutual 상호의   (D) reluctant 주저하는

> **해설** 형용사 어휘 선택: 목적어인 story line의 보어로 가장 자연스럽게 의미가 통하는 형용사를 골라야 합니다. 따라서 '예상 가능한, 너무 뻔한'이라는 의미의 (B) predictable이 정답입니다.

> **번역** 대체로 극장 관객들은 그 영화의 빠른 속도를 좋아했지만 줄거리는 너무 뻔하다고 생각했다.

> **어휘** in general 일반적으로, 대체로 theatergoer 극장에 자주 가는 사람 story line 줄거리

121

Since she joined the company very early on, Ms. Elliott was able to experience all stages of its development.

(A) joins   (B) joined   (C) has joined   (D) will join

해설   동사 시제: 빈칸은 주어 She 뒤에 나오는 동사 자리입니다. 주절의 동사(was)가 과거이므로 since가 이끄는 부사절의 동사도 과거 시제가 되어야 합니다. 따라서 (B) joined가 정답입니다.

번역   아주 초창기에 입사했기 때문에 엘리엇 씨는 회사의 모든 발전 단계를 경험할 수 있었다.

어휘   experience 경험하다   development 발전

122

After months of difficult negotiations, Essane Ltd.'s acquisition of Channing Perfumery was finally completed yesterday.

(A) finally 마침내   (B) repeatedly 거듭   (C) knowingly 빈틈없이   (D) strongly 강하게

해설   부사 어휘 선택: 수개월 간의 협상 후이기 때문에 인수가 '마침내' 마무리되었을 것입니다. 따라서 빈칸 뒤의 과거분사 completed를 수식해 가장 자연스럽게 의미가 통하는 부사 (A) finally(마침내)가 정답입니다.

번역   수개월 간의 어려운 협상 끝에, 에세인 사의 채닝 향수 인수가 어제 마침내 완료되었다.

어휘   negotiation 협상   acquisition 인수   perfumery 향수

123

Linville Market will celebrate its opening on May 1 by offering 10 percent off all purchases.

(A) where   (B) although   (C) by   (D) for

해설   전치사 어휘 선택: 빈칸 뒤에 동명사 offering이 있으므로, 접속사 (A) where와 (B) although는 빈칸에 들어갈 수 없습니다. '할인을 제공함으로써 개업을 축하하다'라는 의미가 자연스러우므로 전치사 (C) by가 정답입니다.

번역   린빌 마켓은 모든 구매품에 10퍼센트 할인을 제공해 5월 1일 개업을 축하할 예정이다.

어휘   celebrate 축하하다   opening 개업   purchase 구매(품)

124

The Stockler Group sponsors numerous sporting events, including the Shishi Marathon.

(A) happens 일어나다, 발생하다   (B) becomes 되다   (C) cooperates 협력하다   (D) sponsors 후원하다

해설   타동사와 자동사: 빈칸 뒤 명사구 numerous sporting events를 목적어로 취하는 타동사 자리이므로, 타동사 (D) sponsors(후원하다)가 정답입니다. 자동사 (A) happens, (B) becomes, (C) cooperates는 목적어를 취할 수 없습니다.

번역   스토클러 그룹은 시시 마라톤을 포함해 수많은 스포츠 행사를 후원한다.

어휘   numerous 수많은

125

The software includes a video that provides instructions for customizing documents.

(A) who   (B) this   (C) that   (D) what

해설   주격 관계대명사: 빈칸 뒤에 동사 provides가 또 있으므로, 빈칸에는 접속사가 들어가야 합니다. 빈칸이 이끄는 절은 앞에 있는 사물 명사 video를 수식하므로 사물 명사 video를 대신하여 동사 provides의 주어 역할을 하는 주격 관계대명사 (C) that이 정답입니다.

번역   그 소프트웨어에는 문서를 맞춤 제작하는 것에 대한 설명을 제공하는 동영상이 포함되어 있다.

어휘   instructions 사용 설명(서)   customize 맞춤 제작하다

126

The workshop focused on common strategies for increasing sales in a variety of businesses.

(A) each 각각의   (B) fascinated 매료된   (C) willing 기꺼이 하는   (D) common 일반적인

> 해설   형용사 어휘 선택: 빈칸 뒤 명사 strategies를 수식하는 형용사 자리로, 전치사구 for increasing sales 또한 명사 strategies를 수식합니다. 문맥상 '매출을 늘리기 위한 일반적인 전략'이라는 의미가 자연스러우므로, (D) common이 정답입니다.

> 번역   워크숍은 다양한 사업에서 매출을 늘리기 위한 일반적인 전략을 중점으로 다루었다.

> 어휘   strategy 전략   increase 늘리다   a variety of 다양한

127

Niagara Space Ventures will send an exploratory satellite to Jupiter within the next five years.

(A) explore   (B) explored   (C) explores   (D) exploratory

> 해설   명사를 수식하는 형용사 선택: 빈칸 앞의 부정관사 an과 빈칸 뒤 명사 satellite 사이에서 명사를 수식하는 형용사 자리이므로, (D) exploratory(탐사의)가 정답입니다. 과거분사 (B) explored도 형용사 역할을 하지만 '탐사된 위성'이라는 의미는 문맥상 자연스럽지 않습니다.

> 번역   나이아가라 스페이스 벤처스는 앞으로 5년 안에 목성에 탐사 위성을 보낼 것이다.

> 어휘   exploratory 탐사의   explore 탐사하다

128

At the end of the training session, participants will be presented with a certificate of completion.

(A) Along   (B) At   (C) Except   (D) Between

> 해설   전치사 어휘 선택: 문맥상 '교육 세션 종료 시 수료증을 받을 것이다'라는 의미가 자연스럽고 빈칸 뒤에 the end of가 있으므로 '~의 끝에'라는 의미를 완성할 수 있는 (B) At이 정답입니다.

> 번역   교육 세션 종료 시 참가자들은 수료증을 수여받을 것이다.

> 어휘   participant 참가자   certificate 증서   completion 수료

129

Trelstem researchers will spend one month evaluating the fuel-efficiency data and then write up the results.

(A) evaluation   (B) evaluated   (C) evaluative   (D) evaluating

> 해설   분사구문: 빈칸 앞에 완전한 구조의 절이 왔으므로 빈칸 뒷부분은 수식어구 역할을 한다는 것을 알 수 있습니다. 빈칸 뒤 the fuel-efficiency data를 목적어로 취하면서 분사구문을 만드는 (D) evaluating이 정답입니다

> 번역   트렐스템 연구진은 한 달을 보내며 연비 데이터를 평가한 후 결과를 기록할 예정이다.

> 어휘   fuel-efficiency 연료 효율, 연비   result 결과   evaluate 평가하다

130

Ryou Fujita has leased the entire ground-floor space at 480 Shaw Boulevard to exhibit contemporary art.

(A) paid 지불하다   (B) leased 임대하다   (C) trained 교육하다   (D) advanced 나아가다, 개선하다

> 해설   동사 어휘 선택: 빈칸 뒤 명사구 the entire ground-floor space를 목적어로 취하는 타동사 자리로, the entire ground-floor space와 어울리는 동사를 선택해야 합니다. 문맥상 '1층 전체를 임대했다'라는 의미가 자연스러우므로, (B) leased가 정답입니다.

> 번역   류 후지타는 현대 미술을 전시하기 위해 480 쇼 불러버드 1층 공간 전체를 임대했다.

> 어휘   entire 전체의   exhibit 전시하다   contemporary 현대의

Questions 131-134 refer to the following e-mail.

From: United Lamps, Inc. <customerservice@unitedlampsinc.
      com>
To: Shannon Cohen <scohen@britemail.com>
Date: January 31
Subject: Your order
Attachment: Mail form

Dear Ms. Cohen,

Thank you for your order from United Lamps, Inc. We will be shipping your lamps **131.** shortly and will send a confirmation e-mail at that time.

Occasionally, items arrive at their **132.** destination damaged. **133.** If this happens, please use the attached label to return the item. We will **134.** provide a replacement as soon as we receive the original items.

Thank you for your continued patronage.

Customer Service Team

131-134 이메일

발신: 유나이티드 램프 사 <customerservice@
      unitedlampsinc.com>
수신: 섀넌 코헨 <scohen@britemail.com>
날짜: 1월 31일
제목: 귀하의 주문
첨부: 우편 양식

코헨 씨께,

유나이티드 램프 사에서 주문해 주셔서 감사합니다. 저희가 곧 램프를 발송하고 그때 확인 이메일을 보내드리겠습니다.

가끔 물건이 손상된 상태로 목적지에 도착합니다. 이런 일이 발생하면, 첨부된 라벨을 사용해 물건을 반품하세요. 저희가 원래 물건을 받는 대로 교체품을 제공해드리겠습니다.

계속 애용해 주셔서 감사합니다.

고객 서비스 팀

어휘 ship 발송하다 confirmation 확인 occasionally 가끔, 때로는 replacement 교체(품) patronage 애용

131 (A) short

(B) shortly

(C) shorter

(D) shortest

해설 **동사를 수식하는 부사 자리:** 빈칸은 미래진행형 동사 will be shipping을 뒤에서 수식하는 부사 자리이므로 (B) shortly(곧)가 정답입니다.

132 (A) estimate

(B) storage

(C) destination

(D) appointment

(A) 견적

(B) 보관

(C) 목적지

(D) 예약

해설 **명사 어휘 선택:** 빈칸 앞에 '물건이 ~에 도착한다(items arrive at)'라는 표현이 나옵니다. 따라서 도착하는 장소를 나타내는 명사가 나오는 것이 자연스러우므로 정답은 (C) destination입니다.

133
(A) If this happens, please use the attached label to return the item.
(B) Your lamps should arrive within the next week.
(C) Our lamps have won awards for outstanding craftsmanship.
(D) Shipping costs have gradually increased.

(A) 이런 일이 발생하면, 첨부된 라벨을 사용해 물건을 반품하세요.
(B) 램프는 다음 주 안에 도착할 것입니다.
(C) 당사 램프는 뛰어난 솜씨로 상을 받았습니다.
(D) 배송비가 점차 증가되어 왔습니다.

해설 문장 삽입 문제: 빈칸 뒤 문장에서 원래 물건을 받는 즉시 교체품을 제공한다고 했습니다. 따라서 빈칸에는 물건 반품에 관련된 내용을 언급하는 것이 내용 전개 면에서 자연스러우므로 정답은 (A)입니다.

어휘 attached 첨부된 outstanding 뛰어난 craftsmanship 솜씨 gradually 점차 increase 오르다

134
(A) recommend
(B) provide
(C) design
(D) purchase

(A) 추천하다
(B) 제공하다
(C) 디자인하다
(D) 구매하다

해설 동사 어휘 선택: 빈칸 뒤 목적어 a replacement를 목적어로 취해 가장 자연스럽게 의미가 통하는 동사를 선택해야 합니다. 문맥상 '교체품을 제공할 것이다'라는 의미가 자연스러우므로 정답은 (B) provide입니다.

Questions 135-138 refer to the following e-mail.

To: Jin-Hee Yang <jyang@herongifts.ca>
From: Tom Vermette <tvermette@vermettehca.ca>
Date: 16 May
Subject: Installation Information
Attachment: Proposal

Dear Ms. Yang:

Thank you for trusting Vermette Heating, Cooling, and Air with your service needs. I **135.** have attached the proposal for the new air-conditioning system. Please let me know if you have any questions about **136.** it. You will find that this unit will function more efficiently than your current system. **137.** Consequently, you should see a decrease in your monthly electric bills. **138.** You can save even more money by signing up for our maintenance plan. It includes annual tune-ups of your system. For more information, call our office at 613-555-0164. We can answer any questions about the plan and payment options.

Sincerely,

Tom Vermette

135-138 이메일

수신: 양진희 <jyang@herongifts.ca>
발신: 톰 버메트 <tvermette@vermettehca.ca>
날짜: 5월 16일
제목: 설치 정보
첨부: 제안서

양 씨께:

귀사의 서비스 요구 사항을 버메트 냉난방 공조에 믿고 알려주셔서 감사합니다. 새로운 에어컨 시스템에 대한 제안서를 첨부했습니다. 그것에 관해 문의 사항이 있으면 알려주세요. 이 장치는 현재 시스템보다 더 효율적으로 작동할 것입니다. 따라서 매달 전기 요금이 줄어드는 것을 보실 겁니다. 당사의 유지관리 플랜에 가입하시면 훨씬 더 많은 비용을 절약할 수 있습니다. 여기에는 연례 시스템 튜업이 포함됩니다. 더 자세한 정보는 613-555-0164번 저희 사무실로 전화 주십시오. 플랜과 결제 방식에 관한 어떠한 질문에도 답변해 드릴 수 있습니다.

톰 버메트

어휘 trust 믿고 이야기하다　proposal 제안(서)　function 작동하다　efficiently 효율적으로　current 현재의　decrease 줄다
tune-up 튠업, 성능 향상 조정　payment 결제

135 (A) attaches

(B) attaching

(C) had attached

(D) have attached

해설 현재완료 시제: 빈칸은 주어 I 뒤의 동사 자리이고 문맥상 '제안서를 첨부했다'라는 뜻으로, 과거에 시작된 일이 완료되었다는 의미이므로 현재완료 (D) have attached가 정답입니다. 과거완료 (C) had attached는 과거의 특정 시점 이전에 일어난 일을 나타냅니다.

136 (A) him

(B) it

(C) them

(D) anyone

해설 인칭대명사 선택: 빈칸은 전치사 about의 목적어 역할을 하는 자리로 문맥상 앞 문장의 the proposal을 대신하는 목적격 인칭 대명사 (B) it이 정답입니다.

137 (A) Nevertheless　　　　　　　　　　(A) 그럼에도 불구하고

(B) Otherwise　　　　　　　　　　　(B) 그렇지 않으면

(C) Consequently　　　　　　　　　　(C) 따라서

(D) In contrast　　　　　　　　　　　(D) 반대로

해설 접속부사 선택: 빈칸 앞 문장에서 제안하는 장치는 현재 시스템보다 더 효율적이라는 내용을, 빈칸 뒤에서 전기 요금이 줄어들 것이라는 내용을 언급했습니다. 따라서 인과 관계를 나타내는 '그 결과로, 따라서'라는 의미의 접속부사 (C) Consequently가 정답입니다.

138 (A) You can save even more money by signing up for our maintenance plan.

(B) You may submit your payment through our online system.

(C) Many businesses in the area are upgrading their heating systems now.

(D) I read your proposal with great interest.

(A) 당사의 유지관리 플랜에 가입하시면 훨씬 더 많은 비용을 절약할 수 있습니다.

(B) 당사 온라인 시스템을 통해 결제할 수 있습니다.

(C) 지역에 있는 많은 업체들이 현재 난방 시스템을 개선하고 있습니다.

(D) 귀하의 제안서를 매우 흥미롭게 읽었습니다.

해설 문장 삽입 문제: 빈칸 앞 문장에서 전기 요금이 줄어들 것이라고 했습니다. 따라서 빈칸에는 요금이나 절약 관련 내용을 언급하는 것이 내용 전개 면에서 자연스러우므로 정답은 (A)입니다.

어휘 sign up for ~에 가입하다　maintenance 유지 (관리), 정비

Questions 139-142 refer to the following letter.

Mr. Adam Weisberg
37 Autumn Road
Nyack, NY 10960

June 24

Dear Mr. Weisberg,

This letter is being sent to remind you **139.** that it is time for your dental appointment with Dr. Shuyama. During your last visit, you scheduled an appointment to have your teeth cleaned on Tuesday, July 16, at 3:00 P.M. If you need to reschedule, please call us **140.** at your convenience at (845) 555-0162.

We would like to take this opportunity to inform you about our latest giveaway campaign. Throughout the month of July, **141.** we will keep a jar filled with toothbrushes on the registration desk. Patients are asked to guess the number of toothbrushes in the jar. Whoever comes closest to the actual number will win a True Smile electric toothbrush valued at $135. **142.** True Smile is the best electric toothbrush available.

We look forward to seeing you soon.

Shuyama Dental Associates

139-142 편지

애덤 와이즈버그
37 어텀 로드
나이액, 뉴욕 주 10960

6월 24일

와이즈버그 씨께,

슈야마 선생님과 잡은 치과 예약 시간이 되었음을 상기시켜 드리고자 이 편지를 보냅니다. 지난 방문 시, 7월 16일 화요일 오후 3시에 스케일링을 예약하셨습니다. 일정을 다시 잡으시려면 편한 시간에 (845) 555-0162로 전화 주십시오.

이 기회를 빌어 새로운 경품 캠페인에 대해 알려드리고자 합니다. 7월 한 달 동안, 저희가 칫솔이 가득한 병을 접수처에 두겠습니다. 환자들은 병에 들어 있는 칫솔의 개수를 알아맞히도록 요청받습니다. 실제 숫자에 가장 근접한 사람은 누구나 135달러짜리 트루 스마일 전동 칫솔을 받게 됩니다. <u>트루 스마일은 최고의 전동 칫솔입니다.</u>

곧 뵙기를 고대합니다.

슈야마 치과

어휘 appointment 예약 latest 새로운 giveaway 증정품, 경품 jar 병 patient 환자 actual 실제의

139 (A) that
(B) how
(C) unless
(D) whenever

해설 명사절 접속사 that: 빈칸 앞에 동사 remind가 있으므로 빈칸은 to부정사의 간접목적어 you 다음의 직접목적어인 명사절을 이끄는 접속사가 들어가야 합니다. 따라서 (A) that이 정답입니다.

140 (A) instead   (A) 대신에
(B) as if   (B) 마치 ~인 것처럼
(C) nevertheless   (C) 그럼에도 불구하고
(D) at your convenience (D) 편한 시간에

해설 전치사구: 빈칸 앞 문장은 you가 생략된 명령문으로 〈동사(call) + 목적어(us)〉의 완전한 절이 있으므로 수식어구가 들어가야 합니다. 문맥상 '편한 시간에 전화를 하라'는 의미가 적합하므로, 전치사구 (D) at your convenience가 정답입니다.

141

(A) we

(B) you

(C) one

(D) they

> **해설** 인칭대명사 선택: 빈칸은 동사 will keep의 주어 자리입니다. 문맥상 병을 접수처에 두는 주체는 편지를 작성한 Shuyama Dental Associates이므로 인칭 대명사 (A) we가 정답입니다.

142

(A) Contact our front desk for a free consultation.

(B) We recommend that you see the dentist twice a year.

(C) True Smile is the best electric toothbrush available.

(D) A fee of $25 will be charged for canceled appointments.

(A) 프런트에 연락해 무료 상담을 받으세요.

(B) 1년에 두 번 치과에 가는 것을 권장합니다.

(C) 트루 스마일은 최고의 전동 칫솔입니다.

(D) 취소된 예약에 대해서는 25달러의 수수료가 부과됩니다.

> **해설** 문장 삽입 문제: 빈칸 앞 문장이 트루 스마일 전동칫솔을 받을 수 있는 방법을 설명하고 있습니다. 따라서 빈칸에는 트루 스마일 전동칫솔에 대해 언급하는 것이 내용 전개면에서 자연스러우므로 정답은 (C)입니다.

> **어휘** consultation 상담 recommend 추천하다, 권장하다 charge 부과하다 cancel 취소하다

Questions 143-146 refer to the following passage.

Event Calendar

August 18–19

The popular Antique and Vintage Trade Show returns for its tenth consecutive year. Sponsored by the Fullman Antique Dealers Association, the show offers a chance to view private collections from around the country. **143.** Exhibits will be divided into three categories. The first, located in East Hall, includes collectibles such as jewelry, toys, silverware, and dishes. A second area, in South Hall, will **144.** feature handcrafted furniture. Finally, rare books, vintage signs, and historical artifacts will be displayed in West Hall. The first day is limited to **145.** registered association members only. Doors will be open to the public **146.** on August 19. All tickets must be purchased in advance on our Web site or by calling 555-0142.

143-146 문단

행사 일정

8월 18-19일

인기 있는 골동품 및 빈티지 상품전시회가 연속 10년째 다시 찾아온다. 풀먼 골동품상 협회가 후원하는 이 전시회는 전국의 개인 소장품을 관람할 수 있는 기회를 제공한다. 전시품은 세 가지 범주로 나뉜다. 이스트 홀에 위치하는 첫 번째 범주에는 장신구, 장난감, 은식기류, 접시와 같은 수집품이 포함된다. 사우스 홀에 있는 두 번째 구역에서는 수공예 가구들을 선보일 것이다. 마지막으로, 웨스트홀에는 희귀 도서, 빈티지 간판, 그리고 역사적인 공예품이 전시될 예정이다. 첫날은 등록된 협회 회원만으로 입장이 제한된다. 일반인들에게는 8월 19일에 공개될 예정이다. 모든 티켓은 웹사이트에서 미리 구매하거나 555-0142번으로 전화해 구입해야 한다.

> **어휘** consecutive 연속되는 collectible 수집품 handcrafted 수제의, 수공예품인 rare 희귀한 artifact 공예품 purchase 구매하다 in advance 미리

143 (A) There are several steps to get signed up.

(B) Exhibits will be divided into three categories.

(C) The director has shared a few of her favorite memories.

(D) A number of changes have been made to the event.

(A) 신청하려면 몇 가지 단계가 있다.

(B) 전시품은 세 가지 범주로 나뉜다.

(C) 이사는 가장 좋아하는 몇 가지 추억을 공유했다.

(D) 행사에 많은 변경이 이루어졌다.

[해설] **문장 삽입 문제:** 빈칸 뒤 문장들에서 첫 번째 범주에 속하는 전시품과 두 번째 및 세 번째에 속하는 전시품을 나열하고 있습니다. 따라서 빈칸에는 전시품이 세 가지로 나뉘어지는 사실을 언급하는 것이 자연스러우므로 정답은 (B)입니다.

[어휘] exhibit 전시품   divide 나누다

144 (A) polish

(B) determine

(C) feature

(D) charge

(A) 닦다

(B) 결정하다

(C) 선보이다

(D) 부과하다

[해설] **동사 어휘 선택:** 빈칸은 명사구 handcrafted furniture를 목적어로 취하는 동사 자리로 문맥상 '수공예 가구를 선보이다'라는 표현이 되는 것이 자연스러우므로 정답은 (C) feature입니다.

145 (A) register

(B) registers

(C) registered

(D) registration

[해설] **형용사 역할을 하는 분사:** 빈칸 뒤 명사 association members를 수식하는 형용사 자리이므로, 형용사 역할을 하는 과거분사 (C) registered가 정답입니다.

[어휘] register 등록하다

146 (A) about

(B) except

(C) after

(D) on

[해설] **전치사 선택:** 빈칸 뒤 시간 표현 August 19을 목적어로 취하는 전치사 자리입니다. 문맥상 '8월 19일에 공개된다'라는 의미가 자연스러우므로 '(특정 날짜)에'라는 뜻의 전치사 (D) on이 정답입니다.

Questions 147-148 refer to the following advertisement.

147-148 광고

147 Mishri's, located at 1077 Cedar Avenue, is a thriving department store that has been serving the San Francisco area for more than two decades. Mishri's offers everything from work uniforms to the latest fashions, indoor and outdoor furniture, electronics, and sporting goods. **We currently have an opening for an experienced sales consultant in the furniture department. The full-time position includes a competitive salary with paid holidays. Take a look online at mishris.com/jobs to learn more. 148**Interested applicants should contact Vikas Tawde, sales manager, at 415-555-0185 to arrange an interview.

1471077 시더 애버뉴에 위치한 미슈리즈는 20년 이상 샌프란시스코 지역에 서비스를 제공해 온 번창하는 백화점입니다. 미슈리즈는 직장 유니폼부터 최신 패션, 실내 및 실외 가구, 전자제품, 스포츠 용품에 이르기까지 모든 것을 제공합니다. **현재 가구부에 경력직 영업 컨설턴트 자리가 비어 있습니다. 이 정규직에는 경쟁력 있는 급여와 유급 휴가가 포함됩니다. 자세한 내용은 mishris.com/jobs에서 온라인으로 확인하세요. 148**관심 있는 지원자들은 영업부장 비카스 타우드에게 415-555-0185번으로 연락해 면접 일정을 잡아야 합니다.

어휘 thriving 번창하는 decade 10년 currently 현재 experienced 경력이 있는 competitive 경쟁력 있는, 뒤지지 않는 paid holiday 유급 휴가 applicant 지원자

147 What is suggested about Mishri's?

(A) It recently reorganized the store layout.

(B) It has sold a variety of goods to customers for many years.

(C) It is opening a new location in another city.

(D) It plans to expand its current location.

미슈리즈에 관해 시사되는 것은?

(A) 최근 매장 배치를 개편했다.

(B) 여러 해 동안 고객에게 다양한 상품을 판매해 왔다.

(C) 다른 도시에 새로운 지점을 열 것이다.

(D) 현 매장을 확장할 계획이다.

해설 추론: 첫 번째와 두 번째 문장에서 미슈리즈는 20년 이상 유니폼부터 스포츠 용품까지 모든 것을 제공해 온 백화점이라고 했으므로 정답은 (B)입니다.

Paraphrasing 지문의 offers everything → 정답의 has sold a variety of goods

어휘 reorganize 개편하다 location 지점 expand 확장하다

148 Why are readers encouraged to call Mr. Tawde?

(A) To place an order

(B) To provide feedback

(C) To arrange a delivery

(D) To set up a meeting

독자들이 타우드 씨에게 전화하라고 권유받는 이유는?

(A) 주문을 하기 위해

(B) 의견을 제공하기 위해

(C) 배송을 준비하기 위해

(D) 면담 일정을 잡기 위해

해설 세부 사항: 마지막 문장에서 지원자들은 타우드 씨에게 연락해 면접 일정을 잡아야 한다고 했으므로 정답은 (D)입니다.

Paraphrasing 지문의 to arrange an interview → 정답의 to set up a meeting

Questions 149-150 refer to the following text-message chain.

149-150 문자 메시지

Jamal Kirby [9:15 A.M.]

Hi, Paula. I'm working at home today. ¹⁴⁹Could you please send me the Torvale Enterprises contracts and let me know when to expect them? I would like to review them as soon as possible.

Paula Lahti [9:16 A.M.]

Of course. I can have our expedited delivery service pick them up later this morning, so you should get them this afternoon. ¹⁵⁰The address I have on file for you is 140 Riverside Drive.

Jamal Kirby [9:17 A.M.]

¹⁵⁰No, sorry, that is my old place. I'm now at 35 Elston Avenue, Apartment 103.

Paula Lahti [9:18 A.M.]

Got it. It'll send the documents you need there.

Jamal Kirby [9:19 A.M.]

That sounds good. ¹⁵⁰Be sure to update your records, too. Thanks, Paula.

자말 커비 [오전 9:15]

안녕, 폴라. 저는 오늘 집에서 근무해요. ¹⁴⁹토베일 엔터프라이즈 계약서를 보내주시고 언제 받아 볼 수 있는지 알려주실래요? 가능한 한 빨리 검토하고 싶어요.

폴라 라티 [오전 9:16]

그럼요. 긴급 배송 서비스를 불러 오늘 오전 늦게 그것들을 가져가게 할게요. 그러면 오늘 오후에 받아보실 수 있을 거예요. ¹⁵⁰제가 갖고 있는 당신 주소는 140 리버사이드 드라이브예요.

자말 커비 [오전 9:17]

¹⁵⁰아니요, 미안하지만 그건 예전 집이에요. 지금은 35 엘스턴 애비뉴 아파트 103호에 있어요.

폴라 라티 [오전 9:18]

알겠어요. 필요하신 서류를 그쪽으로 보낼게요.

자말 커비 [오전 9:19]

좋아요. ¹⁵⁰기록 수정도 꼭 하세요. 고마워요, 폴라.

어휘   contract 계약(서)   expedited 신속한, 긴급한   delivery 배송, 배달   on file 기록으로 보관 중인   document 문서, 서류

149   What is most likely true about Mr. Kirby?

(A) He is currently on a business trip.

(B) He wants to receive some documents soon.

(C) He plans to move his office.

(D) He is writing an article about Torvale Enterprises.

커비 씨에 대한 설명으로 맞는 것은?

(A) 현재 출장 중이다.

(B) 빨리 서류를 받고 싶어한다.

(C) 사무실을 옮길 계획이다.

(D) 토베일 엔터프라이즈에 대한 기사를 쓰고 있다.

해설   Not / True: 커비 씨는 오전 9시 15분 메시지에서 계약서를 언제 받아 볼 수 있는지 알려 달라(Could you please ~ when to expect them?)면서 가능한 한 빨리 검토하고 싶다(I would ~ as soon as possible.)고 했습니다. 이 말은 계약서를 빨리 받고 싶다는 의미이므로 정답은 (B)입니다.

Paraphrasing   지문의 contracts → 정답의 documents

150   At 9:19 A.M., what does Mr. Kirby mean when he writes, "Be sure to update your records, too"?

(A) Ms. Lahti should note the new value of a property.

(B) Ms. Lahti should revise an address on file.

(C) Ms. Lahti needs to destroy a client report.

(D) Ms. Lahti must use a different delivery service.

오전 9시 19분에 커비 씨가 "기록 수정도 꼭 하세요"라고 쓸 때 의미하는 것은?

(A) 라티 씨는 부동산의 새로운 가치에 주목해야 한다.

(B) 라티 씨는 보관 중인 주소를 수정해야 한다.

(C) 라티 씨는 고객 보고서를 파기해야 한다.

(D) 라티 씨는 다른 배송 서비스를 이용해야 한다.

해설   의도 파악: 오전 9시 16분에 라티 씨가 자신이 갖고 있는 커비 씨의 주소를 말하자 9시 17분에 커비 씨가 그것은 예전 주소라며 새 주소를 알려주었습니다. 따라서 주소를 변경하라는 의미로 한 말이므로 정답은 (B)입니다.

Paraphrasing   property 부동산   revise 수정하다   destroy 파기하다

Questions 151-152 refer to the following coupon.

A Special Offer from Spee-Dee Long-Term Parking

Present this coupon to get a 10 percent discount on our long-term parking rates!

- **151**We're just minutes away from Kingston Airport.
- Our complimentary shuttle bus leaves on the hour to drop passengers off at their flight terminals.
- We're open 7 days a week, 24 hours a day.

Reserve your space in advance at www.spee-dee.com!
No charge if you need to cancel.

Only one coupon accepted per visit. Cannot be combined with other coupons.
152 Expires 31 December.

151-152 쿠폰

스피-디 장기 주차의 특별 할인

이 쿠폰을 제시하고 저희의 장기 주차 요금을 10퍼센트 할인 받으세요!

- **151**킹스턴 공항에서 불과 몇 분 거리에 있습니다.
- 무료 셔틀 버스가 정시에 출발해 승객들을 항공편 터미널에 내려드립니다.
- 연중무휴 24시간 영업합니다.

www.spee-dee.com에서 미리 자리를 예약하세요!
취소해야 할 경우 수수료를 부과하지 않습니다.

1회 방문 시 쿠폰 1장만 받습니다. 다른 쿠폰과 함께 사용할 수 없습니다.
15212월 31일 만료.

어휘 offer (단기간) 할인 long-term 장기의 complimentary 무료인 on the hour 정시에 in advance 미리 cancel 취소하다 expire 만료되다

151 What is suggested about Spee-Dee Long-Term Parking?

(A) It is closed on holidays.

(B) It is near an airport.

(C) It does not accept reservations.

(D) It charges a cancellation fee.

스피-디 장기 주차에 관해 시사되는 것은?

(A) 공휴일에는 휴무이다.

(B) 공항 근처에 있다.

(C) 예약을 받지 않는다.

(D) 취소 수수료를 부과한다.

해설 추론: 쿠폰 초반부에 킹스턴 공항에서 몇 분 거리(minutes away from Kingston Airport)에 있다고 했으므로 정답은 (B)입니다.

152 What is true about the coupon?

(A) It is valid at other locations.

(B) It is offered to first-time customers only.

(C) It expires at the end of the year.

(D) It includes a discount on a shuttle-bus ticket.

쿠폰에 관해 사실인 것은?

(A) 다른 영업장에서도 유효하다.

(B) 처음 방문하는 고객에게만 제공된다.

(C) 연말에 만료된다.

(D) 셔틀버스 이용권 할인이 포함되어 있다.

해설 Not / True: 쿠폰에서 12월 31일 만료를 확인할 수 있으므로 정답은 (C)입니다.

어휘 valid 유효한

Paraphrasing 지문의 31 December → 정답의 at the end of the year

Questions 153-154 refer to the following flyer.

WE MISS YOU!

¹⁵⁴All of us on the staff here at Mike's Workout Center in Taylorville miss seeing you!

^{153,154}If you are ready to renew your membership, we are offering one-half off the standard monthly membership rate for the next three months. This offer will expire at the end of July.

Come enjoy our regular sessions featuring dance fitness, cycling, and strength training. In addition, take time to check out our recently updated athletic boutique, featuring top-quality exercise apparel, tote bags, and more. Many boutique items are now branded with the Mike's Workout Center logo!

Contact the membership office today. We will help you keep on track with your fitness plan and do it in style!

153-154 광고지

여러분을 보고 싶습니다!

¹⁵⁴테일러빌의 마이크스 워크아웃 센터 저희 직원 모두는 여러분을 정말 보고 싶습니다!

^{153,154}회원권을 갱신할 준비가 되셨다면 앞으로 3개월 동안 표준 월 회원가에서 반값 할인을 제공합니다. 이번 할인은 7월 말에 만료됩니다.

오셔서 댄스 피트니스, 사이클, 근력 운동 같은 정규 수업을 즐기세요. 덧붙여 시간을 내서 최근 새로 단장한 운동복 부티크를 구경하세요. 최고 품질의 운동복, 토트백 등을 선보이고 있습니다. 이제는 많은 부티크 상품들에 마이크스 워크아웃 센터 로고가 상표로 붙어 있습니다!

오늘 회원권 사무실로 연락하세요. 여러분이 피트니스 플랜을 순조롭게 진행하시고 멋지게 하시도록 도와드리겠습니다!

어휘 renew 갱신하다 expire 만료되다 recently 최근 apparel 복장 keep on track 순조롭게 진행하다 in style 멋지게

153 For whom is the flyer written?

(A) New residents of Taylorville

(B) Exercise class instructors

(C) Current members of a fitness club

(D) Frequent customers of a boutique

광고지가 작성된 대상은?

(A) 테일러빌의 새 주민

(B) 운동 수업 강사

(C) 피트니스 클럽의 현재 회원

(D) 부티크 단골 고객

해설 추론: 두 번째 단락 첫 번째 문장에서 회원권을 갱신(renew your membership)하면 회원가를 반값 할인해 준다고 했으므로 현재 회원을 대상으로 한 광고지임을 알 수 있습니다. 따라서 정답은 (C)입니다.

어휘 resident 주민, 거주자 instructor 강사 frequent 자주 오는

154 What is suggested about Mike's Workout Center?

(A) Its branded apparel sells well.

(B) Its discount offer will no longer be available in August.

(C) It has introduced new classes recently.

(D) It has seen an increase in membership.

마이크스 워크아웃 센터에 관해 시사되는 것은?

(A) 자체 브랜드 의류가 잘 팔린다.

(B) 8월에는 더 이상 특가 할인을 받을 수 없다.

(C) 최근 새로운 강좌를 도입했다.

(D) 회원 수가 증가해 왔다.

해설 추론: 마이크스 워크아웃 센터가 광고지를 작성한 것을 첫 단락에서 확인할 수 있고 두 번째 단락에서 회원가 할인은 7월말에 만료된다고 했으므로 정답은 (B)입니다.

어휘 introduce 도입하다 increase 증가

Questions 155-157 refer to the following blog post.

Fariba Khan, 28 April

Although I travel to Bartonsburg for work several times a year, this was the first time I stayed at the Lazy Lilac Inn. I normally reserve a room at a hotel next to my company's Bartonsburg location, but it was unable to accommodate the four-night visit I needed, so I opted for the Lazy Lilac Inn at the suggestion of a colleague. [156]It was extending a special promotion when I made the reservation, and I received a discounted rate.

[155]Overall, my stay was pleasant enough. Though the inn was farther from my company's office than my usual lodging, it was closer to the airport, which was convenient. It has an exercise room as well as a space that functions as a business center. [157]There was also a room where I could wash a load of dirty clothes. My main qualm about the Lazy Lilac Inn was that it does not have a full-service breakfast. Though I ate most of my meals with my colleagues, it would have been nice to eat at the inn in the morning. However, it had just pastries and hot beverages available. I certainly recommend it for any of you who may take a similar trip.

155-157 블로그 게시 글

파리바 칸, 4월 28일

바턴스버그에 업무차 1년에 몇 번씩 오지만 레이지 라일락 인에 묵은 건 이번이 처음이었습니다. 보통은 바턴스버그 회사 사무실 옆에 있는 호텔에 방을 예약하지만 나흘 밤을 묵어야 하는데 그곳이 수용할 수가 없어 동료가 추천해준 레이지 라일락 인을 선택했습니다. 제가 예약할 당시 [156]그곳에서 특별 판촉을 제공하고 있어서 요금을 할인 받았습니다.

[155]전반적으로 체류는 충분히 즐거웠습니다. 인이 늘 묵는 숙소보다는 회사 사무실에서 더 멀었지만 공항에서 더 가까워서 편리했습니다. 비즈니스센터 기능을 하는 공간뿐 아니라 운동실도 있었습니다. [157]더러워진 많은 옷을 세탁할 수 있는 방도 있었습니다. 레이지 라일락 인에서 가장 꺼림칙했던 것은 풀서비스 조식이 없다는 점이었습니다. 식사는 대개 동료와 함께 먹었지만 아침에 인에서 먹었으면 좋았을 겁니다. 하지만 그곳에는 빵과 뜨거운 음료밖에 없었습니다. 비슷한 여행을 하실 분이라면 물론 누구에게나 이 그곳을 추천합니다.

어휘 normally 보통 accommodate 수용하다 extend 제공하다 promotion 판촉, 홍보 overall 전반적으로 lodging 숙소 convenient 편리한 function 기능하다 a load of 많은 qualm 거리낌, 꺼림칙한 full-service breakfast 메인 메뉴를 따로 주문할 수 있는 뷔페형 조식

155 For whom most likely is the blog post written?

(A) Tour companies
(B) Residents of Bartonsburg
(C) Business travelers
(D) Family vacationers

블로그 게시물이 작성된 대상은?

(A) 관광업체
(B) 바턴스버그 주민
(C) 출장 여행객
(D) 가족 휴가객

해설 추론: 두 번째 단락에서 체류가 즐거웠고 회사 사무실에서 더 멀었지만(farther from my company's office) 공항에서 가까워서 편리했다고 했습니다. 따라서 출장가는 사람들을 대상으로 한 글임을 유추할 수 있으므로 정답은 (C)입니다.

156 The word "extending" in paragraph 1, line 5, is closest in meaning to

(A) delaying
(B) stretching
(C) offering
(D) moving

첫 번째 단락 5행의 'extending'과 의미상 가장 가까운 것은?

(A) 지연시키다
(B) 늘리다
(C) 제공하나
(D) 움직이다

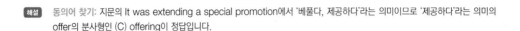

해설　동의어 찾기: 지문의 It was extending a special promotion에서 '베풀다, 제공하다'라는 의미이므로 '제공하다'라는 의미의 offer의 분사형인 (C) offering이 정답입니다.

157 What is mentioned as an amenity of the Lazy Lilac Inn?

(A) Laundry facilities
(B) An outdoor patio
(C) Airport limousine service
(D) An event room

레이지 라일락 인의 편의시설로 언급된 것은?

(A) 세탁 시설
(B) 옥외 테라스
(C) 공항 리무진 서비스
(D) 행사장

해설　Not / True: 두 번째 단락 네 번째 문장에서 더러운 옷을 세탁할 수 있는 방이 있다고 했으므로 정답은 (A)입니다.

Questions 158-160 refer to the following memo.

158-160 회람

MEMO

From: Fred Stiller, President, ROE Smart Solutions
To: All Staff
Subject: All-staff meeting
Date: June 4

The next all-staff meeting will be on Tuesday, June 11, at 1:00 P.M. in Conference Room A. On-site employees are expected to attend in person. Those of you working remotely will be receiving a link that, once activated, will enable you to participate in the meeting over the Internet.

As you know, earlier this year we acquired Greer Technologies and merged its management, products, and operations with our company. At the all-staff meeting, **159**I will be focusing on some key issues stemming from this development, including changes within company management. **160**Among other things, I will be introducing Mr. Paul Oberweis, the former director of finance at Greer Technologies and now our new chief financial officer. **158**He will be reviewing our financial projections for the year.

If you have questions that you would like to have answered during the meeting, please submit them to Adrienne Petruso (a.petruso@roe.org) by June 10.

발신: 프레드 스틸러, 사장, ROE 스마트 솔루션즈
수신: 전 직원
제목: 전 직원 회의
날짜: 6월 4일

다음 전 직원 회의는 6월 11일 화요일 오후 1시 A 회의실에서 열립니다. 현장 근무 직원들은 직접 참석해야 합니다. 원격 근무하는 직원들은 활성화되면 인터넷으로 회의에 참여할 수 있게 하는 링크를 받게 됩니다.

아시다시피, 올해 초에 우리는 그리어 테크놀러지스를 인수해 경영, 제품 및 운영을 우리 회사와 합병했습니다. 전 직원 회의에서 저는 회사 경영진 내의 변화를 포함해 **159**이러한 발전에 따른 몇 가지 핵심 문제를 중점적으로 다룰 예정입니다. **160**무엇보다 그리어 테크놀리지스의 전임 재무이사이자 현재 우리 회사의 신임 최고 재무 책임자인 폴 오버와이스 씨를 소개할 것입니다. **158**그가 올해 우리의 재정 전망을 검토할 것입니다.

회의 도중에 답변 받고 싶은 질문이 있으시면 6월 10일까지 아드리엔 페트루소(a.petruso@roe.org)에게 제출해 주십시오.

어휘　on-site 현장의　be expected to ~해야 한다　in person 직접　remotely 원격으로　participate in ~에 참여하다　acquire 인수하다　merge 합병하다　stem from ~에 기인하다　projection 전망

158 What is one item on the agenda for the June 11 meeting?

(A) A course offered to employees

(B) A managerial job opening

(C) A budgetary forecast

(D) A merger procedure

6월 11일 회의 안건의 한 항목은?

(A) 직원에게 제공되는 강좌

(B) 관리직 공석

(C) 예산 예측

(D) 합병 절차

> **해설** 세부 사항: 먼저 첫 단락에서 이 회람이 6월 11일 회의에 대한 것임을 확인합니다. 두 번째 단락 마지막 문장에서 올해 회사의 재정 전망을 검토할 것(reviewing our financial projections)이라고 했으므로 정답은 (C)입니다.
>
> **Paraphrasing** 지문의 financial projections → 정답의 budgetary forecast
>
> **어휘** managerial 관리(자)의 budgetary 예산의 procedure 절차

159 The word "issues" in paragraph 2, line 3, is closest in meaning to

(A) publications

(B) reasons

(C) matters

(D) titles

두 번째 단락 3행의 'issues'와 의미상 가장 가까운 것은?

(A) 간행물

(B) 이유

(C) 문제

(D) 직함

> **해설** 동의어 찾기: 지문의 I will be focusing on some key issues에서 issues는 '문제들, 쟁점들'이라는 의미이므로 '문제들'이라는 의미의 (C) matters가 정답입니다.

160 What is true about Mr. Oberweis?

(A) He wrote the memo.

(B) He purchased a company.

(C) He has developed new technologies.

(D) He has a new position.

오버와이스 씨에 관해 사실인 것은?

(A) 회람을 작성했다.

(B) 회사를 매수했다.

(C) 신기술을 개발했다.

(D) 새로운 직책을 맡았다

> **해설** Not / True: 두 번째 단락 후반부에서 Mr. Paul Oberweis라는 이름이 등장하며 그리어 테크놀리지스의 전임 재무이사(former director of finance)이자 현재 회사의 신임 최고 재무 책임자(new chief financial officer)라고 말했습니다. 따라서 오버와이스 씨는 이직을 하여 직책이 바뀌었음을 알 수 있으므로 정답은 (D)입니다.

Questions 161-163 refer to the following e-mail.

To: Caiaro Realty Employees

From: Sean Patrick

Date: January 29

Subject: Real Estate Agent of the Year finalist

Dear Colleagues:

161-163 이메일

수신: 카이아로 부동산 직원

발신: 션 패트릭

날짜: 1월 29일

제목: 올해의 부동산 중개인 최종 후보

동료 여러분께:

I am pleased to announce that our colleague, Shanice Walker, is a finalist for the Real Estate Agent of the Year award that is being presented by the California Board of Real Estate Agents. Ms. Walker has had an outstanding year and is very deserving of this honor. **161**She has been a real estate agent for fifteen years, the last ten with Caiaro Realty. **163**The winner will be announced at the awards banquet, which will be held on February 28 at the High Lingon Hotel from 6 p.m. to 10 p.m. Caiaro Realty will be hosting several tables at the banquet. I encourage everyone to attend and support Ms. Walker. **162**If you do plan to attend, please e-mail my assistant, Mingzhe Zhou, to reserve your spot. Make sure to congratulate Ms. Walker when you see her.

Best,

Sean Patrick
President, Caiaro Realty

우리 동료인 샤니스 워커가 캘리포니아 부동산 중개인 협회가 수여하는 올해의 부동산 중개인상 최종 후보라는 것을 알려드리게 되어 기쁩니다. 워커 씨는 뛰어난 한 해를 보냈으므로 이 영예를 누릴 자격이 충분합니다. **161**그녀는 15년 동안 부동산 중개인으로 일했고, 마지막 10년 동안은 카이아로 부동산에서 일했습니다. **163**수상자는 2월 28일 오후 6시부터 10시까지 하이 링곤 호텔에서 열리는 시상식 연회에서 발표됩니다. 카이아로 부동산은 연회에서 테이블 몇 개를 맡을 예정입니다. 모두 참석해서 워커 씨를 지원해 주실 것을 권합니다. **162**참석할 계획이면 제 비서인 밍제 주에게 이메일을 보내 자리를 예약하십시오. 워커 씨를 보면 꼭 축하해 주십시오.

션 패트릭
사장, 카이아로 부동산

어휘 real estate 부동산　outstanding 두드러진, 뛰어난　deserve 받을 자격이 있다

161 What is indicated about Ms. Walker?

(A) She just received an award.

(B) She has been a finalist for an award in the past.

(C) She recommended a colleague to become a board member.

(D) She has worked for Caiaro Realty for ten years.

워커 씨에 관해 명시된 것은?

(A) 얼마전에 상을 받았다.

(B) 과거에 최종 수상 후보였다.

(C) 동료를 이사가 되도록 추천했다.

(D) 카이아로 부동산에서 10년 동안 일했다.

해설 Not / True: 첫 번째 문장에서 Shanice Walker라는 이름을 확인할 수 있습니다. 세 번째 문장에서 부동산 중개인(real estate agent)으로 15년간 일했고 카이아로 부동산에서는 10년을 일했다고 말했으므로 정답은 (D)입니다.

Paraphrasing 지문의 the last ten with Caiaro Reality → 정답의 has worked for Caiaro Reality for ten years

162 What should someone who wants to attend the banquet do?

(A) Reply to Mr. Patrick's e-mail

(B) Visit a Web site

(C) Call the High Lingon Hotel

(D) Send an e-mail to Ms. Zhou

연회에 참석하려는 사람은 어떻게 해야 하는가?

(A) 패트릭 씨의 이메일에 답장하기

(B) 웹사이트 방문하기

(C) 하이 링곤 호텔에 전화하기

(D) 주 씨에게 이메일 보내기

해설 세부 사항: 지문 후반부에 연회에 참석할 계획이면 밍제 주에게 이메일을 보내라고 했으므로 정답은 (D)입니다.

Paraphrasing 지문의 e-mail my assistant, Mingzhe Zhou → 정답의 Send an e-mail to Ms. Zhou

163 In which of the positions marked [1], [2], [3], and [4] does the following sentence best belong?

"Caiaro Realty will be hosting several tables at the banquet."

(A) [1]

(B) [2]

(C) [3]

(D) [4]

[1], [2], [3], [4]로 표시된 곳 중에서 다음 문장이 들어가기에 가장 적합한 곳은?

"카이아로 부동산은 연회에서 테이블 몇 개를 맡을 예정입니다."

(A) [1]

(B) [2]

(C) [3]

(D) [4]

> **해설** 문장 삽입: '카이아로 부동산은 연회에서 테이블 몇 개를 맡을 예정이다'라는 말이 들어가야 하므로, 맥락상 빈칸 앞에 연회 관련 내용이 나와야 합니다. 따라서 2월 28일 오후 6시부터 10시까지 하이 링곤 호텔에서 열리는 시상식 연회에서 수상자가 발표된다고 말하는 문장 다음에 이어지는 [3]에 들어가는 것이 가장 적절합니다.

Questions 164-167 refer to the following article.

164-167 기사

CRESTWOOD (March 22)— **164**A pipe on the top floor of the Crestwood Theater burst open on Wednesday morning, causing flooding that soaked the antique wood flooring and several interior walls. Nathan Therriault, a spokesperson for Gilliam Associates, which owns and operates the historic theater building, said the issue was discovered when a maintenance team arrived to perform routine cleaning. Mr. Therriault said that given the considerable damage, **165**Gilliam Associates is already in the process of selecting a company to tackle the repairs.

"The Crestwood Theater is one of our town's treasures, so we are committed to maintaining the beauty and character of the original interior as we plan for this restoration work," Mr. Therriault said. He added that he is hopeful the theater will be able to reopen for the autumn/winter performance season.

Crestwood Theater staff are now determining whether the performances slated for the spring and summer will be postponed or canceled entirely. **166**The theater had been seeing unprecedented levels of attendance since hiring a new artistic director who began a strong outreach campaign in the local community. Many performance dates were already sold out.

크레스트우드 (3월 22일) – **164**수요일 아침 크레스트우드 극장의 최상층 배관이 갑자기 터지면서 물이 넘쳐 고풍스러운 나무 바닥과 내벽 몇 개가 흠뻑 젖었다. 이 유서 깊은 극장 건물을 소유하고 운영하는 길리엄 어소시에이츠의 대변인 네이선 테리얼트는 정비팀이 정기 청소를 하기 위해 도착했을 때 그 문제가 발견됐다고 말했다. 테리얼트 씨는 상당한 피해 상황을 감안해 **165**길리엄 어소시에이츠는 이미 수리 작업에 착수할 회사를 선정하는 과정에 있다고 말했다.

"크레스트우드 극장은 우리 도시의 보물 중 하나이므로 우리는 이 복구 작업을 계획하면서 원래 내부의 아름다움과 특징을 유지하는 데 전념하고 있습니다." 테리얼트 씨는 말했다. 그는 극장이 가늘/겨울 공연 시즌에 다시 개관할 수 있기를 바란다고 덧붙였다.

크레스트우드 극장 직원들은 지금 봄과 여름에 계획된 공연들을 연기할지 아니면 전면 취소할지 결정하고 있다. **166**지역 사회에 활발한 지원 활동을 시작한 신임 예술 감독을 채용한 이후 극장은 전례 없는 수준의 많은 관객을 보게 되었다. 많은 공연 날짜들이 이미 매진되었다. 제니스 머숀 극장 지배인은 공연에 대한 결정은 시간이 좀 걸린다며 입장

Theater manager Janice Mershon warned that decisions about the performances will take some time to make and [167]asked that ticket holders remain patient. When the schedule is finalized, the box office will contact ticket holders directly to issue new tickets or to make arrangements for full refunds, she said.

권 소지자들에게 참고 기다려 달라고 당부했다. 일정이 확정되면, [167]매표소에서 티켓 소지자들에게 직접 연락해 새 티켓을 지급하거나 전액 환불을 위한 조치를 할 것이라고 그녀는 말했다.

어휘 burst open 갑자기 터지다   soak 흠뻑 적시다   routine 정례적인   considerable 상당한   tackle 착수하다   repairs 수리 작업   treasure 보물   be committed to ~에 전념하다   maintain 유지하다   restoration 복구   determine 결정하다   slate 계획하다   postpone 연기하다   unprecedented 전례 없는   attendance 참석자 수, 참석률   outreach (지역 사회 대상) 지원 활동   patient 인내하는

164 What is one purpose of the article?

(A) To report on changes to a building's construction schedule

(B) To present historical facts about a building

(C) To describe recent damage to a building

(D) To provide information about a building's sale

기사의 한 가지 목적은?

(A) 건물의 공사 일정 변경을 알리려고

(B) 건물에 대한 역사적 사실을 제시하려고

(C) 최근의 건물 손상을 설명하려고

(D) 건물 매각 정보를 제공하려고

해설 주제 / 목적: 글의 목적이나 주제를 묻는 문제는 주로 서두에 단서가 나옵니다. 첫 문장에서 배관이 터져 나무 바닥과 내벽이 흠뻑 젖었다고 했고 이후 이 상황의 해결에 관련된 내용이 계속되고 있습니다. 따라서 정답은 (C)입니다.

165 What has Gilliam Associates begun to do?

(A) Search for a company to do restoration work

(B) Conduct a safety inspection

(C) Find an alternate space to host performances

(D) Increase the size of the maintenance team

길리엄 어소시에이츠가 하기 시작한 일은?

(A) 복구 작업을 할 업체 물색하기

(B) 안전 점검 실시하기

(C) 공연을 주최할 대체 공간 찾기

(D) 정비팀 규모 확대하기

해설 세부 사항: 지문에 길리엄 어소시에이츠라는 이름이 언급된 부분에서 정답의 단서를 찾아야 합니다. 첫 번째 단락 마지막 문장에서 Gilliam Associates가 수리 작업에 착수할 회사를 선정하는 과정에 있다고 했으므로 정답은 (A)입니다.

어휘 inspection 조사, 점검   alternate 대체하는

166 What is indicated about the Crestwood Theater?

(A) It is seeking a new artistic director.

(B) It is typically closed during the summer months.

(C) Its shows have become popular among Crestwood residents.

(D) Its ticket prices have been criticized for being too high.

크레스트우드 극장에 관해 명시된 것은?

(A) 새로운 예술 감독을 구하고 있다.

(B) 보통 여름철에는 문을 닫는다.

(C) 공연이 크레스트우드 주민들 사이에서 인기를 얻고 있다.

(D) 티켓 가격이 너무 비싸다는 비판을 받아 왔다.

해설 세부 사항: 세 번째 문단 두 번째 문장에서 활발한 지역 사회 지원 활동을 시작한 신임 예술감독 채용 후 극장이 전례 없는 수준의 많은 관객을 보게 되었다고 했습니다. 따라서 극장이 지역 주민에게 인기가 많다는 것을 알 수 있으므로 정답은 (C)입니다.

어휘 criticize 비판하다

167 According to the article, what are all ticket holders advised to do?

(A) Check the theater's Web site for updates

(B) E-mail the theater's management to request a refund

(C) Visit the box office to exchange their tickets

(D) Wait for a theater employee to contact them

기사에 따르면 모든 티켓 소지자가 하도록 권고받는 것은?

(A) 극장 홈페이지에서 최신 소식 확인하기

(B) 극장 경영진에게 이메일을 보내 환불 요청하기

(C) 매표소를 방문해 티켓 교환하기

(D) 극장 직원이 연락할 때까지 기다리기

> **해설** 세부 사항: 지문의 마지막 단락에서 티켓 소지자들에게 참고 기다려 달라고 하며 새 티켓 지급이나 환불을 위해 매표소에서 연락할 것(the box office will contact ticket holders)이라고 했으므로 정답은 (D)입니다.

> **Paraphrasing** 지문의 remain patient → 정답의 wait for
> 지문의 the box office will contact ticket holders → 정답의 a theater employee to contact them

---

Questions 168-171 refer to the following advertisement.

168-171 광고

Aiyar's Cleaning Services

One way of making your office look its best is by keeping your carpeting clean and bright. **168**Aiyar's Cleaning Services (ACS) is a full-service commercial carpet cleaning company. We use specialized equipment to remove dirt, dust, and stains from carpeting. **171**We can also clean area rugs and upholstery on chairs and sofas. We are experienced at handling cotton, wool, and synthetic fabrics. **169**Area rugs can be cleaned either at your facility or at ours.

To avoid disruption to your employees' schedules, our technicians can work after hours, overnight, or during weekends. They will move office furniture as needed and return everything back to its place when cleaning is complete.

Located in Troy, ACS serves businesses within the greater metropolitan area. **170** Visit our Web site at www.acs.com to get a price quote or to schedule an appointment. To speak with a customer service agent about special service requests, call us at 555-0101. New customers receive a ten percent discount on their first service.

아이야르 청소 서비스

사무실을 최고 상태로 보이게 만드는 한 가지 방법은 카펫을 깨끗하고 밝게 유지하는 것입니다. **168**아이야르 청소 서비스(ACS)는 풀 서비스 상업용 카펫 청소 전문 업체입니다. 저희는 카펫에서 흙, 먼지, 얼룩을 제거하기 위해 특수 장비를 사용합니다. **171**또한 작은 러그와 의자나 소파의 커버도 청소할 수 있습니다. 저희는 면, 양모, 합성 직물을 다룬 경험이 풍부합니다. **169**작은 러그는 고객님 시설에서든 저희 시설에서든 청소할 수 있습니다.

직원들의 일정에 방해가 되지 않도록 저희 기술자들은 근무 시간 이후, 야간 또는 주말에 일할 수 있습니다. 그들은 필요에 따라 사무용 가구를 옮기고 청소가 끝나면 모두 제자리에 놓려놓을 것입니다.

트로이에 위치한 ACS는 대도시권 내의 기업들에 서비스를 제공합니다. **170**저희 웹사이트 www.acs.com을 방문해 가격 견적을 받거나 예약 일정을 잡으십시오. 특별 서비스 요청 건으로 고객 서비스 담당자에게 통화하시려면 555-0101로 전화하십시오. 신규 고객은 첫 서비스 시 10퍼센트를 할인 받습니다.

> **어휘** specialized 특수한 equipment 장비 remove 제거하다 dirt 흙(먼지) stain 얼룩 upholstery (소파 등의) 커버 avoid 피하다 disruption 방해 quote 견적(서) appointment 약속

168 According to the advertisement, what is one service ACS provides?

(A) Carpet repair

(B) Trash removal

(C) Window washing

(D) Furniture cleaning

광고에 따르면 ACS가 제공하는 한 가지 서비스는?

(A) 카펫 수선

(B) 쓰레기 치우기

(C) 창문 세척

(D) 가구 청소

> **해설** 세부 사항: 첫 번째 단락 두 번째 문장에서 아이야르 청소 서비스(ACS)는 상업용 카펫 청소 전문 업체라고 소개했으므로 정답은 (D)입니다.

> **어휘** trash 쓰레기   removal 치우기

169 What is mentioned about area rugs?

(A) They can be moved offsite for cleaning.

(B) They are more durable than carpeting.

(C) They are easier to clean than carpeting.

(D) They require the use of special chemical cleaners.

작은 러그에 관해 언급된 것은?

(A) 청소를 위해 외부로 옮길 수 있다.

(B) 카펫보다 내구성이 좋다.

(C) 카펫보다 청소하기 쉽다.

(D) 특수 화학 세정제를 사용해야 한다.

> **해설** Not / True: 첫 번째 단락 마지막 문장에서 작은 러그는 고객의 시설이나 ACS의 시설에서 청소할 수 있다고 했으므로 정답은 (A)입니다.

> **Paraphrasing** 지문의 can be cleaned ~ at ours → 정답의 can be moved offsite for cleaning

> **어휘** durable 내구성이 좋은

170 According to the advertisement, why might customers want to visit the ACS Web site?

(A) To file a complaint

(B) To find an office location

(C) To obtain a cost estimate

(D) To read customer reviews

광고에 따르면, 고객들이 ACS 웹사이트를 방문하려는 이유는?

(A) 불만을 제기하려고

(B) 사무실 위치를 찾으려고

(C) 비용 견적을 얻으려고

(D) 고객 리뷰를 읽으려고

> **해설** 세부 사항: 광고의 세 번째 단락에서 업체 웹사이트를 방문해 가격 견적을 받거나 예약 일정을 잡으라고 했으므로 정답은 (C)입니다.

> **Paraphrasing** 지문의 to get a price quote → 정답의 To obtain a cost estimate

> **어휘** estimate 견적(서)

171 In which of the positions marked [1], [2], [3], and [4] does the following sentence best belong?

"We are experienced at handling cotton, wool, and synthetic fabrics."

(A) [1]

(B) [2]

(C) [3]

(D) [4]

[1], [2], [3], [4]로 표시된 곳 중에서 다음 문장이 들어가기에 가장 적합한 곳은?

"저희는 면, 양모, 합성 직물을 다룬 경험이 풍부합니다."

(A) [1]

(B) [2]

(C) [3]

(D) [4]

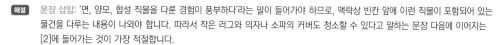

해설 문장 삽입: '면, 양모, 합성 직물을 다룬 경험이 풍부하다'라는 말이 들어가야 하므로, 맥락상 빈칸 앞에 이런 직물이 포함되어 있는 물건을 다루는 내용이 나와야 합니다. 따라서 작은 러그와 의자나 소파의 커버도 청소할 수 있다고 말하는 문장 다음에 이어지는 [2]에 들어가는 것이 가장 적절합니다.

어휘 experienced 경험이 풍부한 synthetic 합성의 fabric 직물

Questions 172-175 refer to the following online chat discussion.

Carlene Ramirez (11:02 A.M.)

172Regina and Alfonso, I need some help this afternoon. A school group is coming at 1:00, and I just found out that Charles Toskin is out with a cold.

Regina Marcum (11:04 A.M.)

Isn't Lydia available to take them around?

Carlene Ramirez (11:07 A.M.)

No. She's away at a conference. 173Can one of you fill in for Charles?

Alfonso Vesga (11:08 A.M.)

172,173Since my specialty is modern photography, I'm not sure I feel comfortable discussing Impressionist painting. Regina, you have knowledge in that field, right?

Regina Marcum (11:09 A.M.)

Actually, I deal mostly with Renaissance painting. 174I am familiar enough with the Impressionists, though. I could talk about them.

Carlene Ramirez (11:11 A.M.)

174Looks like we've got it covered then. The group plans to eat in the café and then gather in the first-floor lobby at 1:00.

Regina Marcum (11:12 A.M.)

I'll meet them there and show them the Impressionist collection. After that, I'll bring them to the Asian sculpture exhibit for you to take over, Carlene.

Carlene Ramirez (11:14 A.M.)

175Great, Regina. I'll let you get back to work. Alfonso, I'll bring the students to you around 4:00.

Alfonso Vesga (11:15 A.M.)

Sounds good, Carlene.

172-175 온라인 채팅

칼린 라미레스 (오전 11:02)

172레지나, 알폰소, 오늘 오후에 도움이 필요해요. 학생 단체가 1시에 오는데 찰스 토스킨이 감기로 자리에 없는 걸 방금 알았어요.

레지나 마컴 (오전 11:04)

리디아가 그들을 안내할 시간이 없나요?

칼린 라미레스 (오전 11:07)

아니요. 콘퍼런스에 가서 외부에 있어요. 173당신들 중에 한 명이 찰스를 대신해줄 수 있나요?

알폰소 베스가 (오전 11:08)

172,173제 전공은 현대 사진이라, 인상주의 회화를 편안하게 논할지 모르겠어요. 레지나, 그 분야에 지식이 있죠, 그렇죠?

레지나 마컴 (오전 11:09)

사실은 저는 주로 르네상스 회화를 다뤄요. 174그래도 인상주의 화가들도 웬만큼은 알아요. 그들에 대해 얘기할 수는 있을 거예요.

칼린 라미레스 (오전 11:11)

174그럼 그건 해결된 것 같네요. 그 단체는 카페에서 식사한 뒤 1시에 1층 로비에서 모일 계획이에요.

레지나 마컴 (오전 11:12)

제가 그들을 거기서 맞이하고 인상주의 화가 소장품을 보여줄게요. 그런 다음 당신이 넘겨받도록 아시아 조각 전시회로 데려갈게요, 칼린.

칼린 라미레스 (오전 11:14)

175좋아요, 레지나. 제가 다시 일하러 가게 해줄게요. 알폰소, 제가 학생들을 4시쯤에 데려다줄게요.

알폰소 베스가 (오전 11:15)

좋아요, 칼린.

어휘 fill in for ~을 대신하다 comfortable 편안한 familiar with ~을 잘 아는 sculpture 조각 exhibit 전시(회) take over 넘겨받다

172 Who most likely is Ms. Ramirez?

(A) A university professor
(B) A professional photographer
(C) A museum educator
(D) A conference organizer

라미레스 씨는 누구이겠는가?
(A) 대학 교수
(B) 전문 사진가
(C) 박물관 교육자
(D) 회의 주관자

해설 추론: 11시 02분에 라미레스 씨가 학생 단체가 오는데 찰스 토스킨이 결근이라며 도와 달라고 하자 11시 08분에 베스가 씨가 인상주의 회화를 편안하게 논할지 모르겠다고 대답했습니다. 따라서 이들은 미술관이나 박물관 종사자라는 것을 알 수 있으므로 정답은 (C)입니다.

173 What most likely is Mr. Toskin's area of specialization?

(A) Asian sculpture
(B) Renaissance painting
(C) Impressionist painting
(D) Modern photography

토스킨 씨의 전문 분야는?
(A) 아시아 조각
(B) 르네상스 회화
(C) 인상주의 회화
(D) 현대 사진

해설 추론: 11시 07분에 라미레스 씨가 찰스 (토스킨)을 대신해줄 수 있는지 묻자 11시 08분에 베스가 씨가 인상주의 회화를 편안하게 논할지 모르겠다고 대답했습니다. 따라서 토스킨 씨의 전문 분야는 인상주의 회화임을 유추할 수 있으므로 정답은 (C)입니다.

174 At 11:11 A.M., what does Ms. Ramirez most likely mean when she writes, "Looks like we've got it covered then"?

(A) She understands Mr. Vesga's concern.
(B) She accepts Ms. Marcum's offer.
(C) She knows why an exhibit is closed.
(D) She plans to pay for a group's admission.

오전 11시 11분에, 라미레스 씨가 "그럼 그건 해결된 것 같네요"라고 쓸 때 의미하는 것은?
(A) 베스가 씨의 걱정을 이해한다.
(B) 마컴 씨의 제안을 받아들인다.
(C) 전시회가 문을 닫은 이유를 안다.
(D) 단체의 입장료를 지불할 계획이다.

해설 의도 파악: 라미제스 씨의 말은 11시 09분에 마컴 씨가 인상주의 화가들도 웬만큼 알아서 그들에 대해 얘기할 수 있겠다고 한 말에 대한 대답입니다. 따라서 마컴 씨가 토스킨 씨 대신 설명하는 것으로 결정한다는 의미로 한 말이므로 정답은 (B)입니다.

175 What will Ms. Marcum most likely do next?

(A) Call Ms. Ramirez for advice
(B) Return to her usual duties
(C) Go to the lobby to wait
(D) Eat lunch in the café

마컴 씨는 다음에 무엇을 하겠는가?
(A) 라미레스 씨에게 전화해 조언을 구한다
(B) 평상시 업무로 복귀한다
(C) 대기하러 로비로 가기
(D) 카페에서 점심 먹기

해설 추론: 11시 14분에 라미레스 씨가 레지나 (마컴)에게 자신이 학생들을 넘겨받아 다시 일하러 가게 해주겠다고 했으므로 정답은 (B)입니다.

Paraphrasing 지문의 get back to work → 정답의 return to her usual duties

교재 p.296

Questions 176-180 refer to the following e-mails.

176-180 이메일 + 이메일

To: [177]Rita May
From: Jason Woyimo
Date: September 13, 10:20 A.M.
Subject: Request for information

Hello Ms. May,

Could you provide me with some information, please? [176]I just had a call from Ms. Linda Bandasack with the Kirkwood Corporation. [177,179]She wants to place an order for 1,000 fine-point gel pens but is unable to reach Christopher Warren, her assigned sales representative here at Executive Stationery, Inc. I was unable to find his name in our employee database, possibly suggesting that Mr. Warren has left the company. [177]I happened to come across an organizational chart, though, that indicates that Mr. Warren reports to you. With this in mind, and so that I can provide Ms. Bandasack with the correct information, can you confirm that Mr. Warren has left the company, and if so, which sales representative is now serving his clientele?

Thanks,

Jason Woyimo
Customer Service Specialist
Executive Stationery, Inc.

수신: [177]리타 메이
발신: 제이슨 워이모
날짜: 9월 13일, 오전 10:20
제목: 정보 요청

안녕하세요, 메이 씨,

저한테 정보를 좀 주시겠어요? [176]방금 커크우드 사 린다 반다삭 씨의 전화를 받았어요. [177,179]그녀는 심아 가는 젤펜 1,000개를 주문하려고 하는데, 그녀에게 배정된 이그제큐티브 문구사의 이곳 영업 담당자인 크리스토퍼 워런과 연락이 닿지 않는다고 합니다. 제가 직원 데이터베이스에서 그의 이름을 찾을 수 없는 걸 보니 아마도 워런 씨가 퇴사한 것 같아요. [177]그런데 우연히 조직도를 발견했는데, 워런 씨가 당신의 부하 직원으로 나와 있네요. 이 점을 염두에 두고, 제가 반다삭 씨에게 정확한 정보를 제공할 수 있도록 워런 씨가 퇴사했는지, 만약 그렇다면 지금은 어떤 영업 담당자가 그의 고객들을 돕고 있는지 확인해 주시겠어요?

감사합니다.

제이슨 워이모
고객 서비스 전담 직원
이그제큐티브 문구사

어휘 unable to ~할 수 없는 reach 연락하다 assign 배정하다 representative 담당자 clientele 고객들, 의뢰인들

To: linda.bandasack@kirkwoodcorp.com
From: kgrainer@esi.com
Date: September 13, 1:04 P.M.
Subject: Your order

Hello Ms. Bandasack,

[178]My name is Kenyatta Grainer, and I am a sales representative from Executive Stationery, Inc. (ESI). I understand that you have been trying to contact Mr. Warren. Please note that Mr. Warren

수신: linda.bandasack@kirkwoodcorp.com
발신: kgrainer@esi.com
날짜: 9월 13일, 오후 1:04
제목: 귀하의 주문

안녕하세요, 반다삭 씨,

[178]제 이름은 케냐타 그레이너이고 저는 이그제큐티브 문구 사(ESI) 영업 담당자입니다. 워런 씨에게 연락하려고 애쓰셨다고 알고 있습니다. 워런 씨는

retired from our company on September 1. [178]I have been assigned his clients and will do my utmost to provide you with the same excellent service he provided to you.

I have been informed about your order. According to the information I have, [179,180]you are looking to place the same order as last year. Can you verify that this is correct?

Please feel free to contact me by e-mail or telephone at any time. I look forward to a long, successful business relationship with you.

Sincerely,

Kenyatta Grainer
Sales Representative
Executive Stationery, Inc.
Phone: 416-555-0149
E-mail: kgrainer@esi.com

9월 1일 회사에서 퇴사하셨다는 것을 유의하십시오. [178]제가 그의 고객들을 배정받았으며, 그가 제공해드렸던 것과 똑같은 훌륭한 서비스를 제공해드리기 위해 최선을 다하겠습니다.

고객님의 주문에 대해 들었습니다. 제가 갖고 있는 정보에 따르면, [179,180]고객님은 지난해와 같이 주문하려고 하신다고요. 이것이 맞는지 확인해 주시겠어요?

언제든지 제 이메일이나 전화로 연락하십시오. 고객님과 오랫동안 성공적인 거래 관계를 유지하기를 고대합니다.

케냐타 그레이너
영업 담당자
이그제큐티브 문구사
전화: 416-555-0149
이메일: kgrainer@esi.come

어휘 do one's utmost 최선을 다하다   verify 확인하다

176 According to the first e-mail, what is Ms. Bandasack's problem?

(A) She cannot find ESI's organizational chart.
(B) She cannot get access to some reports.
(C) She cannot place an order online.
(D) She cannot contact a sales agent.

첫 번째 이메일에 따르면, 반다삭 씨의 문제는?

(A) ESI의 조직도를 찾을 수 없다.
(B) 일부 보고서에 접근할 수 없다.
(C) 온라인으로 주문할 수 없다.
(D) 영업 직원에게 연락할 수 없다.

해설 세부 사항: 두 번째와 세 번째 문장에서 반다삭 씨가 젤펜을 주문하려는데 배정된 영업 담당자와 연락이 닿지 않는 문제가 있다고 했으므로 정답은 (D)입니다.

Paraphrasing 지문의 reach Christopher Warren, her assigned sales representative → 정답의 contact a sales agent

어휘 get access to ~에 접근하다

177 What most likely is Ms. May's role at ESI?

(A) Recruiter
(B) Sales manager
(C) Database administrator
(D) Product designer

ESI에서 메이 씨의 역할은?

(A) 채용 담당자
(B) 영업부장
(C) 데이터베이스 관리자
(D) 제품 디자이너

해설 추론: 메이 씨는 이메일의 수신자임을 확인합니다. 첫 번째 메일의 세 번째 문장에서 워런 씨는 ESI의 영업 담당자라고 했고 지문 후반부에서 워런 씨가 메이 씨의 부하 직원이라고 했습니다. 따라서 메이 씨는 영업부장임을 알 수 있으므로 정답은 (B)입니다.

어휘 administrator 관리자

178 What is a reason why Ms. Grainer contacted Ms. Bandasack?

(A) To introduce herself

(B) To inform her of a policy change

(C) To ask her for her contact information

(D) To thank her for being a loyal customer

그레이너 씨가 반다삭 씨에게 연락한 이유는?

(A) 자신을 소개하려고

(B) 방침 변경을 통보하려고

(C) 연락처를 문의하려고

(D) 충성 고객이 되어준 것에 감사를 표하려고

해설 세부 사항: 그레이너 씨가 반다삭 씨에게 보낸 두 번째 이메일의 첫 번째 단락에서 그레이너 씨는 자신이 영업 담당자(sales representative)라고 소개한 후, 워런 씨 고객을 배정받았고 훌륭한 서비스 제공을 위해 최선을 다하겠다고 했습니다. 따라서 정답은 (A)입니다.

179 What is suggested about Ms. Bandasack?

(A) She wanted to find an affordable supply company.

(B) She ordered 1,000 pens the previous year.

(C) She regularly met with Mr. Warren.

(D) She was contacted by Ms. May.

반다삭 씨에 관해 시사되는 것은?

(A) 가격이 적당한 납품업체를 찾고 싶어했다.

(B) 지난해에 펜 1,000개를 주문했다.

(C) 워런 씨를 주기적으로 만났다.

(D) 메이 씨가 그녀에게 연락했다.

해설 연계: 첫 번째 이메일의 첫 번째 단락에서 반다삭 씨는 1,000개의 젤 펜을 주문하려고 한다고 했습니다. 두 번째 이메일의 두 번째 단락에서 반다삭 씨가 지난해와 같이 주문하려고 한다(you are looking to place the same order as last year)는 언급이 있으므로 정답은 (B)입니다.

어휘 affordable 가격이 적당한 previous 이전의

180 What is Ms. Bandasack asked to do?

(A) Comment on ESI's service

(B) Assign a different representative

(C) Confirm the accuracy of an order

(D) Send Mr. Warren a thank-you note

반다삭 씨가 하도록 요청받은 일은?

(A) ESI 서비스에 관해 의견 말하기

(B) 다른 담당자 배정하기

(C) 주문이 정확한지 확인하기

(D) 워런 씨에게 감사 편지 보내기

해설 세부 사항: 두 번째 이메일의 후반부에서 반다삭 씨에게 지난해와 같이 주문하려 하는 것이 맞는지 확인해 달라고 요청하고 있으므로 정답은 (C)입니다.

Paraphrasing 지문의 verify that this is correct → 정답의 Confirm the accuracy of an order

어휘 accuracy 정확(성)

Questions 181-185 refer to the following memo and article.

MEMO

From: Anja Biermann, CEO

To: All Stamitz Group Employees

Date: June 6

Subject: Company honored

181-185 회람 + 기사

발신: 안자 비에르만, 최고 경영자

수신: 슈타미츠 그룹 전 직원

날짜: 6월 6일

제목: 회사 수상

[181]I am pleased to announce that on June 4 the National Federation of Civil Engineers (NFCE) awarded its highest honor, the Platinum Engineering Achievement Award, to the Stamitz Group. Our success is the outcome of the hard work you have done over the last few years. [181,184]I know that some of you were skeptical about our move into the business of designing apartment complexes, given our longtime reputation as designers of office buildings. [182]This acknowledgment clearly shows the value of business diversification.

On June 30, the NFCE will be holding an awards banquet, where I will formally accept the award. Since most employees will not be able to attend that event, [183]we will hold a reception at our headquarters on June 22. An invitation for this gathering will be sent later today. Please respond to the invitation by June 15 so that we know how many people plan to attend.

[181]6월 4일 전국 토목기사 연맹(NFCE)이 스타미츠 그룹에 최고 영예인 플래티넘 엔지니어링 공로상을 수여했음을 발표하게 되어 기쁩니다. 우리의 성공은 지난 몇 년 동안 여러분이 열심히 일한 결과입니다. [181]사무용 빌딩 설계 업체로서 우리의 오랜 명성을 감안할 때, [184]우리가 아파트 단지 설계 사업으로 진출한 것에 회의적인 분들도 있었다는 것을 알고 있습니다. [182]이번에 인정 받은 건 사업 다각화의 가치를 여실히 보여줍니다.

6월 30일, NFCE가 시상식 연회를 열 예정인데, 제가 그곳에서 정식으로 상을 받을 것입니다. 대부분의 직원은 그 행사에 참석할 수 없기 때문에, [183]6월 22일 본사에서 축하연을 열 예정입니다. 오늘 늦게 모임 초대장이 발송됩니다. 몇 명이나 참석할 계획인지 알 수 있도록 6월 15일까지 초대장에 응답해 주시기 바랍니다.

> **어휘**　civil engineer 토목기사　achievement award 공로상　outcome 결과　skeptical 회의적인　reputation 명성
> acknowledgment 인정　diversification 다각화

NFCE Announces Awards
By Zulfiqar Nawaz

June 10—The National Federation of Civil Engineers (NFCE) has announced the winners of its annual Engineering Achievement Awards. [184]It bestowed its highest honor, the Platinum Award, to the Stamitz Group, which received glowing praise for its work on the Venice Tower building in downtown Kayleb City. The Stamitz Group had been expected to win the award last year for its design of the new headquarters of Helios Bank; however, the award went to MCL Contractors, a well-known architectural firm that designs department stores.

The NFCE Awards are different from other engineering awards in that their focus is not on innovation. [185]"Our evaluation of a structure is solely based on its longevity," said NFCE president Laura Fordham. "We are keenly interested in the materials used and features added that will result in the long-term existence of an architectural work. Thus, the structures we honor are not necessarily the ones that are most eye-catching or trendy;

NFCE, 수상자 발표
줄피카르 나와즈

6월 10일–전국 토목기사 연맹(NFCE)이 연례 엔지니어링 공로상 수상자를 발표했다. [184]최고 영예인 플래티넘 상은 카일렙 시 중심가에 있는 베니스 타워 빌딩 작업으로 극찬을 받은 스타미츠 그룹에 수여했다. 스타미츠 그룹은 지난해 헬리오스 은행 본점 신사옥 설계로 그 상을 받으리라 예상되었지만, 상은 백화점을 설계하는 유명 건축 회사인 MCL 컨트랙터즈에게 돌아갔다.

NFCE 상은 혁신에 중점을 두지 않는다는 점에서 다른 엔지니어링 상과 다르다. [185]로라 포드햄 NFCE 회장은 "구조물에 대한 우리의 평가는 오로지 수명에만 근거를 둡니다"라고 말했다. "우리는 사용된 자재와 추가된 기능이 건축 작품의 장기적인 생존으로 이어질지에 지대한 관심을 둡니다. 따라서 우리가 영예를 주는 구조물은 반드시 가장 눈길을 끌거나 최신 유행을 좇는 구조물만은 아닙니

rather, they are the ones we believe are more likely to still be standing in one hundred years' time."

다. 오히려 100년 후에도 여전히 서 있을 가능성이 높다고 우리가 믿는 구조물들입니다."

어휘 bestow 주다 architectural 건축의 evaluation 평가 longevity 수명 keenly interested 지대한 관심을 두는 existence 생존 not necessarily 반드시 ~는 아니다 eye-catching 눈길을 끄는

181 What kind of business most likely is the Stamitz Group?

(A) An investment bank

(B) An architectural firm

(C) A department store

(D) A software engineering firm

스타미츠 그룹은 어떤 종류의 업체이겠는가?

(A) 투자 은행

(B) 건축 회사

(C) 백화점

(D) 소프트웨어 엔지니어링 회사

해설 추론: 첫 번째 지문의 첫 문장에서 전국 토목기사 연맹이 스타미츠 그룹에 플래티넘 엔지니어링 공로상을 수여했다고 했고 세 번째 문장에서 사무용 빌딩 설계 업체(designers of office buildings)라고 언급했으므로 정답은 (B)입니다.

182 In the memo, the word "acknowledgment" in paragraph 1, line 7, is closest in meaning to

(A) contract

(B) example

(C) admission

(D) recognition

회람에서 1번째 단락 7행의 'acknowledgment'와 의미상 가장 가까운 것은?

(A) 계약

(B) 사례

(C) 입장

(D) 인정

해설 동의어 찾기: 지문의 This acknowledgment clearly shows the value에서 acknowledgment는 '인정, 승인'이라는 의미이므로 '인정, 인식'이라는 의미의 (D) recognition이 정답입니다.

183 When will an event be held at the office of the Stamitz Group?

(A) On June 4

(B) On June 15

(C) On June 22

(D) On June 30

스타미츠 그룹 사무실에서는 언제 행사가 열리는가?

(A) 6월 4일

(B) 6월 15일

(C) 6월 22일

(D) 6월 30일

해설 세부 사항: 회람의 두 번째 단락 두 번째 문장에서 6월 22일 본사에서 축하연을 열 예정이라고 했으므로 정답은 (C)입니다.

184 What is most likely the primary use of Venice Tower?

(A) Residential

(B) Medical

(C) Governmental

(D) Cultural

베니스 타워의 주된 용도는?

(A) 거주지

(B) 의료

(C) 정부

(D) 문화

해설 연계: 회람 첫 번째 단락에서 스타미츠 그룹이 아파트 단지 설계 사업으로 진출했고 이 사업으로 인정을 받았다고 했습니다. 기사 첫 단락의 두 번째 문장에서 플래티넘 상은 베니스 타워를 작업한 스타미츠 그룹에 수여했다고 했으므로 베니스 타워가 아파트 단지임을 유추할 수 있습니다. 따라서 정답은 (A)입니다.

185 According to the article, what does the NFCE look for in a building?

(A) Durability

(B) Profitability

(C) Stylishness

(D) Innovation

기사에 따르면 NFCE가 건물에서 찾는 것은?

(A) 내구성

(B) 수익성

(C) 멋스러움

(D) 혁신

[해설] 세부 사항: 기사 두 번째 단락의 두 번째 문장에서 NFCE 회장은 구조물의 평가는 수명에만 근거를 둔다고 했으므로 정답은 (A)입니다.

[Paraphrasing] 지문의 longevity → 정답의 Durability

Questions 186-190 refer to the following brochure and e-mails.

186-190 안내 책자 + 이메일 + 이메일

186Stony Hill Museum of Art (SHMA) Yearly Membership Levels

Student Membership: For full-time students of any age with a current student identification. $30.00

Individual Membership: Includes one guest pass. $50.00

Dual Membership: For two adults living in the same household. Includes two guest passes. $70.00

185Family Membership: For two adults and up to four children. Includes four guest passes and priority registration for children's summer camps. $90.00

Contributor Membership: Includes four guest passes, two museum posters, and early admission to all exhibitions. $110.00

187Sustainer Membership: Includes all the benefits of the contributor membership plus complimentary single admission to over 1,000 museums in the United States. $250.00

186All membership levels include unlimited admission to SHMA, invitations to members-only programs, a 10 percent discount at the Museum Shop and Café, and a free subscription to the SHMA newsletter. To purchase or renew a membership, please fill out the from at www.shma.org/membership. If you have questions, send an e-mail to the museum's member services coordinator, Jeff Hill, at jhill@shma.org or call him at 518-555-0158.

186스토니 힐 미술관 (SHMA) 연간 회원 단계

학생 회원: 현재 학생증이 있는 모든 연령의 정규 학생. $30.00

개인 회원: 손님 1인 무료 입장 포함. $50.00

2인 회원: 한 집에 사는 성인 2인. 손님 2인 무료 입장 포함. $70.00

188가족 회원: 한 집에 사는 성인 2인과 자녀 최대 4인까지. 손님 4인 무료 입장 및 어린이 여름 캠프 우선 등록 포함. $90.00

기여자 회원: 손님 4인 무료 입장, 미술관 포스터 2장, 모든 전시회 조기 입장. $110.00

187지지자 회원: 기여자 회원의 모든 혜택에 미국 내 1,000여 개 미술관 1회 무료 입장 추가. $250.00

186회원 전체 단계에 SHMA 무제한 입장, 회원 전용 프로그램 초대, 미술관 숍 앤드 카페 10퍼센트 할인, SHMA 소식지 무료 구독이 포함됩니다. 회원권 구매나 갱신은 www.shma.org/membership에서 양식을 작성해주십시오. 문의 사항이 있으시면 미술관 회원 서비스 코디네이터, 제프 힐에게 jhill@shma.org로 이메일을 보내거나 518-555-0158로 전화하십시오.

어휘 identification 신분증 priority 우선(권) contributor 기여자 sustainer 떠받치는 사람, 지지자 benefit 혜택 complimentary 무료의 subscription 구독 purchase 구매하다; 구매(품)

To: Jeff Hill <jhill@shma.org>
188 From: Nadia Amari <namari@thrumail.com>
Date: December 10
Subject: Membership

Dear Mr. Hill,

My current membership at SHMA expires at the end of the month and is set up for automatic renewal. **188** However, I want to upgrade my dual membership to the next level, which includes priority registration for summer camps, but I am unable to do so on your Web site. I cannot figure out how to pay the additional cost for the upgrade. I called your number, and the automated system immediately transferred me to voice mail. I left a message on December 5, but my call has not been returned. Please let me know how to proceed. **190**I want to resolve this issue before the beginning of January, when the special exhibition of Marco Stellitano's work opens.

Thank you,

Nadia Amari

수신: 제프 힐 〈jhill@shma.org〉
188발신: 나디아 아마리 〈namari@thrumail.com〉
날짜: 12월 10일
제목: 회원권

힐 씨께,

현재 제 SHMA 회원권이 이달 말에 만료되어 자동 갱신 예정입니다. **188**하지만 저는 제 2인 회원권을 여름 캠프 우선 등록이 포함된 다음 단계로 업그레이드하고 싶습니다. 그런데 미술관 웹사이트에서 그렇게 할 수가 없네요. 업그레이드를 위한 추가 비용을 어떻게 지불해야 할지 모르겠습니다. 당신의 번호로 전화를 걸었더니 자동 시스템이 즉시 음성 메일로 전환됐습니다. 12월 5일에 메시지를 남겼는데, 아직 답신 전화가 안 왔어요. 어떻게 진행해야 하는지 알려주세요. **190**마르코 스텔리타노 작품 특별 전시회가 열리는 1월이 시작되기 전에 이 문제를 해결하고 싶습니다.

감사합니다.

나디아 아마리

어휘 expire 만료되다 renewal 갱신 figure out 알아내다 additional 추가의 immediately 즉시 proceed 진행하다 resolve 해결하다

To: Nadia Amari <namari@thrumail.com>
From: Jeff Hill <jhill@shma.org>
Date: December 12
Subject: RE: Membership

Dear Ms. Amari,

Thank you for contacting me regarding your membership. To upgrade to the next membership level, you will need to stop your automatic payment and then reenroll at the next level. This can be done online or over the phone with me at 518-555-0158.

수신: 나디아 아마리 〈namari@thrumail.com〉
발신: 제프 힐 〈jhill@shma.org〉
날짜: 12월 12일
제목: Re: 회원권

아마리 씨께,

회원권 관련해 연락 주셔서 감사합니다. 다음 회원권 단계로 업그레이드하려면 자동 결제를 중지하고 다음 단계에 다시 등록해야 합니다. 온라인으로 하셔도 되고 518-555-0158번으로 저에게 전화 주셔서 함께 하셔도 됩니다.

Please accept my apologies for the difficulty you experienced. **189**I was out of the office for a week, and, unfortunately, I neglected to forward my messages to another staff member. As a token of our appreciation for your understanding, **190**we will be sending you a coffee mug that has a painting from our special exhibition opening on January 1.

Please let me know if I can be of further assistance.

Sincerely,

Jeff Hill, Member Services Coordinator
Stony Hill Museum of Art

고객님이 겪으신 어려움에 대해 사과 드립니다. **189**제가 일주일 동안 사무실을 비웠는데, 안타깝게도 제게 오는 메시지를 다른 직원에게 자동 전송시키는 것을 잊어버렸습니다. 양해해 주신 것에 대한 감사 표시로, **190**1월 1일 개막하는 특별 전시회에 나오는 그림이 있는 커피 머그잔을 보내드리겠습니다.

제가 더 도와드릴 일이 있으면 알려주십시오.

제프 힐, 회원 서비스 코디네이터
스토니 힐 미술관

어휘 reenroll 다시 등록하다 unfortunately 안타깝게도 neglect (할 일을) 잊어버리다 as a token of ~의 표시로 appreciation 감사

186 What is included with an SHMA student membership?

(A) A museum guest pass
(B) Discounts on museum programs
(C) Unlimited museum admission
(D) A museum poster

SHMA 학생 회원권에 포함되는 것은?

(A) 미술관 손님 1인 무료 입장
(B) 미술관 프로그램 할인
(C) 미술관 무제한 입장
(D) 미술관 포스터

해설 세부 사항: 안내 책자 제목에서 스토니 힐 미술관(SHMA) 회원권에 대한 내용임을 확인합니다. 마지막 단락에서 회원 전체 단계에 SHMA 무제한 입장을 확인할 수 있으므로 정답은 (C)입니다.

187 How much is an SHMA membership that includes free entry to other museums?

(A) $70
(B) $90
(C) $110
(D) $250

다른 미술관 무료 입장권이 포함되는 SHMA 회원권은 얼마인가?

(A) 70달러
(B) 90달러
(C) 110달러
(D) 250달러

해설 세부 사항: 안내 책자 후반부 지지자 회원란에서 250달러로 미국 내 1,000여 개 미술관 1회 무료 입장 추가를 확인할 수 있으므로 정답은 (D)입니다.

188 What membership level does Ms. Amari want to purchase?

(A) Individual
(B) Family
(C) Contributor
(D) Sustainer

아마리 씨는 어떤 단계 회원권을 구매하고 싶어하는가?

(A) 개인
(B) 가족
(C) 기여자
(D) 지지자

해설 연계: 아마리 씨가 보낸 첫 번째 이메일 두 번째 문장에서 2인 회원권을 여름 캠프 우선 등록이 포함된 다음 단계로 업그레이드하고 싶다고 했습니다. 안내 책자에서 가족 회원권이 어린이 여름 캠프 우선 등록을 포함하고 있으므로 정답은 (B)입니다.

189 According to the second e-mail, what did Mr. Hill forget to do?

(A) Have a coworker receive his messages

(B) Inform colleagues about his absence

(C) Stop Ms. Amari's automatic renewal

(D) Send a membership card to Ms. Amari

두 번째 이메일에 따르면 힐 씨가 깜박 잊고 하지 않은 일은?

(A) 동료 직원이 자신의 메시지를 받게 하기

(B) 직장 동료에게 결근 알리기

(C) 아마리 씨의 자동 갱신 중지하기

(D) 아마리 씨에게 회원증 보내기

해설 세부 사항: 두 번째 단락 두 번째 문장에서 사무실을 비우면서 자신에게 오는 메시지를 다른 직원에게 자동 전송시키는 것을 잊어버렸다고 했으므로 정답은 (A)입니다.

Paraphrasing 지문의 forward my messages to another staff member → 정답의 Have a coworker receive his messages

어휘 absence 결근

190 What is suggested about the coffee mug that Ms. Amari will receive?

(A) It is sold in the Museum Shop.

(B) It is being discontinued.

(C) It features a work by Mr. Stellitano.

(D) It holds more coffee than most mugs.

아마리 씨가 받게 될 커피 머그잔에 관해 시사되는 것은?

(A) 박물관 상점에서 판매한다.

(B) 생산이 중단될 것이다.

(C) 스텔리타노 씨의 작품이 들어 있다.

(D) 대부분의 머그잔보다 커피가 더 많이 담긴다.

해설 연계: 두 번째 이메일 두 번째 단락 마지막 문장에서 1월 1일 개막하는 특별 전시회에 나오는 그림이 있는 머그잔을 아마리 씨에게 보내주겠다고 했습니다. 첫 번째 이메일 마지막 문장에서 마르코 스텔리타노 작품 특별 전시회가 열리는 1월 전에 문제를 해결하고 싶다고 했으므로 커피 머그잔에 스텔리타노의 그림이 있다는 것을 유추할 수 있습니다. 따라서 정답은 (C)입니다.

어휘 discontinue (생산을) 중단하다

Questions 191-195 refer to the following article, e-mail, and invitation.

191-195 기사 + 이메일 + 초대장

Magazine Changes Chief

NEW YORK (January 21)—**194,195**It has just been announced that Rina Talbot will assume the editorial leadership of *Financial Age Magazine*. Her predecessor, Finn Cobb, made the announcement at a press conference this morning.

"I have full confidence that Ms. Talbot will continue to deliver the quality reporting on world financial markets that has made *Financial Age Magazine* as respected as it is today," Mr. Cobb said.

Ms. Talbot is no newcomer to the magazine. **191**In fact, she started there 22 years ago as a staff writer, filing numerous financial news stories from Asia. Later she was named to head the magazine's European bureau.

잡지, 편집장 교체

뉴욕 (1월 21일)—**194,195**리나 탤벗이 〈파이낸셜 에이지 매거진〉 편집장직을 맡게 된다고 방금 발표되었다. 전임자인 핀 콥이 오늘 아침 기자 회견에서 그렇게 발표했다.

저는 탤벗 씨가 〈파이낸셜 에이지 매거진〉이 오늘날처럼 높이 평가받게 만든 세계 금융 시장에 대한 수준 높은 보도를 계속 제공하리라 전적으로 확신합니다." 콥 씨가 말했다.

탤벗 씨는 이 잡지에 새로 온 사람이 아니다. **191**사실, 그녀는 22년 전 그곳에서 전속 기자로 출발해 아시아로부터 수많은 금융 보도 기사를 전송했다. 나중에 그녀는 그 잡지 유럽 지국장으로 임명되었다.

Kosuke Higa, chair of ASBI Media, which owns the magazine, said that he is sad to see Mr. Cobb leave. "For 25 years, Mr. Cobb has led the magazine to major success," Mr. Higa said. "However, I have complete confidence in Ms. Talbot's ability to build on his very successful record."

이 잡지를 소유하고 있는 ASBI 미디어 회장 코스케 히가는 콥 씨가 떠나는 것을 보게 되어 애석하다고 말했다. "25년 동안 콥 씨는 잡지를 크게 성공하도록 이끌었습니다."라고 히가 씨는 말했다. "하지만 저는 그의 아주 성공적인 기록을 토대로 성장할 능력이 탤벗 씨에게 있다고 전적으로 믿습니다."

> **어휘** assume 맡다 editorial 편집의 predecessor 전임자 press conference 기자 회견 confidence 확신 numerous 수많은 bureau 국

To: Finn Cobb
From: Kosuke Higa
Subject: Your career
Date: January 22

Dear Mr. Cobb,

We both know where *Financial Age Magazine* was 25 years ago and where it is today. **192,193**You led the publication through some very challenging periods, and I am proud to have witnessed your success. And now you are retiring. **194**I know that at first you were hesitant about the person selected to assume your role, so I was pleased to learn that you fully support this choice. This is deeply appreciated.

192 Soon you will be receiving an invitation to a celebration in honor of your work. We haven't informed the rest of the company yet, but I thought it appropriate for me to let you know in advance of the announcement. **195**In addition to inviting current employees and colleagues, we will also have a very special guest as the keynote speaker: your first supervisor at the magazine and the person who held this position before I did! It will be quite a night.

Yours,

Kosuke Higa

수신: 핀 콥
발신: 코스케 히가
제목: 당신의 커리어
날짜: 1월 22일

콥 씨께,

우리 두 사람 모두 〈파이낸셜 에이지 매거진〉이 25년 전 어디에 있었고, 오늘 어디에 있는지 알고 있습니다. **193**당신은 아주 힘든 시기에 이 출판물을 이끌었고 **192**저는 당신의 성공을 목격해 온 것을 자랑스럽게 생각합니다. 그리고 이제 은퇴하시네요. **194**당신의 역할을 맡도록 선발된 사람에 대해 처음에는 망설였다고 알고 있습니다. 그래서 당신이 이번 선택을 전적으로 지지한다는 것을 알게 되어 기뻤습니다. 그 점을 깊이 감사드립니다.

192곧 귀하의 업적을 기리는 축하 행사 초대장을 받으실 겁니다. 회사의 나머지 사람들에게는 아직 알리지 않았지만 발표 전에 당신에게 미리 알려드리는 게 적절하다고 생각했습니다. **195**현 직원과 동료를 초대하는 것 외에도 기조연설자로 아주 특별한 손님도 모십니다. 그 잡지에서 당신의 첫 번째 상사였고 저 이전에 이 직책에 있었던 분입니다! 근사한 저녁이 될 겁니다.

코스케 히가

> **어휘** publication 출판(물) witness 목격하다 retire 은퇴하다 hesitant 망설이는 appreciate 감사하다 celebration 축하 행사 in honor of ~을 축하하는 appropriate 적절한 supervisor 상사

You are cordially invited to a celebration in honor of Finn Cobb ¹⁹⁵**Keynote speaker**: Thomas Jean-Pierre **Date**: Friday, February 12 **Time**: 7:00 P.M. to 10:00 P.M. **Place**: Morvyn Manor, 787 Manor Drive Confirm your attendance by sending an e-mail to feb12rsvp@morvynmanor.com by February 5.	**핀 콥을 기념하는 축하 행사에 당신을 정중히 초대합니다** ¹⁹⁵기조연설자: 토머스 장-피에르. 날짜: 2월 12일 금요일 시간: 오후 7시에서 오후 10시 장소: 모빈 매너, 787 매너 드라이브 2월 5일까지 feb12rsvp@morvynmanor.com 으로 이메일을 보내셔서 참석 여부를 확인해 주십시오.

어휘 cordially 진심으로, 정중히 confirm 확인하다 attendance 참석, 출석

---

191 What does the article state about Ms. Talbot?

(A) She has written many articles for a magazine.

(B) She is responsible for issuing press releases.

(C) She will soon head a magazine's European office.

(D) She arrived late to a news conference.

기사에서 탤벗 씨에 관해 언급한 것은?

(A) 잡지에 기사를 많이 썼다.

(B) 보도 자료 발행을 책임지고 있다.

(C) 곧 잡지의 유럽 지국을 이끌 것이다.

(D) 기자 회견에 늦게 도착했다.

해설 Not / True: 세 번째 단락 두 번째 문장에서 22년 전 전속 기자로 출발해 수많은 금융 보도 기사를 전송했다고 했으므로 정답은 (A)입니다.

Paraphrasing 지문의 filing numerous financial news stories → 정답의 has written many articles

어휘 responsible for ~을 책임지는 press release 보도 자료

---

192 What is the purpose of the e-mail?

(A) To get advice on career development

(B) To respond to a question about an article

(C) To describe a change in business strategy

(D) To offer congratulations to an employee

이메일의 목적은?

(A) 커리어 개발에 대한 조언을 얻으려고

(B) 기사에 관한 질의에 응답하려고

(C) 사업 전략의 변화를 기술하려고

(D) 직원에게 축하 인사를 전하려고

해설 주제 / 목적: 첫 번째 단락 두 번째 문장에서 콥 씨의 성공을 목격해 온 것이 자랑스럽다고 했고 두 번째 단락 첫 문장에서 그의 업적을 기리는 축하 행사가 열린다고 언급했습니다. 따라서 정답은 (D)입니다.

---

193 In the e-mail, what does Mr. Higa note as one of Mr. Cobb's achievements?

(A) Hiring a number of successful editors

(B) Guiding a magazine through difficult times

(C) Expanding *Financial Age Magazine* to cover the global market

(D) Writing quality articles about Asian financial markets

이메일에서 히가 씨가 콥 씨의 업적 중 하나로 꼽은 것은?

(A) 수많은 성공한 편집자를 채용한 것

(B) 어려운 시기를 거치면서 잡지를 이끈 것

(C) 〈파이낸셜 에이지 매거진〉을 확장해 글로벌 시장을 취재한 것

(D) 아시아 금융 시장에 대한 수준 높은 기사를 작성한 것

해설 세부 사항: 첫 번째 단락 두 번째 문장에서 콤 씨가 아주 힘든 시기에 출판물을 이끌었고 성공했다고 했으므로 정답은 (B)입니다.

Paraphrasing 지문의 led the publication through some very challenging periods → 정답의 Guiding a magazine through difficult times

194 What made Mr. Cobb doubtful initially?

(A) The appointment of Ms. Talbot

(B) The choice of a place for a celebration

(C) The rapid growth of a magazine

(D) The plans for a new publication

처음에 콤 씨가 의구심을 갖게 한 것은?

(A) 탤벗 씨의 임명

(B) 축하 장소 선정

(C) 잡지의 빠른 성장

(D) 신간 계획

해설 연계: 이메일 첫 번째 단락 중반부에서 콤 씨가 처음에는 후임자로 선택된 사람에 대해 망설였다고 했습니다. 기사 첫 번째 단락에서 탤벗 씨가 편집장직을 맡게 되었고 전임자가 핀 콤이라는 내용을 확인할 수 있으므로 정답은 (A)입니다.

Paraphrasing 지문의 Rina Talbot will assume the editorial leadership → 정답의 The appointment of Ms. Talbot

어휘 appointment 임명

195 What can be inferred about Mr. Jean-Pierre?

(A) He organized a press conference.

(B) He has worked for *Financial Age Magazine*.

(C) He was hired by Mr. Higa 25 years ago.

(D) He works at Morvyn Manor.

장-피에르 씨에 관해 추론할 수 있는 것은?

(A) 기자 회견을 준비했다.

(B) 〈파이낸셜 에이지 매거진〉에서 일한 적이 있다.

(C) 25년 전에 히가 씨에게 채용되었다.

(D) 모빈 매너에서 일한다.

해설 연계: 초대장에서 장-피에르 씨가 기조연설자임을 확인할 수 있습니다. 이메일 두 번째 단락 후반부에서 기조연설자가 그 잡지에서 콤 씨의 첫 번째 상사라고 했습니다. 기사 첫 단락에서 콤 씨의 직장은 〈파이낸셜 에이지 매거진〉이라는 것을 알 수 있으므로 정답은 (B)입니다.

Questions 196-200 refer to the following Web page, e-mail, and form.

196-200 웹페이지 + 이메일 + 양식

https://www.continuousgrowth.com.au

https://www.continuousgrowth.com.au

200 Continuous Growth offers training for aspiring agricultural specialists who want to explore the latest technological advances in the field.

200지속 성장은 농업 분야의 최신 기술 발전을 탐구하기 원하는 야망 있는 농업 전문가를 위한 교육을 제공합니다.

We offer four online prerecorded video modules, each led by a guest expert. The topics covered are as follows:

우리는 사전 녹화된 온라인 동영상 모듈 4개를 제공하는 데, 모두 초빙 전문가가 지도합니다. 다루는 주제는 다음과 같습니다:

- **197**Creative Water Catchment Systems, with Samir Wadekar
- Advanced Soil Health Strategies, with Garth Martin
- Tree Care, with Jessica Chin
- Animal Systems, with Dawn Brown

- **197**창의적인 집수 시스템, 사미르 와데카
- 선진 토양 건강 전략, 가스 마틴
- 나무 관리, 제시카 친
- 동물 시스템, 돈 브라운

Modules can be purchased individually for $150 each. Access to any courses purchased is good for two years.

199 Additionally, we offer a comprehensive and intensive programme consisting of 80 total hours of instruction. The four online modules described above make up the core of the intensive programme curriculum. But also included are multiple in-person workshops at our training centre where attendees will participate in hands-on projects. In addition, students will be responsible for reading key selections from research journals. **196**Enrollment in the two-month programme is capped at fifteen students and costs $1200. Certificates are awarded to students upon successful completion of the programme.

모듈은 각 150달러에 개별 구입 가능합니다. 구매한 강좌 이용은 2년 동안 유효합니다.

199덧붙여, 우리는 총 80시간 강습으로 구성된 종합적이고 집중적인 프로그램을 제공합니다. 위에 설명한 온라인 모듈 4개는 집중 프로그램 교과 과정의 핵심을 구성합니다. 하지만 우리 교육 센터에서 직접 참여하는 다수의 워크숍도 포함되어 있어 참석자들이 실습 프로젝트에 참여하게 됩니다. 또한 학생들은 연구 잡지에서 선정된 핵심 글들을 읽을 책임을 지게 됩니다. **196**2개월 프로그램 등록은 학생 15명으로 상한이 있으며 비용은 1,200달러입니다. 프로그램을 성공적으로 이주한 학생들에게는 수료증을 수여합니다.

어휘 continuous 지속적인 aspiring 야망 있는 agricultural 농업의 expert 전문가 purchase 구매하다 individually 개별적으로 access 접근, 이용 comprehensive 종합적인 intensive 집중적인 consist of ~로 구성되다 instruction 강습 describe 설명하다 in-person 직접 참여하는 attendee 참석자 hands-on 실습의, 직접 해보는 responsible for ~을 책임지는 enrollment 등록 cap 상한을 정하다 certificate 증서

To: Intensive Programme Students
From: Darlene Stein
Date: 22 October
Subject: Apprenticeship

Students,

I am sure you are busy working on your final projects, but I wanted to take a moment to pass on to you some important information. **197**Our expert trainer who specializes in water collection systems is looking to hire two apprentices at his agricultural engineering firm. Those interested should let me know.

198 Also, all those seeking employment should read the latest article on the Australia Eco-Farming Web site that explains how to effectively market yourself to agricultural-industry employers.

Best,

Darlene Stein

수신: 집중 프로그램 학생들
발신: 달린 스타인
날짜: 10월 22일
제목: 수습직

학생 여러분께,

최종 프로젝트를 진행하느라 바쁘시겠지만, 잠시 중요한 정보를 전달하고자 합니다. **197**집수 시스템을 전공하는 우리 전문 교육자가 자신의 농업 엔지니어링 회사에 수습생 두 명을 채용하려고 합니다. 관심 있는 분들은 제게 알려주셔야 합니다.

198또한 취업을 원하는 모든 분들은 호주 생태 농업 웹사이트에 올라온 최신 기사를 읽어야 합니다. 이 기사는 농업 고용주들에게 효과적으로 자신을 홍보할 수 있는 방법을 설명하고 있습니다.

달린 스타인

어휘 apprenticeship 수습직 pass on to ~에게 전달하다 apprentice 수습생 article 기사 effectively 효과적으로

199 Congratulations on completing all 80 hours of our intensive programme. Please take a moment to comment about your experience.

199 Name: Jack Nguyen

I enjoyed everything about these courses. The workshops were incredibly helpful, and I had a wonderful time getting to know the other students. **200**I suggest that students be shown examples of farms that have actually implemented some of the techniques presented in the readings. That is the only thing that I felt was lacking. Overall, the tuition was money well spent, and I would recommend it to anyone interested in the agricultural field.

199집중 프로그램 80시간을 모두 수료하신 것을 축하합니다. 잠시 시간을 내주셔서 당신의 경험에 관한 의견을 주십시오.

199이름: 잭 응우옌

이 강좌들에 관한 모든 게 즐거웠습니다. 워크숍은 엄청나게 도움이 됐고 다른 학생들을 알게 되어 멋진 시간을 보냈습니다. **200**읽을거리에서 제시된 기법을 실제 실행한 농장들의 사례를 학생들에게 보여줄 것을 제안합니다. 그점이 제가 부족하다고 느낀 유일한 사항입니다. 전반적으로 수업료만큼 값어치가 있었으며 농업 분야에 관심 있는 사람이라면 누구에게나 추천하겠습니다.

어휘 experience 경험 incredibly 엄청나게 implement 실행하다 lack 부족한 tuition 수업(료)

196 What does the Web page indicate about the intensive program?

(A) It requires students to publish research.

(B) It takes about two years to complete.

(C) There is an established class-size limit.

(D) Students must take a comprehensive written examination.

웹페이지에서 집중 프로그램에 관해 명시하는 것은?

(A) 학생들이 연구 결과를 발표하도록 요구한다.

(B) 수료하는 데 약 2년이 걸린다.

(C) 정해진 강좌 규모 제한이 있다.

(D) 학생은 종합 필기시험을 치러야 한다.

해설 Not / True: 웹페이지 마지막 단락 후반부에서 프로그램 등록은 학생 15명으로 상한이 있다고 했으므로 정답은 (C)입니다.

Paraphrasing 지문의 Enrollment in the two-month programme is capped → 정답의 There is an established class-size limit

197 Who is hiring apprentices?

(A) Mr. Wadekar

(B) Mr. Martin

(C) Ms. Chin

(D) Ms. Brown

수습생을 채용하는 사람은?

(A) 와데카 씨

(B) 마틴 씨

(C) 친 씨

(D) 브라운 씨

해설 연계: 이메일 첫 번째 단락 두 번째 문장에서 집수 시스템 전문 교육자가 자기 회사에 수습생 두 명을 채용한다고 했습니다. 웹페이지 중반부의 강좌 소개에서 집수 시스템 전문가는 사미르 와데카임을 확인할 수 있으므로 정답은 (A)입니다.

198 According to the e-mail, why should people visit the Australia Eco-Farming Web site?

(A) To read training-program reviews

(B) To find resources for completing projects

(C) To learn more about available courses

(D) To take advantage of career-related advice

이메일에 따르면, 사람들이 호주 생태 농업 웹사이트를 방문해야 하는 이유는?

(A) 교육 프로그램 수강 후기를 읽기 위해

(B) 프로젝트 완성을 위한 자료를 찾기 위해

(C) 이용 가능한 강좌에 대해 자세히 알아보기 위해

(D) 직업 관련 조언을 활용하기 위해

> **해설** 세부 사항: 마지막 단락에서 호주 생태 농업 웹사이트에 들어가 농업 고용주에게 효과적으로 자신을 홍보할 수 있는 방법(how to effectively market yourself)을 설명하는 기사를 읽어야 한다고 학생들을 독려하고 있으므로 정답은 (D)입니다.

> **어휘** resource 자료 take advantage of ~을 활용하다

199 What is most likely true about Mr. Nguyen?

(A) He viewed all four online modules.

(B) He gardens as a hobby.

(C) He recently accepted a new position.

(D) He still has coursework to finish to earn a certificate.

응우옌 씨에 관해 사실인 것은?

(A) 4개의 온라인 모듈을 모두 보았다.

(B) 취미로 정원을 가꾼다.

(C) 최근 새로운 직책을 수락했다.

(D) 아직 수료증을 얻기 위해 끝내야 할 수업 과제가 있다.

> **해설** 연계: 응우옌이라는 이름은 양식에서 확인할 수 있고 양식 첫 문장에서 집중 프로그램 80시간 수료를 축하한다고 했습니다. 웹페이지 마지막 단락 첫 번째와 두 번째 문장을 통해 온라인 모듈 4개는 80시간 집중 프로그램 교과 과정의 핵심을 구성한다는 것을 알 수 있으므로 정답은 (A)입니다.

200 What does Mr. Nguyen want Continuous Growth to do?

(A) Provide hands-on workshops instead of online modules

(B) Show how some methods are being used in the real world

(C) Reduce the cost of the program

(D) Offer courses for those wanting to work in a different field of study

응우옌 씨가 '지속 성장'에 하도록 원하는 것은?

(A) 온라인 모듈 대신 실습 워크숍 제공하기

(B) 일부 방식들이 현장에서 어떻게 사용되고 있는지 보여주기

(C) 프로그램 비용 인하하기

(D) 다른 연구 분야에서 일하고 싶은 사람들을 위한 강좌 제공하기

> **해설** 연계: 웹페이지 첫 문장에서 '지속 성장'이 교육 제공 기관을 확인합니다. 양식에서 응우옌 씨는 읽을거리에서 제시된 기법을 실행한 농장들의 사례를 학생들에게 보여줄 것을 제안했으므로 정답은 (B)입니다.

> **Paraphrasing** 지문의 be shown examples of farms that have actually implemented some of the techniques → 정답의 Show how some methods are being used in the real world